HORARY ASTROLOGY RE-EXAMINED
The Possibility or Impossibility of the Matter Propounded

Barbara Dunn

The Wessex Astrologer

Published in 2009 by
The Wessex Astrologer Ltd
4A Woodside Road
Bournemouth
BH5 2AZ
England

www.wessexastrologer.com

Copyright © Barbara Dunn

Barbara Dunn asserts the moral right to be recognised as the author of this work

ISBN 9781902405353

A catalogue record of this book is available at The British Library

Cover design by Dave at Creative Byte, Poole, Dorset

Unless otherwise stated in the text, astrological charts produced from Solar Fire Deluxe v.6.0.32 by
Esoteric Technologies Pty Ltd.

All rights reserved. No part of this work may be used or reproduced in any manner without written permission. A reviewer may quote brief passages.

Saint Chrystom says, 'By a STAR did God direct the Gentiles, not by an ANGEL, not by a PROPHET, not by a VOICE from heaven, because he would condescend to their weakness and teach them by such things as they were most acquainted with', and here because these Arabians were Astrologers, and well versed in the stars, he calleth them to himself by a STAR. [1]

Dedication

This book is dedicated to my friend and teacher Olivia Barclay,
to my partner Victor
and to my children Tremayne and Emmeline.

Acknowledgements

I thank the Urania Trust for their generous grant, which helped make this book possible.

I also thank my family, friends and colleagues for their input and support, particularly:
  Victor Downer
  Tremayne Bidgood
  Emmeline Downer
  Dr Amanda Hilmarsson-Dunn
  Babs Kirby
  Ian Lewis
  Margaret Cahill
  Paul F Newman

I am grateful for permission to use material from the following:

Dr Nicholas Campion, *Astrology Quarterly* and his introduction to the *Carter Memorial Lecture 1996*.

Robert Hand and ARHAT, *Night & Day Planetary Sect in Astrology, On Reception* by Masha'allah, *The Correspondence Between the Rabbis of Southern France and Maimonides about Astrology*, tr. Meira B Epstein.

Charles Burnett *The Abbreviation of the Introduction to Astrology* by Abu Ma'shar.

Quotations from the following are reprinted by permission of the publishers and the Trustees of the Loeb Classical Library, Cambridge, Mass.: Harvard University Press. The Loeb Classical Library ® is a registered trademark of the President and Fellows of Harvard College.

> Ptolemy: *Tetrabiblos*, Loeb Classical Library Vol.435, translated by F.E. Robbins, 1940.

> Manilius: *Astronomica*, Loeb Classical Library Vol. 469, translated by G.P. Goold, 1977, 1992.

The American Federation of Astrologers and James Holden *The Judgments of Nativities* by Abu 'Ali Al-Khayyat.

Annabella Kitson *Astrology Quarterly* and *Astrological Journal*.

Deborah Houlding *Tools & Techniques of the Medieval Astrologers*, by Robert Zoller.

Sunday Mirror and Trinity Mirror plc for the use of my photograph on the cover.

Both the author and the publisher have made every effort to contact the publishers of work quoted in this book. Where we have been unable to trace the copyright we apologise, and where we have established the copyright we have acknowledged it.

Contents

	Foreword	vii
	Introduction	ix
	Terms of Art	xxi

PART ONE - Methodology: Ancient and Medieval Astrological Doctrine

1.	The Planets	1
2.	The Houses	33
3.	Signs of the Zodiac and their Divisions	57
4.	Planetary Sect	76
5.	Planetary Movement and Aspect	90
6.	An Evaluation of Planetary Strengths and Weaknesses: Essential Dignities and Debilities	111
7.	An Evaluation of Planetary Strengths and Weaknesses: Accidental Dignities and Debilities	135
8.	Reception	167
9.	Almuten	185
10.	Signification	195
11.	Considerations before Judgement	229
12.	The Question	240
13.	Planetary Testimony Preceding Judgement	261
14.	The Possibility of the Matter Propounded	293
15.	The Impossibility of the Matter Propounded	321

PART TWO - The Possibility or Impossibility of the Matter Propounded: Questions and Judgements

16.	Second House Matters: Wealth and Possessions	349

17.	Fourth House Matters: Land and Property	373
18.	Fifth House Matters: Pregnancy	393
19.	Sixth House Matters: Health and Sickness	414
20.	Seventh House Matters: Marriage and Relationships	438
21.	Seventh House Matters: Lawsuits and Disputes	464
22.	Tenth House Matters: Career and Achievement	485
23.	Tenth House Matters: Sport	506
	Afterword	521
	Bibliography	523
	Index	527

Foreword

Astrology is the interface between humanity and destiny. By observing the ever-changing cycles of the Sun, the Moon and the planets we understand the times we live in and are offered clear insights into the future. The power of astrology has been understood for thousands of years, since at least the time of the Babylonians. Over the centuries and millennia, each generation of astrologers has passed their knowledge down to the next.

Yet over the last few centuries astrology has had a bumpy ride. The Age of Reason hit this ancient art very hard. Scientists pored scorn and ridicule over astrology, conveniently forgetting that some of their own heroes, for example Ptolemy, Copernicus and Galileo, were thoroughly versed in the art of astrology, taking its validity for granted.

Matters became even worse in the twentieth century. Although there was a renewed interest in astrology, the astrology practised was downgraded in order to fit in with the new age geist, which was tightening its grip over twentieth and even twenty-first century astrology. The old techniques were frequently ignored, as astrology evolved into a psychological talking shop, where the horoscope became a pretty mandala next to the counsellor's couch.

As modern astrologers lost touch with ancient techniques, either through ignorance or lack of skill, they had to start inventing their own system. Not content with the additional planets Uranus, Neptune and Pluto, discovered between 1781 and 1930, many astrologers started incorporating a plethora of dwarf planets, planetoids and asteroids into their work. In spite of its minuscule size, the astronomical body Chiron grabbed everyone's attention for a long time. Whole books were written about its significance. More recently, there was the arrival of the dwarf planet Eris. Within a couple of years of its official 2005 discovery, Eris emerged as a rival for Chiron in terms of its pride of place in the open-ended canons of new age astrology.

There are advantages in using an ever-expanding list of astronomical bodies in one's chart judgement. The astrologer is playing with so many factors that it is easy to find an explanation for everything. The same Nativity can be fitted to a nun or a war criminal, a brain surgeon or a chimpanzee. The astrologer doesn't have to worry about making precise predictions, because new age astrology is about free will rather than destiny: clients can supposedly live happily ever after, leading their lives according to amorphous, self-interpreted trends.

Fortunately the tide is slowly turning. In the 1980s, *Christian Astrology*, William Lilly's seventeenth century masterpiece, was republished in an unadulterated form. This is an astrological textbook and casebook, which has relevance in a fundamental and unambiguous way, to the issues and concerns of the twenty-first century.

The main focus of *Christian Astrology* is the techniques of horary astrology. Horary astrology is the means by which questions are asked and answered. An astrologer sets up a chart for the precise moment a question is asked and by using traditional techniques an accurate answer can be produced. Questions are wide-ranging: When will I get married? Where is my lost dog? Will my business venture succeed? Should I buy the house? Will I recover from my illness? Will I find the secret of eternal life?

The astrologer who did most to publicise Lilly's work was Olivia Barclay. Born in 1919, she became an astrologer late in life and up until her death in 2001 was an uncompromising advocate of traditional, horary astrology. She set up a demanding correspondence course which often took students several years to complete. It was through this course that she transmitted the wisdom of William Lilly, together with the writings of many of the great astrologers before him.

One of Olivia Barclay's students was Barbara Dunn. Already familiar with horary astrology when she first met Olivia, Barbara used the course to hone her skills and by the early 1990s was a sought after teacher and lecturer of astrology, with a growing list of private clients. At the same time, she started making accurate, unambiguous predictions on radio and television, as well as in magazines and newspapers.

Inheriting Olivia Barclay's course (Qualifying Horary Practitioner) in 2001, Barbara has carried on the tradition, being Britain's foremost teacher and practitioner of horary astrology. Over the course of her career, Barbara has maintained a meticulous record of her work and in this book she shows us the secrets of accurate judgement. She makes it clear that an astrologer needs to have humility. Astrologers cannot simply make up the rules as they go along. Instead, astrologers must have respect for the long tradition of their craft. Their judgements must, therefore, be guided by the wisdom of their forebears. For this reason, Barbara spends the first part of the book looking at the works of earlier astrologers, for example Ptolemy, Masha'allah, Abu Ma'shar, Guido Bonatus, Al Biruni, Morin de Villefranche and William Lilly. In the second part of the book, Barbara shows us how to judge Questions and Nativities, using the time-honoured methods of the ancients.

The journey Barbara takes us on is exhilarating, as we realise how accurate astrology can be if it is taken seriously. She gives us the real stuff, free from the gentle euphemisms of new age astrology. However it's not for everyone – psychological platitudes can often be more acceptable than the cold truth. It's your call. If you think the journey might be too exhausting or too disturbing, you can, if you so wish, stop right here.

ARCHIE DUNLOP
Bratislava October 2008

INTRODUCTION

If births are natural things then interrogations are natural things.²

Horary astrology is a language of symbols developed thousands of years ago. It is part of an ancient tradition, which has, at its very core, the Question. The Question is asked at a moment of deep and sincere thought, perhaps when all alternatives have been exhausted. The time to proceed with judgement is when the astrologer has a complete understanding of that Question, whether the astrologer is the Querent, or another person.

It is the various testimonies (indications) in the chart, which reveal the answer to the Question. In the process of producing this answer, the chart provides confirmation that the pattern in the heavens produces a corresponding pattern of events on earth.

> ...it is not the solution to the question asked that is of major importance... [but] the affirmation of the universal laws of astrology, the deciphering of the code.³

In Meira Epstein's translation of *The Correspondence Between the Rabbis of Southern France and Maimonides about Astrology*, Moses Maimonides, the great Jewish philosopher of the Middle Ages, tells us about the intelligence of the stars

> In the same way that we say that God delivers his miracles through the angels, so do those philosophers say that all things that happen on earth are brought about by the spheres and the stars. They also say that the spheres and the stars have a living soul and intelligence. All these things are true...⁴

The wonder of astrology is that "the smallest and seemingly insignificant object is comprised of the same pattern that permeates all existing things..."⁵ This is why a Question can be asked about anything on earth, because every single person, object or matter enquired about belongs to one of the houses, signs or planets.

This book examines the methods by which astrologers through the centuries evaluated planetary strengths and weaknesses and how these evaluations provide a platform for judgement today just as they did in the past. My source material is derived from a number of authors, among whom Ptolemy, Masha'allah, Abu Ma'shar, Al Biruni, Ibn Ezra, Bonatti, Morin and William Lilly are referred to extensively.

Some of the texts were written by astrologers who practised the art of Questions, others by astrologers who objected to Questions and wrote mainly about Nativities or Elections. However, it is William Lilly's *Christian Astrology* which is my inspiration and which provided the starting point for my studies many years ago. William Lilly followed the medieval tradition and was probably the greatest horary astrologer of his time. In the words of my teacher and great friend, Olivia Barclay

> I am indebted to William Lilly for nearly all I write – and so are most English-speaking astrologers, whether they know it or not.[6]

The republication of *Christian Astrology* represented something of a turning point in the modern history of astrology. This we owe almost entirely to Olivia Barclay. It was Barclay's photocopied editions of Lilly's 1647 masterpiece, which facilitated Regulus's 1985 republication of this work. *Christian Astrology* was the first astrological textbook to be written in English. Worsdale calls Lilly

> ...the greatest professor of the Mundane, and Horary departments of this science, that ever wrote in the English language; his precepts and judgement prove his abilities to every unprejudiced reader.[7]

As Nicholas Campion explains, it was Olivia Barclay who introduced us to *Christian Astrology*, and who was, therefore, instrumental in "restoring a direct line of astrological interpretation extending back in the classical world".[8] That line had been broken when astrology went out of fashion in the late seventeenth century. The republication of *Christian Astrology* took place at a time when, Campion believes, "the consensus was that the future of astrology lay in its marriage with depth psychology". He tells us that Barclay drew people back to the realisation that there was a very precise way of working with astrology. According to Geoffrey Cornelius, the two hundred and twenty eight titles listed in Lilly's bibliography, represent "virtually the entire corpus of the European tradition extant in his day".[9] Patrick Curry confirms that *"Christian Astrology* was the most thorough, detailed and authoritative textbook of astrology that had hitherto appeared in English".[10]

Whether the chart under consideration is a Nativity, Election, Question, Mundane or Ingress, the process of evaluation is broadly the same; what Coley calls the "short comprehensive and approved rules of Art".

Astrology is comprised of six areas of study, to which the tools and techniques of the tradition apply universally. Coley tells us that, "Amongst those things that appertain to giving judgment in questions of Astrology, there are six to be chiefly considered:"

- Nations, and their particular kinds.

- Families, and the constitutions and ordinations of Families and Houses.

- Rich and potent persons, Dispositions and Affairs.

- Individuals of human kind.

- Elections or times proper for the beginning of any Work or Enterprise.

- Questions as well universal as particular, pertinent and fit to be demanded.[11]

Although the method of planetary evaluation in this book can be applied to any chart, the principal focus is Questions. *Horary Astrology Re-Examined* is a comprehensive reference work, as well as a casebook, giving judgement on over fifty Questions as to the 'possibility or impossibility of the matter propounded'. Like Lilly, I do not make any attempt to develop the religious or philosophical theme in the text. As in *Christian Astrology*, where our understanding is derived from the examples which Lilly brings before us, I attempt to explain the process of horary astrology through practice rather than debate.

Although an understanding of the development of astrological technique is essential, it is also important to apply these principles on a practical level. My aim, therefore, is to find out what actually happens to a person, situation, event or development, when significators are, for example, combust, under rays, applying to Fortunes or separating from Infortunes. What sort of person is actually signified by Jupiter dignified or Saturn peregrine? As in *Christian Astrology*, I hope that the student or reader will see that it is the Questions (horary charts) themselves which allow us to observe horary astrology in action. In *Tools & Techniques of the Medieval Astrologers* Robert Zoller tells us that the complete study of astrology consists in "not merely digging up the writings of the ancients and assiduously studying them so much as penetrating to their inner meaning..." He doesn't advocate that we should do this to the exclusion of our modern perceptions. But he does say that we should be able to "see in both worlds". Ultimately, therefore, this task "is a practical one, not merely a theoretical one". In view of this, I have included over fifty practical examples of horary judgements in *Part Two* of this book.

In *Part One*, I consider the work of different authors, focusing on tools and techniques, together with any differences of opinion between them. I hope to present a clear comparison between Arabic and medieval techniques and the practices of later authors. I do not pretend that my writing constitutes anywhere near a full examination of the material available. My source material is mainly in the form of translation. I accept that in some instances I may have relied on a poor translation or even a mistranslation; however with careful cross-referencing I hope to have highlighted any ambiguity. In an attempt to clarify certain issues, I have separated and categorised where it seems appropriate. However, in a study of techniques which are interdependent, there is inevitably some overlap.

In various places in *Christian Astrology*, Lilly himself comments upon the methods of earlier authors, stating where he agrees or disagrees and where he is uncertain. In this way he offers the reader or student the benefit of his experience. This is a theme, which I attempt to expand upon in *Horary Astrology Re-Examined*. Robert Hand tells us that although Bonatti was influenced by Zael (Sahl) and Haly on a number of occasions, he also includes new material in his writings, which must have arisen from his anecdotal experience. These appear to have been his own discoveries. After the time of Pico, we see further changes in astrological doctrine. By the time of Morin and his *Astrologia Gallica* a whole new system of philosophy is emerging. Morin rejects various traditional techniques such as the terms and the faces. He changes the triplicity rulerships and does not consider the debility of peregrine to be unfortunate.

Lilly does not agree with Ptolemy in assigning the eleventh house to children. He rejects the notion by Al-Kindi and others that the Querent is co-signified by the planet from whom the Moon is separating and the Quesited by the Planet to whom the Moon is applying. Regarding Questions about marriage Lilly mentions

> An Arabick Aphorism not overmuch to be credited without consent of other Significators...[12]

He disagrees about the placement of the significator for who loves most in a marriage and states that his experience in this regard is "Contrary to all the rules of the Ancients..." In relation to planetary orbs (more specifically "the quantity of their Orbs") Lilly includes the thoughts of those whom he believes are the best authors, as well as his own experience. Lilly draws upon the work of two hundred and twenty-eight authors in *Christian Astrology*. He acknowledges his sources by saying he gives every author their due, but explains that "the Method is my owne, it's no translation..."

Lilly tells us that in his Horary section in *Christian Astrology* he consulted with "Bonatus, Haly, Dariot, Leopoldus, Pontanus, Avenezra and Zael". In his section on Nativities, Lilly's sources include Origanus, Albubater, Montulmo, Judeus, Ptolemy, Cardan and Lindholt.[13] Lilly also studied the manuscripts of "Ancient and Reverend Professors in this Art, who lived more remote from these corrupt Times..." telling us

> I have with some trouble reconciled their disagreements, and reformed and corrected what might have led the Reader into an errour.[14]

This, he explains was largely down to poor translations of their work, because the translators "did not understand the Art or the Terms thereof..." Referring to Nativities, Lilly admits that in some places he disagrees with Ptolemy because

> I am more led by reason and experience, then by the single authority of any one man...

However, it is clear that Lilly's intention in *Christian Astrology* is, as he himself claims, to "advance this Art, and make even a slender wit capable hereof". I would agree with Geoffrey Cornelius when he says

> ...we may trust Lilly's own report of the patient thought he put into satisfying himself on the main points of art...[15]

Clearly there are differences of opinion through the tradition, for example between the authors of the Arabic era, such as Masha'allah, writing in the eighth/ninth century and later authors such as Morin in the seventeenth century.[16] It is clear that astrologers through the centuries disagreed amongst each other just as they do now. The crucial difference however, is that our predecessors, "knowing they were dealing with the truth, did not seek to change it so much as understand it".[17]

One might argue that astrologers of the past simply followed the tradition without attempting to question it, or that some simply did not understand it and failed to pass on the correct teachings. However, at the other end of the scale are the modern astrologers, who feel free to invent new techniques which contradict the tradition entirely. As a consequence, the philosophy behind astrology is being eroded, and the horoscopic tradition is losing ground as against the psychological approach. Furthermore, the practical application of our Art is becoming dangerously close to relegation. In order to understand anything at all about astrology, we must understand what went before, but with each successive generation the astrological knowledge of the centuries has been "watered down, distorted and misunderstood".[18]

Robert Zoller, referring to astrology's development in the twentieth century and its revisions by new age philosophies, explains that they are

> ... characterised by a lack of method, integrated philosophical or metaphysical vision and a patchwork of 'techniques' drawn from wholly unconnected traditions...[19]

Robert Hand confirms that "if everything means everything, then nothing means anything".[20] He suggests that there is a need for what he calls "rigour" in our use of symbols. We should have an exact knowledge of their meaning. Despite attempts by modern psychological astrologers to change or modify our traditional "celestial apparatus", Annabella Kitson tells us

> ...this apparatus does not change in the sense that the material of other crafts does; doesn't become antiquated like an ancient weapon does for a modern soldier; so we are peculiarly fitted to learn from history and about the astrology of history itself, and if we gain historical perspective, we may be better able to understand our roles as astrologers...[21]

The transmission of knowledge from our ancestors is fundamental to any proper study of astrology. We have inherited a vast body of information and although we can build upon our heritage, in the first instance we must have a thorough understanding of that heritage. This lack of understanding appears to have been a problem common to many astrologers. In 1886, William Eldon Serjeant notes

> The science of the stars has of late years fallen into disrepute, chiefly owing to imposters, but also to zealous persons endeavouring to practise an art in which they have not been sufficiently well read to give correct judgements.[22]

Today it is unfashionable to make predictions, as modern astrologers continue to emphasise the psychological aspects of a client's Nativity. Even horary astrologers themselves question the validity of making predictions. It has been claimed that "the idea of prediction is far from adequate as an expression of the core process of horary".[23] Astrologers may not wish to embrace the idea of prediction, but astrology is about prediction. Robert Hand confirms that "Questions demand answers. Answers demand rigorous and logical interpretation of symbols".[24] Coley tells us that the aim of astrology is to

> ...truly foretell future accidents; for this art has its peculiar rules and Aphorisms and its end is judgement...[25]

Modern astrologers continually talk about "specialisation". Even astrologers who are acquainted with traditional methods discuss the various "branches" and apply different "techniques" to each. For example, many astrologers use traditional methods for Questions (horary) but not for Nativities. More than once, in his excellent book *The Moment of Astrology*, Geoffrey Cornelius refers to the reading of a chart in a "natal style", implying that there is a difference between the methods used to evaluate a Question, as contrasted to a Nativity. Some astrologers, who prefer to mix psychology with astrology, have even called for a "radical revisioning of our own tradition". Regardless of context, it would be absurd for an astrologer to evaluate Saturn, peregrine, in his detriment and in square with the Sun as fortunate testimony, or Jupiter in Sagittarius in trine with the Sun as unfortunate.

Bonatti rarely makes a distinction between Questions and Nativities in the majority of his 'considerations'. Al Biruni explains that

> ... in the case of an idle request or one for a general prognostic the custom of the majority of astrologers is to follow the same procedure as in other questions, namely to ascertain the ascendant of the time of the query. They then examine the aspects as they would at a nativity and make conclusions...[26]

Obviously the outcome revealed by the planetary patterns in a Question is more immediate and only relevant in terms of that particular Question, whereas in a Nativity the entire life pattern is revealed. But the method of planetary evaluation remains the same. In *Christian Astrology* Lilly examines the strengths and weaknesses of the planets and allocates each of them a score.[27] This process is the same in his section on Horary as in his section on Nativities.

Even those astrologers who rejected the validity of Questions showed in the main only small differences in their method of planetary evaluation. In a Question concerning wealth for example, strong and fortunate signification produces an affirmative outcome for the Querent. In a Nativity the same signification brings wealth during the Native's lifetime. This is agreed by all.

From a reading of this book it will become clear that all charts are inextricably linked together. Both the Question and the Election are intimately connected with the Nativity: some would say that they are dependent on the Nativity. Certainly, the Nativity takes precedence over the Question and the Election. In *Christian Astrology*, Lilly himself reminds the reader that no promising Horary can contradict the testimony of an unfortunate radix (Nativity).[28] The Nativities of the parents are also important. Lilly tells us that in determining the length of life of the Native

> ...that which is principally considerable, and ought if possible to be obtained, is, judiciously to examine the Nativities of the Parents of the Childe, and whether the Significators of Children in them are strong yea or not;[29]

He explains that in the same way "as the goodnesse of fruit depends on the temperament of the root" so does a child's health and well-being depend on the significators in the parents' Nativity. Ramesey explains that an Election should only be drawn up with knowledge of the person's Nativity (if that is available).

> ...there can be no time elected... advantagious to anyone whose nativity or time of birth is not exactly known; for according unto it must you frame your election, together with respect to the revolution of the year...[30]

However, if the testimonies in a Nativity contradict those in the chart of a nation it is the latter which is thought to be pre-eminent. This is the area of study which Coley refers to as "nations, and their particular kinds". In Meira Epstein's translation of *Sefer Ha'Moladot*, by Ibn Ezra, she tells us: "his unambiguous conclusion is that the general prevails over the individual".

Traditional methods remain as fundamental and indispensable today as they were two thousand years ago. Accurate judgement based on these methods supplies clear evidence that the movement of heavenly bodies affects life on earth, that a synchronicity exists between them showing that life is one: as above, so it is below. As Barclay explains, "even if your motivation is not prediction, it is the accurate prediction which supplies such evidence".[31]

There is no denying that psychological astrology can be of immense help in counselling work, but it does not follow that psychology's more ego-based discipline should be merged with the very structured and practical methods of the tradition. I suggest that for the psychological astrologers the real dilemma lies in their inability, or reluctance, to accept the notion of determinism. Although recognising the value of Questions, proponents of the non-deterministic school feel uncomfortable with the idea of prediction. Their solution is to mix Horary with psychology, in order to circumnavigate this awkward issue. Rather than accepting that an astrological chart inevitably produces a prediction of some sort, the preferred option is to believe that the chart testimony provides only the possibility of an outcome, a possibility which the Querent may or may not choose to take up. This is explored further in chapter twelve.

According to Geoffrey Cornelius in *The Moment of Astrology*, the fact that astrology has had a marvellous history is no guarantee of its future survival. Indeed, the majority of modern astrologers appear to have little or no understanding of the tradition. Annabella Kitson tells us that for the few who do have an understanding, their methods are more reliable, their practice is enriched and their role as astrologers is more rewarding.

If astrologers are ever going to "establish the verity of Stellar power on mankind" or "convince the unbelievers, of the truth of Astronomical computations, and predictions..."[32] there must indeed be a radical revisioning of our art, but not in the way envisaged by the psychological astrologers. Annabella Kitson is correct when she suggests that astrologers need to

> ...come to grips with their history, complex as it is... like an isolated ethnic group, they need the courage of their identity in a hostile world.[33]

References

1. Doctor Swadling, in *Divinity an Enemy to Astrology*, London, 1653.
2. Roger Bacon, *Speculum Astrologiae* cited in Olivia Barclay's *Horary Astrology Rediscovered*, Schiffer, PA, 1990, p. 23.
3. Olivia Barclay, her original notes.
4. *The Correspondence Between the Rabbis of Southern France and Maimonides about Astrology*. Translation and commentary by Meira Epstein, ARHAT Publications, 1998, p. 16.
5. Olivia Barclay, her original notes.
6. Olivia Barclay Introduction to *Horary Astrology Rediscovered*, p. 25.
7. John Worsdale, 1798 *Celestial Philosophy or Genethliacal Astronomy*, Ballantrae Reprints, p. vi, author's address.
8. Nicholas Campion, his introduction to *The Need for Traditional Astrology* by Olivia Barclay, a transcript of the Carter Memorial Lecture delivered at the 1996 Exeter Conference.
9. Geoffrey Cornelius, *A Modern Astrological Perspective*, from *Christian Astrology*, Regulus, 1984, p. 865.
10. Patrick Curry in *Christian Astrology* by William Lilly, Bibliographical Appendix p. 862.
11. Guido Bonatus, *The Astrologer's Guide or Anima Astrologiae*, translated by Henry Coley 1675, republished by W.C.E. Serjeant 1886 and republished 1953 by The National Astrological Library, Washington, USA. Henry Coley's address to the reader p. xi and xii.
12. William Lilly, *Christian Astrology*.
13. ibid, To the Reader.
14. ibid
15. Geoffrey Cornelius, *A Modern Astrological Perspective*, from *Christian Astrology*. p. 865.
16. Mainly on the issue of triplicities, dignities, and planetary placement. Masha'allah claims that house rulers are more important in terms of outcomes even if they are not positioned in the house that they rule. Morin claims that even if a planet is not the ruler of a house, it has more power if positioned in that house than an absent ruler.
17. Olivia Barclay, 'Two Thousand Years of Houses', *The Astrologer's Quarterly*, Summer 1984, Vol. 58, No. 2, p. 70.
18. Olivia Barclay, *The Need For Traditional Astrology*, transcript of the Carter Memorial Lecture 1996, Exeter Conference.
19. Robert Zoller from his website, quoted by Martien Hermes, 'The need for traditional astrology', *The Astrological Journal*, January 2002, Vol. 44, No.1, p. 31.
20. Robert Hand in his foreword to *Horary Astrology Rediscovered* by Olivia Barclay, p. 16.
21. Annabella Kitson, 'Lodge Astrologers and the History of their Art', *The Astrology Quarterly*, Summer 1986, Vol. 60, No.2, p. 82.
22. W M Eldon Serjeant, in his preface to *Anima Astrologiae* by Guido Bonatus.

23. Geoffrey Cornelius, *The Moment of Astrology*, Arkana, London, 1986, p. 164.
24. Robert Hand in his foreword to *Horary Astrology Rediscovered* by Olivia Barclay.
25. Guido Bonatus, *Anima Astrologiae*, Henry Coley's address to the reader, p. xii.
26. Al Biruni, *The Book of Instruction in the Elements of the Art of Astrology*. Tr. by Ramsay Wright, Luzac and Co., 1934 (originally written in 1029), p. 332.
27. William Lilly, *Christian Astrology*, pp. 178-181 and pp. 744-745.
28. ibid p. 240.
29. ibid p. 525.
30. William Ramesey, 1653 *Astrologia Restaurata or Astrology Restored*, Ascella, p. 122.
31. Olivia Barclay, 'The Need for Traditional Astrology', Carter Memorial Lecture 1996 Also in *The Astrological Journal*, Volume 39, no 1, January/February 1997.
32. John Worsdale 1798, *Celestial Philosophy or Genethliacal Astronomy*, Longman & Co., p. iv.
33. Annabella Kitson, 'Lodge Astrologers and the History of their Art', *The Astrology Quarterly*, p. 82.

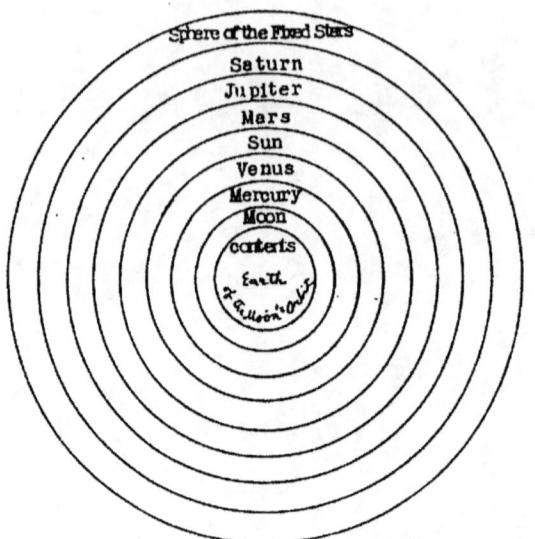

Al Biruni's Celestial Spheres

Signs of the Zodiac

Aries	♈	Libra	♎
Taurus	♉	Scorpio	♏
Gemini	♊	Sagittarius	♐
Cancer	♋	Capricorn	♑
Leo	♌	Aquarius	♒
Virgo	♍	Pisces	♓

Luminaries

Sun ☉   Moon ☽

Planets

Saturn ♄   Venus ♀
Jupiter ♃   Mars ♂
Mercury ☿

Classifications

Effect	Gender	Sect
Beneficent ♃ ♀ ☽	Masculine ☉ ♄ ♃ ♂	Diurnal ☉ ♃ ♄
Maleficent ♄ ♂	Feminine ☽ ♀	Nocturnal ☽ ♀ ♂
Common ☿	Common ☿	Common ☿

Terms of Art

Accidental Debility
A planet or luminary, which is accidentally debilitated, exerts an unfortunate influence or reduces the good fortune in terms of the chart under consideration. This can be due to its house placement, its motion and direction, or through its relationship with other planets and/or the luminaries and the nodes. A planet accidentally debilitated experiences a decrease in its strength and power.

Accidental Dignity
A planet or luminary, which is accidentally dignified, exerts a fortunate influence in terms of the chart under consideration. This can be due to its house placement, its motion and direction, or through its relationship with other planets and/or the luminaries, the nodes or the Lot of Fortune. A planet accidentally dignified experiences an increase in its strength and power.

Afflicted
A planet, a luminary, a cusp of a house, or one of the Lots, which is badly aspected by an Infortune, or other malefic, is said to be afflicted. An Infortune, not in his essential dignities, or other malefic, can afflict a house by its presence.

Almuten
Almuten is an Arabic term for the planet or luminary which has most counts of dignity in a particular place: the chief ruler of a house or chart.

Almuten of a Chart
The strongest planet or luminary in the chart, in terms of both its accidental and essential dignity (usually the most elevated), is referred to as the almuten of that chart. Some authorities believed that the luminaries could not be considered almuten of a chart.

Almuten of a House
The planet or luminary, which has the most essential dignities in the sign in a house cusp, is referred to as the almuten of that house. The almuten has a rulership of that house, together with the domicile ruler.

Angle
The first, fourth, seventh and tenth houses are angular houses.

Antiscium
If an imaginary line is drawn from 0 degrees Cancer to 0 degrees Capricorn, the planets can be reflected across that line to the corresponding degree on the other side. This is a planet's antiscium or antiscion.

Antiscia
This is a collective term for more than one antiscium point.

Application
When a planet, or luminary, is approaching a conjunction or aspect with another planet, luminary or point, it is said to be applying towards that planet. This is referred to as application. For the application to be effective, the distance between the planets should be within the moiety of their joint orbs.

Ascendant
The eastern horizon and the cusp of the first house, which starts at that point, is referred to as the ascendant.

Ascending Degree
The degree in the cusp of the first house is the ascending, or the rising, degree.

Aspect
An angle or fractional division between planets, luminaries or points in the chart is an aspect. The only aspects used in Questions (horary) are the opposition, square, trine and sextile. The conjunction is not really an aspect, but is included for convenience. Aspect means the beginning of the aspect. If, for example, a planet is separated from another by 54 degrees, this is what Ibn Ezra calls "the force of the sextile aspect". When this distance is 60 degrees, the aspect is perfect and signifies "completion of all that which they prognosticate".[1]

Benefic
In this book a benefic refers to the Sun, Jupiter, Venus, the Moon and Mercury (unless afflicted by a conjunction, square or opposition with Mars or Saturn) or Mars and Saturn in their domicile, exaltation or triplicity. Any of the foregoing in conjunction, square or opposition with the Sun experience a reduction in their power.

Besiegement
A point, a planet, a luminary or a house which is positioned between two or more other planets is besieged, or contained. Besiegement can take place through conjunction or aspect. If this takes place between Fortunes it is fortunate, but if between Infortunes, the reverse applies.

Cadent House
A house furthest from an angular house is a cadent house: the third, sixth, ninth and twelfth houses are cadent houses.

Cadent Planet
A planet or luminary in the third, sixth, ninth or twelfth house is a cadent planet. A

planet can also be cadent from its own domicile: Mars in Aries is considered to be angular, but if Mars is in Taurus, he is said to be succedent. Lilly tells us that if Mars is in Gemini "he is then Cadent as from his owne House; and so doe the rest: for ever a Planet is Angular in any of his owne Houses [domicile]".[2]

Caput Draconis*

The dragon's head, or north node, is another term for Caput Draconis. The dragon's head is masculine and was thought to be of the nature of Jupiter and Venus. Not all authorities agree on its precise influence, but in this work the north node is considered to be fortunate.

Cauda Draconis*

The dragon's tail, or south node, is another term for Cauda Draonis. The dragon's tail is feminine and thought to be of the opposite nature to the head. Not all authorities agree on its precise influence, but in this work the south node is considered to be unfortunate.

Cazimi

A planet or the Moon in the heart of the Sun, within 16 or 17 minutes of a conjunction, is said to be cazimi (not all authorities agree on the exact distance which defines cazimi). In this book the distance is considered to be 17 minutes or less.

Chart

An astrological representation of the celestial houses and the celestial bodies in those houses is referred to as a chart, circle, figure or map. The houses begin at the eastern horizon (the ascendant) and are numbered one to twelve.

Collection

When two planets or luminaries are not in aspect with each other, but they both aspect another, usually slower moving, planet, it is this planet which collects their light and helps to achieve the desired outcome (bring the matter to perfection).

Combust

A planet or other celestial body within about eight and half degrees of the Sun is combust. The exact distance thought to be necessary for combustion to take place varies among past authorities, but it is somewhere between six and eight and a half degrees. A planet is more afflicted when moving towards combustion than when moving away.

Commit Disposition

Any planet or luminary when applying to another planet commits its disposition to that planet. In other words, it sends its characteristics forward on to that planet.

Common Sign

Gemini, Virgo, Sagittarius and Pisces are common, double-bodied, or bi-corporeal signs.

Conjunction
A planet, luminary, house cusp, Lot or fixed star in the same sign and degree as another, forms a conjunction. The allowable distance for a conjunction to be effective or to be in operation is dependent on the moiety of the joint orbs belonging to a planet or luminary.

Contra-antiscium
The degree opposite to an antiscium is the contra-antiscium. A planet in conjunction with the contra-antiscium of an Infortune may become unfortunate.

Contra-antiscia
This is the collective term for more than one contra-antiscium point.

Co-significator
This is a planet or luminary in aspect or conjunction with the principal significator, a planet placed in the house of the matter enquired about, or a planet ruling intercepted degrees in the house of the matter enquired about. I refer the reader to chapter ten, Signification.

Cusp
The exact point in the chart where a house begins is the cusp of a house. The cusp of any house is the most powerful part of that house.

Day
The day started at dawn in previous centuries and this is where the sequence of planetary hours begins.

Debility
See essential debility and accidental debility.

Declination
The distance between a planet or luminary and the equator, in a northerly or southerly direction, is its declination.

Decumbiture
A chart drawn up for the moment when a sick person lies down or goes to bed is a decumbiture. The chart is drawn up as an Event.

Degree
The circle of the chart is divided into three hundred and sixty degrees, with thirty degrees allocated to each sign.

Detriment
The sign which is opposite to a planet or luminary's domicile is the sign of its detriment. This is a very weak position for a planet or luminary. Mars in Taurus, Venus in Scorpio and the Moon in Capricorn are in their detriment.

Dexter
An aspect made against the flow of signs is a dexter aspect: a trine between the Moon in Leo and Jupiter in Aries is a dexter trine.

Dignity
See essential dignity and accidental dignity.

Direct
A planet or luminary moving forwards from one degree to two degrees to three degrees is said to be moving in direct motion.

Dispositor
A planet or luminary ruling one (or more) of the dignities in which another planet is placed is the dispositor of that planet. For example, if Saturn is in Libra, his dispositor (by domicile) is Venus. If Saturn is in Aries, his dispositor (by domicile) is Mars and his dispositor by triplicity during the day is the Sun. A planet or luminary can be a dispositor of the domicile, exaltation, triplicity, term or face of another planet or luminary.

Diurnal Chart
A chart drawn up during the day, when the Sun is above the horizon, is a diurnal chart.

Diurnal Planet
The Sun, Jupiter and Saturn are diurnal planets. Mercury was thought to be diurnal when rising before the Sun. Diurnal planets exercise their power during the day.

Diurnal Sign
Aries, Gemini, Leo, Libra, Sagittarius and Aquarius are the diurnal signs.

Domicile
Another term for the sign over which a planet or luminary has rulership is domicile or house. Jupiter's domiciles are Sagittarius and Pisces. Mercury's domiciles are Virgo and Gemini.

Election
A chart drawn up for a particular (auspicious) moment, which is selected by the astrologer, is called an Election. This might relate to a time chosen for the beginning of an enterprise, for getting married, for building a house and so on.

Elevated
A planet or luminary in the upper part of a chart (above the horizon) is said to be elevated. This is an important consideration in all charts, but particularly those relating to sickness. In a general sense, planets elevated are stronger than those below.

Essential Debility**
A planet or luminary placed in a sign or part of a sign, where it is weak, is said to be in its debility or is debilitated. The essential debilities are detriment and fall. These are the places opposite to a planet's domicile (sign) or exaltation. Mercury in Sagittarius is in his detriment. Mercury in Pisces is in his fall.

Essential Dignity**
A planet or luminary placed in a sign or part of a sign, where it is strong and which belong to them, is said to be in its dignity or dignified. The essential dignities are domicile, exaltation, triplicity, term and face (decanate). Jupiter in Cancer is placed in his exaltation; Saturn in Gemini is placed in his diurnal triplicity.

Exaltation
A planet or luminary positioned in a sign where it is strong, such as Venus in Pisces or the Sun in Aries, is said to be exalted. A planet in its exaltation is not usually as strong as a planet in its own domicile (sign), but in certain instances the exaltation is stronger, for example in Questions relating to law-suits or disputes.

Face
One of a planet or luminary's weaker essential dignities is face. This is a subdivision of a sign, which contains ten degrees. Each face is ruled by a different planet or luminary.

Fall
The sign occupied by a planet or luminary, which is opposite to its exaltation, is the sign of its fall. The Moon in Scorpio is in her fall. Jupiter in Capricorn is in his fall.

Feminine Quarter
The quarter or quadrant from the cusp of the tenth house to the cusp of the seventh house and the quarter opposite to it, are the feminine or decreasing quarters.

Feminine Sign
Taurus, Cancer, Virgo, Scorpio, Capricorn and Pisces are the feminine signs.

Feral
If the Sun, Moon or planet makes no aspect at all throughout the whole sign where it is placed, it is said to be feral. Some authorities considered a planet to be feral if it did not make any conjunction in a sign.

Fixed Sign
Taurus, Leo, Scorpio and Aquarius are the fixed signs.

Fixed Star
A star (as distinct from a planet), which is visible to the naked eye, but so far away that it does not appear to be moving is given the name "fixed" in its constellation.

Fortuna
This is another term for the Lot of Fortune.

Fortune
Venus and Jupiter are the Fortunes.

Frustration
This is a method by which perfection between significators is prevented.

Hayyiz or Hayz
A diurnal planet (or the Sun) correctly placed above the horizon during the day, in a masculine sign, or a nocturnal planet (or the Moon) correctly placed above the horizon during the night, in a feminine sign, is in its hayyiz or hayz. Mars is different in that he is nocturnal and is correctly placed above the horizon during the night, but he is in his hayyiz only when in a masculine sign.

Horoscope
In modern astrology the horoscope refers to the Nativity, but in the classical system it was the term used to represent the ascendant.

House
Each of the twelve divisions within the chart is called a house. In the Regiomontanus system the houses can be of different sizes.

Impeded
A planet or luminary which is unfortunate, because of its position by house, sign, or aspect (or all of them) is impeded.

Inconjunct
A planet or luminary not in aspect with another planet or luminary, nor beholding that planet or luminary through the antiscia, is said to be inconjunct. A planet or luminary is inconjunct the ascendant if it does not behold the ascending sign.

Inferior Planet
Mercury, Venus and the Moon are the inferior planets, or the Inferiors.

Infortune
Mars and Saturn are the Infortunes.

Joy
A planet or luminary's position where it is most comfortable, either by house, by quarter, or by sign, is said to be its joy. Saturn in Aquarius, Mercury in the first house or a Superior in an increasing quarter are places where these planets are in their joy. In addition to the latter, the diurnal planets joy in diurnal houses in the east and oriental of the Sun near the ascendant. The nocturnal planets joy in nocturnal houses in the west and occidental of the Sun, near to the cusp of the seventh house.

Lady of a House
If a feminine planet, or the Moon, is the ruler of a particular house, it is referred to as the lady of the house. For example, if the ascending sign is Cancer, the Moon is lady of the ascendant. If Taurus is the sign found in the fifth house cusp, Venus is lady of the fifth house, or ruler of the fifth house.

Latitude
A planet or luminary's distance north or south of the ecliptic is referred to as its latitude.

Longitude
A planet or luminary's distance along the ecliptic starting at the beginning of the sign of Aries is referred to as its longitude.

Lord of a House
If a masculine planet, or the Sun, is the ruler of a particular house, it is referred to as the lord of the house. For example, if the ascending sign is Aquarius, Saturn is lord of the ascendant. If Pisces is the sign found in the eleventh house cusp, Jupiter is lord of the eleventh house, or ruler of the eleventh house.

Lots
The Lots are another word for Parts. The importance of the Lot of Fortune was emphasised by authorities of the past, especially Ptolemy. By day the Lot of Fortune is calculated using the degrees of the ascendant plus those of the Moon, minus those of the Sun. By night the Lot of Fortune is calculated using the degrees of the ascendant plus the degrees of the Sun, minus those of the Moon. Ptolemy uses the diurnal calculation in both the diurnal and nocturnal chart.

Luminaries
The Sun and the Moon are referred to as the lights, or the luminaries, and have great power in a chart. The Sun has particular power by day; the Moon has particular power by night. In an overall sense the Moon is usually the most important body in a Question (horary).

Malefic
In this book a malefic refers to Saturn or Mars in their detriment, fall or peregrine, or any other planet or luminary afflicted by a conjunction, square or opposition with either of them. Rulership of an unfortunate house may also cause a planet to be malefic.

Masculine Planet
Sun, Mars, Jupiter and Saturn are masculine. Mercury is usually masculine, but Mercury's 'sex' can depend on which planet has an influence over Mercury. If Mercury is in aspect or in conjunction with Venus, Mercury takes on a feminine role. However, if Mercury is with Mars, the role is more likely to be masculine.

Masculine Quarter
The quarter or quadrant from the ascendant to the cusp of the tenth house and the one which is opposite, are the masculine or increasing quarters.

Masculine Sign
Aries, Gemini, Leo, Libra, Sagittarius and Aquarius are the masculine signs.

Moveable Sign
Aries, Cancer, Libra and Capricorn are moveable signs (called cardinal signs by modern astrologers).

Mutual Reception
Where one particular planet or luminary is in a dignity of another and the latter is also in a dignity of the former, this is mutual reception. The strongest mutual reception is between domiciles (signs), but mutual reception can also be mixed between the stronger dignities and possibly between the lesser dignities. Jupiter in Pisces and Venus in Cancer have a mutual reception between their exaltations. Jupiter in Scorpio and Mars in Cancer have a mixed reception between domicile and exaltation.

Nativity
The name which astrologers of the past gave to a natal chart is the Nativity. This is the name referred to in this book.

Natural Rulers
Planets or luminaries which have a natural association with certain things, people or matters are the natural or universal significators of those things. For example, Jupiter is natural ruler of pregnancy, Saturn is natural ruler of elderly people, the Moon is natural ruler of women.

Nocturnal Chart
A chart drawn up during the night, when the Sun is below the horizon, is a nocturnal chart.

Nocturnal Planet
The Moon, Venus and Mars are nocturnal planets and exercise their power during the night.

Nocturnal Sign
Taurus, Cancer, Virgo, Scorpio, Capricorn and Pisces are nocturnal signs.

Occidental
A planet rising after the Sun in the morning is said to be occidental.

Orb
The distance around a planet or luminary, where it is able to exert an influence, is called its orb. Outside its orb, the influence of a planet or luminary comes to an end.

Oriental
A planet rising before the Sun in the morning is said to be oriental.

Partill
An exact aspect between planets, luminaries or other celestial bodies is a partill aspect. The Sun in five degrees of Leo makes a partill trine with Jupiter in five degrees of Sagittarius. A partill aspect is very strong.

Peregrine
A planet or luminary in a sign and degree, where it has no essential dignity, either through its domicile, exaltation, triplicity, term or face, nor any dignity through one of the stronger mutual receptions, is referred to as peregrine.

Perfection
When two or more planets, or luminaries, which are significators in the Question, make an exact or partill aspect with each other, this signifies a perfection of the matter enquired about (other testimonies supporting).

Platick
An aspect, which takes place within the moiety of the joint orbs between planets or luminaries, is called platick. The platick aspect is weaker than the partill aspect.

Prohibition
This is a method by which the perfection of an aspect between significators is prevented.

Querent
This is the term used to describe the person asking the Question. The Querent is usually signified by the ascendant and the ruler of the ascendant.

Quesited
This is the term used to describe the person, thing or matter enquired about. In any Question concerning a husband or wife, for example, the seventh house and the ruler of the seventh house would usually represent the Quesited.

Reception
Where a planet or luminary is positioned in the dignity of another, it is received by that planet. Jupiter in Libra is received by Venus being in her domicile. Venus in Leo is received by the Sun, being in his domicile. Reception can take place between any of the dignities of the planet. The receiving planet is the dispositor of the received planet. To be effective, reception usually requires an applying aspect to be in operation.

Refranation
This is a method by which the perfection of an aspect between significators is prevented. See also chapter fifteen.

Regiomontanus
This is a method of house division thought to have been created by Regiomontanus, although some authorities claim that the method was in use for centuries before and that he simply popularised the mathematical concepts of Abraham Ibn Ezra.[3] The Regiomontanus house system is frequently used in Horary astrology and is the system used in this book.

Retrograde
A planet moving backwards from three degrees to two degrees to one degree is retrograde. A planet retrograde can be unfortunate in its effect.

Sect
A sect is a division between planets and luminaries, according to whether they belong to the solar diurnal sect (the Sun, Jupiter, Saturn and Mercury), or the lunar nocturnal sect (Venus, Mars, the Moon).

Separation
When two planets, or luminaries, have been in a conjunction or an aspect and are moving away from each other, they are separating. An aspect between two bodies which has passed exactitude even by just one minute, but is still within orbs, is separating.

Significator
A planet, luminary, house or sign, which is associated with the matter enquired about, is a significator. The Querent's significator is usually the ascendant, the ascendant ruler and the Moon. A significator is a "symbol of" the person enquiring and of the person, thing or matter enquired about.

Sinister
An aspect made forward in the order of the signs is a sinister aspect: the Sun in Aries makes a sinister trine with Jupiter in Leo.

Stationary
When a planet does not move at all, neither forwards nor backwards, it is stationary. Thereafter, the planet's direction will change: either from direct motion to retrograde motion or from retrograde motion to direct motion.

Succedent House
The second, fifth, eighth and eleventh houses are succedent houses.

Sunbeams
A planet or other celestial body within about eight to seventeen degrees away from the Sun is said to be under sunbeams. The exact distance, which was thought to be necessary for a planet to be under sunbeams, varies between different authorities. But it is agreed that any planet (or the Moon) is more afflicted when moving towards sunbeams than when moving away.

Superior Planet
Mars, Jupiter and Saturn are the superior planets, or the Superiors.

Terms
Subsections within each sign, where each of the planets has a rulership, are called a planet's terms.

Testimony
The circumstances particular to a planet or luminary in the chart are referred to as the testimony (or indications) of that planet. For example, the Moon in Cancer in the tenth house has two testimonies of good fortune, being in her own domicile and angular. If however, she is in conjunction with Saturn, this is a testimony of misfortune.

Translation of Light
Where two planets or luminaries are not in aspect, but a swifter planet (or luminary) separates from one and moves to an aspect with the second, this helps to bring about perfection and is called translation.

Triplicity
A group of three signs, which are all of the same nature, form a triplicity. Aries, Leo and Sagittarius belong to the fire triplicity; Taurus, Virgo and Capricorn belong to the earth triplicity; Cancer, Scorpio and Pisces belong to the water triplicity; Gemini, Libra and Aquarius belong to the air triplicity.

Via Combusta
This is the area of the zodiac somewhere between fifteen degrees of Libra and fifteen degrees of Scorpio, although not all astrologers agree on the exact distance. It is believed to be an area of misfortune. When the Moon is found in this position the astrologer must be cautious when giving judgement. Some authorities believe that the Moon in the Via Combusta renders the chart unreadable.

Void of Course
If the Moon, the Sun or any planet has separated from an aspect and makes no further aspect in the sign where it is placed, before departing and moving into the next sign, it is void of course.

Wild
If a planet or luminary makes no aspect whatsoever in any particular sign it is called wild. This is more likely to occur with the Inferiors and very unlikely with the Superiors, especially Saturn.

Zodiac
The ecliptic is divided into twelve signs, the first of which is Aries, the last of which is Pisces.

References

1. Abraham Ibn Ezra, *The Beginning of Wisdom*. Ed. Raphael Levy and Francisco Cantera. John Hopkins Press and Oxford University Press, 1939, reprinted by Ascella Publications, pp. 210-211.
2. William Lilly, *Christian Astrology*, p.227.
3. J. D. North, *Horoscopes and History*, pp. 33, 44, Warburg Institute, London, 1986.

*   The nodes are the points where the ecliptic is intersected by the orbits of the planets, particularly by that of the Moon. Where the moving body crosses from north to south is the descending node (cauda draconis). Where the moving body crosses from south to north it is called the ascending body (caput draconis). These points are not fixed. They have a motion of their own in the zodiac.

** In this book, Lilly's table of dignities is the point of reference (based on Ptolemy).

PART ONE

METHODOLOGY: ANCIENT AND MEDIEVAL ASTROLOGICAL DOCTRINE

We learn from the unanimous consent of Philosophers and Professors of Theology, as well as from the Egyptians, Arabians, Persians, Medes, and other very extensive nations, that this science was cultivated, in the first place, among all the natural sciences, by kings and the greatest princes, and it was also held in the highest honour; the truth of which is found in several places among their historical annals.

Placidus de Titus, Primum Mobile

1

THE PLANETS

Referring to Placido's *Fourth Thesis*, Michael Baigent[1] tells us about an ancient idea originally put forward by the Babylonians and repeated by Ptolemy much later: "If the stars or other celestial phenomena cannot be seen then they cannot have any effect". According to Baigent, Placido's reasoning appears to be that if the stars are not visible to mankind, it follows that their light cannot be falling upon us: there is "no connection so there is no effect". The ancient astrologers believed that celestial bodies could only have an influence over the places from where they could be seen. As a consequence, only the seven bodies which could be seen from earth were used in their astrology (the five planets and the two luminaries).* I would suggest that these planets are the only ones which should be used today, despite the growing number of new celestial bodies presented in journals and periodicals from time to time, not to mention the old faithfuls, Uranus, Neptune and Pluto.

In this book I only consider Saturn, Jupiter, Mars, Venus, Mercury, the Sun, the Moon, Dragon's Head, Dragon's Tail (the north and south nodes) and the Lot of Fortune. With only these as their main points of reference, William Lilly, as well as astrologers before and after him, produced beautiful and masterly judgements.

Saturn, Jupiter and Mars are called the *superior* planets, because they are placed above the orb of the Sun. They are the ponderous, heavier, slow moving planets. Venus, Mercury and the Moon are called the *inferior* planets, because they are placed under the orb of the Sun. The Inferiors move more swiftly than the Superiors. Saturn, Jupiter and the Sun are *diurnal* planets, exercising their power during the day. Mars, Venus and the Moon are *nocturnal* planets, exercising their power during the night. Mercury can be either one or the other depending on his sign or aspect with other planets.

Al Biruni tells us that every planet assists those which resemble it. The diurnal planets ask for assistance from the diurnal planets; the nocturnal planets ask for assistance from the nocturnal planets. He also explains that

> The sun is lord of the day and the moon of the night, because their influence is exerted during these periods. Every planet which is under the horizon during its own period is without influence.[2]

---

* In this book, where the text refers to planets, this includes luminaries unless stated otherwise.

Planetary Nature

By nature Saturn is cold and dry, Jupiter is hot and moist, Mars is hot and dry, the Sun is hot and dry, Venus is cold and moist, Mercury is cold and dry and the Moon is cold and moist. According to Al Biruni, "The planets always influence whatever is receptive under them... the results of their actions incline in different directions":[3]

Saturn	extreme cold and dryness
Jupiter	moderate heat and moisture
Mars	extreme heat and dryness
Sun	not immoderate heat and dryness, less than characterizes Mars, the heat being greater than the dryness.
Venus	moderate cold and moisture, the latter predominant.
Mercury	cold and dryness, the latter rather stronger, which influence however may be altered by association with another star.
Moon	moderate cold and moisture, the one sometimes dominating the other. For the moon alters in each quarter in accordance with the extrinsic heat it is receiving from the rays of the sun.

Morin suggests that it is difficult to discover the true nature and the essential properties of any planet because its manifestations are modified by so many other factors. Morin tells us, however, that a planet passing through its own zodiacal sign and not connected to any other planet through a conjunction or other aspect, "manifests its true nature free from modifying influences". In this instance a planet's specific effects appear to be reinforced as though they were doubled.

Morin tells us that a planet also produces different effects according to its position by house. In the example of the Sun these effects are of a "Solar nature". As a result, "whatever is common to all these effects must be due to the specific nature of the Sun" and similarly with the other planets. Presumably with the Moon the effect would be of a lunar nature. Morin explains that this sort of procedure is less complicated with the Sun and the Moon because each only rules one sign. However, the remaining planets each rule two signs, both of which are different in their nature.[4]

Planetary Joys

Planetary joys are explored later in this book in chapter six, but I include just a brief summary here.

A planet is said to have joy when it is in a position where it is particularly strong and comfortable. Bonatti tells us that the planets can have joy by house position, by position in a sign, by chart position and by position in a particular quarter of the chart.[5]

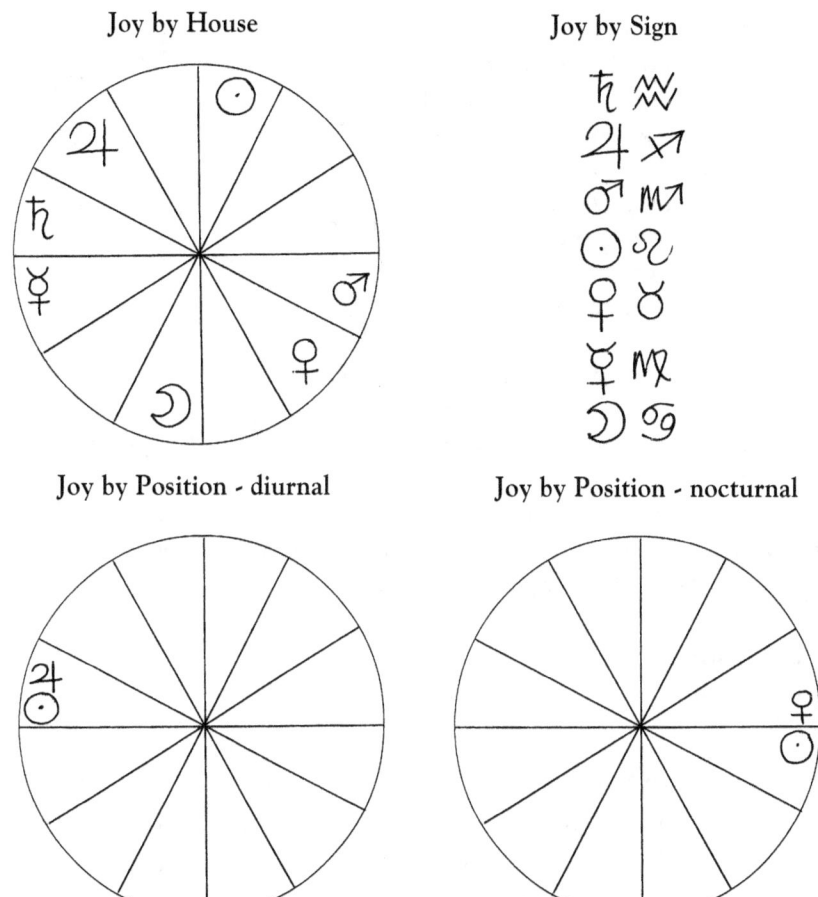

Joy by House Position
Mercury has joy in the first house, the Moon in the third house, Venus in the fifth house, Mars in the sixth house, the Sun in the ninth house, Jupiter in the eleventh house and Saturn in the twelfth house.

Joy by Sign Position
Saturn joys in the sign of Aquarius, Jupiter in Sagittarius, Venus in Taurus, the Moon in Cancer, Mercury in Virgo, Mars in Scorpio and the Sun in Leo. The assignation of joy by sign differed among various astrologers.

Joy by Chart Position
The diurnal planets, Saturn, Jupiter, Sun and Mercury joy in diurnal houses in the east and oriental of the Sun near the ascendant. The nocturnal planets, Mars, Venus, Moon, Mercury, joy in nocturnal houses in the west and occidental of the Sun, near to the cusp of the seventh house. Note that Bonatti implies here that Mercury can be assigned to either the diurnal or nocturnal sect.

Joy by Quarter or Quadrant

The Superiors, Saturn, Jupiter, Mars have joy in masculine quarters (the cusp of tenth house to the cusp of ascendant and from the cusp of the fourth house to the cusp of the seventh house). Among the Inferiors, Venus and the Moon have joy in feminine quarters (the cusp of the ascendant to the cusp of the fourth house and from the cusp of the seventh house to the cusp of the tenth house). Bonatti confirms that Mercury "delights" when with masculine planets in masculine quarters and with feminine planets in feminine quarters.

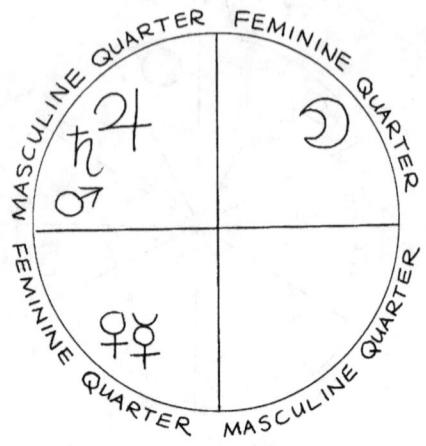

Among these planetary joys there appear to be some contradictions, mainly because Mars is Superior but is nocturnal. As a Superior, Mars prefers to be oriental, but as a nocturnal planet, Mars prefers to be occidental.

Planetary Motion

According to Lilly, the average daily and maximum daily motion of the planets is as listed below.[6]

Planet	Average daily motion	Maximum daily motion
Saturn	2 minutes 1 second	about 6 mins
Jupiter	4 minutes 59 seconds	about 14 mins
Mars	31 minutes 27 seconds	about 44 mins
Sun	59 minutes 8 seconds	about 61 mins 6 secs
Venus	59 minutes 8 seconds	about 82 mins
Mercury	59 minutes 8 seconds	about 1 degree 40 mins
Moon	13 degrees 10 mins 36 secs	about 15 degrees 2 mins

Planets and Colours[7]

Saturn	black
Jupiter	a colour mixed with red and green
Mars	red, or iron colour
Sun	yellow or yellow purple
Venus	white or purple
Mercury	sky-colour or blue-ish
Moon	a colour spotted with white and other mixed colours

Fortunes and Infortunes

In his *Tetrabiblos*, Ptolemy tells us that Jupiter, Venus and the Moon are beneficent because of their "tempered nature and because they abound in the hot and the moist…" Saturn and Mars produce the opposite effects: Saturn because of his excessive cold and Mars because of his excessive dryness. Ptolemy tells us that the Sun and Mercury have "both powers, because they have a common nature…"[8]

A *Fortune* is a planet whose natural influence is that of moderation and balance. An *Infortune* is a planet whose natural influence is that of extremes and imbalance. In this book a Fortune refers to Jupiter or Venus; an Infortune refers to Saturn or Mars. However, where the text refers to a benefic, in a general sense this refers to any planet well placed in essential dignity. A malefic refers to an Infortune in its detriment, fall or peregrine. A Fortune not essentially dignified doesn't necessarily become unfortunate, just less fortunate. I refer the reader to Terms of Art which precedes this chapter.

Al Biruni tells us that "any planet which has its two qualities in an extreme degree is maleficent; in a moderate degree, beneficent".

On the whole the effects of the beneficent planets may be described as virtue, peace, plenty, good disposition, cheerfulness, repose, goodness and learning. On the other hand

> …the maleficent effect destruction, tyranny, depravity, covetousness, stupidity, severity, anxiety, ingratitude, shamelessness, meanness, conceit and all kinds of bad qualities.[9]

Bonatti explains that Saturn and Mars are naturally unfortunate, Saturn because of an excess of cold, Mars because of an excess of heat. They signify "evil and damage and hindrance" unless he says, they receive the significator or the Moon through domicile, or exaltation, or two of the smaller dignities. If Saturn or Mars themselves are significators, in this instance they "bridle their malice" and will not weaken or hinder another planet if they are in reception with that planet, no matter what the aspect is between them. However, if there is no reception, "their malice is increased" especially if they have an opposition or square with that planet.[10]

If the aspect is with a sextile or trine "the mischief is less…" Bonatti quotes Zael who has suggested that although in this instance (with a sextile or trine) the Infortunes "lay aside or restrain their malice" in fact claims Bonatti, his meaning was "only that they were not then so violent, and intended not that their malice was wholly abated".[11]

Bonatti explains that Jupiter and Venus are fortunate by nature. They are temperate and have no malice. They do not wish to hurt anyone, although it can happen now and again by accident. Their intention is always to help, whether they have any type of reception or not. However, it is, of course, a lot better if they are have a reception. A trine or sextile with one of the Fortunes is more advantageous than the square. The square is better than the opposition.[12]

Al Biruni confirms that Saturn and Mars are "maleficent", especially Saturn. Jupiter and Venus are "beneficent", especially Jupiter. According to Al Biruni "Jupiter confronts Saturn in clearing-up unfortunate complications as Venus does Mars". He tells us that the Sun can be either beneficent or maleficent. The Sun is fortunate when distant from another planet and when in a trine or sextile aspect. The Sun is unfortunate when near to another planet and in conjunction.[13]

Bonatti claims that the Sun is generally fortunate and can be called a Fortune, no matter what aspect he makes with another planet. However, the opposition of the Sun with a planet is unfortunate and if the aspect is a conjunction, the Sun becomes an Infortune. This is because any planet in conjunction with the Sun is combust. If, however, the planet is in the heart of the Sun the planet is "fortified" and is particularly strong, being *cazimi* of the Sun. I would agree that in harmonious aspect the Sun is most fortunate and I have not found an author who disagrees.[14]

In the case of either Mercury or the Moon, Bonatti explains that it is important to consider which planets they are joined to, because in these instances they will have the same signification as that planet. This is because they are "of a convertible nature".[15] Al Biruni agrees that Mercury can be either very fortunate or the reverse. Mercury assists whatever planet is near to it. He tells us that when Mercury is alone, he is inclined to "beneficence". This increases in proportion to the proximity between Mercury and the other planet and decreases in proportion to the distance between them.

Referring to the Moon, Al Biruni confirms that "in virtue of its own nature the moon is fortunate..." However, the Moon's position in relation to the other planets changes quickly owing to her speed of motion. In a general sense, however, the Moon should be considered as a Fortune because she does a lot of good if well-placed and only a little bad if poorly placed.[16]

Change in Planetary Indications

Whether a planet exerts a malefic or benefic influence depends on a number of factors: planets that are naturally either a Fortune or Infortune can be converted into their opposite by particular circumstances in the chart. It cannot be assumed that Venus and Jupiter will always produce good results, nor that Saturn and Mars will always produce bad results. In *Carmen Astrologicum* Dorotheus tells us that each planet is benefic when in its own domicile, triplicity or exaltation, so the beneficial effects of the planet are amplified. In the same way, when a malefic is in its own domicile, exaltation or triplicity, its malefic influence is decreased.[17]

Al Biruni tells us that the *indications* of a planet do not always remain constant. This, he says, is because a planet is dependent on its relations to the various signs, to the other planets, to the fixed stars, to the Sun and to its distance from the earth. For example, Al Biruni explains that Saturn which is dry when rising, becomes moist when setting.

In a general sense Al Biruni tells us that the effects attributable to the various "situations" of a planet, take two forms: one fortunate, the other unfortunate. If, for example, Saturn which rules matters of the land, is in a fortunate condition, it follows that issues relating to agriculture will improve: there will be good luck and increased profits. However, if the condition of Saturn is unfortunate, there will be disappointment, together with no profit and failure.[18]

Morin tells us that the "manifestations" of each planet are not always constant. Each planet produces different effects on, for example, metals, plants, animals and men. A planet's action also "varies in form" depending on its sign, aspect and so on. Each planet produces different effects according to the planets it is connected to. The effects of any planetary connection are further modified according to the aspect connecting the two planets. A planet's action also differs according to each house and also according to its rulership over any particular house.[19]

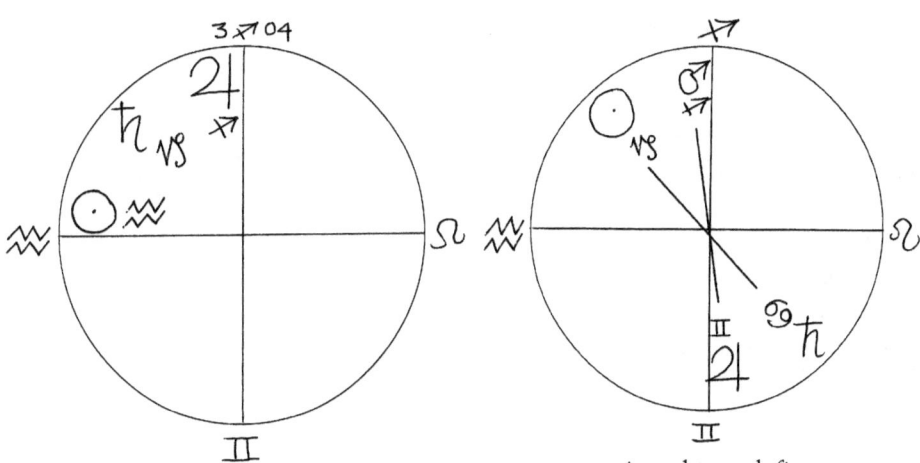

Changes in Indications for Saturn and Jupiter

♄ and ♃ benefic
♄ in his domicile ♃ in his domicile

♄ and ♃ malefic
♃ in his detriment and afflicted by his opposition with ♂.
♄ in his detriment and afficted by his opposition with ☉

Friendship or Enmity between Planets

Although friendship or enmity between planets can be in accordance with the sign they rule, Al Biruni explains that there are different theories on the matter. Some astrologers, for example, base friendship or enmity on the *temperament and nature* of the planets themselves. In this instance, Saturn and Jupiter would be regarded as inimical because

> ...the one is dark, maleficent and extremely distant, while the other is shining, beneficent and only moderately distant.

He tells us that other astrologers base it on their *elementary qualities* for example, the fiery ones being "inimical" to the watery, the airy to the earthy. He adds that other astrologers base the issue of friendship or enmity on the relative situations of the domicile or exaltation of the planets. If their aspects in this instance are "inimical" it follows that "their lords are also inimical".

> The astrologers of our day however, lay little stress on the friendship or enmity of the planets in the matter of judicial astrology. The Hindus on the other hand regard them as equally important or more so than the domiciles and exaltations...[20]

These are set out below[21] and it is important to note that they differ significantly from those used by William Lilly in *Christian Astrology*.[22]

Saturn
Al Biruni
Friends: Venus, Mercury
Enemies: Mars, Sun, Moon
Indifferent: Jupiter

Lilly
Friends: Jupiter, Sun, Mercury
Enemies: Mars, Venus

Jupiter
Al Biruni
Friends: Mars, Sun, Moon
Enemies: Venus, Mercury
Indifferent: Saturn

Lilly
Friends: Sun, Venus, Mercury, Moon, Saturn
Enemies: Mars

Mars
Al Biruni
Friends: Jupiter, Sun, Moon
Enemies: Mercury
Indifferent: Saturn, Venus

Lilly
Friends: Venus
Enemies: Sun, Mercury, Moon, Saturn, Jupiter

Sun
Al Biruni
Friends: Jupiter, Mars, Moon
Enemies: Saturn, Venus
Indifferent: Mercury

Lilly
Friends: Mercury, Mars, Jupiter, Venus, Moon
Enemies: Saturn

Venus
Al Biruni
Friends: Saturn, Mercury
Enemies: Sun, Moon
Indifferent: Jupiter, Mars

Lilly
Friends: Sun, Moon, Mercury, Mars, Jupiter
Enemies: Saturn

Mercury
Al Biruni
Friends: Sun, Venus
Enemies: Moon
Indifferent: Saturn, Jupiter, Mars

Lilly
Friends: Jupiter, Venus, Saturn
Enemies: Mars, Sun, Moon

Moon
Al Biruni
Friends: Sun, Mercury
Enemies: None
Indifferent: Saturn, Jupiter, Mars, Venus

Lilly
Friends: Venus, Sun, Mercury, Jupiter
Enemies: Saturn, Mars

Harmony or Disharmony between Planets

Morin refers to "harmony and disharmony" among planets. This harmony or disharmony results either in their "constructive or destructive cooperation". There is harmony between planets sharing one of the *vital qualities*, for example hot and wet. From this point of view, the Sun and Jupiter harmonise, Jupiter and Venus harmonise, Venus and the Moon harmonise. Planets which contain *antagonistic qualities* are mutually hostile, for example, the Sun and Saturn (one is hot, the other is cold), Saturn and the Moon (one is dry, the other is wet), Saturn and Venus (one is dry, the other is wet) and most especially the Moon and Mars, which he claims are "totally opposite in terms of elemental qualities". In a similar fashion, the 'cooperation' of two planets which produces a harmful excess of one of these qualities is also destructive, such as the Sun and Mars (excess of hot and dry) Saturn and the Moon (excess of cold), Saturn and Mars (excess of dry).

However, Morin explains that there is *accord* between the Sun and Jupiter with regard to life and success, between Jupiter and Venus with regard to good luck and wealth or children and friends, between the Moon and Venus with regard to affairs of love, marriage and the spouse. The 'cooperation' of Jupiter and Saturn can also be beneficial in that it brings about prudence, a serious intellect and the ability to achieve great things. 'Cooperation' between Mercury and Saturn gives a profound and penetrating mind; between Mercury and Mars an active mind.

On the other hand, Morin confirms that the 'cooperation' of Mercury and the Moon can be harmful, because it provokes deceitful habits, impudence and rash behaviour. 'Cooperation' between the Sun and Mars can result in arrogance. 'Cooperation' between Venus and Mars is not easy, because Venus rules love affairs, peace, and tranquillity, whereas Mars "incites hatred, quarrels and toil". 'Cooperation' between Saturn and Venus does not promote physical beauty. 'Cooperation' between the Sun and Saturn is unhelpful from the point of view of reputation and success, unless, claims Morin, Saturn is "specially determined in the Chart and in good Zodiacal state". What Morin calls the 'mutual cooperation' between the two Infortunes Saturn and Mars is very destructive, because of the dangers it can cause, as well as the moral depravity, the bad luck and so on.[23]

Principal Signification and Analogies

In the same way as each zodiacal sign and house is inherently associated with a particular part of the body, a particular colour, event, item, group of people, or individual and so on, each planet has similar sorts of associations, which remain the same regardless of that planet's position in the chart.

However, each planet can also take on the signification of a particular person, matter or event by virtue of its specific placement by house and by rulership of a house (whether it rules the house where it is located and/or whether it rules another house). A planet's essential dignity does not change whatever its location in the chart, whereas accidental dignity depends totally on a planet's location in the chart. Accidental dignity is dependent on a planet's relation with other planets, houses, its position by house, aspects with the Sun, Moon, nodes and the Lot of Fortune. Essential and accidental dignity is explored further in chapters six and seven.

In the following section[24] I consider the various planetary significations put forward by different authorities. This is by no means a comprehensive listing of the significations; it merely serves as a guide to highlight some of the similarities or differences between various authors. Where a planet or luminary is referred to as being in good or bad "zodiacal state", this is attributable to Morin. Morin's definition of a planet in a good zodiacal state is when it has dignity in its domicile, exaltation, or triplicity, when it is oriental of the Sun, occidental of the Moon, free from any bad aspects of the

Infortunes and is in rapid or direct motion. Such a planet is regarded as a benefic, whatever house it occupies and even more so if it is helped by good aspects with the Fortunes. A planet in bad zodiacal state is in the opposite condition.[25]

Family Ties and Social Connections

Saturn	Old people: ancestors, the grandfather, the father, servants, secret enemies. Older brothers (Abu Ma'shar)[26]
Jupiter	People that direct and manage. Sometimes children. Grandchildren (Abu Ma'shar).
Mars	The husband, older brothers, open enemies. Middle brothers (Abu Ma'shar).
Sun	Father, the husband.
Venus	The wife, mother, sisters, daughters, mistresses. Younger sisters (Abu Ma'shar).
Mercury	Younger brothers, servants, domestics.
Moon	The mother, wife, daughters, widows. Maternal aunts, older sisters, (Abu Ma'shar).

Occupation and Profession

Saturn *According to Morin*
In good zodiacal State: Men of science and research: theologians, philosophers, mathematicians, treasurers, sculptors, architects, mining engineers.
In mediocre zodiacal state: Farmers, metallurgists, potters and brick makers, curriers, monks, hermits.
In bad zodiacal state: Sorcerers, chiropractors, beggars, all work which is mean and dirty, hang-men.
According to Lilly[27]
Miners, potters, brick makers, shepherds, plumbers and funeral directors, beggars, labourers, clowns, monks.
According to Abu Ma'shar
Eunuchs, slaves, the rabble.

Jupiter *According to Morin*
In good zodiacal state: Men in government, statesmen, governors, advisors, chancellors, diplomats, politicians, magistrates, prefects, mayors. Great dignitaries of the church: popes, cardinals, archbishops and bishops, abbots, leaders of religious orders, dignitaries of the court.
In bad zodiacal state: School-masters, gym-teachers (coaches).

	According to Lilly
	Judges, senators, councillors, bishops, priests, ministers, cardinals, chancellors, young scholars and students in a university or college, lawyers.
Mars	*According to Morin*
	In good zodiacal state: Military men, hunters, lawyers, doctors, foundry workers.
	In bad zodiacal state: Butchers, tanners, pirates, robbers, executioners.
	According to Lilly
	Princes ruling by tyranny and oppression, tyrants, usurpers, new conquerors. Generals of armies, all types of soldiers, doctors, apothecaries, alchemists, sergeants, bailiffs, thieves, bakers, barbers, tanners, butchers, watchmakers, tailors, cooks, carpenters.
	According to Abu Ma'shar
	Horsemen, commanders.
Sun	*According to Morin*
	Popes, emperors, kings, princes, governors, magnates, nobles, all those invested with honour and dignity, ambassadors.
	According to Lilly
	Kings, princes, emperors, dukes, earls, barons, lieutenants, magistrates, gentlemen in general, Justices of the Peace, High Sheriffs, majors, huntsmen, stewards of noble-mens' houses, principal magistrate of any town or city, goldsmiths, pewterers, coppersmiths, minters of money.
	According to Abu Ma'shar
	Judges, kings, leaders, nobility, communities of men.
Venus	*According to Morin*
	In good zodiacal state: Artists, musicians, initiates into sacred orders, pharmacists, perfumers, weavers, jewellers.
	In bad zodiacal state: Courtesans, madams and female beggars.
	According to Lilly
	Painters, jewellers, embroiderers, wives, mothers, virgins, musicians, picture-drawers, silk-men, linen-drapers, artists and anything to do with making clothes.
	According to Abu Ma'shar
	Whores, lesbians, dancers, musicians.
Mercury	*According to Morin*
	In good zodiacal state: Mathematicians, geometers, astrologers, astronomers, philosophers, orators, men of letters, poets, painters,

secretaries, writers, merchants, inventors, skilled craftsmen.
In bad zodiacal state: Thieves, forgers, counterfeiters
According to Lilly
All educated people. Philosophers, mathematicians, astrologers, secretaries, poets, school teachers, painters, ambassadors, solicitors, sometimes thieves and messengers. Stationers, printers, exchangers of money, attorneys, solicitors, tailors, carriers, footmen.
According to Abu Ma'shar
Men of science, surveyors, astrologers, poets, sorcerers, writers.

Moon *According to Morin*
Queens, princesses, widows, travellers, fishermen, hunters, the public.
According to Lilly
Queens, countesses, ladies, all manner of women, travellers, sailors, mariners, pilgrims, fishermen, fisherwomen, brewers, messengers, coachmen, huntsmen, millers, drunkards, watermen and water bearers, common people, midwives, nurses.
According to Abu Ma'shar
Noble women, wet nurses, messengers, bookkeepers, fugitives.

Rank, Wealth and Life-events

Saturn *According to Morin*
In good zodiacal state: High office, positions in government, large material resources.
In bad zodiacal state: Social downfall, poverty, servitude, failure and misfortune in all enterprises, secret enemies, infamy, prison, exile, a miserable end.

Jupiter *According to Morin*
In good zodiacal state: Freedom, wealth, rewards, fame, friendship, happy marriage, reputation, renown, numerous offspring and happiness through them. Profits, reward and success in all enterprises.
In bad zodiacal state: Almost the same advantages as in good zodiacal state, but sharply diminished.

Mars *According to Morin*
In good zodiacal state: The friendship of military men, military authority, victory and triumph.
In bad zodiacal state: Enemies, quarrels, duels, battles, unlucky military actions, waste of fortune, money, dissipation, extortion, destruction, ambush, theft, murderers, adulterers, rapists and prisons.

According to Abu Ma'shar
Injustice, oppression, war, haughtiness; punishment, hardship, fugitives, controversy, slander, journeys, absence from home, adultery, indulgence in love-making, abortion. Power, fires and things which happen unexpectedly.

Sun

According to Morin
In good zodiacal state: Glory, renown, high rank, honorary missions, public responsibility, royal distinction, ecclesiastical honour, powerful friends and posthumous fame.
In bad zodiacal state: Powerful enemies, failure in all enterprises. Or, acquisition to a certain extent of the preceding advantages, which become a source of misfortune.
According to Abu Ma'shar
Wealth, eloquence, cleanliness, judgement, religion, the life to come, powers over evil men. The Sun brings good fortune, it brings bad fortune; at one time it raises, another time it brings down.

Venus

According to Morin
In good zodiacal state: Benevolence and sympathy for the whole world, profit and success, lucky love affairs, happy marriage, numerous offspring who will be a source of happiness and satisfaction. Rewards.
In bad zodiacal state: The preceding things, but they will become a source of unhappiness, or will be achieved very incompletely.
According to Abu Ma'shar
Happiness, chivalry, luxury, love of amusement, love-making, wearing of crowns, religious devotion, adherence to religion and the practice of piety.
Weakness of the soul.

Mercury

According to Morin
In good zodiacal state: Profitable enterprises and transactions, lucrative missions, advantageous contracts, remarkable and profitable inventions, rewards and profit from public responsibility, numerous and useful friendships.
In bad zodiacal state: The contrary of the preceding: secret but useless research, deceptions and general misfortune, forgery, instability in a position which always fluctuates, a doubtful end.
According to Abu Ma'shar
Divinity, revelation to prophets, omens by birds, sorcery, receiving and giving, patience, friendliness with one who is suitable, assistance.
Little joy, corruptions to wealth, swindling.

Moon   *According to Morin*
In good zodiacal state: Renown, even fame, wealth, happiness, honorary and fruitful missions, numerous offspring, happy marriage, royal honours, friendship of magnates and powerful people.
In bad zodiacal state: The preceding things, but greatly diminished, and becoming a source of unhappiness. Life in general, full of changes and uncertainty.
According to Abu Ma'shar
The beginning of all activities, good fortune in one's livelihood, jurisprudence, the upbringing of children.
Rumours, lying, slander, a friend does not keep his secret, profusion in food.

Natural Properties and Signification

Each planet moves along the zodiac at a different speed and completes a three hundred and sixty degree cycle over a different length of time. At the same time the earth continues its daily rotation, causing each planet to appear as if it is rising or setting on a daily basis.

The information below is a brief listing of the properties, influences or effects of the Sun, Moon and planets. In an overall sense, astrologers of the past agreed on these significations, with just a few small differences, some of which I have included. In fact Lilly and Sibley's significations are very similar, almost identical in places!

Saturn

Saturn takes about twenty-nine and a half years to complete a cycle, spending about two and a half years in each sign. Gadbury refers to Saturn as "Superiorum Altissimus, the highest of all the seven".[28]

Sibley tells us that Saturn is "the most supreme, or most elevated, of all the planets, being placed between Jupiter and the firmament..."

> ... if this planet is well dignified at the time of birth, the native will be of an acute and penetrating imagination; in his conduct, austere; in words, reserved; in speaking and giving, very spare; in labour, patient; in arguing or disputing, grave; in obtaining the goods of this life, studious and solicitous; in his attachments, either to wife or friend, constant and unequivocal; in prejudice or resentment, rigid and inexorable.[29]

The opposite is true if Saturn is ill-dignified. Dariot tells us that in this instance, Saturn is "an enemy and destroyer of the nature and life of man..."[30] However, Sibley explains that if a kingdom, city, town, principality or family "take its rise" when Saturn is essentially and accidentally dignified, it is probable that they will "continue in honour and prosperity, without any material alteration for the space of four hundred and sixty five years".[31] Lilly states that

> Saturn Oriental and well disposed, that is strong and in Reception, gives great fortune in building, planting trees requiring a long growth, in manuring ground, erecting waterworks and the like.[32]

Diurnal Motion[33]	3, 4, 5 or 6 minutes.
Rules	Capricorn by night, Aquarius by day, the air triplicity by day. Has his exaltation in Libra (his degree of exaltation is 21), his fall in Aries, his detriment in Leo.
Nature	Diurnal, cold and dry, melancholy, earthly, masculine, solitary. Saturn is called the *Greater Infortune*. Al Biruni calls Saturn "extremely cold and dry... disagreeable and astringent... offensively acid, stinking".[34]
When well-dignified	Profound, reserved, patient, studious, austere. Abu Ma'shar associates Saturn with trustworthiness in speech, intelligence, profundity of thought and much wealth.[35]
When ill-dignified	Envious, jealous, mistrustful, sluggish, suspicious, stubborn, malicious, never content, cares little for the church, eats too much, has big shoulders, is seldom rich.
	Hatred, cunning, artifice, perfidy, every activity of evil, fear, grief, sadness (Abu Ma'shar).
Appearance	Pale complexion, small eyes, broad forehead, dark hair, sometimes stooping when walking or standing. Thin, rough skin, hairy body, lean, sometimes knock kneed, coughing.
Sickness	Illnesses of the right ear, teeth, fears and fantasies.
	Melancholy and nervous affections, pains in limbs and joints, gout, rheumatism, insanity, fractures, deafness (Sibley).[36]
Tastes	Sour, bitter, sharp.
Herbs	Hemlock, poppy, nightshade.
Plants and trees	Willow, yew tree, pine tree.
Animals	Cat, dog, elephant.
	Ass, cat, hare, mouse, dog, wolf, bear, elephant, scorpion, adder, serpent, toad, hog, all creeping things produced by putrefaction, tortoise, eel, shell fish (Sibley).
Birds	Crow, lapwing, owl, bat, crane, peacock, thrush, blackbird, ostrich, cuckoo (Sibley).
Places	Woods, obscure valleys, caves, dens, holes, mountains, places where people have been buried, churchyards, ruins, coalmines, sinks, dirty or stinking muddy places and wells.
	Subterranean places, mines, pits, cesspools, prisons, cemeteries, the wilderness, the desert (Morin).

	Deserts, pinewoods, places near yew trees, caves, dirty or dark places in houses, doors and thresholds (Barclay).[37]
Minerals	Lead.
	Diamonds and all hard black stones, as well as ordinary stones that are grey (Barclay).
Weather	Cloudy, dark and cold.
Orb	Nine or ten degrees before and after an aspect.
Countries	Germany, Emilia Romana in Italy.
Day of the week	Saturday
Age	Old men and anything else which is old like old trees, plants and living creatures.

Jupiter

Jupiter takes just under twelve years to complete a cycle of the zodiac passing through one sign per year. Sibley calls Jupiter the *Greater Fortune* and tells us

> When he presides over a nativity, he gives an erect and tall stature, a handsome rosy complexion, an oval visage, high forehead, large grey eyes, soft thick brown hair... his speech sober and manly, and his conversation grave and commanding.

If well dignified at birth, Sibley explains that Jupiter

> ... betokens most admirable manners and disposition to the native. He will be in general magnanimous, faithful and prudent, honourably aspiring after high deserts and noble actions, a lover of fair dealings, desirous of serving all men, just, honest, and religious... of affable manners and conversation; kind and affectionate to his family and friends; charitable and liberal... wise, prudent and virtuous...

Gadbury also refers to Jupiter as the "greater Fortune and the Author of Moderation, Justice, Temperance and Sobriety".[38] Dariot tells us that Jupiter is a "friend and preserver of the life and nature of man..."[39] Lilly states that Jupiter gives good luck in sciences such as the law or religion or perhaps through being made a bishop or a judge. This is of course, assuming that he is well placed.[40]

Diurnal Motion	8, 10, 12 or 14 minutes.
Rules	Sagittarius and Pisces, the fire triplicity during the night. Has his exaltation in Cancer (his degree of exaltation is 15), his fall in Capricorn, his detriment in Gemini and Virgo.
Nature	The Greater Fortune. He is the author of temperance, modesty, sobriety and justice.
When well-dignified	Magnanimous, faithful, honourable, a lover of fair dealings, religious, wonderfully indulgent, full of charity and godliness, just, liberal, indulgent, a reliever of the poor, thankful, virtuous, wise, prudent.

When ill-dignified	Hypocritically religious, ignorant, careless, dull. Abu Ma'shar associates Jupiter with the soul which nourishes, the explanation of dreams, trustworthiness, appetite for wealth, luck in character, the giving of alms, love of buildings and magnificent residences, keeping promises, jesting, adornment and much love-making.
Appearance	Upright, straight and tall, lovely complexion, oval face, full and fleshy, high forehead, large grey eyes, long feet, sober speech and grave. Jovial, thick hair (possibly black when Jupiter is combust), good broad teeth with some difference in the two front teeth. If Jupiter is in a fire sign, the hair gently curls, in a moist sign the body is fleshy and fat, in an air sign big and strong, in an earth sign, usually from a good family.
Diseases	Pleurisy, problems with the liver, left ear, inflammation of the lungs, palpitations of the heart, pain in the back, all diseases of the veins or ribs, wind, putrefaction in the blood. Cramps, fevers, palpitations of the heart (Sibley).
Tastes	Sweet or well scented odours. Nothing extreme or offensive. Sweet, bitter-sweet, delicious (Al Biruni).
Colours	Sea green or blue, ash colour, purple, a mixture of yellow and green.
Herbs	Cloves, sugar, nutmeg, strawberry, violet, pimpernel, flax, liquorish, mint, saffron.
Plants and trees	Cherry tree, olive, almond tree, pear tree, gooseberry, beech tree, fig tree. Sweet scents, large gentle animals, horses and whales. Figs, lime trees, mulberry and acanthus (Barclay).
Animals	Sheep, stag, doe, ox elephant, dragon, tiger, unicorn, mild and gentle beasts. Unicorn, doe, hart, stag, elephant, horse, sheep and all domestic animals (Sibley).
Birds	Lark, eagle, partridge, hen, peacock, bees, the stork.
Places	Altars of churches, wardrobes, courts of justice. Monuments and palaces, places used for the service of justice, churches, barracks, arsenals, forts, slaughter houses (Morin).
Mineral	Tin.
Precious stones	Amethyst, sapphire, hyacinth, topaz, marble and crystal.
Weather	Pleasant and healthy not windy.
Orb	Between nine and twelve degrees before and after any aspect.
Age	Of middle age.
Countries	Iran, Spain, Hungary.
Day of the week	Thursday.

Mars

Mars is the first of the Superior planets, whose orbit lies outside that of the earth. Because of this, Mars can be positioned at any angle with the Sun in the zodiac. Sibley tells us that "Mars is next located to Jupiter, and is the first planet above the Earth and Moon's orbit..." On average Mars spends about two months in each sign. Sibley explains that if Mars is well-dignified

> ...the native will inherit a courageous and invincible disposition; unsusceptible of fear or danger; hazarding his life on all occasions, and in all perils; subject to no reason in war or contention; unwilling to obey or submit to any superior... and yet prudent in the management and direction of his private concerns.

Gadbury refers to Mars as

> Superiorum Insimus, the lowest of the three highest planets... the lesser infortune... and indeed the Author of Strife, Quarrels, Controversies and Contentions.[41]

When well placed, Mars is associated with the leading forth of armies and good fortune in military affairs.[42]

Diurnal Motion	Between 32 and 44 minutes.
Rules	Aries and Scorpio, the water triplicity during the day and night. Has his exaltation in Capricorn (degree of exaltation 28), his fall in Cancer, his detriment in Taurus and Libra.
Nature	Masculine, nocturnal, hot and dry, cholerick and fiery. He is the *Lesser Infortune*, the author of quarrels, strife, and contention.
When well-dignified	Invincible in feats of war and courage, bold, confident, immovable, valiant, lover of war, obeys nobody.
When ill-dignified	Lover of slaughter and quarrels, murder, thievery, treacherous, furious, violent, a traitor, unthankful, a cheat.
Appearance	Strong, sturdy, big boned, lean, brown ruddy complexion, high colour, round face, red or sandy hair, sharp hazel eyes, bold, confident, active and fearless. Eyes sparkling and sharp, hair is reddish (this varies according to sign): in fire or air and with fixed stars of his own nature, the hair is a deep sandy red; in watery signs, the hair is sandy or fair; in earth signs, the hair is brown or sad chestnut.
	In the sign of Venus, there is flirting and womanising; in the signs of Mercury he could be a thief; in his own sign he quarrels; in the sign of the Sun he is lordly; in the sign of the Moon he is a drunkard.

Diseases	The gall, left ear, fevers, migraines, spots, pimples, blisters, jaundice, wounds, diseases in men's genitals, stones, scars, pock marks in the face, all wounds from iron, shingles.
	Blisters, ringworm, burnings, hot and feverish complaints in the head, small-pox, diabetes, diseases of the genitals, wounds, bruises by iron or fire, all effects proceeding from anger and passion (Sibley).
Tastes	Bitter, sharp.
Colour	Red or yellow fiery and shining.
	Dark red (Al Biruni).
Herbs	Pointed leaves, sharp, burning taste. Nettles, thistles, onions, brambles, garlic, radish, ginger. Plants which are red or reddish. Plants with sharp pointed leaves which taste hot and grow in dry places. Nettles, thistles, radish and prickly thorn trees (Barclay).
Trees	Thorn, Chestnut.
Animals	Panther, tiger, vulture, fox, ostrich, goat, wolf, leopard, ass, gnats, bear. Beasts which are ravenous and wild.
Birds	Hawk, owl, vulture, raven, crow. All ravenous fowle.
	Hawk, kite, raven, vulture, owl, cormorant, crow, magpie and all birds of prey (Sibley).
Places	Slaughter houses, places where bricks or charcoal are burned, chimneys, forges.
	Foundries, smithies, weapons, factories, metallurgical factories (Morin).
Minerals	Iron, antimony, arsenic, brimstone.
Stones	Red lead, blood stone.
Weather	Red clouds, thunder, lightning often after a long period of dryness.
Orb	Seven to seven and a half degrees before or after an aspect.
Years	The time of youth.
Countries	Italy, Netherlands and Sweden.
Day of the week	Tuesday.

The Sun

Sibley calls Sol, or the Sun, an "immense globe or body of fire, placed in the common centre, or rather in the lower focus, of the orbits of all the planets and comets..." He tells us that if the Sun is well dignified at birth, the native will be

> ...of a noble, magnanimous, and generous, disposition; high-minded but very humane; of a large and benevolent heart, affable, and courteous; in friendship, faithful and sincere; in promises, slow, but punctual. The solar man is not of many words; but when he speaks, it is with confidence... he is usually

thoughtful, secret, and reserved, his deportment is stately and majestic; a lover of sumptuousness and magnificence.

Gadbury refers to the Sun as

> Oculus Mundi, the Eye of the World; and Fons Lucus the Fountain of Light... he is indeed Rex Planetarum, the King of the Planets.[43]

Although all the other planets can change direction from forwards to backwards and sometimes don't move at all, "This Princely Body is never found to deviate..." Lilly tells us that when well placed the Sun brings luck "in Lay Preferments, as Kingdoms, Governments, etc".[44]

According to Ramesey in *Astrologia Restaurata*, the Sun is placed "in the midst of all the planets, being the chief light and president of them all, sitting as a Judge or King amongst his Nobles..." He reports that some of the ancient astrologers "have ascribed to him chief rule, and made him, as it were, an Emperor amongst the Stars".

> Saturn is his Vice-roy, for that all Planets give unto him their light, or do homage and reverence unto him, by reason of his slowness.
> Jupiter hath assigned him chief rule and dominion in the Realm, for that he is of a temperate, sober, good, honest and religious inclination.
> Mars is his chief Captain, or General of all his Forces.
> Venus is Receiver, or Master-Comptroller of his house, by reason she is nearer Sol than any other.
> Mercury hath assigned him chief Secretary of State, by reason when the King goeth any Progress or Journey, he goeth; and when the King stayeth, so doth also Mercury, for he is never far from his beck.
> Luna is his Standard-bearer, being furthest from him; she is also, as I may say, Embassador, Messenger, &c. to do his business.[45]

Ramesey tells us that the fixed stars of differing magnitudes are officers and commanders under these. This is particularly relevant with fixed stars of the first, second and third magnitude. The others are subjects to the above, equivalent to the common people.

Diurnal motion	Between 57 minutes 16 seconds and 61 minutes 6 seconds.
Rules	Leo and the fire triplicity during the day. Has exaltation in Aries (his degree of exaltation is 19), his detriment in Aquarius and fall in Libra. The Sun is always direct and can never be retrograde. The Sun has no terms.
Nature	Hot and dry but more temperate than Mars, masculine and diurnal.
	According to Abu Ma'shar the Sun is associated with the animal soul, light, brightness, the intellect, knowledge, intelligence, conquering, fighting and mastery.
When well-dignified	Equivalent to a Fortune. Very faithful, keeps promises, incomparable judgement. Speaks seriously and deliberately but

	not with many words, full of thought, big heart, affable, very humane, loves magnificence.
When ill-dignified	Arrogant, proud, poor judgement, domineering, foolish, extravagant, troublesome, snobbish.
Appearance	Large and strong, round large forehead, large protruding eyes, yellow hair and quickly bald, honest, sincere high-minded and has a big heart. Comely body, curly hair, white and tender skin. Likes praise and fame, is held in high regard amongst friends. Clear voice, uneven teeth, slow speech, outwardly composed, but inwardly inclined to many vices.
Diseases	Pimples in the face, disease of the brain or heart. Problems with the eyes, diseases of the mouth, fevers, right eye, in women the left eye, palpitations, trembling, cramps, swooning. Trembling of the heart, fainting, weakness of sight, violent fevers, disorders of the brain, foul breath (Sibley).
Colours	Yellow, gold, scarlet, clear red, purple.
Tastes	Mixture of sour and sweet together – bitter a little sharp.
Herbs and plants	Those which smell pleasant and have a good flavour, yellow or reddish flowers, herbs which strengthen the heart and comfort, which give clear eye sight and dissolve malignant influences (resist poison). They love to grow in open and sunny places: vine, st johns wort, musk, barley, marigold, rosemary, cinnamon, celandine, pyony.
Trees	Ash, palm, cedar, laurel, orange and lemon trees.
Animals	Lion, horse, goat, glow-worm.
	All stately bold, strong, furious and invincible animals as the lion, tiger, leopard, hyena, crocodile, wolf, ram, bull, boar, horse, baboon (Morin).
Birds	Eagle, nightingale, cock, phoenix, peacock, buzzard, fly, swan. Hawk, lark. (Sibley).
Places	Houses, courts, palaces, theatres, dining rooms, magnificent structures.
	Princely palaces and churches (Morin).
	Grand buildings, such as theatres and palaces (Barclay).
Minerals and metals	Gold.
Stones	Ruby, hyacinth.
Weather	According to the season: gentle moist showers, autumn mist, small winter rain, extreme heat in summer if with Mars.
Orb	Fifteen to seventeen degrees before or after an aspect.
Countries	Italy, Sicily, Lebanon, Southern Iraq, Czech Republic.
Day of the week	Sunday.
Years	Youth or when a person is at his strongest.

Venus

Venus, like Mercury lies between the earth and the Sun and cannot therefore be more than about forty eight degrees from the Sun. Venus spends approximately four weeks in one zodiacal sign. Gadbury refers to Venus as the "lesser fortune; the Author of pleasure, mirth and jollity".[46] Lilly tells us that the "lower planets" that is the Inferiors, "bestow their gifts inherent to men and more durable: as Venus, in the attempts of women, their ornaments, courting them, etc".[47] Sibley tells us that if Venus is well dignified at birth the Native is

> ...of a quiet, even, and friendly, disposition, naturally inclined to neatness, loving mirth and cheerfulness, and delighting in music; amorous, and prone to venery; though truly virtuous, if a woman; yet she will be given to jealousy, even without cause.

According to Sibley, when Venus appears west of the Sun

> ...she rises before him in the morning, and is called the morning-star; but, when she appears east of the Sun, she shines in the evening after he sets, and is then called the evening-star...

Robert Hand tells us that in Babylonian astrology, depending on whether Venus rises before or after the Sun, she is referred to as the warrior goddess when a morning star and the feminine goddess of love when an evening star.[48] Lilly tells us that the "vulgar" call Venus the evening star, or *Hesperus*, when she appears after the Sun has set. He explains that the common people call her the morning star, but the learned call her *Lucifer*, when she is visible before sunrise.

Diurnal Motion	Between 62 minutes and 82 minutes a day.
Rules	Taurus and Libra, and the earth triplicity by day. Has her exaltation in Pisces (degree of exaltation 27), her detriment in Scorpio and Aries, her fall in Virgo.
Nature	A feminine planet, cold and moist, nocturnal, the *Lesser Fortune*, associated with mirth and jollity.
When well-dignified	A quiet person not given to quarrelling or wrangling. Pleasant, neat, clean, might drink too much rather than eat too much, often entangled in love matters. Musical, cheerful, likes entertaining and being entertained.
When ill-dignified	Riotous, vulgar, extravagant, bad reputation, adulterer or adulteress, no credit, spends too much in pubs, an atheist, lazy, careless.
Appearance	Fair, not tall, lovely eyes, plenty of smooth fair hair, lovely mouth, well shaped body, neat clothes and body, amorous. A fair and round face, full eyes even goggle eyed, red lips, a delightful body, dimples, amorous, lovely hair colour, mostly according to the sign Venus occupies.

Diseases	In the stomach, kidneys, reins, naval, loins, back, genitals, sexually transmitted diseases, impotency, hernias, diabetes. Disorders of the belly and womb, suffocation, heart-burn (Morin).
Tastes	Pleasant tastes, moist or sweet, nice smell, aromatic.
Colours	White or milky sky colour mixed with brown, or a little green.
Herbs and plants	All herbs with a sweet flavour, pleasant smell, white flowers and smooth leaves. Lilly, lilly of the valley, white and yellow daffodil. Sweet apples and white roses, peaches and apricots (Barclay).
Trees	Sweet apple, white rose, fig, sycamore, olive, almonds, thyme, walnut, coriander, plums.
Animals	Panther, small cattle, calf, goat. Animals of a hot and amorous nature such as dog, bull, coney, sheep, goat, calf, panther (Sibley).
Birds	Sparrow, dove, hen, nightingale, thrush, pelican, partridge, wren, eagle, swan, swallow, owl, blackbird.
Places	Gardens, fountains, bridal chambers, beds, dancing schools. Gardens, meadows, groves, places of pleasure, theatres (Morin).
Metals and minerals	Copper and brass.
Stones	White and red coral, alabaster, lapiz lazuli.
Weather	South wind because it is hot and moist, in summer still clear weather, in winter, rain or snow.
Orb	Seven to eight degrees before or after any aspect.
Years	Youth from 14 to 28 years of age.
Countries	Arabia, Austria, Cyprus.
Day of the week	Friday.

Mercury

Mercury is the closest planet to the Sun. He can never be more than twenty-seven degrees away from the Sun and, therefore, is not often visible. Mercury moves quickly and can spend as little as three weeks in one zodiacal sign. Mercury can be masculine or feminine, lucky or unlucky as determined by his position. Abu Ma'shar confirms that "Mercury inclines his nature to the natures of the planets and the signs with which it mixes". Sibley tells us that if Mercury is well dignified in the Nativity

> ...the person will inherit a strong subtil imagination, and retentive memory; likely to become an excellent orator and logician, arguing with much eloquence of speech, and with strong powers of persuasion. Is generally given to the attainment of all kinds of learning; an encourager of the liberal arts; of a sharp, witty, and pleasant, conversation... curious in the search of all natural and occult knowledge: with an inclination to travel or trade in foreign countries.

Lilly explains that Mercury brings good fortune through trading and writing.[49] Refering to Nativities and Questions, Bonatti tells us if Mercury is either the principal significator or co-significator and is fortunate and strong, in either Capricorn or Aquarius, the Native will be "of profound and piercing wit, and great understanding..." This is particularly true if Saturn is well-placed and makes a good aspect to Mercury. This is even better if Mercury is in Aquarius, which is the "delight" of Saturn and even more so if a Fortune is in conjunction with Mercury and one of the "propitious" fixed stars. However if Mercury is in either Aries or Scorpio, the native will be

> ...bold, Perfidious, inconstant, arrogant, and yet quick of apprehension; rather nimble to repeat or find out things said by others than invent them himself.[50]

Cardan tells us about Mercury in conjunction with Mars.

> Mars is seldom joined with Mercury for good, for he makes people haughty and impudent, yet industrious in Art, whence it comes to pass that the best Artists are too often the worst men.[51]

Diurnal motion	Between 66 and 100 minutes a day.
Rules	Gemini and Virgo. Has exaltation in Virgo (his degree of exaltation is 15), his detriment in Sagittarius and his fall in Pisces. He rules the air triplicity by night.
Nature	Neither masculine nor feminine. He can be either one or other depending on which planet he is joined to, but his own nature is cold and dry. If joined to good planets he can bring about good, with evil planets evil. He rules subtlety, tricks, devices, perjury.
When well-dignified	Subtle and astute brain, very logical, arguing with learning and discretion. A researcher, able to learn almost anything without a teacher, great eloquence in speech, a researcher, sharp and witty, a natural traveller, curious in the search for occult knowledge, inventive, prone to divination. In trading or inventing no one can outperform him.
When ill-dignified	Too much talking, no purpose, a tell tale, an idiot, cheating and thieving, no solid learning, no judgement, a liar, inconstant and a boaster, likes wicked arts, ungodly knowledge, a cheat, a thief, not a real scholar, poor judgement, easily perverted, idle words.
Appearance	Tall and thin, high forehead, narrow long face, thin lips and nose, long nose, brown or black hair, little hair on chin but not much on head, long arms, fingers and hands. Slender body, small legs, nimble and light footed, full of action. More than any other planet, Mercury is influenced by other planets and takes on the characteristics of a planet in aspect. If Mercury is

	in aspect with Saturn, the appearance is more heavy; if with Jupiter more temperate; if with Mars more rash; if with the Sun, more genteel, with Venus more jesting.
Diseases	Vertigo, giddiness in the head, madness or any disease of the brain, stammering, over-active imagination, defects in the memory and dry coughs, sniffing in the nose, dumbness, evil tongue.
	Disorders of the brain, convulsions, asthmas, imperfections of the tongue, whatever impairs the intellectual faculty, gout in the hands and feet (Sibley).
Colours	Grey mixed with sky colour.
	Sky blue mixed with a darker colour (Al Biruni).
Tastes	Of all things mixed together, complex flavour and colour, subtle and penetrating.
Herbs and plants	Planets which don't have much smell, or a very subtle smell, grow in sandy barren places, have a connection with the tongue, brain, lungs or memory. They dispel wind and can lift the spirits. Beans, three leafed grass, walnut and walnut tree, elder tree, dragon wort, marjoram, herbs used for divination.
Animals	Ape, fox, weasel, spider, hyena, squirrel, spider, greyhound. All cunning creatures.
	All sagacious animals: dog, mule, squirrel, serpent and adder (Sibley).
Places	Shops, markets, fairs, halls, bowling alleys, schools, tennis courts.
	Places of instruction, schools, universities, fairs (Morin).
Mineral	Quicksilver.
Stones	Millstone, malachite, topaz, any stones of diverse colours.
Weather	Windy, stormy and violent weather, the wind in the direction appropriate to that planet and the planet he is applying to. Sometimes rain or hail and lightning; in hot countries, earthquakes.
Orb	Seven degrees before and after any aspect.
Year	In pregnancies Mercury rules the sixth month.
Day of the week	Wednesday.

Moon

The Moon is the only celestial body used in astrology who does not orbit the Sun. She moves around the earth, taking twenty-nine and a half days to complete her cycle. During this time she forms different angular relationships with the earth and the Sun. These are called phases of the Moon, the most obvious being the New Moon and the Full Moon. All the planets move through the zodiac (a band extending about eight degrees either side of the apparent path of the Sun, which is referred to as the *ecliptic*). The Moon has a path similar to that of the Sun, but this path has a five degree deviation. This means that the Moon's path will cross the Sun's path twice a year. At these times the Sun, Moon and Earth are in exact alignment. The "nodal" points are where these two paths cross. The north node and the south node are very important in astrological judgement, whether the chart is a Question, Nativity, Ingress, Election and so on. The exact alignments of the Sun, Moon and Earth result in the lunar and solar eclipses. As in chess, the Moon, which can represent Queens, is usually the most important celestial body. Certainly in terms of Questions the Moon takes precedence, especially during the night. Because the Moon's motion changes quickly and, therefore, her sign and house location, Sibley tells us that

> Her influence, in itself, is neither fortunate or unfortunate, but as she happens to fall in with the configurations of the other planets, and is then either malevolent or otherwise as those aspects happen to be.

The Moon is either fortunate or unfortunate according to her aspects and position. Sibley claims that the Moon is

> ...the most powerful of all the heavenly bodies in her operations, by reason of her proximity to the Earth, and the swiftness of her motion, by which she receives and transmits to us the light and influence of all the superiors by her configurations with them.

Abu Ma'shar explains that the Moon is a benefic and although her own nature is cold, moist and moderate, she acquires "accidental heat", because her light is from the Sun. Lilly tells us that the Moon brings good fortune through navigation, planting vines, using drinks, selling wine, etc. As with all other planets, however, these advantages only derive from the Moon if she is "advantageously posited".[52]

Diurnal Motion	Never exceeds 15 degrees and 2 minutes in 24 hours.
Rules	Cancer and the earth triplicity during the night, has her exaltation in Taurus (her degree of exaltation is 3) her detriment in Capricorn, her fall in Scorpio. She has no terms.
Nature	Feminine, nocturnal, cold and moist.
When well-dignified	Soft tender creature, composed, honest, moves around a lot, lives in the present. Easily frightened, peace loving, free from cares of life, learns many occupations, always investigating different ways of earning a living. According to Sibley, if the Moon is well dignified in a nativity, the native "....will be of soft engaging manners and disposition, a lover of the polite arts, and of an ingenious imagination, fond of novelties, and given to travelling, or rambling about the country..."
When ill-dignified	Idle, dislikes work, a drunkard and careless, no spirit.

Appearance	Fair round face, grey eyes, much hair on the head, face and other parts of the body, sometimes one eye a little larger than the other, short fleshy hands, fleshy and plump. If the Moon is afflicted by the Sun in a Nativity or Question, there is usually some blemish near the eye. Weight and shape fluctuates. Round face, white and red mixture for complexion, but usually pale. If in fiery signs the person speaks quickly, in watery signs there are freckles on the face. Not a very handsome person. Unless well dignified, the Moon signifies a very ordinary or common person.
Diseases	Colic, bladder, liver, problems with menstruation, rheumatism, worms in children or men, coughs, small-pox, measles, convulsions. Complaints of the bowels, dropsy, cold and rheumatic complaints, worms, disorders of the eyes, coughs, convulsions, small pox, vertigo, lunacy, she governs the stomach, bowels, left eye in a man, right eye in a woman, the whole expulsive faculty (Morin).
Colour	White, or pale yellow with white, pale green, silver. Blue and white or some deep colour not unmixed with reddish yellow (Al Biruni).
Tastes	Fresh or without any flavour, herbs before they are ripe. Salt or insipid, somewhat bitter (Al Biruni).
Herbs, plants and trees:	Soft and thick juicy leaves, a little sweetish or watery taste, grow in watery places. Cabbage, melon, onion, poppy, lettuce, mushrooms, linden tree. Trees or herbs with round shady and great spreading leaves. Plants without much flavour, such as unripe fruits. The plants have thick, soft, juicy, round leaves (Barclay).
Animals	Those that live in the water. Frogs, otters, snails, seal fowl, duck and night owl (and fish of course like oyster, cockle, crab, shelf fish). All amphibious animals, or those that love the water. Chameleon, dog, hog, frog, baboon, panther, cat, mice, goat, rat (Morin).
Birds	Goose, swan, duck, moor-hen, night owl, night-raven, bat and water fowl (Sibley).
Places	Fields, fountains, baths, havens of the sea, highways, rivers, fish ponds, boggy places, brooks, springs and harbours for ships or docks. Woods, the sea, water in general and public places (Morin).
Mineral	Silver.

Stones	Selenite, crystal.
Weather	If the Moon is with Saturn there is cold air, with Jupiter serene, with Mars winds and red clouds, with the Sun according to the season, with Venus and Mercury showers and winds.
Orb	Twelve or twelve and a half degrees before or after any aspect.
Year	In pregnancies the Moon rules the seventh month.
Countries	Holland, Denmark and Belgium.
Day of the week	Monday.

Shared Signification

In reality it is rare to find only one planet that is significator of one object. In general, according to Al Biruni, two or more planets will be associated with that object. This takes place when "two elementary qualities are present obviously related to two different planets". Al Biruni explains that the onion is related by its warmth to Mars and by its moisture to Venus. Opium is related by its coldness to Saturn, and its dryness to Mercury.

He tells us that, in addition, there are groups of objects, which have as their general significator one particular planet, while other planets are associated with the individuals of the group. For example, Venus is significator for all sweet-smelling flowers, but Mars is associated with the rose because of its "thorns, colour and pungent odour". Jupiter shares signification with Venus over the narcissus, Saturn shares with Venus over the myrtle, the Sun shares with Venus over the water-lily, Mercury shares with Venus over royal basil and the Moon over the violet.

Similarly, the various parts of a plant are associated with different planets. The stem of a tree is signified by the Sun, its roots by Saturn, its thorns, twigs and bark by Mars, its flowers by Venus, its fruit by Jupiter, its leaves by the Moon and its seed by Mercury. Even in the fruit of a plant like a melon, its various parts are divided among several planets.

> ...the plant itself and the flesh of the fruit belong to the sun, its moisture to the Moon, its rind to Saturn, smell and colour to Venus, taste to Jupiter, seed to Mercury and the skin of the seed and its shape to Mars.[53]

Each planet in itself also has a natural association with more than one thing object or person, for example, the Sun is associated with fathers, kings, health and achievements, the Moon is associated with the mother, queen, the people and so on.

Unlike most authorities of the past, however, Morin believes that the ancients "abused the analogical nature of the Planets". He tells us that one planet in itself cannot simultaneously signify more than one thing. He claims that Cardan himself made this admission, when he stated that "Ptolemy introduced a new confusion by attributing many meanings to one Significator". Morin claims that, following Cardan, if the Moon signifies the wife, mother, servants, daughters and sisters and so on, how would the Moon be placed in the chart of, for example, a man

...who himself will live long, but whose wife will die in child-bed; who will see some of his daughters die and others spared; whom his servants will betray; whose mother will die early; who will nevertheless have good health for himself, but also a moody disposition with bad instincts?[54]

Morin finds the concept of general or universal significators unacceptable unless other factors in the chart agree. This is examined in more detail in chapter ten.

Description

Ptolemy gives a wonderful description in the *Tetrabiblos* of "bodily form and temperament" as signified by the planets. I include his description from Saturn

> Saturn if he is in the orient, makes his subjects in appearance dark-skinned, robust, black-haired, curly-haired, hairy-chested, with eyes of moderate size, of middling stature, and in temperament having an excess of the moist and cold. If Saturn is setting, in appearance he makes them dark, slender, small, straight-haired, with little hair on the body, rather graceful, and black-eyed; in temperament, sharing most in the cold and dry.[55]

Descriptions derived from the planets are explored further in chapter ten.

Planetary Ruler of the Hour

The Sun, Moon and planets are also the rulers of the days of the week and their hours. Whichever planet is ruler of a particular day is also the ruler of the first hour of that day. Following from that, the planet which is below it in the sphere is the ruler of the second hour. The one following that is the ruler of the third hour. This process carries on until the completion of twenty-four hours. For example, Saturday belongs to Saturn and so Saturn rules the first hour of that day. Jupiter which follows Saturn is ruler of the second hour, Mars, ruler of the third hour and so on. This information is contained in the planetary hour tables in *Christian Astrology*.[56]

> The planetary ruler of Sunday is the Sun
> The planetary ruler of Monday is the Moon
> The planetary ruler of Tuesday is Mars
> The planetary ruler of Wednesday is Mercury
> The planetary ruler of Thursday is Jupiter
> The planetary ruler of Friday is Venus
> The planetary ruler of Saturday is Saturn

> If one begins in the morning at sunrise on Monday, when the Moon is the ruler of the first hour, this is the order in which to proceed:

Moon, Saturn, Jupiter, Mars, Sun, Venus, Mercury, Moon, Saturn, Jupiter, Mars, Sun, Venus and so on...

> As we progress through the chapters I hope that the process of signification and evaluation will become clear and that the reader or student will gain an understanding

of the role of the planets in terms of astrological judgement. Although the modern astrologer is probably more familiar with the zodiacal signs and aspects, it is (as I hope to demonstrate throughout this book), the position and dignity of a planet which is the most important factor in chart judgement.

References

1. Placidus de Titis, 1657, *Primum Mobile*, Introduction by Michael Baigent, translated by John Cooper, The Institute for the study of Cycles in World Affairs, Bromley, Kent, 1983.
2. Al Biruni, p.234.
3. ibid pp.231-232.
4. *Astrosynthesis: The Rational System of Horoscope Interpretation according to Morin de Villefranche*. Taken from 21st Book of *The Astrologia Gallica* by Morin de Villefranche. Trans. Lucy Little, Emerald Books, New York, 1974, p.14.
5. Guido Bonatus, *The Astrologer's Guide or Anima Astrologiae*, p.5, 8th consideration.
6. William Lilly, *Christian Astrology*, pp.57-83.
7. ibid p.86.
8. Claudius Ptolemy, *Tetrabiblos*, Trans. F E Robbins, Loeb Classical Library, William Heinemann Ltd, 1980, p.39.
9. Al Biruni p.233.
10. Bonatus p.9, 11th consideration.
11. ibid p.10, 11th consideration.
12. ibid p.10, 12th consideration.
13. Al Biruni p.232.
14. Bonatus p.10, 13th consideration.
15. ibid p.10, 14th consideration.
16. Al Biruni p.233.
17. Dorotheus, *Carmen Astrologicum*. Trans. David Pingree, Teubner Verlagsgesellschaft, 1976, pp.164-165.
18. Al Biruni p.235.
19. Morin p.13.
20. Al Biruni p.260.
21. Al Biruni, Table of Friendship and Enmity according to the Hindus, p.261.
22. Lilly pp.57-83. (Planetary friends and enemies).
23. Morin pp.154-155.
24. Morin, references to Morin in this section taken from pp.158-160.
25. ibid p.34.
26. Abu Ma'shar, *The Abbreviation of the Introduction to Astrology*. Any references in this section from pp.38-40.
27. Any references to Lilly in this section taken from pp.57-83.
28. John Gadbury, *The Doctrine of Nativities*, Giles Calvert, William Larnar and Daniel White, London, 1658, p.66.

29. Ebenezer Sibley, from the Appendix in Morin, pp.176-177.
30. Claudius Dariot, *A breefe and most easie Introduction to the Astrologicall judgement of the Starres*, p.9.
31. Sibley, from the Appendix in Morin, p.178.
32. Lilly's note in Bonatus p.52.
33. Lilly, references in this section are from *Christian Astrology*, pp.57-83 and p.84.
34. Al Biruni, all references to Al Biruni in this section are from p.240.
35. Abu Ma'shar, all references to Abu Ma'shar in this section are from pp.38-40.
36. Sibley, all references to Sibley are from *Astrosynthesis*, pp.176-192 and p.161.
37. Olivia Barclay, all references to Olivia Barclay in this section are from *Transit*, the Magazine of the Astrological Association, August 1983.
38. Gadbury p.67.
39. Dariot p.9.
40. Lilly's note in Bonatus pp.52-3.
41. Gadbury p.68.
42. Lilly's note in Bonatus p.53.
43. Gadbury p.69.
44. Lilly's note in Bonatus p.63.
45. William Ramesey, p.56.
46. Gadbury p.70.
47. Lilly's note in Bonatus p.53.
48. Robert Hand, *Night and Day, Planetary Sect in Astrology*, citing Knappich p.8.
49. Lilly's note in Bonatus p.53.
50. Bonatus p.42, 126th consideration.
51. Cardan in *Anima Astrologiae* p.69, no.66.
52. Lilly's note in Bonatus p.53.
53. Al Biruni pp.235-236.
54. Morin pp.15-16.
55. Ptolemy p.309.
56. Lilly, *Christian Astrology*, pp.474-481.

2

THE HOUSES

> There is nothing appertaining to the life of man in this world, which in one way or other hath not relation to one of the twelve Houses of Heaven ... the twelve houses represent not onely the severall parts of man, but his actions, quality of life and living, and the curiosity and judgment of our Fore-fathers in Astrology, was such, as they have alotted to every house a particular signification...[1]

Houses are a symbolic description of the heavens: usually a division of a circle or square. They should not be confused with the positions of the stars, planets and luminaries, which are measurable concrete phenomena. For modern astrologers, there are three different systems of house division: ecliptic-based, time-based and space-based. In each of these systems the planets may be located in different houses. There has been much discussion among astrologers, both today and in the past, as to the most reliable house system. Some of the house systems available include:

Alcabitius	A time-based system used in the late Middle Ages.
Campanus	A space-based system, possibly the same system as that used by Al Biruni in the 11th century and perhaps by Manilius in his *Astronomica*.
Equal	An ecliptic-based system. Here, the midheaven may not coincide with the cusp of the tenth house.
Morinus	A space-based system.
Placidus	A time-based system and probably the most commonly used system in modern astrology.
Porphyry	An ecliptic-based system.

Regiomontanus

Regiomontanus is a space-based system and the standard house system used in the later Middle Ages. It is named after Johannes Müller (Joannes de Regio Monte), who has been credited with its invention, although it seems probable that this system was devised in the Arabic era. In the Regiomontanus system the equator is divided into twelve equal parts. Great circles are drawn through these divisions and between the north and south points on the horizon. The intersection points of these circles with the ecliptic represent the house cusps. Lilly uses this system of house division. If one has to use a house system at all, I would suggest that Regiomontanus is the most reliable.

In fact, the modern problem of house division did not exist for the ancients; they did not see the signs as separate from the houses. The houses were simply the roles which the signs took on in relation to a particular point. This point determined which of the individual signs should occupy the first house or *place*. That marking point was called *horoskopos* in Greek. The word horoscope is derived from horoskopos.

In *The Judgments of Nativities*, James Holden tells us that the author, Abu 'Ali Al-Khayyat, seems to have used what we call the Equal House method of house division. He tells us that underlying this system is the more ancient system which Holden calls *Sign-House*. Here, the rising sign is considered to be the first house, the next sign is the second house and so on. The cusp is usually at the beginning of the sign. Each house comprises exactly 30 degrees. There are no intercepted houses and no two houses with the same sign in the cusp. For example in the Regiomontanus house system, in popular use centuries later, if early degrees of Cancer are ascending in the cusp, both the second and third house cusps have Leo ascending. Similarly, with an Aquarius ascendant, the entire sign of Pisces is intercepted in the first house. Holden explains that the originators of astrology also counted houses from places other than the ascendant, for example from the Sun, the Moon, the Lot of Fortune, the other Lots, or a planet.[2]

Shepherd Simpson explains that the three house systems in classical astrology were based on temples, cardinal points and quadrants, and Lots. He tells us

> Houses and house systems seem to have taken a long and obscure road since the time of the early Classical Astrologers.[3]

He believes that "the lack of a rigorous choice of house system is one of the most fundamental problems in modern astrology". He goes on to tell us that in his opinion none of the usual house systems should be used.

> I think we should return to the Temples, Cardinal Points and Quadrants and Lots system that we appear, inexplicably, to have moved away from over the centuries. Classical astrologers used these three systems – basing their work on several hundred years of astrology; by what right do we think we should be doing something different?

By way of illustration, I include some of the writings of Ptolemy and Manilius below. It is also interesting to observe a chart which has no house divisions. Here, the astrologer can only observe the cardinal points (angles) together with the luminaries, the planets, the Lot of Fortune and their rulers. The important point is to note where in the circle the planets are located in relation to the points, most especially the ascendant. For example, in the diagram below there are no house divisions, but it is clear that the Moon and Venus, although not close to a cardinal point, make an aspect with the ascendant. Any planet aspecting the ascendant acquires more strength in itself and in terms of that chart, especially if the aspect is a trine or sextile.

Charts with no Houses

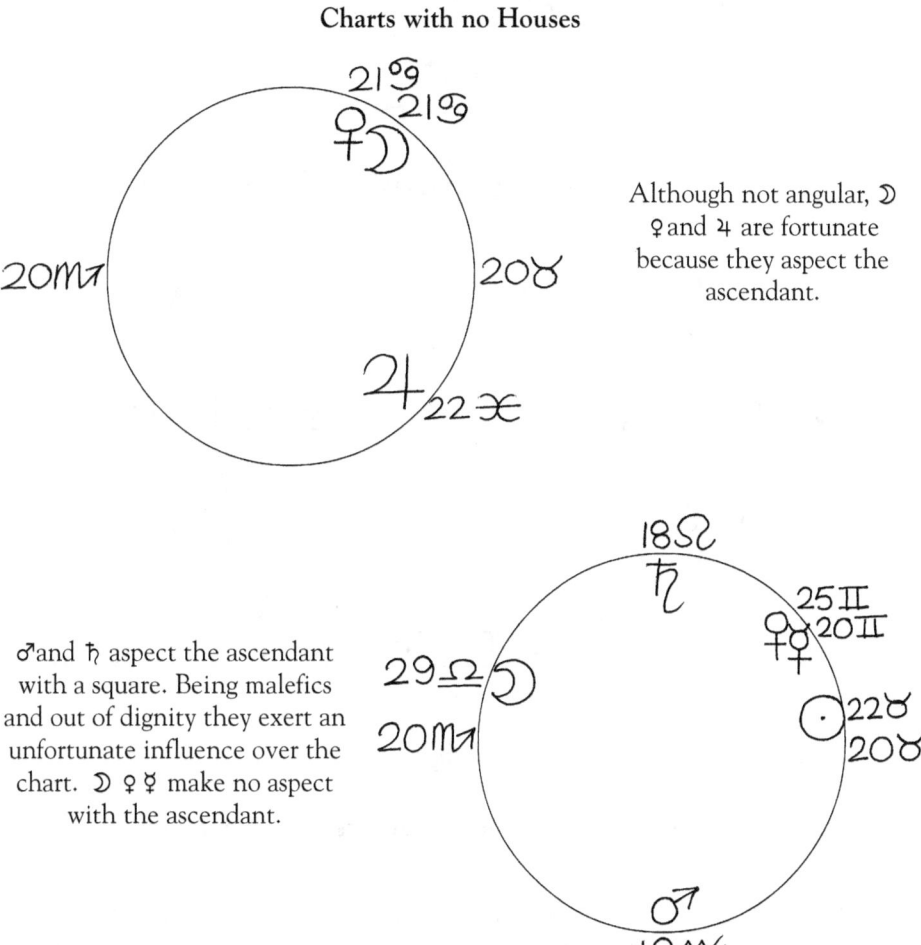

Although not angular, ☾ ♀ and ♃ are fortunate because they aspect the ascendant.

♂ and ♄ aspect the ascendant with a square. Being malefics and out of dignity they exert an unfortunate influence over the chart. ☾ ♀ ☿ make no aspect with the ascendant.

Ptolemy and Manilius

Ptolemy in his *Tetrabiblos* refers to *places* or *parts* which appear to correspond with the areas which modern astrologers refer to as houses.[4] Manilius refers to the four cardinal points which have "positions in the firmament permanently fixed". He tells us that these points have exceptional powers. Of these cardinal points (ascendant, midheaven, seventh house cusp and the point opposite the midheaven or *nadir*) priority is given to the midheaven in terms of its strength and virtue.

> First place goes to the cardinal which holds sway at the summit of the sky and divides heaven in two with imperceptible meridian...[5]

Manilius explains that there are *spaces* in between these points, which extend over a larger range and have special powers. These are the quadrants which are discussed later in the chapter. These quadrants link the cardinal points. They have associations with the quarter periods of human life as discussed on p.39.

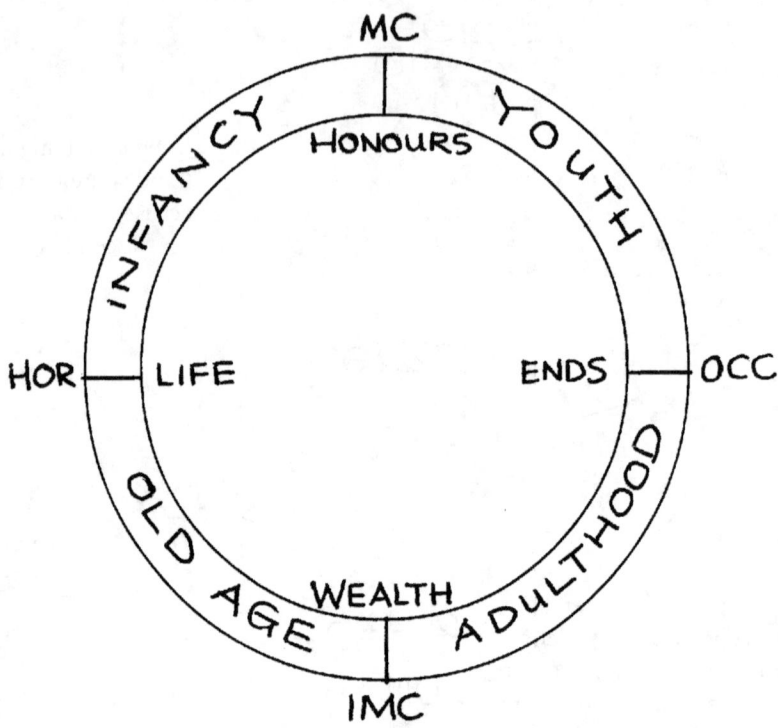

Cardines and Intervalla [Quadrants] from Manilius

Manilius also divides the circle into twelve divisions called *temples*. Four of these temples are associated with the cardinal points and the intervening segments are bisected to provide a further eight segments or temples. Manilius does not assign any numbers to these segments, but he gives each of them a name, confirms which planet has a special honour in that place (if there is one) and tells us the area of human experience associated with it.

> In any geniture every sign is affected by the sky's division into temples; position governs the stars, and endows them with the power to benefit or harm; each of the signs, as it revolves, receives the influences of heaven and to heaven imparts its own.[6]

When discussing the most important places in the circle (in terms of determining the length of life), Ptolemy starts his explanation by referring to the area we would consider the first house, that is, the twelfth part of the zodiac which surrounds the

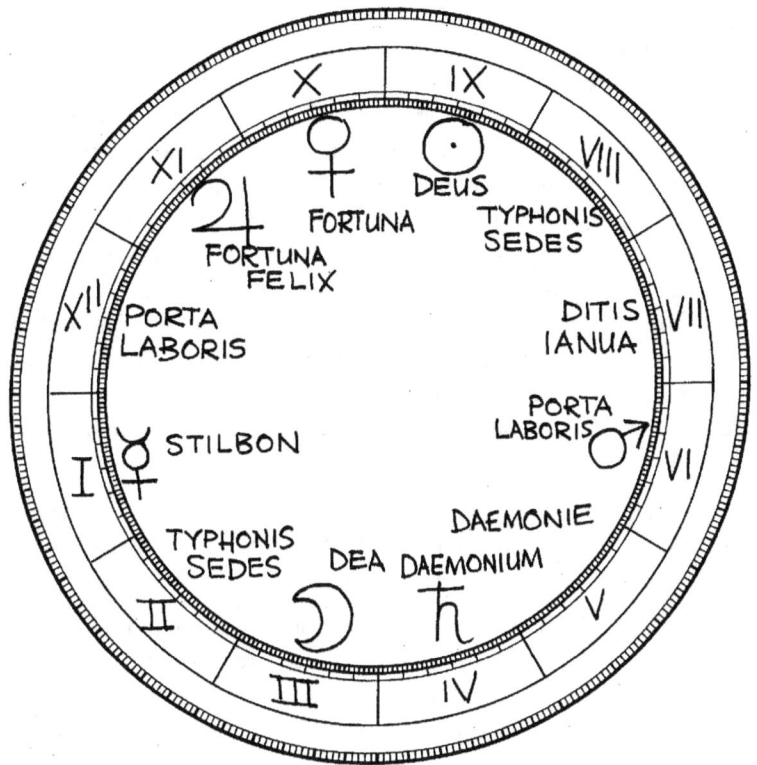

The Dodecatropos from Manilius

horoscope (ascendant) from five degrees above the actual horizon up to twenty five degrees the other side and "which is rising in succession to the horizon".[7] The part which is in dexter sextile with the horizon (the ascendant) is the house of the *Good Daemon* (the eleventh house). This is shown in the diagram on p.43.

Manilius calls this "the temple immediately behind the summit of bright heaven" and gives it the name *Fortuna Felix*. Ptolemy calls the part in quartile (square) with the horizon the *Midheaven* (the tenth house). The part in trine with the horizon is the house of *God* (the ninth house).

> Among these there are to be preferred, with reference to power of domination, first those which are in the mid-heaven, then those in the orient, then those in the sign succedent to the mid-heaven, then those in the occident, then those in the sign rising before the mid-heaven; for the whole region below the earth must, as is reasonable, be disregarded when a domination of such importance is concerned, except only those parts which in the ascendant sign itself are coming into the light.

The seventh house is called the *Occident* by Ptolemy, the fourth house the *Lower Mid-heaven*. Manilius tells us that here the "universe subsides, occupying the foundations, and from the depths of midnight gloom gazes up at the back of the Earth..." He calls this temple *Daemonium*.

The area that we refer to as the fifth house is called *Good Fortune* by Ptolemy and is associated with pleasure and merriment. The area corresponding to the second house is called the *Gate of Hades*. Although it is associated with wealth or poverty, goods and possessions, it was not considered a fortunate house by certain authorities. The area corresponding to the third house is called *Goddess* by Ptolemy and *Dea* or *Brothers* by Manilius. Ptolemy calls the place which we refer to as the eighth house *The Beginning of Death*; Manilius associates this area with violence and war.

The sixth house is the part called *Bad Fortune* by Ptolemy and *Laboris* by Manilius. The misfortune associated with the areas corresponding to the sixth, eighth and twelfth houses is partly due to the fact that these places do not usually aspect the ascendant. The area we call the twelfth house is called the *Bad Daemon* by Ptolemy, whereas Manilius compares it to the sixth house and calls it *Laboris, the Portal of Toil*.

> Of the part above the earth it is not fitting to consider either the sign that is disjunct from the ascendant, nor that which rose before it, called the House of the Evil Daemon. (Eighth and twelfth houses).

The meaning of the houses has remained constant throughout history, with one or two occasional deviations. The houses were considered more potent than the signs. Every house has a particular signification and everything on earth belongs to one of the houses. It is important to understand the signification associated with each house, because to a certain extent, astrological judgement depends on this. This is important to all charts, whether a Nativity, Question, or Election. According to Wharton

> ... amongst all other Foundations of Astrology, this of dividing the Heavens into 12 houses, is the first and chiefest; in that thereupon principally depends the whole Art of Predictions.[8]

Although a proper understanding of the houses is necessary for astrological judgement, in more recent times some sort of mistaken correlation between the houses and their planetary rulers has arisen: the outer planets are assigned house rulerships. Pluto is said to rule the eighth house, Uranus the eleventh house and Neptune the twelfth house. These rulerships have no place in the classical system.

There has also been confusion over the relationship between the signs and the houses. Although Aries may have co-signification over the first house, Aries does not have signification over the life of the native. This is signified by the first house only. Aries has signification over the head. In the same way, Gemini may have co-signification over the third house, but does not have signification over brothers. The third house signifies brothers. Gemini signifies, among other things, the arms and hands. In the past there was little identification of houses with signs, except perhaps with parts of the body and even then there were exceptions. Lilly confirms that the "...twelve Signes are appropriate to the particular members of mans body".[9]

It must be emphasised that the history and derivation of the houses and signs were quite separate. The houses were always considered more important than signs. Houses occasionally have similar properties to signs, but not always. For example, the stomach belongs to the fourth sign (Cancer) but to the fifth house. Barclay tells us that this may be because the solar plexus is associated with the fifth house. However, she urges caution in this matter, when she reminds us that they are not identical.[10] Culpeper, writing in the seventeenth century, declares

> ... some Authors hold an opinion that the signs carry the same signification in order that the houses of heaven do, and that Aries should signifie life; Taurus estate; Gemini bretheren and short journeys, you know the rest. Truly my own opinion is, many Authors invented whimsies, and when they had done, set them down to posterity for truth...[11]

I would suggest that the planets' relationship to the cardines (angles) principally to the ascendant, is possibly more important than their position within a 'house'.

Quarters (Quadrants)

Following earlier authorities, Lilly teaches that the whole horoscope (figure or map) is divided into four equal *quadrants* (or quarters) by the meridian and horizon.[12] Each quarter comprises three smaller parts, which in total gives twelve equal parts. These are the houses, which start at the east. In *The Book of Instruction in the Elements of the Art of Astrology* Al Biruni explains that the quarter between the ascendant and the tenth house and the quadrant between the seventh house and the fourth house are known as *excesses*, because both day and night (respectively) are on the increase here, whereas day and night are on the decrease in the remaining quarters.[13] He tells us that the Superiors are "joyous" when positioned in the increasing quarters or quadrants. The Inferiors are joyous when positioned in the decreasing quarters.[14]

The first quarter begins at the east, from the cusp of the first house and ends at the midheaven at the cusp of the tenth house. It contains the twelfth, eleventh and tenth houses. Lilly calls this the *orientall, vernall, masculine, sanguine, infant* quarter. This quarter corresponds to an "increasing" part, where daylight is on the increase and where the Superiors are more comfortable.

The second quarter starts at the cusp of the midheaven and ends at the cusp of the seventh house. It contains the ninth, eighth and seventh houses. Lilly calls this the *meridian, estivall, feminine, youthful, cholerick* quarter. This quarter corresponds to a "decreasing" part, where daylight decreases and where the Inferiors are more comfortable.

The third quarter starts at the cusp of the seventh house and ends at the cusp of the fourth house. It contains the sixth, fifth and fourth houses. Lilly calls this the *occidentall, autumnall, masculine, melanchollique, manheod, cold and dry* quarter. This quarter corresponds to an "increasing" part, where darkness increases and where the Superiors are more comfortable.

The fourth quarter starts at the cusp of the fourth house and ends at the cusp of the first house. It contains the third, second and first house. Lilly calls this the *northern, feminine, old age, of the nature of winter, phlegmatique* quarter. This quarter corresponds to a "decreasing" part, where darkness decreases and where the Inferiors are more comfortable.

Houses and Directions

First house	East
Second house	Northeast by east
Third house	North northeast
Fourth house	North
Fifth house	Northwest by north
Sixth house	West northwest
Seventh house	West
Eighth house	Southwest by south
Ninth house	South southwest
Tenth house	South
Eleventh house	Southeast by south
Twelfth house	East southeast

Angles, Succedents and Cadents

The first, tenth, seventh and fourth houses are called *angles*. The eleventh, second, eighth and fifth houses are called *succedents*. The third, twelfth, ninth and sixth houses are called *cadents*, or what Dariot calls "falling" houses.[15] Robert Hand tells us, in Masha'allah's *On Reception*, that Masha'allah does not use the word cadent in the same way as other authors. He uses the word cadent to indicate a house which is unfortunate. According to Hand there is a similar usage in Valens, where the expression "fallen amiss" describes planets which are located in either the twelfth, sixth, eighth or other unfortunate house.[16]

Lilly confirms that the angles are most powerful, the succedents next and the cadents last. He lists the houses in order of strength, as follows: 1, 10, 7, 4, 11, 5, 9, 3, 2, 8, 6, 12. In Lilly's system if two planets are equally dignified, one in the ascendant, the other in the tenth house, the planet in the ascendant has more power to bring about a positive result. The reason why Lilly gives the ninth and third houses, which are cadent houses, precedence over the second and eighth houses, which are succedent houses, is that in most instances the third and ninth houses (and/or planets in these houses) make an aspect with the ascendant, whereas the second, eighth, sixth and twelfth houses, (and/or planets placed in them) do not. This is a very important point.

In certain house systems, a planet in the sixth or twelfth house can make an aspect with the ascendant. For example, in the Regiomontanus house system used in horary, a chart with Taurus ascending has Virgo in the sixth house cusp. Virgo makes a trine aspect with the ascendant. Any planets placed in that house in Virgo do the same. The twelfth house and any planet placed close to the twelfth house cusp in Pisces also behaves in the same way. In fact, whichever house system is used these planets will make an aspect with the ascendant (but the houses themselves may not).

Early astrologers appear to draw little or no distinction as to whether the aspecting planet is within its orb of aspect, or merely aspecting the ascendant by sign. For example, if three degrees of Gemini are ascending, but Mercury is in twenty degrees of Libra, Mercury is considered to be aspecting the ascendant by sign. In this instance, Mercury is fortunate and might be acceptable as primary or principal significator of the Querent in a Question (horary) in preference to the Moon (see chapter ten).

Astrologers differed as to the order of the individual houses in terms of their strength and power, but all agreed that the angles are most powerful.

> Prosperity (iqbal) is associated with the cardines [angles], as these indicate a happy mean; adversity (idbar) with the cadent houses, which point to destruction and excess.[17]

In *The Book Of Instruction In The Elements Of The Art Of Astrology*, Al Biruni tells us that a succedent house is "beyond the half-way line to prosperity, for they are the paths leading there from adversity". However, he confirms that the prosperity and adversity assigned to these houses is not all alike. There is a difference in strength between the angular houses themselves, the succedent houses and the cadent houses. He explains that the angles are "higher and lower in glory and dignity". Referring to the cadent houses, he tells us that they are

> ...not alike in their destructive influences, because although the 3rd and 9th houses are cadent, the 6th and 12th are not only cadent but are also inconjunct to the horoscope [ascendant]. [18]

As discussed earlier, houses and planets not beholding the ascendant are unfortunate and I have not yet found an author who holds a different view.

In *Carmen Astrologicum* Dorotheus tells us about the "superiority of the places", confirming that the best position is the ascendant, followed by the midheaven, the eleventh house, the fifth house, which he calls "the house of the child" and finally the seventh house, which he calls "the house of marriage". This is followed by "the cardine of the earth" the fourth house and the ninth house. Finally, he lists in order: the third house (where the Moon joys), the second house, the eighth house and the "worst of the worst" the sixth house and the twelfth house.[19]

A little later in the text where Dorotheus considers "the upbringing of natives" (in other words whether a native would survive childhood), he emphasises the importance of these places being occupied by a diurnal planet in a diurnal chart or a nocturnal planet in a nocturnal chart. This is explored further in chapter four.

In *On Reception* Masha'allah agrees that the planets "are raised up in the four angles". Among these angles he claims that "the most worthy and swiftest in advantage and in the outcome of the matter" is in order: the ascendant, the tenth house, the seventh house (what he calls the house of sexual unions and marriages) and the fourth house.

> ...among the middle houses [succedent] the most worthy is the house of hope, and it is swifter than the house of marriages and [the house] of fathers in the doing of things, and this is the eleventh house.[20]

After this, follow the ninth, fifth and third house. Masha'allah explains that these houses are "good and praiseworthy". However, the houses which are cadent from the angles "are worse than all of the houses". He tells us that the eighth, sixth, twelfth and second are "enemies to the Ascendant because they do not aspect the Ascendant."

In *The Beginning of Wisdom*, Ibn Ezra calls the angular houses "poles", because they look like "points" and agrees that the most powerful poles are the first and the tenth houses. He calls the succedent houses, the second, fifth, eighth and eleventh houses, "supports for the poles", giving most power to the fifth and eleventh house. He gives the third, sixth, ninth and twelfth houses the "common name of wanes". According to Ibn Ezra, the most powerful of these is the sixth house and the ninth house. He tells us that the poles are more powerful than the supports; the supports are more powerful than the wanes.[21]

The Twelve Houses, their Nature and Signification

The following is a brief description of the people, things or matters associated with a particular house, based largely on the writings of the seventeenth century astrologers, particularly Lilly. However, Lilly and his contemporaries mostly followed the reasoning of Ptolemy. I have also included some of Al Biruni's writings on signification from *The Book of Instruction in the Elements of the Art of Astrology*, the section entitled *Indications Relating To Horary Questions*. Here, there are differences between signification as put forward by Al Biruni and that put forward by Lilly. I also include Al Biruni's writings on signification from his section entitled *Special Indications of the Houses Peculiar to Nativities*. Here there are further differences in signification between houses in a Nativity as compared to houses in a Question (horary).[22]

In *Astrologia Gallica*, Morin tells us that when considering the signification taken from a house

> ...it is necessary to say not that the First House signifies life, but that it produces a determination referring to life, and that consequently it is the House of Life.[23]

He explains that the same is true for the other houses, and also that that the zodiacal signs which occupy the houses do not "signify" the things or events attributed to those houses, no more than the planets that are placed there or the planets that rule these houses. Morin claims that "celestial bodies empowered in the first House have a significance *relating to* life, character, and intelligence". Similarly, in the tenth house they have a significance relating to enterprises, profession, honour, achievement and so on. In an overall sense, therefore, Morin suggests that the planets have

> ...in the first place a significance relating to the kind of thing or event, and this by reason of their local determination. In the second place, they indicate whether or not this thing or event will be realised for the Native. Thirdly, they define the quality and extent of this realisation.

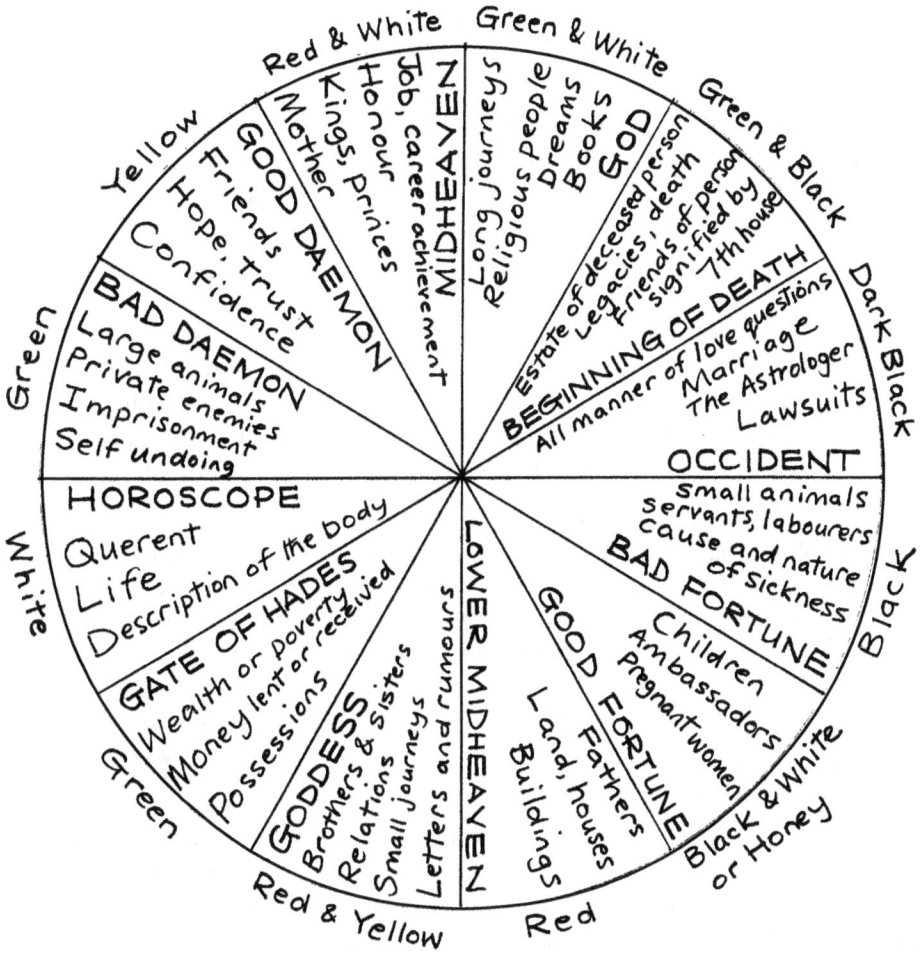

The Twelve Houses
Large Capitals = Ptolemy
Small writing and colours = Lilly

As an example of this, the Sun in the tenth house may amplify an achievement or may produce honours, whereas Saturn or Mars may restrict or prevent it.

First House[24]

General signification: the life of a human being.
Referring to Nativities, Morin gives this house signification over life, physical constitution, temperament, general state of health, morbid predispositions, instinctual, moral and intellectual tendencies.[25] The first house was often called the "horoscope".

The first house signifies the build, colouring and complexion of the person who asks the Question (the Querent) or of the Native in a Nativity. It also signifies the head and face.

Al Biruni tells us that the first house has signification over the asking of horary questions, important public matters, nobility, advancement in rank, witchcraft and spells. In Nativities, however, he gives the first house signification over the soul, length of life, education and native land.[26]

Colours: White. Any planet in this house signifies white, wan, or something near to that colour.

Co-significators: Aries and Saturn. If Saturn is well placed in the first house and in good aspect with Jupiter, Venus, Sun or Moon, it signifies a strong constitution and long life. Mercury has joy in the first house, because he represents the head and the tongue. If Mercury is well placed here, it signifies a good speaker. Bonatti tells us that if Mercury is in conjunction with Saturn in the ascendant, it signifies a person who is a

> ...foolish talkative fellow, that would be counted wise... the greatest wit he hath is to invent many lies; nor doth he ever open his mouth, but something of untruth appears intermixed with his discourse... Saturn give him a foul tongue, and Mercury a sharpness of malice to employ it.[27]

In *Christian Astrology*, in his section on Nativities, Lilly discusses the appearance and shape of the face, explaining that it is Venus and Jupiter which give the best complexions, Mercury and the Moon the next best. Here, I assume that Lilly is referring to planets positioned in the first house or ascendant. The Infortunes can cause "ill Faces or Complexions" but, claims Lilly, if they are in no way afflicted "they declare a good and handsome face." However, if Mars, Saturn or the south node are in a bad aspect with the ascendant, this shows "unhandsomnesse". If any of the foregoing are actually placed in the ascendant there is a "Scarre or blemish in the Face".[28]

Morin claims that the presence of a planet in a house is worth more than the rulership of an absent planet. He tells us that this assertion is confirmed by Garcae and Junctin (among others) when they state that a planet in the first house, whether in the ascending sign or in the intercepted sign, is the principal significator (not the co-significator) of the "moral and intellectual integrity of the Native".[29]

In addition, Morin tells us that the dispositor of that planet "also participates". He confirms that Origanus is of the same opinion. Morin asks why, if this is true for the intellectual characteristics, shouldn't this be equally true for other things such as wealth, marriage, status and so on? Later in his work Morin gives as an example the dispositor of Mercury positioned in the first house. Here, he declares, Mercury gives fine intelligence, even if Mercury himself is not in the first house. This is even better if the dispositor itself is in good condition.[30]

Second House

General signification: The fortune (or otherwise) of the Querent.

Morin gives the second house signification over wealth and moveable possessions. Al Biruni gives this house signification over lending and borrowing, counting friends, arrival of strangers, enemies or friends and winds when they blow. In Nativities, he gives the second house signification over nutriment, disaster to eyes, livelihood, household requisites, assistants and the profession of children.

The second house signifies all moveable possessions, including money in the bank, money lent, profit or gain, loss or damage. The condition of the second house shows the extent of the Querent's wealth in a Question and for the Native in a Nativity. In a lawsuit the second house represents the Querent's friends or allies. It also represents the Querent's neck, as well as the part behind the neck towards the shoulders.

Colour: Green.

Co-significators: Taurus and Jupiter. If Jupiter is placed in the second house, or is the ruler of this house, it signifies a fortune. The Sun and Mars are never well placed in the second house: they show dispersion of wealth and loss of money. However if either the Sun or Mars rule the second house and are placed in the second house, this can be fortunate in terms of money and wealth, or other affairs signified by this house. The reason why the Sun was thought to be unfortunate in the second house may be due to the fact that the Sun is a diurnal planet and when placed in the second house, the chart will, in this instance, be nocturnal. As a diurnal planet the Sun prefers to be located in a diurnal chart. This is explored in chapter four. This rule applies to both a Question and Nativity. Lilly tells us that this "dispersion of substance" is "according to the capacity and quality of him that is either born [Native] or asks the question [Querent]".[31]

Third House

General signification: Brothers and sisters, cousins, relatives, neighbours, short journeys, moving from one place to another, letters, documents, rumours, messengers.

Morin gives the third house signification over brothers, sisters and more distant blood relatives. Al Biruni gives the third house signification over secrets, news, commentaries, well-born ladies and journeys by water. In Nativities, he gives the third house signification over brothers, sisters, relations, in-laws, jewels, friends, migration, short journeys, intelligence, knowledge and expertness in religious law. The third house rules shoulders, arms, hands and fingers.

Colours: Red and yellow.

Co-significators: Gemini and Mars. Mars in this house (unless joined to Saturn) is not unfortunate. The Moon has joy in this house. If the Moon is placed here it indicates a great deal of travel and movement.

Fourth House

General signification: Fathers in general and the father of the Querent. The fourth house signifies land, houses, inheritances, the earth, treasure hidden, the end of a matter, towns, cities and castles, all ancient dwellings, gardens, fields, pastures, the quality and nature of the ground (woody, stony or barren).

Morin gives signification of this house to parents, real estate, inheritance. Al Biruni associates the fourth house with old and hidden things, treasures, thieves' hiding places, schools, fortresses, fetters, dismissal from office, opening abscesses, stepfather and prison. In Nativities he gives the fourth house signification over parents, grandparents, descendants, real estate, fields, houses, water supply, knowledge of genealogy, what succeeds death and what happens to the dead.

The sign in the fourth house cusp signifies the town. The ruler of the sign signifies the Governor of that town. The fourth house rules the breast and the lungs.

Colours: Red.

Co-significators: Cancer and the Sun. It is the angle of the north or *imum coeli*. The Sun by day and Saturn by night also represent fathers. If the Sun is placed in the fourth house, Lilly tells us that the father is of "noble disposition". The fourth house can signify treasure buried in the ground. Gadbury, Lilly, Bonatti and Coley all agree that if Venus, Jupiter and the north node are here, there are valuables in the ground. If the planets are strong in essential dignities it is more certain and gives confirmation that investing in this property or land will bring good fortune.

Modern astrologers often refer to the point opposite to the midheaven as the *nadir* of a chart. According to Robert Hand this is not strictly correct. He cites an example in Masha'allah where the seventh house is referred to as the nadir of the ascendant. Hand explains that there is a similar use of this in Montulmo where the nadir simply means the point opposite.[32] Al Biruni, referring to planets being weak in accidental dignity, explains that one of these conditions is the placement of planets "at the nadir of their joys..."[33] When referring to the eastern quarter of a chart, he tells us that the quarter opposite to this quarter is "its nadir".[34]

Fifth House

General signification: Children, ambassadors, the condition of a pregnant woman, parties, pubs, messengers, the wealth of the father, the ammunition of a town.

Morin gives signification of this house to offspring and worldly pleasures. Al Biruni associates the fifth house with messengers, right guidance, bribery, rectitude, distant places, poor harvests, securing the wealth of the ancients, feasts, food, drink. In Nativities he gives the fifth house signification over children, friends, clothes, pleasure, joy, little acquisition of property, accumulated wealth of father and what was said of him at his burial service. The fifth house rules the stomach, liver, heart, sides and back.

Colours: Black and white or honey colour.

Co-significators: Leo and Venus. Venus has joy in this house. The fifth house is the house of pleasure, delight and merriment. If Saturn or Mars are placed here (unless dignified) it can be unfortunate. These planets can signify disobedient children. Venus gives her characteristics to this house, which is associated with amusements, the arts, theatre, music, sculpture and painting. Jupiter in this house is a strong and definite indication of pregnancy.

Sixth House

General signification: Servants or employees, labourers, farmers, tenants, shepherds, small animals (for example, sheep, goats, cats and dogs), the type and cause of a sickness, whether it is curable, or whether it will last a long time.

Morin gives signification of the sixth house to servants and domestic animals. Al Biruni associates the sixth house with lost and escaped; some lost trifle which does not turn up, affairs of women, suspicion, hatred, violence, dissipation, deceit, terrors, prison, enemy, poverty and moving from place to place. In Nativities he gives the sixth house signification over sickness, defects of the body, overwork, accident to the legs, loss of property, disease of internal organs, slaves, maids and cattle.

The sixth house rules the intestines and the back to the backside. It is an unfortunate house because it does not usually aspect the ascendant.

Colours: Black.

Co-significators: Virgo and Mercury. Mars has joy in this house. If Venus and Mars are in conjunction with each other in the sixth house, this can signify a good doctor. The sixth house is sometimes called the house of labour, deriving its qualities from the Lesser Infortune, Mars, who joys in this house. The sixth house does not signify your professional job. A job or career is always a tenth house matter. The labour which is associated with the sixth house is usually manual or perhaps healing work.

Seventh House

General signification: All manner of love questions, including the Querent's marriage, partnerships and relationships, public enemies, the opposing party in war, quarrels and lawsuits, doctors and thieves, the astrologer (unless it is the astrologer who asks the Question and is, therefore, represented by the first house and its ruler).

Morin gives signification of this house to marriage, the spouse, open enemies, quarrels, fights, lawsuits, contracts and partnerships. Al Biruni associates the seventh house with the absent, a thief, places where travellers assemble, treasure, death of contemporaries, foreign travel, sudden murder (for a trifle), denial, obstinacy, claiming a right, cheapness and dearness. In Nativities he gives the seventh house signification over women, concubines, giving in marriage, marriage-feasts, contentions, partnership, losses and lawsuits. The seventh house rules the area from the navel to the thighs.

Colours: Dark black.

Co-significators: Libra and the Moon. Saturn and Mars are unfortunate in this house.

Eighth House

General signification: The quality and nature of the estate of people deceased, wills and legacies. A partner's wealth and resources, or whatever belongs to another person, for example, loans, tax or a library book. In lawsuits the eighth house represents the opposing party's friends. It signifies the kind of death, fear and anxiety, as well as the heir to the deceased.

Morin gives signification of this house to death. Al Biruni states that this house is associated with buried and hidden treasure, things ruined or lost or old, rubbish heaps, sickness of friends, lawsuits without a case, folly, contention, pride, dullness of the market, leisure. In Nativities, he gives the eighth house signification over death and its causes, murder, poisoning, evil effects of drugs on body, inheritance, wife's property, expenditure, poverty, extreme indigence, feigning death. The eighth house rules the genitals, stones, poisons, the bladder.

Colours: Green and black.

Co-significators: Scorpio and Saturn.

Ninth House

General signification: Long journeys, clergy of any kind (for example, bishops or vicars), dreams, visions, foreign countries, books, learning, the relations of the Querent's partner, husband or wife.

Morin gives signification of the ninth house to religious matters and changes, specifically journeys. Al Biruni associates the ninth house with failure, abandoned business, books, information, ambassadors, miracles, roads, brothers-in-law. In Nativities he gives the ninth house signification over travel, religion, piety, fate, seriousness, attainment of knowledge from the stars, divination, philosophy, surveying, sharp discernment, trustworthiness, and the interpretation of visions and dreams. The ninth house rules the hips and thighs.

Colours: Green and white.

Co-significators: Sagittarius and Jupiter. If Jupiter is placed here it signifies a devout and Christian person. The Sun has joy in this house.

In the Renaissance most astrologers gave signification of the ninth house to travel or journeys. However, in ancient times and to a lesser extent in the Renaissance, the ninth house was considered the house of the Sun God, the house where the Sun joys. Gauquelin discovered that successful athletes tend to have Mars in the ninth house, which supports the ancient belief in the Sun's strength in this house. According to Barclay, this is because Mars is of the same nature as the Sun (hot and dry). She tells us that Mohammed Ali has Mars here and that he is also a man of God.[35]

Authorities of the past differed on the strength and importance of the ninth house. To many ancient astrologers it was primarily a cadent house and therefore it was weak. However, Ptolemy as well as others discussed briefly above, looked at the ninth house a little differently. They took the view that the ninth house is above the horizon, makes a trine with the ascendant, and therefore is not lacking in strength.

Tenth House

General signification: Kings, princes, dukes, earls, senior officers, commanders in chief, magistrates and officers in authority, mothers, honour, dignity, lawyers, profession or job, kingdoms, empires and countries.

Morin gives signification over this house to honours, rewards, elevation of social position, the profession, career, enterprises, the general activity of the Native. Al Biruni associates the tenth house with kings, notables, judges, the celebrated in all classes, things newly legitimised, wine and the step-mother. In Nativities he gives the signification of the tenth house to the rule of the Sultan, government with council of nobles, absolute authority, success in business, commerce, professions, well-behaved children and liberality. The tenth house rules the knees. The tenth house is called the *medium coeli* or midheaven.

Colours: Red and white.

Co-significators: Capricorn and Mars. The Sun and Jupiter are very fortunate in this house. Saturn or the dragon's tail (the south node), in the tenth house usually deny achievement or honour in some way.

Eleventh House

General signification: Friends and friendship, hope, trust, confidence, praise, the trustworthiness of friends, the king's money, courtiers, associates, allies and the government.

Morin gives signification over this house to friendships. Al Biruni associates the eleventh house with the treasury of the Sultan, its officials, trouble in the office, foreigner's child, servant's child, things which are sound, beautiful, advantageous, the beginnings of affairs, friendship of the great, bribery and food. In Nativities he gives the eleventh house signification over happiness, friends, enemies, concern for the next world, prayer and praise, friendship of women, love, dress, perfume, ornaments, commerce and longevity. The eleventh house rules the legs to the ankles.

Colours: Saffron or yellow.

Co-significators: Aquarius and the Sun. Jupiter has joy here. This is probably the most fortunate house for it derives its characteristics from the Greater Fortune, Jupiter. It is the house of reassurance, hopes and wishes; a house from where you could go higher, whereas from the tenth house of glory you could only fall. In antiquity, having Jupiter placed in this house was the greatest good and it probably still is. In his *Tetrabiblos* Ptolemy calls the eleventh house "the house of the good Daemon"[36] and claims that the eleventh house is associated with children, but Lilly and others disagree with Ptolemy in this matter.

Twelfth House

General signification: Private enemies, large animals, such as horses and cows, sorrow, tribulation, all manner of affliction or self-undoing and informers.

Morin gives signification over this house to sicknesses, servitude, imprisonment, exile and secret enemies. Al Biruni associates the twelfth house with fugitives, writers, those who neglect devotion, a precious gem, prisoners, the matter which preceded the question, property of oppressors, thieves, lost property, scorn, envy and fraud. In Nativities he gives the twelfth house signification over enemies, misery, anxieties, prison, debt, fines, bail, fear, adversity, disease, pre-natal fancies of mother, cattle, harbours, slaves, servants, armies, exile and tumults. The twelfth house rules the feet.

Colours: Green.

Co-significators: Pisces and Venus. Saturn has joy here and can do a great deal of mischief especially if he has no dignity.

Triplicity Rulers

Earlier authorities placed enormous emphasis on the triplicity rulers of signs. In Questions regarding health and life, for example, Robert Zoller tells us that Bonatti's Arabic sources require the ascendant and its ruler and the triplicity ruler of the ascendant, to be considered as supporting testimony. Each of the four triplicities had two or more planetary rulers assigned to them. This was the system in use by most astrologers in the ancient world. These rulers included the planets which had the highest dignities in the signs of the triplicity and which were also of the same sect. The triplicities and the triplicity rulers are explored further in chapter four and chapter six. Here I focus on the role of the triplicity rulers in relation to house signification.

Dariot, who follows Dorotheus in his assignation of triplicity rulers, tells us that every house has its "owne proper signification".[37] However Dariot himself, like astrologers before him, attaches great or perhaps greater importance to the triplicity ruler of each house. In his work *A breefe and most easie Introduction to the Astrologicall judgement of the Starres*, it is not until Dariot has explained the signification of the houses from their triplicity rulership that he considers "By what meanes the other signification of the houses may be found out…"

> Having thoroughly considered and wayed the first and principall significations of the houses it is easie to find the rest.[38]

Dariot reports that the "proper Lords of the triplicitie of the houses" is the "Lord of the Triplicitie of the signe" (the ruler of the sign in the cusp of the house).[39] Like astrologers before him, Dariot uses the three planet rulership of the triplicity: a diurnal ruler, a nocturnal ruler and a common ruler, which assists both the diurnal and nocturnal rulers. According to Dariot, each ruler of the triplicity has jurisdiction over particular matters or things, and/or over these things at a particular stage in the Native's life. With regard to the first house for example, this is associated with what Dariot calls the "lyfe and body" of the Native. The first ruler of the triplicity shows the

> ...life and nature of him that is borne, or that demaundeth the Question. By the same is knowne also what he doth love or hate in the beginning of his lyfe.[40]

The second ruler of the triplicity is associated with the force and strength of the body as well as middle age. The third ruler of the triplicity has the same signification as the previous two, but it rules old age. For example, in a Nativity with Taurus ascending in a diurnal chart, Venus (diurnal ruler of the triplicity) has governance over what the Native likes or dislikes in early life, as well as the life in general. The Moon (nocturnal ruler of the triplicity) is associated with the strength of the body in middle age. Mars (common ruler of the triplicity) rules all of these things in old age. However, in a nocturnal chart, the Moon is the "first Lord of the Triplicity", being the ruler of the earth signs during the night.

In the case of the second house, which Dariot calls "hope" and which rules "substance", Dariot explains that whichever is the strongest out of the first or second lords of the triplicity is the "authour or giver of the substance or riches". However, the first lord brings riches in early life, the second lord in middle age and the third lord in old age. Let us suppose as an example, Taurus is the sign in the second house cusp. If the Moon, the nocturnal triplicity ruler, is stronger than Venus the diurnal triplicity ruler, the Moon is the principal significator of the Native's wealth. However, that wealth is associated more with Venus in early life, the Moon in middle life and Mars in old age.

The importance of the triplicity rulers in relation to signification from the houses is discussed by Ibn Ezra in *The Beginning of Wisdom*. With respect to the first house Ibn Ezra explains that the ruler of the first triplicity

> ...prognosticates the life and character of the new-born and of the asker [Querent], his requests, and all that which may befall him early in life whether beneficial or baleful.

He also explains that

> ...the ruler of the second triplicity exerts an influence over the body, over strength, and over middle age. The ruler of the third triplicity shares, jointly with his companions, in all that they dominate and, in addition, he controls the end of the span of life.[41]

In some instances, the more general signification is divided up and assigned to each of the triplicity rulers. For example, in the case of the tenth house, this, according to Ibn Ezra refers to the mother, the government, reputation, and all professions. Here it is the ruler of the first triplicity which "points to the mother, the second to reputation, and the third to professions".

In other instances (as discussed above), the signification remains broadly the same, but each triplicity ruler has governance at a different stage in the Native's life, each ruler being associated with either early, middle or old age.

In *The Judgments of Nativities*, Abu Ali Al Khayyat attaches similar importance to the triplicity rulers. He asks the reader to consider the lords of the triplicity of the 2nd house because they also have signification in matters of wealth in accordance with their own nature and strength.[42]

He explains that if the first triplicity ruler has no aspect to any evil planet, the native will have "good circumstances" during his early life. If the second triplicity ruler is strong, he will be wealthy in middle age. If the third triplicity ruler is strong, good things will happen during old age.

Triplicity Rulers according to Al Biruni (following Dorotheus):[43]
Al Biruni calls the common ruler a *partner*.

Fire   Diurnal ruler the Sun, Nocturnal ruler Jupiter, Common ruler Saturn
Earth Diurnal ruler Venus, Nocturnal ruler Moon, Common ruler Mars
Air   Diurnal ruler Saturn, Nocturnal ruler Mercury, Common ruler Jupiter
Water Diurnal ruler Venus, Nocturnal ruler Mars, Common ruler Moon

Triplicity Rulers according to Dariot:[44]

Fire   Diurnal ruler Sun, Nocturnal ruler Jupiter, Common ruler Saturn
Earth Diurnal ruler Venus, Nocturnal ruler Moon, Common ruler Mars
Air   Diurnal ruler Saturn, Nocturnal ruler Mercury, Common ruler Jupiter
Water Diurnal ruler Venus, Nocturnal ruler Mars, Common ruler Moon

Triplicity Rulers according to Morin:[45]
Morin calls the common ruler a *participating* ruler.

Fire   Diurnal ruler Sun, Nocturnal ruler Mars, Common ruler Jupiter
Earth Diurnal ruler Mercury, Nocturnal ruler Saturn, Common ruler Venus
Air   Diurnal ruler Saturn, Nocturnal ruler Venus, Common ruler Mercury
Water Diurnal ruler Jupiter, Nocturnal ruler Moon, Common ruler Mars

Triplicity Rulers according to Lilly:[46] (from Ptolemy)

Fire   Diurnal ruler Sun, Nocturnal ruler Jupiter
Earth Diurnal ruler Venus, Nocturnal ruler Moon
Air   Diurnal ruler Saturn, Nocturnal ruler Mercury
Water Diurnal ruler Mars, Nocturnal ruler Mars (Moon and Venus have a share)

Morin, who attempted to make reforms to the traditional framework, attaches less importance to the rulers of triplicities.

> ...judgment drawn from the Ruler of a House has a much greater certainty than a judgment based on the Ruler of the Triplicity.

He claims that the ruler of the house is a "primary cause" because "the activity of the Sign depends essentially on it". He claims that the ruler of the triplicity is only a "secondary cause, on which the Sign in itself does not depend".

I would suggest that triplicity rulership is very important, particularly in terms of Nativities. This is especially so in the case of diurnal charts with Aries ascending, or nocturnal charts with Taurus ascending. In the diurnal chart the Sun has a rulership through triplicity and exaltation. In the nocturnal chart the Moon also has particular significance through her rulership of the triplicity and the exaltation. However, it is not always easy to separate the importance of the triplicity ruler from all other factors which may be present in a Question or Nativity.

Triplicity Rulers and Signification according to Dariot
According to Dariot the triplicity rulers have significance over the following:[47]

First House (Life)
First Lord of the Triplicity: Early life of the Native, the Querent
Second Lord of the Triplicity: Strength of body, middle age
Third Lord of the Triplicity: Old age

Second House (Hope)
First Lord of the Triplicity: Wealth in early life
Second Lord of the Triplicity: Wealth in middle age
Third Lord of the Triplicity: Wealth in old age

Third House (Brethren)
First Lord of the Triplicity: Older brothers
Second Lord of the Triplicity: Middle brothers
Third Lord of the Triplicity: Youngest brothers

Fourth House (Parents)
First Lord of the Triplicity: Fathers
Second Lord of the Triplicity: Castles and cities
Third Lord of the Triplicity: The end of all things

Fifth House (Children)
First Lord of the Triplicity: Children
Second Lord of the Triplicity: Love
Third Lord of the Triplicity: Ambassadors
*In contrast to Lilly, Dariot assigns love to the fifth house.

Sixth House (Health or Sickness)
First Lord of the Triplicity: Sicknesses and their cause.
Second Lord of the Triplicity: Servants
Third Lord of the Triplicity: Profit and loss from servants and small cattle.

Seventh House (Marriage)
First Lord of the Triplicity: Marriage and women
Second Lord of the Triplicity: Arguments and quarrels
Third Lord of the Triplicity: Infidelity

Eighth House (Death)
First Lord of the Triplicity: Death
Second Lord of the Triplicity: Ancient or old things
Third Lord of the Triplicity: Inheritances

Ninth House (Religion)
First Lord of the Triplicity: Long journeys and accidents or developments associated with them
Second Lord of the Triplicity: Faith and religion
Third Lord of the Triplicity: Dreams and wisdom

Tenth House (Middle of the Heaven)
First Lord of the Triplicity: Mediocre position at work.
Second Lord of the Triplicity: Dignity of position
Third Lord of the Triplicity: Stability and permanence in position or work.

Eleventh House (Good Spirite)
First Lord of the Triplicity: Confidence and boldness
Second Lord of the Triplicity: Work
Third Lord of the Triplicity: Profit from work.

Twelfth House (Ill Spirite)
First Lord of the Triplicity: Secret enemies
Second Lord of the Triplicity: Work and sorrow
Third Lord of the Triplicity: Beasts and cattle

Dariot does not make it clear whether it is the diurnal or nocturnal ruler which is lord of the triplicity at any given time. In her paper referring to Dariot's triplicities, Lee Lehman does not offer clarification: she appears to assign the diurnal ruler of the triplicity as the first lord of the triplicity, the nocturnal ruler of the triplicity as the second lord of the triplicity and the common ruler (participating ruler or partner) as third lord of the triplicity.[48] However, in a nocturnal chart, the nocturnal ruler of the triplicity must be the first lord of the triplicity, not the diurnal ruler. Robert Hand clarifies the issue in his quotation from Vettius Valens

> Now, for those who are born by day, it will be necessary to consider in what trigon the Sun is found, and the ruler of this trigon by preeminence...[49]

The first ruler of the triplicity is the diurnal ruler during the day or the nocturnal ruler during the night.

Turning the Chart

Dariot also tell us that signification of the houses does not necessarily start at the ascendant, but can take their beginning from any house. This is explored further in chapter ten. Dariot explains that the first house, for example, is the second house from the twelfth house, so it can signify the money or substance of a secret enemy. It is also the fourth house from the tenth house and, he claims, can signify the father of kings and so on.

This is called "turning" the chart, which Lilly uses on occasion in his judgements in *Christian Astrology*. However, any turning of the chart needs to be carried out with care. In my opinion the concept of turning the chart in the way described cannot always be justified. If signification from the radix or original chart (starting from the ascendant), supports the testimony of the "turned" chart, it is possible that starting from a house other than the ascendant can be of some importance. However, if the Question concerns a father, whether or not he is the father of a king, it is the fourth house of the original chart which is important. If the Question concerns the father of kings it is more likely that the tenth house has signification, because royalty are usually signified by the tenth house.

I hope it is becoming clear to the reader or student that a sound knowledge of chart division, angles, houses and their signification is required in order to make a judgement. The position of the planets in relation to the cardines (angles) is especially important. This applies to all charts under consideration, whether a Nativity, Question, Election or any other.

References

1. Lilly p.50.
2. James Holden in *The Judgments of Nativities* by Abu 'Ali Al-Khayyat translated from the Latin version of John of Seville by James H. Holden M.A., The American Federation of Astrologers, AZ., USA, 1988, p.17.
3. Dr Shepherd Simpson, his website.
4. Claudius Ptolemy, *Tetrabiblos*. Trans. F E Robbins, Loeb Classical Library, p.273.
5. Marcus Manilius, *Astronomica*. Trans. G P Goold, Loeb Classical Library, pp.147-149.
6. Manilius p.151.
7. Ptolemy pp.271-275.
8. George Wharton, 1657, *Gesta Britannorum*, p.195.
9. Lilly p.50.
10. Olivia Barclay, 'A Natal Astrologer's Guide To Horary', *Transit*, February 1984, p.3.
11. Culpeper, *Astrologicall Judgment of Diseases*, Ballantrae Reprints, p.68.
12. Lilly, references from this section on Quadrants from pp.47-48.
13. Al Biruni p.112.
14. ibid p.309.
15. Dariot p.40.
16. Robert Hand in *On Reception* by Masha'allah, ARHAT Publications, 1998, p.83.
17. Al Biruni p.309.
18. ibid.
19. Dorotheus pp.164-165.
20. Masha'allah p.46.

21. Ibn Ezra, *The Beginning Of Wisdom*, edited by Raphael Levy and Francisco Cantera, The John Hopkins Press and Oxford University Press, 1939. Reprinted by Ascella Publications, p.192.
22. Al Biruni, throughout this section the references to Horary are from p.276 and the references to Nativities from p.275.
23. Morin p.29.
24. Lilly, the section on houses is largely based on pp.50-56.
25. Morin, all references to Morin in this section from p.142.
26. Al Biruni, all references in this section to Al Biruni are from pp.275 and p.276.
27. Bonatus, *The Astrologer's Guide or Anima Astrologiae*, p.47, 137th consideration.
28. Lilly p.548.
29. Morin p.32-33.
30. ibid p.59.
31. Lilly p.52.
32. Robert Hand in *On Reception* by Masha'allah, p.83.
33. Al Biruni p.316.
34. ibid p.112.
35. Olivia Barclay, 'Traditional Astrology', *The Astrologer's Quarterly*, Autumn 1987, Vol. 61, No. 3, p.123.
36. Ptolemy, *Tetrabiblos*. Trans. F. E. Robbins, Loeb Classical Library, p.409.
37. Dariot p.41.
38. ibid p.46.
39. ibid p.41.
40. ibid p.42.
41. Ibn Ezra, *The Beginning Of Wisdom*, p.192.
42. Abu 'Ali Al-Khayyat p.29.
43. Al Biruni p.259.
44. Dariot p.15.
45. Morin p.69.
46. Lilly, Table of Essential Dignities, p.104.
47. Dariot pp.42–45.
48. Lee Lehman, 'Horary Two Generations before Lilly', *The Astrologers Quarterly*. Spring, 1992, p.29.
49. Robert Hand quoting Vettius Valens in *Night and Day, Planetary Sect in Astrology*, p.29 and footnote.

3

SIGNS OF THE ZODIAC AND THEIR DIVISIONS

The zodiac is divided into twelve equal parts. These are the zodiacal signs. Each sign contains thirty degrees, each degree contains sixty minutes and each minute contains sixty seconds. The signs are divided into unequal segments called the *terms*, each ruled by one of the five planets. The signs are also divided into equal divisions of three called the *faces*, each ruled by one of the five planets or one of the luminaries.[1] The planetary rulership of the terms was the subject of much disagreement among astrologers of the past. In this book, the planetary terms referred to are those put forward by Ptolemy. In chapter six they are examined in a little more depth.

A planet cannot act independently of the sign in which it is placed, nor can the sign act independently of its ruler. In terms of a Question, if a planet symbolises a person or object, the zodiacal sign in which it is placed describes that person or object. The terms of each planet are also important in confirming the description of people or objects in the chart. Morin tells us that

> ...a Planet acts not only according to its own nature, but also according to its Zodiacal state, which changes successively according to the Sign through which the Planet passes, and according to its connections with the other Planets. A Sign thus depends on its Ruler as much with regard to the Ruler's Zodiacal state as with regard to the Ruler's nature.[2]

Signs and Rulers

Aries	ruled by Mars
Taurus	ruled by Venus
Gemini	ruled by Mercury
Cancer	ruled by the Moon
Leo	ruled by the Sun
Virgo	ruled by Mercury
Libra	ruled by Venus
Scorpio	ruled by Mars
Sagittarius	ruled by Jupiter
Capricorn	ruled by Saturn
Aquarius	ruled by Saturn
Pisces	ruled by Jupiter

Signs and Triplicities

Each of the twelve zodiacal signs can be assigned to one of four groups, which are called the *triplicities*. The importance of the triplicities and their rulers in terms of judgement cannot be over-emphasised.

The fire triplicity, which by nature is hot and dry, comprises Aries, Leo and Sagittarius. The earth triplicity, which is cold and dry, comprises the signs Taurus, Virgo and Capricorn. The air triplicity, which is hot and moist, comprises the signs Gemini, Libra and Aquarius. The water triplicity which is cold and moist comprises the signs Cancer, Scorpio and Pisces. Each triplicity is composed of the three signs which are the same in terms of their nature.

> Those signs whose nature as regards two qualities is identical are situated in the zodiac at the angles of right-angled triangles; they are consequently known as triplicities and are recognised as entities, although three in number, the effects of each being identical or similar.[3]

Al Biruni explains that the first triplicity is fiery in nature, what he calls "withering and heavy". He tells us that within each triplicity, each sign has its own special association. For Aries, this is fire in ordinary use, for Leo, fire which is present in minerals and plants, for Sagittarius, "that which is distributed from the heart of animals throughout the body".

The second triplicity is earth, which Al Biruni confirms is "generous with its wealth". Taurus is associated with unsown pastureland, Virgo with plants which have no berries or seeds, as well as small trees, Capricorn with crops which are sown, as well as large, tall trees.

The third triplicity is air and is associated with "sending winds abroad..." Gemini is associated with quiet air which produces and sustains life, Libra is associated with the wind, which causes trees to grow, fertilises them and produces fruit. Aquarius is associated with destructive storms.

The fourth triplicity is water and is "watery in sympathy". Cancer is associated with sweet and pure water, Scorpio with water which is "turbid" and Pisces is associated with water which is "stinking, distasteful and alkaline".

Feminine and Masculine Signs

The signs can be divided into two groups: *masculine, diurnal and hot*, comprising Aries, Leo, Sagittarius, Gemini, Libra, Aquarius, or *feminine, nocturnal and cold*, comprising Pisces, Scorpio, Cancer, Taurus, Virgo, Capricorn. This information can be useful in determining the physical characteristics of an individual when locating significance. For example, a masculine planet in a masculine sign has more masculine qualities. A masculine planet in a feminine sign has less masculine qualities, but more feminine qualities.

Signs and Parts of the Body

It is the zodiacal signs which are associated with parts of the body. Lilly explains that "... the twelve Signs are appropriate to the particular members of mans body".[4]

According to Culpeper the signs which have an association with particular parts of the body are:[5]

> Aries, which has a signification over the head and all its parts, such as the bones, face, brain, hair, beard, eyes, nose tongue, teeth, and whatever in a human being "is above the first Vertebra of the neck".
>
> Taurus is associated with the neck, throat, the vertebrae of the neck (seven in total) and the shoulder blade. Taurus also has signification over the voice, for Culpeper tells us that "he will roar like a Bull".
>
> Gemini has signification over the shoulders, shoulder-bones, arms, hands and fingers "together with their bag and baggage".
>
> Cancer is associated with the breast, ribs, lungs, stomach, the liver and perhaps the spleen.
>
> Leo is associated with the heart, the back and the vertebrae of the breast (twelve in total). Culpeper tells us that some authors give Leo significance over the stomach but that he himself "can scarce believe it". In fact, Culpeper is "perswaded that the appetite is under LEO, and that's the reason such as have that signe ascending in their Genesis are such greedy eaters".
>
> Virgo has a significance over the belly and the bowels, the navel, the spleen and the intestines.
>
> Libra is associated with the kidneys.
>
> Scorpio is associated with "the secrets of both sexes". Culpeper tells us that "it is not very fitting for me to name them..." Nevertheless, he explains that it is the areas of "propagation" for both men and women.
>
> Sagittarius is associated with the thighs and thigh bone.
>
> Capricorn is associated with the "knees, hams, and what belongs unto them".
>
> Aquarius is associated with the legs and "whatsoever belongs unto them," from the skin to the bone marrow.
>
> Pisces "claims the feet and ankles, toes and all the bones". Culpeper explains that every single bit of the foot is included such as the skin of the foot, the flesh and the vessels between the skin and the bones.

Signs, Planets and Parts of the Body

	♄	♃	♂	☉	♀	☿	☽
♈	Breſt Arme	Neck Throat Heart Belly	Belly Head	Thighes	Reines Feet	Secrets Legs	Knees Head
♉	Heart Breſt Belly	Shoulders Armes Belly Neck	Reines Throat	Knees	Secret-members Head	Thighs Feet	Legs Throat
♊	Belly Heart	Breſt Reines Secrets	Secrets Armes Breſt	Legs Ancles	Thighs Throat	Knees Head	Feet Shoulders Armes Thighs
♋	Reines Belly Secrets	Heart Secrets Thighs	Feet	Knees Shoulders Armes	Knees Shoulders Armes	Legs Throat Eyes	Head Breſt Stomack
♌	Secrets Reines	Belly Thighs Knees	Knees Heart Belly	Head	Legs Breſt Heart	Feet Armes Shoulders Throat	Throat Stomack Heart
♍	Thighs Secrets Feet	Reines Knees	Legs Belly	Throat	Feet Stomach Heart Belly	Head Breſt Heart	Armes Shoulders Bowels
♎	Knees Thighs	Secrets Legs Head Eyes	Feet Reines Secrets	Shoulders Armes	Head ſmal guts	Throat Heart Stomack Belly	Breſt Reines Heart Belly
♏	Knees Legs	Thighs Feet	Head Secrets Armes Thighs	Breſt Heart	Throat Reines Secrets	Shoulders Armes Bowels Back	Stomack Heart Secrets Belly
♐	Legs Feet	Knees Head Thighs	Throat Thighs Hands Feet	Heart Belly	Shoulders Armes Secrets Thighs	Breſt Reines Heart Secrets	Bowels Thighs Back
♑	Head Feet	Legs Neck Eyes Knees	Armes Shoulders Knees Legs	Belly Back	Breſt Heart Thighs	Stomack Heart Secrets	Reines Knees Thighs
♒	Neck Head	Feet Armes Shoulders Breſt	Breſt Legs Heart	Reines Secrets	Heart Knees	Bowels Thighs Heart	Secrets Legs Ancles
♓	Armes Shoulders Neck	Head Breſt Heart	Heart Feet Belly Ancles	Secrets Thighs	Belly Legs Neck Throat	Reines Knees Secrets Thighs	Thighs Feet

In the table shown we can see which part of the body is ruled by each planet in each different sign.[6]

Signs and Seasons

The four quarters or quadrants of the zodiac are each associated with different seasons:

- Firstly, there is a quadrant containing the signs of Aries, Taurus and Gemini. These signs are "vernal and changeable". They have rulership over childhood, the east, the east wind, and the first watch of day and night.

- Secondly, there is a quadrant containing the signs of Cancer, Leo and Virgo. These signs are "aestival and restful" and have rulership over youth, the south, the south wind and the second watch.

- Thirdly, there is a quadrant containing the signs of Libra, Scorpio and Sagittarius. These signs are "autumnal and changeable" and have rulership over adult life, the west, the west wind, and the third watch.

- Finally, there is a quadrant containing the signs of Capricorn, Aquarius and Pisces. These signs are "hibernal and peaceful" and have rulership over old age, the north, the north wind and the fourth watch.[7]

When the Sun enters certain signs, it signals a particular time of year:

- In Aries, Cancer, Libra or Capricorn, it signals the new quarter of the year (spring, summer, autumn, winter). In terms of timing in judgement, these signs are *moveable* and are associated with quick movement.

- In Taurus, Leo, Scorpio or Aquarius, the season of the year is *fixed*. At this time, we are more aware of the hot or cold. In terms of timing in judgement, these signs are associated with slow movement.

- In Gemini, Virgo, Sagittarius or Pisces, the season is somewhere between those described above. These signs take on the nature of both the preceding and following sign; they are called *bycorporeall* or double bodied, because they represent two bodies.[8] They are also known as *common* signs. For example, Gemini is associated with the twins and Pisces with the two fish. In terms of timing in judgement, these signs are changeable and the length of time is somewhere in between moveable and fixed.

    In a Question (horary), if the ascendant ruler is in a moveable sign and the sign ascending is also moveable, it suggests that the Querent is unstable, dislikes commitment and is easily distracted and inconstant. If the ascendant is in a fixed sign and the ascendant ruler is also fixed, the Querent is consistent in his or her actions and is firmly committed. This is an individual who says what he means and means what he says. If the ascendant is in a common sign and the ascendant ruler is also in a common sign, the Querent is neither determined nor inconstant, but somewhere between the two.

Bonatti tells us that a significator in a fixed sign signifies stability and continuance. A significator in a common sign indicates a change with a return or a repeat, for example, the matter could be broken off and later begun again, something could be added, or there could be some other alteration. A significator in a moveable sign indicates a sudden change "a quick despatch or end whether good or evil."[9]

Signs and Colours

Each sign is associated with a particular colour or mixture of colours:

Aries	white mixed with red
Taurus	white mixed with citrine
Gemini	white mixed with red
Cancer	green or russet
Leo	red or green
Virgo	black speckled with blue
Libra	black or dark crimson, or tawny colour
Scorpio	brown
Sagittarius	yellow or a "green sanguine"
Capricorn	black or russet or a "swart browne"
Aquarius	sky colour with blue
Pisces	glittering white[10]

Signs and Directions

Each sign is associated with a direction:

Aries	East
Leo	East and by north
Sagittarius	East and by south
Libra	West
Gemini	West and by south
Aquarius	West and by north
Cancer	North
Scorpio	North and by east
Pisces	North and by west
Capricorn	South
Taurus	South and by east
Virgo	South and by west[11]

Signs and Fertility

Cancer, Scorpio, Pisces are signs which are associated with fertility, what Lilly calls "fruitful or prolifical".[12] Al Biruni confirms that these signs favour large families, as well as "the hinder half of Capricorn". He tells us that Aries, Taurus, Libra, Sagittarius and Aquarius are associated with small families. The first part of Taurus, Leo, Virgo and Capricorn indicate sterility. However, "The production of twins is specially in charge of Gemini, but also is favoured by Virgo, Sagittarius and Pisces". He adds that sometimes this can occur in Aries and Libra and the last part of Capricorn.[13] Although Gemini is associated with twins, many authorities, including Lilly, tell us that Gemini, Leo, Virgo are the zodiacal signs which are associated with infertility.[14] I would suggest that where Gemini is a sign of signification, confirming testimony would be needed to support the possibility of twins.

In Questions about pregnancy and children, if the Moon and the principal significators are dignified and in prolific signs, there is a very good chance that the Querent will have children. However, if the same planets are in barren signs, this might represent few or no children.

Signs and Description

Gemini, Libra, Virgo and Aquarius are the zodiacal signs which are associated with sociability and social graces, what Lilly calls "manly or humane, curteous Signes". He tells us that the zodiacal sign of Leo and the last part of Sagittarius are signs associated with what he calls "feral" and that Cancer, Scorpio and Pisces are the zodiacal signs associated with low voice or of not being able to talk at all, what Lilly calls "mute". This is more pronounced if Mercury is placed in any of these signs and is in conjunction, square or opposition with Saturn.[15]

According to Al Biruni, Gemini, Virgo and Libra are "loud-voiced"; Aries, Taurus and Leo are "half-voiced"; Capricorn and Aquarius are "weak-voiced" while Cancer, Scorpio and Pisces are "voiceless".

Al Biruni also claims that the "dark and anxious" signs are Leo, Scorpio and Capricorn, but tells us that there is "a suspicion of trouble in Virgo and Libra".[16]

Referring to Nativities, Bonatti explains that if either the ascendant or ascendant ruler is in a human sign such as Gemini, Virgo, Libra or Aquarius, the native is honest, sociable and neighbourly, especially if both of them are in any of these signs. However, if the ascendant is located in signs of "creatures which men use to labour with" for example, in Aries, Taurus or the last part of Sagittarius and Capricorn, the native is submissive and humble, but is also very sociable.[17] The signs of Aries, Taurus, Leo, Sagittarius and Capricorn are those which represent four-footed creatures, what Lilly calls "bestial or quadrupedian".[18]

Bonatti explains that if the ascendant is in a sign which is "half-feral" for example, Cancer or Pisces, the native is less sociable. If the ascendant is in a "feral, furious or salvane sign", such as Leo or Scorpio, the native will be

...of a brutish temper, delighting in the woods, hunting and living upon spoils and rapine; caring not to associate himself with men, so that he seldom remains long with his own Parents or nearest Relations.[19]

It is unlikely that an astrologer would describe an individual in quite this way! However, the above information can be useful when the astrologer is considering the characteristics of people described in a Question. For example, if a significator is located in the sign of Pisces a person may be unsociable. If a significator is located in the sign of Aries, a person may be more sociable, although according to Lilly they may also have characteristics similar to the animal represented by Aries (rash or foolish). However, if a significator is placed in Gemini, Virgo, Libra, or if Aquarius is ascending, the person in question is civilised, friendly and easy to deal with.

The relevant house and sign in its cusp can also be considered in finding description. If the Question concerns a friend, signification is taken from the eleventh house. The astrologer must consider the sign in the eleventh house cusp, the ruler of that sign and the condition of the Moon. If the sign is human and airy and the ruler of

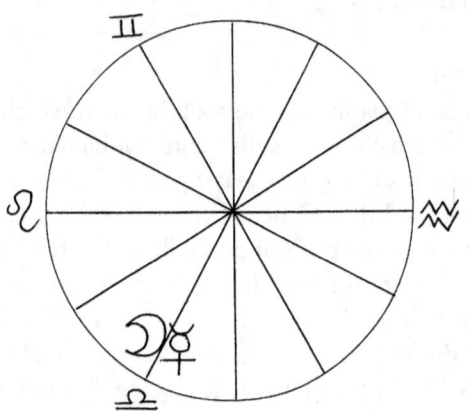

The Friend

Signification of character from a sign

that sign (or the Moon) is in any sign of the same triplicity or nature, the friend is likely to be handsome, sociable and courteous. As an example, the sign in the cusp of a given house is Gemini, Mercury the ruler of that house is in Libra and the Moon is also in Libra.

In a very general way, if the Question concerns an illness and Aries is the sign ascending or in the cusp of the sixth house, the disease is of the nature of Aries. However, in order to work out exactly what the illness might be and how long it might last, the condition of the other significators and the Moon must be taken into account.

There are other parts or degrees of a sign which are associated with different significations. For more information I refer the reader to *The Book of Instruction in the*

Elements of the Art of Astrology, by Al Biruni, where he discusses the male and female degrees of signs, the bright and dark degrees, the degrees increasing or diminishing in fortune, places injurious to the eyes and so on.[20]

Signs of Right or Long Ascension and Signs of Short or Oblique Ascension

Signs of long ascension are Cancer, Leo, Virgo, Libra, Scorpio and Sagittarius. Signs of short ascension are Capricorn, Aquarius, Pisces, Aries, Taurus and Gemini. Signs of long ascension continue their journey in the ascendant for two hours or more. Signs of short ascension complete their ascension in just over one hour and in some cases, less. At various places in *Christian Astrology*, Lilly mentions that a square between signs of long ascension can be equivalent to trine, or that a trine between signs of short ascension can be equivalent to a square.[21] However, Culpeper is very clear about this

> ...why do they hold that a Quartile in Signes of long ascensions is aequivalent to a Trine, and a Trine in Signes of short ascensions as pernicious as a Square? put the rest of the non-sence into the bundel, and when you have done, look upon it a little while; and when you have viewed it a little, tell me I pray; Doth the longness or shortness of the ascensions adde or take away any thing from the quality of the Signs?[22]

The Nature, Place, Country, General Description and Diseases signified by the Signs[23]

Aries

Quality: The fire triplicity, masculine, diurnal, moveable, cardinal, equinoctial, fiery, hot and dry, cholerick, bestial, intemperate and violent, the diurnal house (domicile) of Mars and the exaltation of the Sun in the 19th degree, of the east.
Diseases: Pimples in the face, smallpox, hare lips, polyps, ringworms, tooth ache, head ache, baldness.
Places: Where sheep or cattle feed, sandy or hilly ground, a place of refuge for thieves (some obscure unfrequented place), a stable for small beasts, the plastering, ceiling or covering of a house, newly ploughed land or where bricks have been burned or lime.
Description: Not very tall, lean, strong bones, long face, black eye brows, long neck, thick shoulders, dark complexion.
Countries and Cities: Germany, France, England, Denmark, Syria, Florence, Naples, Padua, Marseilles.

Abu Ma'shar[24] tells us that Aries is royal and is a sign prone to anger. He gives Aries a rulership over the head and the face. Sometimes Aries indicates twins. Abu Ma'shar associates the countries of Babylon, Persia, Azerbaijan and Palestine with the sign of Aries.

Barclay says that Aries people are often distinguished by their love of the colour red and their love of competitive sport.[25] In a house the roof, ceiling and plastering belong to Aries.

Taurus

Quality: The earth triplicity, feminine, nocturnal, fixed, cold and dry, melancholy, bestial, the nocturnal house (domicile) of Venus and the exaltation of the Moon in the 3rd degree, of the south.

Diseases: Sore throats.

Places: Stables for horses, low houses, farm buildings, pastures or feeding grounds where there are no houses, plain ground or where there used to be bushes, where wheat and corn are sown, land where there are some small trees in the distance, cellars, low rooms.

Description: Short but strong and well built, broad forehead, great eyes, big face, large strong shoulders, thick lips, big hands, black rugged hair.

Countries and Cities: Russia, Ireland, Switzerland, Cyprus, Persia, Parthia, Parma, Mantua, Nantes, Liepzig, Novograde.

Abu Ma'shar tells us that Taurus is associated with few children and that sometimes the early degrees of Taurus are barren. Taurus is associated with the neck and the Adam's apple. He gives rulership of "the country of the Kurds" to Taurus.

Barclay explains that Taurus has an association with the throat and all illnesses connected to it, but adds that Taurus can produce fine singing voices. Taureans often like the colour of green grass. Low-ceilinged rooms and cellars belong to Taurus. She quotes Nick Kollerstrom[26] as saying that women have more copper in their bodies than men, which is interesting because Venus (planetary ruler of Taurus) rules both copper and women.

Gemini

Quality: The air triplicity, airy, masculine, diurnal, common or double-bodied, hot and moist, sanguine, the diurnal house of Mercury, of the west.

Diseases: All diseases or infirmities in the arms, shoulders, hands, bad blood, vivid imagination and fancies.

Places: Plastering and walls of houses, halls or where people play, hills and mountains, barns, storehouses for corn, chests, high places.

Descriptions: Upright, tall straight body, not a clear complexion, but obscure and dark, long arms but hands and feet can be short and fleshy, dark hair almost black, strong active body, piercing hazel eyes, perfect sight, excellent understanding, fair in dealings.

Countries and Cities: West and southwest England, Lombardy, Flanders, Armenia, London, Bruges, Cordoba.

Abu Ma'shar says that Gemini is "eloquent, barren, powerful in voice, youthful, beautiful in face, generous, good in its soul." Gemini is associated with the shoulders, the upper arms and the hands. He gives Gemini a rulership over Egypt, Armenia, and Azerbaijan.

Barclay explains that Gemini is a nervous and intellectual sign and that Geminis seem to like the colour emerald green. Gemini is associated with high places, chests and boxes. She tells us that a country with a probable Gemini ascendant is the USA.

Cancer

Quality: The water triplicity, the only sign ruled by the Moon, the first sign of the water or northern triplicity, feminine, nocturnal, watery, cold and moist, flegmatick, moveable, a solstice sign, mute and slow of voice, fruitful, of the north.

Diseases: Problems with the stomach and breast, weak digestion, cold stomach, rotten coughs, cancers in the breast.

Places: The sea, great rivers, navigable waters, in the inland countries places near rivers, brooks, springs, wells, cellars in houses, wash houses, swimming baths, marshy ground, ditches with rushes, sea banks, trenches, cisterns.

Description: Generally short, the upper parts bigger than the lower, round face, sickly, pale, white complexion, sad brown hair, little eyes, many children (if a woman).

Countries and Cities: Scotland, Holland, Algeria, Prussia, Tunisia, Constantinople, Venice, Milan, Genoa, Amsterdam, York, Cadiz.

Abu Ma'shar associates Cancer with having many children, but tells us that Cancer is also a sign of no voice. The chest, the breasts, the heart, the stomach, the flanks, the spleen and the lungs belong to this sign. Lesser Armenia, China and part of Azerbaijan are ruled by Cancer.

Barclay reports that people signified by Cancer usually have Moon shaped faces and small eyes. They are heavier in the upper part of the body than they are in the lower part. Damp basements in houses belong to Cancer.

Leo

Quality: The fire triplicity, masculine, diurnal, the only sign ruled by the Sun, fiery, hot and dry, cholerick, commanding, bestial, barren, of the east.

Diseases: All sicknesses in the ribs and sides, pleurisy, convulsions, pains in the back, problems with the heart, sore eyes and jaundice, burning fevers.

Places: A place where wild beasts frequent, woods, forests, deserts, steep rocky places, inaccessible places, Kings' palaces, castles, forts, parks, in houses where the fire is and near a chimney.

Description: Large round head, big eyes, staring or goggle eyes, quick sighted, full and large body, broad shoulders, narrow sides, curly yellow (or dark sandy) hair, a fierce countenance, ruddy high complexion, strong, valiant, active.

Countries and Cities: Italy, Bohemia, the Alps, Sicily, Turkey, Bristol, Damascus, Rome, Prague.

Abu Ma'shar says that Leo is prone to anger, is barren, "half-voiced", but is also "a master of cleverness..." Leo is associated with slyness, deceit, cunning and having many cares and sadnesses. Leo rules the upper half of the stomach, the heart, sinews, the side, and the back. He gives rulership of Turkey to Leo.

Barclay tells us that Leo has an association with the eyes. Leo rules grand buildings, castles, theatres and palaces. Inside a house the fireplaces and the areas within their vicinity belong to Leo.

Virgo

Quality: The earth triplicity, earthly, feminine, nocturnal, cold and dry, melancholy, barren, the domicile of Mercury, of the south.
Places: A study where books are kept, a closet, a dairy house, corn fields, granaries, malt houses, hay ricks, a place where cheese and butter are preserved and stored.
Diseases: Worms, wind, colic, all obstructions in the bowels and diseases in the belly.
Description: A slender body of average height but well shaped, ruddy brown complexion, black hair, not a beautiful person, small shrill voice, short arms and legs, witty and discreet, fair and well-spoken, studious, good understanding, intelligent.
Countries and Cities: Croatia, Southern Greece, Albania, Mesopotamia, South West France, Africa, Rhodes, Lyons, Paris.

Abu Ma'shar gives Virgo a rulership of all plants. Virgo is also associated with barrenness, but it is "powerful in voice, beautiful in face, generous and good in its soul". Virgo rules the belly, large intestine, small intestine and the diaphragm.

Syria, the Euphrates and Persia belong to Virgo.

Barclay tells us that the people associated with the sign of Virgo are not as tall as those associated with Gemini. People who limp or nearly limp are ruled by Virgo. Virgos can be studious and interested in history. They seem to like small brown patterns. Cupboards, store rooms and things at floor level belong to Virgo.

Libra

Quality: The air triplicity, masculine, diurnal, hot and moist, moveable, equinoctial, cardinal, human, the chief house of Venus, the exaltation of Saturn at the 21st degree, of the west.
Diseases: Diseases in the loins, kidney stones, ulcers, weakness in the back, corruption in the blood.
Places: Grounds near windmills, barn or outhouse, saw pits or where wood is cut, sides of hills, tops of mountains, grounds where hawking and hunting is carried out, sandy and gravelly ground, pure clear air, the upper rooms in houses, bedrooms, attics, one room within another.
Description: A well framed body, straight and tall, slender, a round lovely and beautiful face, a pure sanguine complexion, in youth the face is not excessively red or white, but can be pimples when older or a high colour in the face, long smooth yellow hair.
Countries and Cities: Austria, Lisbon, Vienna, Greece, Thebes.

Abu Ma'shar reports that Libra is associated with having few children, although it can indicate twins. Libra is beautiful in face and generous of soul. Libra is associated with the backbone, lower belly, the naval, genitals, buttocks and waist. Abu Ma'shar gives rulership of the area between Upper Egypt to Ethiopia and Kabul, to Libra.

Barclay tells us that Librans are straight bodied and attractive with well proportioned faces, but sometimes their neck is short. They have soft voices and enjoy pleasant surroundings and melodious music. They like the colour sky blue. Upstairs rooms, attics, bookshelves and high places belong to Libra.

Scorpio

Quality: The water triplicity, feminine, nocturnal, cold, watery, phlegmatic, fixed. The domicile and joy of Mars, of the north. This sign can represent subtle deceit, deceitful men.
Diseases: Bladder, ruptures, piles, gonorrhea and all afflictions of the genitals in either man or woman, stones in the genitals.
Places: Where all sorts of creeping beasts live, like beetles, or poisonous creatures without wings, gardens, orchards, vineyards, ruins of houses near water, muddy ground, stinking lakes, quagmires, sinks, the kitchen or larder, wash house.
Description: A strong able body, broad or square face, a dusky muddy complexion, sad dark hair, hairy body, bow legged, short necked, a squat person.
Countries and Cities: Northern Bavaria, the wooded part of Norway, Catalonia in Spain, Valencia, Vienna, Messina.

Abu Ma'shar confirms that Scorpio is associated with many children, but is "corrupt, cautious, prone to anger, lying, master of cares, beautiful in face, generous of soul, without voice". Scorpio rules the penis, the testicles, the bladder, the rump and the perineum. Abu Ma'shar gives rulership of the desert of the Arabs, places in the vicinity of Yemen and Tangier, to Scorpio.

Barclay says that Scorpio is the natural ruler of reptiles and is associated with places where insects and beetles live. Scorpio people are often slightly bow-legged and their eyes are close under their brows. They do not start quickly but sustain their energy and finish their work thoroughly. Kitchens or rooms with water in them, as well as anywhere damp, belong to Scorpio.

Sagittarius

Quality: The fire triplicity, masculine, diurnal, fiery, hot and dry, cholerick, diurnal, common, bicorporal or double-bodied, the domicile and joy of Jupiter, of the east.
Diseases: Wounds or diseases of the thighs and buttocks, fevers, falls from horses or injuries from them or four-footed beasts, illnesses or problems caused from fire or heat, injury through sports.
Places: A stable for large horses, or horses for war, a house where large four-footed animals are kept, fields, hills, the highest places, land or grounds that rise a little above the rest, in houses upper rooms near the fire.
Description: Long face, full and ruddy, sun burnt, light chestnut coloured hair, taller than average, a strong able body, well shaped limbs.
Countries and Cities: Spain, Hungary, Budapest, Toledo.

Abu Ma'shar tells us the Sagittarius is royal and noble. It is associated with few children and is "half-voiced, master of stratagem, cunning". The thighs are ruled by Sagittarius. Abu Ma'shar gives rulership of Baghdad to this sign.

Barclay tells us that the upstairs parts of buildings, which are near the fireplace, are associated with Sagittarius. Sagittarius people are tall and have large front teeth. They enjoy outdoor life, drive fast and they love nature.

Capricorn

Quality: The earth triplicity, feminine, nocturnal, the domicile of Saturn, cold and dry, melancholy, earthy, cardinal, moveable, domestic, four-footed, the exaltation of Mars, of the south.

Diseases: The knees and any disease of the knees like strains and fractures, leprosy, itches, scabs.

Places: Where ox or cows are kept, where old wood is laid or where farming tools are kept; where sails for ships and such materials are stored. Sheep pens, grounds where sheep are fed, barren fields, bushy and thorny places, dunghills in fields, low places in houses, dark places near the ground or threshold.

Description: Not tall, long, lean and slender face, thin beard, black hair, narrow chin, long small neck. If Capricorn ascends the person often has white hair, but if Capricorn is in the seventh house it is black.

Countries and Cities: Bulgaria, Turkey, Albania, southwest Saxony, West Indies, Oxford, Cleves.

Abu Ma'shar tells us that Capricorn is associated with many children, the twins of children and birds. This sign is "corrupt, beautiful in its way of life, weak in voice, prone to anger, cautious, master of stratagem, of many cares, dark, libidinous". Capricorn rules the knees and the countries of Ethiopia, the Indus, Oman and Bahrain.

Barclay tells us that Capricorns are hard-working and efficient; the men often have beards and the women's hair is often thin. They have narrow chins and they like ladders. In houses, the places near the floor or threshold belong to Capricorn.

Aquarius

Quality: The air triplicity, masculine, diurnal, airy, hot and moist, sanguine, fixed, rational, the principal domicile of Saturn and where he is has his joy, of the west.

Diseases: Legs, ankles, illnesses connected to the legs, blood clots and cramps.

Places: Hilly and uneven places, newly dug ground, stone quarries or areas where minerals have been dug up, the eaves or upper parts of houses, rooves, vineyards or near some little spring or conduit.

Description: Squat thick body, strong well-shaped body, not tall, long face, sanguine complexion, if Saturn (ruler of this sign) is located in Capricorn or Aquarius, the person has black hair, with sanguine complexion, with distorted teeth. If not, the person has a clear white or fair complexion and sandy coloured hair and a very pure skin.

Countries and Cities: Saudi Arabia, Croatia, Westphalia in Germany, Piemont in Savoy, west and southern Bavaria.

Abu Ma'shar tells us that Aquarius is associated with having few children and that sometimes it indicates barrenness. It is weak in voice. Aquarius rules the "two shanks which are below the knees" and it rules parts of Egypt.

Barclay reports that this sign is associated with the roof and upstairs rooms, as well as places off the floor near windows. Aquarian people like waves of any sort and are interested in photography. They seem to like the colour yellow.

Pisces

Quality: The water triplicity, feminine, nocturnal, cold, moist, flegmatick, the domicile of Jupiter and exaltation of Venus, of the north, a bicorporal, common or double-bodied sign, an idle, effeminate, sickly sign, can represent someone who is lazy.
Diseases: All diseases in the feet: gout, lameness and aches in the legs. Scabs, itches, boils, ulcers, colds.
Places: Grounds full of water or where there are many springs and poultry, fish ponds or rivers full of fish, moats around houses, water mills in houses near the water, a well or pump, or where water stands.
Description: Short, not well shaped body, but good large face, pale complexion, fleshy or swelling sort of body, a body which is not very straight.
Countries and Cities: Portugal, North Egypt, Calabria in Sicily, Alexandria, Normandy, Compostella.

Abu Ma'shar confirms that Pisces is associated with many children and is "without voice, cautious, master of stratagem, rash, of many forms." Pisces rules the feet and the countries from the Byzantine Empire to Syria, Egypt, Alexandria and the sea of Yemen.

Barclay tells us that Pisces rules places of meditation, churches, hospitals and prisons. Pisces also rules floors and floor coverings, places where shoes are kept and places near standing water. Pisceans have fine hair, but do not have strong or straight backbones. They have difficulty finding comfortable shoes and often have short legs.

Signs and Missing Items

If the Querent has lost something at home, the sign in which the significator is placed should describe the item. If the Moon or the planetary hour ruler is angular it shows that the item is indoors and probably mislaid. Again, other testimonies must be considered. The chart on the following page is an example. The Querent (the author) is signified by the Scorpio ascendant and its ruler Mars in Cancer. The second house and its ruler do not help in finding the location of the missing item, but show the possibility and time of recovery. In this chart Mercury, natural ruler of books and papers, is in the ascendant. Mercury therefore is principal significator of the papers. With Mercury retrograding back to Mars, significator of the Querent, by less then two degrees and received by Mars in his domicile, I was certain to find the papers.

Mercury in Scorpio and Saturn ruling the fourth house suggest that the papers are in a dark place within the home. However, the Moon, Jupiter and the Lot of Fortune in Sagittarius indicate that they may be in an upstairs room or near a fire.

I found the papers in a large plastic box under a bed in an upstairs room, next to a fireplace, which is no longer used. However, its chimney is still connected to a fireplace below which is in use during the winter.

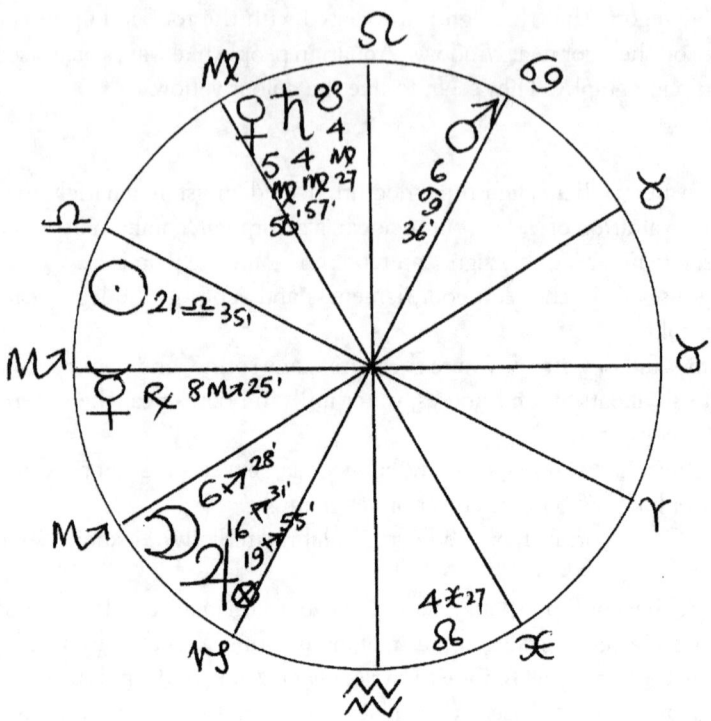

Where are my Papers?

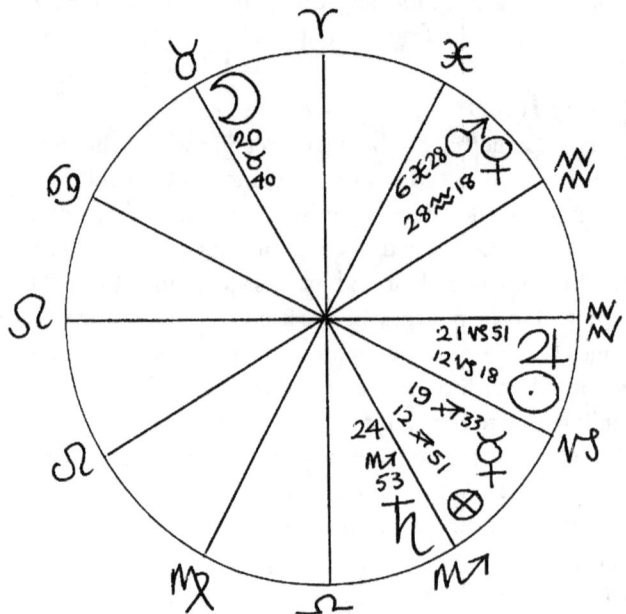

Where is Teddy?

Signs and Missing Animals

The rules for missing animals are slightly different to those for mislaid items. If a pet is missing, for example a cat (which occurs frequently), in the first instance the significator of the cat must be considered. For example, if the significator is in Aries one would look in an Aries type of place, or that part of the house, garden or locality, which is associated with the sign of Aries. The sign should describe the cat and should give a clue as to the direction in which the animal is heading, for example Aries is a sign associated with the east.

Olivia Barclay[27] gives a wonderful description about a missing cat, Teddy. Teddy's significator is the sixth house and the ruler of the sixth house, Saturn in Scorpio. From this Barclay explains that we can derive the "description, condition and whereabouts of the cat".

> I assumed he was black – Saturn and Scorpio have affinities with that colour – and that he had white on his face or head because Jupiter is in the first house and rules white.

Scorpio also shows the sort of place where Teddy is. From this she concludes that he is in a place which is damp, wet, northerly and cold, or a place which contains beetles, perhaps a garden, orchard, kitchen, larder or wash house. He was found the next day locked in the dark basement of a block of flats, in a north-easterly direction.

Signs and Places

In Questions enquiring about the most fortunate part of a country to live, or to travel to, the signs are particularly significant. For example if the Querent asks whether she would be happy in a certain place, or make money there, the sign in which the ascendant ruler is placed is very important. If the significator is placed in Pisces and if Jupiter or Venus are placed in Pisces, the part of the country (or indeed another country) represented by the sign of Pisces would be fortunate. In a similar way, any country or place represented by a sign where the Infortunes are placed (unless they themselves are significators) is likely to be unfortunate (if other testimonies concur).[28] The house involved is also important. For example, if the Question concerns making money, look at the second house as well as the tenth house and its ruler(s).

In these examples the Question is about a move to Ireland and whether it would be fortunate.

A Fortunate Place to Live

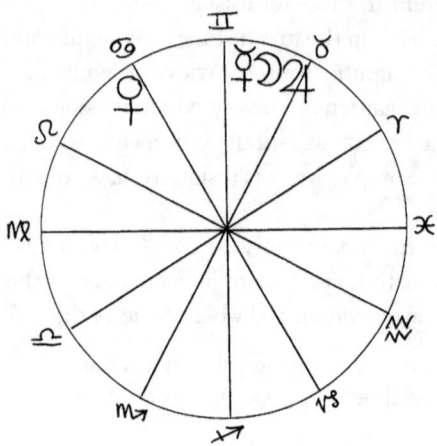

Shall I move to Ireland?
Yes.

An Unfortunate Place to Live

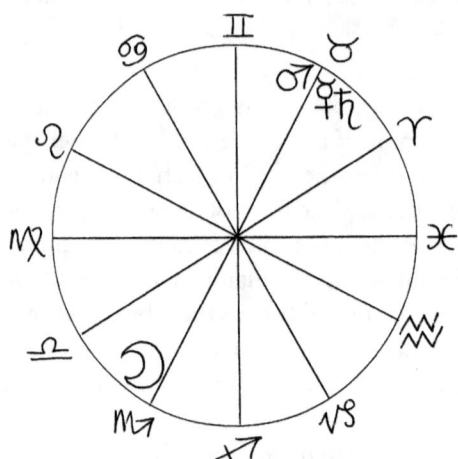

Shall I move to Ireland?
No.

Having discussed the nature of the houses, planets and signs, I hope that a basic framework as to planetary evaluation is starting to take shape. The signs in which the planets are placed are vital in that they provide information about direction, colour, illness, appearance and fertility to name but a few. Moreover, as we will learn in chapter six, the signs provide the information needed to evaluate the essential dignity or debility of a planet, a vital point in judgement.

References

1. See chapter six.
2. Morin p.50.
3. Al Biruni, references in this section taken from p.230.
4. Lilly, p.50.
5. Culpeper, all references to Culpeper in this section from pp.65-68.
6. Lilly pp.119-120.
7. Al Biruni p.230-231.
8. Lilly p.88.
9. Bonatus, *The Astrologer's Guide or Anima Astrologiae*, p.22, 60th consideration.
10. Lilly p.86.
11. ibid p.365.
12. ibid p.89.
13. Al Biruni p.214.
14. Lilly p.89.
15. ibid
16. Al Biruni pp.213-214.
17. Bonatus p.43, 128th consideration.
18. Lilly p.89.
19. Bonatus p.43, 128th consideration.
20. Al Biruni pp.269-272.
21. Lilly p.157.
22. Culpeper p.21.
23. Much of this section from Lilly, pp.93-99.
24. Abu Ma'shar. All references to Abu Ma'shar in this section from pp.2-9.
25. Olivia Barclay, *Horary Astrology Rediscovered*, Schiffer, PA, 1990. References to Olivia Barclay in this section from pp.32-46.
26. Nick Kollerstrom, *Astrochemistry: A Study of Metal-Planet Affinities*, Emergence Press, London, 1984. Cited by Olivia Barclay p.39.
27. Barclay, pp.192-195.
28. Lilly pp.100-101.

4

PLANETARY SECT

The concept of planetary sect has largely disappeared from our present day study of astrology, along with many of our traditional tools and techniques. In his excellent book *Night & Day, Planetary Sect in Astrology*, Hand tells us that the understanding of planetary sect may be "the single most important area of interpretation to have been lost, or at least mislaid, between the Greeks and modern astrology".[1]

The concept behind planetary sect was of fundamental importance and an indispensable piece of information to astrologers of the past. To astrologers of the late classical period, a vital consideration in their judgement was whether an individual was born during the day or night.[2]

Sect

A *sect* is a division. All planets belong to either the *solar diurnal* sect or the *lunar nocturnal* sect. The planets can be put into order within their sect, from most diurnal to most nocturnal, although Hand confirms that there is some doubt as to whether the Moon is more nocturnal than Mars.[3]

The solar and diurnal planets are the Sun, Jupiter, Saturn and Mercury. The Sun is most diurnal. Mercury is the least diurnal. The lunar and nocturnal planets are the Moon, Mars and Venus. The Moon is probably the most nocturnal. Venus is the least nocturnal.

During the day the Sun is above the horizon, so a chart drawn up during that time is a diurnal chart. During the night the Sun is below the horizon, so a chart drawn up during that time is a nocturnal chart. The calculation of most of the Lots, as well as the calculation of the rulers of the triplicities, is affected by this simple phenomenon. The triplicities are ruled by two or more planets which hold the highest dignities in the signs within the triplicity and who are also of the same sect. Hand tells us that this was the system practised by Vettius Valens, Dorotheus of Sidon and others in the ancient world, as well as most of the Arab writers and Guido Bonatti.[4]

Each of the triplicities has a diurnal ruler and a nocturnal ruler, as well as a third ruler, what Al Biruni calls a *partner*, what Dariot calls a *common* ruler or what Morin calls a *participating* ruler. This third ruler was believed to offer assistance to the diurnal and nocturnal rulers. Each of the three triplicity rulers was said to have a governance over certain things or events in a Nativity or Question and/or governance over a certain period of life.

Ptolemy's system is a little different in that he puts forward two rulers instead of three, although he does give co-signification over the water triplicity to Venus and the Moon. He does not include common rulers, nonetheless his rulerships follow the same pattern, being assigned on the basis of the chart's diurnal or nocturnal status. Ptolemy's triplicity system was used by Lilly and other English writers in the seventeenth century. This book is also based on the triplicity rulerships according to Ptolemy.

Any consideration of the triplicities and their rulers must acknowledge the importance of their diurnal or nocturnal status, because each planet, aspect and house position are interpreted differently according to a chart's diurnal or nocturnal nature. Hand explains that in each type of chart the planets have "different capabilities, powers and functions".[5] Diurnal births, although different to nocturnal births, are not more powerful; they are equally powerful.

There are three factors which relate to the sect of a planet.[6] A planet which fulfils all three of these conditions is more comfortable and gains extra strength.

Diurnal or Nocturnal Chart

The most important consideration relating to planetary sect is whether the chart itself is diurnal or nocturnal. A diurnal planet is always more comfortable in a diurnal chart (when the Sun is above the horizon) regardless of where it is placed in the chart, or in what sign. Similarly, a nocturnal planet is more comfortable in a nocturnal chart (when the Sun is below the horizon) regardless of where it is placed, or in what sign. As an example, Jupiter prefers the diurnal chart, Venus prefers the nocturnal chart.

In his *Mathesis*, Firmicus Maternus explains that the Sun, Jupiter and Saturn "rejoice by day". Therefore, "they follow the condition of the Sun". If they are in

Planets Rejoicing in a Diurnal Chart

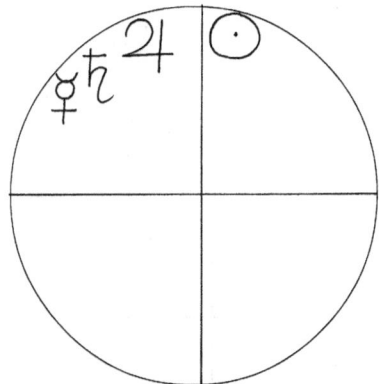

☉ ♃ ♄ rejoice in a diurnal chart.
(☿ can be either diurnal or nocturnal but is probably more diurnal)

Planets Rejoicing in a Nocturnal Chart

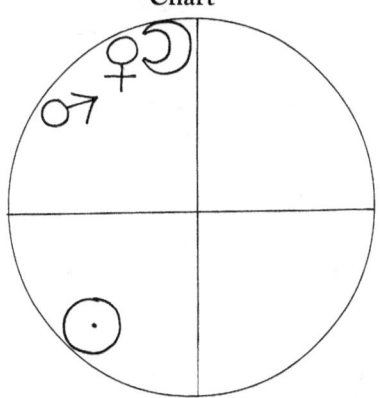

♀ ☽ ♂ rejoice in a nocturnal chart.

favourable positions (important houses and angular) in a diurnal chart, they indicate the "greatest increase in good fortune".[7] Venus, Mercury and Mars "rejoice by night" and therefore follow the Moon. If they are in favourable positions in a nocturnal chart they indicate good fortune. However, if nocturnal planets are located unfavourably in a diurnal chart they indicate "...unending misfortune and constant catastrophe..."[8] The same applies to diurnal planets in the same places in a nocturnal chart.

Diurnal or Nocturnal Placement

Secondly one must consider whether the planet is placed diurnally or nocturnally in the chart.[9] Any planet is considered to be placed diurnally when it is above the horizon during the day or below the horizon during the night. Any planet is placed nocturnally when it is below the horizon by day or above it by night. Venus, for example when above the horizon during the night is nocturnally placed. When she is placed below the horizon at night she is said to be diurnally placed.

Planets placed Nocturnally

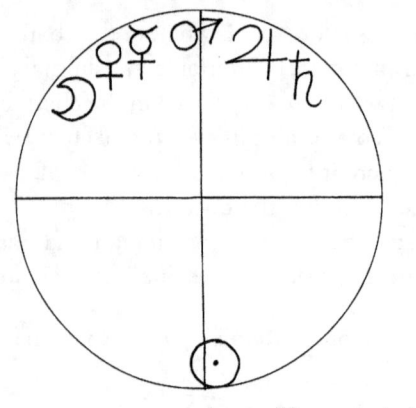
Nocturnal chart

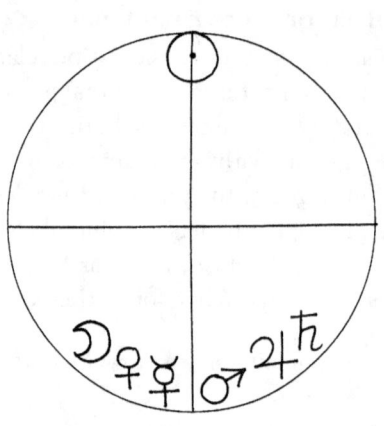
Diurnal chart

Planets placed Diurnally

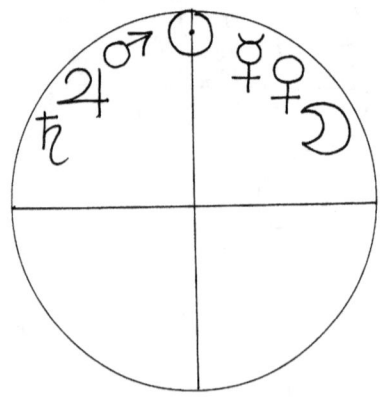
Diurnal chart

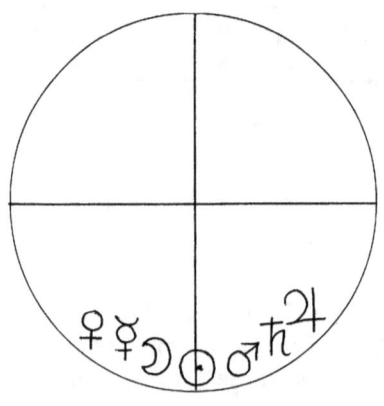
Nocturnal chart

Sect and Sign of the Same Nature

Finally, one must consider whether a planet is placed in a sign of the same nature as his sect.[10] A planet has more strength when placed in a sign agreeing with his own sect. Diurnal planets are optimally placed in Aries, Gemini, Leo, Libra, Sagittarius and Aquarius. Nocturnal planets are optimally placed in Taurus, Cancer, Virgo, Scorpio, Capricorn and Pisces, except Mars who prefers a masculine sign.

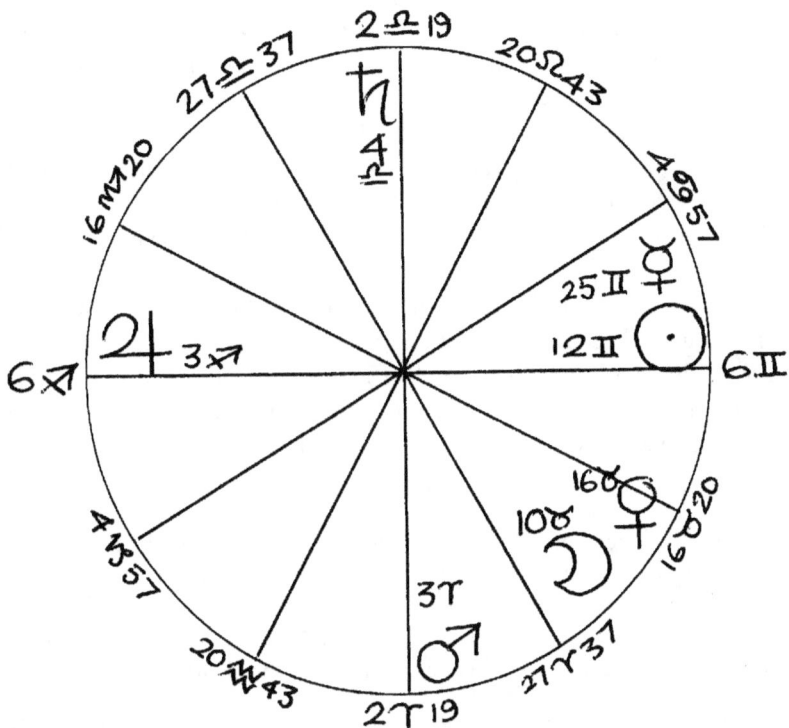

Sign and Sect in Agreement

According to Hand (although he confirms that no ancient writing ever states this explicitly), it seems that the most important of these relationships is that a planet is of the same sect as the chart.[11] Diurnal planets, such as the Sun, Jupiter, Saturn and, to some extent, Mercury, work best in diurnal charts. Nocturnal planets, such as the Moon, Mars and Venus work best in nocturnal charts. In *The Book of Instruction in the Elements of the Art of Astrology*, Al Biruni confirms that Saturn, Jupiter and the Sun exercise their power during the day, whereas Mars, Venus and the Moon exercise their power at night. He tells us that Mercury can be either diurnal or nocturnal, depending on his sign placement or the planet in aspect. As noted in chapter one, "Every planet assists those resembling it, the diurnal asking assistance from the diurnal and the nocturnal from the nocturnal".[12]

Second in importance is that a planet is correctly placed above or below the horizon.[13] Diurnal planets work best above the horizon during the day or below the horizon at night. Nocturnal planets are best above the horizon during the night or below the horizon during the day. As an example, Saturn in the ninth house in a diurnal chart is correctly placed, or Mars in the eleventh house in a nocturnal chart is correctly placed. Even a planet, whose sect is not in accord with the chart, has more strength (or is more effective) if it is correctly placed by "hemisphere".[14]

Bonatti asks the astrologer to carefully consider "whether the significator be in his Light or no"; that is whether a diurnal planet during the day is above the earth, or during the night under the earth or whether a nocturnal planet during the night is above the earth and during the day is under the earth. If this occurs, Bonatti explains that it makes the planet "more strong". However, if a nocturnal planet is a significator in the day above the earth, or if a diurnal planet is a significator in the night above the earth, "the same is thereby weakened and under a kind of impediment, that he can scarce accomplish what he signified".[15]

Al Biruni tells us that the Sun is the lord (ruler) of the day and the Moon is lady (ruler) of the night, because it is at these times when their influence is exerted. He confirms that "Every planet which is under the horizon during its own period has little or no influence".[16] Lilly follows this line of thought in *Christian Astrology*, where he quotes Dariot in the context of a Question about illness.

> If the Party be sicke of whom the Question is Demanded
>
> A diurnall Planet being Signifcator, and he under the earth, ill affected, Combust, Retrograde, in his Fall or Detriment, weak, or in Termes of malevolents, or with violent fixed Stars, or besieged by the two Infortunes, these things happening, the party is sick. What was spoken of a diurnall Planet, must be understood of a nocturnall one (consideratis considerandis).[17]

Third in importance is that a planet is placed in a sign whose sect is in agreement with its own.[18] For example, when the Moon is in Cancer, Venus is in Pisces, or when Jupiter is in Leo and the Sun is in Aries. Here each planet is in a sign whose sect agrees with its own. The exception to this appears to be Mars. Although Mars is nocturnal in terms of his sect, he was considered to be masculine and therefore performs better in a masculine sign, such as Gemini, Leo or Aries.[19] I have a little difficulty with this, as it would be more logical for Mars, as a nocturnal planet, to be located in a feminine sign.

Hayyiz

Clearly if all three factors are in operation, a planet has particular strength. For example, when a planet's sect is in accordance with the type of chart (diurnal or nocturnal), as well as its placement in the chart (above or below the horizon at the appropriate time) and with the sect of its sign (masculine planets in masculine signs and feminine planets in feminine signs), it acquires a special dignity. This was called "*Hayz, Haim,* or *Aym*". Hand explains that these are Latin corruptions of the Arabic word Hayyiz.[20]

Al Biruni tells us about *hayyiz* and *halb* which refer to the same phenomena.[21] He explains that these terms are related in their meaning and they share one condition: When a diurnal planet is above the ground during the day and beneath it during the night, or when a nocturnal planet is above the ground during the night or beneath the ground during the day, it is said to be in its halb. In addition to the above conditions, Al Biruni tells us that if a planet is masculine and is placed in a masculine sign or is feminine and placed in a feminine sign, it is said to be in its hayyiz. However, with regard to hayyiz, Al Biruni confirms that Mars, as discussed previously, is different to the other planets because "it is both male and nocturnal". If he is above the earth by night or below the earth by day and in a masculine sign, he is said to be in his hayyiz. From the above, Al Biruni confirms it is clear that every planet in its hayyiz must be in its halb, but not every planet in its halb is in its hayyiz.

Lilly defines *Hayz* as a masculine, diurnal planet which is above the earth during the day and in a masculine sign, or a feminine, nocturnal planet which is above the earth during the night and in a feminine sign.

> ...in Questions it usually shews the content of the Querent at time of the Question, when his significator is so found.[22]

A diurnal planet is at its strongest when in a diurnal chart, diurnally placed and in a diurnal sign. Examples of this in a diurnal chart are the Sun and Mercury in Leo in the ninth house, Jupiter in Sagittarius in the twelfth house and Saturn in Libra in the tenth house. A nocturnal planet is at its strongest when in a nocturnal chart, nocturnally placed and in a nocturnal sign. Examples of this in a nocturnal chart are the Moon and Venus in Scorpio in the eleventh house. To be in his hayz Mars could be in Gemini in the seventh house.

Nocturnal Planets in their Hayyiz

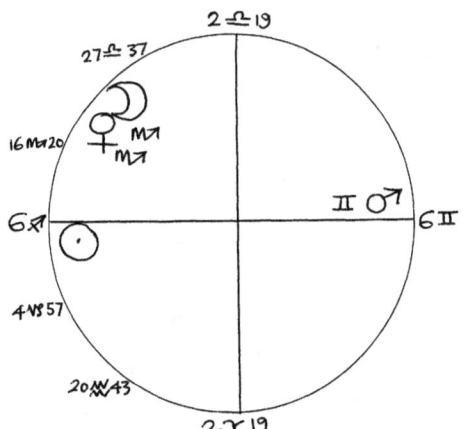

Nocturnal chart

Nocturnal planets nocturnally placed in a nocturnal chart in a feminine sign except ♂ who prefers a masculine sign.

Diurnal Planets in their Hayyiz

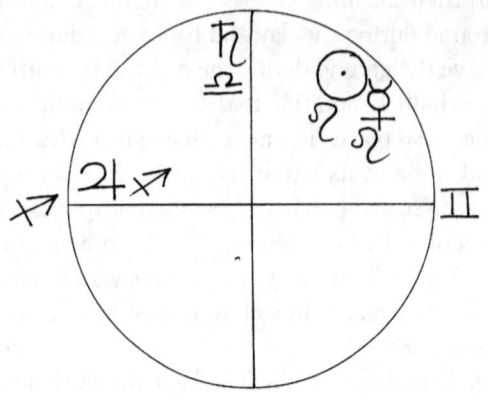

Diurnal chart

Diurnal planets diurnally placed in a diurnal chart in a masculine sign.

Out of Sect

If a planet does not satisfy any of these three conditions, the planet is said to be out of sect, it is somehow altered in its expression. Al Biruni calls a planet in this condition "in a contrary hayyiz" which he says is a place where a planet is weak. He also tells us about a condition called *contention* which he claims "is nearly the reverse of hayyiz".[23]

When a planet is debilitated because it is out of sect, it is inhibited in its expression and experiences a reduction in its power. However, it appears that some planets, especially the Infortunes, become more malefic in quality and not lessened in their quantity of power at all. Examples of this might be Mercury, Jupiter and Saturn in Scorpio in the eleventh house in a nocturnal chart. An example of this in a diurnal chart might be the Moon in Libra in the tenth house, Venus in Sagittarius in the twelfth house, or Mars in Cancer in the eighth house. In these conditions each of the above is considered to be out of sect or in a *contrary* hayyiz.

Diurnal Planets not in their Hayyiz (out of sect)

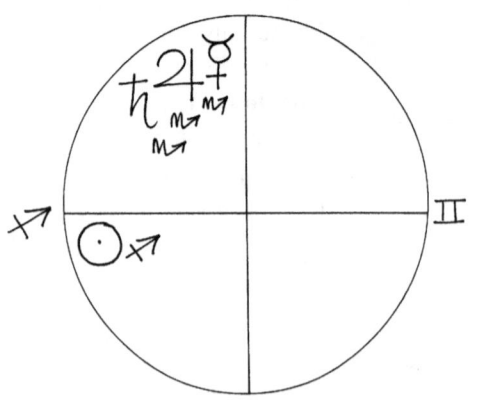

Nocturnal chart

♄ ♃ ☿ diurnal planets in a nocturnal chart, nocturnally placed and in feminine signs.
* ☉ cannot be above the horizon at night.

Nocturnal Planets not in their Hayyiz (Out of Sect)

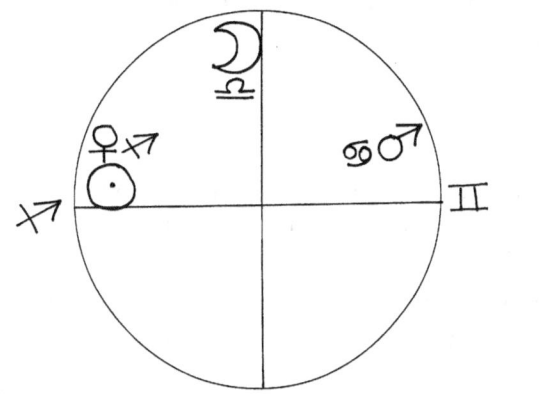

Diurnal chart

☽ ♀ ♂ nocturnal planets in a diurnal chart, diurnally placed and in masculine signs except ♂ in a feminine sign.

Contention

Ramsay Wright's translation isn't totally clear, but Al Biruni tells us that contention is nearly the reverse of hayyiz. Therefore it seems likely that contention simply refers to a diurnal planet in the sign of a nocturnal planet and vice versa. For example, contention takes place when Saturn is in Aries (Saturn, a diurnal planet in the domicile of a nocturnal planet, Mars), or Mars is in Pisces (a nocturnal planet in the domicile of Jupiter, a diurnal planet).

Differences in Interpretation

Maternus tells us that the interpretations of the planets according to their house position are different depending on whether the chart is diurnal or nocturnal. In the following examples Maternus is only concerned with a planet's sect being in accord with the chart, that is a nocturnal planet being placed in a nocturnal chart or a diurnal planet located in a diurnal chart.

Saturn

Maternus explains that if Saturn is in the seventh house in a diurnal chart and in a morning rising, this is favourable and "will grant great possessions", although this won't be until old age.[24] However, if Saturn is in the seventh house in a nocturnal chart (in an evening rising), the Natives are often "grieved by the very painful condition of their wives".[25] Saturn in the first house is fortunate if the chart is diurnal, but not if it is nocturnal. If Saturn has dignity in the first house, especially in his domicile of Aquarius, this does not represent a warning to the astrologer regarding the radicality of the chart.

Jupiter

Jupiter in the seventh house in a diurnal chart indicates "wealth and a happy old age". However, in a nocturnal chart, this is very different, when "the native will lose a beloved wife and see the deaths of his children." [26]

Mars

If Mars is in the ascendant in a diurnal chart this makes men

> ...bold, clever, emotional; wanderers, unstable in every way; never able to complete what they propose...they also lose their whole livelihood...nothing is saved from their paternal inheritance...[27]

However, Mars in the ascendant in a nocturnal chart (providing the ascendant and Mars are in the masculine sign of Mars and in conjunction with Jupiter, or in good aspect), makes men

> ...leaders in war to whom the entire army is entrusted and power of life and death...they will be brave, serious, fortunate..." [28]

The Sun

The Sun in the tenth house in a diurnal chart in his domicile, in the domicile of Jupiter, or in his exaltation, makes "kings, generals, governors, consuls or proconsuls – all of whom inherit their position from their father".[29] However, the Sun in the second house (where the chart must be nocturnal) makes the native seek a livelihood through his own efforts.[30] Although they will be "agreeable and respectable," they are also "sluggish, of small energy, and hindered in many ways". Throughout their lives they will be "anxious and fearful".

Lilly tells us that the Sun in the second house is always unfortunate in terms of wealth, in that the Native or Querent will not hold onto it.[31] If the Sun is in his domicile or exaltation this is less likely to be the case, especially where the Sun is in Leo and has signification over the second house.

Venus

Venus in the ascendant in a nocturnal chart makes

> ...men of divine intelligence, friends of emperors and powerful men, entrusted with the management of their affairs.[32]

However, Venus in the ascendant in a diurnal chart makes the natives "oversexed, unchaste, of ill repute". [33]

Mercury

If Mercury is located in the ascendant in signs where he rejoices in a diurnal chart he makes "philosophers, teachers of the art of letters, or geometers".[34] Mercury in the ascendant in a nocturnal chart makes men "of divine sensibilities, easily attaining their wishes...sober and respectable...in charge of activities..."[35] In regard to Mercury there does not appear to be much difference according to whether the placement is diurnal or nocturnal. Mercury's influence depends on the "different qualities of the signs".

The Moon

If the Moon is in the tenth house in a nocturnal chart

> ...in signs in which she rejoices or is exalted, if she is waxing and protected by a favourable aspect of Jupiter, this will make the greatest emperors and most powerful governors with power of life and death.[36]

In a diurnal chart the Moon placed in the midheaven makes the native "mediocre in life and in all occupations...cheated in various ways". However, with assistance from the Sun and Jupiter this position can make "most powerful emperors"[37]

Hand points out that a nocturnal placement of the Moon seems to give power on its own without requiring assistance from another planet.[38] However, the diurnal Moon has little power unless assisted by the Sun or Jupiter, both of which are diurnal. He points out that in contrast to Mars, the Moon is not malefic in a diurnal chart, just less effective.

Matutine and Vespertine Phase

There is another placement sometimes related to sect and sometimes related to masculine and feminine. This is connected to the concept of a *morning* star (or matutine phase) or to the concept of an *evening* star (vespertine phase). It was believed that a star rising ahead of the Sun (a morning star) acquired some type of masculine or diurnal status. However, a star setting after the Sun (an evening star) was thought to acquire some type of feminine or nocturnal status. According to Knappich, cited in Hand, the morning Star Venus was considered to be "a warrior goddess" whereas the evening star Venus was "the very feminine goddess of love".[39]

Maternus tells us that planets "placed in the light of the Moon are protected by its greatest influence when in any aspect they precede its rising".[40] It was also believed that planets rising ahead of the Sun, especially those within one or two signs of the Sun, are better and more effective if diurnal planets. Planets setting after the Sun or Moon are better if they are nocturnal planets. Maternus explains that certain astrologers believed that Mars was favourable when setting "when he is overwhelmed by the rays of the Sun, for in being subservient to the Sun he loses his natural malefic qualities".[41] This was not agreed by all authorities.

As well as making a distinction between the diurnal and nocturnal planets, it is also useful to make a distinction between the Superiors and the Inferiors. When the Superiors rise before the Sun they are in fewer degrees of the sign than the Sun. In this instance, because they move more slowly than the Sun, the Sun is moving away from them and they are stronger. If the Superiors follow the Sun in the morning rising, they are in more degrees of the sign than the Sun. In this instance the Sun is moving towards them, so they are moving in the direction of sunbeams or combustion and are weaker. The opposite is true of the Inferiors. When rising before the Sun the Inferiors are in fewer degrees than the Sun. Because they move more quickly than the Sun they are moving in the direction of sunbeams or combustion. When the Inferiors rise after the Sun (and set after the Sun) they are in more degrees than the Sun and because they move more quickly than the Sun they are moving away from sunbeams or combustion. Of course this does not apply if any planet is retrograde.

Diurnal Planets rising before the Sun

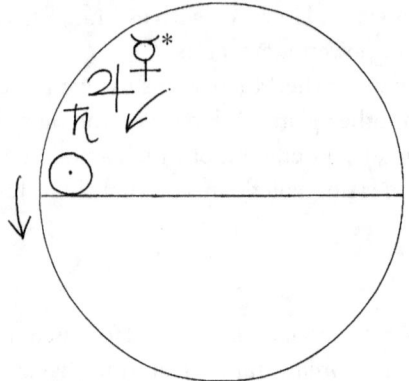

*☿ will become combust

Nocturnal Planets setting after the Sun

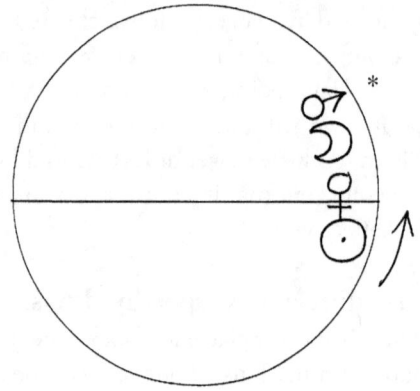

* ♂ will become combust

Superiors rising before the Sun

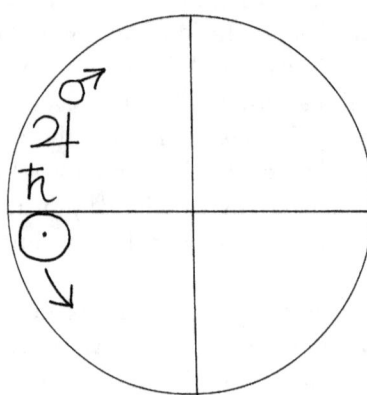

☉ moving away from superiors

Superiors rising after the Sun

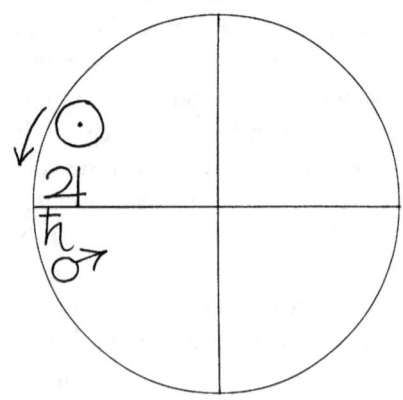

☉ moving towards superiors

Inferiors rising before the Sun

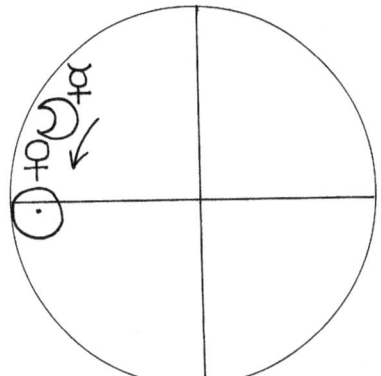

Inferiors moving towards ☉

Inferiors rising after the Sun

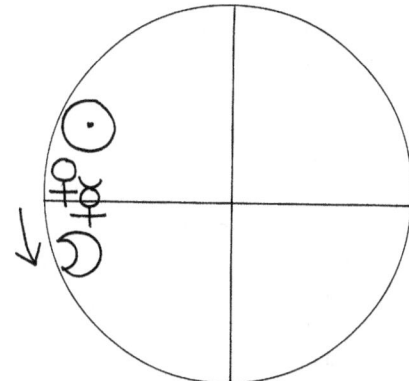

Inferiors moving away from ☉

Of course planets will not rejoice in company with the Sun if they are too close, that is under sunbeams or combust. It is generally agreed that planets are severely weakened when they are close to the Sun, whether they are placed diurnally or nocturnally. There is no doubt that planets moving towards the Sun and approaching sunbeams or combustion are very weak. As I have suggested, much depends on whether the planet is a Superior or an Inferior and, therefore, whether it is moving towards or moving away from the Sun. However, a planet emerging from sunbeams is particularly strong.

We are told by Maternus that in certain conditions the matutine star "rejoices" and in others the vespertine star "rejoices".

> Some planets located with a morning rising rejoice in company with the Sun. For the divine power of the Sun is protected by very favorable influences whenever he is accompanied by the morning rising of planets. But those planets become weakened whenever they follow after the Sun in an evening rising.[42]

Maternus explains that if Saturn rises fifteen degrees before the Sun he is said to be "matutine". Similarly, Jupiter is said to be "matutine" when he precedes the rising of the Sun by twelve degrees, Venus and Mars if they precede the rising of the Sun by eight degrees and Mercury when preceding the rising of the Sun by eighteen degrees. In the same way, these planets are said to be "vespertine" when they follow the rising of the Sun by the same number of degrees.[43]

The concept of sect is absolutely fundamental to the understanding of the planets and to any evaluation of their strength or otherwise. The importance of sect becomes clearer in Part Two when individual charts are examined.

References

1. Robert Hand, *Night and Day Planetary Sect in Astrology*, p.66.
2. Hand p.2.
3. ibid p.5.
4. ibid p.27.
5. ibid p.2.
6. ibid p.5.
7. Firmicus Maternus, *Ancient Astrology Theory and Practice*, *Matheseos Libri VIII*. Trans. Jean Rhys Bram, Noyes Press, New Jersey, 1975, p.38.
8. ibid p.52.
9. Hand p.5.
10. ibid p.5.
11. ibid p.6.
12. Al Biruni, p.234.
13. Hand p.6.
14. ibid p.6.
15. Bonatus, *The Astrologer's Guide or Anima Astrologiae*, p.17, 47th consideration.
16. Al Biruni, p.234.
17. Dariot, cited by Lilly in *Christian Astrology*, p.259.
18. Hand p.6.
19. ibid p.7.
20. ibid p.7.
21. Al Biruni p.308.
22. Lilly p.113.
23. Al Biruni p.316 and 308.
24. Maternus p.77 14.
25. ibid p.77 15.
26. ibid p.81 15.
27. ibid pp.82-83 3.
28. ibid p.82 2.
29. ibid p.93 34.
30. ibid p.90 12.
31. Lilly p.52.
32. Maternus p.94 1.
33. ibid p.94 4.
34. ibid p.99 1.
35. ibid p.99 3.
36. ibid p.114 9.
37. ibid p.114 10.
38. Hand p.16.
39. Wilhelm Knappich in *Night and Day Planetary Sect in Astrology*, Robert Hand, p.8, (*Die Geschichte der Astrologie*, chapter two).
40. Maternus p.39.

41. ibid
42. ibid
43. ibid

5

Planetary Movement And Aspect

The strongest aspects and the only ones used in Questions (horary) are the *opposition* (180 degrees apart), the *square* (90 degrees apart), the *trine* (120 degrees apart), the *sextile* (60 degrees apart) and the *conjunction* (planets in the same place). Apart from one case in his section on Questions, Lilly considered only the major aspects in his judgements.[1] In his writings on Elections, in *Astrologia Restaurata*, Ramesey reports that he will "treat only of those Aspects of the Planets and signs which are most usual and necessary". He is in agreement with Lilly and earlier authors when he states that the conjunction is "not properly termed an Aspect".[2]

Conjunction

When one or more planets are in the same degree and in the same sign, this is a conjunction of the planets. Lilly tells us that conjunctions are either fortunate or unfortunate "as the Planets in conjunction are friends or enemies to one another".[3]

> ...this conjunction is of nature neither good nor bad, but according to the significators and their dispositions and places is both, viz some times good and some times bad.[4]

According to Al Biruni

> When of two planets in aspect, the degrees of the inferior one are less than those of the superior planet, the inferior one is said to be proceeding to conjunction and when greater to be separating from the superior. At the time of conjunction the lower planet is said to be conferring counsel on the higher and the latter receiving counsel from it.* This is conjunction in longitude.[5]

Trine and Sextile

The trine and sextile are aspects of "Love, Unity and Friendship" although Lilly reports that the trine is "more forcible" than the sextile. This is because the trine takes place between signs of the same nature, for example between Aries and Leo or between Pisces and Cancer.

---

*   Perhaps this is another form of *committing disposition*.

...the trine is more forcible and better, for that a Planet in trine with another is out of houses [signs] of the one and the same nature, as fire with fire, earth with earth, water with water, and ayr with ayr.[6]

However, the sextile aspect takes place between signs of different natures, for example fire and air, or earth and water. These signs only agree partly. Leo is hot and dry, Libra is hot and moist so they only agree in heat. Likewise, Scorpio is cold and moist, Capricorn is cold and dry so they only agree in cold. For this reason Ramesey tells us that the sextile "is not altogether so good as a trine" calling the sextile an aspect of "indifferent good".[7]

Square and Opposition

Lilly calls the square a quadrate, stating that the "Quadrate Aspect is a signe of imperfect enmity" but explains that the "Opposition is an aspect or argument of perfect hatred".[8] Ramesey tells us that both the square and the opposition are aspects of "enmity and discord" because each one is "quite contrary to the other" although both Lilly and Ramesey agree that the opposition is the worst.[9]

Relationship with the Luminaries

Authorities of the past believed that the degree of malevolence or benevolence of the planetary aspects was in accordance with their relationship to the luminaries. Ramesey explains that the square aspect is less malefic than the opposition because the domiciles of Mars (the *Lesser Infortune*) behold the "houses [domiciles] of the luminaries with a Quartile". For example, Aries makes a square with Cancer (the domicile of the Moon) and Scorpio with Leo (the domicile of the Sun). However, Saturn (the *Greater Infortune*) beholds the domiciles of the luminaries with an opposition. Capricorn is opposite to Cancer and Aquarius is opposite to Leo. This, explains Ramesey, is the "worst of Aspects by reason he is the worst of Planets". Ramesey explains that another reason why the square aspect is less malefic than the opposition is because Scorpio, the domicile of Mars, makes a friendly aspect with Cancer, the domicile of the Moon.

In the case of Jupiter (the *Greater Fortune*), Ramesey explains that he "beholdeth the houses [domiciles] of the Luminaries with a Trine aspect..." and is therefore said to be the most fortunate of planets. Venus (the *Lesser Fortune*) beholds the domiciles of the luminaries with a sextile aspect, but the sextile is less forcible than the trine, a confirmation that Venus has less power than Jupiter.[10]

Planetary Co-operation

Morin writes about co-operation between planets and states that such co-operation is *constructive* if it is between two planets whose signs are in mutually favourable aspect. The Sun and Mars are favourable because they rule the signs of Leo and Aries respectively, which make a trine aspect with each other. Jupiter and the Moon are favourable because they rule the signs Pisces and Cancer, which make a trine aspect with each other. In the case of Saturn and Mercury, they rule Capricorn and Virgo or Aquarius and Gemini.

However, any co-operation between planets is *destructive* if their domiciles are in mutual opposition or square, such as Saturn and the Sun, who rule Aquarius and Leo respectively; Saturn and the Moon who rule Capricorn and Cancer; Jupiter and Mercury who rule Sagittarius and Gemini, or Mars and Venus ruling Scorpio and Taurus.

Morin claims that co-operation is only *partial* in the case of the Sun and Mars ruling Leo and Scorpio; the Moon and Mars ruling Cancer and Aries; Saturn and Mars ruling Capricorn and Aries or Aquarius and Scorpio.[11]

The Power of the Aspects

> The most influential of all the aspects is that of opposition, next in influence is the quadrature aspect, which in turn is followed by the trine aspect, and the weakest of all is the sextile aspect.[12]

Ibn Ezra, like most authorities of the past, does not consider the conjunction to be an aspect: it is a joining together, which is why planets in conjunction are often referred to as "joyned". Planets which are 'joyned' are more powerful than planets which are in aspect. For clarity, however, I refer to the conjunction as an aspect in this book.

Al Biruni, a generation before Ibn Ezra, lists the order of power of the aspects as follows

1. Conjunction (most powerful)
2. Opposition
3. Dexter quartile (square)
4. Sinister quartile (square)
5. Dexter trine
6. Sinister trine
7. Dexter sextile
8. Sinister sextile [13]

Morin states that the opposition of a planet is in itself more powerful than the square and the trine is more powerful than the sextile. This, he explains, is because the square is half of the opposition and the sextile is half of the trine. However, Morin emphasises that the power of aspects is only according to the condition, position and aspects of these planets in a chart. He gives as an example, Mars as ruler of the eighth house and located in the tenth house which, he claims, has a greater impact on the life of the native by his square with the ascendant than he has on the parents and inheritance of the native by his opposition with the fourth house.

This appears to be logical, but his example is not a good one, because Morin is not comparing like with like. A square with the ascendant is clearly more important than an opposition with the fourth house. However, an opposition with the ascendant is more important than the square, in line with the order of power of the aspects as above. However, Morin is correct when he tells us that the chart in its entirety is the most important consideration.[14]

Morin's claim that an aspect coming from an angle is more powerful than one coming from another house should also be emphasised. A trine from the tenth house is more powerful than a trine from the ninth house. Morin also points out that an aspect coming from an unfortunate house, for example, the eighth house or the twelfth house, is worse than another, especially if it is in itself malefic. However, the dignity of a planet must be considered. In the case of a trine, for example, if this is with Saturn in the twelfth house (and, therefore unfortunate), this is modified if Saturn is in any of his essential dignities, especially in his domicile or exaltation, or if he is in any type of reception with the aspecting planet. A trine with Jupiter in Cancer is, for example, more fortunate than a trine with Jupiter in Scorpio. Clearly a square or opposition with any planet in the twelfth house is less fortunate.[15]

Antiscia

An important and neglected technique is that of the relationship of planets with their own antiscia or with the antiscia of other planets. If an imaginary line is drawn between 0 degrees of Cancer and 0 degrees of Capricorn, this acts as a mirror from one side of the chart onto the other. If a planet is in three degrees of Capricorn, its *antiscium* or *antiscion* is in twenty-seven degrees of Sagittarius. If a planet is in ten degrees of Cancer, its antiscium is in twenty degrees of Gemini.

The antiscium sign of Gemini is Cancer, of Leo is Taurus, of Virgo is Aries, of Libra is Pisces, of Scorpio is Aquarius and of Sagittarius is Capricorn.

The antiscium signs are, therefore, those which are similar and are equally distant from the first degree of the two tropical signs (Cancer, Capricorn), where the days and nights are of equal length. When the Sun is in ten degrees of Taurus, the distance from the Sun to the first degree of Cancer is the same as when the Sun is in twenty degrees of Leo. Therefore, the Sun in ten degrees of Taurus has his antiscium in twenty degrees of Leo and in this instance the Sun has an influence over any star or planet, which, at that time is in the same degree by conjunction (20 degrees of Leo) or is in any aspect with it.

A *contra-antiscium* is the same number of degrees on the other side of that imaginary line. It is like an opposition to the antiscium. The contra-antiscium of twenty degrees Leo is twenty degrees of Aquarius. The contra-antiscium degree area can act like a conjunction, square or opposition. If there are antiscia which are linked with good planets, this may be equal to a sextile or trine. However, the antiscium of Saturn on a promising planet can prevent a good outcome or spoil your hopes.

Maternus attached great importance to the antiscia, telling us "how much force there is in the antiscia…"[16]

> The antiscia of the Greeks have been handed down by tradition. I do not wish anyone to think that this topic has not been discussed by the Greeks. For even Ptolemy followed no other theory but that of the antiscia. Antiochus, when he said that indeed Libra did not see Aries because the Earth was in the middle, as if through a mirror reached the theory of antiscia.

> Dorotheus of Sidon...a very wise man...explained the calculation of the antiscia in clear terms in his fourth book.[17]

Maternus gives an example of a man in whose Nativity the Sun and Jupiter make a conjunction with each other in the fifth house. He claims that anyone not knowing about antiscia on seeing (in the Nativity) the Sun and Jupiter in the house of "Bona Fortuna" would have predicted a father (father of the owner of this Nativity), "fortunate, prosperous, powerful" and of course "the same thing for the native himself". However, in actual fact he suffered an exile and constant plots against him. Maternus confirms that this could not have been predicted unless one considers the theory of antiscia. Not wishing to undermine the theory of antiscia, it must be noted that Jupiter combust is not promising testimony.

If planets do not make an aspect with each other, the astrologer must consider whether they are connected to each other through the relationship of the antiscia.

> For when they send an antiscium in such a way that they are in aspect through the antiscium, in trine, square, sextile, or opposition, they portend just as if they were thus located in the normal arrangement, and all of these various influences fit together in the final calculation.[18]

Ibn Ezra points out that planets being in antiscia must be treated as though they are in conjunction.[19] Morin, referring to the most important points in judgement, observes "four determining factors" which are: the position of a planet in a house, the essential dignities, the aspects and the antiscia.[20]

Table of Antiscia	
♊	♋
♌	♉
♍	♈
♎	♓
♏	♒
♐	♑

Chart showing Antiscia

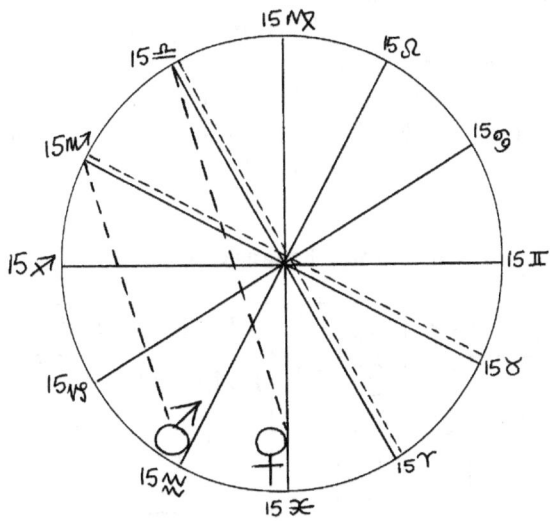

Antiscium of ♂ in 15♒ is 15♏ Contra Antiscium of ♂ is 15♉
Antiscium of ♀ in 15♓ is 15♎ Contra Antiscium of ♀ is 15♈

Al Biruni also makes use of equipollent signs which are similar to the antiscia, but are counted from 0 degrees Aries to 0 degrees Libra. This is not mentioned by Lilly in *Christian Astrology*.

Equipollent Signs

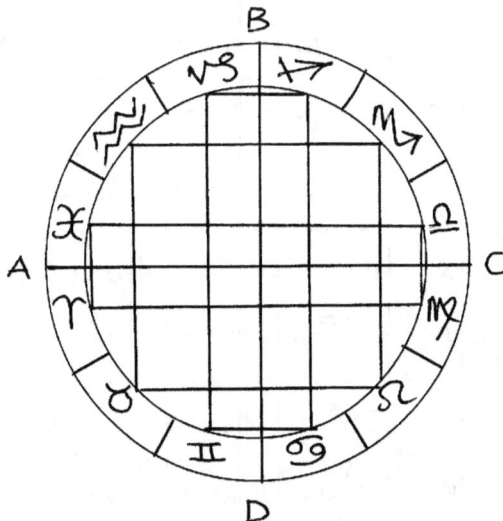

Beholding

If one planet *beholds* another, it means that he is either in aspect with the planet, or is in the place of the antiscium of that planet. If one planet does not behold another it means that it does not aspect that planet, nor is it in the place of that planet's antiscium. Signs not beholding one another are said to be *inconjunct*. They have no aspect with a particular sign, nor are they related through the antiscia. As an example of this, Aries does not behold Taurus or Scorpio. Taurus does not behold Aries, Gemini, Libra or Sagittarius.

Signs Not Beholding One Another

♈	♉	♊	♋	♌	♍	♎	♏	♐	♑	♒	♓
♉ ♏ ♎ ♐	♈ ♊	♉ ♏	♌ ♒	♋ ♍ ♑ ♓	♌ ♒	♏ ♉	♎ ♐ ♈ ♊	♏ ♉	♌ ♑ ♒	♑ ♓ ♋	♌ ♒

Sinister and Dexter

When planets make an aspect with each other, this is either in the order of the signs, or against the order of the signs, starting with Aries. An aspect manifesting with the order

	✶	□	△	☍		✶	□	△	☍		✶	□	△	☍
Dexter ♈	♒	♑	♐		Dexter ♌	♊	♉	♈		Dexter	♎	♍	♌	
Sinister	♊	♋	♌	♎	Sinister	♎	♏	♐	♒	Sinister	♒	♓	♈	♊
Dexter ♉	♓	♒	♑		Dexter	♋	♊	♉		Dexter ♏	♍	♎	♍	
Sinister	♋	♌	♍	♏	Sinister	♏	♐	♑	♓	Sinister	♓	♈	♉	♋
Dexter ♊	♈	♓	♒		Dexter	♌	♋	♊		Dexter	♐	♏	♎	
Sinister	♌	♍	♎	♐	Sinister	♐	♑	♒	♈	Sinister	♈	♉	♊	♌
Dexter ♋	♉	♈	♓		Dexter	♍	♌	♋		Dexter	♑	♐	♏	
Sinister	♍	♎	♏	♑	Sinister	♑	♒	♓	♉	Sinister	♉	♊	♋	♍

of the signs is called *sinister*. An aspect manifesting against the order of signs is called *dexter*. For example, if a planet in Aries is aspecting another planet in Aquarius, this is against the order of signs, because Aquarius is behind Aries. This aspect is called a dexter sextile. Similarly, if a planet in Aries aspects another planet in Capricorn, the aspect is called a dexter square. A planet in Aries aspecting another planet in Sagittarius makes a dexter trine. However, if a planet in Aries aspects a planet in Gemini, this is called a sinister sextile. Aries beholds Cancer with a sinister square and Leo with a sinister trine. According to Lilly and others before him, the dexter aspect is stronger than the sinister.[21]

Planetary Orbs

In Questions (horary), a particular event takes place at the very moment that an aspect becomes exact, that is, when planets are in exactly the same degree through conjunction or any other aspect. For example, when the Sun and Saturn are both in three degrees of Sagittarius, or when the Sun and Saturn are making a trine from three degrees Leo to three degrees Sagittarius, these aspects are partill (exact). However, during the period before the aspect perfects, the two planets are in *application* (moving towards each other) and are said to be within orb of aspect. This orb belongs to the planet, not to the aspect as modern astrologers appear to think. This is what Abu Ma'shar refers to when he states that "Each one of them [planets] in its body has power over a certain number of degrees before and after".[22] Burnett explains that the orb of influence which Abu Ma'shar assigns to each planet "equates quite closely with the later tradition." The orb of influence belonging to a planet measures a certain number of degrees around the planet like a circle.

A Planet's Orb

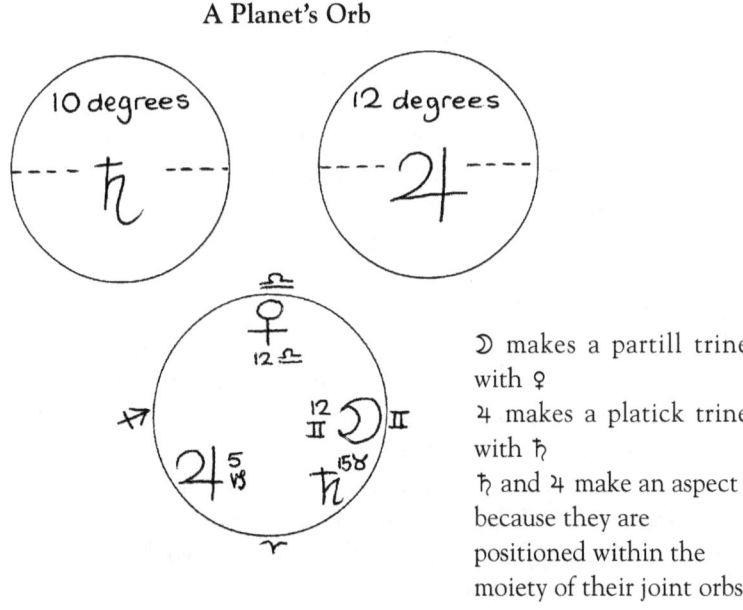

☽ makes a partill trine with ♀

♃ makes a platick trine with ♄

♄ and ♃ make an aspect because they are positioned within the moiety of their joint orbs

Burnett tells us that in Greek astrology there is not a great deal of consistency regarding the question of orbs. In the main they were not used at all. It was merely whether an aspect was being made between signs which was important. However, there are several references to the "allowable distance for planets which are applying and separating from each other..." Burnett gives as an example *Hephaistio of Thebes*, who states that planets apply when they are within three degrees and separate after three degrees. However, the Moon is allowed thirteen degrees. Burnett suggests that Hephaistio may only be referring to the orb of a conjunction. Burnett tells us that Vettius Valens used a three degree orb and that Paulus also describes the application of the Moon as most active when she is within this three degree orb.[23]

From Lilly's table on the next page, we can see that astrologers differed as to their opinion on the exact size of the orb. However, it is the *moiety* (half) of an orb which must be in contact for the aspect to be in operation. Each planet's orb is divided in half (a moiety) and added to the moiety of the orb of the approaching planet. In this way the total number of degrees can be calculated, in order to find out whether or not a planet is within orb. For example, Saturn's orb is ten degrees so the moiety of his orb is five degrees. Jupiter's orb is twelve degrees so the moiety of his orb is six degrees. For Jupiter and Saturn to be within the moiety of their orbs the aspect between them should be no greater than the sum of these moieties, which is eleven degrees.

In practical terms if, for example, Mars in three degrees of Libra is applying to a trine with Saturn in twenty-two degrees of Aquarius, this aspect is well beyond the moieties of their orbs joined together and is ineffective. However, if Venus in three degrees of Cancer is applying to a conjunction with Jupiter in five degrees of Cancer, this is well within the moieties of their joint orbs and is effective in terms of the Question, or Nativity.

However, I would suggest that in terms of a Question, perfection might still be achieved even if significators are slightly out of contact in regard to their joint moieties, as long as the significators are applying to each other (moving towards each other). In this instance, the matter will proceed more slowly. When significators are separating (moving away from each other) the matter enquired about cannot be brought to perfection, unless of course other planets are assisting in some way.

Lilly claims that when six minutes of arc after perfection has taken place separation begins.[24] To be totally separated from each other, the planets must reach the outer limit of their orbs. From this point, they have no further contact with each other. There are several examples in Lilly's work where a planet is said to be afflicted by an Infortune, because it is still within orb, even though it is separating.[25] However, not all astrologers were in agreement about the distance for separation being six minutes of arc. This is discussed later in this chapter.

Masha'allah does not appear to consider the 'allowable distance between planets' as particularly important in his judgements. There are numerous examples in Hand's translation of *On Reception* where a planet which is void is allowed to perfect an aspect many degrees into the next sign.

Lilly's Table of Orbs

	Degrees	Minutes	According to others	Degrees	Minutes
Saturn	10	0	According to others	9	0
Jupiter	12	0	"	9	0
Mars	7	30	"	7	0
Sun	17	0	"	15	0
Venus	8	0	"	7	0
Mercury	7	0	"	7	0
Moon	12	30	"	12	0

Masha'allah also allows an aspect between planets which are many degrees apart in the same sign. As an example, in A *Question Concerning Illness* he allows the Moon in twenty six degrees and twenty five minutes of Taurus to move into the following sign of Gemini and perfect her square with Venus in five degrees and thirty seven minutes of Pisces. In the same Question, Masha'allah allows Venus to perfect her sextile with Jupiter in nineteen degrees and fifteen minutes of Taurus. Of course the aspect between Venus and Jupiter is strong because of their mutual reception.[26]

In a separate example of another *Question Concerning Illness*, Masha'allah notes that the Sun in twenty four degrees and thirty five minutes of Aquarius is "void in course or joined to no-one" and that the Moon is also void in twenty eight degrees and thirty seven minutes of Aries. Masha'allah initially considers the Moon in preference to the Sun in his evaluation, because the Moon will change sign position before the Sun. He considers which of the seven planets the Moon would be joined to "in the first moment of her exiting from the sign in which she was into the following sign". He tells us that the Moon will be joined to Mercury in the next sign, Mercury positioned in two degrees and seven minutes of Aquarius. From this (and a number of other factors such as reception), Masha'allah makes his judgements as to the significators. He then subjects the Sun to the same analysis and later arrives at his conclusion as to the outcome of the Question.[27]

Partill and Platick

Where two planets make an exact aspect, for example, if Venus is in nine degrees of Pisces and Jupiter is in nine degrees of Pisces, this is called a *partill* conjunction. The Sun in one degree of Taurus and the Moon in one degree of Cancer make a partill sextile. This is a strong argument for a positive outcome to the Question asked and/or it signifies that the matter is almost concluded. If the aspect is between Fortunes it signifies good fortune, but if the aspect is between Infortunes it can be a sign of mischief. According to Ramesey "your business signified by those Significators shall be accomplished when they come to the Partil aspect".[28] Lilly, in his examples appears to accept a seventeen minute orb for partill.

Where Venus is in ten degrees of Taurus and Saturn in eighteen degrees of Virgo, Venus has a *platick* aspect or makes a platick trine with Saturn because she is within the moiety of their joint orbs. The moiety of Saturn is five degrees and the moiety of Venus is four degrees. This gives a total of nine degrees. The distance between them in this example is eight degrees. As eight degrees is less than nine degrees, this aspect is within the distance allowed. Ramesey explains that the platick aspect is one "admitting of the Orbs of the Planets in Aspect..."[29]

Planetary Movements

In order to acquire a fuller understanding of the nature of the planetary aspects it is necessary to examine the movements of the planets which are making those aspects. When a planet moves forwards in a sign, when "he moveth in his Natural motion..." for example, from thirteen degrees to fourteen degrees, a planet is in *direct motion*.[30] In terms of judgement, it is fortunate when a planet is moving in direct motion.

When a planet doesn't move at all, when it stands still, it is said to be *stationary*. This happens both before being direct and before being retrograde. For example, the Superiors are stationary about two, three or four days before retrogradation.

A planet has two stations. The *first station* is when it changes from direct to retrograde. In terms of judgement this is unfortunate. The *second station* is when the planet changes from retrograde to direct. In terms of judgement this is fortunate. Ramesey tells us that after separating, if one of the significators is stationary and immediately applies again to another significator, the matter "hangeth in some suspence, and after a while beginnith afresh..."[31]

Retrogradation is a movement which is contrary to the succession of signs, that is, when a planet moves backwards. For example, Venus moving from eleven degrees to ten degrees, to nine degrees and so on is retrograde. In terms of judgement, being retrograde is unfortunate. Bonatti tells us that when a planet that is a significator is retrograde, or stationary to retrogradation, it signifies "mischief and damage, discord, contradiction..." However, he claims that being stationary is not as bad as being retrograde, because being retrograde indicates "the mischief to be, as it were, present and in being", whereas being stationary indicates that it is "past and over". Any hindrance or evil is in the past. This, claims Bonatti, is similar to a time when a person has been sick and is beginning to recover.[32] Bonatti points out that "as the First Station is not so bad as Retrogradation, so the Second Station is not so good as direction".[33]

Lilly agrees that a planet changing direction from being stationary to retrograde (his first station) results in "dissolution and destruction". However, a planet changing direction from being retrograde to stationary (second station), signifies "an aptness, and the renewing and strength of everything".[34] Bonatti tells us that the second station shows that "the affair will be done, but slowly, and intricately, and with pains and trouble".[35] However, the matter will eventually be well done. Barclay explains that she began teaching her course in Horary Astrology (QHP) at such a time. She explains that "Astrology needed reviving from its tragic lethargy".[36] Al Biruni reports that in the second station, "hope of succour is given...delivery being near at hand".[37]

Due to her swiftness of motion, the Moon applies to all planets, but is applied to by no planet. Mercury applies to all the planets except the Moon. Venus applies to all the planets except the Moon and Mercury. The Sun, Mars and Jupiter apply to "those above them". However, Al Biruni explains that "Saturn alone applies itself to no planet because all are below it".[38] When two planets make an aspect and the degrees of the Inferior are less than those of a Superior, the Inferior is said to be applying to a conjunction or aspect with the Superior. When the degrees of the Inferior are greater they will separate (unless the Inferior is retrograde). A Superior cannot apply to an Inferior unless the latter is retrograde.

Application

Application takes place when two (or more) planets "draw neer the rays or bodies of each other by Conjunction or Aspect".[39] Ramesey explains that the application of the planets takes place in three ways:

- By *direct application* (with conjunction or aspect). This occurs when a planet moving more swiftly applies to one that is slower, when they are both direct. For example, when Mercury is in six degrees of Taurus and Venus is in ten degrees of Taurus, Mercury applies to a conjunction with Venus. The weightier planet (Venus) is in later degrees of the sign than the lighter one (Mercury).

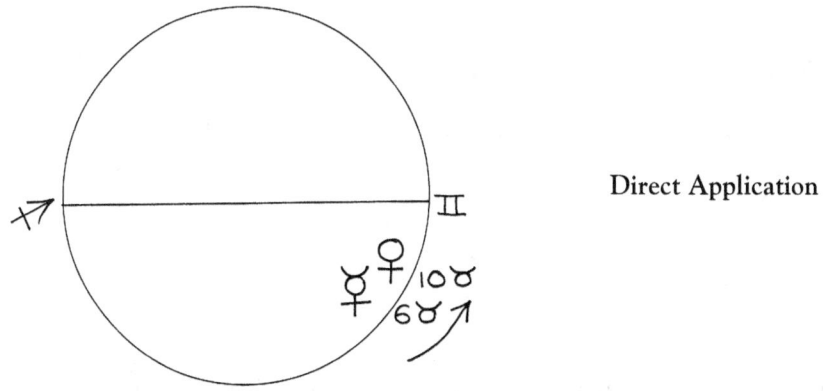

Direct Application

- *Application by retrograde motion* (with conjunction or aspect). This takes place when both planets are retrograde. For example, Venus is in ten degrees of Aries and Mars is in nine degrees of Aries. Venus moves in retrograde motion back towards Mars and does not turn to direct motion until she has made a conjunction with Mars. However, this is an unfortunate application and can mean a sudden negative outcome to the Question (when a positive outcome was expected).

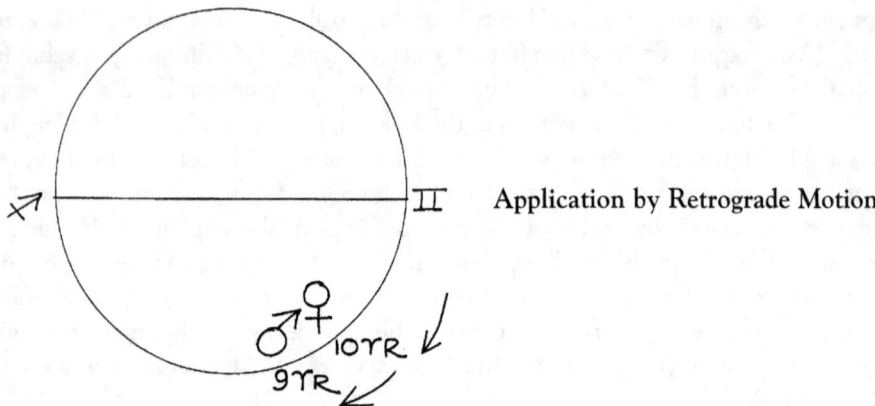

Application by Retrograde Motion

- By *mutual application* (with conjunction or aspect). This takes place when one planet is direct and the other planet is retrograde. The first planet is direct and in fewer degrees than the retrograde planet. For example, Mars is moving forwards in fifteen degrees of Scorpio and Mercury is retrograde in seventeen degrees of Capricorn. Mercury moves towards a sextile with Mars. This is an unfortunate application and signals great changes to be expected in terms of the Question. However, Lilly tells us that if the Moon applies to a good aspect with a retrograde planet this brings matters to an end one way or another and quite quickly.[40]

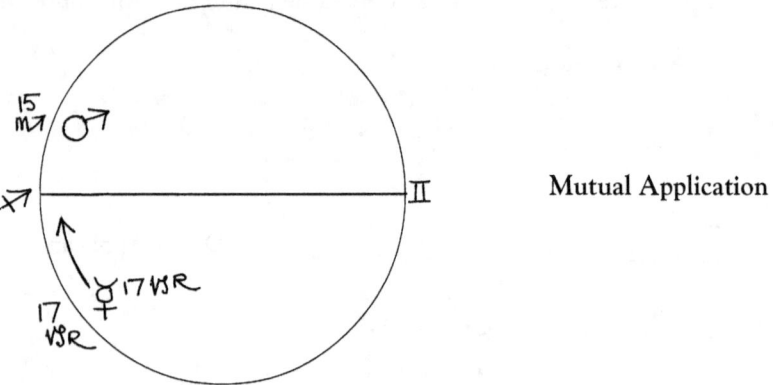

Mutual Application

In a general sense, however, application usually takes place when a planet is moving to a conjunction, sextile, trine, square or opposition with another, where the lighter planet applies to the heavier planet. The true or exact aspect (partill) takes place when one planet arrives in the same degree and minute as the other. Al Biruni tells us that there are significant differences of opinion as to the "amount and limits of completion" (when application begins), for example from five to six degrees, or the average of a planet's terms.

Committing Disposition

Hand, when referring to Masha'allah's methods in *On Reception*, explains that each planet as it applies to another planet *commits its disposition* to that planet, that is, it sends its characteristics forward on to that planet. The applying planet *pushes* its disposition on to the second planet. The second planet in turn can push its disposition on to a third planet and so on. Hand tells us that whichever planet is the last in this chain of applications is very important in determining the outcome to a Question.[41]

This appears to be just one method of committing disposition, but there are others: Bonatti, in the context of the doctrine *translation of light*, tells us that a heavier planet can also commit its nature and disposition to a lighter (translating) planet. This lighter planet is able to "carry it with itself" until it is joined to another planet. At this point the lighter planet will "commit to that planet what it had received". In other words, the nature and disposition of one planet can be carried to another planet, by a third. Bonatti tells us it is unlikely that one planet can commit its virtue or disposition to another, unless it is joined to it from one of its dignities (reception): "A planet gives nothing in a place in which it promises nothing". Bonatti also explains that in certain instances, a planet can return that virtue or disposition if it is debilitated, for example through being cadent, retrograde or combust. This doctrine of the *return of virtue* can be beneficial in terms of achieving perfection, but again, only if some type of reception is in place and if the planets are in good houses.[42] Translation of light and return of virtue or disposition are explored further in chapters fourteen and fifteen.

In *The Abbreviation to the Introduction of Astrology* Abu Ma'shar also tells us about planets "pushing" their power or nature onto other planets.

Pushing Nature

This occurs where a planet, for example, Venus in Scorpio applies to the ruler of the sign in which she is placed, that is, Mars. Here, Venus pushes the nature of Mars back on to Mars. This can also take place if Venus is in the exaltation sign of Mars, for example Venus in Capricorn applying to Mars. Pushing power can take place where a planet is in any dignity of another planet such as its domicile, exaltation, term, triplicity or face.

Pushing Power

If a planet is in its own domicile, exaltation or other dignity and applies to another planet, pushing power takes place. As an example of this, Venus in Taurus pushes her own power onto Jupiter in Virgo, or Jupiter in Sagittarius pushes his own power onto Saturn in Aries.

Pushing Two Natures

Abu Ma'shar tells us that pushing two natures is of two kinds. Firstly, where Venus is in a sign in which she has dignities, for example in Pisces where she is exalted and she applies to another planet, which also has dignities in that sign, for example Jupiter in

Pisces. According to the editors, this is a specific kind of reception called *communion* where one planet has a rulership and the other has exaltation.

Secondly, pushing two natures can take place if a diurnal planet applies to a diurnal planet and the two are in a diurnal place, or a nocturnal planet applies to a nocturnal planet and the two are in a nocturnal place. An example of this would be Jupiter applying to an aspect with Saturn above the horizon during the day or the Moon applying to an aspect with Venus above the horizon during the night.[43]

Pushing Counsel

This occurs when there is an application between two planets. If this is with a trine or sextile, or there is a reception, this pushing is "from compatibility" and is a favourable application. However, if this application is a square or opposition, this pushing is from "antagonism or enmity" and the application is unfavourable.

Separation

According to Lilly, separation takes place when two planets have departed from an aspect by six minutes. For example, if Saturn is in ten degrees twenty five minutes of Aries and Jupiter is in ten degrees and twenty five minutes of Aries, they are in a partill conjunction. Once Jupiter reaches ten degrees and thirty one minutes of Aries, he is said to be separating from Saturn. However, due to the fact that Saturn has a ten degree orb and Jupiter has a twelve degree orb, Jupiter is not totally separated or clear from Saturn's rays until he is beyond the joint moieties of their orbs, eleven degrees away. This is because half of Jupiter's orb is six degrees and half of Saturn's orb is five degrees. When added together they make eleven degrees.[44]

Every planet that applies is allowed half his own orb, as well as half the orb belonging to the planet he is moving toward. When a planet that is a significator is afflicted by an Infortune, at that time the significator is said to be "impeded, hindered or afflicted", until the Infortune has moved away.[45]

Zael (Sahl) explains: "After the ill planet has passed the Planet he did afflict, one whole degree, the Planet shall be said to be freed from him."[46] However, Bonatti himself believes that "after the Malevolent is passed him [only] one minute, he may be said to be free and excepted; for afterwards he can only frighten him..."[47]

In a similar way, Bonatti describes a situation, where a significator is well aspected by a Fortune. At that time, the planet is "safe and guarded ... and signifies the perfection of the thing." However, after the Fortune has separated "by the space of one minute", he confirms that the matter will not be perfected nor accomplished. It only "raises hopes..."

Ramesey explains that planets "shall not be said to be fully separated, neither shall their signification be ineffectual for that time" until they are elongated (separating from conjunction) or separated from an aspect by the number of degrees which comprise the joint moieties of their orbs.[48] Abu Ma'Shar tells us more about separation and application

> Application in longitude occurs only if a planet which is light in movement goes towards a planet which is slower than it, when it is in conjunction with or aspecting it. As long as the degrees of the light planet are less than the degrees of the heavy planet, which is in conjunction with or aspecting it, then it is 'going into application with it'. When it has the same number of degrees, then its application with it is finished. When it has passed it, then it is separating from it.[49]

Paulus tells us

> ...the application or separation of planets, by conjunction or aspect, 3 degrees apart or less is the most powerful in regard to their effects being brought about. Second in strength is when the distance between them is 7 degrees or less. Next when this distance is 15 degrees or less. Lastly when this distance is 30 degrees or less.[50]

In *The Abbreviation of the Introduction to Astrology*, the editors cite Ptolemy and his definition of the application or separation of planets by longitude, which Ptolemy explains is dependent on the interval between them being "not great".[51]

There is of course the question of latitude to consider in the context of application and separation, but for the sake of simplicity I haven't included it in this book.

The Trace of Influence

Despite the fact that after separation a matter cannot usually be perfected, the following point emphasised by Al Biruni is of crucial importance:

> Separation begins when the degree of the inferior becomes even a minute higher than that of the superior, but, on account of the trace of influence which remains, the completion of separation should be determined by the amount assigned to the beginning of the application.[52]

If, for example, ten degrees is the given orb for application, it is the same for separation. This "trace of influence" is of great importance and is the reason why a planet even when separated from an Infortune is still influenced by that planet, although not as much as if applying. The afflicted planet does not perform as well as expected. I have seen examples of this frequently in my practice.

Lilly gives a wonderful example in a Question about a marriage. Here, the significator of the intended marriage partner is Saturn in fourteen degrees and fifty-three minutes of Taurus. Mars, although separating from Saturn in seventeen degrees and forty minutes of Taurus, continues to exert his influence over Saturn.

> Finding Saturn so, as above-said, elevated, and in conjunction with Mars, I judged the Gentleman to be sad, angry, much discontented..."[53]

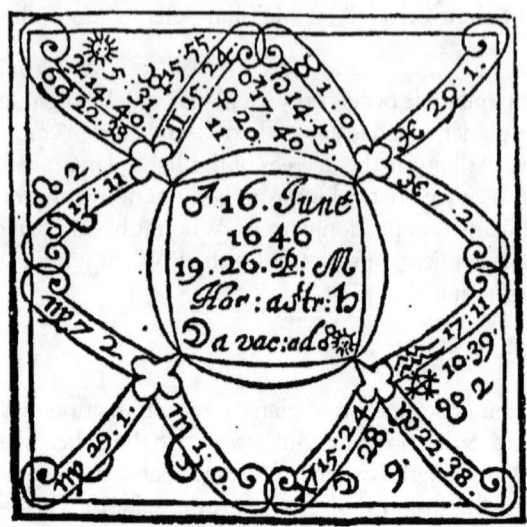

A Lady, if marry the Gentleman desired?

Later in the text he tells us that Saturn is "vitiated by Mars, and made therby chollerick as well as melancholy, so will he be naturally jealous without cause…" Lilly also explains that Jupiter's sextile to both Mars and Saturn is helpful even though Mars has separated from Jupiter, Jupiter being in fourteen degrees and forty minutes of Cancer.

Planetary Motion

Bonatti points out that if a significator is slow in motion it can delay things. If the matter is in its beginning, he explains that this will retard it "so that it will scarce ever be finished". He explains that this can also occur if the significators are in Sagittarius, Capricorn, Aquarius or Pisces, or if their dispositors are slow in motion. In Aries and Scorpio, however "they are not quite so dilatory…" In Leo "they hasten business; more in Taurus or Libra; but most of all in Gemini or Virgo". Significators which are swift in motion are stronger and better able to bring matters to perfection.[54]

Void of Course

A planet (usually the Moon) is considered to be void of course when it makes no further aspects to any other planet before leaving the sign she is in. In this instance, the Moon cannot help in bringing matters to perfection, unless she is in the sign of Cancer, Taurus, Sagittarius or Pisces. In these signs she can sometimes perform, but even here it is dubious and the chart becomes unreliable.

If an aspect to be made by the Moon or other planet can only be perfected by crossing into another sign and the aspect is well within the moiety of their joint orbs, it is possible that the desired outcome will be achieved. However, I believe that this is only possible where the Moon resides in one of the signs where she has strength (Taurus, Sagittarius, Cancer or Pisces) and the aspect is very close (within 3 degrees). Even then, the matter is unlikely to proceed in a smooth or easy manner.

In fact, Al Biruni claims that it is only the conjunction, which prevents a planet from being void. During its course through a particular sign, if a planet does not enter into conjunction with another planet, even if it is in aspect with other planets, Al Biruni claims that this planet is void of course. The planet is regarded as having separated from a conjunction even if that occurred in a previous sign. Apparently this name is given because "the field is empty and it moves without any companion".[55]

As discussed previously, the concept of a planet being void of course was handled rather differently by Masha'allah.

In *Christian Astrology*, in cases where the Moon is void of course, Lilly occasionally allows an aspect across signs. In an example below, concerning the whereabouts of a lady's son he allows the Moon in twenty-six degrees and forty-three minutes of Pisces to perfect her aspect with Saturn in three degrees and twenty-two minutes of Aquarius.[56] In the previous example concerning the marriage of a lady, the chart shows the Moon in twenty-eight degrees and nine minutes of Sagittarius moving into Capricorn to perfect

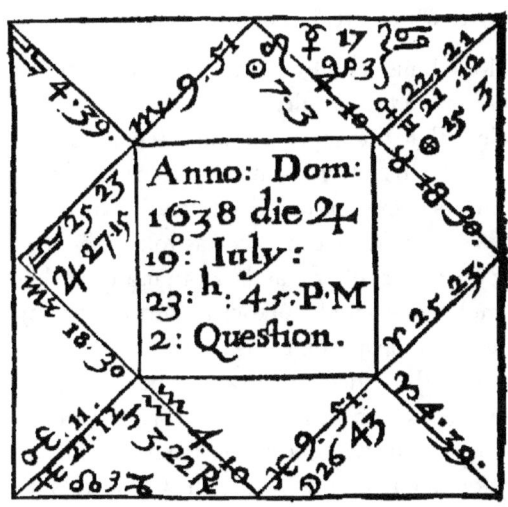

If finde the party inquired of at home.

an opposition with the Sun in Cancer in five degrees and thirty-one minutes. Here, there is a mutual reception between the Moon and the Sun before the Moon moves into the next sign.[57] In both these cases, however, the Moon is well placed in Pisces and Sagittarius. I include another example in chapter twenty, where the Moon is void of course in Sagittarius but has a mutual reception with the Sun.

Feral

When a planet makes no aspect at all from the time of entering a sign until the time of leaving, it is said to be feral in its course. This is almost impossible with the Superiors and the Sun. However, this can take place frequently in the case of the Moon. Morin calls a planet in this condition *solitary*, where it neither "approaches nor departs from any other" so that it has no connection through aspect with any other planet. He tells us that if this planet is in the first house or rules the first house it can make the Native a recluse or cause the Native to "flee the company of others".[58] Abu Ma'shar calls a planet in this condition wild and confirms that this happens most frequently to the Moon.[59]

By way of summation Morin tells us that there are seven points to consider in terms of planetary aspects:

- The planet sending the aspect
- The zodiacal state of this planet
- The planet's determination by position and rulership
- The form of the aspect
- The sign in which the aspect falls and the ruler of that sign
- The house in which the aspect falls
- The circumstances which precede or follow this aspect[60]

One must, as Morin himself notes, also take into account the connection between the planets and the houses and their rulers.

It should be clear that the application and separation of planets is crucial to astrological judgement, both in Nativities and Questions. In order to determine whether an aspect is effective in its operation or less effective in its operation, the concept of orbs was introduced. We are told that in Greek astrology there was not a great deal of consistency regarding the matter of orbs and that in most instances orbs were not used at all. Astrologers simply considered whether an aspect of conjunction, opposition, square, trine or sextile was in operation by *sign only*.[61]

I would suggest that the concept of an aspect being effective simply by sign, can be upheld in regard to aspects with houses, house cusps and angles, more specifically in determining whether or not a planet aspects the ascendant. However, in the context of Questions, an aspect for example, from Venus in two degrees of Taurus to Jupiter in twenty-eight degrees of Taurus, is well beyond the moiety of their orbs. An aspect such as this is unlikely to be effective even if applying and possibly irrelevant if separating.

This is the view I take both in this book and in my practice. However, I believe that the Moon can in certain instances perfect her aspect within a wider orb than is commonly supposed, especially if she has a mutual reception and/or is in her domicile of Cancer, her exaltation of Taurus or in her preferred places of Pisces and Sagittarius.

References

1. Lilly p.390. If She Should Marry The Man Desired?
2. Ramesey p.92.
3. Lilly p.106.
4. Ramesey p.92.
5. Al Biruni p.303.
6. Lilly p.106.
7. Ramesey p.92.
8. Lilly p.106.
9. Ramesey p.92.
10. ibid p.93.
11. Morin p.156.
12. Ibn Ezra, *The Beginning Of Wisdom*, p.190.
13. Al Biruni p.226.
14. Morin pp.86-87.
15. Morin p.92 footnotes
16. Maternus p.68.
17. ibid p.60.
18. ibid p.62.
19. Ibn Ezra, p.211.
20. Morin, p.25.
21. Lilly, p.109.
22. Abu Ma'shar p.18.
23. ibid p.18, editor's note.
24. Lilly, p.110.
25. ibid pp.385-388.
26. Masha'allah, *On Reception*. Includes examples throughout the text where Masha'allah disregards orbs - also pp.12-13 Chapter III.
27. ibid pp.18-19, Chapter IV.
28. Ramesey, p.92.
29. ibid
30. ibid p.110.
31. ibid p.92.
32. Bonatus, *The Astrologer's Guide or Anima Astrologiae*, p.13, 25th consideration.
33. ibid pp.13-14, 26th consideration.
34. Lilly's footnote in Bonatus p.26, 74th consideration.
35. Bonatus, p.26, 74th consideration.
36. Olivia Barclay, *Horary Astrology Rediscovered*, p.94.
37. Al Biruni, p.299.
38. ibid p.303.
39. Ramesey, p.110.
40. Lilly, p.164.
41. Robert Hand, in *On Reception*, p.vii.
42. Robert Zoller, *Tools & Techniques of the Medieval Astrologers*, pp. 98, 105.

43. Abu Ma'shar p.27-28, and Editor's note.
44. Lilly p.110.
45. Bonatus pp.10-11, 16th consideration.
46. Zael cited in Bonatus, p.11, 16th consideration.
47. Bonatus p.11, 16th consideration.
48. Ramesey p.110.
49. Abu Ma'shar p.24.
50. Paulus, chapter 17 pp.37-39, cited in Abu Ma'shar, p.24, editor's note.
51. Ptolemy cited in Abu Ma'shar, p.24, editor's note. *Tetrabiblos Book I*, chapter 24, pp.48-49, (translated by Schmidt).
52. Al Biruni, p.304.
53. Lilly, pp.385-388.
54. Bonatus, p.14, 28th consideration.
55. Al Biruni, p.310, and editor's note p.310.
56. Lilly, p.152.
57. Lilly, p.385.
58. Morin, p.134.
59. Abu Ma'shar, p.25.
60. Morin, pp.98-99.
61. Charles Burnett in *The Abbreviation of the Introduction to Astrology*, by Abu Ma'shar, (editor's note), p.18.

6

EVALUATION OF PLANETARY STRENGTHS AND WEAKNESSES:

ESSENTIAL DIGNITIES AND DEBILITIES

> The exact way of judicature in Astrology is, first, by being perfect in the nature of the Planets and Signes. Secondly, by knowing the strength, fortitude or debility of the Planets, Significators, and a well poysing of them and their aspects and severall mixtures, in your judgement.[1]

Having examined the general nature of the signs, the planets and the houses, it is important to consider how planets are evaluated in terms of their inherent strength or weakness. According to Dariot, the ancient astronomers discovered and proved through experience that the planets have more force and strength in certain places than in others. In these places there is

> ...a certayne sympathie or agreement between the nature of the one and the other. And for this place also they are called the essential dignities of the planets.[2]

Essential dignity refers to a planet's essential strength according to its position in a sign. There are five of these essential dignities: the sign (sometimes called *domicile* or *house*), the exaltation (sometimes called *honor*), the triplicity, the term (sometimes called *limit*) and the face (sometimes called *decanate*). A planet is said to be *dignified* (and therefore, strong and fortunate) when it is placed in one of these essential dignities, or a combination of them. A planet is said to be *debilitated* (and therefore weak or unfortunate) when it is placed in a sign opposite to one of these dignities: when it is placed in its detriment, fall or is peregrine. A planet can be in his detriment or fall and also be peregrine.

In an overall sense, a planet strong in essential dignity becomes moderate and fortunate. A planet with no dignity becomes immoderate and unfortunate. In modern astrology much of this knowledge appears to have been either overlooked or downgraded. However, the fact remains that if a planet has no essential dignity, the chances of a positive outcome to a Question are significantly reduced, unless that same planet is very strong in accidental dignities. The same applies to Nativities: planets which are dignified are fortunate for the Native. It is always best if a planet is strong in both essential and accidental dignities. Referring to Nativities, Maternus tells us

> ...an average chart is that which has a single planet in its own sign, located in an important house of the chart. The man who has a chart with two planets, each in its own sign, is blessed with moderately good fortune. Fortunate and powerful beyond the usual is the one who has three; and he could be near to the gods in happiness who has four planets, each located in its own sign. More than this number the character of the human race does not allow; while on the other hand, he who has no planet in its own sign will forever be unknown, of low-born family, and doomed to a miserable life.[3]

The Fortunes and Infortunes

The ancients believed moderation to be benefic, but excess to be malefic. The Fortunes, Venus and Jupiter are naturally moderate and any lack of dignity can only reduce that moderation. It cannot wipe it out entirely. A Fortune well dignified is fortunate and is of great assistance in any chart. Even a Fortune which is ill-dignified usually does little harm, although cannot in this instance offer the same degree of assistance as aforementioned.

The Infortunes, Saturn and Mars, are naturally excessive. Any lack of dignity increases that excess and they become unfortunate. Their malice appears to increase. An Infortune which is dignified becomes fortunate and can offer assistance in any chart. According to Bonatti an Infortune in his own domicile, exaltation, triplicity or term

> ...loses his sting; and being rein'd in like a wild horse from doing mischief, his malice is converted into good...[4]

This does not apply to the dignity of face. Bonatti explains that face is not as strong as the other dignities and therefore "...'tis necessary it should be assisted with another Dignity, which is Hayz or Light..." Bonatti tells us that if an Infortune is a significator and has strength through domicile, exaltation, term or triplicity or is in an angle or succedent house, "he is fortified and shall be counted strong as a Fortune". Bonatti does not believe that the dignity of face has enough power to bring this about.[5]

If an Infortune is located in signs which are "like him, or of his own nature", this will abate his ill effects

> ...like a cross fellow when he is pleased and has what he will, as Saturn in Capricorn, Aquary, or Libra, or in a cold Sign, especially if he have any Dignities there: and so Mars in Aries, Scorpio, Capricorn, or a hot Sign, etc. But if Saturn be in a hot Sign, or Mars is in a cold Sign, out of their dignities, it will be bad, and the business be no more completed, than oil will mix with water; but if strong and well disposed, they will mix in good, like water and wine, or milk with honey.[6]

A Fortune or an Infortune is also strengthened by being in an angle or succedent house. However, if an Infortune is in his detriment or fall, or peregrine (that is, not in any of his dignities), his malice is increased in this position.

Dignities and Debilities

In ancient astrology, the "thrones" were identified with the dignities of the planets and the debilities of the planets were called their "prisons". When they are on their thrones the planets have "royal power" but when they are in their prisons they are "abased and oppose their own powers".[7]

SIGNS	HOUSES OF THE PLANETS	EXALTATION	TRIPLICITY OF PLANETS Di.	Noc.	THE TERMS OF THE PLANETS					THE FACES OF THE PLANETS			DETRIMENT	FALL
♈	♂ D	☉ 19	☉	♃	♃ 6	♀ 14	☿ 21	♂ 26	♄ 30	♂ 10	☉ 20	♀ 30	♀	♄
♉	♀ N	☽ 3	♀	☽	♀ 8	☿ 15	♃ 22	♄ 20	♂ 30	☿ 10	☽ 20	♄ 30	♂	
♊	☿ D	☊ 3	♄	☿	☿ 7	♃ 14	♀ 21	♄ 25	♂ 30	♃ 10	♂ 20	☉ 30	♃	
♋	☽ N D	♃ 15	♂	♂	♂ 6	♃ 13	☿ 20	♀ 27	♄ 30	♀ 10	☿ 20	☽ 30	♄	♂
♌	☉ N D		☉	♃	♄ 6	☿ 13	♀ 19	♃ 25	♂ 30	♄ 10	♃ 20	♂ 30	♄	
♍	☿ N	☿ 15	♀	☽	☿ 7	♀ 13	♃ 18	♄ 24	♂ 30	☉ 10	♀ 20	☿ 30	♃	♀
♎	♀ D	♄ 21	♄	☿	♄ 6	♀ 11	♃ 19	☿ 24	♂ 30	☽ 10	♄ 20	♃ 30	♂	☉
♏	♂ N		♂	♂	♂ 6	♃ 14	♀ 21	☿ 27	♄ 30	♂ 10	☉ 20	♀ 30	♀	☽
♐	♃ D	☋ 3	☉	♃	♃ 8	♀ 14	☿ 19	♄ 25	♂ 30	☿ 10	☽ 20	♄ 30	☿	
♑	♄ N	♂ 28	♀	☽	♀ 6	☿ 12	♃ 19	♂ 25	♄ 30	♃ 10	♂ 20	☉ 30	☽	♃
♒	♄ D		♄	☿	♄ 6	☿ 12	♀ 20	♃ 25	♂ 30	♀ 10	☿ 20	☽ 30	☉	
♓	♃ N	♀ 27	♂	♂	♀ 8	♃ 14	☿ 20	♂ 26	♄ 30	♄ 10	♃ 20	♂ 30	☿	☿

A Table of Essential Dignities of the Planets

Essential Dignities

The first column shows the planetary rulerships by sign (domicile). Each planet rules two signs (a masculine sign and a feminine sign) except the Sun and Moon. One of these signs is diurnal (D) and the other nocturnal (N). The adjacent column lists the exaltations of the planets and gives the degree of their exaltation. The next column lists the four triplicities, as well as the triplicity rulers by night or day. The term and face of each planet follows on from this. Not all astrologers agree on the triplicity or term rulerships.The table is completed by a list of planets, which have detriment or fall in a particular sign.

Ptolemy tells us that the planets "have familiarity with certain parts of the zodiac, through what are called their houses [domiciles], triangles [triplicities], exaltations, terms and the like".[8] It is Ptolemy's writings upon which most astrologers based their work. Centuries later, the similarities are very obvious. The writings of Ramesey are included later in this section.

Domicile

In line with Ptolemy's assignation of domicile rulership, Al Biruni tells us that the zodiac belt is divided into two halves, the first extending from the beginning of Leo to the end of Capricorn. This half is given to the Sun, whose domicile is the first sign, Leo. The other half, which extends from the beginning of Aquarius to the end of Cancer, is given to the Moon, because Cancer is her domicile. Al Biruni explains that because the remaining planets have two methods of movement, direct and retrograde, they have two domiciles, one which is on the Sun side and one which is on the Moon side. These are at equal distances from the interval between Leo and Cancer.[9]

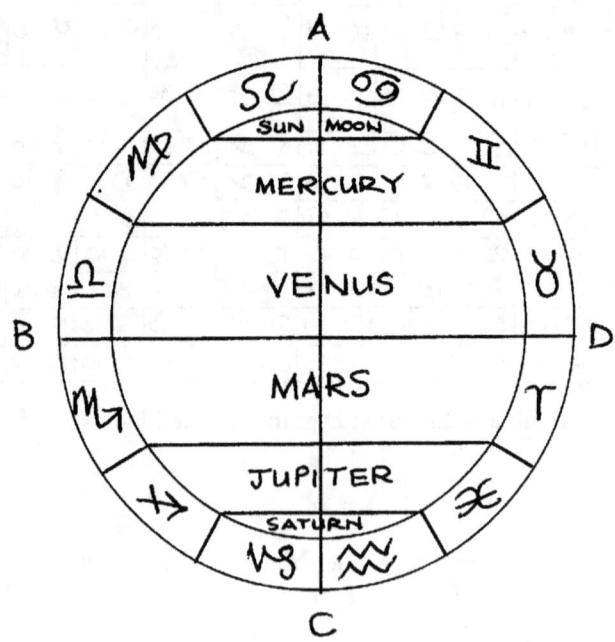

Domiciles of the Planets

Beginning with Mercury which is the planet closest to the Sun, he is given Virgo as his domicile on the Sun side and Gemini on the Moon side. Following on from that, Venus is given Libra on the Sun side and Taurus on the Moon side. Mars is given Scorpio on the Sun side and Aries on the Moon side; Jupiter is given Sagittarius on the Sun side and Pisces on the Moon side. Saturn is given Capricorn on the Sun side and Aquarius on the Moon side. According to Al Biruni one of these domiciles is always more "congenial" to the planets, that is, a place where they are "more joyful on account of temperament, formation, and sex".[10] This is discussed later in the chapter.

There was no disagreement among authorities of the past as to which planet had rulership over which sign. However, the reasons for arriving at these rulerships are interesting. I include Ramesey's thoughts on sign rulership below, based of course on Ptolemy. His writing is beautiful and descriptive.[11]

The Sun
The Sun has his domicile in the sign of Leo because Leo "is most agreeable unto his nature..." Due to the fact that the Sun is naturally hot and dry, he shows his effects "more forcibly" in Leo than in any other sign. Although Aries and Sagittarius are fire signs, the Sun is not as "hot, powerfull nor efficacious therein, as in Leo".

The Moon
The Moon has her domicile in the sign of Cancer for the same reason, because Cancer is "more agreeable with her temper and quality then any of the rest".

Saturn
Saturn is naturally cold, is an enemy to heat and is also the planet which is the "highest and most remote from the Luminaries of all the Planets..." His domiciles therefore are Capricorn and Aquarius, which are in opposition with the signs Cancer and Leo. Due to his opposition with the luminaries, Ramesey tells us that Saturn is said to be hurtful and the "most obnoxious and malevolent of all the Planets". This, as Ramesey explains, is because he opposes the luminaries, which are "the Lamps of light, life and nutrition".

Jupiter
Jupiter is placed underneath Saturn and so he has his domicile in the two signs which go before and after Capricorn and Aquarius, that is, Sagittarius and Pisces. These two signs make a trine with the signs of the Luminaries. Pisces, the "night-house" of Jupiter makes a trine with Cancer the house of the nocturnal luminary, which is the Moon. Sagittarius which is Jupiter's "day-house" makes a trine with Leo the house of the diurnal luminary, which is the Sun. They are temperate and because of the amicable aspect, Jupiter is considered "temperate and good; fortunate and benevolent to mankinde, and the greatest Fortune of all the planets".

Mars

Mars follows Jupiter in order and so Mars has his domicile in those signs which are before and after those of Jupiter, that is, Scorpio and Aries. These signs make a square with the signs of the luminaries. Aries the sign of Mars's "day-house" makes a square with Cancer, the nocturnal luminary. Scorpio, the "night-house" of Mars makes a square with Leo, the diurnal luminary. The square is an aspect of enmity and is considered to be "hurtfull and unfortunate" (although according to Ramesey not as bad as Saturn who makes an opposition with the signs of the luminaries). Mars is, therefore, considered to be the *Lesser Infortune*.

Venus

Venus has a "temperate constitution" and has her domicile in the signs which go before and after the signs of Mars, that is, Libra and Taurus. These signs make a sextile with the signs of the luminaries. The sextile is an aspect of "love and amity, causing generation and multiplication…" However, because the sextile is "not so perfect an aspect as a Trine" Venus is considered to be the *Lesser Fortune*.

Mercury

Mercury is 'below' the rest of the stars, so he has his domicile in the two remaining signs, that is, Gemini and Virgo. These signs either precede or follow the signs of the luminaries. Because Mercury is on neither side and is never more than one sign away from the Sun, he doesn't lean in any direction either good or bad. However, he is said to be "participating of the nature of the planet to which he is joyned".

A planet or significator in his own domicile represents a Querent or Native who is in a very strong position. Lilly tells us that this is a man who is "Lord of his owne house, estate and fortune…"[12] This person is in a good state of mind and is prosperous. This only applies if the significator is well placed, but not when retrograde, combust or afflicted.

Ramesey explains that when a planet is in his own domicile this shows a "good state of the person or thing he signifieth in any scheam whatsoever". For example, he states that if the chart concerns a "Revolution of the year of the World" and that planet is significator of the king, people etc. this signifies that

> …their condition is, and shall be during the time of his being essentially strong, in great esteem, prosperity, health, plenty, &c.

Morin points out that a planet in its own domicile will

> … manifest its power in a complete way, being left only to itself for the production of effects, and independent of all other action. For this reason it is very powerful and always benefic by itself.[13]

In Lilly's scoring system, a planet positioned in his own domicile is assigned FIVE essential dignities. Jupiter in Sagittarius and Saturn in Capricorn are in their domiciles.

Joy

The planets are said to be in their *joy* when they are placed in certain parts of the chart, certain houses or in those signs where they have most strength and power. This has been touched upon in chapter one.

Here, I examine planetary joy by sign. Planets usually have their joy in one of their domiciles. Al Biruni tells us that these are "domiciles preferred". For example, he tells us that Mercury prefers Virgo to Gemini, Venus prefers Taurus to Libra, Mars prefers Aries to Scorpio, Jupiter prefers Sagittarius to Pisces, Saturn prefers Aquarius to Capricorn. He claims that the Hindus agree in some respects but differ in others, for example, they say that Mars finds Aries more congenial, the Moon Taurus, the Sun Leo, Mercury Virgo, Venus Libra, Jupiter Sagittarius and Saturn Aquarius. The Hindus call such situations *mulatrikuna* and believe that a planet occupying this position has more influence than in its own domicile.[14]

Ramesey tells us that Saturn has his joy in Aquarius, not Capricorn. Although these are both his domiciles, Saturn has triplicity rulership over Aquarius during the day. Similarly Jupiter has his joy in Sagittarius, not Pisces, because Sagittarius is his domicile and the sign where Jupiter has triplicity rulership during the night. Mars has his joy in Scorpio, not Aries, because Scorpio is his domicile and the sign where Mars has triplicity rulership during the day and night. Venus has her joy in Taurus, not Libra, because Taurus is her domicile and the sign where she has triplicity rulership during the day. Mercury has his joy in Virgo, not Gemini, presumably because he has both his domicile and exaltation in Virgo, although he has triplicity rulership over Gemini during the night. The Sun joys in Leo. The Moon has her joy in Cancer, although, according to Ramesey she does not enjoy any dignity through a rulership over the water triplicity (in fact various authorities have assigned the Moon a rulership over the water triplicity at night). In any case, Ramesey tells us that Cancer is a sign of "her own nature and complexion".

Exaltation

The Sun

In assigning planetary exaltation, Ptolemy tells us that the Sun is exalted in Aries because at that time, the Sun is "making his transition to the northern and higher semicircle".[15] However, when the Sun is in Libra, he is moving into the "southern and lower one". For this reason, the Sun is said to be exalted in Aries, because during that time the length of the day and the heating power of his nature begin to increase. Ptolemy tells us that the Sun is in his fall in Libra ("his depression") for the opposite reasons.

Saturn

In order for Saturn to have a position opposite to the Sun (being associated with cold), he is exalted in Libra and has his fall in Aries. "For where heat increases there cold diminishes, and where the former diminishes cold on the contrary increases". Ramesey following Ptolemy, explains that Saturn is the planet which is most remote from the Sun, "contrary in houses [domicile], and author of cold, as the Sun is of heat".

The Moon

Ptolemy explains that the Moon, after being in conjunction with the Sun in Aries, is in her first phase and begins to increase in light and in height. This occurs in the first sign of her "own triangle" (triplicity). This is the sign of Taurus. For this reason she is exalted in Taurus and has her fall in the "diametrically opposite sign", Scorpio. Ramesey tells us that Scorpio is also a sign where she is decreasing in light. Using the Sun in Aries as a starting point, Ramesey explains

> ...because the Moon hath her light from him, she being in conjunction with him in Aries, shews herself first unto us in Taurus, the first sign in which she hath Triplicity...

Jupiter

Ptolemy explains that Jupiter, which produces the "fecund north winds, reaches farthest north in Cancer and brings his own power to fullness;" Ramesey following the same line of thought, confirms that Jupiter

> ...delighteth in the Northern part of Heaven, stirring up Northern winds, which causeth fertility, and maketh things to grow, and his greatest declination Northward is in Cancer...

For this reason he is exalted in Cancer and has his fall in the opposite sign, which is Capricorn.

Mars

Ptolemy points out that because Mars is fiery by nature, he "becomes even more so in Capricorn because in it he is farthest south". Ramesey agrees that Mars is naturally hot and dry and that he shows his effects more powerfully in the sign of Capricorn, because Capricorn is a southern sign where the Sun is "most hot" at about noon. Therefore, Mars has his exaltation in Capricorn and his fall in Cancer. By way of contrast to Jupiter, Mars is violent and Jupiter is temperate.

Venus

Ptolemy tells us that Venus is moist by nature and "increases her own proper power all the more in Pisces..." This is the place where we see the beginning of the moist spring. Ramesey explains that Venus is naturally moist and especially in Pisces because this is the time of spring, when Venus is moistened and strengthened. So she is said to be exalted in Pisces, because she is the cause of "generation and procreation". However, during the autumn, "all things wither, and fade" so she has her fall in the sign of Virgo.

Mercury

In contrast to Venus, Ptolemy tells us that Mercury, because he is "naturally drier", has his exaltation in the sign of Virgo, which is the time of the dry autumn. He has his fall in Pisces. Ramesey agrees that because Mercury is dry, he is "contrary in nature to Venus". Mercury also has his domicile and joy in Virgo.

Al Biruni describes the exaltations of the planets "like the thrones of kings and other high positions". He points out that in such signs the "the exaltation is regarded as specially related to a certain degree..." However, he admits that there are many differences of opinion on the matter. For example, he tells us that some astrologers say that it extends for some way either in front or behind the degree in question, while others claim that it extends from the first point of the sign to that degree.[16] Others claim that it is present in the whole sign without any special degree. Al Biruni includes a list of the exaltation signs and degrees "according to the Persians and Greeks" reproduced below.[17]

Saturn	21 Libra
Jupiter	15 Cancer
Mars	28 Capricorn
Sun	19 Aries
Venus	27 Pisces
Mercury	15 Virgo
Moon	3 Taurus
Dragon's Head	3 Gemini
Dragon's Tail	3 Sagittarius

Maternus explains that "...in the doctrine we use, we maintain that all the planets are more favourable in their exaltations then in their own signs".[18]

A planet or significator in his exaltation can represent a person who is arrogant, perhaps overestimating his abilities and talents. However, being in exaltation is a very strong position for a planet. Ramesey explains that a planet in his exaltation shows "a man of a high and majestical carriage and disposition, very high-minded, lofty and proud, taking more upon him than befitteth".

Barclay tells us that Cyril Fagan claimed to have calculated the year when the planets were in their exaltation degrees: 786 B.C. These positions were apparently crystallized to retain the exaltation degrees. Fagan claims that this was an extraordinary year in that there was a great lunar eclipse. The other outstanding event of the year was the removal of Nabu, Mercury, the God of Astrology from one temple to another.[19]

In his scoring system, Lilly gives a planet in his exaltation FOUR essential dignities, whether or not he is near the very degree of exaltation. Venus in Pisces and Jupiter in Cancer are exalted. In Questions about wars or disputes, a planet exalted is usually considered to be stronger than a planet in his domicile.[20]

Triplicity

Ramesey tells us that a triplicity is "three signs of the Zodiack, all of one nature, making a perfect triangle..." The triplicities are fire, air, water and earth. Each triplicity comprises the three signs of its own nature: Leo, Aries and Sagittarius make up the fire triplicity; Scorpio, Pisces and Cancer make up the water triplicity; Gemini, Libra and Aquarius make up the air triplicity and Taurus, Virgo and Capricorn make up the earth triplicity.

Triplicity Rulerships

In regard to the rulers of the triplicities, there were differences of opinion among authorities of the past, as discussed throughout this book.

Traditionally, the four triplicities were ruled by two or more planets. Hand tells us that for various reasons, the fire triplicity was thought to be ruled by the Sun by day, Jupiter by night and Saturn having an equal share by day and by night, but in a "subordinate position" to the Sun by day and Jupiter by night. The same logic is followed in the assignation of the remaining triplicities. For more information I refer the reader to Robert Hand's excellent *Night & Day: Planetary Sect in Astrology*.[21]

> The fire triplicity is ruled in this order:
> By day: Sun, Jupiter, Saturn
> By night: Jupiter, Sun, Saturn

> The earth triplicity is ruled in this order:
> By day: Venus, Moon, Mars
> By night: Moon, Venus, Mars

> The air triplicity is ruled in this order:
> By day: Saturn, Mercury, Jupiter
> By night: Mercury, Saturn, Jupiter

> The water triplicity is ruled in this order:
> By day: Venus, Mars, Moon
> By night: Mars, Venus, Moon

Ptolemy's system, employed by Lilly and other English authorities in the seventeenth century, has two rulers not three, but they are assigned (as those above) on the basis of whether a chart is diurnal or nocturnal. In regard to rulership of the water triplicity, although Mars is the chief ruler both day and night, Ptolemy gives co-rulership to Venus by day and the Moon by night.

Like most seventeenth century astrologers, Ramesey follows the same system as Ptolemy and explains the reasons for the rulerships. He tells us that the Sun is given rulership by day because he is "hot and fiery" which is the exact nature of the fire signs. Jupiter is given rulership of the fire triplicity by night, because Jupiter is temperate and he helps to "...moderate the extremity thereof". Fire is the eastern triplicity.

The reason why Mars was assigned as the chief ruler of the water triplicity was "to cool his courage and abate his heat". Ramesey points out that Mars "is more powerful to work his mischievous pranks in Leo then in Cancer..." Although he confirms that Mars in Cancer is in his fall, Mars in Leo is peregrine and Ramesey tells us that a planet which is peregrine is worse than a planet in his fall. In his work Lilly also gives Mars rulership of the water triplicity. Water is the northern triplicity.

Saturn rules the air triplicity by day and Mercury rules by night. This is because Saturn has his exaltation in the sign of Libra and not only does he rule the sign of Aquarius but he has his joy here also. Mercury rules the sign of Gemini and Gemini is "Mercuries house..." so Mercury rules by night. Ramesey points out that some authorities give Jupiter a rulership over the air triplicity together with Saturn and Mercury (as above) because of his temperate nature. Air is the western triplicity.

Ramesey explains that Venus and the Moon are "chief Governesses of the Earthy-Triplicity, which is Feminine and Southern, cold and moyst, causing South-east winds, cold and moyst Ayr..." For this reason the earth triplicity is assigned to these feminine planets, with Venus ruling by day and the Moon ruling by night. Earth is the southern triplicity.

According to Lilly, a planet in his own triplicity shows a person who is "modestly indued with the Goods and Fortune of this world..."[22] The condition of his or her life at the time of the Question is quite strong, but not as strong as being in one of the previous two dignities (domicile or exaltation). Ramesey claims that a planet in his triplicity shows

> ...a man meanly endued with the goods of this life, not meanly, nor very well descended; yet his present condition to be good.

In his scoring system, Lilly gives a planet in his own triplicity THREE essential dignities.

As discussed in chapter two, Morin follows the three rulership method. He assigns the rulers of the triplicities to those planets which have their domicile in one of the signs composing the triplicity. The diurnal ruler is the planet which has both its domicile and exaltation in the triplicity. For example, the Sun, diurnal ruler of the fire triplicity, has his domicile in Leo and his exaltation in Aries. Saturn, diurnal ruler of the air triplicity, has his domicile in Aquarius and his exaltation in Libra. The nocturnal ruler is the planet which has its domicile in the cardinal sign of the triplicity. For example, Mars is the planet which Morin gives as nocturnal ruler of the fire triplicity. This is because Aries is the domicile of Mars (Aries being a moveable or cardinal sign). Venus is the planet which Morin assigns as nocturnal ruler of the air triplicity, because Libra is the domicile of Venus.[23]

In relation to the judgement of a Nativity, Morin sets out his *Rules for the Predominance of Planets in Triplicity:*[24]

- A ruler of a triplicity physically located in one of the signs belonging to that triplicity is preferred to the absent ruler.
- A triplicity ruler above the horizon outweighs one which is below.
- The diurnal ruler of the triplicity should be preferred during the day if it is above the horizon and the nocturnal ruler during the night if it is above the horizon.
- The diurnal ruler of a triplicity has a certain secondary power during the night if it is above the horizon. A nocturnal ruler of a triplicity has a certain secondary power during the day if it is above the horizon during the day.
- When both the diurnal and nocturnal rulers are below the horizon, the diurnal should be preferred during the day, the nocturnal at night.
- If there are two triplicity rulers in conjunction with each other in a particular sign, it is the one ruling the sign which outweighs the other.
- In a situation where a significator is physically placed in a particular triplicity, the ruler of the triplicity which is also the dispositor of the significator will prevail.
- The participating ruler of the triplicity prevails over the principal ruler of the triplicity if the latter is below the horizon but the former is above the horizon.

Term

A term is a certain number of degrees within each sign where one of the five planets has, what Ramesey calls, "a priority". He says that this "by long study and experience was at the last (by Gods assistance) found out by the Ancients". The Sun and Moon have no terms.

Traditionally, there were two types of term in use: the Ptolemaic terms, sometimes called Chaldean, and the Egyptian. The Ptolemaic terms were used by Lilly and by a great number of other seventeenth century astrologers. Al Biruni tells us that in the matter of terms people differ, for example "some holding to the Chaldean" as Vettius Valens, (the ancient Babylonian method), others to that of Asteratus (perhaps the name of a Greek astrologer) while others again adopt the scheme of the Hindus. However, he confirms that none of these are employed by professional astrologers, who are unanimous in using the Egyptian terms, because, he says "they are more correct". He explains that those astrologers who have "expounded Ptolemy's works" use the terms which Ptolemy apparently found in an old book and which he later inserted in his *Tetrabiblos*.[25]

Al Biruni includes a table which shows both the Egyptian terms and the Ptolemaic terms and says "there is no use in discussing any others". This is reproduced on the following page.

Terms of the Planets

Signs	Egyptian Lords of Terms					Ptolemy's Lords of Terms				
♈	♃ 6	♀ 12	☿ 20	♂ 25	♄ 30	♃ 6	♀ 14	☿ 21	♂ 26	♄ 30
♉	♀ 8	☿ 14	♃ 22	♄ 27	♂ 30	♀ 8	☿ 15	♃ 22	♄ 26	♂ 30
♊	☿ 6	♃ 12	♀ 17	♂ 24	♄ 30	☿ 7	♃ 13	♀ 20	♂ 26	♄ 30
♋	♂ 7	♀ 13	☿ 19	♃ 26	♄ 30	♂ 6	♃ 13	☿ 20	♀ 27	♄ 30
♌	♃ 6	♀ 11	♄ 18	☿ 24	♂ 30	♄ 6	☿ 13	♀ 19	♃ 25	♂ 30
♍	☿ 7	♀ 17	♃ 21	♂ 28	♄ 30	☿ 7	♀ 13	♃ 18	♄ 24	♂ 30
♎	♄ 6	☿ 14	♃ 21	♀ 28	♂ 30	♄ 6	♀ 11	♃ 19	☿ 24	♂ 30
♏	♂ 7	♀ 11	☿ 19	♃ 24	♄ 30	♂ 6	♃ 12	♀ 21	☿ 24	♂ 30
♐	♃ 12	♀ 17	☿ 21	♄ 26	♂ 30	♃ 8	♀ 14	☿ 19	♄ 25	♂ 30
♑	☿ 7	♃ 14	♀ 22	♄ 26	♂ 30	♀ 6	☿ 12	♃ 19	♂ 25	♄ 30
♒	☿ 7	♀ 13	♃ 20	♂ 25	♄ 30	♄ 6	☿ 12	♀ 20	♃ 25	♂ 30
♓	♀ 12	♃ 16	☿ 19	♂ 28	♄ 30	♀ 8	♃ 14	☿ 20	♂ 26	♄ 30

Ramesey offers an explanation as to how the terms are divided. Briefly, the planet with most dignities in a particular sign is calculated. These include exaltation and domicile, triplicity and domicile, or domicile, exaltation or triplicity only. The planet that has two or more dignities is given the first term, whether that planet is a Fortune or Infortune. If an Infortune does not have two dignities in a sign, he is given the last term of a sign. Cancer and Leo are exceptions. Due to the fact that Cancer is the opposite sign to the exaltation of Mars (Capricorn) the first term of Cancer is assigned to Mars. Similarly because Leo is the opposite sign to the domicile and joy of Saturn (Aquarius), the first term of Leo is given to Saturn.

Ramesey goes on to explain how the terms are divided.

> When Jupiter and Venus have not two of the aforesaid dignities in the same sign, nor in the second, third, nor fourth, they have seven degrees alotted them for their term: Saturn and Mars, because they are infortunes... but five; sometimes four, three, and two;

Mercury, because he is of a "mixt nature, and naturally neither good nor bad" is assigned six degrees. However, if a planet has dignity as previously mentioned in a particular sign, he is assigned one more degree. Venus in the first term of Taurus for example has eight degrees.

Ramesey tells us that he does not understand why, exactly, they are divided this way throughout the signs. He explains, like Al Biruni above, that Ptolemy apparently found the information about the terms in an old worm-infested book, in which he claimed there was a long story of the "utility and reasons of the terms" but that because the book was so damaged, the work could not be transcribed. It would appear that the Ptolemaic terms are based upon the information found in this old manuscript, although it is unclear whether Ptolemy himself played any role in the design or arrangement of this system.

Ptolemy himself states that of the two systems in circulation, the first is the Egyptian which is "chiefly based on the government of the houses". The second is the Chaldean, "resting upon the government of the triplicities." He claims that the Egyptian system "does not at all preserve the consistency either of order or of individual quantity". However, he tells us that the Chaldean system, although "more plausible", is

> not so self sufficient with respect to the government of the triangles... and the disposition of quantity...[26]

The system of term rulership believed to be favoured by Ptolemy was used by William Lilly although he, like others, makes no attempt to explain the logic or rationale underlying this particular system. The Ptolemaic terms reproduced on page 113 may or may not have been Ptolemy's preferred option. In fact this system appears to contain a number of inconsistencies, but for simplicity it is the one used in this book. Lilly explains that if a planet only has dignity by term, it shows a person

> ...more of the corporature and temper of the Planet, than any extraordinary abundance in fortune, or of eminency in the Common-wealth...[27]

Ramesey agrees when he says that dignity by term shows a man

> ...rather participating of the temper and shape of the Planet, then of the wealth, power or dignity signified by the nature of that Planet.

Ramesey also tells us that if

> ...a fortunate Planet be in a fortunate term (I say note in general) his goodnesse is the more increased and augmented, having more power and strength to operate in any thing whatsoever he is significator of; as if he have signification of good, he is then so much the better; and on the contrary an evil or malevolent Planet in a malevolent sign and term is the more mischievous.

Lilly gives a planet in his terms TWO essential dignities.

Face

Al Biruni tells us that each third of a sign (ten degrees) is called a *face* (what the Arabs called *wajh*). The rulers of these faces are agreed on by the Persians and Greeks: the ruler of the first face of Aries is Mars, the ruler of the second face is the Sun, the ruler of the third face is Venus. The ruler of the first face of Taurus is Mercury and so on in the order of the planets from "above downwards till the last face of Pisces".[28]

Al Biruni explains that the Hindus call these thirds of a sign *darigan* or *Drikan* (or *decanate*). However, their rulers are different to the rulers of the faces, because the ruler of the first third of the sign (decanate) is the ruler of the whole sign. The ruler of the second decanate is the ruler of the fifth sign from that sign. The ruler of the third decanate is the ruler of the ninth sign from it.[29]

Faces of the Planets

Signs	Lords of faces			Of darijan		
	10°	20°	30°	10°	20°	30°
Aries	Mars	Sun	Venus	Mars	Sun	Jupiter
Taurus	Mercury	Moon	Saturn	Venus	Mercury	Saturn
Gemini	Jupiter	Mars	Sun	Mercury	Venus	Saturn
Cancer	Venus	Mercury	Moon	Moon	Mars	Jupiter
Leo	Saturn	Jupiter	Mars	Sun	Jupiter	Mars
Virgo	Sun	Venus	Mercury	Mercury	Saturn	Venus
Libra	Moon	Saturn	Jupiter	Venus	Saturn	Mercury
Scorpio	Mars	Sun	Venus	Mars	Jupiter	Moon
Sagittarius	Mercury	Moon	Saturn	Jupiter	Mars	Sun
Capricorn	Jupiter	Mars	Sun	Saturn	Venus	Mercury
Aquarius	Venus	Mercury	Moon	Saturn	Mercury	Venus
Pisces	Saturn	Jupiter	Mars	Jupiter	Moon	Mars

Ramesey tells us that each face shows the "nature and inclination of the Planets in them". He explains that Mars is given the first face of Aries, because Mars is the ruler of Aries. The second face of Aries is assigned to the Sun because "he followeth Mars in course, and is located under him in the Heavens..." The third face of Aries is assigned to Venus "who successively followeth the Sun". Mercury, who follows Venus is assigned to the first face of Taurus, the second face is assigned to the Moon, being under Mercury, and the third face to Saturn, because he is the first of the planets and follows the Moon, the last planet, in that order. This order carries on through the faces.

As an example, Ramesey explains that Mars, ruling the first face of Aries indicates "the face of boldness, strength, magnanimity, unshamefastness, resoluteness and confidence". The Sun rules the second face of Aries, which is "the face of nobleness, might, majesty, power, renown and authority..." In this face (which includes nineteen degrees of Aries) the Sun has his exaltation, in fact his very degree of exaltation. Venus rules the third face of Aries, which is "effeminate, milde, joyfull, merry, full of sport and play".

If a planet has dignity in its face, he cannot be peregrine. However, if a planet only has dignity by face, Lilly tells us that this is

> ...almost like a man ready to be turned out of doores, having much adoe to maintain himselfe in credit and reputation...[30]

Ramesey says that a planet having dignity in its face shows a man to be "at the last gasp, not knowing how to bestow himself, nor what course to take..." In this instance, he advises the reader to "so judge of anything signified, to be either in a good or bad condition, according to the strength of the significator". Lilly gives a planet in his decanate or face ONE essential dignity.

Reception

A planet located in a dignity of another planet is said to be received by that planet. Jupiter in Libra is received by Venus in Aquarius. When two planets are each located in one of the dignities of the other, such as Venus in Sagittarius and Jupiter in Libra they have a mutual reception between their domiciles. Reception or mutual reception can also take place between exaltation, triplicity, term and face. A planet in mutual reception with another between domicile or exaltation has the same strength as if located in his own domicile or exaltation. This can be seen in Lilly's table of scores for essential and accidental dignities, part of which is included below.[31]

Although some astrologers are probably more familiar with mutual reception than reception, the fact that a planet is received by another, even if the reception is not mutual, is an extremely positive feature. Cardan tells us that

> Not only Trines and Sextiles may be counted friendly aspects, but even Squares and Oppositions too, if there happen a Reception.[32]

Bonatti explains that if a Fortune is the significator and has a reception "its signification will thereby be much bettered". If an Infortune is a significator "its impediment and mischief much lessened".[33] Reception is explored in more detail in chapter eight.

Order of Precedence of Dignities

The dignities have a certain order or precedence. Although Lilly gives the order of strength as domicile, exaltation, triplicity, term and face,[34] Al Biruni, centuries before Lilly, gives the order: domicile, exaltation, term, triplicity, face.

He tells us that these figures can be added up in order to find out which planet is "pre-eminent". He attributes a higher score to a planet being in term than in triplicity.

Essential Dignities		Debilities	
A planet in his domicile or having a mutual reception between domicile.	5	In his detriment	-5
In his exaltation, or reception between exaltation.	4	In his fall	-4
In his own triplicity	3	Peregrine	-5
In his own term	2		
Decanate or face	1		

The Essential Dignities and Debilities of the Planets

Essential Dignities and Debilities 127

Will I be awarded a grant?

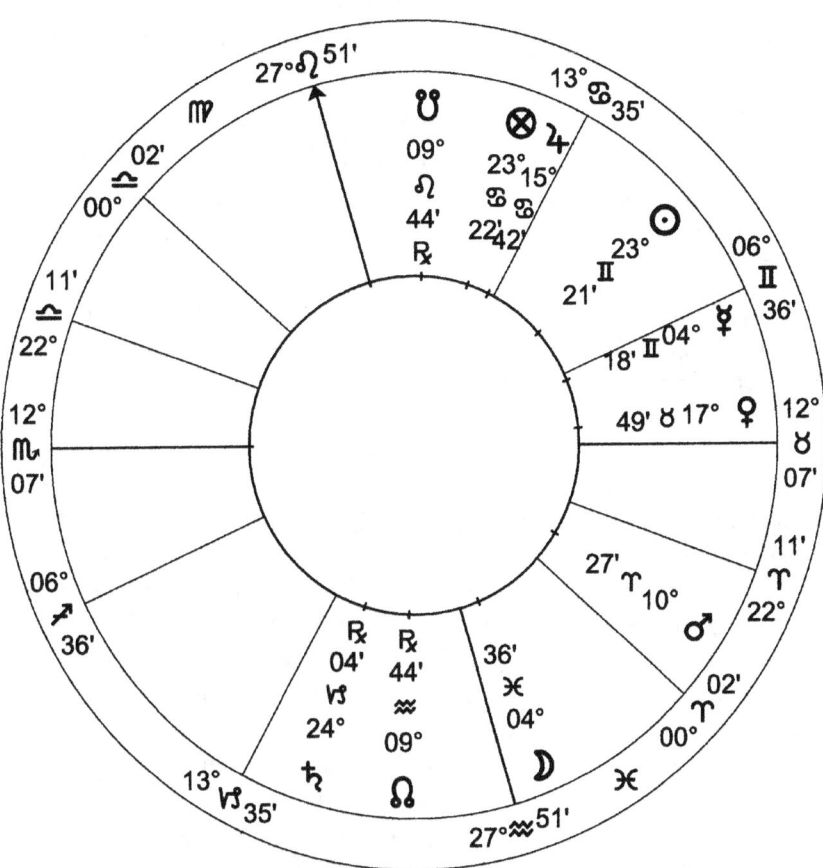

> Most important is the lordship of the house, next, exaltation, then, term, then triplicity, lastly, face; and so, a certain scale of numbers has been assigned to them, viz. 5 to the house, 4 to exaltation, 3 to term, 2 to triplicity and 1 to face.[35]

Al Biruni tells us about an authority on the subject who actually assigns

> 30 to the lordship of the ascendant, 20 to exaltation, 10 to lordship of face, 5 to that of term, 3.5 to that of triplicity, 4.5 to that of the hour, and finally to the sun or moon, whichever is lord of time, as much as to the lordship of the ascendant.

He explains that this is the practice of the astrologers of Babylon and Persia who regard the rulership of the face as highly important. However, he acknowledges that among his contemporaries, the triplicity takes precedence over term and face and that the face is often considered "of no account". He also discusses certain changes in this order in certain situations. For example, the ruler of the exaltation may take precedence over the ruler of the domicile in matters connected to "empire and government in high places". In Questions about disputes, Lilly claims that a planet in his exaltation is stronger than a planet in his domicile.[36]

In addition, these dignities may be strengthened by aspect, or other conditions particular to a given chart. Al Biruni points out that if the scorings of two planets are equal, but one of the planets is in aspect and the other inconjunct, the planet in aspect is "preferred even if its favourable positions and testimonies amount to less than those of the latter".[37]

The chart on p. 127 is a rare example of all planets in their domiciles (except the Sun, having dignity in his face and the Moon having a mutual reception with Jupiter between domicile). Having enrolled for a post-graduate diploma, I needed a grant, but the local council informed me that any such grant would be discretionary and that they were seldom awarded. The fact that all planets (except the Sun) are positioned in their domiciles or have a mutual reception between domiciles, is very promising testimony. Jupiter at the very degree of his exaltation in conjunction with the Lot of Fortune and beholding the ascendant with a trine is almost sufficient to bring about perfection. In addition, the Moon applies to a trine with Jupiter and they have a mutual reception between domiciles. I received a full grant, the first student to receive one for many years.

Essential Debilities

A planet can be essentially dignified if it is placed in its own domicile, in its exaltation, or in any other position "congenial" to it, such as triplicity, term or face. In these instances it has one or more dignities and it occupies a fortunate position. If a planet is not in a favourable situation and is placed in a sign which is opposite to its domicile or exaltation, it is said to be in its detriment or fall. If a planet is placed in a sign where it has no dignity at all, it is peregrine. If that planet is also in his detriment or fall, Al Biruni tells us that "calamity is added to the alien situation".[38]

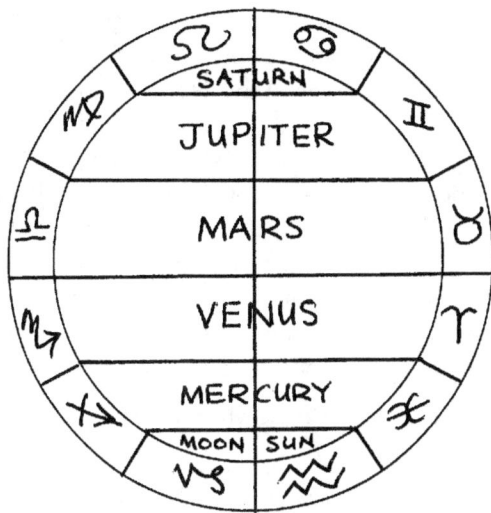

Detriments of the Planets

Detriment

The signs opposite to the domiciles of the planets are said to be signs of their detriment or debility. For example Mars rules Scorpio but has his detriment in Taurus. Venus rules Libra but has her detriment in Aries. According to Lilly, a planet in detriment can also be peregrine. Al Biruni explains that although the Hindus recognise the domiciles, they "do not know this expression" (the detriments).[39]

When in detriment, Morin points out that a planet's action is "found to be corrupt..."[40] He explains that its activity is thwarted and obstructed, its constructive power is weakened, whereas its power to destroy is increased. He points out that a planet in its detriment is also subject to the influence of another planet, for example its dispositor. If that planet is also in its detriment or fall the planet is rendered even more unfortunate. Morin tells us that a planet's influence is "hurt" even more if it is located in a sign whose sex differs from its own, for example Saturn is more "pernicious" in Cancer than in Leo, Jupiter is more harmful in Virgo than in Gemini, Mars more in Taurus than in Libra, Venus more in Aries than in Scorpio, Mercury more in Sagittarius than in Pisces. Morin believes that a benefic in its detriment can still produce some good, but in a much smaller quantity and with more difficulty.[41] In Lilly's system, a planet in its detriment scores MINUS FIVE.

Fall

The opposite condition to a planet being in its exaltation is being in its fall. Venus is exalted in Taurus, but has her fall in Scorpio. Jupiter is exalted in Cancer, but has his fall in Capricorn. According to Lilly, a planet in his fall can also be peregrine.[42] Al

Biruni explains that the opposite signs and degrees are regarded as "places of dejection" for the planets. In such places, they are "confined and their condition deteriorated".[43] The ancient astrologers usually considered the debility of fall to be more serious than that of detriment.

Morin calls a planet in its fall "weakened as if benumbed"[44] and tells us that a planet in its fall loses its power.[45] He claims that Saturn in his fall is harmful because of his malefic nature, the malefic nature of his dispositor Mars, as well as the "excess of Dry" which arises out of the combination of Saturn and Aries. Mars in his fall is "only weaker" and its activity does not become worse. The activity of the Sun in Libra is "only weakened". However, the Moon's position in Scorpio becomes "pernicious" due to its "surplus of Wet and the malefic nature of its Dispositor".

> ...no Planet delights to be in the Signe wherein he Fals, or is he able therein to express the strength of his influence.[46]

Al Biruni explains that if a planet is in its fall, or in a sign in which it has "no proper section", it is similar to being "confined to a tight place or cave".[47] However if a planet which is friendly towards that planet can give it a helping hand to deliver it from its "calamitous situation", it is described as "conferring a favour" on it, and is called a *benefactor*. Hand confirms that Masha'allah considered the debility of fall to be more harmful than that of detriment.[48] In Lilly's system, a planet in its fall scores MINUS FOUR.

Peregrine

A planet is said to be peregrine when it has no essential dignity whatsoever. For example, Saturn in ten degrees of Aries is peregrine, because Aries is not his domicile, exaltation, or triplicity, nor are these the degree areas where Saturn has his terms or face. For example, if Saturn is in twenty seven or twenty eight degrees of Aries, he is not peregrine because he has his terms in this degree. The Sun in any part of Cancer is peregrine, because he has no dignities at all in that sign.

A planet's peregrine status is very important in all Questions, especially those concerning theft. In a Question, the thief can be signified by a peregrine planet in an angle, or second house. Bonatti is quite clear about the dangers of a peregrine significator

> ...for then the person whom he signifies, either in a Nativity or Question, etc., will be subtle, crafty, malicious, one that shall know how to act both good and evil, but more inclinable to the latter.[49]

Bonatti confirms that if an Infortune is peregrine, whether he is a significator or not, "his malice is increased". However, when in his dignities "it somewhat abates it" especially when he is in his domicile, exaltation or term. However, if he is in his triplicity or face, this malice only decreases "very little" and in Hayz "least of all". Bonatti considers the dignity of term to be stronger than that of triplicity.[50]

Referring to the issue of peregrine planets, Morin disagrees with most authorities when he tells us

> Peregrinity alone does not constitute an essential debility, for neither the elemental nature of the Planet nor its properties (at least influential ones) experience opposition.[51]

He explains that a peregrine planet merely finds itself not to be in its domicile, exaltation, nor in the signs opposite to them, but "simply in another sign". Morin believes that a peregrine planet "holds the middle line, in its influence, between the way it acts in dignity and the way it acts in debility".

Morin claims that a planet can only be peregrine when not in any dignity or debility, that is, when it is "neither in essential honor nor in essential dishonor".[52] This is doubtful. According to Lilly, a planet can be peregrine, as well as being in detriment or fall.

Morin claims that the activity of a peregrine planet is not necessarily harmed as much as when in detriment, nor weakened as much as being in fall. In fact, he states that the activity of a peregrine planet located in the domicile of a friendly planet "hardly ever suffers any loss in terms of its own nature". For example, Saturn in a domicile of Jupiter is good for wealth, but in a domicile of a "hostile planet" its activity loses its energy and becomes corrupt, likewise Mercury in Scorpio and Mars in Gemini. Morin claims that the latter causes an "argumentative and nit-picking intellect, one which deceives and lies".[53]

He argues that the influence of the sex is also important in determining the "degree of malignity". The influence of a masculine planet in a masculine sign or a feminine planet in a feminine sign will be more constructive. It will be less constructive when the sexes differ.

Reception

A planet which has a mutual reception between its domicile or exaltation is not peregrine. All the texts I have read support this. The remaining mutual receptions between triplicity, term and face (or combinations of them) may prevent a planet becoming peregrine.[54] I believe that they do. Unfortunately there does not appear to be any consistent evidence to support this theory. Lilly does not include mutual receptions between the lesser dignities in his table, but he includes the occasional example of mixed reception in *Christian Astrology*.[55]

Even if a mutual reception between lesser dignities can prevent a planet from being peregrine, the planet in question is still fairly weak in terms of dignity. However, it can be of some assistance in terms of bringing about a positive outcome in a Question or of providing strength in a Nativity or Election. Even a weak mutual reception can reduce the maleficity of a square or opposition between planets

In chapter eight the issue of planets in mutual reception when they are in their detriment or fall is discussed in more detail. Suffice it to say here that such planets appear to offer some help in terms of achieving a desired outcome, but the matter may not turn out as well as expected. A job offer signified by Mars in Cancer even if Mars has a mutual reception with the Moon in Scorpio, may not be a job that the Querent enjoys or may turn out to be a job not worth having.

The importance of a planet's essential dignity in chart evaluation cannot be underestimated. Morin's writings on essential dignities and debilities, especially those relating to peregrine planets, are very interesting. I would agree that a planet in the domicile of a Fortune, even if peregrine, is probably less unfortunate than a peregrine planet in the domicile of an Infortune.

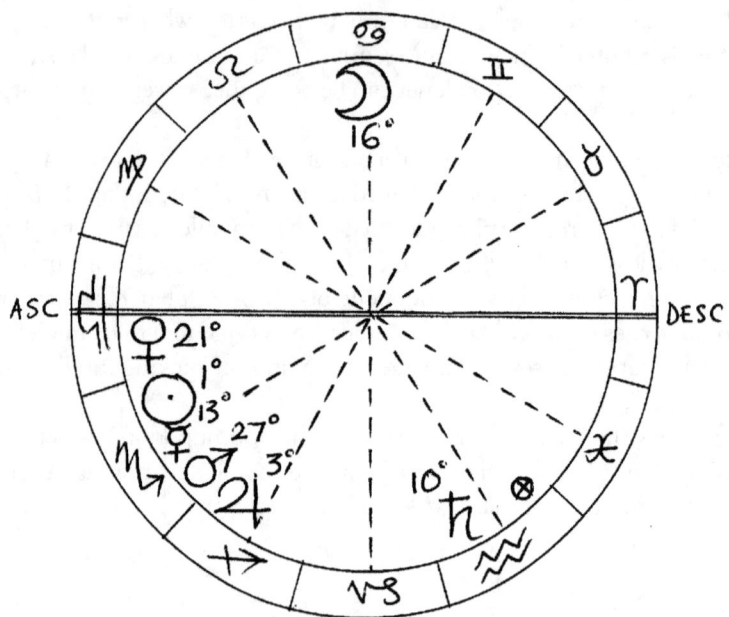

An Eminent Man

In the context of modern astrology, the dignity or debility of a planet is barely taken into consideration. Instead of the huge focus we have today on the outer planets and the asteroids, an emphasis on the essential dignities and other traditional tools would be very welcome. I would like to emphasise once more that it is the position and dignity of a planet which is a vital point in judgement.

I include here the Nativity of "an eminent man". This chart is from the collection of Vettius Valens, and reproduced by Olivia Barclay[56] in *Horary Astrology Rediscovered*. It is an example of a Nativity where a number of the planets are very well dignified and, as a result, the individual has a noble and prosperous life. This chart shows the importance of the Moon in nocturnal charts especially when correctly placed above the horizon. The chart also demonstrates that judgement can be derived without the need for houses cusps, as discussed in chapter two.

References

1. William Lilly, *Christian Astrology*, p.101.
2. Claudius Dariot, *A breefe and most easie Introduction to the Astrologicall judgement of the Starres*, p.11.
3. Firmicus Maternus, *Ancient Astrology Theory and Practice. Matheseos Libri VIII*, p.53, Liber Secundus XXI.
4. Guido Bonatus, *The Astrologer's Guide or Anima Astrologiae*, p.17, 44th consideration.
5. Bonatus, p.16, 41st consideration.
6. Bonatus, p.15, 35th consideration.
7. Claudius Ptolemy, *Tetrabiblos*, Loeb Classical Library, p.111 notes.
8. Ptolemy, pp.79-83.
9. Al Biruni, *The Book of Instruction in the Elements of the Art of Astrology*, p.256.
10. Al Biruni, p.257.
11. William Ramesey, 1653, *Astrologia Restaurata or Astrology Restored: Being An Introduction to the General and Chief Part of the Language of the Stars*. All references to Ramesey in this section from pp.67-75.
12. Lilly, p.101.
13. Morin p.53.
14. Al Biruni p.257.
15. Ptolemy p.89 and 91.
16. Al Biruni, p.258.
17. Al Biruni, Table of Exaltations p.258.
18. Maternus, Liber Secundus, p.34.
19. From a talk by Olivia Barclay.
20. Lilly p.369.
21. Robert Hand, *Night and Day: Planetary Sect in Astrology*, p.27.
22. Lilly p.102.
23. Morin, Appendix p.145.
24. Morin, Appendix p.147.
25. Al Biruni p.265 and editor's footnote.
26. Ptolemy pp.91,93,97,99.
27. Lilly pp.102-103.
28. Al Biruni Table of Faces, p.263.
29. Al Biruni pp.262-263 and editor's footnote.
30. Lilly p.103.
31. Lilly Table of Dignities, p.115.
32. Cardan in Bonatus p.61, no.23.
33. Bonatus p.16, 39th consideration.
34. Lilly p.115.
35. Al Biruni pp.306-307.
36. Lilly p.369.
37. Al Biruni p.307.
38. ibid p.306.

39. ibid p.257.
40. Morin p.70.
41. ibid p.150.
42. Lilly, Table of Dignities p.115.
43. Al Biruni p.258.
44. Morin p.70.
45. ibid p.150
46. Lilly pp.254-255.
47. Al Biruni p.310.
48. Robert Hand, *On Reception*, p.84.
49. Bonatus p.20, 55th consideration.
50. ibid p.16, 40th consideration.
51. Morin p.70.
52. ibid p.146.
53. ibid p.151.
54. See chapter eight.
55. Lilly, Table of Dignities, p.115.
56. A chart from Vettius Valens reproduced by Olivia Barclay in *Horary Astrology Rediscovered*, p.261. Schiffer, 1990 Pennsylvania, USA.

7

EVALUATION OF PLANETARY STRENGTHS AND WEAKNESSES:

ACCIDENTAL DIGNITIES AND DEBILITIES

As well as being strong or weak in terms of their essential dignity or debility, planets can be strong or weak in terms of their accidental dignity or debility. Here, the dignity of a planet or luminary is almost like an accident, it is transient and not necessarily lasting. Dignity in this instance depends entirely on a planet's position in the chart.

The position of a planet in relation to the Sun and Moon, to the ascendant, its house position and its interrelationship to other planets, the Lot of Fortune and the nodes, is a primary consideration. The relationship of a planet to the Sun and Moon (the luminaries) and of the Sun and Moon to each other is of particular importance.

Accidental Fortitudes		Accidental Debilities	
In the midheaven or ascendant	5	In the 12th house	-5
In the 7th, 4th or 11th houses	4	In the 8th and 6th	-2
In the 2nd and 5th	3		
In the 9th	2		
In the 3rd house	1		
Direct (the ☉ and ☽ are always direct)	4	Retrograde	-5
Swift in motion	2	Slow in motion	-2
♄ ♃ ♂ when oriental	2	♄ ♃ ♂ ocidental	-2
☿ and ♀ when occidental	2	♀ ☿ oriental	-2
☽ increasing, or when occidental	2	☽ decreasing in light	-2
Free from combustion and ☉ beams	5	Combust of the ☉	-5
In the heart of the ☉, or cazimi	5	Under the ☉ beams	-4
In partill conj. with ♃ and ♀	5	Partill conj. with ♄ or ♂	-5
In partill conj. with ☊	4	Partill conj. with ☋	-4
In partill trine with ♃ and ♀	4	Besieged between ♄ and ♂	-5
In partill sextile with ♃ and ♀	3	Partill opp. with ♄ or ♂	-4
In conj. with Cor Leonis	6	Partill square with ♄ or ♂	-3
or in conj. with Spica	5	In conj. with Caput Algol	-5

To be *accidentally dignified* means that a planet is well placed in relation to the aforementioned celestial bodies and to the ascendant. To be *accidentally debilitated* means the opposite. The table on the previous page sets out the scoring system for strengths and weaknesses of planets used by William Lilly in *Christian Astrology*. Lilly does not include a positive score for a planet in partill conjunction or aspect with the Lot of Fortune, nor for a planet beholding the ascendant, although I would suggest that this is important.[1]

This evaluation has relevance for all types of astrological charts, whether a Nativity, Question, Election, Ingress or Mundane.

Al Biruni explains that in regard to the strength or weakness of a planet, there is "considerable difference between the sun and moon on the one hand and the other planets on the other".

> When both of the luminaries are in aspect to each other, and to the benefics, and are in their own sections of the signs [in dignity] or those of the benefics, both of them are strong.[2]

However, if they are in situations which Al Biruni calls "unstable" both of them are weak, for example when

> ...the malefics full of enmity are above them, and the benefics below, or are eclipsed, or near the dragon's head or tail, especially the latter by less than 12 degrees.

The Moon is the most important celestial body in a Question, particularly in a nocturnal chart. In certain instances the Sun can be as powerful, for example in a diurnal chart. However, the Sun does not transfer the light or influence between the planets or other celestial bodies in the same way as the Moon. This is due to the fact that the Moon moves more quickly than the Sun or any other planet. However, it must be emphasised that it is the position of the Moon and the remaining five planets in relation to the Sun, which is of critical importance.

Accidental Dignity and Debility in Relation to the Sun

Al Biruni tells us that the various positions of the planets in relation to the Sun are responsible for

> ...the most complete changes which closely resemble changes in their indications, due to the vicissitudes of natural conditions.[3]

Aspects with the Sun
Trine or Sextile
Any planet making a good aspect, that is, a trine or sextile, with the Sun is deemed fortunate, even more if there is a reception or a mutual reception.

Square and Opposition
A square aspect with the Sun is unfortunate, but if there is a reception or mutual reception

this can be quite helpful and would not necessarily prevent the achievement of perfection between significators. However, a planet in opposition with the Sun is always unfortunate. Even a strong mutual reception cannot totally undo the harm from the opposition.

Conjunction

When a planet or the Moon makes a conjunction with the Sun within an eight degree orb (either forward or backward), it is said to be combust and is greatly weakened. The exact orb for combustion is not agreed by all authorities. Combustion can only take place by conjunction and in one sign, not by any aspect. Although the opposition of a planet with the Sun is also unfortunate, this does not cause a planet to be in combustion. Combustion causes a planet to lack power (as opposed to a lack of moderation, or excess). In an overall sense, authorities of the past agree that in combustion, the benevolence of the Fortunes is wiped out and the malevolence of the Infortunes reduced significantly. If the Moon or Venus are combust, in opposition with the Sun or under sunbeams they are very weak. Any planet combust scores MINUS FIVE in Lilly's system. In practice, a combust significator can totally prevent the achievement of the matter enquired about.

Bonatti cites Al-Qabisi (Alchabitius) who reports what the wise say

> ...from the moment a planet enters under the rays of the Sun so that it is touched by them, it is called combust, until he goes forth from his rays and appears. And when he begins to enter under the rays he is said to be burned up, or to have fallen into combustion, and while he is under the rays within 12 degrees of the Sun, applying to him or the planet is one of the inferiors or having been separated, receding from the Sun by two degrees or less. When he is called oppressed.[4]

A planet not within an eight degree orb of the Sun is said to be free from combustion and is stronger. However, if that planet is applying to the Sun, he will soon become combust. The combustion rule, therefore, has to be considered with care. For example, if Venus is in two degrees of Libra and the Sun is in twelve degrees of Libra, technically speaking Venus is not combust (although she is under sunbeams). However, she will move into combustion, where she is severely weakened. A planet free from combustion scores FIVE in Lilly's scoring system.

Under Sunbeams or under Rays

In *Christian Astrology* Lilly tells us that a planet within a seventeen degree orb (forward or backward) of the Sun is said to be under sunbeams or 'under rays' and is weakened.[5] However, inserting a note in *Anima Astrologiae*, Lilly appears to put forward a slightly different definition, where he says that a planet is under sunbeams when it is within twelve degrees of the Sun. Here, Lilly tells us that when a planet is separating from the Sun and is between twelve and fifteen degrees away, it is said to be "going from under the Sun's beams".[6]

In the case of the Inferiors, when they are separating from combustion, they themselves move away from the Sun, but in the case of the Superiors, the Sun itself is moving away. A planet not within a seventeen degree orb of the Sun is not under sunbeams and is stronger.[7] However, the same care must be applied here as in the case of combustion: if Mercury is in three degrees of Sagittarius and the Sun is in twenty-two degrees of Sagittarius, when Mercury reaches five degrees of Sagittarius he is under sunbeams and becomes debilitated.

Whether or not a planet is applying or separating from a conjunction with the Sun is very important. Hand points out that when a planet is emerging from sunbeams (greater than sixteen degrees) the ancients believed that this was an extremely powerful position.[8] Morin agrees when he explains that

> ...in a general way, effects produced by oriental Planets are more remarkable, straightforward, and apparent than those produced by occidentals, especially when they have just emerged from Solar rays.[9]

A planet under sunbeams scores MINUS FOUR in Lilly's scoring system.

Cazimi

Any planet within a seventeen minute orb (behind or in front) of the Sun is said to be greatly strengthened.[10] Gadbury tells us that a planet in this position is said to be *cazimi* or *corde solis* and that all astrologers believe a planet to be "fortified" in this position.[11] It is, without doubt, a very fortunate position for a planet. It's possible that Mercury in this position in a Nativity confers high intelligence. According to Bonatti, if Sagittarius, Taurus or Pisces ascend and if Jupiter, Venus and Mercury are in the ascendant (or if Jupiter and Venus are in *zaminium* [cazimi] whatever sign the ascendant is in), the native shall be "admired as a Prophet, and all his words received as Oracles, or the dictates of destiny".[12] Bonatti confirms that if the Moon is in conjunction with the Sun in a Nativity in exactly the same minute both in longitude and latitude, together with a Fortune in the ascendant, it signifies that the Native "shall be happy in getting a great estate and heaping up of money".[13]

Al Biruni calls a planet within sixteen minutes of the Sun (before or after) *samim*. He explains that the Superiors are only in such a position in the middle of their direct course. The Inferiors are samim in the middle of their direct and retrograde courses.[14]

I would suggest that most planets are very strong being cazimi, but I do not have an example which would confirm that the Moon and Venus acquire this extra strength being cazimi.

Bonatti reports that a planet is *camino solis* (cazimi, or in the heart of the Sun) when there are only 16 minutes between them "by latitude and by longitude" which he points out "rarely occurs". He tells us that Al-Qabisi believes that when the Sun has separated from the Superiors by five degrees and when the Inferiors have separated from the Sun by five degrees, this is called evasus (escaped).[15] Bonatti himself holds a different view

> I, however, believe that a planet has escaped from the moment when he has separated from the Sun by two degrees or more whether he is before or behind [the Sun].

In *The Abbreviation of the Introduction to Astrology*, Burnett tells us that the condition of being cazimi is found in Antiochus. However, Antiochus himself states that none of the ancients were aware of this phase.[16] The condition of being under the rays or under sunbeams is found in Dorotheus, where the number of degrees assigned for

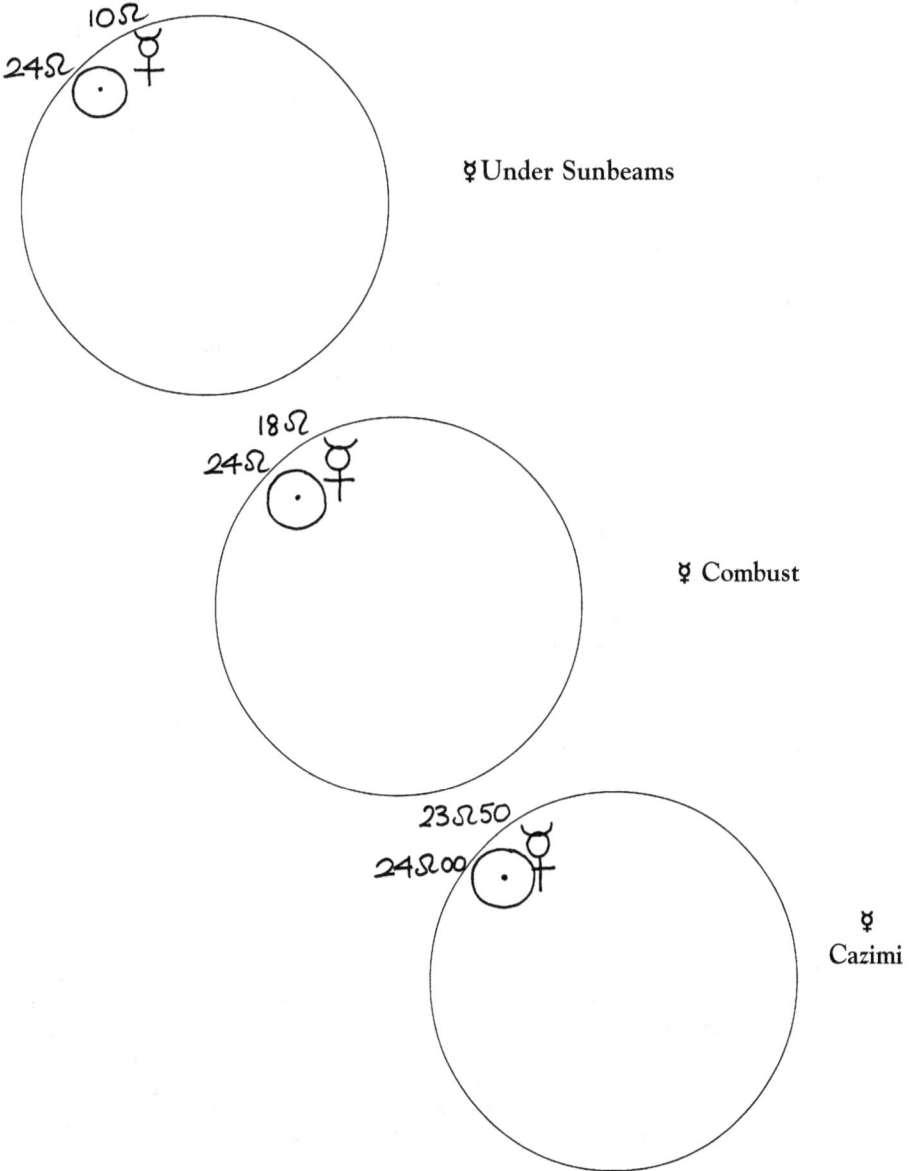

a planet being under the rays differs according to each planet. Dorotheus gives the distance between the Sun and Saturn as fifteen, between Mars and the Sun eighteen, between Mercury and the Sun nineteen. "...whenever you find them behind the Sun by these degrees, then say concerning them that they have the power of being eastern".

According to Burnett, neither Abu Ma'shar nor Dorotheus draw any distinction between being under sunbeams or being combust which, he explains, forms part of the later tradition.

The Moon

Al Birnui tells us that the position of the Moon with regard to combustion and cazimi is similar to that of the other planets. According to Al Biruni the Moon is combust within seven degrees of the Sun. Beyond seven degrees and up to twelve degrees she is under sunbeams. During this stage, it is approximately the time of the New Moon. After that, the Moon's various distances from the Sun result in the phases of the Moon. He confirms that these distances between the Sun and the Moon produce the "quarter, half, three quarters and complete illumination…and are followed at the same distances on the other side of opposition by similar figures".[17]

If the Moon is unfortunate in the Question, the degree of success expected will be diminished significantly or a positive outcome will not happen at all. If the Moon is unfortunate in a Nativity it is unhelpful for the individual.

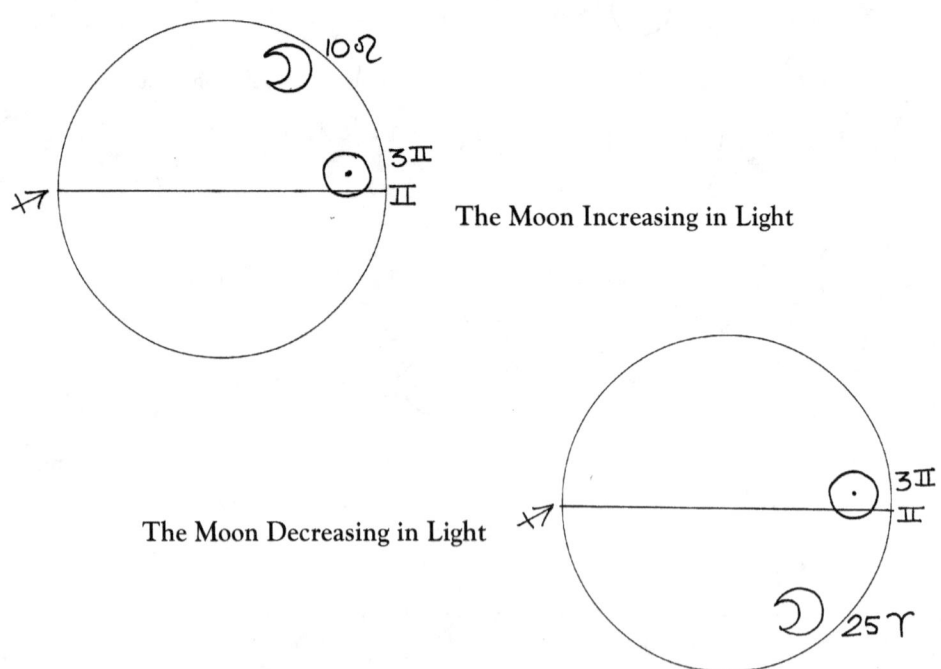

Increasing in Light
The Moon is occidental of the Sun from the time of her conjunction to her opposition and is strengthened in this position, that is, when she is moving away from the Sun. In this position she is said to be increasing in light.

Decreasing in Light
When the Moon is in "want of light, so that no part or very little of her is seen", this is unfortunate for the Moon. This happens about the end of the lunar month. The Moon is oriental of the Sun from the time of her opposition to her conjunction and is weakened in this position. Here, she is said to be decreasing in light.[18]

Oriental and Occidental
Al Biruni claims that any planet which has exceeded those sixteen minutes from samim (cazimi) is said to be combust until its distance from the Sun is six degrees. The Superiors can only be cazimi in the middle of their direct course while the Inferiors can be cazimi in the middle of their direct and retrograde course. They are said to be combust until six degrees away from the Sun. After that, they are no longer combust but are under the rays of the Sun (sunbeams). In this condition Al Biruni tells us that the planets "remain like prisoners in confinement" until, in the case of Venus and Mercury their distance from the Sun is twelve degrees, in the case of Saturn and Jupiter fifteen degrees and in the case of Mars eighteen degrees. This point is described as "the beginning of tashriq, orientality," although he says that they are not necessarily visible at this time (this varies according to country and climate).

He explains that the Superiors differ from the Inferiors in that they continue moving eastward until they are thirty degrees away from the Sun. After this point they are said to be "weakly oriental". When a distance of ninety degrees is reached, they are still oriental, but thereafter they are not. He points out that the stationary point (the first station) is then reached and thereafter the retrograde movement begins. When this is finished, the planet is stationary (the second station) and then direct. The planets' opposition with the Sun takes place in the middle of their retrograde path.

After their station, Al Biruni tells us that the Superiors, until they are ninety degrees away from the Sun, are in the east at sunset, but when they are less than ninety degrees "incline to the west". When this distance is thirty degrees, Al Biruni explains that this is the beginning of occidentality, that is, until Mars is eighteen degrees away from the Sun; Saturn and Jupiter fifteen degrees away from the Sun. Thereafter, they are under sunbeams until they are within those six degrees when they are combust and at sixteen minutes cazimi.[19]

Lilly explains that Saturn, Jupiter and Mars are oriental of the Sun from the time of their conjunction with the Sun until they come to an opposition with the Sun. From that point, until they come to a conjunction again, they are said to be occidental. Lilly tells us that "to be Orientall is no other thing than to rise before the Sun". Saturn, Jupiter and Mars are strengthened by being oriental (when the Sun is moving away from them). Venus and Mercury are oriental of the Sun when they are either in fewer degrees of the sign in which the Sun is placed, or they are in the sign preceding that of the Sun. Venus and Mercury are weakened when they are oriental of the Sun (when they are moving towards the Sun).[20]

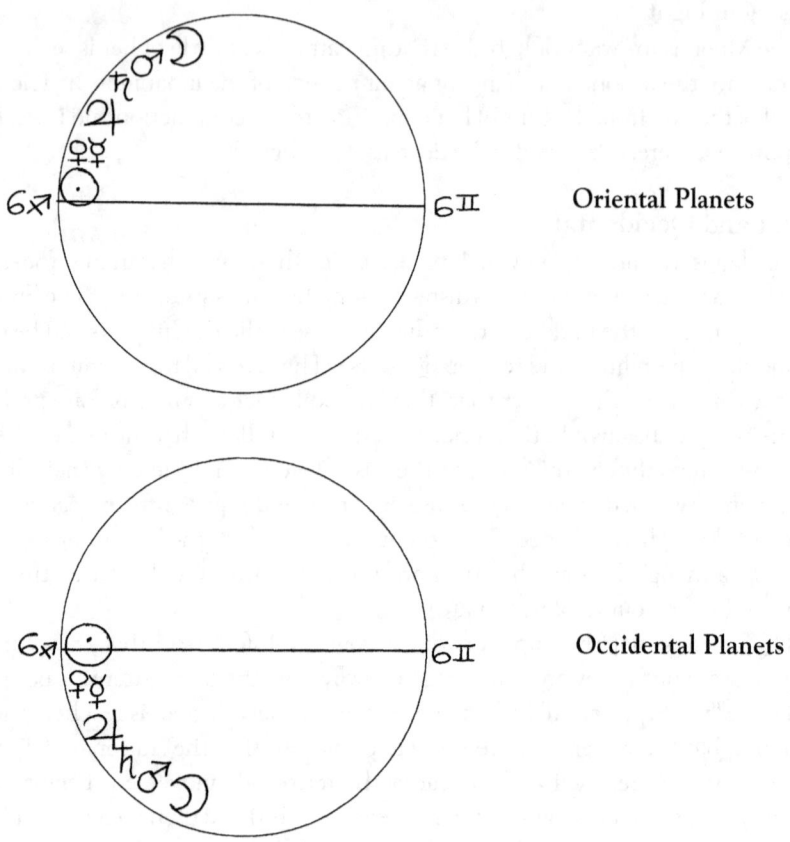

Oriental Planets

Occidental Planets

With regard to *occidentality*, this means that a planet can be seen above the horizon, in other words it sets after the Sun is down. Mercury cannot be further than about twenty seven degrees from the Sun, nor Venus more than about forty five degrees. They are occidental when they are located in more degrees of the sign in which the Sun is placed, or if they are located in the sign following the Sun. Mercury and Venus are strengthened by being occidental (when they are moving away from the Sun). Jupiter, Saturn and Mars are weakened when they are occidental of the Sun (when the Sun is moving towards them).

Al Biruni explains that because the orientality of the Superiors takes place on the direct course after combustion, they are said to be more powerful at that point because, "they are escaping from distress and calamity". He points out that this is comparable to the "vespertine visibility" of the Inferiors, which also occurs after combustion on their direct course. The occidentality of the Superiors also takes place on their direct course, but they are on their way towards combustion. So this is comparable to the "matutine occultation" of the Inferiors also on their direct course. The orientality of the Inferiors resembles that of the Superiors in as much as this takes place after combustion in both cases. At that time however, the Inferiors are not direct so, according to Al Biruni, there is not "entire agreement" here in the matter of orientality.[21]

	INDICATIONS WHILE ORIENTAL	INDICATIONS WHILE OCCIDENTAL
♄	Beginning of old age, happy in farming and art of irrigation, profound and effective judgment, sharp and authoritative dispatch of all business matters.	Advanced old age, miserable standard of living, business mean and small in extent, work in connection with irrigation and wells, poor food, fraud.
♃	Beginning of manhood and maturity, good conduct, beauty, elegance, desirous of office as vizir or qāḍī so as to insure justice, many possessions, good reputation, joy in children.	Advanced middle age, occupations of moderate importance, position as prefect or law-agent, and all things connected with religion such as copying books of traditions; immoral acts, pilgrimage, sufficient wealth.
♂	Leading in battle, commanding armies, reputation for courage. Eagerness for conquest; quickness in business; success in mining.	Mean positions in the army such as butcher, cook, smith, farrier, surgeon; theft; work to do with fire and iron.
☉	Tashrīq and taghrīb indicating position relative to sun are inapplicable to the sun itself.	
♀	Actions when oriental are less effective than when occidental.	Beauty, hatred, love, joy, gladness, pleasure, marriage, gifts; as to crafts, forbidden pleasures, work with colours, pictures, brocades, embroidery.
☿	Intelligence, reasoning power long consideration, wise decisions, poetry, eloquence, clerk of taxes, surveyor, orderliness, affability, medicine, astrology.	Same as under tashrīq but less efficient; occidentality occasions little harm to it and to Venus.
☽	From middle of month to 22nd denotes mature manhood, thereafter to conjunction, old age.	From conjunction to 7th day, childhood, from there to opposition, youth; when the moon is under the rays it points to things secret and concealed, and especially it points to the ill condition of creatures resembling the light at that stage.

Planetary Indications when Oriental or Occidental

Al Biruni tells us that the occidentality of the Inferiors, when their movement becomes slow is "a much more injurious and weakening influence than the occidentality of the Superiors..." This is because the Inferiors are now retrograde and also heading for combustion. In view of this, Al Biruni explains that when the Superiors are in their occidental phase, they are "safer" than the Inferiors, because this phase is only followed by their occultation. He explains that the planets are in general powerful when oriental, but weak when occidental although any differences "do not amount to being exact opposites".[22]

Changes in Situation and Action

Al Biruni asks whether the changes in the situation of the planets coincide with a change in their action. He claims that "If their action did not change, there would be no advantage in paying attention to these situations". All astrologers agree that

> ...the maximum influence of the planets is at tasmim, and during this the indications are of happiness and good news.

Al Biruni tells us that there is also agreement that

> ...such influence is at its minimum in combustion, until it arrives at a point where unluckiness changes to ruination.

There are other factors which exert an important influence. We are told about the distinctions which are made in relation to the "concord and discord of the nature of the planets..." For example, in certain circumstances heat may increase and moisture may decrease. So it appears that what Al Biruni calls the "injurious influence of combustion" has less affect on some planets than on others. Al Biruni tells us that nearness to the Sun causes dryness, whereas distance from the Sun causes moisture. Combustion also changes the nature of a planet. Other conditions such as rising and setting also cause changes. A planet positioned in

> ...moist places of the signs or terms gives friendliness; again in the matter of maleness and femaleness they change, becoming male when oriental and female when occidental.[23]

As discussed in chapter four, the influence of the planets can change according to whether they are placed in a diurnal or nocturnal chart, above or below the horizon.

After conjunction, when a planet is under sunbeams it is, according to Al Biruni, like a person who is sick "advancing to convalescence" and when that planet is oriental it acquires its full strength and is then in a position to "bestow all its benefits". The Persians call this its *vazirate* (position of authority).[24] Apparently, anyone who wishes to do a good act does it at this time. This name of vazirate is given to the whole of the distance to the right of the Sun, until the point of thirty degrees away from the Sun is reached, where this beneficial action comes to an end and the "indications of happiness become moderate".

At sixty degrees the situation changes again. This is what Al Biruni calls the "minor unlucky point". At seventy five degrees is the "middle unlucky point" and combustion (taking place on the retrograde course) is the "major unlucky point". At the first "resting place" (station) Al Biruni reports that a planet seems to be "strangled...hopeless". In the first stage of its retrograde course a planet is "sluggish and depressed". In the second section "hope of succour is given", where Al Biruni claims delivery is near at hand. The direct course signifies "prosperity and power".

What is not clear from a reading of the various sources is how the Sun is advantaged or disadvantaged from planets in conjunction with him. It is clear that the Moon and Venus are particularly weakened by combustion, but can the Moon or Venus exert any beneficial influence on the Sun? An exact conjunction with benevolent planets is fortunate, but if those planets are combust this good fortune presumably disappears. I would suggest that if a planet is cazimi and therefore strengthened, this is beneficial for both the Sun and those planets who are cazimi.

Accidental Dignity

According to Aspect, Position and Motion

Each planet has a most favourable situation, and when some advantage is lost, its power is diminished to a like extent. The converse is true with regard to unfavourable situations.[25]

Summarising the main points from Al Biruni, it is clear that a planet is at the height of its power when the following conditions are present

Motion direct, rapid and increasing, far from the sun's rays, oriental if superior, occidental if inferior, in aspect to both the sun and moon, and these in a fortunate state, besieged by fortunes or aspecting them, relieved of infortunes, associated with fixed stars of the same character, rising in its own orbit, passing above the infortunes and below the fortunes...in domiciles of the fortunes, or their huzuz...in houses most congenial to it, in its own hayyiz, at an angle or succedent... in a quadrant of the same nature, and increasing, elevated high above the malefics and conquering.

The opposite applies to a planet when its power is diminished. However, it is important to note that in all conditions of the planets, there is always

...an admixture of good and bad, often difficult to interpret, and requiring all the resources of the art as well as experience and industry.[26]

Abu Ma'shar tells us that a planet is fortunate if it is: in aspect with the Fortunes through either sextile, square or trine, in conjunction with the Fortunes, if the Infortunes "are cadent from them", separating from one Fortune and applying to another Fortune, contained between two benefics, in the heart of, or in an aspect with, the Sun either through a trine or sextile, in aspect with the Moon when the Moon is fortunate, swift in motion, increasing in light, in their halb, or in places where they have dignity or joy. It is interesting that, unlike other authorities, Abu Ma'shar states that a square with the Fortunes is fortunate. I would certainly agree with this.[27]

Planets Strong in Accidental Dignity

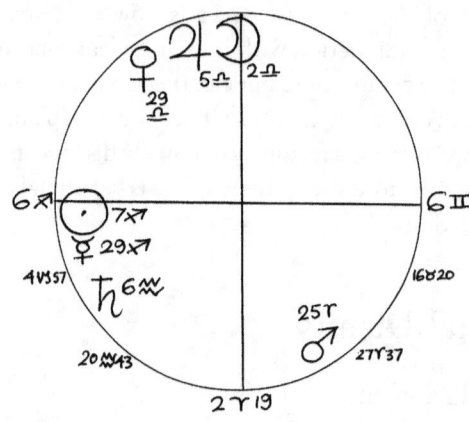

☽ ♃ ♀ angular and aspect ascendant
♂ aspects the ascendant from a good house
☿ emerging from sunbeams
♄ sextile ascendant from a good house
☉ conjunct ascendant

The Moon is strong when she is in a good position in relation to the Sun, in good houses, or aspecting the Fortunes with a trine or sextile. She is especially strong in Pisces, Sagittarius, Cancer and Taurus. She is the most powerful planet in a Question and exercises her power to the maximum during the night in a nocturnal chart.

Position by House
A planet's accidental dignity is related to its location in the chart. The effect of a planet at the "cardine" (angle) is "simply to increase the influence of a planet, so that good fortune at a cardinal point is increased". This is more pronounced in fixed signs. Al Biruni points out that "calamity and adversity are also intensified in a fixed sign, especially if cadent to the cardines..."[28] Most authorities would say that a planet's power would be weakened when it is cadent, either from its domicile, or in terms of its house position. I would suggest that an Infortune at the cardine is fortunate if dignified but unfortunate if not.

A planet in an angular house is said to have accidental strength, that is, strength by virtue of its position in the chart, not strength by virtue of its essential dignity. For example, a planet in the first, tenth, seventh or fourth house experiences an increase in strength because of its angularity. In Lilly's table a planet positioned in the midheaven or ascendant scores FIVE points.

Any planet in conjunction with the cusp of a house is at its most powerful in relation to that house and is even more powerful if that house is angular. A planet within five degrees of a house cusp exerts its influence in the following house. Cardan explains that a planet within five degrees of the cusp of any house "shall be accounted to have virtue in that house though actually posited behind the cusp in another house".[29] Morin confirms that a planet closest to a house cusp is very powerful with respect to the signification of a house. The cusp of a house is the place where "the properties of the whole House manifest themselves with the most effectiveness".[30]

Ibn Ezra tells us

> Any planet at the beginning of a sign is considered weak until it is five degrees away. Likewise, if the planet should be less than five degrees away from one of the houses, it will be considered to be in the force of the house; if it is further away, then it falls beyond the force of the house.[31]

As discussed previously, a planet is fortunate when beholding the ascendant either through a trine or sextile aspect, a conjunction (if that planet is a Fortune or an Infortune strong in essential dignity), or through the antiscia.

Planetary Motion

The motion of a planet is an important factor in the evaluation of planetary dignity. Any planet moving at a rate which is faster than his mean daily motion is said to be *swift in motion* and, therefore gains strength. For example, the Moon's average daily motion is thirteen degrees ten minutes and thirty six seconds. Her maximum speed is about fifteen degrees and two minutes, so any speed between the average and the maximum is said to be swift. This applies in the same way to the Sun, Moon and all the planets. A planet swift in motion scores TWO points in Lilly's system.

When a planet moves forwards in motion, for example from three to four to five degrees of a sign, it is said to be in *direct motion*. This is a strong position and a planet scores FOUR points when direct. In terms of a Question concerning, for example, the second house (money and wealth), if all the planets are direct and swift in motion, this is, according to Lilly (together with other positive testimonies), an indication of wealth.[32] A planet is also strong when stationary, if changing from retrograde motion to direct motion. This is called a planet's second station and in Questions can be an indication of a change for the better.

Planetary Joy

Al Biruni tells us that the planets are

> ...joyful, powerful, happy and in good spirits when they are in congenial sections [huzuz] of the signs, in their halb or hayyiz; the quarters friendly to them N.S.E. or W. and also when far from the sun those which were previously in distress, like the superior planets when oriental and the inferiors when occidental in their direct course.[33]

In addition to the above, the planets are, as discussed in chapter one, "joyous" when located in one of their preferred houses, one of their preferred domiciles and when in an increasing quarter if a Superior and a decreasing quarter if an Inferior. Gadbury explains that being in hayz is "an accidental fortitude they delight in".[34]

In Congenial Quarters

The planets are comfortable or joyous when they are in congenial quarters, that is, quarters that are friendly to them. The Superiors are comfortable when they are positioned in the increasing quarters and the Inferiors comfortable in decreasing quarters. Dariot tells us that the force and strength of the *masculines* is increased in masculine degrees, in a masculine quarter (quadrant) and when they are oriental. The force and strength of the *feminines* is increased when they are in feminine degrees, in a feminine quarter (quadrant) and when they are occidental.[35]

In Hayyiz

A diurnal planet placed above the horizon during the day and in a masculine sign is in its hayyiz or hayz. Likewise, a nocturnal planet placed above the horizon during the night and in a feminine sign is in its hayyiz. The exception to this is Mars, a nocturnal planet who prefers to be in a masculine sign.

Conjunction with Benevolent Fixed Stars

When a planet is in conjunction with a benevolent fixed star such as Regulus (Cor Leonis) currently at around twenty-nine degrees and fifty-five minutes of Leo or with Spica at about twenty-three degrees and fifty minutes of Libra, it is said to be strengthened. These fixed stars have moved on some five or six degrees from their positions in the seventeenth century. Lilly writes that Regulus is a star of great virtue and influence and that it shows the native to be "magnanimous, that he is of generous and civill condition, desires to beare rule, or is ambitious of dominion over others".[36] According to Al Biruni

> The fixed stars are those which stud the whole heaven, whose distance from each other is fixed to all eternity, so that they neither approach each other nor separate from each other. In Persian they are called the desert stars biyabani, for finding the right way through deserts depends on them.[37]

Bonatti, referring to Nativities, points out that the benefits derived from the fixed stars do not appear to be as lasting as those from the planets. Quoting from Ptolemy in his *Centiloquium*, he states "The Fixed Stars sometimes confer exceeding great benefits; but oftentimes they end ill". However, he also tells us that

> 'Almansa' in his Treatise to the Great King of the Saracens, says that the Fixed Stars bestow notable gifts, and raise from poverty to happiness and high degree more than any of the seven planets...[38]

The reason why Bonatti claims that the benefits derived from the fixed stars are not as long lasting as those from the planets, is due to the motion of the fixed stars, which he notes, is so slow that they need to be acting upon something "of the same nature" that is, something more lasting. He explains that the revolution of the fixed stars is about 36,000 years, but that the life of man does not generally exceed three revolutions of Saturn (about ninety years). It is because of this, he claims, that "their gifts or the good promised by them continue no longer with men, because men are of so small a duration..." It is best, therefore, to make use of the fixed stars in the foundation of cities and to use planets in the erection of houses. This is because cities are "generally of the longest continuance amongst corruptible things, and far more durable than particular Houses".[39] In his paper 'From Baghdad to Civitas Solis', Jean-Patrice Boudet gives an example of an Election by Campanella where the fixed star Caput Algol is in conjunction with the Lot of Fortune and Mars. This is an interesting deviation from the tradition, where Algol is usually considered most unfortunate.

However, certain fixed stars do appear to be associated with good fortune and in the case of Regulus, can be associated with royalty. Princess Diana had the north node in conjunction with Regulus, which perhaps brought some benefits but was it a contributing factor to her later misfortune? Lilly gives a planet in conjunction with Regulus a score of SIX points and a planet in conjunction with Spica a score of FIVE points, allowing an orb of up to five degrees.

Conjunction, Sextile or Trine with Jupiter or Venus

A planet in partill conjunction, sextile or trine with a Fortune is greatly strengthened, especially if the Fortune has essential and/or accidental dignity. It has already been noted that Abu Ma'shar claims that a square with one of the Fortunes is also fortunate. Lilly gives a score of FIVE points for a planet in this position.

Conjunction with the North Node

Astrologers of the past disagreed on the influence of the nodes, but my experience would certainly support the idea that the north node is fortunate. Lilly tells us that "The Head of the Dragon is Masculine, of the nature of Jupiter and Venus, and of himselfe a Fortune".[40] However, Lilly explains that the ancients did not all agree on this, some of them claiming that when in conjunction with the Fortunes the north node is fortunate, but when in conjunction with the Infortunes the north node is unfortunate. Partridge is very clear

> ...the Dragons-head is accounted a Fortune and doth increase the good of the fortunate Stars, and abateth the force of evil ones.[41]

I would suggest that any planet in exact conjunction with the north node is greatly strengthened. Lilly gives a score of FOUR points to a planet in this position.

Besieged between Fortunes

When a planet is besieged, that is, sandwiched between two Fortunes, it is very fortunate. Al Biruni confirms that when a planet is besieged between Fortunes, the influences are "extremely good".[42] A planet positioned between two Fortunes, which are in the same sign, is probably what he means here, rather than a planet moving between aspects with Fortunes. For example if Venus is in twelve degrees of Pisces, the Moon in fourteen degrees of Pisces and Jupiter in sixteen degrees of Pisces this would be an example of the Moon "besieged" and, therefore, in a position of enormous strength. If the Moon in Pisces is separating from a trine with Venus in Cancer and applying to a trine with Jupiter in Scorpio, this is also extremely fortunate, but probably not as fortunate as in the former example. Abu Ma'shar tells us more about the containment or besiegement of a planet or a sign (corresponding to a house). This is explored further in chapters fourteen and fifteen.

Conjunction with the Lot of Fortune

A conjunction with the *Lot of Fortune* is always advantageous for a planet, especially in matters concerning money. In *Christian Astrology* Lilly includes a table listing the dignities and debilities belonging to the Lot of Fortune. However, he does not appear to assign the same level of importance to the Lot of Fortune as previous authorities. Earlier authors, for example Ptolemy and Bonatti, place a huge emphasis on the importance and power of the Lot of Fortune. In Ptolemy's astrology, the Lot of Fortune is assigned as one of the most important places, together with the Sun, Moon, ascendant and their rulers

> ...we must take as prorogatives the four regions of greatest authority, sun, moon, horoscope, the Lot of Fortune, and the rulers of these regions.[43]

The Lot of Fortune is of course stronger in certain signs and places than others. On his website, Robert Hand explains that the Lot of Fortune is a primary indicator of prosperity. However, he tells us that it is more than that, because it is created out of the longitudes of the Sun, Moon, and ascendant. It is, therefore, composed of the three most important places in the chart. As a result, the Lot of Fortune becomes as important as they are. Although modern astrologers tend to regard the Lot of Fortune as a minor point in the chart, this was not the case with ancient astrologers. Hand includes a quotation from Paulus Alexandrinus a fourth century author

> And Fortune signifies everything that concerns the body, and what one does through the course of life. It becomes indicative of possessions, reputation and privilege.

Robert Zoller tells us that the Lot or Part of Fortune signifies among other things "the life, the body, and also its soul, its strength, fortune, substance, and profit".[45] If the Lot of Fortune is well placed in a Nativity, Question or Election in a good sign, a good

Strengths and Weaknesses Belonging to the Lot of Fortune

Lot of Fortune is strong and fortunate in the signs of:
    ♉ ♓, dignities: 5
    ♎ ♐ ♌ ♋: 4
    ♊ : 3
    ♍, or in the terms of ♃ or ♀: 2

Lot of Fortune is strong by conjunction or aspect:
    In conjunction with ♃ or ♀: 5
    In trine with ♃ or ♀: 4
    In sextile with ♃ or ♀: 3
    In conjunction with ☊: 3

Lot of Fortune is strong in houses:
    5th or 10th: 5
    7th, 4th, 11th: 4
    2nd or 5th: 3
    9th: 2
    3rd: 1

In conjunction with any of these fixed stars:
    With Regulus: 6
    With Spica Virginis: 5

Not combust or under the ☉ beams: 5

Lot of Fortune is weak in:
    ♏ ♑ ♒, debilities: -5
    In ♈ : no score

Lot of Fortune is weak by conjunction or aspect:
    In conjunction with ♄ or ♂: -5
    In conjunction with ☋: -3
    In opposition with ♄ or ♂: -4
    In square with ♄ or ♂: -3
    In terms of ♄ or ♂: -2

Also in houses:
    In the 12th: -5
    In the 8th: -4
    In the 6th: -4

    With Caput Algol: -4
    Combust: -5

house, or in good aspect with a Fortune, the fortune or the estate of the Querent is equal to that planet's strength. For example, if the Lot of Fortune is well placed in an angle or in signs where it is fortunate, the Querent will be prosperous. If the Lot of Fortune is placed otherwise, the opposite will be true. The dispositor of the Lot of Fortune is also important and must be considered.

Almuten

The almuten of a chart is the planet which has the most essential and accidental dignities and is, therefore, the most powerful planet in that whole chart. An example of almuten is a planet which is angular, in its own domicile, swift in motion, free from combustion and free from any bad aspect with an Infortune. This could be Jupiter in Sagittarius in conjunction with the ascendant and in good aspect with Venus in Libra.

> Almuten of a Figure is that Planet who in Essentiall and Accidentall dignities, is most powerfull in the whole Scheame of Heaven.[46]

The almuten of a house is the planet which has the most counts of dignity in a particular house cusp.

> Almuten of any house is that Planet who hath most dignities in the Signe ascending or descending upon the Cusp of any house...

This planet is probably the strongest in relation to matters concerning that particular house. This is explored more fully in chapter nine.

Almuten of a Chart

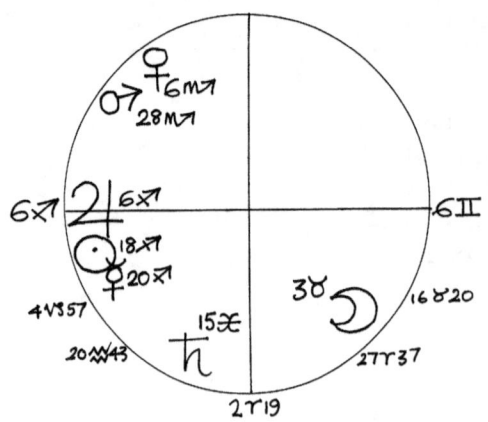

♀ debilitated in ♏ not beholding ascendant and succedent
♂ strong in ♏ but not beholding ascendant and succedent
☿ combust
☉ strong in 1st in ♐
♄ cadent house
☽ strong in ♉ in 5th but not beholding ascendant

♃ ALMUTEN   ♃ strongest: oriental, in very minute of cusp in ascendant, in his domicile and triplicity. Square with ♄ but ♃ disposes of ♄ in his domicile.

Accidental Debility

Al Biruni states that a planet's power is diminished when

> ...slow, retrograde, under the rays, occidental if superior, and if inferior moving slowly westward towards retrograde, inconjunct to sun and moon, or in an unfriendly aspect to them, without reception, the infortunes in an inimical aspect, or besieged by them, associated with fixed stars of a contrary nature, setting in own orbit, so that the malefics pass above and the benefics below... in unlucky houses... in detriment or fall, in a contrary hayyiz, distant from the angles or succedent houses, in a quadrant of different nature, at the nadir of their joys, and conquered by the malefics high above them;[47]

Planets Weak in Accidental Dignity

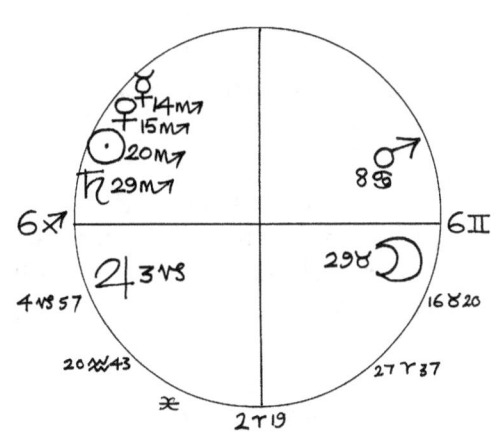

♀ ☿ combust
♂ in 8th house not aspecting ascendant
☽ opposite ☉ ♄ and both cadent
♃ not aspecting ascendant and opposite ♂
♄ under sunbeams

Al Biruni tells us that the name *suspicion* is given to a planet upon which

> ...a number of unfavourable conditions is heaped, and in evil case on account of being combust or retrograde, or in its detriment or fall or in a cadent house, or inconjunct, or antagonized by infortunes, or whose aspects are inimical.[48]

A planet in this condition is said to be *suspect* (what the Arabs called *muttahim*) in its significance: if it shows any promise, it is unable to carry it out.

The Sun and Moon

As discussed previously, the Sun and Moon are of critical importance in judgement: if they are in poor condition, a positive outcome is far less likely. If the luminaries are eclipsed, or near the dragon's head or tail, this means that both of them are weak. The Moon is especially weak when near to the Sun, in conjunction or on the wane, under the earth, or combust. The last part of the signs, where the terms are ruled by the

Infortunes, is a situation which is unfortunate for the Moon and for all the other planets. However, if Saturn or Mars are themselves in these places (where they have rulership by term) they are fortunate.

Afflictions from the Sun

A planet's relationship with the Sun was examined earlier in the chapter, but it is worth emphasising the importance of this relationship. Bonatti tells us that "according to that Aphorism of the Philosopher"

> A Planet Retrograde and Combust, has no strength in signification. The Fortunes when Combust and under the Sun's beams, signify none or very little good; and the Infortunes in like case have little or no virtue to signify ill.[49]

By way of contradiction, the editor's footnote confirms that "An Infortune should be regarded as having very evil signification under the circumstances". However, a little later in the text Bonatti tells us

> ...[a] significator...under the Sun beams...will be of small efficacy in anything as aforesaid; yet the Malevolents will be something more strong in evil than the Benevolents in good.[50]

Does the combination of the retrogradation and the combustion wipe out the strength of the Infortunes or, as the editor states, does it increase their evil? In the latter example, Bonatti appears to be saying that an Infortune under sunbeams does more evil (than when it is combust) or is this simply a poor translation?

The Moon

Bonatti looks at the ways in which the Moon can be "ill-affected", which he believes are "generally reckoned to be Ten", but in his opinion seven more may be added. In these circumstances, he explains that "hindrances and damage happen in all Questions, Nativities, Elections, and actions ..."[51]

- Approaching combustion, which starts from fifteen degrees when the Moon is applying to the Sun, up to twelve degrees when the Moon is separating from the Sun. The impediment is greater in application than separation. When the Moon has separated by five degrees she is said to have escaped, although she is not entirely free.

- In the degrees of her *descensions*, which Bonatti explains are three degrees of Scorpio, or in any part of Scorpio or Capricorn. Also if the Moon is joined to any planet who is also in the degrees of their descensions, for example the Sun in Libra or Aquarius, or Mars in Taurus or Libra.

- In any of the combust degrees which are opposite the Sun. Bonatti points out that the worst degrees in this respect are the twelve degrees before and after the opposition with the Sun.

- In conjunction, opposition or square with either of the Infortunes, Saturn or Mars. If this is without a perfect reception, this is a "grand impediment". However, if the Infortune is positioned in at least two of his smaller dignities, for example, triplicity and term, or face and triplicity, the situation improves. Saturn in twenty three degrees of Gemini, for example, is in his terms and triplicity. Mars has his face and triplicity in the last ten degrees of Pisces.

- In conjunction with the dragon's head or tail (north or south node).

- In Gemini, because this is the twelfth sign from her own domicile.

- At the end of the signs, because these are the terms of the Infortunes, except for the last six degrees of Leo, which Bonatti claims belong to Jupiter, (this does not apply in Ptolemy's system). However, he explains that in the first eight degrees of Leo the Moon is weakened because these are the terms of Saturn (only the first six belong to Saturn in Ptolemy's system). Aside from her location in the signs of Cancer, Taurus, Pisces and Sagittarius, it is doubtful whether the Moon can perform in late degrees of the remaining signs. In addition, if a planet is in the very last minutes of a sign, its influence moves into the next sign.

- In the sixth, eighth, ninth, twelfth or third houses, unless she is in reception with the ascendant, or joined to any planet in the ascendant, or any other planet aspecting the ascendant. Here the Moon is cadent from angles, but because she has her joy in the third house, Bonatti believes that she is not afflicted here as much as in other cadent houses.

- In the *via combusta*, which according to Bonatti, is from the fifteenth degree of Libra to the fifth degree of Scorpio. It is probable that he actually means fifteen degrees of Scorpio, not five, because he goes on to explain that these "30 degrees are called the Combust Way". Al Biruni tells us that the last part of Libra and the first part of Scorpio form the "combust way". This is because these two signs are not congenial to the Sun and Moon because of the "obscurity and ill luck connected with them, and because each of them is the fall of one of the luminaries". Not only that, but he explains that they each contain the two Infortunes, one by exaltation (Libra and Saturn) the other by sign (Scorpio and Mars). Libra is the sign where the Sun has his fall and Scorpio is the sign where the Moon has her fall, while the "adjacent parts of both signs are occupied by terms of Mars" (the last six degrees of Libra and the first six degrees of Scorpio).[52] Dariot claims that the via combusta, or the "burnt way," extends from thirteen degrees of Libra to nine degrees of Scorpio.[53]

- Void of course, that is, "not joined to any planet by body or aspect..." Similarly, when she is *feral*, or when she is *desart*, that is, in a place where she has no dignity.[54] The Moon is void when she makes no further aspects during her stay in one particular sign. Bonatti also claims that even if the Moon is joined to the

Infortunes and not to the Fortunes, if she is in Cancer, Taurus, Pisces or Sagittarius it "signifies good in the business". He believes that when the Moon is void, she is not prejudiced as much in the aforementioned signs as she is in the other signs. However, this is only providing that she is not combust, because in this situation, her position in those fortunate signs "will advantage her little or nothing".[55]

Although he allows a void planet to perfect an aspect in the next sign, Masha'allah explains that if the Moon and the lord of the ascendant are void of course "joining themselves to none", they "proclaim the retardation of and prolongation of the matter and that the matter should be less esteemed according to what you see".[56]

- Slow in motion. Here, the Moon is likened to a planet retrograde and loses strength.
- "...in want of light, so that no part or very little of her is seen..." This happens around the end of the lunar month.
- Besieged by the Infortunes. In this instance, the Moon is most unfortunate.
- In *azimene* degrees, *pitted* degrees, *smoky* degrees and degrees which are called *dark*. For more on this, I refer the reader to Bonatti's *considerations*, which can be found in Anima Astrologiae.

According to Aspect, Position and Motion
Position by House
A planet's position is crucial in the evaluation of accidental dignity. If a planet is cadent or is in any other unfortunate house, it loses strength. For example, in Lilly's scoring system, a planet loses FIVE points if located in the twelfth house. In the eighth and sixth houses a planet loses TWO points. The dangers of being cadent have already been examined in this work, principally the danger of not aspecting the ascendant.

Planetary Motion
A planet moving backwards, or retrograde, is said to be weak, for example if it is moving from ten to nine to eight degrees. A planet retrograde loses FIVE points in Lilly's scoring of planetary strengths. According to Ibn Ezra "The planet which retrogrades denotes rebellion and the destruction of any project".

> If the planet is about to reverse its motion, it forecasts unsuccessful consultation, difficulty, and destruction; if its motion becomes direct, it will better the luck in the matter, its strength, and its uprightness.[57]

Dariot tells us that it is unfortunate when "the good doe apply unto the evil being retrograde".[58] With regard to a stationary planet, Lilly does not include it in his scoring system. He states that because it is not direct it does not score five, but because it is not retrograde it doesn't lose five. However, as noted throughout the book, there is a significant difference between a planet stationary, about to move in direct motion, and a planet stationary, about to move in retrograde motion. Ibn Ezra tells us that the planet, which is in its first station

> ...is like a man who does not know what he will do, and its result is bad; if it is in its second station, it is like a man who expects something and whose hope will not be in vain.[59]

A planet which is moving more slowly than his mean (average) daily motion is said to be slow in motion and is weakened.

In Uncongenial Quarters

The planets are not comfortable or joyous when they are in uncongenial quarters, that is, quarters that are not friendly to them. The Superiors are uncomfortable when they are positioned in decreasing quarters and the Inferiors uncomfortable in increasing quarters. Dariot tells us that the force and strength of the *masculines* is diminished in feminine degrees, in a feminine quarter (quadrant) and when they are occidental. The force of the *feminines* is diminished when they are in masculine degrees, in a masculine quarter (quadrant) and oriental of the Sun.[60]

Contention

Al Biruni explains that a planet is in *contention* when it is in a condition which is "nearly the reverse" of being in its hayyiz. This takes place when a diurnal planet is in the domicile of a nocturnal planet, or a nocturnal planet is in the domicile of a diurnal planet. As an example, Saturn in Aries is in contention (Saturn, a diurnal planet being in the domicile of Mars, a nocturnal planet). Mars in Pisces is in contention (where Mars a nocturnal planet is in the sign of Pisces, the domicile of Jupiter a diurnal planet). Mars does however have dignity in his triplicity in Pisces.[61] As mentioned previously, Ramsay Wright's translation is ambiguous here.

Conjunction with Malevolent Fixed Stars

When a planet is in conjunction with malevolent fixed stars for example *Caput Algol* (about twenty six degrees of Taurus at present), it is greatly weakened. Lilly allows a five degree orb for this unfortunate star.[62] A planet loses FIVE points when in conjunction with a malefic fixed star. According to Richard Proctor

> The Arabian name Algol is the same as Al-ghul, the monster or demon. And to this star most evil influences were attributed by astrologers... the old astronomers had found out how ominously the star looks upon our system...[63]

Conjunction, Square or Opposition with Saturn, Mars or South Node

Any planet in exact (partill) conjunction, opposition or square with Saturn or Mars is greatly weakened, especially the conjunction and the opposition. Any planet in partill conjunction with the south node is weakened. Any house containing Mars, Saturn (not in their essential dignities) or the south node is also unfortunate. I would suggest that a planet becomes unfortunate even when the conjunction with the south node is not partill. This is especially so in the case of the Moon, whose motion is swift, because even when several degrees distant the Moon can quickly reach a conjunction with the south node.

Some authorities believe that when the south node is in conjunction with either of the Infortunes, its malice is doubled or trebled and when joined with the Fortunes, it reduces the good that was expected: the outcome, which may have been expected to be positive, actually comes to nothing. Lilly tells us that "The Tayle of the Dragon is Feminine by nature, and cleane contrary to the Head". Lilly means that where the head of the dragon (north node) is fortunate, the tail of the dragon (south node) is unfortunate. If the dragon's tail is joined to a Fortune, which is a significator in the Question, even though perfection seemed likely

> ...yet did there ever fal out many rubs and disturbances, much wrangling and great controversie, that the business was many times given over for desperate ere a perfect conclusion could be had; and unless the principall significators were Angular and well fortified with essentiall dignities, many times unexpectedly the whole matter came to nothing.[64]

Partridge tells us that the dragon's tail is an Infortune and "doth increase the Evil of the Infortunes, and abateth the good of the fortunate Stars..." [65] Lilly subtracts a score of FOUR points from a planet in conjunction with the south node.

Besieged between Infortunes

A planet positioned between Saturn and Mars is said to be besieged between the Infortunes and is greatly weakened. For example, where Mars is in seven degrees of Aries, Venus is in nine degrees of Aries and Saturn is in eleven degrees of Aries, here, Venus is besieged between Mars and Saturn and is in a very unfortunate place.

Al Biruni gives as another example, planets in different signs where "a planet in sign 1 is surrounded by others in signs 2 and 12".[66] This could be Mars in Taurus (12), Mercury in Gemini (1) and Saturn in Cancer (2). Abu Ma'shar puts forward a similar example which is explored in chapters fourteen and fifteen. However, besiegement usually takes place when three or more planets are in one sign as in the first example above. Here, Venus in Aries is said to be "corporally besieged". According to Al Biruni a planet can be besieged by "rays". He claims that this takes place where a planet has separated from another with a sextile or square aspect and applies to another planet with the same aspect. If the planets in question are Infortunes the influences are "extremely bad" but if they are Fortunes they are "extremely good".

Void of Course

Being void of course is a condition which usually affects the Moon. Masha'allah does not believe that a void of course Moon necessarily prevents the achievement of the desired outcome to a Question. Much depends on the first aspect the Moon makes when she changes sign position.

> ...look at which planet the Moon is joined to first after its going forth from the sign in which it is, and judge the outcome of the matter according to that planet.[67]

However, Masha'allah also explains that a "swifter planet is more worthy in being moved than a ponderous one". He explains that a planet like Saturn for example, when void of course

> ...will be worse than all of the others because the emptiness of the course of planets indicates the evil nature and tardiness of the matter.

Any planet which is void of course indicates that the matter will be delayed. In addition, the astrologer must consider the number of degrees a planet must travel before exiting a sign and moving into another. According to Masha'allah, the greater the number of degrees remaining, the slower the matter moves along. Generally speaking, the Inferiors move more swiftly and cause less delay than the Superiors, but in an overall sense, any planet which is void causes delay and difficulty.

Feral

Morin explains that if a planet neither approaches another planet nor departs from another planet, so that it has no connection through aspect with any other planet, it is called *feral* or *solitary*. He tells us that if this planet is in the first house or rules the first house it can make the Native a recluse, or cause the Native to "flee the company of others".[68] Abu Ma'shar calls a planet in this condition *wild* and confirms that this happens most frequently to the Moon.[69] Morin also refers to a planet as feral when it is in its detriment or fall.

The following chart outlines the way in which Lilly weighed up the testimonies in a Question. These rules provide us with a framework for adding up the strength (or otherwise) of each planet in any given chart.

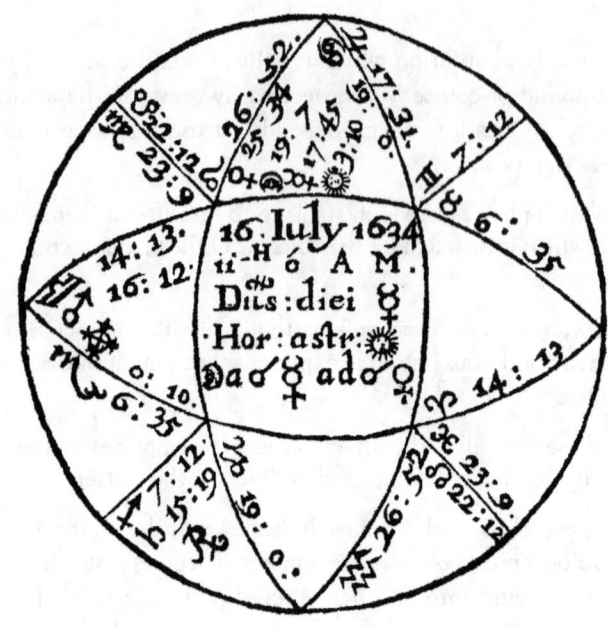

If he should be rich, or subsist of himselfe without Marriage? [70] 16 July 1634 11.00am

Average diurnal motion

Saturn	2 minutes 1 second
Jupiter	4 minutes 59 seconds
Mars	31 minutes 7 seconds
Sun	59 minutes 8 seconds
Venus	59 minutes 8 seconds
Mercury	59 minutes 8 seconds
Moon	13 degrees 10 minutes 36 seconds

Diurnal motion of the planets in the figure

Saturn	2 minutes (slow)
Jupiter	13 minutes (swift)
Mars	35 minutes (swift)
Sun	57 minutes (slow)
Venus	1 degree 13 minutes (very swift)
Mercury	1 degree 44 minutes (very swift indeed)
Moon	11 degrees 54 minutes (slow)

The Strengths and Weaknesses of the Planets
Saturn
Accidental and essential dignities

In the third house	1
Free from combustion	5
Total	6

Accidental and essential debilities

Peregrine	minus 5
Retrograde	minus 5
Slow	minus 2
Occidental	minus 2
Total	minus 14

Total **minus 8**
Weak by dignities and therefore unfortunate

Jupiter
Accidental and essential dignities

In exaltation	4
Tenth house	5
Direct	4
Swift	2
Free from combustion	5
Total	20

Accidental and essential debilities	None	
Some hindrance because Mars is square Jupiter but the aspect is platick*		*In fact this is only just over 1 degree
Total (Strong)	**20**	

Mars
Accidental and essential dignities

In the ascendant	5
Direct	4
Swift	2
Free from combustion	5
In conjunction with Spica or within 5 degrees	5
Total	21

Accidental and essential debilities

In detriment	minus 5
Peregrine	minus 5

Occidental of the Sun	minus 2
Total	minus 12
Total Strength	**9**

Sun

Accidental and essential dignities

Own sign	5
Midheaven	5
Total	10

Accidental and essential debilities

Slow	minus 2
Total	minus 2
Total	**18**

Venus

Accidental and essential dignities

Eleventh house	4
Direct	4
Swift	2
Occidental of the Sun	2
Free from combustion	5
Conjunct Regulus or within six degrees	6
Total	23

Accidental and essential debilities

Peregrine	minus 5
Total	minus 5
Total (Strong)	**18**

Mercury

Accidental and essential dignities

Tenth house	5
Direct	4
Swift	2
Occidental	2
Free from combustion	5 (is Mercury under the sunbeams here?)
Total	18

Accidental and essential debilities

Peregrine	minus 5
Total	minus 5
Total	**13**

Moon

Accidental and essential dignities

Tenth house	5
Increasing in light	2
Free from combustion	5
Total	12

Accidental and essential debilities

Slow	minus 2
Peregrine	minus 5
Total	minus 7
Total	5

From this scoring system it would appear that Jupiter is the strongest planet in the figure and, therefore, *almuten* of the chart, closely followed by Venus.

Lot of Fortune

The Lot of Fortune placed in Scorpio has 5 debilities and being in the second house has only 3 testimonies of strength. It is WEAK by MINUS 2.

Antiscia of Planets in the Figure

	Antiscium	Contrantiscium
Saturn	14° 41' Capricorn	14° 41' Cancer
Jupiter	12° 29' Gemini	12° 29' Sagittarius
Mars	13° 48' Pisces	13° 48' Virgo
Sun	26° 50' Taurus	26° 50' Scorpio
Venus	4° 26' Taurus	4° 26' Scorpio
Mercury	12° 15' Taurus	12° 15' Scorpio
Moon	10° 53' Taurus	10° 53' Scorpio

Lilly summarises

- The majority of planets (especially the two Fortunes) are swift in motion and well placed in houses with no affliction.

- Venus, ruler of the ascendant is near to *Cor Leonis* (Regulus) a star of great fortune and power.

- The Moon is increasing in light.

- Jupiter is almost in the midheaven.

From this information, Lilly considers that the Querent should have a high standard of living. And so it was.

I would suggest that Lilly's framework, although very useful in determining planetary strengths and weaknesses, is best followed as a guide only. I say this because, on a practical level, a planet which is combust, for example, especially applying to combustion, can be totally ineffective in terms of achieving the desired outcome in a Question, or in terms of producing good fortune in a Nativity. A significator which is combust can actually prevent the achievement of the desired outcome. In the scoring system above, this debility might appear to be outweighed if that planet were dignified by sign and angular. Combustion is one of the most important, but unfortunate, chart testimonies. Similarly, if the chart contains a New Moon, Full Moon or Eclipse the chart as a whole is unfortunate, no matter what the scores of the remaining planets.

It is clear that certain testimonies need to be evaluated with care. As an example, a planet in its detriment is less afflicted if its dispositor is well dignified essentially and/or accidentally. A peregrine planet is probably less afflicted if in the domicile of a Fortune. In the chart examples in Part Two, I include a positive score for planets who have a mutual reception between the lesser dignities, as well as a score for a planet aspecting the ascendant. In *Gesta Britannorum*, George Wharton gives a score of TWO points to any planet in the terms of the Fortunes, Venus or Jupiter.[71]

Lilly's scoring system is very useful and provides a comprehensive guide, but we should proceed in the way that Lilly himself tells us and "mix Art and Reason together..."[72]

References

1. Lilly, Table of Dignities, p.115.
2. Al Biruni p.316.
3. Al Biruni p.296.
4. Zoller, *Tools and Techniques of the Medieval Astrologers*, Bonatti citing Al-Qabisi (Alchabitius), p.115.
5. Lilly p.113.
6. Lilly's note in Guido Bonatus, *The Astrologer's Guide or Anima Astrologiae*, p.19, 53rd consideration.
7. The orb for sunbeams varies between different authors. Lilly himself puts forward different orbs in different publications.
8. Robert Hand, *Night and Day: Planetary Sect in Astrology*, p.10.
9. Morin p.154.
10. Lilly in Bonatus where he puts forward 16 minutes for cazimi, not 17 as in *Christian Astrology*.
11. Gadbury p.44.
12. Bonatus pp.37-38, 112th consideration.
13. ibid p.40, 123rd consideration.
14. Al Biruni p.296.
15. Zoller, citing Bonatti p.115.
16. Abu Ma'shar p.19 editor's note (referring to Antiochus Part I p.4).

17. Al Biruni p.298.
18. Bonatus p.3.
19. Al Biruni p.296.
20. Lilly p.114.
21. Al Biruni p.300.
22. ibid p.301.
23. Al Biruni pp.298-300.
24. Al Biruni p.299 and editor's note.
25. Al Biruni p.315.
26. Al Biruni p.316.
27. Abu Ma'shar p.31.
28. Al Biruni p.300.
29. Cardan in Bonatus p.60 no.22.
30. Morin p.66.
31. Ibn Ezra *The Beginning Of Wisdom*, p.218.
32. Lilly, also chapter sixteen.
33. Al Biruni p. 309.
34. Gadbury p.45.
35. Dariot p.38.
36. Lilly p.537.
37. Al Biruni p.46.
38. Bonatus p.48, 141st consideration.
39. Bonatus p.49, 141st consideration.
40. Lilly p.83.
41. Partridge John, 1679, *Vade Mecum*, William Bromwich, London. Reprinted by Ascella Publications p.18.
42. Al Biruni p.309.
43. Ptolemy, *Tetrabiblos*. Trans. F E Robbins, Loeb Classical Library, p.275.
44. Lilly, A table of Fortuna's strengths and weaknesses, p.145.
45. Zoller, *The Lost Key to Prediction. The Arabic Parts in Astrology*, Inner Traditions, New York, 1980, p.85.
46. Lilly p.49.
47. Al Biruni p.316.
48. ibid p.310.
49. Bonatus p.17, 43rd consideration.
50. ibid p.19, 53rd consideration.
51. ibid pp.2-3, 5th consideration.
52. Al Biruni p.317.
53. Dariot p.38.
54. Bonatti does not explain feral here, see definition later in this chapter.
55. Bonatus p.23, 64th consideration.
56. Masha'allah pp.8-9.
57. Ibn Ezra pp.218-219.
58. Dariot p.39.
59. Ibn Ezra p.218.

60. Dariot p.38.
61. Al Biruni p.308 and editor's footnote.
62. Lilly p.115, Table.
63. Richard Procter, 1882, *Easy Star Lessons*, Chatto and Windus, Piccadily, p.127.
64. Lilly p.83.
65. Partridge p.18.
66. Al Biruni p.309.
67. Masha'allah pp.8-9.
68. Morin p.134.
69. Abu Ma'shar p.25.
70. Lilly pp.178-181.
71. George Wharton, *Gesta Britannorum*, London, pp.244-245.
72. Lilly p.184.

8

Reception

Whether a planet has either a reception or mutual reception with one or more planets is perhaps one of the most important considerations in chart evaluation. This applies equally to a Question, Nativity, or any other chart. Where the planetary testimony appears to be unfavourable, either because of aspect, dignity or other factors, the presence of a reception (especially mutual reception) can bring about a positive outcome. Reception substantially reduces the impact of any unfortunate testimony and strengthens the power of fortunate testimony.

Astrologers of the past, especially Masha'allah, placed a huge emphasis on reception, whereas modern astrologers have mostly discarded it. For centuries after Masha'allah, the use of reception continued. Robert Hand reports that he has found this sort of emphasis in Bonatti and later authors, even up to Henry Coley in the seventeenth century. However, Robert Hand reports that most of these later authors did not use it as systematically as Masha'allah.[1]

Reception takes place where one particular planet is located in the dignity of another planet, for example, when Venus is in Sagittarius she is said to be "received" by the other planet, Jupiter, because Jupiter rules the sign of Sagittarius. A planet can be received by any of the dignities in which it is placed. If Venus is located in eleven degrees of Cancer she is received by the Moon (being in her domicile), by Jupiter (being in his exaltation), by Mars (being in his triplicity by day or night), by Jupiter (being in his term) and by Mercury (being in his face). These are examples of a single or one-way reception.

If each of the planets involved is also placed in a dignity of the other, this is called mutual reception. This is stronger than reception, for example, Venus in Sagittarius and Jupiter in Libra are in each other's domicile, Venus in Cancer and the Moon in Taurus are in each other's domicile. Venus in Capricorn and Mars in Pisces are in each others exaltation. The Sun in Libra and Saturn in Aries are in each other's exaltation, as well as in each other's triplicity during the day.

Astrologers of the past usually required an applying aspect to be in operation between planets, in order for a single or simple reception to take place. However, with mutual reception it appears that in most cases an aspect between planets is unnecessary (although the relationship between the two planets would of course be a lot stronger in

Reception

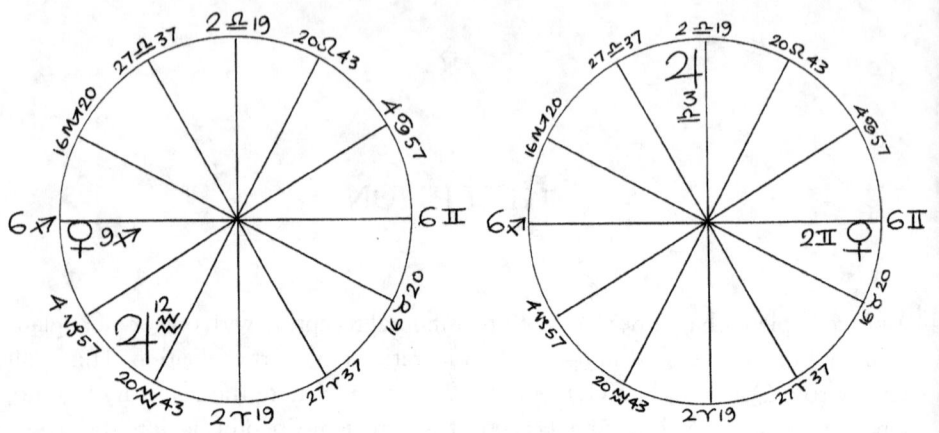

♀ received by ♃
being in his domicile

♃ received by ♀
being in her domicile

Mutual Reception

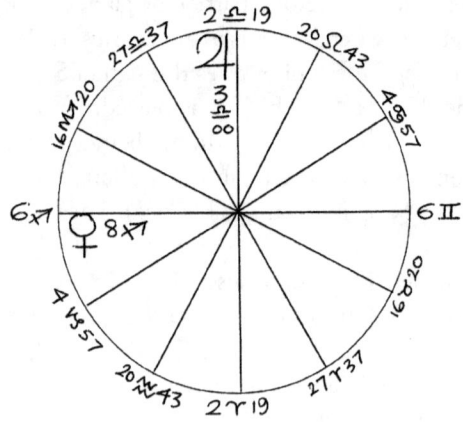

♀ and ♃ received by each other
being in each other's domicile

this instance). As far as I can ascertain, all authorities agree that a mutual reception involving domicile or exaltation is the strongest of receptions. If there is also an aspect between them this is even better. If each planet also has some dignity of its own, this is the very best of indications. However, there are slight variations in the definition of reception and mutual reception. Some authors allow a mutual reception between the lesser dignities, for example Mercury in Aries has a reception with Jupiter in Libra. Here, Mercury is positioned in the nocturnal triplicity of Jupiter and Jupiter is positioned in the nocturnal triplicity of Mercury. This is mutual reception between triplicity. In the case of a simple reception between the smaller or lesser dignities, this was usually dependent on a planet being in two of these dignities simultaneously. However, the texts are not totally consistent or clear on this. An example of the aforementioned would be the Moon in five degrees of Leo applying to a trine with Saturn in six degrees of Sagittarius. Here the Moon is in the term and face of Saturn and makes an applying aspect. The Moon is, therefore, received by Saturn.[2]

Masha'allah
Masha'allah tells us

> ...in the causing of whether things will be or will not be reception occurs because of exaltations and domiciles; that is, in such a manner that one of the seven planets is in the exaltation or domicile of a second planet, and that first planet is being joined to the second according to one of the seven recognised aspects; or they are both in one sign, and one of them is in the exaltation [or domicile] of his comrade and joined to it. Consequently then it will be joined to that planet by its body.[3]

Masha'allah only recognizes reception involving domicile or exaltation. It also appears as if the planets must be either in a conjunction or in one of the seven aspects* for reception to be allowed. However, it does not appear to matter whether or not the planets involved are within 'allowable distance'. In *On Reception* Masha'allah gives an example of the Sun in one degree of Libra and Saturn in thirty degrees of Aries. Here, the Sun and Saturn are considered to have a reception between exaltation providing that there are no planets in the sign of Aries, nor placed closer to Saturn by aspect than the Sun. In addition, Saturn cannot leave the sign of Aries until the Sun "is joined to him by degree according to degree". If these conditions are satisfied, they both receive each other in their exaltations. Masha'allah also tells us that in certain instances, the dignity of exaltation is stronger than that of domicile

> ...exaltations are of greater authority in kingship, to wit, if something is done by a king, the lord of the exaltation is stronger then the lord of the domicile.[4]

---

* The conjunction was not thought to be an aspect, so the seven aspects are the dexter and sinister sextile, the dexter and sinister trine, the dexter and sinister square and the opposition.

Abu Ma'Shar

Abu Ma'shar tells us that when a planet, for example, Venus applies to another planet, Jupiter, from either the domicile, exaltation, triplicity, term or decan of Jupiter, in this instance Jupiter is said to receive Venus. Or if Jupiter is in one of the dignities of Venus, Venus receives Jupiter. He tells us that a reception between domicile and exaltation is the strongest and that the term, triplicity and decan are weak, unless two or more of these lesser dignities are joined together. Abu Ma'shar clearly requires an aspect to be in operation. However, he explains that one planet may receive another also "by aspect without application," although of course a reception with application is stronger.[5]

Reception therefore has varying degrees of strength. Charles Burnett tells us that there is more information on this in Adelard's Latin translation, corresponding to a section in the *Great Introduction*

> ...in generosity [reception] some are found stronger, some weaker, some of medium strength. The greatest generosity is between the Sun and the Moon. For the Moon takes from the Sun in any sign, except opposition, which is harming. Therefore, when the Moon comes into a sign in which the Sun enjoys some dignity, its benefit is doubled: for one gift is from the sign, the other from the nature. Mercury, when another planet is in Virgo, provides two benefits for it. But a medium benefit is what each star receives from another, either from its house or from its exaltation or its decan or its triplicity or its term. If two of these are given, it will be greater. Whatever is other than the aforesaid, will be weak.[6]

A similar passage is found in Ibn Ezra's writings some two hundred years later

> The reception may be strong, moderate, or weak. The strong reception always applies to the Moon with the Sun, because the former receives it from any sign and because its beams come from the Sun; from the opposition, however, it will be in pain and sorrow; if it should be in a sign lacking all power, then there are two receptions, as in the case of Mercury when it receives the planet in the sign of Virgo, because that is its house and the house of its honor; therefore, that reception is perfect. The reception of the house is moderate. The reception of the triplicity, or of the limit [term], or of the face, is weak.[7]

Al Biruni

> When an inferior planet arrives in one of the dignities proper to a superior one, and makes known to it the relation thus established, there is an exchange of compliments such as 'your servant' or 'neighbour'. If further the superior planet happens to be in a situation proper to the inferior one, mutual reception takes place, and this is fortified, the richer the situation is in dignities, especially when the aspects indicate no enmity or malevolence.[8]

Al Biruni also tells us that when reception does not take place the result is "negative". In his example of a single reception at the beginning of the piece, he explains that this occurs when an Inferior is in the dignities of a Superior. I would suggest that Al Biruni's definition of a single reception would also include a situation where a Superior is in the dignities of an Inferior. He also implies that an aspect is required and that the strongest mutual reception occurs when the aspect is with a trine or sextile.

Abraham Ibn Ezra

> Reception is noticed when a planet enters into conjunction or into aspect with a planet which is the master of its house [domicile], the master of the house of its honor [exaltation], the master of the house of its triplicity, its limit [term], or its face, and it receives that planet.[9]

For example, when Mercury in Capricorn makes a conjunction with Saturn in Capricorn, Mercury is received by Saturn (a Superior receives an Inferior). When Mercury in Capricorn makes a trine with Saturn in Taurus, Mercury is received by Saturn. It is of course the same the other way around, when one planet makes a conjunction with another planet and the latter is in the dignity of the former. For example, when Venus in Libra makes a conjunction with Mars in Libra, Mars is received by Venus (an Inferior receives a Superior). The same would apply when Mercury in Gemini makes a conjunction with Mars in Gemini. Here Mars is received by Mercury.

However, Ibn Ezra points out that if a planet is only received in one of its lesser dignities, for example the triplicity, the term or the face, this is "not a perfect reception". He only allows reception between the lesser dignities if two influences join together, for example, the triplicity with the term or the face. In addition to this, both planets should make a trine or sextile aspect. An example of this is Mars in twelve degrees of Virgo in a nocturnal chart, in trine with Venus in ten degrees of Taurus, where Mars is in the term and face of Venus. Here Mars is received by Venus in her triplicity.

We are also told that Mars and Saturn can only receive each other when they make a conjunction, sextile or trine with each other, but not with the other aspects (square and opposition). Ibn Ezra tells us that the reception between domicile "is moderate", but that the reception between triplicity, term or face is "weak". Ibn Ezra gives the name *liberality* to mutual reception. This takes place where

> ...each of two planets is in the house of its companion, or in the house of its honor, or in any of its influences, and, even though they do not enter into conjunction or aspect with each other, still there will be reception between them.

In his definition of mutual reception any of the dignities are allowed and no aspect between the planets is required. In Ibn Ezra's reception it appears that with a single or simple reception, an aspect between planets is required, whereas with mutual reception no aspect between the planets is necessary.

Dariot

Dariot divides reception into two types: *strong* and *weake*. His strong reception is mutual reception

> ...when a Planet doth applye to the Lord of a house, or Exaltation, or Triplicitie...and that likewise hee hath some dignitie in the place where the Lord is placed, and if both two be in dignities one of another, having also dignitie in the place where they are, and that their application bee by a trine or sextill aspect, the reception shall be the better and the more perfite.[10]

As an example of mutual reception, Dariot includes the Moon in Cancer in sextile with Venus in Taurus. Both of these planets have dignity in their own position and receive each other. The Moon receives Venus in her exaltation and Venus receives the Moon in her triplicity (Dariot gives rulership of the water triplicity to Venus during the day). Dariot's weak reception takes place when the application between the planets takes places in their lesser dignities, for example when they are in their term or face. Dariot calls their reception "weake and impotent". In both his examples, reception can only take place if the planets make an aspect.

Morin

Morin tells us that any planet in a domicile other than one of its own is received by another. Clearly, if a planet is not located in its own domicile, it must be located in the domicile of another. The planet which does the receiving has a rulership over the sign in which the other planet is placed. Morin only considers the three more important dignities in his definition of reception: domicile, exaltation or triplicity, what might be called the "triple point of view".[11]

Morin divides reception into reception with presence or absence. With presence, the planet which receives the other, itself occupies the sign in which the other planet is found. For example, when Mars and Mercury are in Gemini, Mars is received by Mercury and Mercury is present in the same sign as Mars. In absence, the planet which does the receiving is itself located in a different sign. For example, Venus in Sagittarius is received by Jupiter in Aries. Here, Jupiter is absent from that sign (Sagittarius).

In absence, Morin makes a division between simple reception and mutual reception. With simple reception, the planet receiving the other in its domicile is not itself located in a place of honor of the received planet. For example, Venus in Sagittarius received by Jupiter in Aries, where Jupiter is not located in a dignity of Venus. However, with mutual reception, the receiving planet itself occupies a sign in which the received planet has dignity, for example Venus in Sagittarius received by Jupiter in Pisces (Pisces being the exaltation of Venus).

Presumably, mutual reception with presence can take place in Morin's system. As an example, both Mars and Saturn in Capricorn have a mutual reception where Mars is in the domicile of Saturn and Saturn is in the exaltation of Mars. Apparently this was a special type of reception called *communion* where two planets are located in the same sign, one being in the domicile of the other, the other in the exaltation of the former.[12]

Morin tells us that mutual reception can take place between planets located in the same dignity, or between a mixture of dignities (for example domicile and exaltation). For example, Mars in Taurus and the Moon in Capricorn have a mutual reception between exaltation. Jupiter in Taurus and the Moon in Pisces have a mutual reception between exaltation and domicile.[13]

Saunders

Saunders also divides reception into two different types, what he calls "perfecta and imperfecta".

> ...perfect Reception, otherwise called mutual Reception, is when two Planets aspect one another, either of them being in the Dignity of the other; as if Mars were in Leo and the Sun in Aries, here Mars receiveth the Sun and the Sun also receiveth Mars.

His *imperfect* reception, what I have called a simple or single reception, is when a planet

> ...beholds another in his Dignity; as if the Moon were in Gemini and Mercury in Pisces, here the Moon doth receive Mercury with a square.[14]

He explains that the Moon receives Mercury, presumably because Mercury is in the triplicity of the Moon. However, the Moon is also in the domicile of Mercury. This is a little confusing. This is really a mutual reception, but the aspect is a square so it appears as if this cannot be a strong reception.

Saunders divides his reception into two other kinds, "fortis and debilis". *Fortis receptio* is when two planets receive each other between domicile or exaltation. *Debilis receptio* is when two planets receive each other between triplicity, term or face. Saunders allows a mutual reception between the lesser dignities, although it is of course weaker than mutual reception between domicile or exaltation.

It would seem that among seventeenth century astrologers only Saunders followed Dariot in distinguishing strong (fortis) and weak (debilis) types in mutual reception. However, Dariot's strong mutual reception also includes the dignity of triplicity as well as that of domicile and exaltation. According to Saunders, a strong mutual reception is only allowed between domicile and exaltation; he does not include the dignity of triplicity. In both systems a fortunate applying aspect is also required. Dariot's weak mutual reception is between term or face, whereas that of Saunders is between triplicity, term or face.

Hand

In *On Reception*, Robert Hand puts forward his own definition of reception

> Reception exists when a planet applies toward one of its dispositors according to the five essential dignities, or the dispositor applies towards it.

As an example of this, Venus in Capricorn applies to a trine with Saturn in Virgo. Saturn disposits or receives Venus in his domicile. Similarly, Mercury in Libra applies to a trine with Jupiter in Gemini. Here Mercury, the dispositor of Jupiter is the applying planet. Mercury disposits or receives Jupiter. Hand tells us that the received planet commits *disposition* to the receiving planet. This is one example of the doctrine of committing disposition.

Hand explains that the receiving planet takes on the responsibility for handling or arranging the affairs of the received planet. He adds that in some of the texts there is also the notion that the "receiving planet may gain the dignity it would have had were it in the location of the received planet..." However, he explains that this is not consistently taught.[15]

Lilly

In *Christian Astrology*, Lilly explains that a mutual reception can take place between two planets in each others' domicile, exaltation, triplicity, term or face. He tells us that reception can take place between "any essentiall dignity..."[16] However, in his scoring system referring to a planet's strength in essential dignity, Lilly only gives a score to planets who have a mutual reception between domicile or exaltation.[17]

Lilly does not require an aspect to be in place between planets who have a mutual reception. In fact he puts forward as an example, the Sun in Taurus and Venus in Aries who have a mutual reception between triplicity during the day. Lilly also gives an example of planets who have a mutual reception between their terms. In *Christian Astrology* he does not put forward a definition of single reception, but there are examples of reception throughout the text.

Ramesey

In his definition, Ramesey only includes mutual reception, which he claims can take place between all dignities. He doesn't divide reception into strong or weak

> Reception is, when two Planets are in each other's dignities; for then they are said to receive one the other; and this may be accomplished as many ways as there are dignities of a Planet;

Ramesey does not appear to require an aspect to be in operation for a mutual reception to take place. He puts forward an example of a mutual reception between Jupiter in Capricorn and Mars in Cancer, where both planets are in their fall and make an opposition with each other. This is quite unlike some of the earlier authorities.[18]

In chapter five, certain aspects which included reception were examined, such as pushing nature, pushing two natures, pushing power and pushing counsel.[19] Whatever definition of reception or mutual reception is preferred, there is no doubt that a reception or better still, a mutual reception, is extremely powerful in a chart and can make the difference between the Querent being successful or being defeated, between a Native being successful in a particular area of their life or unsuccessful. In some instances the presence of reception can mean the difference between life and death. A planet which has the strongest dignity of all in a chart has

- Dignity in its own position.
- A mutual reception between domicile or exaltation.
- An applying harmonious aspect with the received or receiving planet and from good houses.

Mutual Reception in Debility

In a situation where each planet is in its detriment, even if they are mutually received, certain authors believed that this was not very helpful. In fact, Morin claims that this is harmful. If for example, Saturn is in Cancer and the Moon is in Capricorn, both planets are in their detriment, but they have a mutual reception, because Saturn is placed in the domicile of the Moon and the Moon is placed in the domicile of Saturn. Morin believes this type of configuration to be unfortunate, especially the opposition, but less so the square. If the planets are in one of their debilities but have a mutual reception

Mutual Reception in Debility

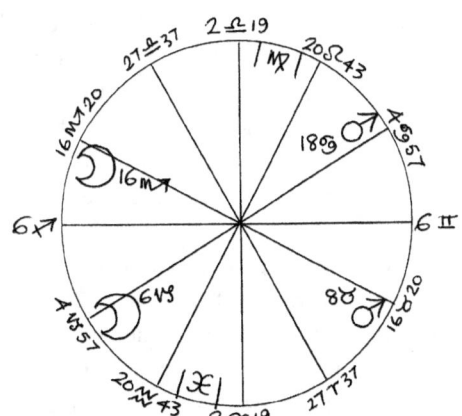

Mutual reception between domicile and exaltation

and are applying to each other with a trine, he suggests that the reception is more favourable, but only in "an average way". Here, he explains, it becomes necessary "to determine which of the two planets has the most power to do good or ill".[20]

It is tempting to accept this theory, given that it appears to be a logical assumption. However, in practice this type of mutual reception can be fairly helpful and the Querent can achieve the desired outcome, as long as the aspect is fortunate. I have a number of charts where the principal significators are in their detriment and/or fall. The Moon in Scorpio in mutual reception with Mars in Cancer is an example. However, in these instances I have noted that although the Querent might achieve the desired outcome, this has not always worked out to the Querent's advantage. In this particular example of course, it is clear that Mars may gain strength through his triplicity rulership over Cancer. The Moon (according to some authors) also has a triplicity rulership over Scorpio. In addition the Moon makes a harmonious aspect with Mars.

I would suggest that significators in their detriment or fall, even if they have a mutual reception between one of the stronger dignities, also need an applying and harmonious aspect between them in order to produce the outcome desired. Where planets have dignity in their own right this does not appear to be necessary. Masha'allah himself states that with reception

> ...all of the fortunate planets with fortunate planets increase the good, and the malefics with the malefics are made good...their evil and impediment recedes...[21]

This occurs unless of course the aspect between them is a square or opposition. However, in a chart concerning a Kingship from Masha'allah in *On Reception*, we are told that the Moon is in her detriment in Capricorn; Mars is in his fall in Cancer. It is a diurnal chart and as a consequence the Moon has no dignity by virtue of her rulership over the earth triplicity. However, the Moon receives Mars in her domicile and Mars receives the Moon in his exaltation. The Moon is placed in the second house, which has signification over people assisting the Querent, as well as "substance".[22] Although this reception is strong, Robert Hand tells us because of the fact that the planets are in signs where they have "a major debility" this is taken as an indication that the rebel lord's troops would not get all their back pay from the rebel lord. But if the Querent were to pay the troops their back pay, or part of it, this would work to the advantage of the Querent.[23] Hand tells us that in this text the debility of fall is taken much more seriously than the debility of detriment.

Hand, from a reading of Masha'allah, believes that a planet in a major debility can receive, but that its receiving is not very useful to the received planet.[24] Hand notes that in one of his Questions concerning a Kingship, Masha'allah is not much concerned by the fact that Jupiter is placed in his detriment of Virgo when receiving other planets.[25] However, in a separate example where the Querent is hoping to acquire a Kingship, Hand notes that Masha'allah does pay attention to the issue of whether a planet in a major debility can receive. In the latter, the Moon is in four degrees and twenty-two minutes of Libra in the fourth house and in opposition with Saturn in twenty-nine degrees and ten minutes of Aries in the tenth house. Here, there is a reception, but the aspect is an opposition, which is the worst of all aspects, whereas in the previous example, Jupiter is receiving other planets with a square.[26] In the example, which includes the opposition, Masha'allah tells us that in terms of acquiring this kingship

> ...this would not be until it would be begged for by the lord of the interrogation, and there will be some difficulty or suffering because Saturn receives the Moon by opposition or contrariety:; and the spirit of the one who seeks the matter will be made anxious because of Saturn's placement; because Saturn which receives the Moon is in his descension or fall, and in vileness. Thus Saturn is distressed in its own place.

If there is no reception, for example, where the Sun is in Aries and Saturn is in Libra, Masha'allah claims there will be "hostilities and contrarieties, ignorance, and denials because neither one of these receives its associate".[27] Hand calls this a war between equals because both planets are in their exaltations and there is no reception between them.[28]

Reception and Aspect

Masha'allah explains that if the reception is through a square or opposition, it signifies "hardship, error, anxiety, and contrariety..." However, with the trine, sextile and

War Between Equals

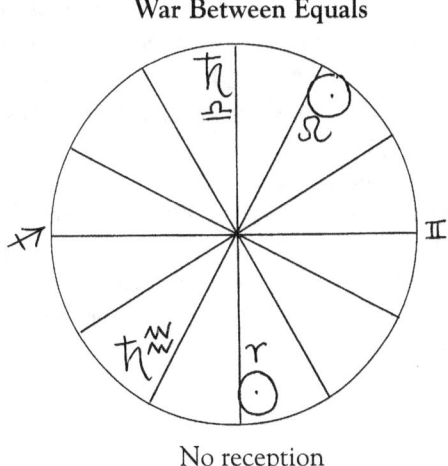

No reception

conjunction, reception signifies "gentleness, piety, loftiness". In all cases of reception he claims that any aspects between fortunate planets will increase the good that is expected, whereas any difficulties expected from aspects between the malefics will be reduced.[29] This takes place unless the aspects are the square or opposition. Later in the work Masha'allah tells us that an Infortune can "destroy the matter" unless there is reception, but a Fortune produces a good outcome, whether there is reception or not. If, for example, the ascendant ruler or the Moon makes a conjunction with a malefic, if the malefic receives this planet "the matter will be perfected" but if the malefic does not receive it, "it will destroy the matter..." This is because a malefic planet causes the destruction of things if there is no reception. However "fortunes render matters more advantageous...even if they do not receive nor are received". If there is reception "the good will be the greater" and even if there is no reception, "they nevertheless work good and do not impede..." In a similar way if a Fortune commits its disposition to a malefic which does not receive it, the matter ruled by it will "endure harm". However, if the malefic receives the Fortune, the matter will be perfected "without harm".[30]

Reception and Planetary Strength

In Lilly's table where he examines the dignities and debilities of the planets, it is clear that he only allows a mutual reception between domicile or exaltation (or a mixture of the two) in order for that planet to achieve the same strength as if the planet itself had dignity in the place where it is located.[31] For example a mutual reception between Venus in Sagittarius and Jupiter in Taurus is given a scoring of FIVE to each planet, which is the same score assigned to a planet which has dignity in its own right. One has to assume, therefore, that Lilly does not believe that other types of weaker mutual receptions, or mixed mutual receptions, allow a planet to achieve the same level of strength which they acquire when located in that particular dignity. For example, Venus in Sagittarius and the Sun in Virgo have a mutual reception between triplicity in the diurnal chart but they not allocated a score of three points which they would have been given had they been located in their own triplicities.

Even so, in his earlier definition of mutual reception, Lilly explains that this can take place between any of the dignities.

A planet which has a mutual reception between triplicity is not included in Lilly's table nor allocated a score. Similarly, a planet in one of the more important dignities of domicile or exaltation, in mutual reception with a planet in one of the lesser dignities, is not included nor given a score. However, there are instances in *Christian Astrology*, where Lilly talks of a mixed reception between planets, which helps bring about a positive outcome.[32]

Simple Reception

How strong or effective planets were thought to be when they have a single or simple reception between the lesser dignities is unclear. However, because the simple reception usually requires an applying aspect to be in operation, this configuration must be helpful. For example, Mercury in Pisces applying to a trine with Mars in Cancer, where Mercury is received by Mars in his triplicity, must be more helpful than Mercury in Pisces applying to a trine with Saturn in Cancer, where there is no reception. Simple reception between one of the stronger dignities can be very helpful, where for example Venus in Cancer applies to a trine with Jupiter in Scorpio.

Mutual Reception
How effective a planet which has a mutual reception between the lesser dignities might be is not totally clear. I would suggest that it is certainly quite helpful, especially where the planets have a harmonious and applying aspect between them. Where the aspect is a square or opposition the mutual reception helps to alleviate the difficulties caused. Clearly a mutual reception between the stronger dignities gives a planet much more strength and helps reduce the negative impact of a square or opposition quite substantially. Where there is a square between significators, which might have prevented the achievement of the desired outcome, a strong mutual reception can help towards achieving that outcome.

Mutual Reception and Peregrine Planets
It is clear that a planet which has a mutual reception between domicile or exaltation cannot be peregrine. Whether a mutual reception between the lesser dignities of triplicity, term or face would prevent this is not clear from the texts. Similarly, it is unclear whether a mutual reception between mixed dignities of both the stronger or weaker kind would prevent a planet having peregrine status. From experience I would suggest that a mixed reception between planets in any of their dignities is enough to prevent a planet from being peregrine.

However, even if this can be achieved it is doubtful that a mutual reception of this manner contains much strength in the chart in an overall sense, unless there is an applying and harmonious aspect in operation, in which case this would be quite a strong application. In a similar manner, if a planet with a weak mutual reception between lesser dignities is the afflicting planet in a Question or Nativity, even if it can only do a little good, at least it may do the good of doing no harm.

Lehman suspects that the classification of strong and weak receptions by various authors, as in my earlier examples, supports the idea that a mutual reception between triplicity would prevent a planet from being peregrine. Unfortunately she has not located a text which states this clearly. Nor have I.[33] However, in terms of a Question attempting to locate a thief, for example, a planet with no dignity nor reception whatsoever must be the preferred choice of significator for the thief, as compared with a planet which has a reception between the lesser dignities.

Dispositor
A dispositor is simply another name for the planet which does the receiving. This is the very essence of reception. Maternus tells us that if the ruler (dispositor) of a sign is well located, the planet in question "shares in a part of the good fortune of the host's joy". But if the ruler of the sign is "dejected in any way" the planet in question (even if it is located in a fortunate house) is "hindered by the dejection of that other planet".[34]

Morin tells us that it is important in judgement to ascertain if and how a planet, which is located in a sign other than its own, is connected with its dispositor.

For its impact, a planet will depend more on its Dispositor, and will be more directly ruled by it when in conjunction or aspect with it.

He adds that in this instance, their "co-operation is then more effective, especially if this connection is powerful and harmonious". He explains that if the planet in question is in a bad zodiacal or terrestrial state, but its dispositor is in a good state, this means that things go badly in the beginning, but will later take a turn for the better, especially if this planet approaches its dispositor with a good aspect. However, if the planet is in good state, but its dispositor is not, "the success or happiness at the beginning will turn into failure or sadness, and all hope will have to be abandoned".[35]

If both planets are in a good zodiacal state, this is the very best of all indications and there will be good fortune if the planet disposed of is in a good house. Similarly, it's likely that something bad will be suppressed, even if the planet disposed of is in a bad house, as long as both planets are in a good zodiacal state. If both planets are in a bad zodiacal state, their effect is unfortunate. If the planet being disposed of is in an

The Strength or Weakness of a Planet in Relation to its Dispositor

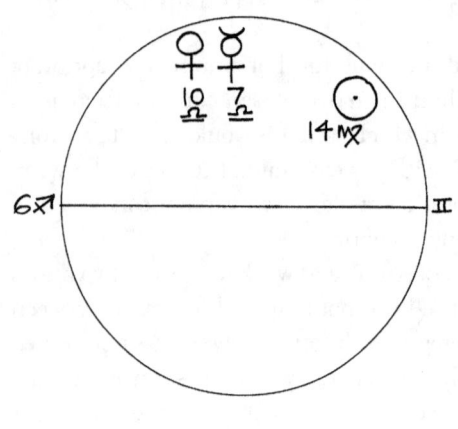

☿ is strong in accidental dignity and the conjunction of ☿ with his dispositor (♀) is fortunate because ♀ is in a good state. This is beneficial.

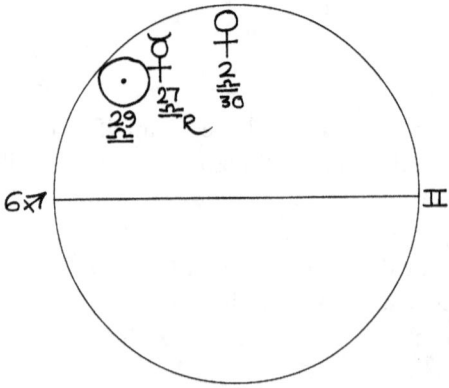

☿ is weak being retrograde and combust, but his dispositor ♀ is in a good state. This indicates that things start badly but take a turn for the better.

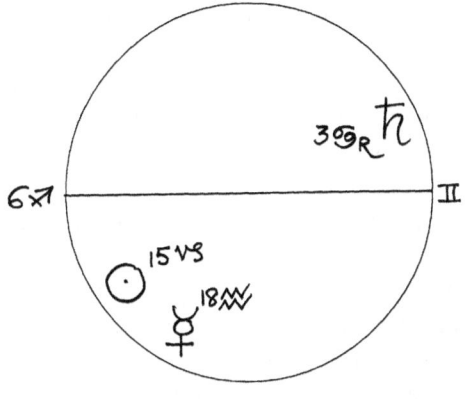

☿ is strong being in his triplicity, direct and free from combustion. However his dispositor ♄ is weak being in his detriment and retrograde. This indicates that an early success could turn into failure.

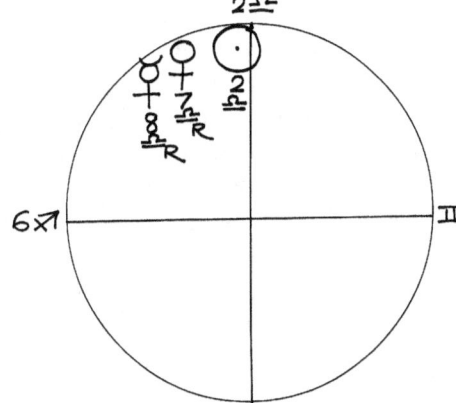

Both ☿ and his dispositor ♀ are weak, being retrograde and combust. This is unfortunate.

unfortunate house, there will be misfortune. Even if both planets are in fortunate houses, they will still "destroy or impede" any advantages which might have been possible.

Exchanging Places

Planets which have a reception or mutual reception do not swap places as some commentators have suggested. Clearly it is not possible for planets to move their position within the heavens, so how could they do this in the chart? Earlier authorities did not mention an exchange of places, nor did Lilly, Ramesey, Saunders, Gadbury, Coley, Partridge or Dariot. More importantly, this concept is not supported by anecdotal evidence. Al Biruni called it "an exchange of compliments" not an exchange of places![36] I agree with Lehman, who states that "given what we know now, the concept of swapping positions cannot be supported as a classical concept".[37]

The Importance of Reception

From a reading of various sources, it appears that to certain authors, the presence or absence of reception between significators is more important to the outcome of a

Question than even the kind of aspect being formed. There is no doubt that reception was considered a major factor in the condition of a planet by the astrologers of the Arabic era (between about the eighth and eleventh centuries). However, it seems clear that the importance of reception has gradually declined until today only mutual reception is in use. I would argue that even mutual reception is barely in use among modern astrologers.

On Reception contains exceptionally clear and vivid examples of how Masha'allah uses reception in order to arrive at his judgements. The text demonstrates in a simple yet concise way how interrogational astrology was practiced in the eighth century. In "A Question Concerning a Kingship", Masha'allah tells us that the Sun and Venus being in Sagittarius are joined to Jupiter from his domicile (sign) and that Jupiter receives them "with respect to his domicile, a strong reception".[38] He goes on to say that this, along with the fact that Jupiter is located in the house of the matter enquired about (the tenth house) and the fact that the Sun receives Jupiter according to his light, signifies "the strength of the lord of the interrogation over his enemy, the firmness of his honor and that he would obtain the kingship..."[39]

In many of Masha'allah's charts in On Reception, Hand confirms that Masha'allah is not overly concerned with the type of application between the significators. He is more interested in whether or not there is any reception between them. Masha'allah shows us a chart where the Moon in Libra applies to an opposition with Saturn in Aries. Despite the fact that any opposition between the Moon and Saturn is unfortunate, due to Saturn's position in the house of the matter enquired about and being the dispositor of the exaltation of the sign where the Moon is placed (Libra), Masha'allah tells us that the Querent will achieve the desired outcome, although he accepts that this may not be easy.[40]

Hand explains that Masha'allah "makes reception a centerpiece of his method".[41] In Masha'allah's astrology, it would appear that on occasion, no reception can mean no hope.

Lilly is also very clear about the importance of reception. He tells us that if the prospect of achieving the desired outcome to a Question "seems doubtful", either because it is denied by the aspects, there is no aspect, or the aspect is a square or opposition (which is always dubious), if there is a mutual reception between the significators "the thing is brought to passe...without any great trouble, and suddenly to the content of both parties".[42]

Referring once again to the chart from *Christian Astrology* in chapter five, where a lady hopes to marry a particular gentleman, Lilly notes that the principal significators, the Sun and Saturn, are applying to a sextile. However, this application by itself gives "little hopes", because there is no reception between them. Lilly finds a mutual reception between the Moon, co-significator of the Querent, and Jupiter, as well as a reception between the Sun and the Moon, which gives part of the supporting testimony required.[43]

The presence of reception can completely change an outcome, making the difference between life and death, a win or a defeat, a pass or a fail, a distinction or a merit. If an aspect is with a square or opposition, the presence of reception can substantially mitigate whatever negative outcome might otherwise have been expected. Bonatti asks the reader to take notice

> ...whether the planet to which the Moon or Significator joins, receives them; for then there will be a good laudable end: and the matter will be accomplished with success, if the receiver be a Fortune.[44]

References

1. Robert Hand in *On Reception* by Masha'allah, p.iv.
2. See later in this chapter.
3. Masha'allah, Introduction, p.2.
4. Masha'allah p.3.
5. Abu Ma'shar p.30.
6. Abu Ma'shar, editor's note p.30.
7. Ibn Ezra, *The Beginning Of Wisdom*, p.214.
8. Al Biruni pp.312-313.
9. Ibn Ezra p.214.
10. Dariot p.31.
11. Morin p.152.
12. Abu Ma'shar editor's note p.27 referring to *Antiochus* Book I chapter 30, p.26.
13. Morin p.152.
14. Richard Saunders, *The Astrological Judgement and Practice of Physick* (1677). Ballantrae Reprints, Canada. p.5.
15. Robert Hand in *On Reception* by Masha'allah p.iii.
16. Lilly p.112.
17. ibid p.115.
18. Ramesey p.111.
19. Abu Ma'shar pp.27-28.
20. Morin p.152.
21. Masha'allah p.4.
22. ibid p.64.
23. Robert Hand in *On Reception* by Masha'allah p.84.
24. ibid p.43.
25. ibid p.61.
26. ibid p.43.
27. Masha'allah p.4.
28. Robert Hand in *On Reception* by Masha'allah p.4.
29. Masha'allah p.4.
30. ibid p.25.
31. Lilly p.115.
32. ibid p.387.

33. Lee Lehman, *Astrology Quarterly*, Spring 1992, vol 62, no.2, 'Horary Two Generations before Lilly: A review and discussion', p.28.
34. Maternus p.52.
35. Morin pp.94-95.
36. Al Biruni p.312.
37. Lee Lehman, 'A Note on Reception', *Astrology Quarterly*, Summer 1994, Vol. 64/3, p.57.
38. Masha'allah p.61.
39. ibid, editor's footnote p.61.
40. ibid pp.42-43.
41. Robert Hand in *On Reception* by Masha'allah pp.iii–iv.
42. Lilly p.112.
43. ibid p.385.
44. Bonatus p.12, 20th consideration.

9

ALMUTEN

Ramesey explains that the almuten is the planet which "bears Chief Rule of any sign, or in any figure..." [1] In an overall sense the planet with most counts of essential dignity in a particular degree is the almuten. However, the almuten can vary, depending on which triplicity system or term system is used in the calculation.

Almuten of a Chart

The almuten, or ruler of the chart, is the planet or luminary which is very strongest in terms of its accidental and essential dignity. It may, or may not, be the ascendant ruler. Various names have been assigned to the strongest planet: Lilly, in the context of Questions, calls this planet the almuten.[2] In Nativities Lilly refers to this planet as the lord of the geniture.[3]

> Almuten of a Figure, is that planet who in Essentiall and Accidentall dignities, is most powerfull in the whole Scheame of Heaven.[4]

In *Clavis Astrologiae Elimata*, Coley, following Lilly, asks "What Planet is Almuten, or Lord of the Geniture?" He answers

> Modern Astrologers do rather accept of that Planet which surmounts all the rest in Essential and Accidental Fortitudes; (which is most rational)...[5]

Referring to Nativities, Alexandre Volguine points out that

> The Birth Governor or ALMUTEN is one of the fundamental, indispensable concepts of the horoscope...[6]

Volguine is very clear when he tells us

> Astrological experience proves daily that the lord of the Ascendant is not always the strongest planet or the most important in its effects. The expression 'governing planet' or 'ruler' which is currently applied to the lord of the Ascendant ought to actually refer to the latter, which one may call the birth governor and which the astrologers of olden times called Maitre de Geniture, or birth ruler, or Lord of Geniture.[7]

In order to discover the almuten, all the essential and accidental dignities of the planets must be calculated as in chapter seven. For example, a planet which is

Choosing the Almuten of a Chart

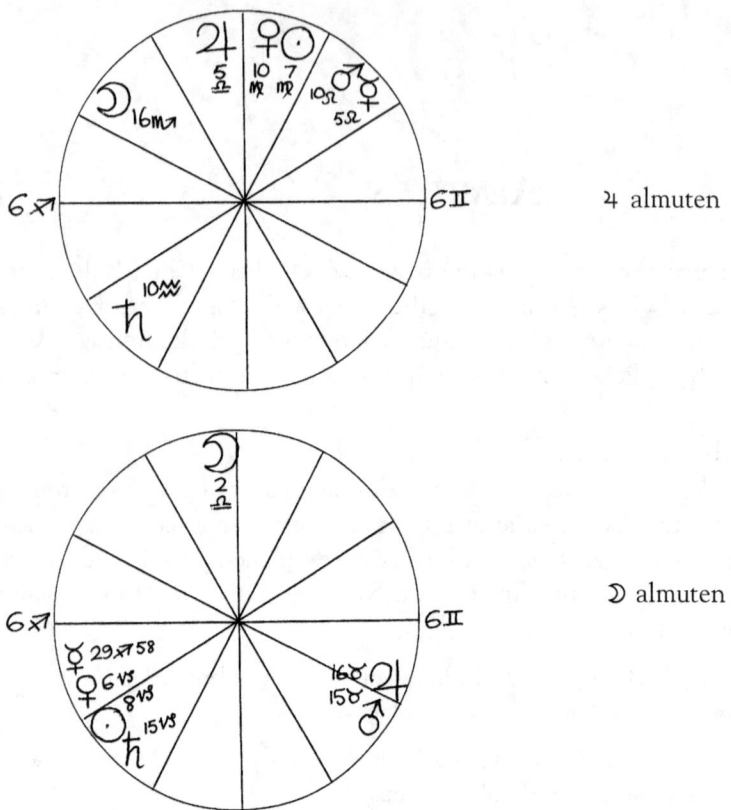

♃ almuten

☽ almuten

angular, in its own domicile, direct, swift in motion, free from combustion and free from any bad aspect with an Infortune, is a likely contender for the almuten.

However, caution is needed in the calculation of the almuten. Although Lilly's scoring system is extremely useful, one must proceed carefully as I advised previously. For example, let us suppose that a planet in a cadent house produces a higher score in terms of all dignities than one in an angular house, in this instance it is more likely that the angular planet is almuten. Cadent planets have far less strength. In a similar way, planets elevated and above the horizon are generally stronger than those below.

Volguine's calculation of the almuten is very interesting. This is produced from his exact mathematical calculations. Unfortunately, he includes the outer planets, Uranus, Neptune and Pluto. In fact, Volguine criticises Morin

> There exist several systems for determining the birth governor, the most well known being that of Morin de Villefrance. The principal error of the latter is that it does not correspond to our present state of knowledge, as we now work with ten planets and no longer with seven, as in the 16th century.[8]

According to Michel Bustros, it is an error to believe that the ruler of the ascendant automatically represents the "dominant" of the chart. The ruler of the ascendant "may well be found in the third or fourth position, if not even farther down the scale". Bustros reports that there is the same distinction in Hindu astrology, where the ruler of the ascendant is one thing *Lagnadi-pathi* and the planet called *Atmakaraka* is quite another. He explains that the latter means "significator of the Atman", also called the "greater significator...the most elevated..." Bustros reminds us that in every chart there is the ruler of the ascendant, a solar ruler (dispositor of the Sun) and finally there is a ruler of the Nativity. The three of them may be different planets.[9]

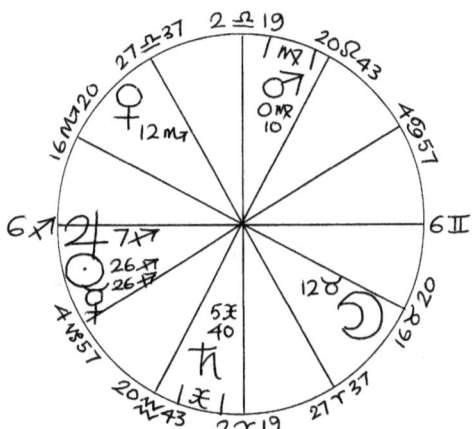

Chart Rulers

ascendant ruler ♃
solar ruler ♃
almuten ♃
(not ☽ because not aspecting the ascendant nor in an angle).

Maternus in the context of Nativities, asks the reader to carefully observe the ruler of the chart, that planet which the Greeks call *oecodespotes*. He tells us why the chart ruler is so important in judgement

> He himself controls the sum of the whole chart and from him the individual planets take their power of forecasting. If he is well located – in signs in which he rejoices, or is exalted, or in his own house, and the chart is of his condition, and he is not attacked by malefic planets or lacking protection of benefic – he predicts all good things, according to the quality of his nature and the whole number of the years of life. But if he is impeded by malefic planets or deserted by benefic, then he languishes and his efficacy is weakened.[10]

Due to the fact that the chart ruler (or almuten), is chosen because of his strength in terms of essential and accidental dignity, it is more likely that this planet will be strong and unafflicted. However, in certain Nativities or Questions, where there are many planets, or a majority of planets, in poor condition, a weak chart ruler (almuten) is possible.

Maternus explains that the ancients have different opinions as to the choice of chart ruler. Some say it is the planet which is located in favourable houses and in his own domicile or term. Others, however,

...have figured from the Sun and Moon, arguing that the ruler of the chart is the one in whose terms the Sun and Moon are found, that is, the Sun in the daytime and the Moon at night.

Other authorities claim it is the ruler of the exaltation of the Moon, or the planet whose domicile the Moon enters after leaving the one where she is positioned in the Nativity. Maternus himself follows the latter method and explains that although "the Sun and Moon never accept the rulership of the chart", when they are in conjunction, favourable aspect, or positioned in the domicile or term of the chart ruler, they have a lot of influence over the forecast.[11] Al Biruni outlines the two ways in which the ruling planet or "Al-Muten" can be chosen

> 'Mubtazz' means a victorious planet and victory may be arrived at in two ways; 1/ mutlaq absolute, dependent on dignities due to position in the orbit, or in relation to other planets or to the horizon; 2/ muqayyad limited, when these dignities are referred to one of the characteristic properties of the twelve houses.[12]

Ibn Ezra refers to the *Almutem* as

> ... the planet having dominion over the entire chart which the Saracens call the Almutez. Its testimony according to its condition is equally as powerful as all the other planets taken together.[13]

However, Ibn Ezra tells us that the method of selecting the almutem is not agreed. Out of the five principal places, the Sun is first, the Moon is second and the conjunction or opposition of the luminaries, which precede a birth, are third. Apparently, it is here that the wise disagree. At this point I refer the reader to Zoller's excellent book *Tools and Techniques of the Medieval Astrologers*.

Referring to Nativities, Lilly tells us that there was some difference among the ancients as to the choice of planet who is lord of the geniture. He confirms that all the ancients reject the judgement of Maternus, as discussed above. Lilly explains that Maternus believes that if the Moon is in a particular sign at birth, for example Aries, it is the planet who is the ruler of the next sign who should be nominated as lord of the geniture. In this instance it will be Venus as ruler of Taurus. If the sign is Leo it will be the ruler of the next sign Virgo (Mercury), who is lord of the geniture. Lilly explains that the Greeks nominated the planet as lord of the geniture which had the most dignities in the place of the Moon and Mercury. This is because "Mercury is the Lord, or hath dominion of the spirit and vigour of the mind, the Moon swayeth the body". Lilly himself calculates the ruler of a Nativity in the same way as he calculates the almuten in a Question

> I am cleerly of this opinion, viz. That Planet who hath most essentiall and accidentall dignities in the Figure, and is posited best, and elevated most in the Scheame, that he ought to be Lord of the Geniture, and am confident the whole actions of the Native will more or less pertake of the nature of that Planet...[14]

The lord of the geniture is the planet which has particular significance for the entire life of an individual in terms of the Nativity. The almuten has particular significance for the Querent in terms of a Question.

Almuten of a House

> Almuten, of any house is that Planet who hath most dignities in the Signe ascending or descending upon the Cusp of any house, whereon or from whence you require your jugement.[15]

Ramesey tells us that

> Saturn in Libra is Almuten, or is Almuter of Libra, because he hath both exaltation and triplicity therein, and Venus hath onely house [domicile], so that Saturn bearing chief rule, is of this sign Almuten.[16]

The almuten of a house is the planet which has most dignities in the cusp of any given house, that is, the planet which has the greatest strength in that place in terms of essential dignity. In Ramesey's example, Saturn has dignity through both exaltation and triplicity in Libra during the day, whereas Venus only has dignity in her domicile. Therefore Saturn can acquire chief rulership over a house which has Libra in its cusp in a diurnal chart.

Choosing the Almuten of a House

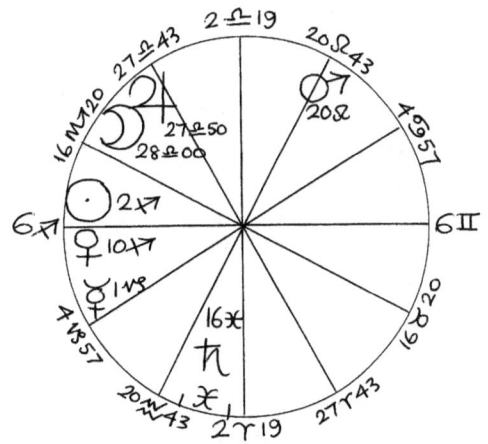

Here the 10th house is under consideration with 2♎19 in its cusp in a DIURNAL chart.

♄ has exaltation	= 4 points
♄ has triplicity	= 3 points
♄ has term	= 2 points
Total	= 9 points
♀ has domicile rulership	= 5 points
☽ has face	= 1 point

♄ has 9 points and therefore is almuten of the 10th house

Let us suppose that the astrologer is assessing the wealth of the Native or Querent. Here, the second house is the area under consideration. The planet with the most counts of dignity (through rulership over the domicile, exaltation, triplicity, term or face), in that particular degree of that sign in the house cusp is the almuten of the house. In a nocturnal chart with Taurus in the cusp of the second house, the almuten of the second house is the Moon not Venus, because the Moon has dignity in Taurus both by exaltation, as well as triplicity, during the night. If the second house has twelve degrees of Taurus in the cusp, the Moon also scores a point for having dignity in her face.

Similarly, in a diurnal chart, the Sun can be almuten of a house which has Aries in its cusp. This is because the Sun has dignity through both exaltation, as well as triplicity during the day. In a diurnal chart with seventeen degrees of Aries in the second house cusp, the points are allocated in the following way:

5 points are allocated to Mars (domicile ruler of Aries).
4 points are allocated to the Sun (exaltation ruler of Aries).
3 points allocated to the Sun (triplicity ruler of the fire signs during the day).
2 points are allocated to Mercury (ruler of the term).
1 point is allocated to the Sun (ruler of the face).

The Sun scores 8, Mars scores 5, Mercury scores 2

The Sun, therefore, is almuten of that house and might be considered as ruler in preference to Mars, or at least to an equal degree. The same procedure can be adopted for all houses.

Dariot tells us that the ruler of a house is called the Almuten by the Arabs, in Latin it is called *Dominium* and in English it is called the *Lord*. He explains that the lord of the ascendant or any other house "is the planet which hath most dignities, or greatest strength in that place".[17] Dariot reports that if two planets have the same dignities in the same place, it is the planet which is also positioned in that house which becomes the ruler. The planet closest to the cusp takes precedence over a planet further away and also over a planet which is absent from that house. If neither planet is positioned in that house, it is the planet aspecting that house with the strongest aspect which is almuten. If neither planet is in aspect, it is the planet in the strongest position which is almuten, for example in an angular house as opposed to a succedent house. If they are both in a similar position in the chart, Dariot asks us to

> ..looke whiche of them is in degree most agreeable to his nature, as if it shoulde bee a masculine planet in a masculine degree, a feminine in a feminine, or in a light, darke, deepe, boyd, azemene, or degrees that both increase fortune, then which of them shall appeare strongest, shall be the Lord.[18]

Finally if the planets still score equal points Dariot asks us to consider their strengths in order of domicile, exaltation, triplicity, term and then face.

Almuten of a House
The choice of almuten from two planets

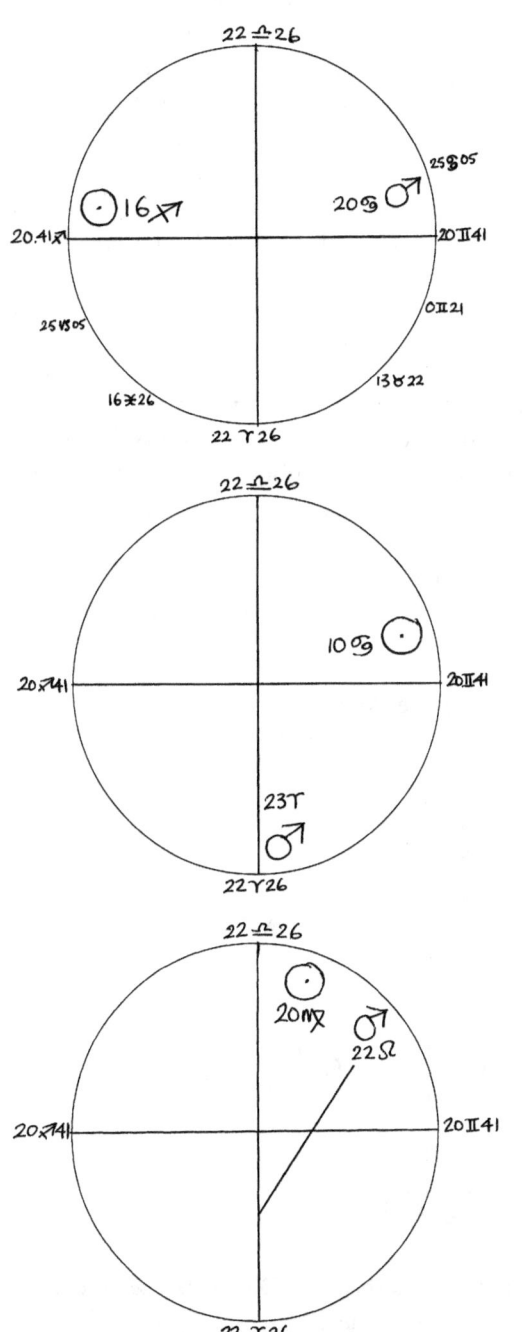

Fourth house
☉ exaltation   4 points
   triplicity   3 points
♂ domicile   5 points
   term   2 points

Both ☉ and ♂ score 7 points. But ☉ is almuten here because he is positioned close to the ascendant in his triplicity and makes a trine with the 4th house.

Fourth house
Here the scores are also equal but ♂ takes precedence because he is positioned in the 4th house.

Fourth house
The scores are equal but ♂ aspects the 4th house with a trine so is almuten.

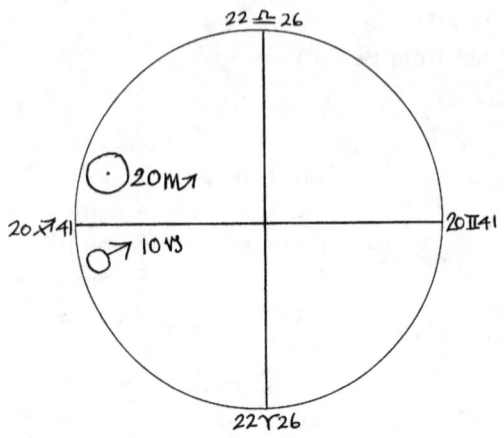

Fourth house
The scores are equal but ♂ is almuten because he is stronger being in a succedent house than ☉ in a cadent house. He is also stronger in dignities being in his exaltation and makes an aspect with the fourth house.

Dariot gives a similar example of a diurnal chart with twenty two degrees of Aries in the ascendant. Here, the Sun scores a total of seven points, having four for his exaltation and three for his triplicity. Mars as ruler of Aries scores a total of seven points also, having five for domicile rulership and two for his term. Venus scores one for her rulership of the face.

Due to the fact that the Sun is near to the tenth house cusp and aspects the ascendant with a square, but Mars is in the sixth house "having no participation

**Choosing the Almuten
An example from Dariot**

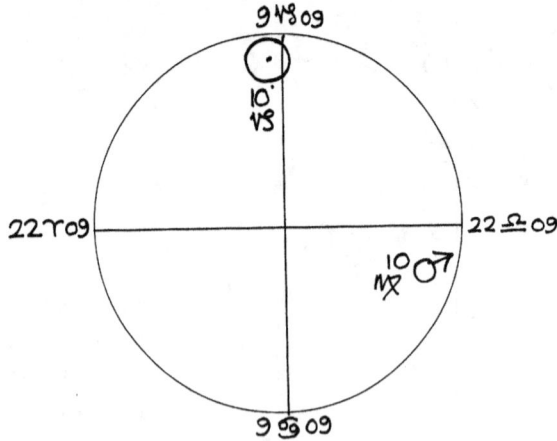

The ☉ is almuten of the ascendant not ♂ because ☉ aspects the ascendant, is elevated and close to the 10th cusp.

with the ascendant", that is, not beholding the ascendant, Dariot gives chief rule of the ascendant to the Sun not Mars. The Sun is almuten of the ascendant. However, he says that "Mars shall bee partaker with the sunne" because of his rulership over Aries.

It is clear from a reading of various sources that authorities of the past did not necessarily consider the ascendant ruler to be the chart ruler as modern astrologers today. I would agree that in many instances the ascendant ruler is not the strongest planet and cannot be considered as ruler. The almuten should always be considered in chart evaluation.

In all charts it is also useful to consider the almuten of a house, as well as the ruler of the sign in the house cusp. In terms of my own Nativity I had considered Venus in Libra to be the ruler of my Taurus ascendant and ruler of my chart. However, Venus is cadent and does not aspect the ascendant so she cannot be chart ruler, nor is she the ruler of the ascendant, because the chart is nocturnal and the Moon has more dignities in the ascendant.

In this example, the Moon is not only almuten of the ascendant but is also almuten of the chart. The Moon is almuten of the ascendant scoring four points for her exaltation in Taurus plus three points for her triplicity rulership. Venus scores five points only for her rulership of Taurus. The Moon is positioned in Capricorn in the midheaven in her triplicity, well supported by the Sun, Mercury, Mars and Jupiter, receiving no afflictions. It is the Moon, therefore, who is almuten of the ascendant and in my case, almuten of the chart.

In any chart it is important to observe: the domicile ruler of a house, the triplicity ruler of a house, the almuten of a house, the ascendant ruler, the solar ruler (dispositor of the Sun) and the almuten of the chart. They all play a vital role in judgment.

References

1. Ramesey p.111.
2. Lilly p.49.
3. ibid pp.531-532.
4. ibid p.49.
5. Coley pp.579-580.
6. Volguine, Alexandre. *The Ruler of the Nativity*. ASI Publishers Inc, New York, 1973. p.3.
7. ibid p.13.
8. ibid pp.18-19.
9. ibid, afterword by Michel Bustros, pp.115-116.
10. Maternus p.138.
11. ibid p.142.
12. Al Biruni p.308.

13. Robert Zoller, *Tools & Techniques of the Medieval Astrologers*, pp.124-126.
14. Lilly pp.531-532.
15. ibid p.49.
16. Ramesey p.111.
17. Dariot p.49.
18. ibid p.50.

10

SIGNIFICATION

General Signification

Signification in general is derived from a house, planet or sign associated with a particular person, thing, or matter enquired about. In a Nativity or Question for example, a pregnancy is associated with the fifth house, marriage and relationships are associated with the seventh house, achievement or career with the tenth house. Likewise, Jupiter has a natural association with pregnancy, Venus with marriage and the Sun with achievement. The signs of Scorpio, Pisces and Cancer are associated with fertility, whereas Virgo and Leo are associated with infertility. Lilly tells us that the "Prolificall Signes" such as Scorpio, Pisces and Cancer are associated with marriage, as well as signs or parts of the signs which are in the dignities of Venus.[1] The signs are also associated with the directions north, south, east or west.

For the sake of clarity, when I refer to a *significator*, this is usually a planet, luminary or other celestial body, which represents or co-represents the person, thing or matter enquired about: it is a *symbol*. In the examples above, Jupiter has a signification (or partakes in the signification) over pregnancy, Venus has a signification over marriage and the Sun has a signification over career or achievement.

In a Question, Nativity or any other chart, signification is derived more specifically from the planet ruling the house which is associated with a particular matter, thing or person. For example, if the degrees of Aries are found in the cusp of the fifth house in a Question about pregnancy, Mars has a rulership over the pregnancy (as well as the Sun during the day, being almuten of the house). If Aries is found in the cusp of the seventh house, Mars and the Sun have a rulership over the relationship or marriage. If Aries is found in the cusp of the tenth house, Mars and the Sun have a rulership over achievement or career.

A planet located in the house of the matter enquired about is also important, whether or not it rules that house, and can sometimes be considered as principal significator. Any planet aspecting that planet (in the house of the matter enquired about), or the ruler of that house, is also important and has signification to a greater or lesser extent. However, it is important to emphasise that the Moon has signification over the entire chart.

The Nativity
In an overall sense, a significator in a Nativity is any planet or luminary, or place in the chart, which represents (has a signification over) any person, matter, or thing connected to the Native, including physical appearance and character, the life, status, wealth and any other event or matter that happens either inwardly or outwardly to the Native. This might also include a description of people, who are related to, or connected to, the Native during the lifetime.

The Question
In an overall sense, a significator in a Question is any planet or luminary, or place in the chart, which represents (has a signification over) any person, matter, or thing connected to the Question. This might include the physical appearance and character of the Querent, as well as the appearance and character of others, who are in any way connected to the Querent and/or the Question.

The Places of Greatest Authority
Ptolemy assigns the ascendant, the Sun, Moon, the Lot of Fortune and their rulers as the places of most important signification in a Nativity. He calls them "the four regions of greatest authority".[2] Lilly takes a similar view, but he includes the midheaven. He tells us that ascendant, the Medium Coeli, the Sun, the Moon and the Lot of Fortune are "the principall Hylegiacall places of the Nativity."[3] Directions to these places cause all sorts of events (or "Accidents") both fortunate and unfortunate, depending on whether these significators make a conjunction or aspect with the Fortunes, Infortunes, benevolent or malevolent fixed stars. Lilly tells us that directions to the above mentioned places will allow most events to be predicted from a Nativity, but not all.

> ...by direction whereof most of the affaires and contingencies belonging to every man or woman in a naturall course of life are found out, both in quality What, and in measure of time When.[4]

The places of greatest authority also differ slightly in importance, according to whether a Nativity is diurnal or nocturnal, with the Sun usually having more power during the day and the Moon by night. In a Question the same applies.

Since the time of Ptolemy, further additions were made to these places of signification and included the planets (as distinct from the luminaries): Saturn, Jupiter, Mars, Venus, and Mercury. The cusps of the houses also became important in signification. For example, the second house in terms of riches, the seventh house in terms of marriage and so on.

The evolution of signification is an interesting phenomenon but is beyond the scope of this book. Ptolemy also gives consideration to the rulers of the luminaries (and the ascendant and the Lot of Fortune), but they were perhaps of less importance. I would suggest that in line with Ptolemy, a judgement can be produced solely from his places of authority. This is because afflictions to these important places will reduce the level of good fortune in a Nativity. If these places are free from affliction and well-supported they increase the good fortune. The same applies to the important places in a Question. However, in the following discussion I give consideration to all types of signification, including the planets and houses, drawing also on the writings of the seventeenth century astrologers.

Selecting the Correct Significator

Story, in his Preface to Simmonite's *Horary Astrology*, tells us that the astrologer should

> Exercise great care to select the right Ruler and Significator of the question propounded. This is the primary and fundamental rule, which, if violated or misunderstood, is the cause of so many of those false predictions which are taken as a basis for argument against the truth of Horary Astrology.[5]

Locating the significators is important, because each house in the chart has a particular significance, as does each sign and each planet. In terms of a Question, the relevant houses, signs and planets are determined by the particular enquiry under consideration. In a Question about the Querent's dog, for example, the sixth house, the sign in the sixth house cusp, planets in the sixth house and planet(s) ruling the sixth house are the primary areas of focus. In a Question about a pregnancy, the same applies, but it is the fifth house and the Fortunes which are the primary area of focus. In a Question about property it is the fourth house which is under focus.

Signification from the houses, planets and signs has already been examined in a general way. In this chapter the emphasis is more specific: on signification from the planets in the houses, planets ruling houses and aspects to these planets.

I would like to add a note of caution here: it is important not to become too caught up with individual significators. It is the chart in its entirety which must be evaluated, with chief significance taken from the Moon. As discussed previously, Ptolemy considers the places of chief significance to be the luminaries, ascendant, the Lot of Fortune and their rulers. A judgement can be produced from these significators only.

The role of the Fortunes and Infortunes also holds great importance. In any chart, if a Fortune is found in powerful places, whether or not it is a principal significator or co-significator, this is a testimony of good fortune. The contrary is true if an Infortune is found in the same places, unless he is in his essential dignities. Broadly speaking, significance is taken from the following

- A house
- A planet
- A sign
- A planet in a house*

---

*   the house of the matter enquired about

- Two or more planets in a house
- A planet ruling a house
- A planet aspecting a planet in a house
- A planet aspecting the ruler of a house
- A planet's dispositor
- The dispositor's aspect with that planet
- The dispositor's aspects with other planets

Like Morin, I believe that a planet positioned in a house, whether it rules that house or not, has greatest power in signification. It certainly appears to have more power than an absent ruler. With regard to the almuten of a house and therefore the chief significator of that house, Dariot would agree.

The Significators

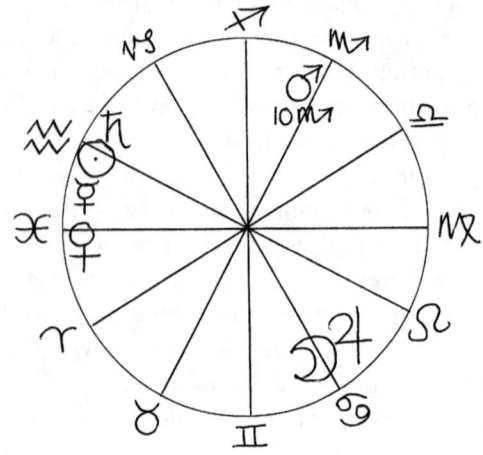

Am I Pregnant?

Fortunate and positive signification.

☽ ♃ are fortunate in the 5th house.

Significators:
☽ ruler of 5th house, positioned in 5th house.
♃ ascendant ruler, positioned in 5th house.
♀ a Fortune in the ascendant.
♃'s dispositor is ☽.
♀'s dispositor is ♃.
♂ casts trine with degree ascending and the degree in the 5th cusp, therefore is important in signification.
♀ becomes co-significator of the Querent, being in the ascendant.

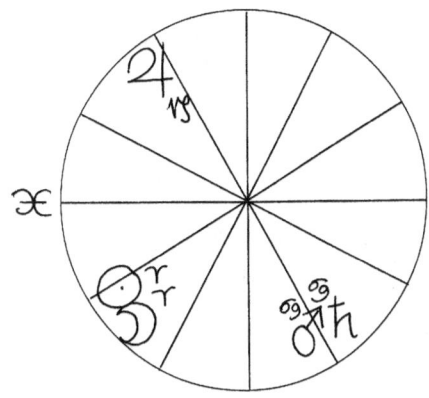

Am I Pregnant?

Unfortunate signification.

♂ and ♄ are unfortunate in the 5th house.

Significators:
♃, ascendant ruler in his fall, opposition ♂♄.
♂ and ♄, Infortunes debilitated, afflict the 5th house.
☽, 5th house ruler and dispositor of ♂ and ♄, afflicted being combust and in square with ♂♄.
♃'s dispositor is ♄.
☽'s dispositor is ♂.

Multiple Signification

A planet or planets usually have signification over more than one matter or thing enquired about. In an overall sense

- One planet can signify one thing
- One planet can signify more than one thing
- Two or more planets can signify one thing
- Two or more planets can signify two or more things

This can be confusing in terms of chart analysis. For example, in a Question concerning a pregnancy let us suppose that Pisces is ascending and Cancer occupies the degrees in the fifth house cusp. If the Moon is in the ascendant in Pisces, the Moon is firstly the principal significator of the pregnancy, but is also co-significator of the Querent. If the Moon is in good condition, this signification is fortunate for the Querent. If instead of the Moon this planet is Saturn, the signification is less fortunate.

If more than one planet is found in the house of the matter enquired about and they are Fortunes, well dignified, the chart testimony is positive; if they are Infortunes and ill-dignified it is negative. If it is a mixture, the astrologer must take care in weighing up the testimonies. This is examined a little later in the chapter.

A planet can at the same time be a significator, as well as the cause of an affliction

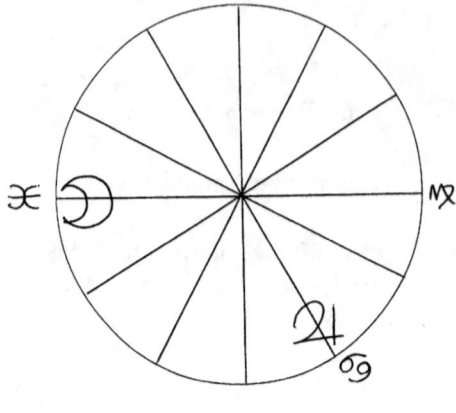

Am I Pregnant?

☽ is significator of the pregnancy and of the Querent

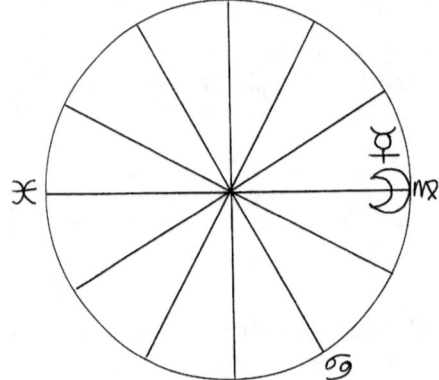

Am I Pregnant - Will our Relationship Continue to go Well?

☽ is significator of the pregnancy and of the relationship.

or assistance, depending on its position and dignity. A planet, therefore, can rule one house, taking on the role of significator or co-significator for that house and at the same time can be located in a different house, having the role of significator or co-significator for that house also. On p. 201, details from a chart in chapter twenty-three are included to illustrate the point.

Will Arsenal win the Champions League (2006)
16 May 2006, 8.32am, 51N30 04W48

Mars, co-ruler of the tenth house and co-significator of the win, is located in the ascendant. Mars is an Infortune and being in his fall, afflicts the ascendant. At the same time as he is co-significator of the win, Mars is also co-significator of the team (Arsenal) by virtue of his position in the ascendant. Being an Infortune, his presence is unfortunate for the team and in terms of the outcome. Had the ascendant and Mars been positioned in one of the domiciles (signs) of Mars, Aries or Scorpio, instead of being in his fall in Cancer, the chart testimony would have been more positive. In this case, however, the team lost the match.

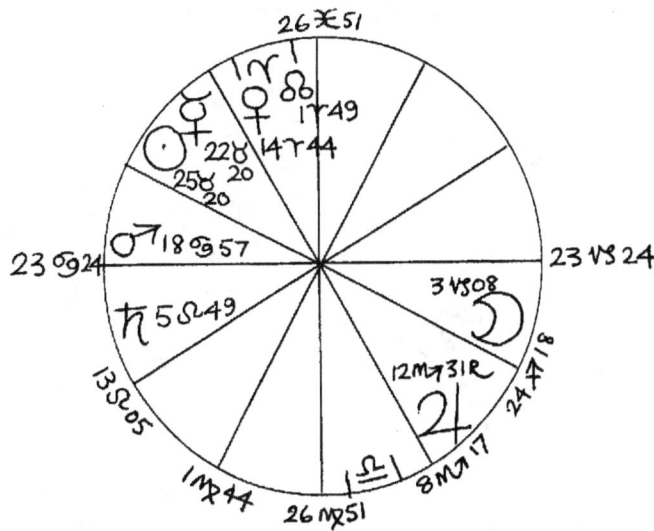

Will Arsenal win the Champions League against Barcelona?

The Querent

> ...the word Querent, signifies no more, but that Man or woman, who propounds any thing to an Artist by way of inquiry; the word comes from the Latin Quere... the quesited is no more than the thing sought, and that doth spontaneously emerge from the same Radix...[6]

The Querent is the person asking the Question. The Quesited is the thing, person or matter enquired about. Lilly explains that in any Question a significator is the planet ruling the house, which signifies the thing or matter enquired about. The sign ascending and the ruler of that sign are usually the significators of the Querent. The sign ascending partly signifies the "corporature, body or stature" of the Querent. The ruler of the ascendant, the Moon, and any planet in the ascendant (or any planet aspecting the Moon or the ruler of the ascendant) shows the "quality or conditions [of the Querent] equally mixed together".[7]

Very occasionally the ascendant ruler may not signify the Querent, even if it is a Question directly concerning the Querent. In a Question from my practice about an unfaithful husband, the ascendant ruler (usual significator of the Querent) is the Sun ruling Leo, the sign ascending. The Querent's husband is Saturn, ruler of the seventh house. However, on finding that the Sun is in conjunction with Venus and that Venus accurately describes the woman with whom the husband was suspected of having an affair, the signification is different. In this case the Sun is taken as co-significator of the husband, the Moon as the Querent, Venus as the other woman.

Is my Husband having an Affair?

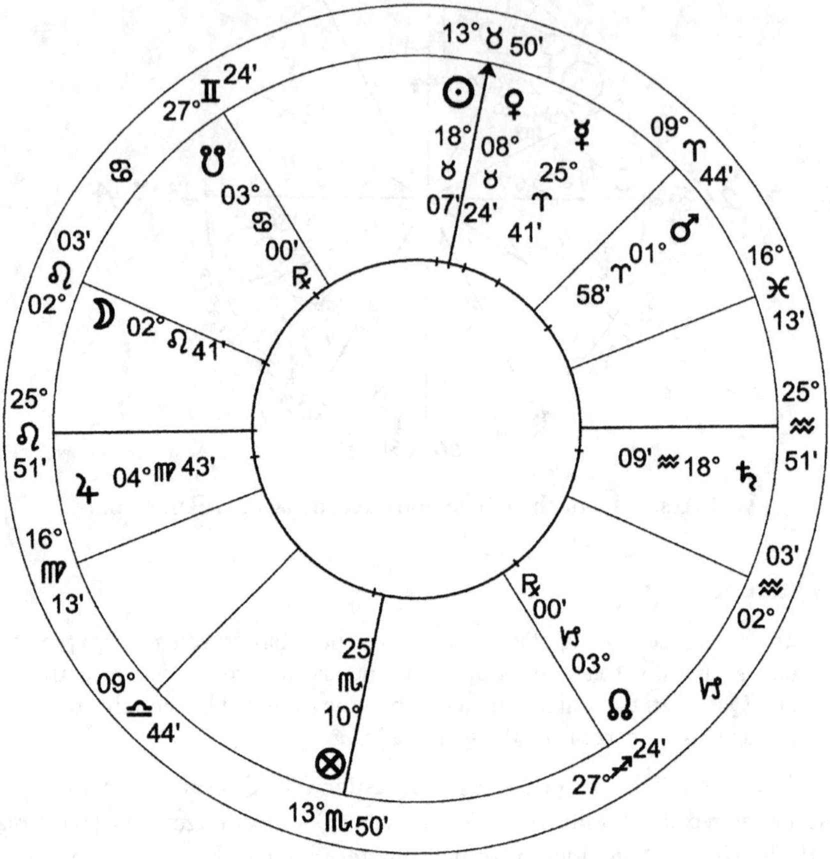

ESSENTIAL DIGNITIES					
	Ruler	Exalt	Trip	Term	Face
☽	☉	—	☉	♄	♄
☉	♀	☽	♀	♃	☽
☿	♂	☉	☉	♂	♀
♀	♀	☽	♀	☿	☿
♂	♂	☉	☉	♃	♂
♃	☿	☿	♀	☿	☉
♄	♄	—	♄	♀	☿
⊗	♂	—	♂	♃	☉

MUTUAL RECEPTIONS
☽ ☉ Ruler-Exalt
☽ ☉ Ruler-Face
☉ ☽ Exalt-Trip
☽ ☉ Trip–Face
☉ ♃ Term-Face
♀ ☿ Term-Face
☿ ♀ Face-Face

In third party Questions about illness, the ascendant can signify a sick person, in which case the Querent does not feature at all in the Question. Over the years I have asked a number of third party Questions and I have not featured in the signification. Similarly, in Questions about sport, the ascendant signifies the team asked about by the Querent. Here, the asker or the Querent, simply drops out of the chart and is not relevant to the Question. This happens frequently with third party Questions, unless the Querent is asking about a person, thing or matter, with whom there is a connection, such as a relative, friend or family member. Even in these instances, the Querent can drop out of the Question. The point to note is that the chart in its entirety describes the Question, and, as a consequence, the ascendant and its ruler will always be significant to the Question, but not necessarily to the Querent.

For example, I might ask a Question about my mother's dog, who is sick. Here the sixth house is important as principal significator of the dog, but the ascendant is equally important in terms of the overall good fortune or misfortune for the dog, but not necessarily for the Querent.

The Moon

The Moon is usually co-significator of the Querent, unless by signification she clearly belongs to another person or matter enquired about. For example, in a relationship Question with the sign of Cancer in the seventh house cusp, the Moon is the ruler of the person enquired about (the Quesited), rather than ruler of the Querent. Even so, the Moon still has a rulership over the Question

> ...for the asker, [the Querent] you should observe the ascending sign with its rulers, and for the request, [the thing or person asked about] the seventh sign with its rulers, and always put the Moon in contact with it.[8]

Referring to Nativities, Bonatti tells us

> ...the Moon in Nativities is the general Significatrix of the native's Person; and the planet to whom she is joined of his faculties and powers...[9]

However, Lilly confirms that the Moon also has general signification in terms of a particular Question

> In every question we doe give the Moon as a Cosignificator with the querent or Lord of the Ascendant...[10]

Masha'allah also tells us that "the Moon will be made a sharer with the lord of the Ascendant in whichever place the Moon may be".[11]

From this it is important to note that the Moon, as well as being significator of the Querent, is also co-significator with the lord of the ascendant (in other words, she also has co-rulership of the Question and, therefore, of the chart). Both Masha'allah and Lilly are stating that the Moon can share with the lord of the ascendant, whether or not the lord of the ascendant is significator of the Querent. As discussed below, Masha'allah did not always consider the ascendant ruler to be significator of the Querent.

Lilly also tells us that earlier astrological writers assigned the planet from whom the Moon separates as significator of the Querent. Similarly, they assigned the planet to whom the Moon applies as co-significator of the thing or matter enquired about.[12] However, I, like Lilly, have not found this to be good practice.

Whatever type of chart is under consideration, the Moon is the most important celestial body, even more so in a nocturnal chart. Lilly confirms that the Moon is cosignificator in all Questions, moving quickly and transferring the light from one planet to another.

> Have speciall regard to the strength or debility of the Moon, and it's farre better the Lord of the ascendant be unfortunate than she, for she brings unto us the strength and vertue of all the other Planets, and of one Planet to another.[13]

The Role of the Ascendant Ruler and the Moon

It is general practice in a Question to regard both the ascendant ruler and the Moon as significators of the Querent, with the ascendant ruler as principal significator and the Moon as co-significator, or what Robert Hand calls a "participating or sharing" significator. What is not clear, explains Hand, from a reading of various sources, is the relative contribution of each significator to the outcome of a Question. Hand reports that the Moon's contribution in terms of bringing about the desired outcome to a Question appears to be "somewhat lesser" than that of the ascendant ruler. Hand also asks when, if ever, would you use one to the exclusion of the other?

Hand tells us that Masha'allah is quite clear on how to arrive at a decision relating to the ascendant ruler, or Moon, as significator.[14] Masha'allah does not add up points as in Lilly's scoring system, but instead he uses some type of chain of application:

- If the ruler of the ascendant makes an aspect by sign with the ascendant, the ascendant ruler is used as the significator, because in this instance it is more powerful. In this respect Hand confirms that Masha'allah agrees with most other sources.

- If the ruler of the ascendant does not aspect the ascendant by sign, but makes an application to another planet which does aspect the ascendant by sign (the very next aspect), the ruler of the ascendant may still be used as the principal significator.

- If the planet to whom the ruler of the ascendant applies does not make an aspect to the ascendant by sign, but in turn makes an immediate application to yet another planet which does aspect the ascendant by sign, one may still use the ruler of the ascendant as principal significator of the Querent.

- If the ascendant ruler makes no such applications, it is considered to be "impeded". In this instance, the state of the Querent is "rendered more doubtful and insecure".

However, Hand confirms that this is not an absolute indication of the failure of the Question.

- If the ruler of the ascendant does not meet any of the foregoing criteria one should then consider the Moon and subject it to the same kind of analysis.
- If neither the Moon nor the ascendant ruler can fulfil the conditions as outlined above, and they are both void of course, it is the one which is nearer the end of the sign, which becomes principal significator. Hand points out that here the text is ambiguous. Is this "nearness" measured in time or distance? Hand suspects that Masha'allah was most concerned with the one that first exits the sign in time.
- If the significator chosen is void, one must consider the first aspect it makes on changing sign position. Throughout *On Reception*, Masha'allah appears to be unconcerned about allowing a planet to cross into another sign in order to make an aspect.

I would suggest that the selection of a planet which is void as significator casts doubt over the entire chart. In terms of achieving perfection through a void significator, I would suggest that this is also doubtful. I have only witnessed a perfection of this manner a few times. In these instances the aspect perfected almost immediately in the next sign and the signficators were strong in dignity.

Signification through Rulership and Position

The principal significators of the matter enquired about are usually the ruler(s) of the relevant houses. For example the seventh house ruler is the significator of a husband or

Choosing Significators: the Ascendant or the Moon

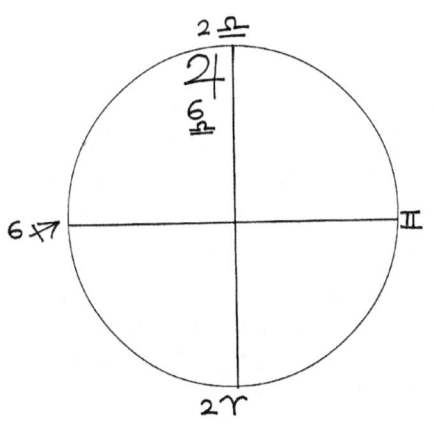

♃ can be chosen as principal significator because he aspects the ascendant

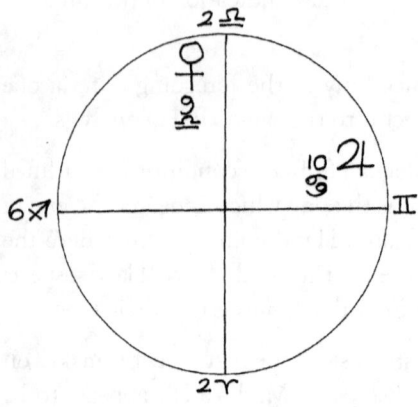

♃ does not aspect the ascendant but can still be considered as principal significator because his very next aspect is with ♀ who does aspect the ascendant.

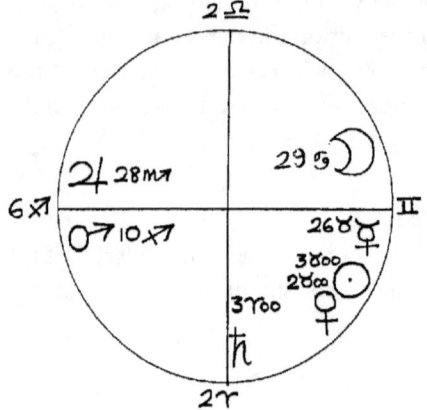

Neither ☽ nor ♃ aspect the ascendant, nor do they aspect another planet who aspects the ascendant.
☽ exits first in time and makes a trine with the ascendant, and a trine with ♄ who also aspects the ascendant.
☽ is also in her domicile and therefore must be the preferred choice of significator.

wife, the fifth house ruler is the significator of a child. Any planet ruling a particular house is important for the Native or Querent in terms of that house. However, a planet positioned in a house is equally, if not more, important. As an example, if Venus is positioned in the seventh house, even if she does not rule the seventh house, she is important in terms of the seventh house. Clearly, the influence of Venus over a seventh house matter is likely to be fortunate, whereas Saturn's position in the seventh house is likely to be unfortunate. Examples of this are included in chapter twenty. Morin explains

> The Planets have in the first place a significance relating to the kind of thing or event, and this by reason of their local determination. In the second place, they indicate whether or not this thing or event will be realized

for the Native. Thirdly, they define the quality and extent of this realization.[15]

The influence of a planet positioned in a house, aspecting a house or ruling a house can be worked out from its essential and accidental dignities. Aspects with the planet are also important. As an example, Morin considers a chart where the Sun is the significator of friends in a Nativity. The Sun's signification of friends in this instance is either due to

- The Sun's position in the eleventh house.
- The Sun's rulership of the eleventh house.
- The Sun's aspect with the eleventh house.

Morin explains that the Sun's position in the eleventh house indicates that any friends will be "persons of royalty, or in high position, or otherwise very prominent". He tells us that the same can be applied to the rulers of any particular house, because rulers of houses signify the same thing as if they were physically located in a house.[16] However, any planet in aspect will modify the effects of a planet which rules, aspects or is positioned in a particular house. In this example, if the Sun is aspecting Jupiter with a trine, the influence of the Sun is extremely powerful and fortunate. If the Sun is aspecting Saturn with a square the reverse applies.

If the Sun is in the tenth house this gives the Sun a significance relating to achievement, career and status. Any planet which is in the tenth house, or is ruler of the tenth house, gives an indication of whether or not these matters will materialize, the ways in which they will not materialise, or the ways in which they will be lost once they have materialized. This can be applied to all houses. From this, it is clear that the Sun in the tenth house and in some of his dignities (assuming he is unafflicted) would produce a high achiever in terms of a Nativity, or would produce one testimony of perfection in terms of a Question about achievement. However, Saturn or Mars could prevent it, destroy it, or cause obstacles and misfortunes. This is modified if either of them is placed in one of their stronger dignities.

Morin believes that a planet physically positioned in a house is more important than the planet ruling that house

> ..the determination of a planet by its physical position is more powerful than that by Rulership alone: in fact, 'the presence of a Planet in a House is worth more than the Rulership of an absent Planet'.[17]

He tells us that "since the determination by physical position is immediate, it is consequently the most effective". I would certainly agree with Morin. Lilly also follows this line of thought in his chart "If Presbytery shall stand?" Here, Lilly does not assign Venus, ruler of the ninth house, as principal significator of presbytery, but instead, he assigns principal signification to Saturn in Taurus positioned in the ninth house. The physical position of Saturn in the ninth house is more important than the absent ruler

The Giving and the Taking

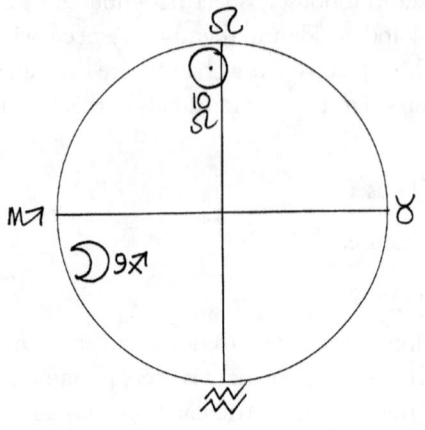

The achievement of honours

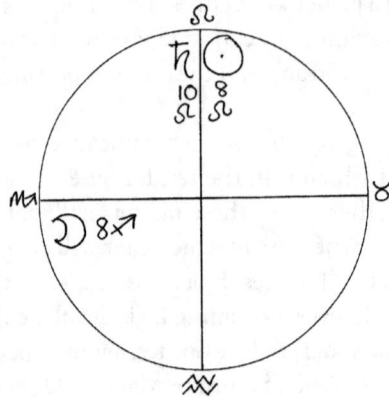

The achievement of honours with difficulty

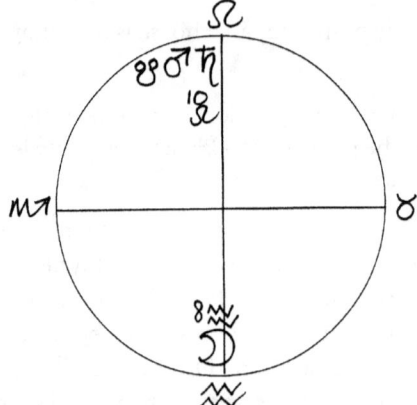

The prevention of honours or the taking of them if achieved

Venus. In this instance because Saturn is an Infortune and not well placed in Taurus, he is unfortunate in terms of the Question.

> The positure of Saturn in the ninth who is naturally of a severe, surly, rigid and harsh temper, may argue, the Presbytery shall be too strict, sullen and dogged for the English Constitutions...[18]

Masha'allah appears to take a different view, when he assigns only the role of sharer to a planet positioned in the house of the matter enquired about

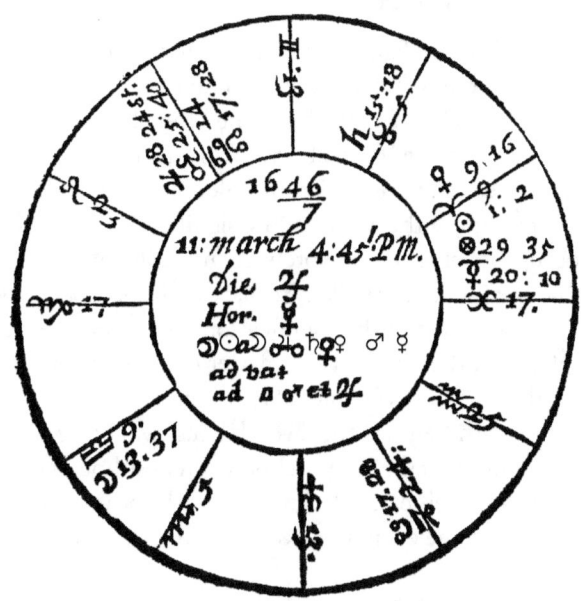

If Presbytery shall stand?

> ...[any] planet which is in the Ascendant should be made a sharer with them [lord of the ascendant or the Moon] in the work...

He explains that the same applies to any planet which is in the house of the matter enquired about. If this planet is helpful in the matter in terms of the sign where it is located and it is received, it indicates the "goodness and worthiness of the matter." If the planet is not helpful in terms of the sign where it is located, nor is it received, it indicates an "impediment in that same matter and the matter's lack of worth".[19]

Unlike Morin, it would appear that Masha'allah does not believe that a planet positioned in a house (but not ruling that house) can take on the role of principal significator. I would suggest that in the majority of cases a planet positioned in the house of the matter enquired about is not just a sharer or co-significator, but can often take on the role of principal significator and is, therefore, extremely important in terms of bringing about the desired outcome (or not, as the case may be). Masha'allah claims that the ruler of a house is more important in bringing about the desired outcome than a planet positioned in a house.

> ...the outcome of a matter and its prohibition does not happen according to a planet which is in the Ascendant but happens in the name of the lord of the Ascendant, or in the name of the Moon, and according to the stars to which they are being joined, and the joining together, reception, and the rendering of the reception of these stars. [20]

Hand agrees with Masha'allah when he confirms that rulers of houses in general are more important to outcomes than occupants of houses.[21] I have seen little evidence for this. As an example, in a Nativity which has the Moon located in the midheaven in Capricorn in a nocturnal chart, the Moon clearly takes on the role of principal significator in matters relating to career and status. Saturn, ruler of the tenth house, is absent and therefore is not as important as the Moon in the signification.

Although occupants of houses are probably more important than absent rulers, it is worth noting that an absent ruler is likely to disposit the occupant. Clearly, therefore, an absent ruler has a large share in the signification. However, there is no doubt that the presence of a planet in the house of the matter enquired about can bring about a positive outcome, with or without the ruler of that house being involved. For example, the Moon's conjunction with Venus in the seventh house will bring about a relationship, no matter what the condition of the seventh house ruler (although it is best of course if that planet is dignified and well placed). Similarly, an Infortune in the seventh house can prevent a positive outcome even if he does not rule the seventh house.

Will I Get Married to him Next Year?

This is a really interesting chart from my practice in that it provides an excellent illustration of our discussion above. The Moon's application to a conjunction with Venus in the seventh house shows the marriage; the opposition between the significators of the first and seventh houses shows the divorce.

The Querent married the following year and divorced two years after that. In this example, both the rulers of the relevant houses, as well as the planets positioned in the house of the matter enquired about, take on the role of significators. The point to note, however, is that Venus brings about the desired outcome to a seventh house matter, even though she is not the ruler of the seventh house. She is, of course, the natural ruler of love and relationships.

Signification 211

Will I get married to him next year?

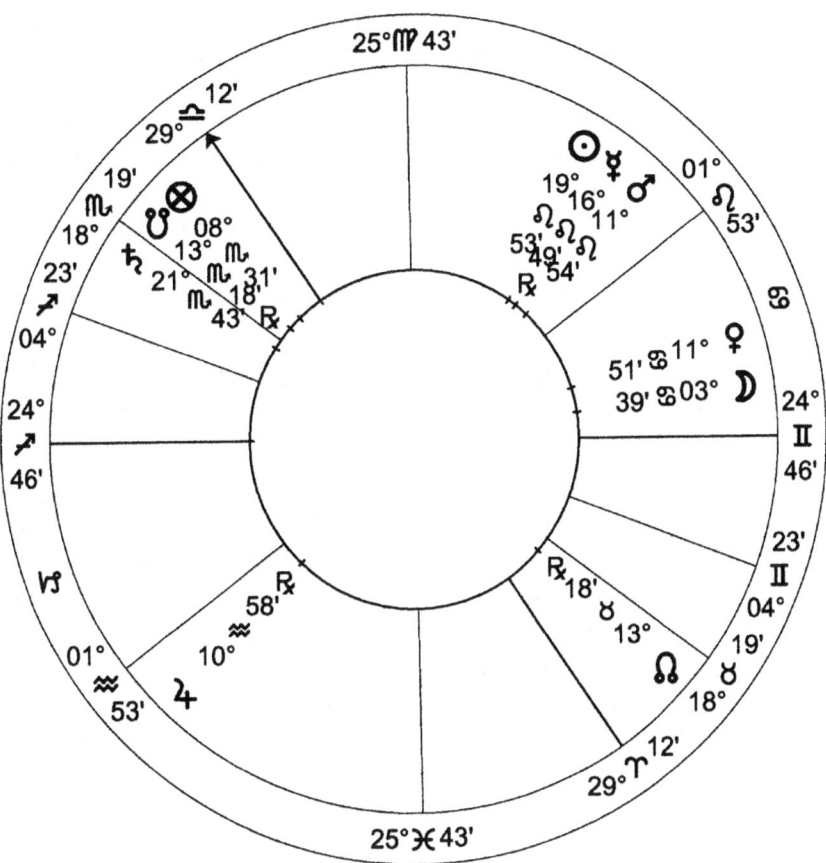

Signification through Aspect

Planets in aspect with significators are also important. Lilly states that if another planet is in aspect with, or in conjunction with, the planet that is the principal significator, this planet also has signification over the matter (to a greater or lesser extent). This planet may either help or hinder in bringing about the desired outcome. At the very least, this planet has "something to doe in the Judgement, and ought to be considered". If this planet is friendly it is a positive indication, but if this planet is an Infortune it can bring about the opposite result, that is "the destruction of the thing, or disturbance in it".[22]

Discussing the profession of the Native, Lilly tells us that if there is more than one planet in aspect with the significator (of the profession)

> ...always the most powerfull aspect is preferred before the weak, and if two planets have dominion in designing Magistery, the most fortified planet is first preferred.[23]

There are two points to consider here. Firstly, let us suppose that the tenth house has Capricorn in the cusp and its ruler Saturn in Sagittarius makes a sextile aspect with Venus in Libra. In this instance Venus has some importance in the signification of tenth house matters. If at the same time, Jupiter is applying to a trine with Saturn, Jupiter also has signification in matters relating to the profession. However, if Saturn receives an opposition from Mars, for example, this will be more important in the signification than a sextile with Venus or a trine with Jupiter, because an opposition is a stronger aspect than the trine or sextile. The opposition will certainly reduce some of the benefits derived from the trine and sextile.

Constructive and Destructive Aspects with a Significator

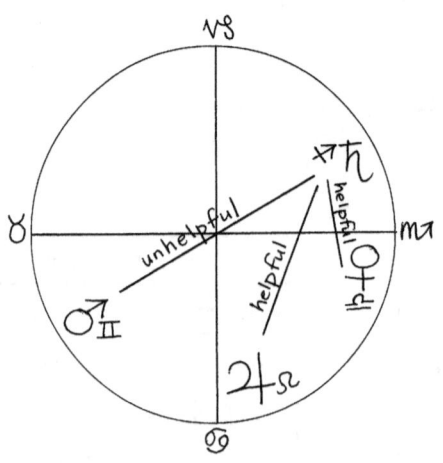

♄'s sextile with ♀ and trine with ♃ is very helpful. However, his opposition with ♂ is unhelpful and unfortunate.

The opposition has more power than the trine or sextile.

Secondly, in a chart where there are two planets in the midheaven such as Venus in Pisces and Mercury in Pisces, Venus would be the preferred significator of tenth house matters, because of her exaltation in Pisces. In this instance Venus has more power to bring about the desired outcome in a Question relating to tenth house matters. The same applies to tenth house matters in a Nativity.

Signification and Radicality

In Questions, the ascendant and ascendant ruler should describe the Querent. This is one way of establishing radicality. This is explored further in chapter eleven.

> When the sign Ascending, and the planet in the ascendant, &c, shall describe the person of the Querent exactly, you may conclude that figure Radical, and the Question propounded fit to be judged.[24]

Partridge tells us

> In all manner of Questions, the first House signifies the person inquiring, and should according to the Rules of Art (and it will if the figure be Radical) represent the Corporature, Complexion, and Condition of the Querent, as it is at the time of asking, according to the Nature of the sign ascending, and the Constitution of the Lord thereof.[25]

Although the astrologers of the past used (among other things) a description of the Querent as confirmed by the principal significators to confirm radicality, here Partridge appears to do it the other way around, stating that if the figure is radical, the first house should describe the Querent. According to Ball,

> ...if the Sign ascending, or the Lord of the Ascendant and Planets therein, do truly describe the Querent then is the Question fit to be Judged.[26]

In order to establish radicality, the astrologer must confirm that the sign ascending in part signifies the Querent's body, shape and physical description.

> ...the Sign ascending shall in part signifie his [Querent] corporature, body or stature, the Lord of the Ascendant, the Moon and Planet in the Ascendant, or that the Moon or Lord of the Ascendant are in aspect with, shall shew his quality or conditions equally mixed together...[27]

Finding a physical description of the Querent (and others) in a Question, or of the Native in a Nativity is extremely complicated and some guidelines are included towards the end of this chapter. Partridge tells us that in terms of a Nativity, the "Temperature and Complexion of the Body" is a mixture of the "four primary humours...Blood, Phlegm, Choler, and Melancholy..." Significators of the complexion include the ascendant and its ruler, any planets in the ascendant or in a partill aspect with the ascendant (including the nodes), the Moon and any planet aspecting the Moon as long as it is within orbs, the quarter of heaven and the ruler of the Nativity. He explains that the sign in which these significators are placed must be carefully examined.[28]

Signification and Intercepted Signs

A planet or planets positioned in a house can take on the role of principal significator, or at the very least, the role of co-significator of that house. In addition to this, a co-significator can be a planet which rules a sign intercepted in a house. For example, a chart with an Aquarius ascendant in the Regiomontanus house system produces the whole sign of Pisces intercepted in the first house. The planetary ruler of Pisces, which is Jupiter, consequently becomes a co-significator of the first house.

If the majority of degrees are contained within a house, the ruler of those degrees may be considered as co-significator, although to a lesser extent than if wholly intercepted in a house. For example, if twenty six degrees of Leo are contained within a house, the Sun is important in judgement. According to Al Biruni

> When a house is formed of two signs, if these are about equally represented, the lords of the signs are also the lords of the house; if both are in aspect...[29]

It is important to note that in order to acquire rulership of a house, these planets must make an aspect with the house that they rule. Al Biruni also tells us that in the case of two planets ruling a house, if only one planet is in aspect, this planet becomes the more important. If both planets are inconjunct, the one which is "superior" is the one with the most dignities. For example, if Scorpio and Sagittarius have the same number of degrees contained within the fifth house, both Mars and Jupiter are the house rulers. If Mars is positioned in Cancer and Jupiter in Pisces, they are both aspecting the sign (Scorpio) in the fifth house. Therefore, they have signification over matters relating to that house. In this example, some authorities would say that Jupiter has precedence over Mars by virtue of his dignity in Pisces. If Mars is in Aries and Jupiter is in Leo and they both aspect the degrees in Sagittarius, they are both house rulers, but some would say that Mars takes precedence over Jupiter by virtue of his rulership over Aries. If neither planet is in aspect by sign, nor aspecting a sign through the antiscia, it is the stronger of the planets in dignities which is given signification. In an overall sense, however, the "victory must always be given to that one which has the highest number of degrees in the house".

Morin tells us that where there are two rulers of a house it is the planet ruling the cusp of that house which should take precedence over the other, although the other ruler should not be neglected. He explains that it is the house cusp where the "properties of the whole House manifest themselves with the most effectiveness..." This, he explains, is due to the fact that the degree of the zodiacal sign occupying that very place is "active in the direction of its Ruler's power". It follows, therefore, that the ruler of the house prevails over the other rulers.[30]

The Preferred Significator

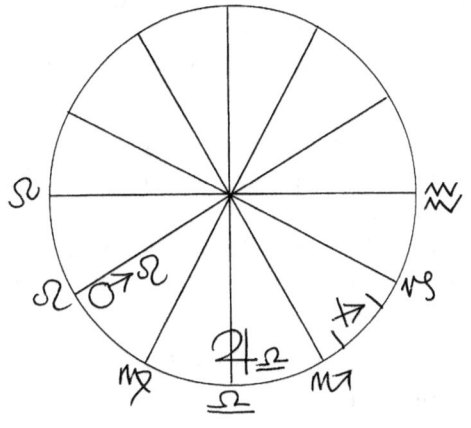

♃ has more degrees in the fifth house than ♂ so must at the very least be considered as co-significator.
If ♃ were in the fifth house in ♐ he becomes principal significator.
♂ is the preferred choice of significator due to his rulership of Scorpio and his aspect with the cusp.

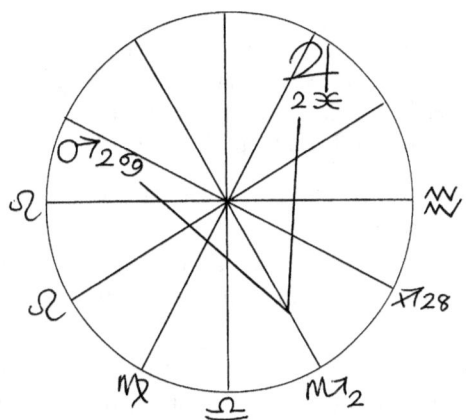

Here there are 28 degrees Scorpio in the fifth house and 28 degrees of Sagittarius. Both ♃ and ♂ make an aspect with the fifth house cusp. Although ♃ is stronger being in his domicile, most authors would consider ♂ to take precedence due to his rulership of the cusp, together with his aspect with the cusp.

Natural Significators

Lilly, as well as authorities before him, believes that each planet has a natural signification. Mercury and Jupiter make famous orators, lawyers and judges,

> ...exercising their faculties with men of great renowne, viz. with the most eminent of that Country wherein they live, whether King, Prince or Nobleman, &c.[31]

Lilly tells us that these natural significations are slightly modified when in configuration with other planets. For example

> ...if Saturn with his malignant aspect be commixed with Mars in designing of the profession, instead of Souldiers, he makes slavish Souldiers, poor, vulgar, common Souldiers, Scullions, Drudges, slaves, and such inferior fellows...

However, if Jupiter makes an aspect with Mars, he

> ...designs more noble Professions, as Captaines, Officers of War, Men of kingly thoughts... If the Sun behold Mars he addes to the quality of the profession, making it more neat civill, and to trade in better and more famous Commodities.

The planets certainly have a natural rulership over a multitude of things and matters, as discussed in previous chapters. For example, the Sun in itself signifies the father, husband, leaders, nobles, the King. The Moon signifies the mother, a queen and the people. Jupiter signifies wealth, Mercury signifies the intellect. These natural significators discussed by Lilly, are what Morin calls "universal significators". However, Morin disagrees with the concept of natural significators:[32]

> ...this doctrine deviates greatly from the truth, and that in this tradition the Ancients have abused the 'analogical nature' of the Planets.

He explains that in reality

> ...even though the Planets possess essentially an analogy with different categories and kinds of beings or sublunary affairs, as, for example, the Sun with life, the father, and honors, nevertheless, the Sun in itself does not signify the life more than the father, nor the husband more than honors.

Morin goes on to say that when interpreting the meaning of the Sun in a Nativity one should not give preference to any of these analogies over any of the others. In addition, he claims that one cannot assign all these meanings to the Sun simultaneously, otherwise the astrologer is in danger of making judgements of "the same quality" for all categories and this would be "completely absurd".

Morin claims that Cardan himself made this admission when he stated that "Ptolemy introduced a new confusion by attributing many meanings to one Significator..." Ptolemy's claim that the Moon signifies the body, also the moral faculties, the life, the wife, mother, servants, daughters and sisters is unacceptable to Morin. According to Morin, Ptolemy (in his Third Book of the *Tetrabiblos*) connects the Sun and Saturn with the father, the Moon and Venus with the mother. From this, Morin explains that astrologers have made judgements on the father in a Nativity based on the condition of the Sun and Saturn, on the mother from the Moon and Venus. However, Morin claims that they have done this without taking into account which house in the Nativity they rule, or which house they occupy. In addition, they have not considered the aspects between them. Although he concedes that the planets have a "particular affinity in virtue of a natural analogy", Morin claims that because this determination is "so universal in itself" it does not apply any more to a man than to an animal, or among many men born at the same instant in time.

In conclusion, he claims that no planet signifies, in itself, life more than death, the father more than the husband, friends more than enemies, unless it is "specially determined towards these significations" in the Nativity. This can take place either through its position by house, by its rulership of such houses, or by its connection with the ruler(s) of these houses. However, it sometimes happens that this "specific and accidental determination agrees with the essential determination of the Planet". For example with regard to the father, the Sun in a diurnal Nativity might be the ruler of the fourth house, or with regard to achievement and career, the Sun might be placed in, or be the ruler of, the tenth house. In such cases

> ...this cooperation will reinforce the efficacy of the planetary action in the direction of a particular determination, while the quality of this action will derive from the favorable or unfavorable state of the Planet in question.

Morin claims that this possible coincidence of two determinations happens fairly frequently and in his opinion is the source of the error by the ancient astrologers.

Morin's claims as outlined above are not quite clear. For example, if the Moon is in the seventh house at night, Morin would claim that it is necessary to make exactly the same predictions regarding the mother, the wife and so on, but this is untrue. As he himself says, the aspects made by the Moon, as well as her rulerships, must also be considered. Moreover, a wife is signified by the seventh house, the ruler of the seventh house, planets in the seventh house and aspects made. The mother is signified by the tenth house, the ruler of the tenth house, planets in the tenth house and the aspects made. However, if in a Nativity, for example, the ruler of the seventh house is positioned in the tenth house, the planet in question may be describing both the wife and the mother, at least to some extent. In a Question asking about a wife, the ruler of the seventh house positioned in the tenth house describes the wife. It may also describe the mother, but only if this line of enquiry is explicit or implicit in the Question. If not, it is probable that this planet only describes the wife.

There is no doubt that the planets have certain, natural associations and that the more precise associations become clear in the context of a specific Question. For example in a Question about a relationship, Venus is always important. In this instance the astrologer is not going to consider Venus as significator of the mother, unless this is related to the Question. In addition, one meaning usually stands out. For example, the Moon's application to a conjunction with Venus in an angle is one positive testimony of a relationship for the Querent, particularly a male Querent. Jupiter in the fifth house is a certain indication of pregnancy even if Jupiter is not a ruler of the fifth or first house. Venus in the fifth house might also signify a pregnancy.

We must remember however, that Venus and Jupiter are Fortunes and as such, are naturally associated with good luck, with money, with fertility, love and so on. It is also important to note that although there is clearly a natural association between certain planets and certain places, people, professions, matters or things, this association is, as Morin explains, reinforced when the planets are positioned in houses which are also associated with the same phenomena.

In a Question, if the house rulers do not have enough strength to bring about the desired outcome, it is probable that the natural rulers, if well-placed, can assist. Morin's claim that the natural analogies of the planets represent only a very general determining

Assistance from Natural Significators

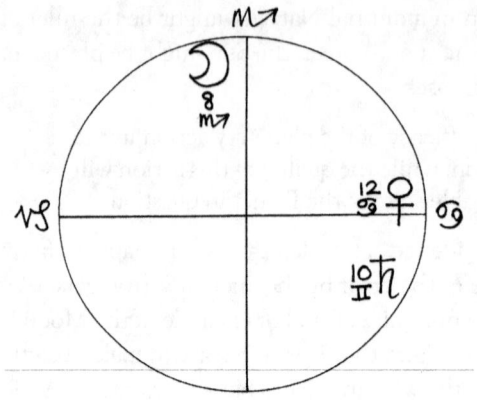

Will we have a relationship?

No aspect between ☽ and ♄, rulers of the 1st and 7th house, but the ☽ applies to a trine with ♀ in the 7th.
This is a testimony of good fortune in the matter.

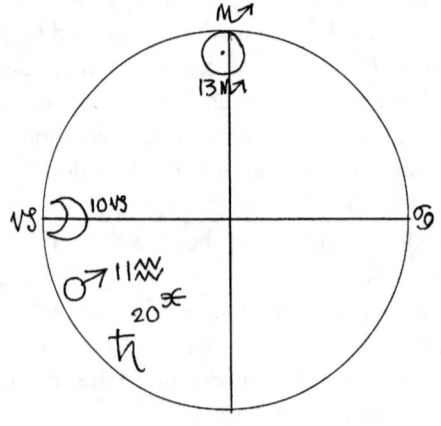

Will I get the job?

No aspect between ♄ and ♂, rulers of the 1st and 10th house, but the ☽ applies to a sextile with ☉ in the midheaven.
This is a testimony of good fortune in the matter.

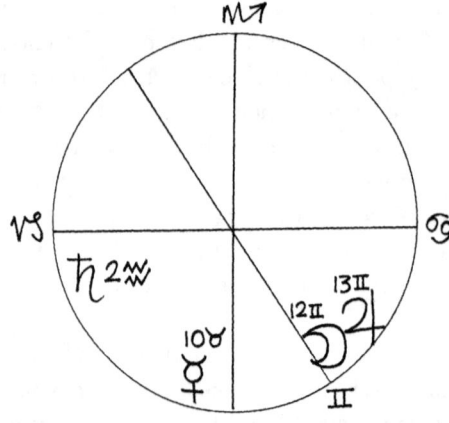

Am I pregnant?

No aspect between ♄ and ☿, rulers of 1st and 5th house, but the ☽ makes a conjunction with ♃ in the 5th house.
This is a testimony of good fortune in the matter.

Natural Significators coinciding with Accidental Significators

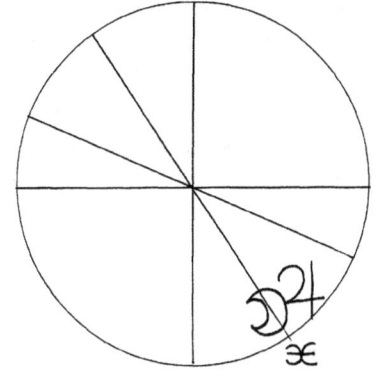

A Question about pregnancy.

♃ rules 5th house and is natural significator of pregnancy.

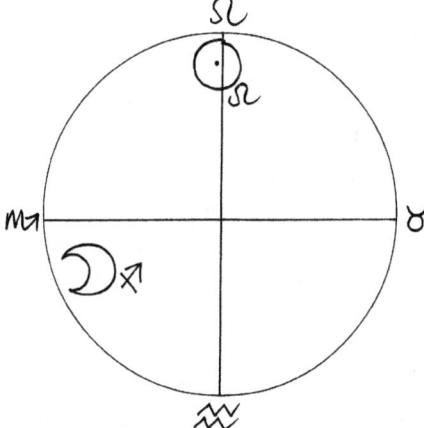

A Question about a job.

☉ rules 10th house and is natural significator of 10th house matters.

factor and that they are "unable to constitute a particular one" is very interesting. Whatever opinion one might like to adopt, the fact remains that any planet well-dignified and well placed, especially a Fortune, is going to offer assistance in the chart, whether a Nativity, Question, Election and so on. In view of this, *it can be difficult to establish whether it is a planet's role as a natural significator, which is important and is also assisting in terms of the outcome, or whether its status as a Fortune is the source of the assistance.* However, there is no doubt as to Morin's claim that if these analogies (of natural rulers) are in harmony with a particular accidental determination, they confirm this determination.

In *Clavis Astrologiae Elimata* Coley tells us about the nature, significations and descriptions of the planets

> These Descriptions being perfectly learn'd and understood, the Artist cannot be to seek in making an Artificial Description of any Significator in all Questions.[33]

Signification and the Houses

Signification associated with the houses has been examined in chapter two, where it was demonstrated that despite occasional differences between authorities of the past, in an overall sense house signification is generally straightforward. The problem arises when (usually in the case of a Question) the astrologer decides to turn the chart. For example, if the Querent asks about her husband's money, it is simply the second house from the seventh house (husband's resources). However, if the Querent asks about her friend's husband's money it is less straightforward. Some would argue that, as a third party Question, this should not be accepted for judgement. It is certainly true that locating significators here requires much more skill.

A common error is to turn the chart when it is unnecessary. In the above example, one might be tempted to turn the chart and consider the eleventh house as the friend and the seventh house from the eleventh house (fifth house) as her husband. Here, the fifth house becomes the starting point for signification of the husband. Providing that the chart is radical and that this house and its ruler describe the person under consideration, it may be acceptable to take this house as co-significator of the Quesited. However, caution is required. Lilly turned the chart on occasion but it is the unturned, original chart, which carries most weight and must be given priority. It is after all, from this original unturned chart, that the triplicity rulers and the Lots are calculated.

Lilly tells us that if a Question is asked about an absent or missing person and the Querent has no relationship with that person, the first house, the ruler of the first house and the Moon should be taken as significators of the absent person. Here, Lilly does not even consider turning the chart.[34]

To ensure clarity, it is always best if the Querent asks a question about him or herself, not about a third party. However, when a third party Question is asked and the chart is radical, I invariably find that the testimony of the original chart and the turned chart are in accord. In *Christian Astrology* in the chart of a missing brother, Lilly considers both the original eighth house and the turned eighth house for supporting testimony as to whether the brother is dead or alive.

> For as much as Venus significatrix of the Quesited is no manner of way afflicted either by Mercury who is Lord of the eight in the figure, or by Mars who is Lord of the eight as to the ascendant of the quesited... I judged the absent Brother was alive...[35]

I would suggest that the following house rulerships remain the same, no matter who asks the Question, nor in what context the Question is asked. These rulerships usually take precedence over turned houses and their rulerships.

> Children and pregnancy belong to the fifth house
> Small animals belong to the sixth house
> Large animals belong to the twelfth house
> Property belongs to the fourth house

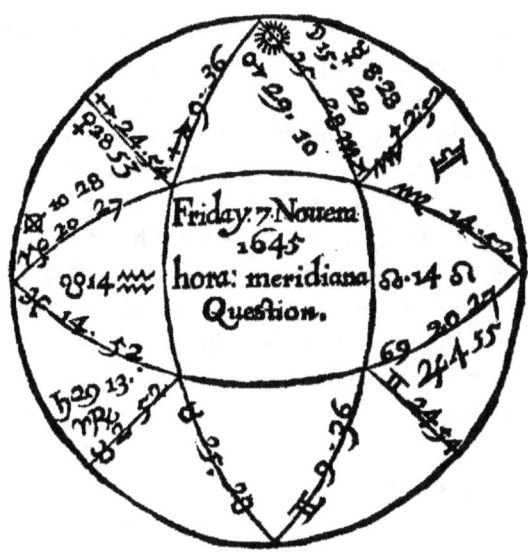

Where an absent Brother was?

Jobs and career issues belong to the tenth house
Sickness belongs to the sixth house
Death belongs to the eighth house

If there are doubts as to the correct house signification, the significators should describe the people asked about. If this does not occur, it is best to consider another significator. For example, a young fair-haired girl is unlikely to be described by Saturn. In this case signification should also be taken from the Moon.

However, the resources of a particular person always belong to the adjacent house. For example, the Querent's husband's money is the second house from the seventh house (eighth house). The Querent's child's money is the second house from the fifth house (sixth house). As with the examples above, however, the astrologer should carefully consider the second house of the unturned chart also.

Although Dariot assigns house signification in the usual way, that is, starting from the ascendant, he (like others) also assigns signification to the rulers of the triplicity of the sign in a house cusp. This is explored in chapter two. In his assignment of house signification, Dariot also appears to be fond of turning the chart, starting from a house other than the ascendant. For example, he claims that the second house, being fourth house from the eleventh house, can signify the fathers of friends, or even the children of Kings, being the fifth house from the tenth house.[36] There is some merit in turning the chart, but care must be exercised: the children of kings are princes or princesses and are more likely to be signified by the tenth house in a Question, unless they ask the Question themselves, when the ascendant is the most likely significator.

In certain charts, especially those concerning sickness, the ascendant and ascendant ruler are usually taken as significators of the sick person. In a chart of this nature, the Querent, unless that is the sick person, simply drops out of the chart. In Part Two, I show examples to illustrate this point. Coley tells us that the Moon is said to be a general significator of all sick people.[37]

I would suggest that in many charts where the Querent asks about another person or situation (a third party Question), the house signification is derived from the original chart. Turning the chart in these instances can produce an incorrect answer. In a Question about a friend's relationship, for example, the seventh house must be considered, not just the seventh house of the friend. Examples are included in chapter twenty. In Questions about pregnancy it is the fifth house which takes precedence, not the fifth house of the friend, sister or relative. Examples are included in chapter eighteen. Whether or not a third party Question should be judged at all is another matter entirely and is discussed in chapter twelve.

Signification and Appearance

The "form and Stature" of a person is, according to Partridge, more difficult to work out from a chart than a person's intelligence or the qualities related to a person's mind. This, he explains, is because the shape and constitution of a person's body depends as much on the parents and their "Progenitors" as it does on the celestial bodies. Not only that, but there is also the place of birth, education, diet and exercise to take into account, which he claims "much alter the favour and form of the Body". Nevertheless, Partridge tells us that

> ...the well placing of the Planets, do add much to the beauty and lustre of the Body; and on the contrary, the ill placing of the Significators do disfigure and as much deform the same.[38]

He explains that the stature of the body is described by the ascendant and the ascendant ruler, as well as the planet or planets beholding the ascendant, plus the planet or planets in the ascendant, together with the luminaries and the fixed stars. His table of descriptions according to whether a planet is oriental or occidental, is reproduced on p.223.[39] Lilly also takes into account the orientality or occidentality of Mercury, Venus, Mars, Jupiter and Saturn in his descriptions.[40]

Coley tells us that descriptions can be derived solely from the planet who is the ascendant ruler. He also explains that these observations can be applied not only to the physical characteristics of a person but also to a person's "Conditions and Qualities".[41]

- If no planet aspects the ascendant ruler, the description is derived from the ascendant ruler only, but the sign placement is not considered.

- If the ascendant ruler is in detriment, fall or is retrograde, the sign placement is used for description.

- If the ascendant ruler beholds the ascendant, the description is derived from the sign ascending.

Orientality and Occidentality and its Affect on Appearance

♄	Oriental	gives	a mean stature inclining to brevity.
	Occidental		short.
♃	Oriental	gives	a high tall stature.
	Occidental		a mean, yet rather tall.
♂	Oriental	shows	a tall stature.
	Occidental		a mean, inclining to tallness.
♀	Oriental	affords	a mean, inclining to tallness.
	Occidental		a mean stature.

- If two planets aspect the ascendant, it is the planet in closest aspect or the planet in its own domicile that holds more importance than a planet in its exaltation.

Partridge tells us that when a significator is Mercury, whether Mercury is oriental or occidental, Mercury "partakes of the Nature of his Dispositor…" However, if Mercury is placed in the ascendant in his own domicile, or in the domicile of either the Sun or Moon, "he partakes of the Nature of the Sign he is in". Partridge explains that the luminaries appear to behave in the same way, but the Sun gives a "large Body" and the Moon if she is increasing in light gives "a pretty tall stature", but if she is decreasing in light "a short ill-composed Body".[42]

Lilly explains that Mercury, more than any other planet, is influenced by the aspects he makes. If Mercury is in aspect with Saturn the person is "more heavy", with Jupiter "more temperate" with Mars "more rash" with the Sun "more genteele" with Venus "more jesting".[43] Partridge continues with a brief description of stature according to the signs

> Aries, Taurus, Libra and Scorpio "give a mean stature, inclining to tallness."
> Leo, Virgo and Sagittarius produce a tall person
> Cancer, Capricorn and Pisces produce a short person
> Gemini gives a tall straight body
> Aquarius gives a "mean Body, rather short."

In addition to the above, if Venus or Mercury are placed in their own domicile or exaltation and behold the ascendant ruler, this gives a tall stature, but if they are in their detriment or fall, the contrary. If Saturn, Jupiter or Mars are in their domicile or exaltation they give "one kind of stature; Peregrine and Retrograde another…" but Partridge does not explain what this might be. He explains that Leovitius only considers the ascendant ruler and its dispositor in this kind of judgement and that he neglects the ascending sign. Partridge disagrees with Leovitius and tells us that he considers both the ascending sign, the ascendant ruler and the Moon as principal significators. Furthermore, he states "and I have good reason for so doing".

Referring to the "Corpulency of the Body" Partridge explains that here, there are differences of opinion, for example, Ptolemy thinks that corpulency is associated with south latitude and leanness is from north latitude. Leovitius on the other hand attributes it to the signs. In this respect, he assigns "grossness" to the first half of Aries, Taurus and Leo, but "leanness" to the latter half. He assigns the first part of Gemini and Scorpio to leanness and the latter fat; the first half of Cancer and Capricorn are "mean", but the latter "tending to grossness", the first part of Sagittarius lean, the latter fat; Virgo, Libra, Aquarius and Pisces give a "mean proportion" but the latter part of Aquarius "inclines to grossness..." Partridge attributes the cause of "fatness" to the Moon and to other significators being placed in "moist and aery Signs, in good Ray with Jupiter or Mercury..." He attributes leaness to significators placed in earth signs and in aspect with Saturn or Mars.

Lilly in his section on Nativities explains that the stature of the body is either tall or short depending on the planet that is in exact aspect with the ruler of the ascendant. If more than one planet aspects the ruler of the ascendant, the strongest one is associated with the type of stature. Lilly produces a table describing the stature of the body according to the orientality or occidentality of the five planets, omitting the Sun and Moon. He confirms that the influence of Mercury depends to a great extent on his dispositor.[44]

In calculating the "proportion of the Members", that is the form and shape of the body, Lilly considers the sign ascending, the ruler of that sign, any planet in the ascendant or any planet aspecting the ascendant, the luminaries, the season of the year and any fixed stars in the ascendant or near the cusp of the ascendant. In relation to the zodiacal signs, Lilly explains that Aries, Taurus, Libra and Scorpio denote a person of "moderate Stature, but more long"; Leo, Virgo and Sagittarius denote "a Body more tall"; Cancer, Capricorn and Pisces make the body "short"; Gemini "indifferent" and Aquarius "a moderate proportion".

Lilly explains that there are five things which are "considerable" when judging the "proportion of the Face and members"[45]

- the sign ascending
- the ruler of that sign
- the planets in the ascendant (or the configurations these planets have in the ascendant)
- the Sun and the Moon
- the quarter of the year
- any fixed stars in the ascendant

Human signs ascending, such as Gemini, Virgo and the early part of Sagittarius and Aquarius signify "faire and cleer complexions". Taurus, Cancer, Scorpio, Capricorn, Pisces and the latter parts of Aries and Leo, show "deformity". Of all the planets it is Venus and Jupiter which give the best complexions; Mercury and the Moon the next best. The Infortunes can show "ill Faces or Complexions" but if they are in no way afflicted "they declare a good and handsome Face". However, if Mars, Saturn or the south node are in bad aspect to the ascendant, they are associated with "unhandsomness". If any of the foregoing is located in the ascendant there is a "Scarre or blemish in the Face".

I would agree that much of the above is true. Jupiter in the ascendant especially in Sagittarius gives great height and good looks (other things being equal). Venus in the ascendant gives great attractiveness and beauty. The south node in the ascendant gives a scar on the face. Lilly tells us

> Where the Lights are both impeded, there's some hurt in the Eyes, when the Infortunes are joined together, or in conjunction with the Lights; [46]

As discussed in chapter two, the second house is also associated with problems to the eyes.

In Lilly's discussion of the "grossenesse or leannesse of Bodies" he explains that this affects our bodies "after a full age, or about thirty years, or somewhat after." Here, judgement is derived from the sign ascending and its ruler, that is, from the planet which has most dignities in the sign ascending (almuten).

Aries, Taurus, Leo	first part grossenesse, the latter part leannesse
Gemini, Scorpio	first part leannesse, the latter grossenesse
Cancer, Capricorn	first part mediocrity, rather lean, the latter part tending more to grossenesse
Sagittarius	the first part lean, the latter part grossenesse
Aquarius, Pisces Libra, Virgo	a moderate proportion, but the latter part of Aquarius tends to leannesse.[47]

Lilly also includes the stations of Saturn in describing a person. If Saturn is in his first station the person will be "a little fat" but in his second station the person will be fat, with "ill favoured Bodies, and weak..." Lilly points out that this type of description derived from planetary stations can be applied to all the other planets.[48] The terms of the planets are also important in deriving physical description. Lilly makes frequent use of the terms in his descriptions in *Christian Astrology*.

In an overall sense, working out the description of a person from either a Nativity or Question is very difficult and far more complicated than it would appear from the above. Physical descriptions derived from the planetary dignities and from the rulers of the degrees in the house cusps are also a method of confirming signification. However, this is complicated and mistakes easily made. I doubt there is any astrologer today who could derive descriptions in the way that William Lilly was able to do in his masterpiece *Christian Astrology*.

A Lady, if marry the Gentleman desired?

> The ascendant and Sun are for the querent; Saturn Lord of the Seventh, is for the man quesited after. The querent was moderately tall, of round visage, sanguine complexion, of a cheerful, modest countenance, gray eyed, her haire a light browne, occasioned, as I conceive, by the Sun Lord of the ascendant, in the Termes of Mars, she was well spoken and sufficiently comely.
>
> Finding Saturn in the angle of the South, and in conjunction with Mars, and both in Taurus, a fixed, earthly Signe, I judged the corporature of the quesited party to be but meane, and not tall, or very handsome, his visage long and incomposed, a wan, pale or meagre complexion, dark haire, or of a sad, chestnut colour, curling and crisp, his eyes fixt, ever downward, musing, stooping forward with his head, some impediment in his going, as treading awry, &c. [this was confessed] Finding Saturn so, as above-said, elevated, and in conjunction with Mars, I judged the Gentleman to be sad, angry, much discontented, and scorning his former slights (as ever all Saturnine people doe)...[49]

Almuten

Lilly explains that in Nativities it is important to establish the planet who is "Lord of the Geniture", because

> ...the whole actions of the Native will more or less pertake of the nature of that Planet and so his Conditions, Complexion, Temperament and Manners shall be much regulated unto the properties assigned that Planet.

If, however, there is another planet almost as strong as this planet in the Nativity

> ...he shall much participate, and a kind of mixture must be framed according to the severall fortitudes each planet hath, together with the aspects good or evill of the other Planets intervening...[50]

Signification is taken from a whole range of sources: through the signs, houses and planets and their interrelationships. The Moon of course has overall signification. The very strongest and most fortunate signification is produced when a planet, strong in dignity, who is natural significator of a thing, person or matter, is placed in a house which also has an association with that particular matter. For example, the Sun in Leo in the tenth house, Venus in Taurus in the fifth house or Jupiter in Pisces in the fifth house. In a Question, Venus would not necessarily be fortunate when placed in the seventh house, because when the ruler of the seventh house is placed in the seventh house in some of its dignities, this often signifies a person who is not interested in a relationship or marriage.

Evaluating any chart requires experience, as well as a thorough knowledge of signification derived from the houses, planets and signs. However, I believe that Ptolemy is correct in assigning the places of principal significance as the ascendant, the Sun, the Moon, the Lot of Fortune and their rulers.

What should be very clear by now is that when the Fortunes are well placed and not afflicted, they produce good fortune in any type of chart: in a Question they help in bringing about the desired outcome; in a Nativity they produce good fortune for the individual. In addition, it appears that the Fortunes produce physical attractiveness in a Nativity, while the Infortunes produce the reverse, unless they are strong in dignity. From this it surely follows that those planets which combine to produce physical beauty (other things being equal) also produce good fortune for the individual in a Nativity. So is it true that an individual who is very attractive ought to have a fortunate life and vice versa? I leave this with you.

References

1. Lilly p. 307.
2. Ptolemy *Tetrabiblos*, F E Robbins Loeb Classical Library p. 275.
3. Lilly pp. 507-508.
4. ibid p. 508 .
5. Simmonite, W. J. *Horary Astrology, the key to scientific prediction, being the prognostic astronomer*. Additions by John Story and further edited by Ernest A Grant. American Federation of Astrologers, AZ.,1950. Preface by John Story.
6. Partridge p. 48.
7. Lilly p. 123.
8. Ibn Ezra, *The Beginning Of Wisdom* p. 215.
9. Bonatus p. 44 130th consideration.
10. Lilly p. 124.
11. Mash'allah p. 6.
12. Lilly p. 124.
13. ibid p. 298 Aphorism 5.
14. Robert Hand in *On Reception* by Masha'allah pp. iv-v.
15. Morin p. 29.
16. ibid p. 30.
17. ibid p. 32.
18. Lilly pp. 439-442.
19. Masha'allah p. 9
20. ibid
21. Robert Hand, in *On Reception* p. 9.
22. Lilly p. 49.
23. ibid p. 633.
24. Gadbury p.237.
25. Partridge p.48.

26. Richard Ball 1697 *An Astrolo-Physical Compendium or A Brief Introduction to Astrology* Ballantrae Reprint, Ontario, Canada p.59.
27. Lilly p.123.
28. Partridge pp.84-86.
29. Al Biruni p. 279.
30. Morin p. 66.
31. Lilly pp.633-634.
32. Morin, references to Morin in this section from pp.15-17.
33. Coley p.42.
34. Lilly p.151.
35. ibid pp.196-199.
36. Dariot pp. 46-48.
37. Coley p.42.
38. Partridge, references to Partridge from pp. 98-99.
39. ibid p.99 Table.
40. Lilly pp.59-78.
41. Coley p.43.
42. Partridge, all references to Partridge in this section from pp.99-101.
43. Lilly p.78.
44. ibid references to Lilly in this section from pp.546-547.
45. ibid p.548.
46. ibid
47. ibid pp.549-550.
48. ibid p.59.
49. ibid p.386.
50. ibid pp.531-532.

11

Considerations before Judgement

Radicality

Before the astrologer is able to proceed with the judgement of a Question, consideration must be given as to whether the chart is radical, that is, whether it complies with certain rules. With regard to a Nativity, it is obvious that radicality has been established or assigned at the very moment of birth. However, in terms of a Question, the situation is different. Here, there are two issues to consider. Firstly, the chart must describe the situation and the parties involved. I would agree with Geoffrey Cornelius when he explains that "Radicality is the assumption that the horoscope is a true symbolic representation of its subject".[1] Secondly, there should be no warnings produced by the chart, indicating that it might be disadvantageous for the astrologer to give judgement. Both of these conditions must be satisfied if the chart is to be termed radical. There are several possible reasons why a warning might be produced from the chart testimonies.

- The answer might not please the Querent.

- The astrologer may be in danger of compromising her/his reputation.

- The Querent is insincere or dishonest in the asking of the particular Question.

- There are circumstances surrounding the Question which the astrologer picks up on and unwittingly upsets the Querent.

- It is too early or too late to ask the Question.

- The Querent is trying to test the astrologer.

- The Querent has already asked the same Question to a number of other astrologers.

In order to avoid any of the above, the chart may produce certain planetary patterns, which advise the astrologer not to proceed with judgement, or at least advise caution in proceeding. These are what Lilly calls *considerations before judgement*.[2] In his *Tractatus Quintus* Bonatti also writes about testimonies produced by the chart which must be diligently observed. Gadbury explains that before proceeding, the astrologer

> ...ought first to consider, whether it be proper and fit to be judged: For many times, Persons propound impertinent Questions, with an intention to disgrace Art; in doing which, they do nothing but create shame to themselves.[3]

Gadbury gives more advice

> ...the Artist shall sometimes meet with Persons that know not how to propound their desires aright, it's an Argument when such Queries are made, that (although they may be asked with a good intent,) yet they are not ripe for a resolve; and the Astrologer in such Cases ought to defer judgement until another time.

Bonatti puts forward a list of those instances where the astrologer is likely to make a mistake.[4]

- When the Querent is so silly that he doesn't know how to ask a Question and doesn't really know what he wants.

- When the time for the setting up of the Question is incorrect.

- When the Fortunes and Infortunes are of equal strength. At this time judgment isn't possible and the astrologer cannot proceed.

- When the Querent comes only to trick the astrologer. Bonatti tells us that such people say to themselves something along the lines of "Let us go to such an Astrologer, and ask him such a thing, and see if he can tell us the truth or not."

- When the Querent is not serious about the Question, for example, when a person meets an astrologer by chance or is going to meet him about something else and on a whim that person thinks of something to ask, "wherein 'tis a thousand to one but mistakes happen".

Bonatti asks: "How shall I know whether the Querent come out of a solid intention, or only to try me?" He answers this himself by saying that what he has often experienced and found to be true is, if at the time of the Question

> ...the Ascendant then happened very near the end of one sign and beginning of another, so that it seemed as between both; I said they did not ask seriously, or that they came to try me;[5]

Gadbury believes that the considerations are in place in order for the astrologer to discover the "knavery of the one, and the unfitness or unpreparedness of the other..."[6]

Description and Radicality

The ultimate test of radicality, that is, whether a chart is representative of the Question and fit to be judged, must be to find description in the chart. The chart should describe the circumstances, as well as the parties involved. This applies particularly to the Querent (if the Question concerns the Querent), whether the Querent is a client of the astrologer, or whether the Querent is the astrologer. However, if the Querent is asking a third party Question, particularly one concerning a sick person, the ascendant and its ruler may describe the sick person, not the Querent. The house ruling the Quesited (the matter enquired about) should also produce a planet describing the person or matter asked about.

The Moon is co-ruler of the Querent and usually shows where the true interest lies. This may be useful if you are not judging your own Question. Barclay claims that the ascendant ruler states fact and that the Moon indicates the real interest. She tells us that the literal placement of the significator will describe the literal placement of the person or thing asked about. If a planet is isolated, a person is alone. If a planet is with another planet, the Querent or Quesited is with another person. Barclay believes that the position of a significator can describe location. If it is in the fourth house, the person represented by that planet is at home, if it is in the fifth house, the person is out having fun. If a significator is in the sixth house that person may be unwell.[7]

I would suggest that in the most fortunate and clear charts, the significator of the Querent (who Ibn Ezra calls the 'asker') or the Moon, will be positioned in the house of the matter enquired about (the 'request'). If this does not occur, it usually casts some doubt over radicality, or it can simply be an indication of misfortune for the Querent. For example, in a Question about a job, career or promotion, the astrologer would expect to find the Sun, Moon or principal significator in at least one of the following positions:

- in the tenth house
- ruling the tenth house
- aspecting the tenth house
- aspecting a planet in the tenth house
- aspecting the ruler of the tenth house

Similarly, in a Question about buying or selling property the principal significator and/or the Moon should have a connection with the fourth house, or with the first house or the seventh house of the buyer or seller.

It is important that the significators describe the parties involved, otherwise there may be some doubt regarding radicality. According to Gadbury

> When the sign Ascending, and Planet in the Ascendant, &c, shall describe the person of the Querent exactly, you may conclude that figure Radical, and the Question propounded fit to be judged.[8]

In certain instances this data is not available, for example I have had clients who are unwilling to put forward a description of themselves, or of another party involved in the Question. In this case the astrologer must be guided by other factors in the chart.

Lilly's Question concerning the death of Canterbury is an excellent example of his method of establishing radicality. As Canterbury is a religious man, Lilly assigns Saturn, ruler of the ninth house as his significator. Saturn, in his fall in Aries, positioned in the twelfth house is a wonderfully clear and appropriate significator for an imprisoned old man and confirms radicality in the chart. Once radicality is established, the chart can be judged.

> ...there is not any amongst the wisest of men in this world could better have represented the person and condition of this old man his present state and condition, and the manner of his death, than this present Figure of heaven doth.[9]

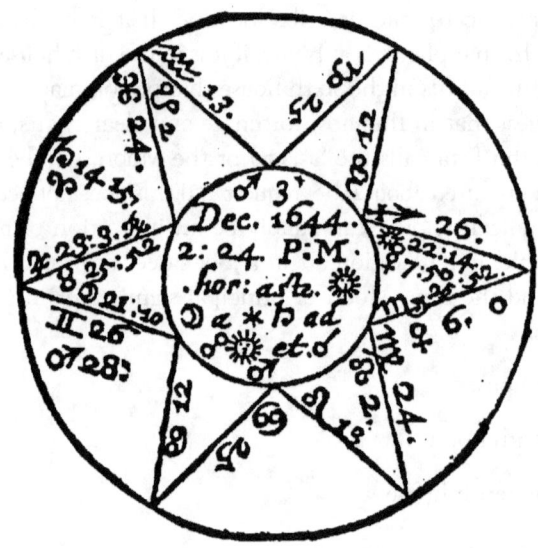

What manner of Death Canterbury should dye?

Combustion

A planet combust can represent a very sick person, in the same way that a planet departing from combustion can represent a sick person recovering from illness. I have several examples of a combust planet representing a sick person, where this planet did not have a rulership over the house expected, nor over the ascendant. In a Question concerning a sick person, a planet in combustion might be taken as confirmation of the radicality of the Question.

Harmonising with the Ruler of the Hour

It is best if the ascendant or ascendant ruler harmonises in some way with the planetary ruler of the hour. This harmonisation can be according to the nature of the signs, the planetary ruler of the sign, or the planetary ruler of the triplicity. As an example, if the ascendant is Leo and Mars is ruler of the hour, the Question is radical, because the Sun, ruler of the ascendant and Mars, ruler of the hour, are "both of one nature", that is, hot and dry. If the ascendant is Cancer and Venus is the ruler of the hour, the Question is radical because the Moon, ruler of the ascendant, and Venus, ruler of the hour, are the same nature, that is, cold and moist.[10] Ball explains that

> Some Authors hold the Question to be Radical, when the Lord of the Ascendant and Lord of the Hour, are of one Nature and Triplicity.[11]

Lilly and others also tell us that if the ruler of the hour is Mars, where Scorpio, Pisces or Cancer are the degrees ascending, the Question is radical, because Mars, ruler of the hour is also the ruler of the triplicity (water triplicity). Likewise, if the ruler of the hour is Venus and the degrees of Virgo, Taurus, or Capricorn are ascending in a diurnal chart, the chart is radical because Venus rules the earth triplicity in a diurnal chart. In a nocturnal chart the Moon has triplicity rulership over the earth signs.[12]

If the ruler of the hour is Mars and Aries is ascending, the Question is radical, because Mars is ruler of the hour and ruler of the sign ascending. If the ruler of the hour is Jupiter and the sign ascending is Sagittarius, the chart is radical because Jupiter rules that sign.

In the most fortunate charts there is usually some sort of sympathy between the ascendant and the ruler of the hour. I would suggest that a chart can be judged if the ruler of the hour does not harmonise with the ascendant in the ways outlined above. Bonatti however, does not agree

> ...when the Lord of the Ascendant and the Lord of the Hour are not the same, nor of the same Triplicity, or be not of the same Complexion with the Ascendant; for then the Question is not radical, as I have frequently found by experience.[13]

Early or Late Degrees Ascending

> When in a Question, either the very beginning, or latter end of a Sign ascend, it is not safe to give Judgement, for if the beginning of a Sign ascends, the question is improperly propounded; if the latter end thereof ascend, the Querent has either been tampering with others about the matter, or the Question is forged.[14]

When either 0, 1, or 2 degrees of a sign are ascending, especially in signs of short ascension like Capricorn, Aquarius, Pisces, Aries, Taurus or Gemini, "you may not adventure judgment" unless, says Lilly

> ...the Querent be very young, and his corporature, complexion and moles or scarres of his body, agree with the quality of the Sign ascending.

When either 27, 28 or 29 degrees of a sign are ascending, "it's no wayes safe to give judgment" unless, explains Lilly "the Querent be in yeers corresponding to the number of degrees ascending" (or unless it is an Election).[15]

The Moon in Late Degrees

According to Lilly, when the Moon is in the later degrees of a sign, especially in Gemini, Scorpio or Capricorn, it is not safe to judge a Question. Lilly does occasionally judge a chart when the Moon is in late degrees. However in these instances, the Moon is usually positioned in the sign of Taurus, Cancer, Sagittarius or Pisces. In *Christian Astrology* Lilly judges a chart with the Moon in late degrees of Aquarius, but perhaps this is because the Moon has dignity in her face and also because the Moon applies immediately to a sextile with Saturn in 0 degrees 36 minutes of Taurus.[16]

Although there are no charts in *Christian Astrology* with the Moon in late degrees in Gemini, Scorpio or Capricorn, there are examples in Lilly's workbooks, according to Sue Ward. This may not necessarily mean that Lilly disregarded this rule, but perhaps he judged accordingly. These degree areas are in the terms of the Infortunes and are unfortunate. Sue Ward points out that there was a significant gap in the workbooks after Lilly had judged three charts with the Moon in late degrees of Gemini. She explains that he restarted work after the Moon had changed signs. This, she believes, might imply that in this instance he refused to judge a chart with the Moon in a late degree.[17]

Bonatti tells us

> ...when a planet that is Significator, or the Moon shall have past the 29th degree of a Sign wherein it is, and touches the 30th, and especially if it have passed one minute of that degree; for then it shall have no strength in that Sign, but in the next.[18]

The Via Combusta

Although not all astrologers agree on the exact area contained in the via combusta, it is approximately the degrees between fifteen of Libra and fifteen of Scorpio.

> When the Moon is in a Combusta, the Combust way, or void of Course, the matter propounded goes unluckily on; therefore at such times, let the Artist defer his judgement.[19]

I would suggest that this is a consideration which can sometimes be waived, especially if the Querent has a planet in the same sign and degree in the Nativity. However, in other instances the chart can be unreliable and the matter may not work out in the way expected. I have not seen enough evidence to confirm that the Moon in the via combusta necessarily produces a chart which is not radical. The Moon close to the fixed star Spica (around twenty three degrees and fifty minutes of Libra) is certainly an exception and in this position the Moon can be fortunate. Lilly gives a planet in conjunction with Spica FIVE points in his scoring system.

Void of Course

The Moon is said to be void of course when she does not aspect any planet further on in the sign at the time of drawing up the chart. If the Moon is void of course, it is unlikely that anything will go forward in a positive manner. As discussed previously, the Moon can sometimes perform in Taurus, Cancer, Sagittarius and Pisces even if void. Lilly is quite clear on this when he tells us

> All manner of matters goe hardly on (except the principall Significators be very strong) when the Moon is voyd of course; yet somewhat she performes if voyd of course, and be in either Taurus, Cancer, Sagittarius or Pisces.[20]

In *On Reception*, Masha'allah does not allow a void of course planet to interfere with any of his judgements. In many of his examples he simply allows the void planet (usually the Moon) to perfect an aspect in the next sign. This is something which Lilly occasionally makes use of in *Christian Astrology*. I would argue that if the Moon makes another aspect very soon after changing sign and that aspect is within orb, a perfection can take place, but only when she is in Taurus, Cancer, Sagittarius or Pisces. Even in this instance, the matter may not turn out as well as might have been expected.

According to Robert Hand, "if the applications that next occur in the new sign are good ones, the matter may still come out well for the querent".[21] Masha'allah believes that even if the Moon is void, it may not necessarily be a serious setback in terms of the Question, but it simply reduces the good fortune anticipated.

Seventh House or Seventh House Ruler Afflicted

Ball explains that if the seventh house is afflicted, or if the seventh house ruler is retrograde or combust, (unless the Question is about a seventh house matter)

> ...the Astrologer doth (by giving Judgement at such times) disgrace both the Art and himself; and if he adventureth to judge, the more Discredit he is liable to...[22]

Ptolemy tells us that

> "The astrologer will be entangled in a labyrinth of error, when the seventh house and its lord shall be afflicted."[23]

Ball claims that if the Moon, or the ascendant ruler, are in opposition with the seventh house ruler (which he takes as the significator of the astrologer)

> "the Querent may then be concluded a Knave, or Fool or both, and comes to abuse both the Art and the Artist..."[24]

Lilly tells us that in this instance, the astrologer's judgement will not please the Querent, because the seventh house is usually the house signifying the astrologer. Lilly goes on to quote "The Arabians, like Alkindus and others" who claim that if the seventh house ruler is unfortunate, in his fall or in the terms of the Infortunes, "the Artist shall scarce give a solid judgement". This serves as a warning to the astrologer, in order to offer protection, but is not applicable when the astrologer asks the Question.[25] Gadbury tells us that if the seventh house is "hindered" or the ruler of the seventh house is retrograde, combust or afflicted in any other way

> ...let not the Astrologer judge any thing: for by how much the more he shall adventure to judge at such a time, by so much the more shall he disgrace himself, and disparage the Art he professeth.[26]

If the Question concerns a seventh house matter, this rule is not applicable, because in this instance any afflictions to the seventh house ruler are describing matters connected to the seventh house. The astrologer can proceed with a judgement, but the outcome is unlikely to be positive.

Saturn in the Seventh House

Most authorities agree that finding a chart with Saturn in the seventh house can either corrupt the judgement of the astrologer, or is an indication that the matter will lurch from one misfortune to another. However, as discussed above, the seventh house considerations only appear to be significant when it is not a seventh house matter under scrutiny. If the Question does concern a seventh house matter, judgement can be given, but the outcome is likely to be unfortunate for the Querent. I would suggest that if Saturn is in the seventh house, but not in the sign adjacent to the one in the cusp and far from the cusp, this may not invalidate the chart. This would also apply to Mars in the same position.

Saturn in the Ascendant

Gadbury tells us

> When Saturn is in the Ascendant of a Question, and infortunate, the Matter propounded is either false, and without ground, or else 'tis past all hope: And if at the same time, the Lord of the Ascendant be Combust or Retrograde, the Querent is either a knave or a fool.[27]

Lilly is of the same opinion when he says "If Saturn be in the Ascendant, especially Retrograde, the matter of that Question seldome or never comes to good."[28] However, this depends on whether Saturn is in his dignity and whether the chart is diurnal or nocturnal. Bonatti asks the reader

> To mind in Questions or Nativities, whether the Significator of the business be an Infortune and Lord of the Ascendant, and in the Ascendant; direct, not vitiated, and in good condition; for then he would both affect the same and bring it to a good conclusion.[29]

Bonatti claims that even if Saturn is not a significator, nor the ascendant ruler, but is positioned in the ascendant and in his exaltation, "he lays aside all his malice, and is restrained from mischief". However, if he is weak and afflicted "his malice and contrariety is increased so as to destroy the business wholly".

As discussed in chapter four, Saturn in the first house can be fortunate if the chart is diurnal, even more so if Saturn is in his dignity. In his chapter on tenth house matters, Lilly states that

> If the Lord of the tenth be joyned to Mars or Saturn, and they or either of them in the ascendant, in their owne house or exaltation, and themselves Orientall and Direct, and not one opposite to another, this doth argue obtaining the Preferment, though with much importunity.[30]

However, the opposite applies where Saturn is in his detriment or fall. In Lilly's chart 'If he should obtain the Parsonage desired', Saturn is in the first house in his fall in Aries.

> Saturn is impeded in the ascendant, and by his presence infortunates the question, causing the querent to despaire in the obtaining it.[31]

The fact that Saturn is in his fall makes the matter turn out badly. In addition, the chart is nocturnal, which adds to the misfortune.

Mars in the first house does not appear to invalidate the chart, but is unfortunate for the Querent unless placed in some of his essential dignities.

I would suggest that Saturn in the first house or the ascendant, placed in either Capricorn or Aquarius (and in this instance probably being the ascendant ruler), can be fortunate for the Querent. In a selection of Questions from the early 1990s when Saturn was in Aquarius, and if positioned in the first house, the matter usually progressed very well for the Querent.

Ascendant Ruler Combust

When the ascendant ruler is combust, judgement cannot be given. There are a number of reasons why this might occur, such as the Querent not disclosing all facts to the astrologer, or perhaps being unaware of them. Occasionally the Querent is in fear and distress.

> If the Lord of the Ascendant be Combust, neither question propounded will take, or the Querent be regulated.[32]

This is good advice, because a combust ascendant ruler is a warning. It may be difficult to be objective about the matter, or perhaps the Querent is being economical with the truth.

Nonetheless, Lilly did answer some Questions like this. Archie Dunlop claims that some astrologers view this as evidence that Lilly did not take his own rules seriously, but this shows a "complete misunderstanding of his work". Dunlop explains that *Christian Astrology*, Lilly's "magnum opus", was never intended as a bible, but that he wrote it firstly as a textbook on astrology and secondly as a casebook. Lilly allowed these considerations to guide his practice. They were part of the grammar of his astrology and like him, we should endeavour to learn and apply this grammar. This, he tells us, may take years of practice.[33]

A Planet in Opposition with its own Domicile

Bonatti points out that if the ascendant ruler or the Moon is in opposition with its own domicile, this implies that the Querent does not wish for the thing to be accomplished but is, in fact, "rather against it". This would take place in the following instances: when the Moon is in Capricorn, the Sun in Aquarius, Jupiter in Gemini or Virgo, Saturn in Cancer or Leo, Venus in Scorpio or Aries, Mercury in Sagittarius or Pisces and Mars in Taurus or Libra.[34] Although this does not render a chart invalid, it is not a positive chart testimony, especially if the planet concerned is a principal significator.

Fortunes and Infortunes Equally Strong

Bonatti tells us that when the Fortunes and the Infortunes are equally strong in the Question, it signifies "no positive judgement, either good or ill; but a kind of indifferency, and that the business will bring neither gain nor loss".[35] Authorities of the past refused to make a judgement in a case like this, but preferred to defer until a better time presented. Ball explains that when the testimonies are equal

> ...the matter propounded ought not to be judged, by reason the Artist then knows not which way the Scales may turn, therefore ought to defer Judgement till a more proper time.[36]

Lilly agrees, saying that in this instance it is not possible to know which way "the Balance will turne" so you must "deferre you your opinion till another question better informe you."[37] In any case, judgement should not be given without more than one testimony: two strong and concurring testimonies are a minimum requirement.

Even though Lilly on occasion proceeds to judge charts which strictly speaking are not radical, this does not show that he disregards the considerations. In cases where he proceeds with judgement despite the warnings, the outcome is unfortunate for the Querent, or brought about with difficulty.

> ...if my Judgements doe vary from the common Rules of the Ancients, let the Candid Reader excuse me, sith he may still follow their Principles if he please; and he must know, that from my Conversation in their Writings, I have attained the Method I follow.[38]

However, for the astrologer, reader or student, these considerations are a very useful guide and should be observed in all Questions, until we are as proficient as Lilly and other authorities of the past! Attempting to proceed with judgement when a chart is not radical, either through a warning, or because it simply does not describe the Question, will inevitably lead to errors and poor judgement.

References

1. Geoffrey Cornelius, *The Moment of Astrology* p.243.
2. Lilly p.121.
3. Gadbury pp.237-238.
4. Bonatus pp.4-5, 7th consideration.
5. ibid p.5, 7th consideration.
6. Gadbury p.237.
7. Barclay p.132.
8. Gadbury p.237.
9. Lilly pp.419-420.
10. ibid p.122.
11. Ball p.60.
12. Lilly p.121.
13. Bonatus p.5, 7th consideration.
14. Ball p.59.
15. Lilly p.122.
16. ibid p.471.
17. Sue Ward, *Astrology Quarterly*.
18. Bonatus p.14, 30th consideration.
19. Ball p.59.
20. Lilly p.122.
21. Robert Hand in *On Reception* by Masha'allah, ARHAT, 1998, p.vi.
22. Ball p.60.
23. Ptolemy, 'The Centiloquy', *Tetrabiblos* trans. J.M.Ashmand, Foulsham, London p.154.
24. Ball p.59.
25. Lilly pp.122-123.
26. Gadbury p.237.
27. ibid
28. Lilly citing the Arabians p.122.
29. Bonatus p.15, 34th consideration.
30. Lilly p.445.
31. ibid pp.437-438.
32. ibid p.123.
33. Archie Dunlop, 'Combust Horaries', *The Astrological Journal*, March/April 1994, Vol.36, No.2, pp.129-133.
34. Bonatus p.28, 77th consideration.
35. ibid p.28, 83rd consideration.
36. Ball p.60.
37. Lilly p.123.
38. ibid p.142.

12

THE QUESTION

The moment of the question is a moment of contact with a greater intelligence. To that extent it is divine. The planetary and fixed star position then extant is an expression of that greater intelligence. From that pattern, that state of the universe, we understand to the best of our ability the outcome of the moment...[1]

The planetary configuration at the moment of a Question has its practical expression in reality. Ball tells us that a chart drawn up for that very moment contains the "possibility or impossibility of the matter propounded".

Whatsoever is Propounded, carrieth in the face thereof, both a Negative, and an Affirmative, that is to say, it may either be brought to pass by a wished Conclusion or not, for all things under the Sun are contingent.[2]

Within the Question, the planetary testimonies (indications) reveal whether the matter enquired about is possible or whether it is impossible. Testimonies which reveal that the outcome is impossible are usually easier to pinpoint than those which reveal that the outcome is possible. Just a single unfortunate testimony such as a Full Moon can render an outcome impossible, whereas the testimonies inclining towards possibility usually need more thought and careful assessment. Occasionally a chart is produced which reveals very strong, clear and fortunate testimony, but this is rare.

Referring to "interrogations", Masha'allah tells us

A certain man who was one of the sages found a book from among the books of the secrets of the stars; and from those books, which kings have treasured, he has expounded upon this subject matter. And he has explained its design concerning questions in all of those matters which mankind might require in its affairs...[3]

From this, the sage puts forward the following, which are relevant to all matters connected to interrogations

- whether something will be or not
- when it will be if it should come to pass

- when it will become apparent that it will not be if it should not come to pass
- what prohibits the matter in case it should not be
- through whom, and from whence it should be if it should come to pass.

Masha'allah explains that the "knowledge and setting forth" of this is due to the conditions of the seven planets, including their essential dignities and debilities, house position, conjunctions, applications or separations, receptions and the pushing of their dispositions. Masha'allah does not imply that there is any free-will involved in a Question or that a Querent can in any way change the course of events. This is only, "according to the command of God".

Direct or Indirect Questions

There are many ways in which a Question might be asked. A Question can be asked directly, for example: Will my son get a place at that school? Alternatively, the Querent can ask whether a certain course of action will bring about the desired outcome: If I take this course of action will my son get a place at that school? Finally, the Querent can ask whether a certain course of action is advisable: Is it a good idea for my son to go to that school?

Is it Good to Proceed?

Lilly tells us that having considered the testimonies in response to the Question and decided whether or not the desired outcome can be achieved, the astrologer must consider whether it is advisable for the Querent to proceed further.

> Having well considered the severall applications and separations of the Lords of those houses signifying your question ... you may begin to judge and consider whether the thing demanded will come to passe yea or no; by what, or whose means, the time when and whether it will be good for the querent to proceed further in his demands yea or no.[4]

Lilly's meaning is slightly ambiguous here, but there are a number of possibilities:

- If the chart testimonies are fortunate, the Querent can expect a favourable outcome, or can proceed with a course of action, if it is action which the Querent has proposed. If the Querent has not proposed action, implicit in the testimony is that the matter enquired about will be achieved, but not necessarily through the Querent's own efforts (this depends on the application of the significators).

- If the chart testimonies are unfortunate, the Querent should not expect to achieve the desired outcome, nor can the Querent proceed further in the matter.

- If the chart testimonies are mixed, the Querent might expect to achieve the desired outcome, but this may or may not be advantageous for the Querent.

The outcome may or may not be achieved through the Querent's own efforts, depending on the application of the significators. Perhaps this is the point at which a decision could be made as to whether or not the Querent should proceed.

Referring to the earlier example: Will my son get a place at that school? Here, the chart can reveal a number of different possibilities. However, it must be emphasised that the strength of the significators will reveal whether or not the school is a good choice, even if this is not directly enquired about. In addition, if the significator of the school applies to an aspect or conjunction with the significator of the Querent and/or her son, the desired outcome will be easily achieved. If not, there will be some difficulty or struggling. There are various scenarios, of which the following are just a few:

- Significators are Fortunes in some of their dignities and well placed. The Querent's son will be offered a place at the school of his choice and this will turn out to be a good choice both for the Querent and her son.

- Significators are Fortunes in their stronger dignities and they have a mutual reception. The Querent's son will be offered a place at the school and this will be an excellent choice both for the Querent and her son.

- Significators are Infortunes weak, in their fall, detriment or peregrine and badly placed. The Querent's son will not be offered a place at the school of his choice.

- Significators are Infortunes in their detriment or fall, but they have a mutual reception. The Querent's son may be offered a place at the school of his choice, but this may turn out to be a poor choice for her son and possibly the Querent. The mutual reception may facilitate a desired outcome, but the debility of the planets is unfortunate.

From the above, it is clear that any action (or inaction) on the part of the Querent, advisable or not, as well as any outcome, is implicit in the chart, even if it is not directly enquired about. This is explored later in this chapter. Significators strong in their dignities produce the desired outcome and this outcome will be to the Querent's advantage. Significators out of their dignities indicate that obtaining the desired outcome is not to the Querent's advantage (or may even prevent the achievement of the desired outcome). Let us suppose that the Question is "Will I marry this man?"

- Principal significators are Fortunes in some of their dignities. This is fortunate for the Querent. In addition to bringing about the desired outcome, the marriage is something which will be to the Querent's advantage. An example of this might be the Moon in Cancer applying to a sextile with Venus in

Virgo in a diurnal chart. The Moon is her domicile and Venus is in her diurnal triplicity. The Querent gets married and the marriage is a happy one.

- Principal significators are Fortunes in one of their stronger dignities and they have a mutual reception. This is the very best indication of all. If the Moon is in Cancer applying to a trine with Jupiter in Pisces, both planets have dignity in their domicile, added to which the Moon is in the exaltation sign of Jupiter and Jupiter is in the triplicity of the Moon (if one allows the Moon a rulership of the water triplicity). This is the very happiest of marriages.

- Principal significators are Infortunes in their detriment, fall or peregrine. This is unfortunate for the Querent. An example of this might be the Sun in Libra applying to a square with Saturn in Cancer. A marriage is most unlikely, but if it takes place it would be a very unhappy one. The Querent might achieve the desired outcome, but this turns out to be far less beneficial than expected.

- Principal significators are a Fortune and an Infortune, but they have a mutual reception. The indications are mixed for the Querent. An example of this might be the Moon in Scorpio applying to a trine with Mars in Capricorn in a nocturnal chart. There is a possibility of achieving the desired outcome, but the marriage is likely to be less beneficial than expected.

In his translation of *On Reception* by Masha'allah, Robert Hand tells us that in a Question about acquiring a Kingship, the principal significator is Saturn in Aries in his fall. Due to Saturn's unfortunate condition, Hand explains that this is "not entirely a Kingship worth having". He confirms that the Moon's opposition with Saturn with a reception signifies that the Querent will acquire the Kingship, but that this will be difficult and the Querent will not get much pleasure having acquired it.

> ... this man will be distressed in his work and will hate it because of the hatred which Saturn has toward this place.[5]

Perfection through opposition is not something which later authors would have allowed, especially with Saturn in such a weak condition.

In a separate Question about a Kingship or Dukedom, Jupiter, principal significator of the Querent, is in the tenth house and receives the Sun and Venus. This is a positive testimony that the Querent will get his wish, according to Masha'allah.[6] However, Jupiter is in his detriment, which, according to Hand, might have prompted later authors to consider that "the dukedom might have some flaw". However, we are told that this would not be an indication that the Querent would fail to get the desired outcome, that is, the Dukedom.[7]

In *Christian Astrology*, Lilly takes a different view regarding both the nature of the aspect and the dignities of the planets involved. For perfection to take place even through a harmonious aspect such as a trine or sextile, significators must be "...out of good Houses and places where they are essentially well dignified..."[8]

With perfection through square, each planet must have "...dignity in the Degrees wherein they are, and apply out of proper and good Houses, otherwise not".

When significators make an opposition, Lilly states, "I have rarely seen any thing brought to perfection by this way of opposition". If perfection does take place, there must be a mutual reception between domicile or exaltation, out of good houses and a translation of light by the Moon.

We cannot be certain just how advantageous – or otherwise – the matters mentioned above really turned out for the Querent in Masha'allah's horoscopes. Significators applying to an opposition with each other, when one of them is in his detriment or fall cannot be considered fortunate. It is clear, however, that in this instance, although the chart testimonies suggest that it is disadvantageous for the Querent to proceed, the application of the Moon towards the significator of the matter enquired about provides confirmation that he will proceed in any case.

The Querent

Masha'allah tells us that the person who makes the enquiry should either do this in person, or write a letter to the astrologer. If he does not know how to write, he should send someone to the astrologer who is "solicitous concerning his matter". Masha'allah also explains that the Querent should only put one Question to the astrologer and not ask a second Question until the first Question has been examined. The Question should be about a matter which is of great concern or a matter of great necessity. Finally he states that "it is not suitable for a sage to look on his own behalf. It is necessary that he asks of another".[9]

Clearly, a Question should only be asked when it is of great importance for the Querent, but whether an astrologer can make an enquiry on his own behalf is probably a matter for debate. This is not something that later authors insisted on.

The Time Frame

It is always best if a Question is framed specifically and within a defined time period. Questions such as "Will I ever get married?" or "Will I ever have a baby?" should be discarded. It is better to ask "Will I be pregnant within two years?" "If I have this treatment will I get pregnant?" In this way, the prospect of a Querent being told that she may never have children or never get married is avoided. Just as importantly, however, is the fact that the chart may not be potent or reliable in describing events far into the future. I do not usually ask, nor accept, Questions from clients beyond a two-year time frame.

Radicality

The way in which a Question is asked and the moment of asking is of crucial importance. If the moment is not right, or the Querent insincere, the chart may include a warning against judgement, in other words, the chart is not radical. If there is a consideration which obviously invalidates the chart, it is best to discard it. If the chart is not a true representation of the situation, or does not describe the people and/or things enquired about, the chart is not radical or perhaps it is unfortunate. It is also important to be aware that the same Question cannot be asked twice. If the answer is likely to displease the Querent or the astrologer, it is always tempting to manipulate the chart, in order to find some pleasant reply. However, if the Querent waits until a period of time has elapsed, when circumstances surrounding the Question have progressed or changed in some way, he or she may then ask a similar Question.

The Question Itself

It is often the day to day concerns of our life that clients enquire about, as well as the bigger Questions about relationships and pregnancies. Every possible Question asked in the context of horary astrology has its potential "moment", but the Question should be asked with sincerity and perhaps when other avenues have been exhausted. It must feel "right" to be asking at that particular moment, whether the Querent is a client or the astrologer. As it is with the Question having an affinity with the moment, so it is this very same moment, which provides an answer given by the heavens. Geoffrey Cornelius tells us that the Question and the answer are one single entity of the same quality of the moment itself.[10] This is what Bonatti means when he talks about "the superior and celestial bodies so they at that time [of the Question] imprint on the thing inquired after, what shall become of it..."[11]

It is interesting to study some of the old Greek horoscopes and discover the type of enquiries which occupied earlier minds. These include a Question asking whether a small lion can be tamed, about the safety of a ship lost at sea and a journey to Athens. These charts date from the first five centuries AD and many were written on papyrus. Masha'allah in about the eighth century AD has several 'clients' who ask whether or not they would acquire a Kingship or Dukedom in that particular year; another asks about things left by a dead person; another about an illness.[12]

There are astrologers who believe that we should not ask large Questions, but only small personal ones. This depends on where your mind ranges. We ask Questions, with which we are deeply concerned. If the heavens do not sympathise with the Question or the Querent, there will be features in the chart which invalidate it. Barclay claims that great matters may be better decided from Event charts, but concedes that William Lilly solved some very great and important Questions in *Christian Astrology*.

The Act of Asking

Bonatti asks the reader to observe what it is that moves a person to ask a Question of an astrologer. He tells us that there are *three motions* to consider

> ... the First, of the mind, when a man is stirred up in his thoughts and hath an intent to enquire; a Second, of the superior and celestial bodies; so that they at that time imprint on the thing inquired after, what shall become of it; the Third, of the free will which disposes him to the very act of enquiring; for although the mind be moved to inquire, 'tis not enough, unless the superior bodies sympathise therewith, nor is such motion of the stars enough, unless by the election of his will the person does actually enquire.[13]

From this we can suppose that if there are certain features within the chart that warn against judgement, this is because the superior bodies do not sympathise with the Question, or the Querent. The astrologer would be wise to take note of the warnings and perhaps discard the chart until a better moment presents itself. Bonatti evidently believes in a certain amount of free will, but also explains that once a Question has been asked, no answer can be given unless the heavens "sympathise". Of particular interest here is the possibility that the motion of the stars is not enough in itself to produce any type of analogous event, unless the person actually asks the Question. This immediately raises the issue of whether a particular event may not occur at all unless the Querent actually goes through the motion of asking.

Sincerity

Lilly counsels his students and readers

> ...not to judge upon every light motion, or without premeditation of the Querent, nor upon slight and trivial Questions, or when the Querent hath not wit to know what he would demand.[14]

Centuries earlier, Bonatti advises the Querent only to approach the astrologer

> ...with a serious intent of being satisfied in some certain and particular doubt, and this not on trifling occasions, or light sudden emotions, much less in matters base or unlawful...[15]

Bonatti tells us that any Questions should only be concerned with

> ...matters of honest importance, and such as have possessed and disturbed his mind for the space of a day and night or longer; unless in sudden accidents which admit not of delay.

Lilly confirms that

> ...a foolish Querent may cause a wise Respondent to err, which brings a scandal upon Art amongst inconsiderate people, whereas the Astrologer is not blameable, but the ignorant silly Querent.[16]

As discussed in the previous chapter, this is the function of the *considerations before judgement*, where the planets signal a warning to the astrologer.

Will my sister pass her viva today and get her PhD?
Will Arsenal beat AC Milan in the Champions League tonight?
Will my daughter pass her cornet and piano exam?

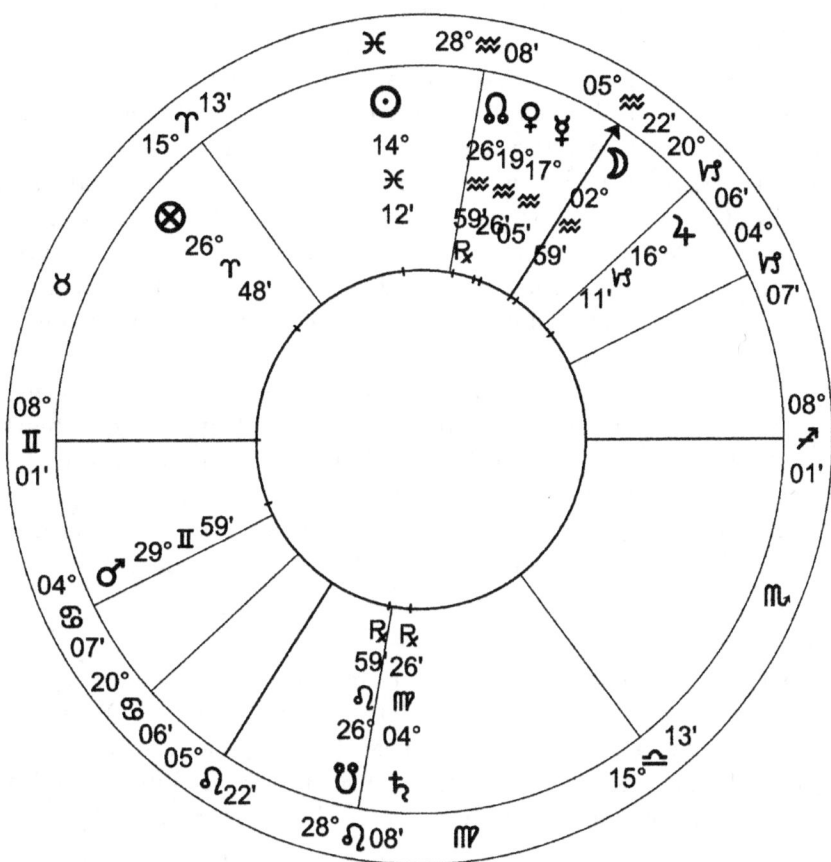

Multiple Questions

It is possible to ask more than one Question if they are all in the Querent's mind at the same time. One chart could also answer more then one Querent. It will describe every event that is happening in that place at that time and will yield a variety of answers according to the Question and significators. The chart on page 247 is an interesting example of three Questions, asked at the same time. For all these Questions it is the tenth house which is the house of the matter enquired about. The Moon in conjunction with the cusp of the tenth house is one testimony of achieving the desired outcome in all three Questions. Mercury, ascendant ruler, positioned in the tenth house is further positive testimony. Mercury applies to a conjunction with Venus, a Fortune in the tenth house. The Moon, Mercury and Venus in the tenth house aspect the ascendant with a trine. However, it is the mutual reception between Mercury and Saturn and between Venus and Saturn which is a most important testimony and without which the matter could not be perfected. Saturn rules the tenth house and as an Infortune might be viewed as unfortunate. Both Saturn and the south node afflict the fifth house by their presence. This is the house of children and of the football game. However, Saturn's mutual receptions remove any malice and help to facilitate a positive outcome. My sister passed her viva, Arsenal beat AC Milan and my daughter passed both exams, the cornet with a distinction. Three planets in the tenth house produce three successes!

Time and Location

The astrologer draws up the chart for the time he or she understands the Question. The astrologer is the medium through which the client is asking the Question, that is, the person who consults the stars. It is clear therefore, that it is the astrologer's location which should be used for the calculation of the chart. Lilly certainly used his own location, as well as the time when he himself understood the Question.

> ...let us suppose a Letter is sent or delivered unto me, wherein I am desired to resolve some doubts; perhaps I receive the Letter into my hands at three of clock in any day of the week, but in regard of some occasions, doe not read it untill four or five hours after; that very hour and minute of hour when I break it open, and perceive the intention of the Querent, is the time to which I ought to erect my Figure, and from thence to draw mine Astrologicall Judgement.[17]

Determinism

There are astrologers who believe that a requirement of the Question is not necessarily prediction. Geoffrey Cornelius explains that if horary is to become part of mainstream astrology

> A barrier that has to be crossed, however, is the notion that a worldly and specific craft method like horary is therefore necessarily fatalistic.[18]

Cornelius is not content with a perfection-type predictive judgement and claims that the requirement to come up front with a yes or no answer to a Question is too strong a demand...[19]

Finding a correct judgement from any chart is not easy, but this is the requirement of a Question. Instead, Cornelius believes that at the point where the chart reveals that the desired outcome is possible, the free will of the Querent can be exercised. This is what he calls "the katarache, or astrology of initiatives".[20] Here, Cornelius tells us that the thing or matter enquired about cannot be brought to pass unless the Querent, taking heed of the symbolism, makes a move. In other words, if the chart is fortunate and reveals the possibility of the Querent attaining what she or he has asked for, the Querent can take steps to fulfil the promise of the chart testimonies.

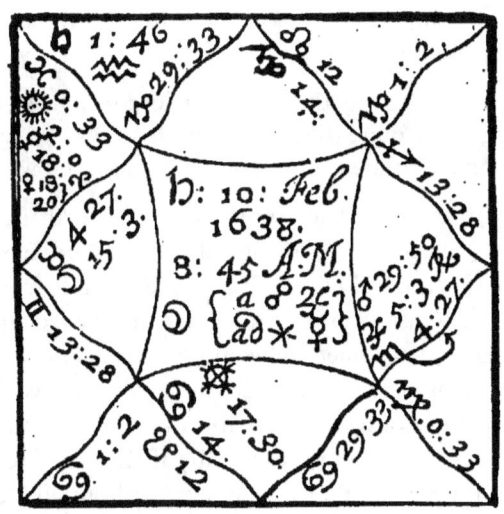

Fish Stolen

Referring to Lilly's chart in *Christian Astrology* depicting the stolen fish, Cornelius argues that

> Lilly's fish will never come back to him on the technical perfection shown unless Lilly embodies the leading symbolism to bring the promise of the horary to pass.[21]

Lilly finds his fish and gets most of them back. Cornelius claims that in these instances

> ...the astrologer has intervened successfully to transmute the pattern of events to bring about good fortune for the client.

Cornelius explains that once Lilly realises that he has a horary perfection of significators to work with, he knows that his actions are likely to succeed.

As Cornelius states himself, however, this presupposes positive chart testimony. Even if his theory were correct, this can only take place where there is perfection between the significators (and of course supporting testimonies). What would Cornelius suggest to the Querent if the chart testimony were negative?

Let us suppose that instead of the Querent's (Lilly) significator applying to the significator of the fish as in Lilly's chart, the significator of the fish applies to the significator of the Querent. Here, it is clear that the fish will be returned to the Querent without any action on the Querent's part. As emphasised in previous chapters, astrologers have demonstrated that in those Questions where the Querent gets what he desires easily and with no effort, the symbolism shows the significator of the thing enquired after applying to the significator of the Querent. Here, the matter is brought to perfection without any involvement on the Querent's part at all.

For example, in *On Reception*, Masha'allah puts forward a Question about the acquisition of Kingship. In this case, if the ruler of the house asked about (in this case the ruler of the tenth house)

> ...itself seeks a joining together with the lord of the Ascendant, then the one asking will acquire the kingship without his own having to seek; it will even come to him sitting in his own house and without effort.[22]

It is the application of the significator of the thing demanded to the significator of the Querent which brings about the positive outcome, with no involvement by the Querent. However, if the ruler of the ascendant is applying to the ruler of the tenth house, this will not happen. Instead, the Querent himself "would seek the kingship, or someone [would] on his behalf".

Dariot gives a similar example, but his perfection takes place through the position of the planets in houses. He explains that if the significator of the matter enquired about is in the first house, especially if there is a reception, it signifies that the Querent will get what he wants easily "without any labour". However, if the ascendant ruler, the Moon, or any of the significators of the Querent, are in the house of the matter enquired about, the Querent will get what he wants but "with much labour".[23] This is a theme which is repeated throughout *Christian Astrology*. Hand in his translation of Masha'allah's On Reception, notes that

> ...things come more easily, i.e., without active 'seeking,' when the... significator of a sought for matter... applies to the lord of the Ascendant rather than the other way around.[24]

Lilly gives another example, where he states that the ruler of the seventh house located in the ascendant shows that the Quesited loves best and the ruler of the ascendant in the seventh house shows the opposite, "for those that apply argue most love..."[25]

Referring once again to the lost fish, let us suppose that instead of Lilly asking the Question, a third party asks the Question instead. A friend of Lilly is concerned about the lost fish so the Question is asked "Will Lilly get his fish back?" If the significator of the fish applies to the significator of the Querent's friend (Lilly), the fish will be returned, without Lilly doing anything at all. If Lilly's significator applies to the significator of the fish, Lilly will get the fish back, through his own efforts. If the testimonies are negative (no application between significators), Lilly won't get the fish back at all, perhaps because he is not prepared to look for them, or because he looks and doesn't find. Whatever the case, Lilly is unaware of the fact that a Question has been asked and, therefore, cannot take up the promise of the symbolism.

These are examples of objective fate, where "the superior and celestial bodies... at that time imprint on the thing inquired after, what shall become of it".[26] Bonatti does not state that the celestial bodies imprint a symbolic possibility, which the Querent may or may not choose to take up. Moreover, it is obvious the Querent cannot, nor would want to, make a move if the chart testimony were negative. The concept of a Querent who embodies the chart testimony (symbolism) is, therefore, undermined at the outset.

Although the concept of *katarche* seems attractive in the context of the positive testimony of the stolen fish, quite how the Querent would, or could, choose to participate in a chart which signifies an illness, or any other type of misfortune, is difficult to envisage. Perhaps the psychological horarists will take up the promise of positive testimony but ignore the warnings of negative testimony? I would agree that in some Questions, the symbolism appears to describe this concept of katarche. But here, I would argue that the course of action to be taken by the Querent is implicit in the chart testimony, as discussed earlier in this chapter.

Cornelius claims that Lilly's marriage Question in *Christian Astrology* is an example of horary astrology "being used not to predict the outcome but to change it". In this chart, where Lilly predicts a positive outcome for the lady, Cornelius claims that the "stars were not even inclining this way".[27] I would suggest that in fact, the chart testimonies are very clear and do indeed signify the possibility of achieving the desired outcome.

Lilly himself explains the reason. The marriage, he confirms, is due to the application of the principal significators with a sextile (and from good houses) and the application of the Moon to the ascendant ruler the Sun, which although through opposition has a strong mutual reception. However, the most important testimony, says Lilly, and without which there could not have been a positive outcome, is

> ...the application of Jupiter to a sextile aspect of Saturn, Lord of the seventh, receiving his virtue which Saturn did render unto him, and he again transferred to the Sun, Lord of the ascendant...[28]

This is an example of the rendering of virtue, which is explored further in chapter fourteen. The symbolism is positive for the lady, so she will be married. The chart shows the lady's significator, the Sun, applying to the significator of the person sought after, Saturn. She is the applying planet, so she makes the move. If the significator of the person enquired about had been applying to her significator,

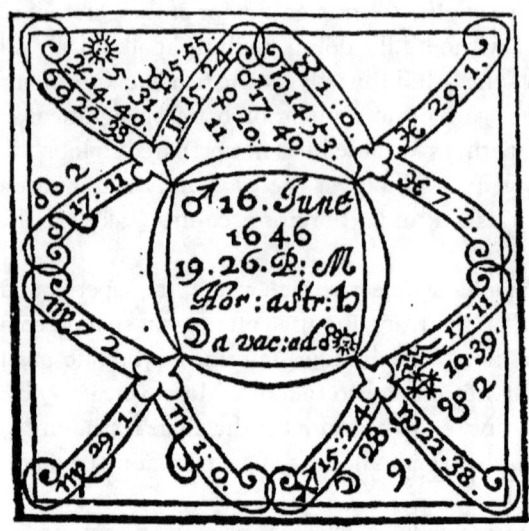

A Lady, if marry the Gentleman desired?[29]

she would not have had to take any action. In this instance, the matter would have been brought to perfection without any involvement on her part at all.

To illustrate the point about objective fate I include an example of a third party Question. In this instance, whether the testimony is positive or negative, the individual enquired about has no option to take up the symbolism, because he is ignorant of it.

The Querent asks about a divorced friend who is planning to move to Cambridge in the hope of meeting a new partner. The Querent is concerned about the friend moving away. Although the Question does not ask specifically about a new partner, the chart testimonies reveal (to the Querent's surprise) that he will meet a woman fairly soon and close to home, so the possible move to Cambridge won't take place. In fact, the friend met a woman about four weeks later, although he knew nothing about the Question or the chart. It could be argued that asking a third party Question is not legitimate, but if it is well-intentioned, if the planets sympathise and the chart is radical, it is difficult to understand why not.

The Querent's friend is signified by the eleventh house and the ruler of the eleventh house Jupiter. Jupiter in the terms of Mercury describes the friend as tall and quite large. Jupiter's position in the seventh house confirms radicality in that the friend is looking for love. With the Lot of Fortune in conjunction with the eleventh house cusp, he is going to be lucky. Venus in her triplicity applies to a conjunction with Jupiter in the seventh house. She comes to him. The Moon applies to a sextile aspect with Venus from the fifth house with no interference. Venus and Jupiter as Fortunes indicate a harmonious relationship, although Mars on the ascendant could cause a bit of trouble!

Will my friend move to Cambridge?

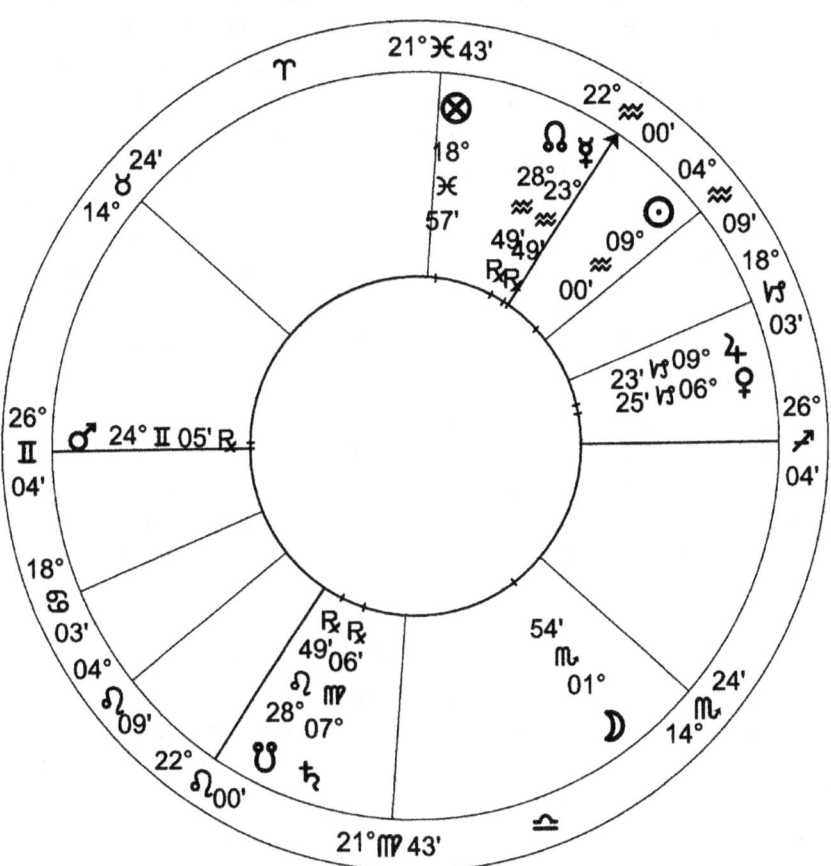

Many modern astrologers appear not to embrace the concept of determinism, or objective fate, presumably because they prefer the idea of free will and that is understandable. However, there are Questions which only reveal an objective fate, as in the example above. In a Question about an illness there can be no free will involved, since it is reasonable to suppose that a Querent would not wish to be ill and would not wish to take up the promise of the symbolism to become ill. Similarly in Questions about love, there is absolutely no possibility whatsoever that a Querent can embody the symbolism in a chart in order to make another person fall in love.

As pleasant as it is to believe that the symbols (chart testimony) in the Question only represent a *possibility* in which the astrologer may or may not choose to participate, the evidence does not support the idea that the stars are *non cogunt*.[30]

Writing in the seventeenth century, Morin himself, although an advocate of free will, tells us

> ...the births and the events of the lives of men are linked by Providence with a view to a coincidence necessary for the common realisation of destinies, so that, for example, someone who is at birth destined to be assassinated does not fail to meet his murderer, and someone who must be unhappy in marriage will always find the woman necessary for this.[31]

The Psychological Horary

Closely linked to the concept of the *katarche* is the notion of the psychological horary. Some astrologers believe that any division between psychological astrology and traditional astrology is unwelcome and that a merger between the two should be embraced. In reality there is only one astrology, the astrology which has been handed down to us from our ancestors.

Geoffrey Cornelius welcomes the idea of a psychological horary. This, he claims, is because the symbolism in a psychological horary moves people and allows them to change. In terms of psycho-analysis this can be viewed as desirable and perhaps achievable. But this is not the purpose of a Question. The act of enquiring is not to ask the heavens to produce chart testimony that the Querent can either choose to accept, to ignore, or use to grow and change. The concept of a psychological horary, therefore, not only represents a contradiction, but is also invalid.

The purpose of a Question is to enquire as to whether the desired outcome is possible or impossible. Proponents might claim that the psychological horary gives a better picture of what is involved. Again, this is not the purpose of a Question. If the Querent needs to have clarification as to what is involved, the Question should not be asked at all. If the matter enquired about needs to be made more explicit through symbolism, it is not clear in the Querent's mind, it may be insincere or perhaps the Querent has come to "vapour" with the art and should not be making an enquiry.[32]

Fortunately, the chart testimonies can warn the astrologer as to the insincerity of a Querent. Having said that, it is quite possible that the advocates of the psychological horary might put a positive spin on the warning, or perhaps ignore it altogether?

The danger of mixing psychology with horary astrology is nowhere better illustrated than in the following chart.

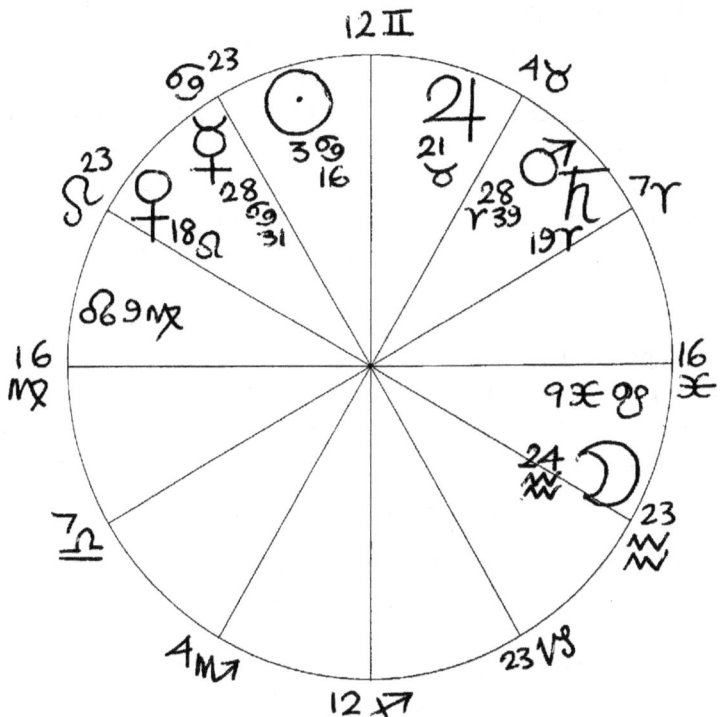

A gentlewoman desired to know if she should have an aged man; yea, or no[33]
14 June 1644 (OS) 10.30am.

In his commentary on Lilly's judgement, Cornelius attempts to mix psychology with astrology and thereby misses the point in Lilly's handling of the matter. A lady asks Lilly if she should marry an old man. Chart testimonies confirm that in fact the lady is not interested in the old man. Lilly reports that the significators show that "the maide's affection was alienated from the old man, and that she desired such a man as Mars..." However, Lilly tells her that, in terms of her affection towards this man, "she should be crossed therein" because the significators are unfortunate. The lady admits to all of this "with teares". Clearly, the lady is hoping the old man has an estate to settle on her, but Lilly, finding the two Infortunes Saturn and Mars in the eighth house (the old man's estate) realises that the old man's estate is encumbered. Consequently, he asks the lady if she could "require a joynture of the aged man..." so that she can discover this for herself. Of course, the old man cannot do this, because, as Lilly has predicted, there is

> ...an incumbrance on his Land, as Saturn with Mars, in his second house of substance doth excellently signifie...

After this, Lilly reports, "they broke off all termes of marriage, directly as I told her". What is in essence a beautiful and, as Cornelius calls it, a "masterly" judgement is now subjected to a lengthy psycho-analysis covering several pages. Cornelius not only equates Mars in the eighth house with "repressed desire", but asks the reader to believe that Lilly did not actually make a prediction here. Lilly's intention, he claims, is to get the Querent to test the situation. The point missed is that Lilly already knows the deal: that the testimonies represent no possibility whatsoever that the lady can have the estate, nor the soldier, whom she prefers to the aged man.

Cornelius, mixing in a little more psychology, informs us that if the lady admits her "repression", there is a slim chance that Mars might then allow a collection of light and subsequently a marriage to the aged man.[34] Just a brief look at the position of Mars tells us that Mars is not only unhelpful, but is actually malefic in terms of the Question. There is no way he can collect light:

- Mars is positioned in the unfortunate eighth house
- Mars afflicts the ascendant ruler with a square
- Mars does not aspect the ascendant
- Mars has reduced strength being in late degrees of his domicile
- Mars is about to move into the sign of his detriment
- Mars, a nocturnal planet, is incorrectly placed above the horizon in a diurnal chart.

As if that was not enough, the principal significators, Mercury and Jupiter, are separating. The testimonies are negative. Achieving the desired outcome is impossible. The chart is a beautiful example of objective fate. The lady is hoping to marry the old man for his money, but there isn't any. She would in reality prefer the soldier, but he is not interested. Lilly asks her to confirm his findings (that is, to enquire about a jointure from the old man). She duly confirms that this is not possible. The chart provides clear and unambiguous evidence that the Querent cannot embody, nor take up, any possibilities produced by the chart testimonies in order to achieve the outcome she desires, because the testimonies are negative.

For serious students of astrology, especially those concerned with Questions, the psychological horary must be viewed with scepticism. It is something of a contradiction in terms and similar to the 'popular astrology' that Gauquelin refers to in his famous book when he states that it is "cut off from its eastern origins...a dismal caricature of what it once was". In the context of modern astrology, Gauquelin states that

> ...all astrological consultation, even the most serious, is today only a caricature of what it once was. Up to a point it can even be claimed that it is no longer astrology.[35]

Third Party Questions

Astrologers of the past did not appear to have an issue about asking third party Questions. They were more concerned that the Querent should be well intentioned and that the Question asked shouldn't be trivial, insincere or unlawful. Although Masha'allah warns the astrologer to accept only "honest and serious questions", he makes it clear, as discussed earlier in this chapter, that the astrologer can also respond to a person

> ...who with much concern and solicitude for himself or for another with whom he is closely involved comes as an anxious inquirer himself or through a messenger.[36]

This is perfectly reasonable. A genuine enquiry about the health of a relative or parent, or the whereabouts of a friend, for example, is acceptable. Some commentators have suggested that third party Questions are generally "weak and voyeuristic". According to Maggie Hyde when we study the Nativity of a public figure, "the timing is given by God or nature". It is another matter, however, when a moment of time is assigned to symbolise a third party or issue, when that moment of time becomes "both the generator and the medium of that moment".[37]

There is no doubt that Questions regarding a person's own concerns are clearer and easier to judge. However, if the Question is sincere and earnest the heavens will provide a radical chart. If the heavens do not sympathise, no answer will be given. Kaye Miller explains

> If the desire 'to know' is truly earnest, then a good, valid and descriptive chart will ensue (no stricture pending). If one's interest is well-intentioned (as I imagine it usually is) then I do not believe that heaven holds itself judge and jury.[38]

Kaye Miller believes that if "as above, so below is applicable, then an objective, non-judgemental display of facts is what you'll get." Rose Elliot agrees and also explains

> ...the issue of intrusion of privacy when using third-party charts is one which all astrologers need to address, not just horary practitioners... if anything, horary charts offer a safeguard in this respect because of the considerations which must be weighed up beforehand.[39]

The issue of third party Questions seems to have occupied the minds of scholars and astrologers for centuries. As far back as the twelfth century in the document *The Correspondence Between the Rabbis of Southern France and Maimonides about Astrology*, the Rabbis ask Maimonides

> What if one has decided in his heart, and made it known that he does not wish to ask nor know his luck, for better and for worse; and then some people, who know of that, go and inquire about him, without his knowledge, which they would not have done, had they not known about his decision. Would our teacher tell us whether such an inquiry is valid like [the] others as instructed by astrologers in the judgement of questions?[40]

In response to the Rabbis' detailed and astrological questions, Meira Epstein tells us that Maimonides makes no response, but instead condemns astrology and pursues the philosophical and religious discussion. The important point here, however, is the actual Question asked by the Rabbis. Meira Epstein tells us that the Rabbis wish to know that if a Question is asked about a person's personal fortunes, does that person need to know that this was done in order for the answer to be valid? Is it necessary for a person to consciously participate in the process of astrological enquiry? Does a person's conscious refusal to know his fortune affect the judgement and negate its validity?[41] This raises a hugely important philosophical and theological issue, which unfortunately is beyond the scope of this book.

I would suggest that in some instances, a third party Question can be valid: well-intentioned third party Questions are acceptable. In this book, it is clearly demonstrated that a person does not have to consciously participate in the process of enquiry. However, if an individual has made it clear that he or she does not wish to know their "fortune", it seems that a Question asking about that person's fortune cannot be well-intentioned. Nicholas Campion tells us more

> Some would doubt whether a question in which the astrologer has no personal involvement can be adequately answered. Others would argue that any question represents a valid enquiry. Others still would say that only the horoscope itself can tell us this.[42]

It is that very moment when the astrologer seeks assistance from the heavens and asks a Question, which carries within it the description of the circumstances, a description of the people contained in the Question, as well as the possibility or impossibility of achieving the desired outcome to that Question. Whether or not an event or development would, or could, take place without the very act of asking, is something we can never know. Does the Querent have to go through the process of enquiring, so that the superior and celestial bodies can, at that very moment in time, "imprint on the thing inquired after, what shall become of it"?[43]

Whatever one's beliefs about determinism, it is clear that the asking of a Question must be sincere, well thought out and something which has occupied the Querent's mind for sometime. It is a Question asked in this manner which will produce a radical chart and a clear answer.

References

1. Olivia Barclay, 1984, 'A Natal Astrologer's Guide to Horary', *Transit*, the magazine of the Astrological Association, February 1984.
2. Ball p.61.
3. Masha'allah p.1.
4. Lilly p.124.
5. Masha'allah p.43.
6. ibid p.61.
7. Hand in *On Reception* by Masha'allah p.82.
8. Lilly pp.124-125.
9. Masha'allah p.6.
10. Geoffrey Cornelius, *The Moment of Astrology*.
11. Bonatus p.1, 1st consideration.
12. Masha'allah. Examples throughout *On Reception*.
13. Bonatus p.1, 1st consideration.
14. Lilly
15. Bonatus p.1, 2nd consideration.
16. Lilly footnote in Bonatus, p.1, 2nd consideration.
17. Lilly p.166.
18. Geoffrey Cornelius, *The Moment of Astrology*, Arkana, p.173.
19. ibid p.153.
20. In this section Geoffrey Cornelius, 'A Modern Astrological Perspective' in *Christian Astrology*, Regulus 1984, pp 869-871 and *The Moment of Astrology*, p.154.
21. Lilly pp.397-399.
22. Masha'allah p.35.
23. Dariot p.62.
24. Hand's footnotes in *On Reception*, p.24.
25. Lilly p.305.
26. Bonatus p.1, 1st consideration.
27. Geoffrey Cornelius, *The Moment of Astrology*, pp.155–156.
28. Lilly p.387.
29. ibid p.385.
30. Geoffrey Cornelius, A Modern Astrological Perspective, in *Christian Astrology*, p.870.
31. Morin p.107.
32. Lilly, his Address in *Anima Astrologiae*.
33. Geoffrey Cornelius, his reproduction of Lilly's chart from *England's Propheticall Merline*, 1644, cited in *The Moment Of Astrology*, p.159.
34. Geoffrey Cornelius, *The Moment of Astrology*, pp.158-164.
35. Michel Gauquelin, 1966, *Astrology and Science*, translated by James Hughes, Peter Davies, London, p.87.

36. Masha'allah, 'On the Rationale of Inquiry and its Method' from *The Book of the Nine Judges* (1508), translated by Graeme Tobyn, (unpublished, COA Latin Translation Group, 1993), quoted by Maggie Hyde, Astrological Journal, Sep/Oct 1995, Vol.37.No.5.
37. Maggie Hyde, *Astrological Journal*, Jan/Feb 1996, Vol.38, No.1, p.43.
38. Kaye Miller, quoted by Maggie Hyde in 'Third Party Horaries', *The Astrological Journal*, September/October 1995, Vol.37, No.5,p.335.
39. Rose Elliot, *Astrological Journal*, Jan/Feb 1996, Vol.38, No.1, p.44.
40. *The Correspondence Between the Rabbis of Southern France and Maimonides about Astrology* p.10.
41. ibid editor's note (Meira Epstein), p.10.
42. Nicholas Campion, *Astrology Quarterly*, Summer 1993, Volume 63, No.3, pp.5-6.
43. Bonatus p.1, 1st consideration.

13

PLANETARY TESTIMONY PRECEDING JUDGEMENT

In William Lilly's publication of *Anima Astrologiae*, containing Bonatti's one hundred and forty six considerations (*Tractatus Quintus*), as well as the "choicest aphorisms" of Jerome Cardan, we are told by Cardan that the astrologer should base his judgements on established and approved rules of Judicial Astrology and not be too eager to form principles of his own with regard to judgements on any possible events and which are not clearly shown in the chart under consideration. Cardan was writing well over four hundred years ago, but the same problem persists today, because modern astrologers have not taken the time to become acquainted with the tools and techniques of the tradition.

> An Astrologer is so far only true and honest, as he depends in his conjectures on principles of natural philosophy...[1]

Cardan also tells us that astrologers should not make absolute or definite predictions

> ... since those Arts which are inherent in their proper subjects, cannot promise any certainty concerning matters to come, the Astrologer ought never to pronounce anything absolutely or peremptorily of future contingencies.

This is good advice, but it is clear that even for astrologers who do attempt to base judgements on these established and approved rules, it is not possible to accurately predict in every single instance, because "prediction is a human activity and hence fallible".[2] However, Coley tells us that despite the difficulties involved in judgement, we should not be discouraged:

> ...to judge of things to come, is no easy task, nor indeed can it always be exactly performed; but we may come near the truth, and differe from it only in some small time or circumstances; which difficulty should not at all discourage us from studying and endeavouring to obtain as great a knowledge therein, as Human minds are capable of..[3]

In this chapter I examine the testimonies which are important to the judgement of a chart in an overall sense. It is these testimonies which, to a certain extent, allow the astrologer to determine "the possibility or impossibility of the matter propounded".[4] This chapter is intended to provide a guide or overview, so that the most important features in evaluation can be identified at the outset. In chapter fourteen, I focus more specifically on those testimonies which produce good fortune and which bring about the desired outcome in a Question. In chapter fifteen I examine the chart testimonies which are likely to prevent the achievement of the desired outcome, or at least reduce the good that might be expected.

The Nativity

In the judgement of any Question, probably the most important information required is the details of the Querent's Nativity. If this is available, the astrologer can subsequently ascertain "what correspondency there is between the Radix and the Question propounded..." and, according to Lilly, be helped in the judgement.[5]

For the individual, a Nativity takes precedence over a Question or Election. Lilly tells us that if the Nativity does not indicate that something is possible, for example, a pregnancy, no promising horary can contradict that significance.

> When women have bin long without children, and propound such a question, see if their Nativity did not originally deny children...for if the Radix affirme Barrennesse, it's impossible any promising Horary Question can contradict its signification...[6]

Coley tells us that if the Querent has details of his own Nativity, what he calls "his own Radical Figure of Birth" he can judge a Question more accurately from this. However, if the details of the Nativity are unavailable, the Question is acceptable.

> ...if the Nativity be but known, an Horary Question is but of small validity, especially in general Questions, such as these, viz, Shall I ever be Rich, or attain to Honour or Preferment in the World?...But if that [Nativity] cannot be procured, a Question is acceptable it being as it were a second Birth, viz. The Birth or motion of the mind.[7]

Lilly explains that when an individual asks a Question of the astrologer (the very first Question),

> ...they have a Signe of the same Triplicity ascending in their Question, agreeable to the nature of the ascendant in their Nativity...[8]

For example, if the Querent has Gemini ascending at birth, it is probable that in the Question the ascendant will be either Libra or Aquarius, which are signs of the same triplicity. This can be a help in establishing radicality. Ramesey, in his discussion of Elections, tells us that

> ...there can be no time elected... advantageous to anyone whose nativity or time of birth is not exactly known; for according unto it must you frame your election, together with respect to the revolution of the year.[9]

Ramesey confirms that past authorities such as "Zahel, Bonatti, Messahalla and Dariot" report that "in case the nativity of a man cannot be obtained, respect must be had to the time of the question".[10] In this instance, a significator in the Question will be of the same nature as one in the Nativity. This will occur if the Question is radical.

The Universal Question

If the Question relates to a year of the Querent's life, or perhaps the whole life, it is called a Universal Question. In *Tools & Techniques of the Medieval Astrologers*, Zoller confirms that if the time of birth of an individual was unknown, a Question would have to be asked instead. This might relate to an individual's fortune for that year, or perhaps for the entire life. Zoller explains that the concept of the Universal Question was a technique developed by Albumasar (Abu Ma'shar).[11] In the Proem in *Anima Astrologiae* we are told that "Questions as well universal as particular" are one of the six areas relevant for astrological study. Gadbury tells us that when it is not possible to obtain the details of the Nativity, astrologers have made use of Questions to "supply the defect"

> From a Question seriously propounded, the Artist may give such satisfaction unto the Querent, as if his Nativity were known. For as the Nativity is the time of the Birth of the Body, the Horary Question is the time of the Birth of the Minde...[12]

In *Christian Astrology* Lilly includes examples of a Universal Question. The chart testimonies relating to this type of Question (concerning wealth), are examined in chapter seven.[13]

- If he should be rich, or subsist of himselfe without Marriage?
- By what meanes he should attaine Wealth?
- The time when?
- If it would continue?

Weighing up the Testimony

Before any attempt at chart evaluation can be made, the astrologer must have a thorough knowledge of the nature of the planets, the signs, the houses, the fortitude or debility of the planets and the strength (or otherwise) of the aspects. All this must be combined in order to arrive at a judgement of planetary strengths and to conclude as to the possibility or impossibility of achieving the desired outcome. The key points are:

- Are the significators and the Moon strong enough to bring the matter to perfection (a positive outcome)?
- If they are weak, do they receive any assistance?

- Are they so weak and lacking in assistance that they have no power to bring the matter to perfection?

The testimonies contained within the chart need careful assessment: in some instances the testimonies support each other, in others the testimonies conflict. More than one indication (testimony) must be found to produce a certain or even probable answer.

In arriving at a correct judgement, experience is the greatest advantage, but a thorough knowledge of horary rules comes first. As Lilly tells us; the astrologer must "mix Art and Reason together..."[14] In my experience clear and very fortunate testimony is uncommon, whereas the opposite is true of less fortunate testimony. It is rare to find a planet very strong in accidental and essential dignities, free from any affliction. From a practical point of view, it is more likely that a client will seek advice from the astrologer when they are at a difficult point in their life. In terms of a relationship for example, it is rare to find a client asking a Question when a relationship is going well. Nevertheless, when the chart testimonies are obviously unfortunate (or fortunate), judgement is simpler. It is the charts where the testimonies are more evenly balanced that require most skill. When the testimonies are very even the astrologer defers judgement.

To reiterate the point made in previous chapters, Bonatti explains that in order to be of the very greatest help in a chart, a planet should be

> ...in his own House; in an Angle on the very minute of the Cusp, direct, swift of course, in reception, and free from all affliction and impediment; which most seldom happens.[15]

Jupiter's Strength in Essential and Accidental Dignity

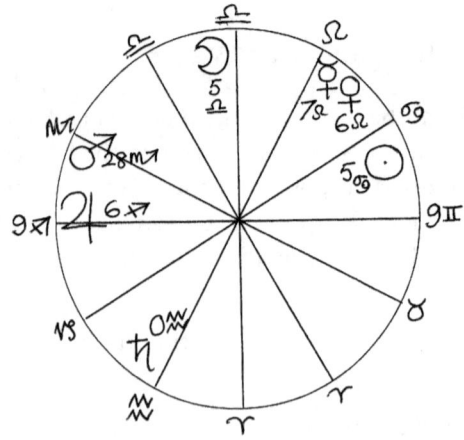

♃ is strong - in the cusp, direct, swift, free from all afflictions or impediments and he has a mutual reception with the ☉.

He is in his own domicile and terms and in his hayyiz.

In a nocturnal chart ♃ would gain strength being in his triplicity but would be incorrectly placed above the horizon.

Bonatti tells us about the "true method of judging" and how the astrologer can work out "the truth of what the stars shall show..." The following points are a summary of the considerations and chart testimonies which, according to Bonatti, should be "considered and heeded":[16]

- Does the Querent propose the Question "really and intentively or not"?
- Is the chart radical?
- What are the aspects of the planets with the significators?
- Are the significators and the Moon angular, succedent or cadent?
- Where does any help for the Querent come from?
- What are the aspects with the Fortunes or Infortunes? If the Fortunes are stronger this is positive, if not it is negative. If the chart testimonies are equal, it is "indifferent".
- Is the ascendant ruler in the house of the thing enquired about, or is it aspecting the ruler of that house?
- Are the signifcators joined together? If not, is there a translation of light?
- Do the significators agree in their nature with each other?
- Is the receiver of the significator's virtue or disposition a Fortune or Infortune? Is that planet strong or weak? Does that planet behold the significator or the Moon with a good aspect or a bad aspect?

Bonatti also asks the astrologer to establish the "mirth of the querent"! He explains that if the ascendant ruler is in the fifth house or in conjunction with the ruler of the fifth house and is free from affliction by the Infortunes, the Querent is happy. However, the Querent will be sad if the significators are in the sixth, seventh, eighth or twelfth houses, unless the Question is connected to something signified by one of these houses.

Morin concludes that there are four determining factors in judgement:[17]

- The position of a planet in a house
- The essential dignities
- The aspects
- The antiscia

The essential dignities, aspects and antiscia have been examined earlier in this book. The position of the planets needs fuller examination.

Position and Rulership of the Planets

The position and rulership of a planet are two very powerful factors, but I would agree with Morin, that a planet's "physical position is more powerful than that by Rulership alone..." [18]

Morin explains that a planet exerts its "complex power" by virtue of its own nature and by virtue of certain accidental conditions such as position in relation to the Sun (oriental, occidental, under sunbeams, combust), and connections with other planets, but principally with the ruler of the house in question and with the ruler of the first house. A planet also exerts its power by virtue of the rulership that it has over other houses, while at the same time it physically occupies a different house (or that same house). For example, Jupiter and Venus in the seventh house would produce a happy marriage, whereas Mars or Saturn might prevent it, or create some sort of misfortune surrounding the marriage. However, if Jupiter at the same time rules the tenth house, this might have different implications for the marriage than if Jupiter rules the twelfth house. Judgements can also be made from the ruler of that house, in this case the ruler of the seventh house.[19]

The Sun and Moon

The condition of the Sun and Moon is of principal importance in terms of the strength or otherwise of any chart. In view of the fact that the Moon is generally the most important body in the chart, it is important to take the advice of Bonatti and

> ...keep a diligent eye to the Moon; for she of all the planets has the greatest similitude and correspondence with inferior things, both in general and particular...she seems a Mediatrix between Superior and Inferior Bodies.[20]

Robert Zoller, in his discussion of the Lot of Fortune, tells us that this Lot or Part (of Fortune) is preferred above all the other Parts in the same way as the luminaries are preferred to all the other stars.[21] Ptolemy in his *Tetrabiblos* states that

> ...the sun and the moon are the marshals and, as it were, leaders of the others; for they are themselves responsible for the entirety of the power, and are the causes of the rulership of the planets, and, moreover, the causes of the strength or weakness of the ruling planets.[22]

A footnote in the *Tetrabiblos* states that the reason why the luminaries exert such power is because they are the ones which "submit to eclipse and thereby determine the places of eclipses and the rulers of these places". There is no doubt that the luminaries are the most important of all celestial bodies and must be given due weight in judgement. In terms of a Nativity, Ptolemy takes as "prorogatives"

> ...the four regions of greatest authority, sun, moon, horoscope [ascendant], the Lot of Fortune, and the rulers of these regions.[23]

According to Morin, when the Sun and the Moon are located in good houses of the Nativity, they

> ...produce marvellous and extraordinary luck, above all when in good Zodiacal state, and likewise by means of their good aspects. But in the bad places... and by their bad aspects, they will effect great calamities, above all if in unfavorable Zodiacal state.[24]

Morin confirms that Saturn and Mars are enemies of the lights or luminaries (Sun and Moon) in practically all affairs, but especially Saturn, who is the most destructive. Jupiter on the other hand is, of all the planets, the one whose "cooperation" is almost always beneficial.[25] In terms of judgement, the strength of the Moon (or otherwise) can mean the difference between a positive outcome and a negative outcome. However, if there is a New Moon, Full Moon or Eclipse in the chart, a positive outcome is almost impossible to expect. Bonatti points out that

> Famous are those persons in whose Nativities the Moon receives the light of many Planets, or is joined to some powerful Royal Fixed Star. (For example Mirach, Rigel, or Sirius).[26]

Lilly asks the student to

> Have speciall regard to the strength or debility of the Moon, and it's farre better the Lord of the Ascendant be unfortunate than she, for she brings unto us the strength and vertue of all the other Planets, and of one Planet to another.[27]

Bonatti explains that the Moon "participates in signification of everything". The Moon is concerned in the signification of "every Question, Nativity, Enterprise and Business, and her good condition to show the good issue of the thing; and so on the contrary".[28]

> ...her Virtue and Power is such and so great, that if the Lord of the Ascendant or other Significator of a business be so weak and afflicted that he cannot bring it about and complete it as he ought: if she be but strong it shall, notwithstanding, be accomplished.[29]

Due to the fact that the Moon moves swiftly and can transfer the fortune of one planet to another, Bonatti calls her

> ...a kind of 'internuncio' between them, carrying their virtues from one to another, by receiving the disposition of one planet and bearing it to another.

Ibn Ezra, referring to Nativities, explains that the Moon "transfers brilliancy from one to the other". He claims that the ancients said that the Moon influences "every deliberation and the beginning of any task".

> If it [Moon] is in its ascendancy and its circumstances are favorable, any thing which one may start at that moment will meet with success, and contrariwise if it is in the unfavorable circumstances.[30]

Gauquelin writing many centuries later in 1969, tells us about the influence of the Moon on life forms.

> At Suez, sea urchins and crabs are called 'full' at the full moon and 'empty' at the new moon. At Nice, Naples and Alexandria it is claimed that the finest sea urchins are those of the full moon.[31]

Gauquelin reports that scientists have confirmed that the sea urchin *Centrechinus setosus* has a rhythm linked to the lunar month. Other sea creatures and mammals have been the subject of further statistical analysis.

Aspects with the Moon

It is important to consider from which planet the Moon has separated and which planet she is moving towards. The planet from whom she separates signifies what has already happened; the planet to whom she applies signifies what is to come. According to Bonatti, in a Question where the Moon separates from an Infortune and applies to a Fortune, it indicates that the worst is past and that whatever happened before will now end happily for the Querent. However, if the Moon separates from a Fortune and applies to an Infortune, the contrary will take place, in other words whatever happened before was good but comes to nothing in the end. If the Moon moves from one Fortune to another, this signifies that it was good before and it will be good in the future. If the Moon moves from one Infortune to another Infortune "it will be an ugly conclusion". This is important whether it is a Question, Nativity or any other chart under consideration.[32]

The First and Tenth House

Any planets ruling the first or tenth houses or placed in the first and the tenth houses have particular importance. If they are in poor zodiacal state "a very harmful influence falls on the meanings of these vitally important houses". This, according to Morin, is especially the case if the planets in these houses, or the rulers of these houses, apply with a bad aspect to other planets in a poor zodiacal state. However, if they apply to planets in good zodiacal state, especially with a good aspect, misfortune will give way to a more fortunate situation.

> By this observation alone of the Planets in I or X or their Rulers one can immediately make a judgment as to whether the Nativity is fortunate or unfortunate...[33]

Planetary Strength

Morin tells us that when two (or more) planets make a conjunction, square, or opposition with each other, in order to find out which of the two "will prevail over the other" there are four factors to consider: The natural rank of planets, their zodiacal state, their terrestrial state and their approach and departure (application and separation).[34]

The Natural Rank of Planets

In regard to the ranking of planets, Morin claims that

> All things being equal, the Sun and Moon... prevail over the others, and the Sun prevails over the Moon. Among the other Planets, the superior ones, Saturn, Jupiter and Mars, prevail over the inferior ones, Venus and Mercury.[35]

In this way, he claims that if, for example, Venus makes a square with Saturn, it follows that Venus is more strongly under the influence of Saturn than Saturn is under the influence of Venus. In other words, an event signified by Venus is strongly influenced by Saturn, but an event signified by Saturn is not very strongly influenced by Venus. This is an extremely important point. A Superior such as Saturn or Mars afflicts an Inferior, such as Venus and Mercury, when making a square or opposition, but an Inferior cannot afflict a Superior to the same extent.

What is unclear from a reading of various texts is whether a Superior derives any benefit from its aspect with an Inferior. In the example above, does Saturn derive any benefit from Venus or does his affliction wipe out any good that can be expected? What is clear, however, is that in most instances a square or opposition with an Inferior does little or less damage than one with a Superior (apart from Jupiter whose aspects are usually fortunate).

Venus and Saturn: their Ranking in a Question

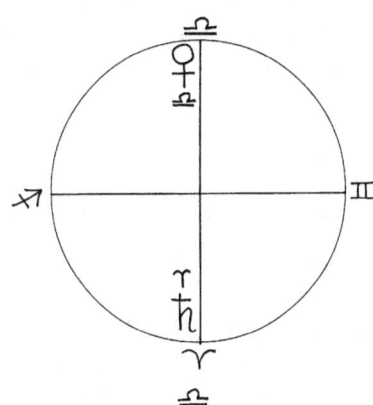

♀ – significator of the job is damaged by her opposition with ♄.

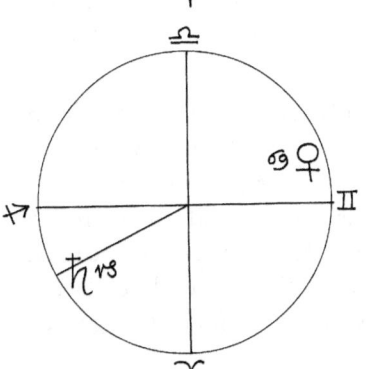

♄ – significator of the money is not damaged much or at all by his opposition with ♀.

Zodiacal State

Morin's definition of a planet in a good zodiacal state is when it has dignity in its domicile, exaltation, or triplicity, when it is oriental of the Sun, occidental of the Moon, free from any bad aspects with the Infortunes, and is in rapid or direct motion. Such a planet is regarded as a benefic, whatever house it occupies and even more so when it is helped by good aspects with the Fortunes. A planet in bad zodiacal state is in the opposite condition. Morin reports that a planet in a better zodiacal state

> ...whether by Domicile [Sign], Exaltation, or Triplicity, its position relative to the Sun, etc., will outweigh one which has a more feeble Zodiacal state.[36]

Morin gives as an example a situation where Mars in Capricorn makes a square with the Sun in Libra. Here, Mars hurts the Sun more than Mars itself is hurt, because the Sun is in his fall. This is somewhat contradictory to the writings of Bonatti and most authors of the past, who claim that a planet dignified does less harm. The Sun in his fall would be expected to hurt Mars more. Moreover, a square with the Sun is always harmful to a certain extent, no matter what sign he is in. It is true that in this example Mars outweighs the Sun by strength, but his power to bring good fortune (or to cause less harm), is also strengthened by the fact that he is in his exaltation. However, a little later in the text, Morin also tells us that the square of one planet with another planet is worse when a planet is in bad zodiacal state. For example, when Saturn is in a bad zodiacal state, he will hurt more than when in a good zodiacal state. Morin explains that when Saturn is in one of his dignities such as domicile, his square is "destructive" but when in his detriment, his square is "disastrous".[37]

Terrestrial State

Morin's definition of a planet's terrestrial state is its "position or Rulership in this or that House" what Morin calls its "local determination in the Natal Figure"[38], in other words its house position and rulership of a house.

> Among many Planets whose aspects fall into one House of the Chart, it is the one determined towards the significations of the House (or towards their contrary) by the most numerous and powerful determining factors which will outweigh the others.[39]

According to Morin if, for example, Jupiter is in Sagittarius in the ascendant, his nature, position and sign determine his influence on the life of the Native. If Jupiter is in conjunction or square with the Moon, ruler of the eighth house (and not afflicted elsewhere), Jupiter's action for life is stronger and, therefore, prevails over the square with the Moon. However, if Jupiter is in his detriment (Virgo) in the ascendant and is in conjunction with Mars, ruler of the eighth house, the action of Mars prevails, because Mars by his nature and rulership afflicts the significator of life, which is Jupiter.

The Prevailing Planet

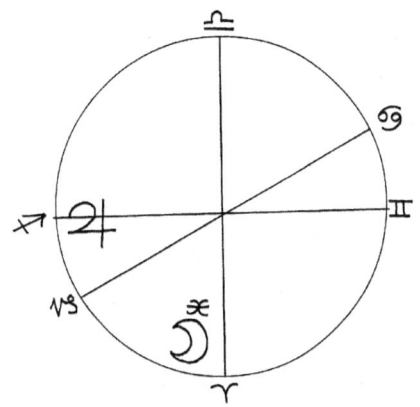

♃ is stronger as significator of life than ☽ is as significator of death.
♃ prevails over the ☽.

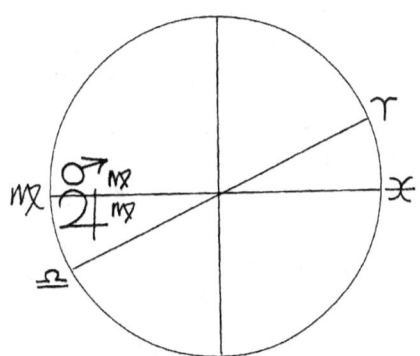

♂ is stronger as significator of death than ♃ significator of life because ♃ is in his detriment.

Clearly Morin believes that ♃'s position in the ascendant, although not ruling the ascendant, gives him the role of significator.

Approach and Departure

According to Morin, any planet approaching another planet with a conjunction or aspect is the more powerful. The application is of course more powerful than the separation. However, Morin tells us that it is necessary to observe the zodiacal and terrestrial states of these planets. In line with previous authorities, Morin explains that the opposition is stronger than the square, the trine more powerful than the sextile.[40] According to Morin, it is best if the planet which applies to another is located in an angle, especially if it is near to the midheaven or ascendant. This is the same even if the planet it applies to is in a cadent house. When the application comes from an angle the result is very powerful and is even greater if the other planet is also in an angle. He also tells us

> An approach towards Planets whose meanings are in harmony with the nature and effect anticipated by the approach, makes this effect even more influential.[41]

Fortunes and Infortunes

In all judgements Bonatti asks us to remember

> ...wherever thou seest the Fortunes, hope for good; and when thou beholdest the Malevolents, fear mischief, unless the same be restrained...[42]

Morin confirms

> ...the Malefics are determined toward the destructive, the Benefics toward the constructive...the Malefics will not directly cause anything favorable, or will cause it accompanied by dangers and difficulties, or will render it imperfect. Benefics, on the other hand, will produce trivial disadvantages, or if, by exception, these prove serious the Benefics will finally remove them.[43]

It is important to weigh up the relative strengths of the Fortunes and Infortunes. Are the Fortunes more powerful than the Infortunes? Are the Infortunes more powerful than the Fortunes? In general, if the principal significators are Fortunes (Venus, and Jupiter) the matter is likely to proceed more advantageously than if they are Infortunes (Mars and Saturn). Bonatti asks the reader to consider

> ...in what House a Fortune shall be fortunate and strong, well disposed, and not afflicted; for in and by these persons or things by that House signified, shall the Native or Querent gain profit, and make his fortune; and so on the contrary of a House that is afflicted.[44]

However, if an Infortune is well dignified, he may be able to offer more assistance than a Fortune ill-dignified. Quoting Sarviator, Bonatti explains

> An ill-planet strong in his own Home or Exaltation, Not joined with any other Infortune to impede or weaken him, is better than a Fortune Retrograde afflicted.[45]

Good aspects with the Fortunes can turn the influence of the Infortunes from negative to positive. Bonatti explains that when an Infortune is a significator, if Jupiter beholds that Infortune, or is in conjunction with him, "this will wholly destroy his malignity and turn his nature into good, how bad soever he be". This is only providing that Jupiter is not afflicted himself, for example, in his fall, combust or retrograde. Even then he can help but not so powerfully.[46] Bonatti confirms that in a similar way

> Venus takes off the fury of Mars, by reason of that endearing intimacy, which is between them, unless the thing be very difficult, as wars and bloodshed, etc

However, he confirms that she cannot as easily remove the mischief of Saturn without the help of Jupiter. The reason for this is that there is no such sympathy between Saturn and Venus: "he is slow, she swift; he heavy, she light; he delights in melancholy, she in mirth". It is important to consider whether the ascendant ruler or the Moon is afflicted by either of the Infortunes with a conjunction, opposition, or square. In this instance Bonatti explains that "the business will be spoiled" unless there is an aspect with a Fortune. However,

> ...if a Fortune, that is, Jupiter, Venus, the Sun or Moon shall behold them, it slackens and dissolves the rigours of such Infortune, and the party signified shall be freed from the danger impending...[47]

Referring to friendships, Simmonite tells us that the Fortunes and Infortunes "make much difference in this question" because the Infortunes always cause something "disagreeable" however well placed they may be. The Fortunes, however poorly placed they may be "never denote a very great degree of malignity".[48]

Position by House

If a significator or the Moon is located in the house of the matter enquired about, this is a strong testimony of achieving the desired outcome. If a Fortune is placed in the house of the matter enquired about or is in the ascendant, this is also a testimony of good fortune, especially if the Fortune is the ruler of that house. Any planet placed in a house over which it has rulership is fortunate. Morin tells us that if the ruler of a house is placed in the house which it rules, it

> ...will realise in a remarkable way the things signified, if good, and above all if these Rulers have an analogy themselves with these affairs.[49]

For example, if the Sun in Leo has rulership of the tenth house and is placed in the tenth house, this is fortunate because the Sun has a natural association with tenth house matters. In a similar manner, if Jupiter in Sagittarius rules the fifth house and is placed in the fifth house, this is fortunate because Jupiter has a natural association with fifth house matters. Gadbury agrees

> When planets dwell in houses proper and convenient, the Matter by that means may be brought to pass, chiefly; if the Moon have a good Defluxion and Application.[50]

As discussed previously, Morin is also of the opinion that "the presence of a Planet in a House is worth more than the Rulership of an absent Planet". According to Morin, "the determination by physical position is immediate, it is consequently the most effective".[51] However, Masha'allah believes that rulers of houses are more important to outcomes than occupants of houses.[52] I have already put forward my opinion on this, but would like to emphasise that from experience it certainly seems to be the case that planets in houses are, in general, more powerful then absent rulers. For example, if the seventh house has Capricorn in its cusp and Saturn, ruler of that house, is in the fifth house, but Venus in Capricorn is in the seventh house, Venus assumes a more important role in matters connected to the seventh house than Saturn. Saturn, in turn, assumes more importance in matters connected to the fifth house.

The Order of Power of the Aspects

For the sake of clarity I include the table below as in chapter five. According to Al Biruni, the order of power of the aspects is: [53]

1. Conjunction (most powerful)
2. Opposition
3. Dexter quartile (square)
4. Sinister quartile (square)
5. Dexter trine
6. Sinister trine
7. Dexter sextile
8. Sinister sextile

I would suggest that the order of aspects as listed above appears to hold true. However, if a planet is afflicted by a square with an Infortune, the malice can be alleviated with a mutual reception between them and/or by assistance given to the afflicting planet because of a good aspect with one of the Fortunes. On the other hand, Al Biruni argues that "When there are two aspects the more powerful renders the weaker one incompetent and takes away its power". Presumably he means that if a planet is afflicted with an opposition, but is also in trine with another planet, the opposition aspect renders the trine "incompetent". This is not necessarily true. Both aspects are still in operation. For example, it is difficult to see how a dexter square with a significator could take away all the power of a dexter trine.

In fact, most authorities agree that a Fortune assisting a badly aspected planet can intervene positively by means of its fortunate rays. In chapter fourteen, Abu Ma'shar tells us that good aspects from a Fortune can relieve the misfortune of a beseiged planet. In *Christian Astrology*, Lilly includes the chart of a lady asking if she is pregnant. The chart is unfortunate and the principal significator Mercury opposes Saturn, but Lilly points out

> Had I found Jupiter either fortunating the cusp of the fifth house, or in any aspect to the Lord of the ascendant, [Mercury] or unto Saturn, or if any reception had been betwixt Saturn and Jupiter, or Jupiter and Mercury, or any collection of light from Mercury to Saturn, and that Planet so collecting had received Saturn or Mercury, I would not have been so peremptory: but when I found no one promising testimony, I gave my judgment in the negative.[54]

Here, Lilly is saying that Jupiter could offer assistance through his aspect with any of the significators, no matter what type of aspect that might be.

Clearly, if there is an unfortunate conjunction in the chart, its power is great and other more fortunate aspects cannot totally remove its maleficity, but they can reduce it. For example, the Moon in conjunction with Saturn in Aries is unfortunate, but if Jupiter in Sagittarius makes a dexter trine with the Moon and Saturn, the maleficity of that conjunction can be reduced (although not totally removed).

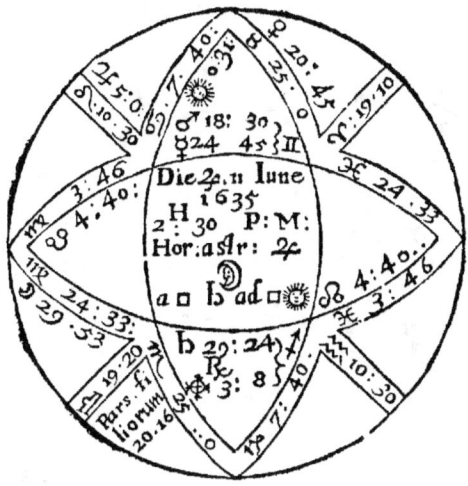

If the Querent should ever have Children?

Helpful aspects from the Fortunes can "abate" malice. In the same way, a malefic making an opposition or square with a conjunction of two Fortunes can reduce their power. However, this does not render the conjunction "incompetent".

Much of course depends on the dignity and position of the planets involved. I would suggest that, other things being equal, conjunctions represent the most powerful configuration in any chart. Conjunctions between Fortunes which are also in some of their stronger dignities represent the very strongest testimony for good fortune and do a great deal to offset negative indications elsewhere. Examples which illustrate this clearly are the charts of Victoria Beckham, who has Venus in conjunction with Jupiter in Pisces; Katie Price (Jordan) who has Venus in conjunction with Jupiter in Cancer, and Kate Moss, who has Venus in conjunction with Jupiter in Aquarius. The opposite applies to conjunctions between Infortunes. Of course there are other important testimonies in these charts, but these are, to some extent, superceded by the power of the conjunction. However, the conjunctions do not render the other aspects incompetent.

In the case of a Nativity from my practice, both the Moon and Jupiter make a conjunction in Sagittarius. This conjunction is in opposition with the Sun, Mercury, Venus and Mars in Gemini. Most of these planets are applying to a square with Saturn (in Pisces). The strength of the Moon and Jupiter in a conjunction with each other and in Sagittarius has evidently been sufficient to mitigate some of the unfortunate affects of the oppositions and squares in terms of the Native's health. However, there is no evidence to suggest that this conjunction renders the opposition or square "incompetent". It merely takes away some its power. In fact, the conjunction of Venus and Mercury with the Sun and Mars is another powerful testimony, but unlike the Moon in conjunction with Jupiter, this conjunction is

The power of the conjunction in a Nativity

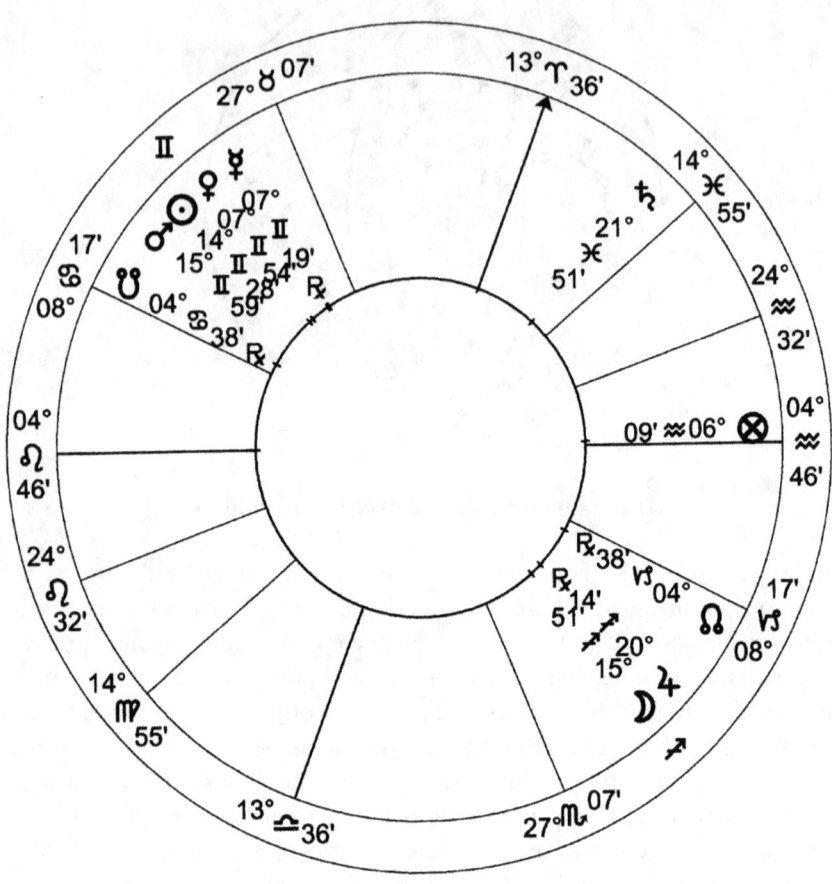

ESSENTIAL DIGNITIES				
Ruler	Exalt	Trip	Term	Face
☽	♃	—	☉	☿	☽
☉	☿	—	♄	♀	♂
♀	☿	—	♄	♃	♃
♀	♃	—	♄	♃	♂
♂	♀	—	☉	♀	♂
♃	♃	♀	♂	♄	♂
♄	♄	—	♄	♂	♀
⊗				

MUTUAL RECEPTIONS
♄ ♃ Ruler-Term
♄ ♃ Ruler-Face
♄ ♀ Exalt-Trip
♄ ♂ Trip-Trip

unfortunate. However, the Moon and Jupiter do a great deal to reduce any difficulties; in fact the Native suffered three major heart attacks in his forties, but he survived and is now in his seventies.

In a separate Nativity (shown on next page), the Moon and Venus make a conjunction in Cancer. Both are applying to a square with Saturn in Libra. Al Biruni might claim that the Moon's merger with Venus would be enough to render the square from Saturn "incompetent". Again, I would argue that the power of the conjunction removes some of the power of the square with Saturn, but not entirely. However, it must be noted that Saturn dignified in Libra does less harm than if he were, for example, in Aries. In this example the Native is now in her mid-eighties having enjoyed good health, although with a few minor problems mainly teeth and bones, probably resulting from the square with Saturn. This Nativity is possibly more fortunate in an overall sense than the one preceding.

There is no doubt that powerful conjunctions involving a Fortune do a great deal to mitigate misfortune elsewhere in the Nativity or Question. Both individuals in the two examples above have many children, surely resulting from the conjunction between the Moon and a Fortune. However, the more difficult aspects elsewhere in their Nativities still have a role to play. This discussion is re-examined later in this chapter, where I discuss the views of Abu Ali Al-Khayyat and James Holden.

Planets Angular and in the Cusp

Bonatti asks us to consider where in a house a planet is positioned, because a planet positioned close to the cusp of an angular house is much stronger than a planet positioned away from the cusp, for example, in the middle of a house.

> ...for how much any Planet is near to the cusp of any Angle so much is he the stronger; how much farther so much the weaker; and by how much sooner he shall be nearer the cusp of a Cadent House, so much shall he be the weaker; how much the farther, so much the less weak.[55]

I have found that in a chart where, for example, the Sun is exactly in conjunction with the tenth house cusp, the signification from the Sun in this chart is stronger than a similar chart with the Sun positioned in the tenth house but away from the cusp. I include an example of this in chapter twenty-three. Morin tells us that where there are two planets ruling the same house (where the degrees of a sign are intercepted), it is the planet ruling the cusp which should take precedence over the other, because "it rules more particularly the meanings of that House", but he emphasises that the second ruler of that house should not be neglected.[56]

Al-Khayyat explains that signification from a cadent house and "mobile" signs (moveable) is weak; from succedent houses and common signs, stronger; from angles and fixed signs, the strongest.[57]

The power of the conjunction in a Nativity

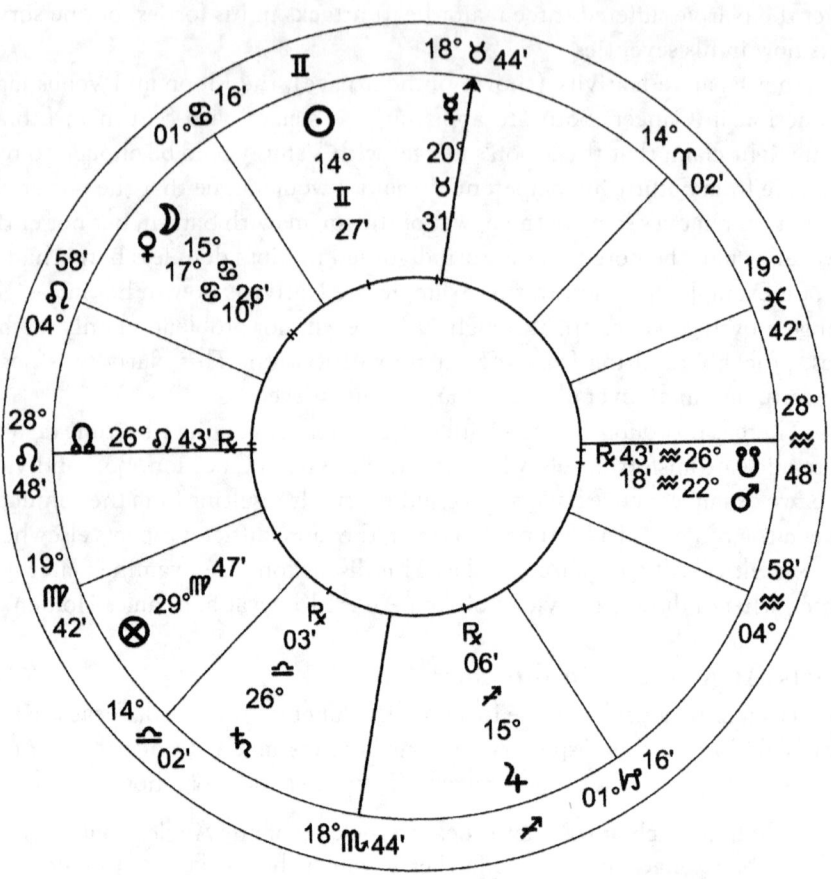

Planetary Aspects

Morin explains that two planets must combine their activity if they want to produce a certain effect. They will only be able to achieve results if they unite their efforts, not if they mutually avoid one another, nor if one comes forward but the other moves away or "recoils". In all aspects which Morin says "are not perfect" it is always worse for a planet to apply to a malefic than to separate from it.[58] The more powerful a planet is in terms of its zodiacal and terrestrial states (whether fortunate or unfortunate) the more important it is to consider in which houses the aspects fall. This is because a planet with this degree of strength will "act more strongly than any other for their good or bad significations, according to the nature of the aspect".[59]

If a planet receives two aspects, it is necessary to examine the relative distance between the significator and the aspects. It is the closest aspect which prevails. A footnote also explains that individuals who are born with exact planetary aspects will, during their life, experience something quite remarkable in terms of good fortune or misfortune relating to this exact aspect (this is in accordance with a planet's rulership and house position).

> Nativities with inexact aspects are mediocre, and those without aspects are base and obscure. Let us add that people whose Rulers receive numerous aspects are distinguished by the variety and multiplicity of their aptitudes.[60]

As discussed earlier in this chapter, the zodiacal state of the aspecting planets is also important. As an example, a trine with Jupiter in one of his domiciles is very good and a square with Jupiter is "inoffensive or at least harmful in a very feeble way". However, when Jupiter is in his detriment, Morin claims that Jupiter's trine is "useless or useful to a very small degree" and his square "damaging".

In a similar way, a trine with Saturn in one of his domiciles is "constructive", but his square is "destructive". On the other hand when in detriment, Saturn's trine "gives no help" and his square is "disastrous." Morin goes on to say that this must be understood from "an intrinsic point of view, and in terms of a condition where all other things are equal".

According to Morin, although squares and oppositions are, in themselves, harmful, they are much worse when they are with the Infortunes, Saturn and Mars. They are even worse when these planets (Mars and Saturn) are in bad zodiacal state, positioned in unfortunate houses or ruling unfortunate houses. In addition, even though all trine and sextile aspects are in themselves constructive, the most helpful are those formed by Jupiter, Venus, the Sun, the Moon and Mercury. These aspects become even stronger when these planets are in good zodiacal state and even better if the planets are associated (either by position or rulership) with fortunate houses.

Finally, this constructive nature is best if, over and above all the aforementioned, the aspects are received or mutually received by the rulers of fortunate houses, or by the planets placed there. This is even better if these planets are Jupiter, Venus, the Moon or Mercury.

Morin reports that the opposition between Saturn in Leo and the Sun in Aquarius is "of all the aspects the worst and the trine from Jupiter in Pisces to the Moon in Cancer, the best". However, in the former example, there is a mutual reception between the Sun and Saturn. I would have thought that an opposition between the Sun in Leo and Saturn in Aquarius might have been equally destructive, what Robert Hand calls a war between equals.

The Order of Aspects in Time

It is important to consider the circumstances in which conjunctions and aspects succeed each other. According to Morin, if a good aspect immediately succeeds another good aspect, the good that is signified is "achieved easily and with certainty". However, if a bad aspect succeeds another bad aspect, "the bad that is signified is equally certain". If a bad aspect follows a good aspect, the good signified by the first will be good only superficially and will give place to "actual harm" and vice versa.[61] Morin's writing is similar to Bonatti's on the aspects of the Moon, as discussed earlier in this chapter. It is also similar to the idea of besiegement or containment by aspect, although the latter more specifically refers to aspects from either the Fortunes or the Infortunes at one time.

The Relaying of Applications

In Masha'allah's astrology the relaying of applications is of fundamental importance in terms of finding perfection and finding signification. In establishing the principal significator of the Querent, it is the applications made with the ascendant by the ascendant ruler, or with other planets aspecting the ascendant, which is important.

In terms of perfection, if the significator of the Querent does not make its first application to the ruler of the matter enquired about, but to another planet, we are told to consider the first application of this second planet. If the latter is applying to the planet that is ruler of the matter enquired about "all is still well" according to Robert Hand. This process carries on. In addition, a series of applications to a Fortune is also a positive indication (unless the Fortune rules the eighth house in a life or death Question and there is no reception between that planet and the significator of the Querent).[62] Along this chain of applications, each planet commits its disposition on to the next planet in the chain. It is the planet which is the last in this chain which can be the most important in determining the outcome of the Question. Due to their slowness of motion, this final planet is likely to be a Superior: Mars, Jupiter or Saturn. Hand suggests that this could be one of the reasons why the Superiors were considered to be more powerful as significators than the Inferiors.[63]

The Ascendant in the Domicile of a Planet Ruling Two Houses

Bonatti explains that in the case of Nativities or Questions it is important to observe whether the ascendant is in the domicile of a planet which rules two houses. If this is the case, he suggests that the

> ...exercises or troubles of the Native or Querent shall be chiefly in those things signified by the other House of the said Planet, which shall lightly happen to him and for the most part through his own means.[64]

For example, if Taurus ascends, the Querent will be challenged by certain things which may cause his own weakness or ill-health, because Libra, the other domicile of Venus is in the sixth house. Bonatti explains that if Venus is in good condition, however, and the Lot of Fortune is in the sixth house, the Querent will be lucky in things connected to the sixth house. If Virgo is ascending, the individual will be challenged by matters connected to the tenth house because Gemini, Mercury's other domicile, is in the tenth house. Bonatti puts forward similar examples for ascendants such as Aries, Gemini, Libra, Scorpio, Sagittarius, Capricorn, Aquarius and Pisces.

Aspects with Houses and House Cusps

Aspects made with houses and house cusps are frequently overlooked in modern astrology. However, Lilly mentions the importance of aspects with house cusps throughout *Christian Astrology*. In terms of sickness charts, good aspects with the ascending degree or with the sixth house cusp from the Fortunes can make all the difference. As discussed previously, planets are more fortunate and powerful when beholding the ascendant.

> ...if I found Jupiter or Venus or the north node in the ascendant, or the Sun in the sixth, or the Moon and Lord of the ascendant in any good aspect, or Jupiter or Venus casting a trine or sextile to the cusp of the ascendant or sixth house, I would directly acquaint the party they were not sick, or that no sickness would succeed upon this Quere...[65]

A planet is also more fortunate when aspecting its own domicile (the sign which it rules). For example, if Jupiter is in Cancer he is aspecting the house which has Pisces (Jupiter's domicile) in its cusp. Affairs signified by that house will prosper in accordance with matters signified by Jupiter. However, matters signified by the house with Sagittarius in its cusp (another domicile of Jupiter) will not prosper to the same extent because, in this instance, Jupiter is not aspecting his own domicile.

Morin

Morin rejected any notion of Questions (horary astrology), although he did include Elections in his work. However, I have included some of Morin's writings here, as I have throughout this chapter, so that the student or reader can see how the evaluation of planetary strengths and weaknesses is carried out in the same way in both in a Question and a Nativity. However, the application of these principles varies slightly between the different sorts of charts. For example, Saturn in the tenth house in a Nativity may operate differently at various times in the life of the

Native, depending on transits or directions. In terms of a Question the position of Saturn in the tenth house may deny success for the Querent on that occasion. Some of this has been touched upon in earlier chapters. Morin claims that in order to work out the particular effects which the celestial bodies produce for a given individual "by virtue of their particular determination", it is necessary to consider four points: [66]

- Firstly, celestial influences can bring about the realisation of a particular matter.

- Secondly, celestial influences can prevent the realisation of a particular matter.

- Thirdly, once this particular thing has been brought about, the celestial influences can destroy it again.

- Finally, the realisation of the matter may affect the Native in different ways. It may become either a source of fortune or misfortune for him.

As an example, Morin tells us that when a celestial body (that is, the Sun, Moon, planet or the Lot of Fortune) causes a failure to acquire wealth, this means that not only will the Native fail to acquire wealth from his own efforts, but that even if he inherits wealth, he will lose it and fall back into poverty.

> ...all the Planets can signify either realisation or obstruction or destruction or the diverse consequences of a previous realisation.

Whilst I agree with Morin, I would suggest that this is a very interesting point to put forward for an astrologer who is non-deterministic. Morin gives as an example the Sun in the tenth house which "confers outstanding honors, considered in itself, because of its natural affinity with them", whereas Saturn in the tenth house will "obstruct honors" for the opposite reason. Of course the Sun can also obstruct if he is in his detriment, fall, peregrine, or in square or opposition with a malefic. Alternatively, the Sun may, in this instance, surround any achievement or honours with difficulties, worries or misfortunes. The worse the zodiacal state of the Sun the greater the difficulties, according to Morin. Any misfortune is of course even worse when the dispositor is also badly placed. Saturn may also confer "honors" if Saturn is located in his own domicile or exaltation and well aspected.

As discussed earlier in the chapter, Morin explains that any planet which is "favourably disposed" must in general terms be considered a benefic whatever house it occupies and particularly when helped by good aspects with Venus or Jupiter. However, Morin explains that this general rule has to be modified in the case of Mars and Saturn in the sense that in favourable zodiacal state and in fortunate houses they can bring good fortune. However, if they are in favourable zodiacal state, but in unfortunate houses (eighth, twelfth and partially the seventh according to Morin) they produce harmful effects. Furthermore, if either Mars or Saturn are found in the ascendant or the midheaven and are in any of their debilities, they can cause "considerable misfortune".

On the other hand, Morin tells us that any planet which is "badly disposed" (in detriment, fall, retrograde, or badly aspected with the Infortunes and has no aspect with the Fortunes) can be considered as "universally malefic" no matter which house it occupies or rules. This destructive character will reveal itself even more energetically in the planets which are malefic by nature.

The action of a planet in mediocre zodiacal state (for example peregrine, but in good aspect with Infortunes or bad aspects with Fortunes) holds the "middle ground", that is, between favourable and unfavourable effects. It is interesting that Morin considers a planet which is peregrine to be in a 'mediocre' state, whereas most authors considered the debility of peregrine to be most unfortunate.

A Planet's Influence when in a Good, Bad or Mediocre State

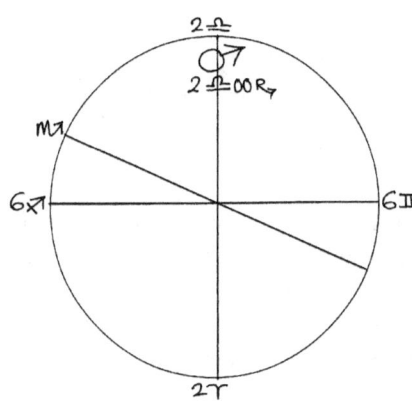

Malefic

♂'s influence is malefic being in his detriment, retrograde, ruling the 12th house and angular.

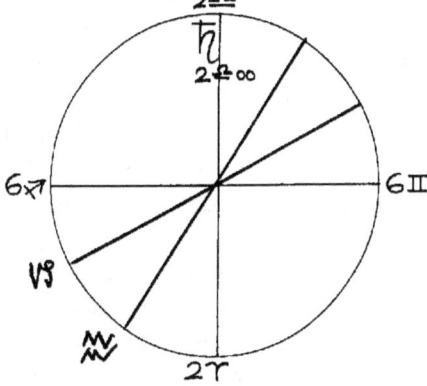

Benefic

♄'s influence is benefic being angular, direct, exalted and in his terms. He rules the 2nd and 3rd houses.

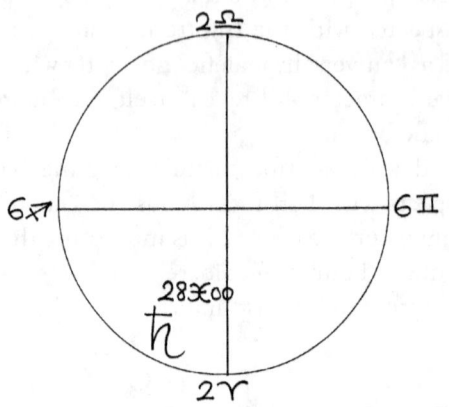

Mediocre
♄ is not in any of his strong dignities, but he is in his terms, in the domicile of a Fortune, ♃, ruling the 2nd and 3rd houses and aspecting the ascendant.

Planets in the Same House

Morin tells us that when there are several planets in the same house (three, four or five), this house must be considered particularly important because it

> ...anticipates something extraordinary in connection with the affairs which it essentially signifies.

According to Morin, the more planets that are positioned in a particular house, "the more the affairs which derive from it will be remarkably good or bad".

Morin explains that "principal significance" is taken from the planet which is the ruler of the house, thereafter from the planet exalted there, then from the one which has closest analogy with the house and finally from the planet which is closest to the house cusp.[67]

The planets also have the power to "increase, diminish or corrupt the power of the meanings of other Planets by their aspects", to a greater or lesser extent. For example, if Jupiter is in the tenth house in Leo, he becomes the significator of achievement (some would say co-significator) and if the Sun aspects Jupiter with a trine, Jupiter's power in terms of that achievement is intensified: the achievement will be that much greater and bring much happiness. However, if Saturn afflicts Jupiter with a square, this same power will not only be diminished, but it will be corrupted. Not only will the achievement be reduced substantially, but there will be some unhappiness connected with the achievement.[68]

Even though each event indicated (in a Nativity) depends to a certain extent on all the planets and their aspects, Morin explains that this dependence is not equal. For example, some planets have a great effect, others less, and others very little. As well as inter-planetary aspects, each house in a chart receives different aspects, that is, the opposition, trine, square and sextile. Among the many aspects falling into each house, Morin claims that "the most powerful ones apparently suppress the action of the weaker ones". I would agree with Morin that to some extent the more powerful aspects might suppress the weaker ones, but unlike Al Biruni, I do not believe that the weaker aspects are rendered incompetent by the stronger aspects. Finally Morin tells us that the astrologer gives judgement "according to those elements in whose favor the scale tips".

Planets in the Same House

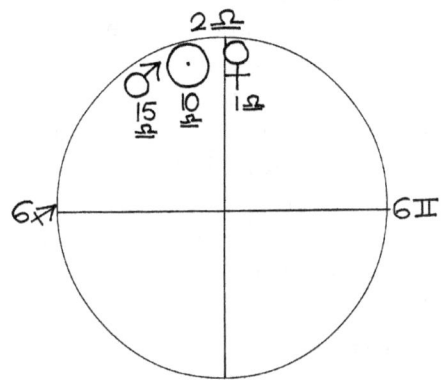

♀ is principal significator being the ruler of the 10th house, being positioned in the 10th house and being closest to the cusp.
☉ is second in importance, having a natural analogy with the 10th house.
♂ is third in importance but is malefic in his detriment.

Caution in Judgement

In terms of a Nativity, Al-Khayyat tells us about "A Caution that must be observed in Judgments". James Holden confirms that this is very important and not consistently stated in texts: if the chart has a single testimony, it is "commonplace", if it has two testimonies, it is "stronger", if it has three testimonies, it is "perfected", but only if the rulers of the significators are strong and not impeded.[69] In other words, the Nativity must contain three concurring testimonies if the matter under consideration is to be important during the lifetime. I would suggest that at least two concurring testimonies are usually enough, but three would make it more certain. James Holden calls this "an important and concise statement of a cardinal principle of astrological interpretation". He suggests that this could be termed "reinforcement", that is, where more than one testimony must be found in order to produce a clear answer.

Al-Khayyat also tells us that if in the chart, both fortunate and unfortunate signification and testimony are produced, the astrologer must compare one testimony with the other, in order to work out which is stronger. The stronger testimony which has more dignities "must be preferred". The other can be discarded. But if the testimonies are equal, both have to be discarded. By following this rule, he believes that "you will judge more surely and much more fortunately". However, Holden believes that this is poor advice, because he explains: "Experience shows that astrological influences act independently".

> Each influence produces its own characteristic effect. If one is stronger, it will produce a greater effect, as compared to a weaker contrary influence, but the weaker influence will still operate.[70]

Holden tells us that if the influences are equal in strength, usually one of these influences will "give" something but the other will take it away. He explains that there many examples of this: big earnings offset by heavy expenses, a happy marriage but a short one, or two marriages, one happy the other unhappy. In the same way, there might be the achievement of an important or high position, followed by its loss, or many illnesses, but good medical treatment. In terms of Nativities I would agree with Holden and I have included examples of two Nativities earlier in this chapter which illustrate this very point. This is of course similar to the writings of Morin discussed earlier, when he tells us that the planets can bring about certain events or things and can subsequently take them away. However in terms of Questions, the situation is a little different, because a malefic in the house of the

Conflicting Planetary Influences

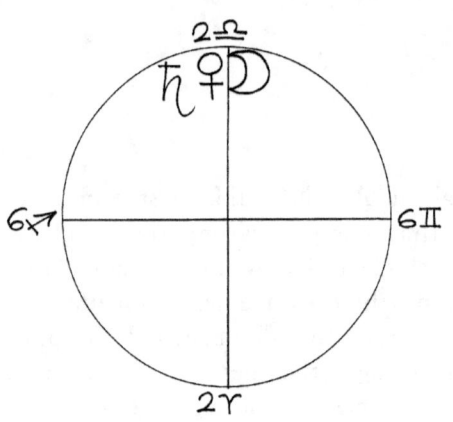

☽ and ♀ produce considerable achievements, but ♄ may reduce them. However he does less harm being in his exaltation.

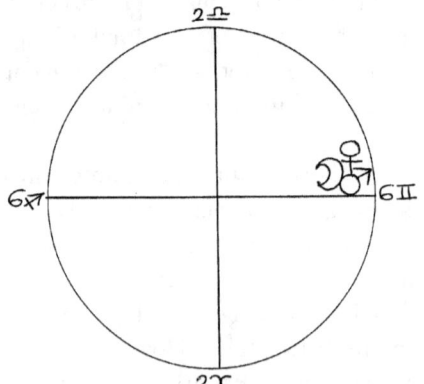

☽ and ♀ would produce happiness in a relationship, but ♂ is certain to reduce that happiness. ♂ always causes difficulties when in the 7th house.

matter enquired about, or any other malefic aspect, may actually prevent the achievement of the desired outcome, but only at that point in time.

As emphasised in this book, at least two concurring testimonies must be found in the Question to produce a possible or even probable outcome. Where the testimonies are very even the chart should be discarded.

Timing

Partridge asks "How long e're the Business will be accomplished – if Probable". He advises the reader to

> Take the distance of your Significators, either of their Bodies [conjunction] or Aspects, and turn the distance into time...[71]

He gives every degree of a fixed sign, a year or month, every degree of a common sign, a month or week, every degree of a moveable sign, a week or day. Partridge claims, along with most authorities, that angles are equal to moveable signs, succedents equal to common signs and cadents equal to fixed signs. If, for example, a significator is in a moveable sign and in an angle Partridge states "you may be positive of the Speed of the matter".

Gadbury in his discussion of marriage and the timing of it, tells us that significators

> ...above the Earth, and swift in Motion, do very much accelerate or hasten the matter; chiefly, if they shall be in moveable Signs. But if they shall be under the Earth, and slow in motion, the Marriage will be retarded.[72]

He observes the degrees, or distance, either by conjunction or aspect between the ascendant ruler and the seventh house ruler, the Sun, or Venus. According to whether their position is in fixed, common or moveable signs, he makes his judgement as to the time of marriage, "chiefly, if at the same time there happen a good transit to bring on the business". Lilly uses the same method.

In practice, the timing of events is complicated and is probably one of the most difficult areas of judgement. However, it is very significant when the application between significators corresponds with the time scale anticipated. This is a positive chart testimony and also confirms radicality in the chart. For example, in Questions about sport I have noticed that if the final of a football match is to be played in, for example, eight weeks, but this does not correspond to the signification, that team is unlikely to win. However, if in another chart the timing matches the signification, that particular team is more likely to win. Here, the astrologer would expect the aspect or conjunction between the principal significators to be about eight degrees and angular. This can be applied to most Questions.

Bonatti discusses the length of time it might take until a matter is perfected, or if the matter has already been perfected, how long it will continue. Questions are often asked about how long an individual may stay in a job, or how long a relationship might last. Bonatti claims that if the significator falls between the ascendant and the twelfth house it signifies days or hours; if it falls between the twelfth house and the tenth house it signifies half-weeks; between the tenth house and the seventh house, months or weeks; between the seventh house and the fourth house, years and between the fourth house and the ascendant, half years.[73] Once the applications and separations of the Moon and significators have been examined, as well as the aspects and the position in houses, it is at this point where Lilly tells us to proceed with our judgement

> ...judge and consider whether the thing demanded will come to passe yea or no; by what, or whose meanes, the time when, and whether it will be good for the querent to proceed further in his demands yea or no.[74]

Will There be a Relationship?

Chart testimonies in this Question illustrate the way in which the timing of an event can be calculated with a fair degree of accuracy. The Moon's conjunction with Jupiter, significator of the person enquired about, takes place within half a degree. The Moon and Jupiter are positioned in an angular house and in a moveable sign. Mercury, principal significator of the Querent, is positioned in a moveable sign in an angular house. The relationship started very quickly in just a few days. However, the application of the Moon and Jupiter to an opposition with Saturn, also in an angular house and a moveable sign, shows the ending of the relationship. This took place in mid-November, just under three months from the time of the Question. Saturn's retrogradation towards the significators indicates that the event may happen more quickly and perhaps more suddenly.

Morin suggests that all of this information

> ...makes the field of predictions extremely vast, and if human intelligence had the necessary power to cultivate this field to its depths, it could predict even the most insignificant details which are produced in the natural order.[75]

However, he explains that because this intelligence is limited, "it is permitted at the most to attain the truth in the prediction of the most important events".

I do not pretend that the testimonies included in this chapter are a comprehensive listing, but they are the most important and they offer a solid foundation upon which to build. It should be emphasised that in a Question, just a single unfortunate and perhaps unsupported chart testimony can be sufficient to prevent the achievement of the desired outcome. A Solar or Lunar Eclipse will prevent the good expected or reduce it substantially. A significator combust, cadent, in his fall and retrograde does the same. On the other hand, it takes at least two, preferably three, strong and concurring chart testimonies to bring about the desired outcome. A chart of this nature is rare. A chart

Planetary Testimony Preceding Judgement

Will there be a relationship?

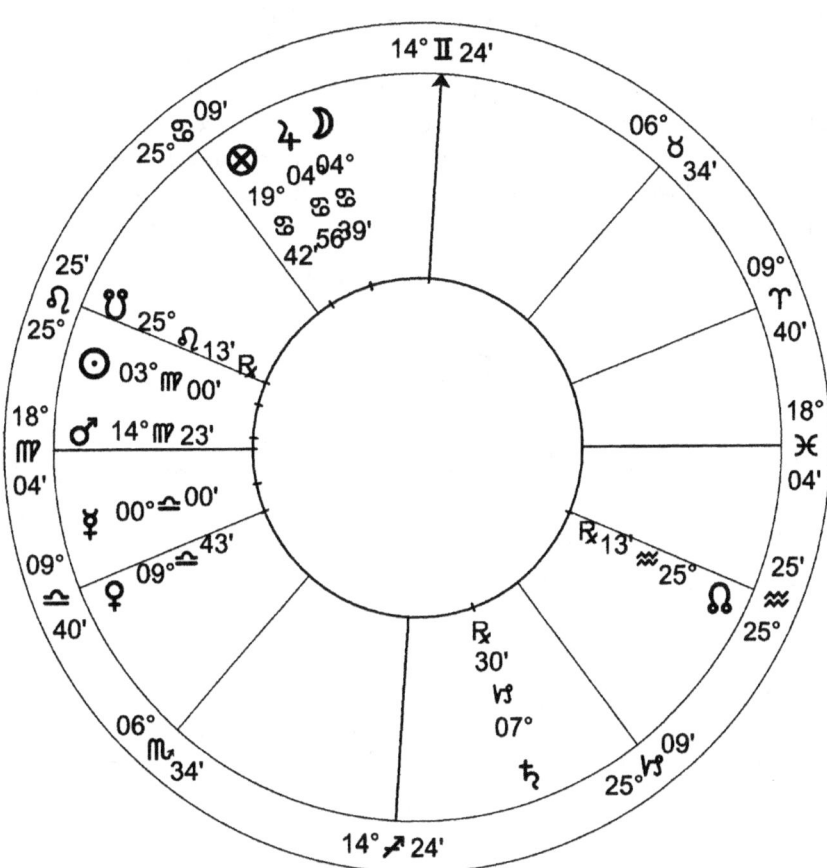

with all planets in their essential dignities is also rare. I only have a handful of Questions which show such exceptionally good fortune for the Querent.

As for Nativities, I think Maternus is correct when he tells us that an average Nativity has one planet in its own domicile located in an important house. The individual with two planets each in its own domicile has moderately good fortune and the individual with three planets each in its own domicile has exceptional good fortune. However, the individual with four planets each in its own domicile "could be near to the gods in happiness... [but] more than this number the character of the human race does not allow..." [76]

References

1. Cardan in Bonatus, p.58 no.8, and the editor's footnote.
2. Nicholas Campion, *Astrology Quarterly*.
3. Henry Coley in Bonatus, PROEM, p.XII.
4. Ball p.61.
5, Lilly p.240.
6. ibid p.223 and p.240.
7. Coley p.131.
8. Lilly p.240.
9. Ramesey p.122.
10. ibid p.122 and repeated in Bonatus p.83, footnote by Lilly.
11. Robert Zoller, *Tools & Techniques of the Medieval Astrologer*, Ascella, p.68.
12. Gadbury p.235.
13. Lilly p.177.
14. ibid p.184.
15. Bonatus p.7, 9th consideration.
16. ibid p.53, 143rd consideration.
17. Morin p.25.
18. ibid p.32.
19. ibid p.30.
20. Bonatus p.8, 9th consideration.
21. Robert Zoller, *The Lost Key to Prediction. The Arabic Parts in Astrology*, Inner Traditions, New York, 1980, p.85.
22. Ptolemy, *Tetrabiblos*, Loeb Classical Library, pp.177-179 and footnote p.178.
23. ibid p.275.
24. Morin p.96.
25. ibid p.156.
26. Bonatus p.67 no.46. Aphorisms relating to Nativities and footnote.
27. Lilly, Aphorisms p.298 no.5.
28. Bonatus p.34, 101st consideration.
29. ibid p.9, 9th consideration.
30. Ibn Ezra, *The Beginning Of Wisdom*, p.215.

31. Michel Gauquelin, 1966, *Astrology and Science*, translated by James Hughes, Peter Davies, London, pp.189-190.
32. Bonatus p.27, 76th consideration.
33. Morin p.97.
34. ibid p.85.
35. ibid p.85.
36. ibid p.85.
37. ibid p.89.
38. ibid p.79 and p.51.
39. ibid pp.85-86.
40. ibid pp.86-87.
41. ibid p.135.
42. Bonatus p.10, 15th consideration.
43. Morin pp.41-42.
44. Bonatus p.38, 118th consideration.
45. ibid p.15, 32nd consideration, quoting Sarviator.
46. ibid p.18, 48th consideration.
47. ibid p.18, 50th consideration.
48. Simmonite p.141.
49. Morin p.53.
50. Gadbury p.239.
51. Morin p.32.
52. Masha'allah, *On Reception*, ARHAT, 1998, p9 and editor's footnote (Robert Hand).
53. Al Biruni p.226.
54. Lilly p.239.
55. Bonatus p.28, 81st consideration.
56. Morin p.66.
57. Abu 'Ali Al-Khayyat p.78.
58. Morin p.136.
59. ibid p.86.
60. ibid pp.88-90.
61. ibid p.91.
62. Robert Hand in *On Reception*, p.vi.
63. ibid p.vii.
64. Bonatus pp.41-42, 125th consideration.
65. Lilly p.259.
66. Morin pp.31-35.
67. ibid pp.45-46.
68. ibid pp.81-82.
69. Abu Ali Al Khayyat p.78, and James Holden's footnote.
70. ibid p.78, Holden's note.
71. Partridge p.52.
72. Gadbury p.274.
73. Bonatus p.25, 71st consideration.

74. Lilly p.124.
75. Morin p.92.
76. Maternus p.53.

14

THE POSSIBILITY OF THE MATTER PROPOUNDED

Now that chart testimonies have been examined in a general sense, this chapter examines and evaluates the testimonies which produce good fortune and which contribute towards the achievement of the desired outcome in a Question. It is these same testimonies which produce good fortune in the Nativity, Election or any other type of chart.

General Testimonies of Good Fortune

In order to achieve the desired outcome, at least two, preferably three, positive, concurring testimonies are required. As discussed in earlier chapters, it is not enough for significators to be applying to a good aspect with each other. They must be in good houses, in some of their dignities and not afflicted by the Infortunes. It is the position and dignity of a planet which is the most important factor in judgement.

It is useful to consider the testimonies an astrologer might choose to include when selecting the moment for an Election. Here, the astrologer has the luxury of choosing an auspicious time, a moment when the planets are lined up in a way which is intended to produce good fortune. One always hopes that the time of a Question, or the time of a birth take place at a similarly auspicious moment.

In the most fortunate charts, the Fortunes are emphasised (angular) and the Infortunes are tucked away (cadent). Al Biruni tells us that when selecting "a suitable time for carrying out some business [an Election]" the astrologer must

> ...insure the presence of fortunes and the absence of infortunes, just as we protect ourselves on the surface of the earth from the rays of the sun, by selecting northern aspects, and shady spots and using moistened pun-kahs and ice-houses.[1]

He explains that when selecting the time for an Election, it is important to

> ...adjust the cardines that the malefics are as distant as possible both in themselves and their rays, while they are to be kept illuminated by the benefics and their light, especially the ascendant and its lord, also the moon and the lord of its house, and the significator of the business...

Al Biruni tells us that it is important that the Moon, the ascendant ruler and the principal significator make an aspect with each other and that all of them aspect the ascendant "lest the election should turn out to have bad effects". This is an equally important consideration in Nativities and Questions. Elections only differ from the aforementioned in that here the astrologer has control over the choice of the moment (the most auspicious moment), which ensures the inclusion of fortunate chart testimonies and the exclusion of unfortunate chart testimonies.

Good Fortune

☾ and ♃ are accidentally dignified
☉ is essentially and accidentally dignified
☿ and ♀ are occidental
♄ is essentially dignified.
all planets make an aspect with the ascendant.

Helpers

Bonatti explains that when it comes to the "judicial part of Astrology" the ancient astrologers did not take much notice of it, nor have they said anything clearly about it apart, he says, from Haly "who seems to have touched a little upon it in his Exposition of the 23rd of Ptolemy's Centiloquium..." Bonatti claims that the ancients were inclined to make their judgements

> ...according as they found the Planets disposed in Houses and Signs, their Fortitudes and Debilities, together with the Part of Fortune, and some few other things.[2]

Bonatti tells us that in any judgement, consideration ought also to be given to "all other circumstances". These other circumstances (among other things) appear to be the influence of the fixed stars, which Bonatti calls *helpers*. Fixed stars which are of the same nature as significators and are in conjunction with these significators offer enormous assistance in terms of the matter enquired about. Bonatti explains very precisely just what position the significators should occupy in relation to the fixed stars, in order to derive maximum assistance. He categorises these helpers according to their strength. Bonatti also tells us about significators out of their dignities, and which are in conjunction with fixed stars of a "contrary nature".

These are given the name *hinderers*. In chapter fifteen, I examine the role and nature of hinderers, that is, the planets who "prejudice, frustrate and hinder business". Bonatti explains that in total there are twenty one helpers and hinderers. He asks the reader to

> ...take notice of the several ways, as well secret as manifest, good and evil, whereby things are helped or hindered to be done or not done...

The following are the 'helpers' which Bonatti refers to: [3]

1. A most strong secret helper
2. A very strong secret helper
3. A strong secret helper
4. A weak secret helper
5. A weaker secret helper
6. A most weak secret helper
7. A most strong manifest helper
8. A very strong manifest helper
9. A strong manifest helper
10. A weak manifest helper
11. A weaker manifest helper
12. A most weak manifest helper

A level of strength or weakness is assigned to these helpers. The secret helpers he refers to are the fixed stars, although it is clear that it is the conjunction of a planet with the fixed star which together produce the good fortune. The manifest or open helpers appear to be the planets only. In terms of a secret helper, Bonatti gives most weight to a fixed star in partill conjunction with a significator, where that significator also has strength by essential dignity. In terms of an open or manifest helper, this is a planet very strong in both essential and accidental dignity.

Secret Helpers
A secret helper does not necessarily have to have strength by angularity; it can be positioned in a succedent or cadent house.

1. A **most strong** secret helper is a fixed star in conjunction to the very minute with a planet (which is a significator). The fixed star should be of the same nature as the significator. This conjunction takes place in the domicile or exaltation of that planet. Here, the matter shall be accomplished "even beyond the Querent's hopes".

2. A **very strong** secret helper is a fixed star in conjunction with a significator of the same nature in the same degree, up to fifteen minutes before or five minutes behind. This conjunction takes place in the domicile or exaltation of that planet. In this case, it will still help but not as much as in example 1.

3. A **strong** secret helper is a fixed star in conjunction with a significator of the same nature in the same degree from sixteen minutes to fifty minutes apart. The conjunction takes place in the domicile or exaltation of that planet. In this case, it will help but to a lesser extent again.

4. A **weak** secret helper is a fixed star in conjunction with a significator of the same nature in the same degree and up to sixteen minutes apart. This conjunction takes place where the planet has two of his smaller dignities. This will help, but to an even lesser extent.

5. A **weaker** secret helper is a fixed star in conjunction with a significator of the same nature in the same degree from sixteen to fifty minutes apart. This conjunction takes place where the planet has two of his smaller dignities. The help offered is even less here.

6. A **most weak** secret helper is a fixed star in conjunction with a significator of his own nature in the same degree from sixteen to fifty minutes apart.[4] This conjunction occurs in a place where the planet has no dignities. The help offered here is even smaller.

Manifest (Open) Helpers

Here Bonatti appears to assign the role of helper to the planet or significator itself. Each helper is assigned a particular position in terms of being in the cusp, angular, succedent or cadent.

7. A **most strong** manifest helper.

    ...the Planet which is Significator of a thing, is in his own House [sign]; in an Angle on the very minute of the Cusp, direct, swift of course, in reception, and free from all affliction and impediment; which most seldom happens.

As discussed earlier in the book, the cusp of a house is the strongest place within that house for a planet to be, especially an angular house.

8. A **very strong** manifest helper. Bonatti gives no details, but this would probably be a planet in the same condition as in point seven, but it would not be in the very minute of the cusp.

9. A **strong** manifest helper is a significator in an angle, in his own domicile or exaltation, within three degrees before the cusp, or five degrees after it.

10. A **weak** manifest helper is a significator in two of his lesser dignities, in an angle within five degrees before or fifteen degrees after the cusp; or is in his domicile or exaltation, in a succedent house and free from affliction.

11. A **weaker** manifest helper is a significator in his own domicile or exaltation, or two of his lesser dignities, but in a cadent house and beholding the ascendant.

A Most Strong Secret Helper

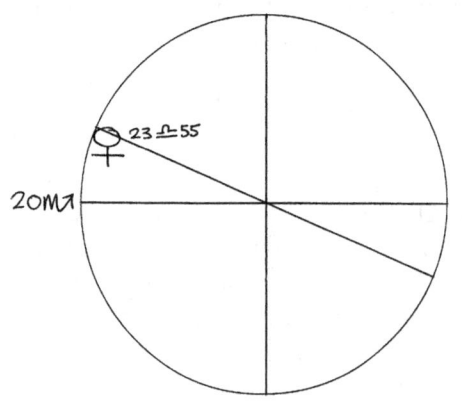

♀ in her own domicile exactly in conjunction with the benefic fixed star Spica.

A Most Strong Manifest Helper

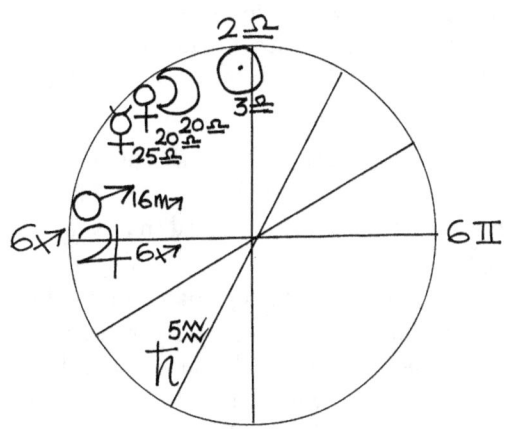

♃ in his own domicile received by the ☉, in an angle in the very minute of the cusp, direct, swift, free from affliction.

12. A **most weak** manifest helper is a significator in one of his stronger dignities or in two of his lesser dignities, not beholding the ascendant. Alternatively the significator can be in one of his lesser dignities and beholding the ascendant, or aspecting a planet who is beholding the ascendant and has some dignities in the ascendant.

In any of the above situations (points 1 - 12), a planet will be of help in bringing about perfection, to a greater or lesser extent. The strongest planet in this regard is of course, a most strong manifest helper. As Bonatti reports, this is a condition which happens infrequently.

Beholding the Ascendant

As discussed in earlier chapters, authors of the past attached great importance to whether or not a planet was beholding the ascendant, either by degree or even just by sign. Any planet aspecting the ascendant (especially if this planet is the ascendant ruler) becomes more fortunate, particularly if the aspect is a trine or sextile, or if the aspect is a conjunction, as long as that planet is a Fortune (or an Infortune dignified). Making an aspect with the ascendant through the antiscia is also acceptable, because in this condition, according to authors of the past, planets can be counted as being in conjunction. Although in various places in *Christian Astrology*, Lilly mentions the importance of a significator aspecting the ascendant, this is not emphasised in his judgements. However, it is clear that certain astrologers of the past would not accept a planet as ruler of the ascendant unless that planet was aspecting the ascendant, or joined to a planet who was aspecting the ascendant.

According to Bonatti and others, an Infortune, or planet badly placed, does less harm if it is cadent and, therefore, not in aspect with the ascendant. He quotes Zael (Sahl)

> ...if a Malevolent planet that would hinder any business be cadent from the Ascendant so that he cannot behold it, he cannot really hinder the matters; but only puts the persons concerned into terrors and frights about it.[5]

Clearly, an Infortune in a harmonious aspect with the ascendant does less harm than an Infortune in a bad aspect with the ascendant. However, a Fortune in a harmonious aspect with the ascendant is always fortunate and in a bad aspect is not necessarily unfortunate, just less fortunate.

Planets aspecting their own domicile (sign) have fortunate implications for the house in question. For example, Venus in Aquarius aspects her own domicile of Libra, so the affairs associated with the house, which has the degrees of Libra in its cusp, will be fortunate. Venus also makes an aspect with her domicile of Taurus, but because this is with a square, any good fortune is likely to be reduced. However, it appears that making any aspect, even a square, is preferable to making no aspect at all, unless the planet is an Infortune. For example, it was thought that the squares of the Infortunes to the fifth house were unfortunate in terms of conception and pregnancy.

Above the Horizon

Referring to Nativities, Bonatti tells us that

> All planets above the Earth, make a man illustrious and generally known far and near, and being all swift in motion, render him dextrous and nimble in the dispatch of affairs.[6]

Having many planets in fixed signs was also believed to produce fame.

Aspects

In regard to aspects made with one planet by another, or others, it is important to consider which planet "impedites" the significator, whether that planet is friendly, what house the planet rules and in what house it is placed. Once that has been established, Lilly explains "from such a man or woman signified by that Planet, shall you be furthered or hindered..."[7] This becomes much clearer with the help of

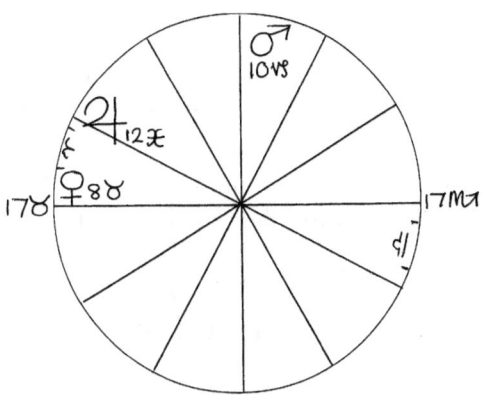

Constructive Aspects

the examples shown and the charts in Part Two of this book. For example, let us suppose that Taurus is the sign ascending. Venus is placed close to the ascendant and is applying to a trine with Mars in Capricorn, ruler of the seventh house. Venus is also applying to a later sextile with Jupiter in Pisces, ruler of the twelfth house (in Regiomontanus). In this instance, Venus is helped by both Jupiter and Mars. This occurs because of the friendly aspects, but also because both Mars and Jupiter

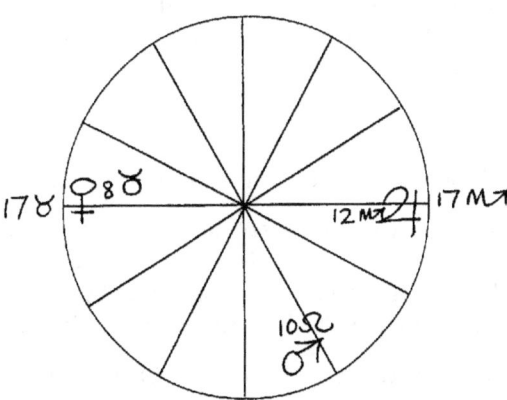

Destructive Aspects

have dignity. Jupiter is also received by Venus in her exaltation. Mars is received by Venus in her triplicity (in a diurnal chart).

However, if Venus is applying to an opposition with Jupiter in Scorpio, ruler of the eighth house, and applying to a square with Mars in Leo, ruler of the seventh house, this is unfortunate. Venus is hindered by both Mars and Jupiter. This is because the aspects are hostile and there are no receptions. Jupiter is also placed in the house of enemies, but more importantly, neither Mars nor Jupiter has dignity in these particular signs. Jupiter as a Fortune is less harmful than Mars as an Infortune.

If the Infortunes are hindering a positive outcome, Bonatti asks us to observe whether

> ...the Fortunes behold them with a Trine or Sextile Aspect; for then their ill-nature will be allayed and mitigated; but much more if these receive them.[8]

In the latter example, a trine from the Sun in Cancer with Jupiter, or a trine from the Moon in Sagittarius with Mars would be helpful.

Perfection

Bringing a matter to perfection implies that the planets have the dignity and position required to being about a favourable outcome. Lilly states that once the significators have been established, the astrologer must consider where they are placed in the chart, in what sign they are positioned and what aspects they receive. For example, if the Question concerns marriage, an applying conjunction between the Moon in Cancer and Jupiter in Cancer, where Jupiter rules the house of the matter enquired about (the seventh house) brings the matter to perfection, or is one positive testimony (indication) of a favourable outcome. The position and dignity of a planet is the most important consideration. In some instances a matter can be brought to perfection with no aspect, for example where planets are very strong in dignity, are in the house of the matter enquired about and have a mutual reception. There are various ways in which a favourable outcome (or perfection) is achieved. The following are probably the most important:

Through Aspect

A matter can be brought to perfection through a strong applying aspect, when

> ...the Planets signifying the Person propounding; and the person or thing enquired after, are going to Conjunction, Sextile or Trine to each other in good places of the Figure, and sometimes by Translation or Collection of Light; or by the Dwelling in Houses or Dignities.[9]

In a general sense the trine and sextile bring positive outcomes, as does the square (but with difficulty). With a square it is important that the planets have dignity and/or that one is received by the other, or they are mutually received. The opposition seldom brings a positive outcome, unless the planets involved have a strong mutual reception and another planet translates the light between them. Even then, the outcome may only be temporary or is something which the Querent later regrets. I have only seen one reasonable outcome brought about by an opposition, where the significators were mutually received and also benefited from a translation of light.

Ibn Ezra tells us that the opposition aspect is one of "complete enmity, the quadrature aspect is semi-enmity, the trine aspect is perfect amity, the sextile aspect is semi-amity".[10] Any aspect which produces good fortune usually takes place from good houses. This is because a planet needs a certain amount of strength to be of assistance. Planets which are in cadent houses are usually weak and cannot bring matters to perfection, nor can they produce good fortune. It is important to emphasise once more that the position and dignity of a planet is more important than the nature of the aspect.

Conjunction

Astrologers of the past believed that a conjunction was the most powerful aspect in a chart. There is no doubting the truth of this. I would agree that a conjunction between planets in a Question, Nativity or any other chart, is of primary importance and is the most powerful of chart testimonies. The power of the conjunction is unrivalled amongst the planetary aspects.

> When the Significators apply to a Conjunction in an Angle, the business may be brought to pass; if the Significator of the thing promised, be fortified, and apply to the Lord of the Ascendant.[11]

If the significators are moving towards a conjunction in the first house or in any angle, meeting with no prohibition or refranation before they come to an exact conjunction, the matter is brought to a successful conclusion. Prohibition and refranation take place when other planets get in the way of the significators. This is explained in chapter fifteen. Perfection happens more quickly if the significators are swift in motion, as well as being essentially or accidentally dignified. If the conjunction of the significators takes place in a succedent house, the matter will be perfected but not so soon. If it takes place in a cadent house, it will be perfected eventually but "with infinite loss of time, some difficulty and much strugling".[12] With the conjunction it is always best if the planets are friendly to each other. Perfection is unlikely to take place if, for example, the Moon is applying to a conjunction with an Infortune, such as Mars or Saturn, especially if they are out of their essential dignities. In a case like this, the matter is more likely to be hindered than brought to perfection. As Lilly tells us "Conjunctions are good or bad, as the Planets in conjunction are friends or enemies to one another".[13] The closer together the planets are, the more power they have. Abu Ma'shar confirms that a conjunction takes place when two planets are in one sign, but that their

> indications are more powerful if there is between them 15 degrees or less [in front or behind them both].[14]

Ibn Ezra explains that a conjunction can only take place if the planets are in one sign. If the planets are in two separate signs, even though they are within orb, what he calls "the force of the other's body" they are not in conjunction.[15]

One must be cautious about a conjunction which takes place across different signs. A conjunction between a planet, which is in late degrees of one sign, with another planet in very early degrees in the next sign, may be capable of helping to bring a matter to perfection. As an example, Mercury in twenty-nine degrees and fifty-nine minutes of Gemini applying to Jupiter in nought degrees thirty minutes of Cancer is a conjunction which is clearly quite strong. However, the greater the distance between significators which are in different signs, the less chance there is of any good fortune being produced from the conjunction. We have seen that a planet positioned after the twenty ninth degree of a sign has no power in that sign, but in the next sign, so this seems entirely possible. However, if Mercury were positioned in twenty-one degrees of Gemini, the outcome would be different. As discussed previously, astrologers of the past, notably Masha'allah, looked well beyond the sign where a planet was positioned and into the adjacent sign for the next aspect.

Morin believes that in general a conjunction with a Fortune produces a favourable effect. To understand the effects produced by a conjunction, he tells us that one must consider the nature of the planets involved and the nature of the sign in which it takes place. Morin lists three conditions where he believes that a conjunction would be favourable:[16]

Constructive Conjunctions

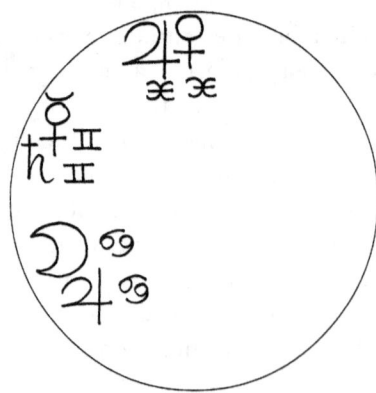

- Where one of the planets is in "honor" (a dignity like exaltation although this varies between different sources) and the other planet is in "dishonor" (a debility like detriment or fall). This might be Jupiter in Pisces in conjunction with Mercury in Pisces.

- Where one of the planets is in dignity, the other peregrine, for example Jupiter in Pisces in conjunction with Saturn in Pisces.

- Where both planets are in dignity, for example when the Sun in Aries is in conjunction with Mars in Aries or Jupiter in Cancer is in conjunction with the Moon in Cancer.

Referring to his first example, it is difficult to envisage how a conjunction between the Moon with Saturn in Cancer could be beneficial.

Fusion

Ibn Ezra tells us about fusion, which appears to be another term for conjunction. When this occurs between two planets, he explains that "there is produced out of their double nature a third nature as, for example, Saturn and Mars, both of which are baleful". According to Ibn Ezra, the ancients declared that when these planets join together, they exert a good influence. However, Ibn Ezra claims that

> The truth is that each one vitiates the action of the other, and thereby the new-born is saved from harm. Therefore they really prognosticate no good except the good of doing no harm.[17]

Clearly, much depends on the dignity of the planets involved. Even so, from my experience, a conjunction between Mars and Saturn in Aries appears to be unfortunate even though Mars has dignity in his own domicile. A conjunction between the Sun and Mars in Aquarius is also questionable. However, a conjunction between Mars and Saturn in Capricorn is more fortunate. In fact, in this conjunction, Mars and Saturn have a mutual reception, a type of mutual reception which the ancients referred to as *communion*. This was noted in chapter five. Charles Burnett tells us more about this in Abu Ma'shar's *The Abbreviation of the Introduction to Astrology*.[18]

Ibn Ezra claims that a conjunction between Jupiter and Saturn is the *great conjunction* because both of them are Superiors. He calls the conjunction between Mars and Venus a *mild conjunction*. The conjunction of all the planets with the Sun is harmful, especially the Moon and Venus. According to Ibn Ezra, Saturn and Mars exert a harmful influence when they are in conjunction with the Sun, but the conjunction of Jupiter with Venus is fortunate and does no harm. The text is a little unclear here, but it appears as if Ibn Ezra is referring to the conjunction of Venus and Jupiter with the Sun, not just with each other. Regarding the conjunction

Strong and Fortunate Trine

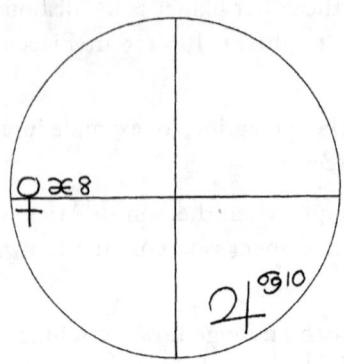

Weak and Less Fortunate Trine

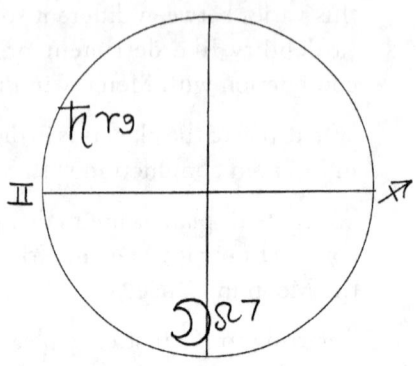

between Mercury and the Sun, he explains

> ...because of the multitude of its [Mercury's] movements and because it is always near the Sun, will do a little harm to it when it is beneath the rays of the Sun or beneath the limit of the scintillation.[19]

Ibn Ezra informs us that the ancients believed that a planet joined (conjunct) with the Sun has "a great force". Ibn Ezra tells us that Ptolemy contradicts them and that he is right. This is because the Sun is harmful to all planets in combustion, except when a planet is in the heart of the Sun (cazimi).

Trine or Sextile

Perfection can take place when the significators apply to each other with a trine or sextile aspect, as long as they are in good houses and in some of their essential dignities. This can only take place if "no malevolent Aspect" intervenes before they perfect the trine or sextile".[20]

> The Sextill and Trine aspects are arguments of Love, Unity and Friendship; but the trine is more forcible,(viz) if the two significators are in Sextill or Trine, no doubt but peace may be easily concluded.[21]

As emphasised throughout this book, in order to achieve the desired outcome (perfection), more than one testimony is required. Even if the principal significators are in aspect, this by itself is not usually sufficient testimony. The significators must be in good houses, preferably angular, in some of their essential dignities and/or have a reception or mutual reception. Lilly tells us that "planets in Angles doe more forcibly shew their effects".[22] Masha'allah also points out that a planet is at its very strongest when in conjunction with a house cusp, especially an angular house.

> ...the angles reinforce matters, and hasten and strengthen matters both good and bad. Therefore, whatever there is that is good is fixed by its

lord and will endure, and whatever there may be of the bad is similarly [fixed and enduring] for the one who suffers.[23]

In terms of sixth house matters connected to sickness, planets in angles do not hasten death: if they are principal significators of the sick person they have the effect of prolonging life. According to Ptolemy

Signs cadent from the ascendant of any kingdom are the ascendants of that kingdom's enemies. But the angles and succedent houses are the ascendants of its friends. It is the same in all doctrines and institutions.[24]

Square

The matter can be brought to perfection when the significators apply to each other with a square aspect, providing each planet has essential dignity and is in a good house. In fact it can be preferable when significators apply to a square with each other in some of their dignities (and with a strong mutual reception), than a trine

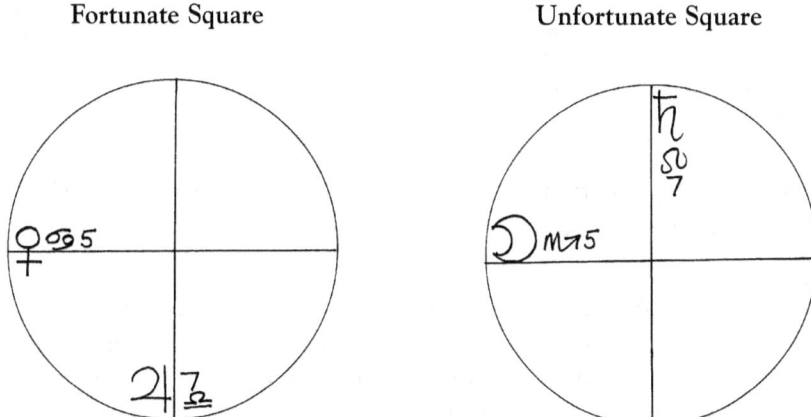

with none of the foregoing. Lilly calls the square an aspect of "imperfect enmity". He tells us that if there is a dispute, the square aspect indicates that the matter is not yet too far gone and that there may be hopes of reconciliation, as long as the other significators or planets are helping a little.[25]

Abu Ma'shar calls the square aspect a "quartile", an aspect of "antagonism".[26] In various places in *Christian Astrology*, Lilly claims that a square aspect in signs of long ascension can be equivalent to a trine and that a trine in signs of short ascension can be equivalent to a square. I have found some anecdotal evidence to support this, but cannot say with any degree of certainty. However, Culpeper is quite clear

> ... why do they hold that a Quartile in Signes of long ascensions is equivalent to a Trine, and a Trine in Signs of short ascensions as pernicious as a Square?.. put the rest of the non-sence into a bundle, and when you

have done, look upon it a little while; and when you have viewed it a little, tell me I pray; Doth the longness or shortness of the ascensions adde or take away any thing from the quality of the Signs?[27]

Opposition

On rare occasions, a matter is perfected when the significators apply to each other with an opposition. However, there must be a strong mutual reception and the

A Promising Opposition

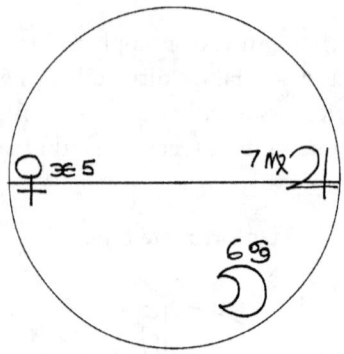

☽ translating the light between ♀ and ♃.
♀ and ♃ have a mutual reception.

A Less Promising Opposition

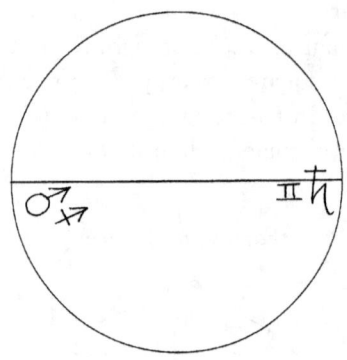

no translating planet and no mutual reception.

planets must be in friendly houses. In addition, it may be necessary for the Moon (or another swifter moving planet) to be separating from one significator and applying to the other significator by way of translation. Even if the matter is perfected in this way, it is often the case that the Querent might have been happier had the thing not happened at all. For example, if the Question concerns marriage, there is a strong possibility of disputes and disagreements later. In a Question about money, even if the Querent recovers his money, it might cost more in legal expenses than the debt was worth in the first instance. Abu Ma'shar calls the opposition an aspect of "enmity".[28]

According to Lilly, the opposition is an aspect of "perfect hatred" and he tells us that it is

> ...impossible to expect a peace betwixt them till the suit is ended, if it be a suit of Law; untill they have fought, if it be a Challenge.[29]

Ramsey explains that any business brought about by either the square or opposition between significators "causeth much discontent and sadness, so that the business had better never been done,&c".[30]

Lilly's Translation

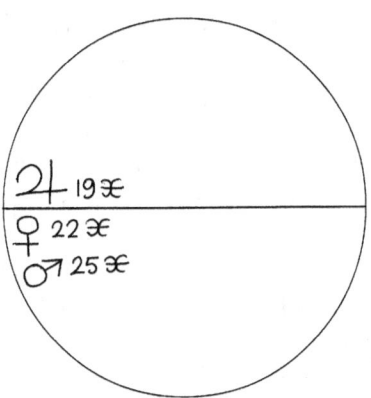

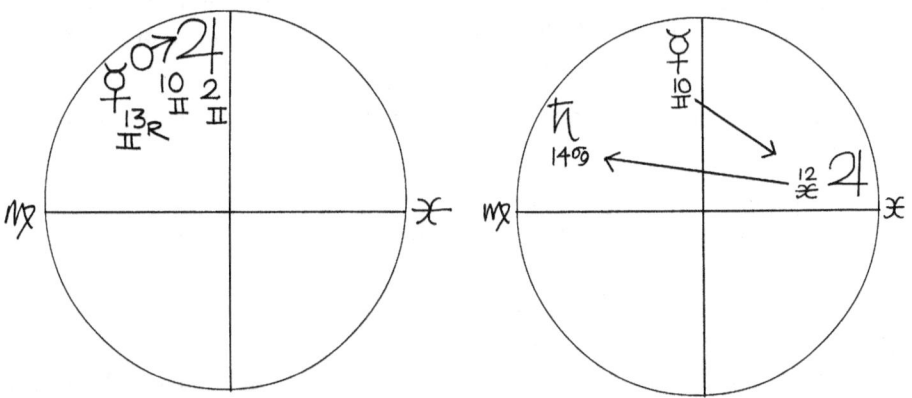

Al Biruni's Translation

Abu Ma'shar's Translation

Translation of Light

According to Lilly, if the significators of both the Querent and Quesited are separating from a conjunction, sextile or trine aspect with each other and another planet is separating from one of these significators and applying to a conjunction or aspect with the other significator, this is called translation of light. In addition, the separating planet should be received by the planet it is separating from by domicile, triplicity or term. Lilly does not include the dignity of exaltation, although this is possibly an error on his part. The translating planet must perfect the aspect before meeting any other planet. In this way, the planet

> ...translates the force, influence and vertue of the first Significator to the other, and then this intervening Planet (or such a man or woman as is signified by that Planet) shall bring the matter in hand to perfection.[31]

For example, Venus in twenty-two degrees of Pisces applies to a conjunction with Mars in twenty-five degrees of Pisces having recently departed from a conjunction with Jupiter in nineteen degrees of Pisces. Here, Venus translates the light from Jupiter to Mars and helps to bring about perfection. Translation can take place by aspect as well as through conjunction. For example, Mercury in twenty degrees of Pisces separates from a sextile with Mars in eighteen degrees of Taurus and applies to a square with Jupiter in twenty-two degrees of Gemini. It is this intervening planet (or the person represented by this planet) who can help to bring about the desired outcome. If this translating planet is, for example, the ruler of the second house, it's possible that some money would help things along. If this planet is the ruler of the fourth house, perhaps a father could help and so on. This might appear to be somewhat contradictory to Masha'allah's chain of applications, but it is simply a different method of seeking perfection.

Al Biruni tells us that translation (like collection) is another condition which is "efficacious besides aspect and conjunction".

> If an inferior planet separates from an intermediate one which is inconjunct [not in aspect] to a superior planet and thereafter conjoins with the superior one the light of the intermediate planet is transferred to the latter. This is called 'naql' or translation.[32]

He explains that "this condition is effective in lieu of conjunction". According to Al Biruni, translation can also take place when

> ...the inferior planet conjoins with the intermediate one, and the latter has already been in conjunction with the superior planet; [this]... is just the same as if the inferior had applied itself to the superior.

However, the examples of translation included by later authors, more specifically by Lilly in *Christian Astrology*, are on the whole, less complicated.

In his 98th Consideration Bonatti explains that if an outcome looks likely to be perfected through either aspect or conjunction, the matter will be brought about by the Querent and the party asked about without any intermediary. However, if perfection takes place through translation, the perfection shall be brought about by "ambassadors, friends, or some person interposing himself..."[33] However, in *Tools & Techniques of the Medieval Astrologers*, Zoller quotes Bonatti (*Liber Astronomiae*) who states

> It does not seem likely that although one planet is joined to another (unless it is joined to it from one of its dignities) that the heavier planet would give its virtue to it, or commit its nature or disposition to the second planet, according to the opinion of the philosophers.[34]

In other words, if one planet (A) cannot give its own nature or virtue to another, lighter planet (B), it does not seem likely, that this planet (B) can carry the nature of planet (A) to planet (C). Even if this 'carrying' of the nature could take place, it does not seem that this planet (B) would give it to another planet (C), unless it is joined to it in some of its dignities. However, Bonatti confirms that if the lighter planet (B) is joined to the heavier planet (A) in one of the dignities of the heavy planet, the latter (A) would commit its nature and disposition to the lighter planet (B). The lighter planet (B) could "carry it with itself" until joining up with another planet (C). This final planet (C), with whom the lighter planet is joined, should also be in some of the dignities of the lighter planet (B). Zoller puts forward an example where the lighter planet Venus, positioned in Sagittarius, the domicile of Jupiter, separates from her conjunction with Jupiter and applies to a sextile with Saturn in Libra, the domicile of Venus. According to Bonatti, Venus might be able to translate Jupiter's virtue to Saturn, but only because Jupiter receives or disposes of Venus when they are in their conjunction. Saturn, the final planet to whom the Venus is joined is in the domicile of Venus. In this example, however, it is clear that Jupiter will make a sextile with Saturn in any case, although there is no reception.

Zoller tells us that this must be looked into, because Bonatti himself is not sure of this doctrine. Bonatti, however, concedes that this doctrine "ought to be sustained" because "these men were wiser than I..." I would suggest that translation is a very straightforward method of achieving perfection and was used extensively by Lilly and his contemporaries.

Abu Ma'shar includes two types of translation. The first is the same as those discussed above, where a light, swifter moving planet, for example Mercury, separates from a slow planet, Jupiter and applies to another, Saturn. Here the nature of Jupiter is transferred to Saturn.[35]

Abu Ma'shar's second type of translation is where a light planet Mercury applies to a slower planet Jupiter and that slower planet Jupiter applies to another planet, Saturn. In this instance, the nature of the light planet Mercury is transferred to Saturn. This appears to be similar to Al Biruni's second example of translation as on page308.

The Yielding, Rendering up, Giving Back or Return of Light or Virtue

Although it is not totally clear from the texts, the doctrine of yielding, rendering or giving back appears to be what Bonatti and others call the 'return'. This doctrine can be divided into two: the *rendering, giving back or return of light* and the *rendering, giving back, or return of virtue*.

In terms of the yielding, rendering up, giving back or return of *light*, Dariot tells us that this occurs

> ..when two planets which do not beholde one another with any aspect, yet both of them do behold some other planet; for that planet doth gather their Lightes and doth cast it back agayne, either to themselves or to some other place of the Zodiack...[36]

Dariot tells us that Mars gathering the light of Saturn and the Sun "doth yield it back agayne unto them".

He goes on to say that if the third planet is heavier than the two other planets "that shall be called a collection or gathering together of the lightes". When *collection* takes place, a heavier planet gathers the light of the two (or more) lighter planets and as Dariot says, casts it back to them. With rendering of the light, it appears that the third planet does not have to be a heavier planet (in Dariot's example Mars is lighter than Saturn) and that the light can also be reflected to some other point in the zodiac. An example from Dariot's work is included below to illustrate this point.

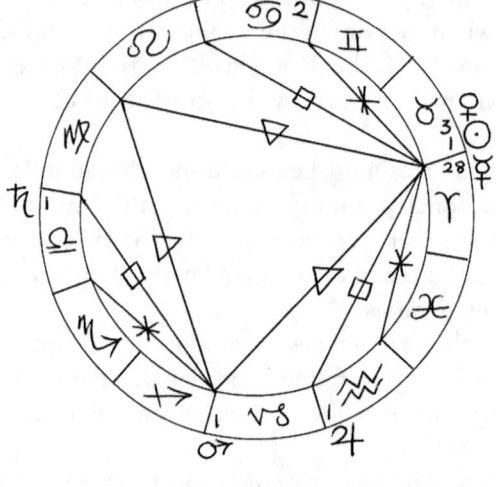

Dariot's Rendering of Light, Collection of Light and Rendering up of Virtue

Bonatti calls this doctrine the return of light, which occurs when, for example, Mercury in eleven degrees of Pisces separates from Venus in ten degrees of Pisces. Both planets make a conjunction with Jupiter in thirteen degrees of Pisces. Jupiter makes no aspect or conjunction with any other planet. Jupiter transfers the light of Venus to a place in the circle which he is aspecting "before him", that is to thirteen degrees of Taurus by sextile, to thirteen degrees of Gemini by square, to thirteen degrees of Cancer by trine, thirteen degrees of Scorpio by trine and thirteen degrees of Sagittarius by square (and presumably thirteen degrees of Capricorn by sextile). The opposition is not included.[37] This doctrine of the *return* or *rendering* of light should not be confused with the *return* of light and its *abscission* which is explained in chapter fifteen. This is very different and can prevent the achievement of a positive outcome.

According to Abu Ma'shar, this mode of perfection is called reflection of light and is of two kinds. Firstly he tells us that if the significators do not apply to a conjunction, or aspect, with each other, but they aspect another planet, which "aspects a place on the zodiacal circle", it appears that this planet can reflect the light of both of them onto that place.[38]

The second way is similar to that of translation: Abu Ma'shar explains that if the ascendant ruler and the significator of the matter enquired about do not aspect each other or are separating from each other, but a planet has moved between them both, it can reflect the light of one of the two onto the other. The doctrine of return or reflection of light seems a little dubious. There is no mention of this in *Christian Astrology* and I can only assume that Lilly having read the work of over two hundred authors and having drawn up thousands of charts, did not feel it warranted his inclusion.

In terms of the yielding, rendering up, giving back or return of *virtue*, Bonatti in his *Liber Astronomiae* (*Tractatus Tertius*), explains that the return of virtue can be 'profitable' if certain conditions are fulfilled. If for example, one planet is joined with another and commits its disposition to that planet and that planet is combust or retrograde, the planet cannot hold on to that virtue, so it gives it back or returns it. However, if both planets are angular or succedent, this return of virtue is "good and useful and with profit". Here we are told that "the thing concerning which the question was asked is perfected..."[39] An example of a satisfactory return and an unsatisfactory return of virtue are included in chapter fifteen on page 331.

Following the same line of thought, Dariot puts forward a very similar example, which he calls the rendering up of virtue. Dariot explains that this takes place when a planet, which is in any of its dignities, beholds another who is combust or retrograde. The weakened planet cannot hold on to the virtue from the stronger planet, which is given to it through the aspect. However, a successful rendering of virtue can take place

> ..where Venus being combuste in Taurus, rendereth up to the Moone her virtue which she did give unto her by a sextile aspect [40]

According to Dariot, this rendering is "good and profitable", but it can only take place successfully if the planets are in angles or succedent houses, or if the applying planet is in an angle and the other in a falling house (with a reception). If these conditions are not fulfilled the rendering will be "unprofitable".

It is difficult to understand why the above example should be deemed fortunate, given that the Moon, the key player, is afflicted by her opposition with Mars. Bonatti tells us that the planet who has the virtue returned, is the planet who perfects the matter. In the former example this is the Moon. In the example included in chapter fifteen, this planet is Mars. Here, Mars receives Jupiter in his domicile of Aries. Mars commits his disposition and virtue to Jupiter, but Jupiter being retrograde and combust, returns this virtue to Mars. Bonatti tells us that "afterwards all of Mars' virtue remains" so that matter enquired about is "perfected by Mars' virtue and from his potency".[41]

Lilly includes an example of what he calls rendering or receiving virtue in *Christian Astrology*. This is the marriage chart, included in chapter twelve. Here, the principal significators are the Sun and Saturn, who apply to each other with a sextile, but since there is no reception of any sort between them, they are not powerful enough alone to bring about perfection. However, Jupiter applies to a sextile with Saturn and the Sun applies to a conjunction with Jupiter. This, according to Lilly, is a rendering of virtue.

> ..the application of Jupiter to sextile of Saturn Lord of the seventh, receiving his vertue which Saturn did render unto him, and he again transferred to the Sun Lord of the ascendant...[42]

Collection of Light

Al Biruni calls translation and collection *substitutes* for conjunction and aspect. He explains that collection takes place when an Inferior and an Intermediate both apply to an aspect with a Superior. The latter is called a *collector*, because it "assembles the light of the others". He explains that if they are in aspect with each other, this is "just as good as conjunction with the collector". If they are not in aspect, the collection of their light is effective in place of the conjunction, even though they might be inconjunct.[43]

Lilly tells us that collection takes place where two significators are not in aspect with each other, but they both aspect a slower moving planet and there is a reception between the two planets and the slower moving planet. This planet can collect their light and bring the matter to perfection. In reality this means that a person interested in these two people or things, or who is friendly with both people described, can bring about a happy conclusion.

> As many times you see two fall at variance, and of themselves cannot think of any way of accommodation, when suddenly a Neighbour or friend accidentally reconciles all differences, to the content of both parties.[44]

However, only a planet well dignified and well placed can bring about perfection through collection. A planet retrograde and combust cannot do this, especially if that planet is an Infortune. In this instance the person signified by the debilitated planet either has no real interest in assisting and would hinder the matter, or is incapable of assisting even if that were the intention. It is always best if the collecting planet is a Fortune, direct, swift, angular and free from misfortune. This is likely to be Jupiter. In practice it is fairly unusual to see a matter being perfected by collection of light.

Reception

Reception is of crucial importance in any chart, whether Nativity, Question or Election. The presence or absence of reception between significators can be more important in bringing about a successful outcome than the kind of aspect being formed between them. As discussed previously, reception between domiciles is the strongest and best of all receptions, followed in order of strength by reception between exaltation, between triplicity, between term and finally between face. For

A Strong Collection	A Weak or Unlikely Collection
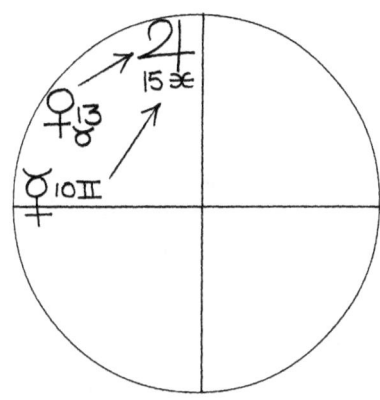	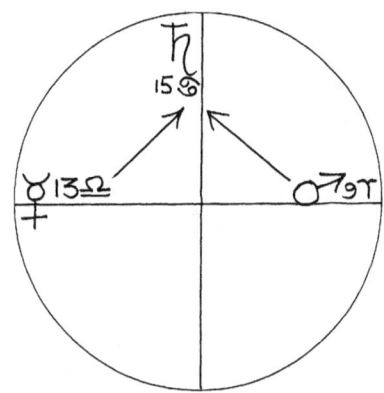

example, Venus in Aries and the Sun in Taurus have a mutual reception between triplicity in the day time. Jupiter in Pisces and Venus in Cancer have a mutual reception between exaltation during the day and night.

With a mutual reception between planets, an aspect is not necessarily required, but if there is an applying aspect the good fortune is increased. With a single reception an aspect between the planets is always required. Where there is any reception or mutual reception, the planets become more fortunate. Planets which are received can help to counteract malefic influences elsewhere. If the perfection of a matter is denied by aspect, if the significators have no aspect with each other, or it is doubtful that what is promised by a square or opposition will bring about the desired outcome, a mutual reception between the significators can help to bring the matter to a successful conclusion. Even if the significators make no aspect, but have a mutual reception, the matter can sometimes be perfected.

House Position

In any Question, a significator placed in the house of the matter enquired about is positive testimony of bringing about the desired outcome, although a second concurring testimony is usually required. Let us use the example of a Querent applying for a job: if the significator of the Querent, or the Moon, is placed in the tenth house, this is positive testimony and can bring matters to perfection, other testimonies supporting. If the significator of the matter asked about (ruler of the tenth house) is in the ascendant or first house, this is even more fortunate for the Querent. If the ruler of the tenth house is in the ascendant and the ruler of the ascendant is in the tenth house, this is even more likely to produce a positive outcome, especially if there is a reception. In the latter example, perfection can take place even if there is no aspect between the significators.

Dariot tells us that if the significator of the thing or person asked about is positioned in the first house, especially if there is reception, it signifies that the

Will they buy the house?

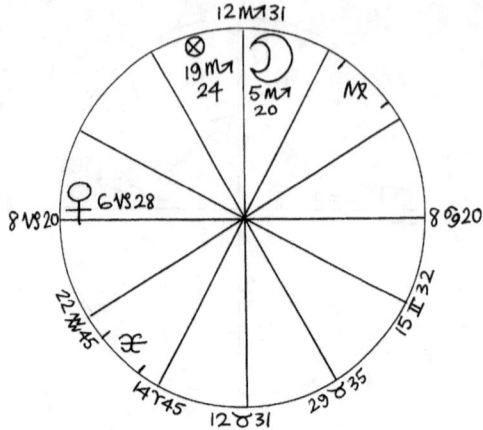

Ruler of the matter enquired about (fourth house) is in conjunction with the ascendant.

Will I get the really good job?

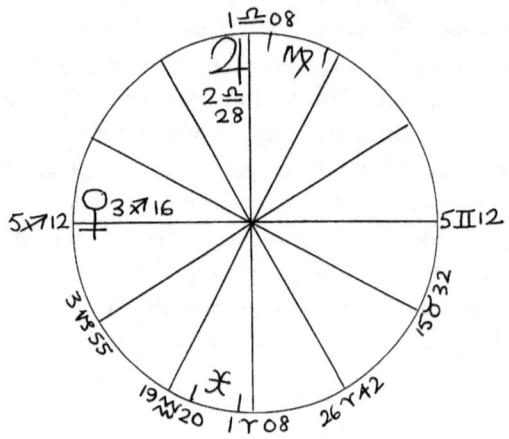

Ruler of the matter enquired about (tenth house) is in conjunction with the ascendant. Ruler of ascendant is in the house of the matter enquired about.

Querent will get what he wants easily "without any labour". However, if the ascendant ruler, or the Moon, or any of the significators of the Querent are in the house of the thing or person asked about, the Querent will get what he wants but "with much labour".[45] Here, I would like to re-emphasise the idea discussed earlier: that things come more easily (without active seeking) when the significator of the matter enquired about applies to the significator of the Querent. Masha'allah in his example of a Querent seeking a Kingship, states that if the ruler of the matter enquired about

> ...itself seeks a joining together with the lord of the Ascendant, then the one asking will acquire the kingship without his own having to seek; it will even come to him sitting in his own house and without effort.[46]

The following chart testimonies are also important and, together with those already discussed, should be carefully considered in any chart evaluation.

Besiegement

Any planet besieged between two Fortunes acquires enormous strength. Besiegement takes place when a planet is positioned in one particular sign, with a Fortune before it and another behind it, or when a planet is separating from a conjunction or aspect with a Fortune and applying to a conjunction or aspect with another Fortune. In *The Abbreviation of the Introduction to Astrology*, Abu Ma'shar refers to containment (besiegement) in both a fortunate and unfortunate sense. With regard to the good fortune of the planets, he tells us that this occurs if a planet is "separating from a benefic and applying to another benefic", or if it is "contained between two benefics..."

Abu Ma'shar also tells us that the besiegement or containment of planets or luminaries can take place across signs (which corresponds to our more modern term of houses) and also that a sign itself or the ascendant can be contained. He explains how this takes place in the case of malefics and causes a planet to be unfortunate, but does not include an example of a similar situation which includes benefics. According to all authors I have researched, it appears that a planet or sign contained by the benefics is the best of good fortune.[47]

Planetary Motion and Movement

The motion of each planet is an important consideration. Morin states that a planet which is stationary brings "Effects which are constant and permanent". A stationary planet is not as favourable as one which is direct, but is more favourable than one which is retrograde. A planet in his first station and about to turn retrograde is unfortunate, but a planet in his second station about to turn from being retrograde to direct is very fortunate. According to Morin, a planet in direct motion indicates "continuity and progression".[48]

The Lot of Fortune

The Lot of Fortune cannot, in itself, bring about the desired outcome, but it has some influence over the matter. Ptolemy assigns the Lot of Fortune as one of the most important places in the Nativity along with the luminaries, the ascendant and their rulers. It is important to consider whether the Lot of Fortune falls in a fortunate house, what its aspects are (from a Fortune or an Infortune) and whether it is received by the aspecting planet.

In his preface to Abu Ali Al Khayyat's *The Judgments of Nativities*, Heller reminds us of the importance of the "lords of the parts, and their strengths and weaknesses...their houses and applications..." He tells us that they should be considered in just the same way as all the other significators.[49] Bonatti asks us to observe

> ...in Nativities and general Questions in what house the Part of Fortune happens; for from the things signified by that House will the Fortune or

gain of the Native or Querent arise, if the same be well disposed, otherwise the same will be [the] cause of his misfortune and loss.[50]

In Questions where a positive outcome seems likely, but the Lot of Fortune is "in an untoward place", for example in a cadent house, making a square or opposition with an Infortune and has no reception, the outcome is likely to be less positive and perhaps less profitable than anticipated, so as to "deceive the Querent's hopes". Alternatively, in Questions where a positive outcome seems unlikely, if the Part of Fortune is fortunate and "joined with a good Planet that receives it" any misfortune will be reduced and "not so much happens to the Querent as the Figure otherwise seems to threaten".[51] Robert Zoller explains that the Lot of Fortune is associated with

> ...praise and good reputation, honours and recognition, good and evil... if this part and the luminaries are well disposed in nativities or revolutions, it will be notably good.[52]

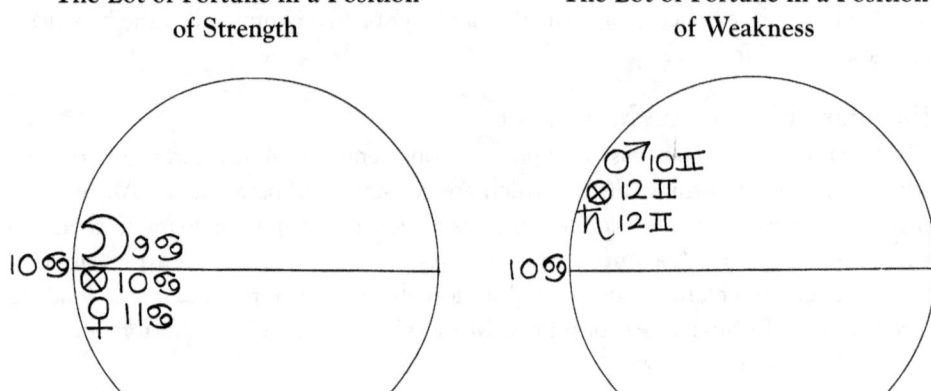

The Fixed Stars

As demonstrated earlier, the fixed stars can be very important in judgement. If a significator is in conjunction with a benevolent fixed star

> ...such star shall so far help the significator, that the thing shall be accomplished and effected, even beyond the Querent's hopes.[53]

This is what Bonatti calls a 'most strong secret helper'. He tells us that the fixed stars sometimes confer "exceeding great benefits".[54] Referring to Regulus (currently positioned at around twenty-nine degrees and fifty-three minutes of Leo), Bonatti asks the reader to observe in diurnal Nativities, whether

Cor Leonis be in the Ascendant... or whether it be in the tenth... without the Conjunction or Aspect of any of the Fortunes; for this alone signifies that the Native shall be a person of great note and power... And if any of the Fortunes behold that place also, his glory shall be the more increased...[55]

In a nocturnal Nativity "his fortune will be somewhat meaner, but not much..." Bonatti tells us that Cor Leonis (Regulus) confers

>...glory, wealth, and great honours, chiefly by military preferment; but the glory promised by such Stars such as Aldebaran, Hercules, Bellatrix, Antares, etc., and all which are of the nature of Mars... is said to be transient.

Concurring Testimonies

As discussed previously, it is crucially important in judgement to consider whether there are at least two supporting or concurring testimonies. James Holden tells us that Al-Khayyat "typically gives the maximum effect" that can be expected from a position or configuration. Holden tells us that this differs considerably from modern astrological practice of stating an average or perhaps a psychological tendency. Holden explains that Al-Khayyat also states quite clearly that many factors have to be present to produce this maximum effect and that the astrologer cannot "assume the maximum effect from a single unsupported position".[56]

I include a chart example below to illustrate the points raised in this chapter. This chart contains very clear and fortunate chart testimony. It is not the most fortunate testimony, but it is certainly good enough to bring the matter to perfection.

Will I get Planning Permission so I can Build a House? When?

The Querent is signified by Mercury, angular, in his own face in the tenth house, and not afflicted by an Infortune or other malefic. Mercury's dispositor is the Moon in Sagittarius, also co-significator of the Querent and the Question. The Moon and Jupiter are aspecting the ascendant. The Moon is increasing in light, approaching the fourth house and applying to a conjunction with Jupiter, ruler of the fourth house, and the seventh house (of an agreement). There is no affliction or impediment before the aspect perfects. Jupiter is in his domicile and is close to the fourth house cusp, although he is retrograde, and incorrectly placed in a diurnal chart, therefore losing some power. The Querent was given the relevant permission at the end of August, just over four weeks later. There are a number of positive and supporting testimonies, but it is in the main the position of Jupiter, strong in essential and accidental dignities, which facilitates this positive outcome.

As emphasised throughout the book, it is the position and dignity of a planet which is of primary importance. It should be clear that perfection is not only achieved through aspect: it can be achieved through dignity, mutual reception, position in a house or a combination of these. For example, in relation to second house matters

Horary Astrology Re-Examined

Will I get planning permission?

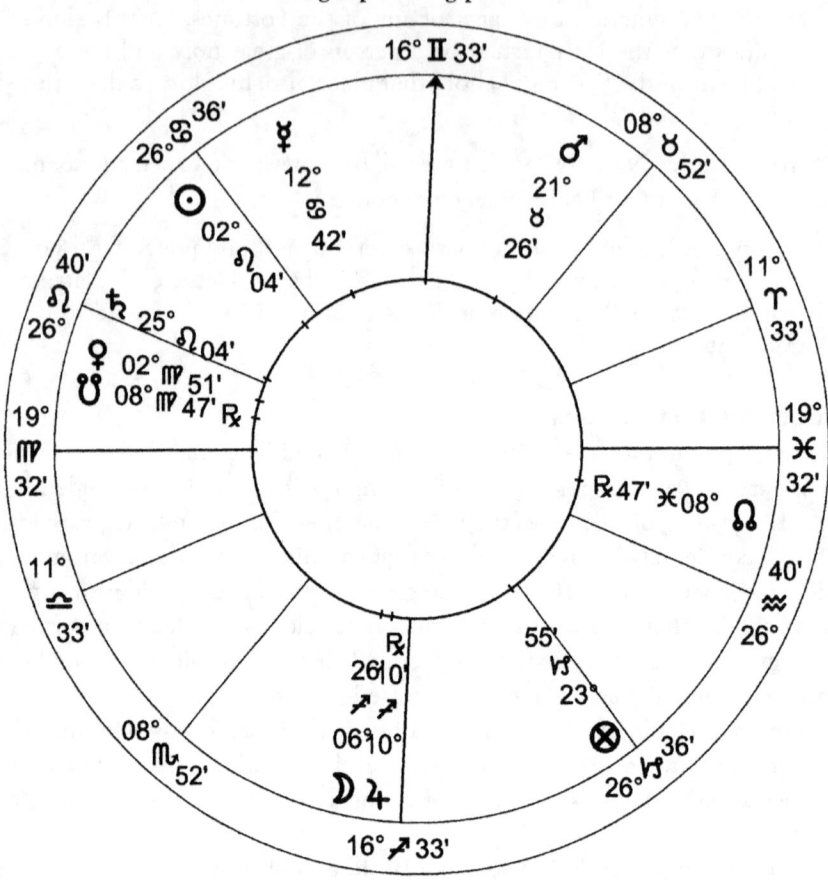

concerning wealth, Lilly tells us that the Querent will not be poor if all planets are angular; if all planets are in succedent houses, direct and swift in motion, or if all planets are in good houses, direct but only moderately dignified. There is no mention of aspect. Lilly tells us that if some or all of these chart testimonies are present, it is "an hopefull argument of an Estate".[57] However, if the chart testimonies are in the main positive, but a significator or the Moon is afflicted by an Infortune, this can reduce the good fortune anticipated or prevent a successful outcome entirely. It is not often that a chart produces a significant number of strong, positive and concurring testimonies. We have learned that a planet which is able to offer the strongest assistance of all, in any type of chart, should be in its domicile, in an angle in the very minute of the cusp, direct, swift in motion, in reception and free from all affliction and impediment. Bonatti confirms that a condition like this "most seldome happens".[58]

References

1. Al Biruni p.331.
2. Bonatus pp.6-7, 9th consideration.
3. ibid p.6, 9th consideration and p.7.
4. ibid not totally clear here on the distance between planet and star.
5. ibid p.11, 16th consideration.
6. ibid p.66, no.40, and editor's footnote.
7. Lilly p.124.
8. Bonatus p.16, 36th consideration.
9. Ball p.61.
10. Ibn Ezra, *The Beginning Of Wisdom*, p.190.
11. Ball p.62.
12. Lilly p.125.
13. ibid p.106.
14. Abu Ma'shar p.23.
15. Ibn Ezra p.209.
16. Morin pp.76-77 and footnote.
17. Ibn Ezra p.210.
18. Abu Ma'shar, editor's footnote (Charles Burnett), p.27. Also see chapter eight.
19. Ibn Ezra p.210.
20. Lilly p.125.
21. ibid p.106.
22. ibid p.48.
23. Masha'allah p.33.
24. Ptolemy, *The Centiloquy*, Ashmand translation, p.154.
25. Lilly p.106.
26. Abu Ma'shar p.23.
27. Culpeper p.21.
28. Abu Ma'shar p.23.

29. Lilly p.106.
30. Ramsey p.93.
31. Lilly p.126.
32. Al Biruni pp.313-314.
33. Bonatus p.32, 98th consideration.
34. Bonatus in *Tools & Techniques of the Medieval Astrologers*, Zoller, p.98 from *Liber Astronomiae* Tractus Tertius.
35. Abu Ma'shar p.25.
36. Dariot p.32.
37. Bonatus in *Tools & Techniques of the Medieval Astrologers*, by Robert Zoller, p.100.
38. Abu Ma'shar pp.25-26.
39. Bonatus in *Tools & Techniques of the Medieval Astrologers*, p.105.
40. Dariot p.32.
41. Bonatus in *Tools & Techniques of the Medieval Astrologers* p.105.
42. Lilly pp.385-387.
43. Al Biruni p.313.
44. Lilly p.126.
45. Dariot p.62.
46. Masha'allah p.35.
47. Abu Ma'shar p.31.
48. Morin p.154.
49. Heller, Joachim, preface to Abu 'Ali Al-Khayyat, *The Judgments of Nativities* p.20.
50. Bonatus p.35 103rd consideration.
51. ibid p.29, 85th consideration.
52. Robert Zoller, *The Lost Key to Prediction. The Arabic Parts in Astrology* p.85.
53. Bonatus p.7 9th consideration.
54. ibid p.48.
55. ibid p.55, 145th consideration and editor's footnote.
56. Abu 'Ali Al-Khayyat, introduction by Holden, p.18.
57. Lilly p.168.
58. Bonatus p.7.

15

THE IMPOSSIBILITY OF THE MATTER PROPOUNDED

This chapter examines and evaluates the testimonies which either produce misfortune, reduce good fortune, and/or prevent the achievement of the desired outcome entirely. It is these same testimonies which produce misfortune in the Nativity, Election or any other type of chart.

General Testimonies of Misfortune

When a planet lacks essential or accidental dignity (or both) and/or is afflicted by the Infortunes, it cannot offer much in the way of assistance. At best, this planet reduces the good fortune expected in a Question. At worst, this planet prevents the achievement of perfection. In terms of a Nativity, this planet either reduces any good fortune for the individual in a particular area of life, surrounds it with disappointment, or prevents it entirely.

If a significator is combust, cadent, in its detriment, fall or peregrine, or if the chart contains a New Moon, Full Moon or Eclipse, this is unfortunate testimony. No amount of planetary dignity elsewhere can fully compensate. Authorities of the past agree that in an overall sense

> When the Significators are Combust, Cadent, or void of Reception, 'tis a Miracle if they bring any thing to perfection...[1]

In the same way

> ...when either the Infortunes, or Cauda Draconis [south node], shall be located in the House signifying the thing enquired after, the business will be brought to an unprosperous end

As well as being weak in "falling houses" (cadent or other unfortunate houses), planets lack strength and are unable to perform if they

> ...doe not beholde the ascendant... are oute of their owne essentiall dignities... in the dignities of the malygne planets as in the tearmes of Mars or Saturne, or that they bee in their falles or in contrarye signes to their owne houses, or else be retrograde or in their first station...[2]

However, there are varying levels of misfortune associated with particular planetary conditions. For example, a planet in the terms of the Infortunes is less malefic than a planet afflicted by a square or opposition with one of the Infortunes.

Misfortune

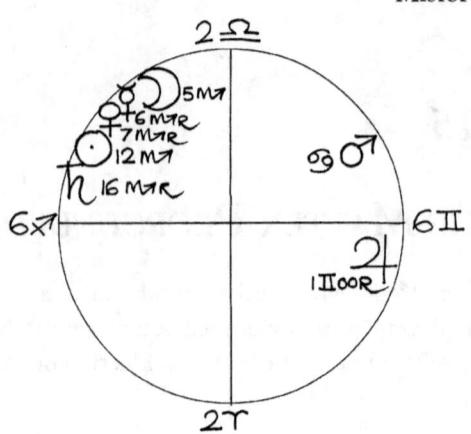

♀ is combust and retrograde. ♃ is in his detriment and retrograde. The ☽ is applying to combustion. ♂ is in his fall. ♄ is peregrine. ☿ is combust and retrograde. No planets make an aspect with the ascendant, except ♃ with an opposition.

Hinderers

As in the previous chapter, where I examined the role of helpers in the chart, here I examine the role of *hinderers*. These are the planets which, according to Bonatti, offer no assistance in terms of bringing about the desired outcome, or can actually prevent it. Similarly, in a Nativity, the hinderers offer no assistance and can cause misfortune. The following are the hinderers to which Bonatti refers: [3]

13. A most strong secret hinderer
14. A very strong secret hinderer
15. A strong secret hinderer
16. A weak secret hinderer
17. A weaker secret hinderer
18. A most weak secret hinderer
19. A most strong manifest hinderer
20. A very strong manifest hinderer
21. A strong manifest hinderer

A level of strength or weakness is assigned to these hinderers. The secret hinderers Bonatti refers to are the fixed stars, although it is clear that it is the conjunction of a planet with the fixed star which together produce the misfortune. The manifest or open hinderers appear to be the planets only. In terms of a secret hinderer, Bonatti gives most weight to a fixed star in partill conjunction with a significator, where that significator also has no essential dignity. In terms of an open or manifest hinderer, this is a planet with no essential or accidental dignity, which is also afflicted. In the same way as fixed stars of the same nature in conjunction with significators become helpers, fixed stars of a "contrary nature" joined with significators become hinderers. They are a weakening influence. If, in addition to this, the significator is out of its dignities, it will "not suffer the thing to come to pass", even if the chart shows a lot of potential. The further away these fixed stars are from the significator, the less influence they have.

Secret Hinderers

A **most strong** secret hinderer is a malefic fixed star in conjunction by only one minute with a significator who has no essential dignity. (Bonatti tells us that this fixed star should be of a contrary nature to the significator.)

A **very strong** secret hinderer is a malefic fixed star of a contrary nature in conjunction by 16 minutes with a significator who has no essential dignity.

Bonatti does not supply all the details of the secret hinderers but tells us that (as in the discussion in chapter fourteen), we go "downward through all the degrees in the same manner" that is, from a **most strong** secret hinderer (as above) until we reach a **most weak** secret hinderer where the influence is at its lowest.

Any planet in conjunction with a malefic fixed star is most unfortunate. The fixed star which probably causes the most damage is Caput Algol. The Moon or principal significator in conjunction with this fixed star or, as Lilly suggests, within a five degree orb, can destroy a successful outcome despite the presence of fortunate testimonies elsewhere.

Manifest (Open) Hinderers

Bonatti does not supply all details of the manifest hinderers but, as in the example of helpers in the previous chapter, the comparison is the same: the helpers produce good fortune to a greater or lesser extent; the hinderers produce misfortune to a greater or lesser extent. A **most strong** manifest (or open) hinderer is a significator

> ...in a place where he hath no Dignity, no delight, is not received; beseiged by the Two Infortunes, Cadent from an Angle, and from the ascendant: and so much the worse if joined with any of the Fixed Stars, of a mischievous nature, etc.

A Most Strong Manifest Hinderer

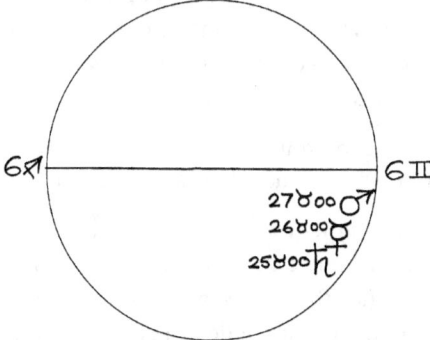

☿ a most strong manifest hinderer in conjunction with Caput Algol, beseiged by Infortunes, cadent from his domicile and from the ascendant.

In contrast to a most strong manifest helper which does the utmost good, a planet in this condition is seriously afflicted and can only cause difficulties and setbacks.

Bonatti explains that in addition to the misfortune that can be brought about by the above-mentioned hinderers there may be other "obstructing causes", both open and secret, relating to the planets, their conjunctions and aspects. He tells us that if this information about helpers and hinderers is carefully observed, it will be "of great use in raising a true and wary judgment; especially if thou hast always a diligent eye to the Moon..."

Not Beholding the Ascendant

It is very important that planets behold the ascendant in some way, whether through aspect (preferably with a trine or sextile), or through the antiscia. If the principal significators or the ascendant ruler do not behold the ascendant, it is less fortunate for the Native or the Querent. The conjunction of a Fortune with the ascendant is fortunate, but the conjunction of an Infortune, unless in some of his essential dignities, is unfortunate. For example, Jupiter in Sagittarius in the ascendant is a very strong and fortunate placement. Saturn in Aquarius in the ascendant is a strong placement, especially in a diurnal chart. Saturn in Aries or Cancer in the ascendant is a weak and unfortunate placement, especially in a nocturnal chart. Mars in Taurus is an unfortunate placement especially in a diurnal chart. Bonatti explains that if a significator is

> ...cadent from an Angle or from the Ascendant, and in none of his Dignities, nor in his Joy: for then he signifies nothing but doubts and mischiefs, and there are no hopes of good or profit from a planet so disposed.[4]

Masha'allah tells us that if the ascendant ruler does not aspect the ascending sign and is not aspecting another planet which in turn is aspecting (or giving its light) to the ascending sign, this is "the downfall of the Lord of the Ascendant".[5] As discussed in earlier chapters, this is a very interesting point and frequently overlooked. The ascendant ruler loses strength to a significant extent if not in aspect with the ascendant. In the same way, a Fortune who is cadent cannot bring about the good that is promised. Quoting Zael (Sahl), Bonatti explains that

> ...if the Fortune be cadent from the Ascendant, so that it cannot behold the same, it only flatters with splendid hopes, but never completes the business.[6]

A planet not aspecting its own domicile is also less fortunate in terms of the house it rules in the chart. Jupiter in Leo, for example, aspects his own domicile of Sagittarius, in which case the affairs associated with that house will prosper. However, Jupiter in Leo does not aspect his domicile of Pisces. So the affairs associated with the house which has Pisces in its cusp may prove to be unfortunate or at least, less fortunate. This applies equally to a Question, or any other chart.

Denial of Perfection

There are several ways in which perfection is denied and the desired outcome prevented.

Significators not Making an Aspect

If the principal significators make no aspect with each other, this is a testimony of misfortune in the Question. In his *Brief Introduction to Astrology*, Ball tells us that if other testimonies do not assist, it may not be possible to achieve the desired outcome.

> If the Significators of the Querent and Quesited, are not beholding each other, it is an Argument the thing enquired after, will not be brought to perfection.[7]

Through Aspect

Conjunction with an Infortune

If a significator perfects a conjunction with an Infortune, out of his essential dignities and in an unfortunate house, this can prevent a positive result. The conjunction of Venus with Jupiter is fortunate, but the conjunction of Venus with Saturn is not. However, a conjunction between Venus and Saturn in Libra, where both have dignity and are mutually received, is less harmful than one where Venus and Saturn are in Aries. Morin lists three types of unfavourable conjunction:[8]

- Where both planets are peregrine, for example Jupiter in conjunction with the Moon in Libra.

- Where one planet is in "dishonor" and the other planet is peregrine, for example, the Sun in conjunction with the Moon in Aquarius.

- Where both planets are in "dishonor" for example the Sun in conjunction with Mars in Libra, or Saturn in conjunction with Mars in Cancer.

Unfavourable Conjunctions

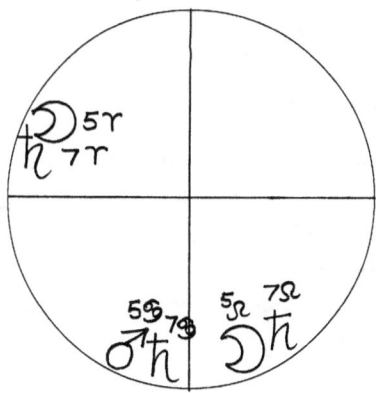

In fact, most authorities would agree that a conjunction with Jupiter, a Fortune, is always fortunate. In *Christian Astrology* in the context of Questions about illness, Lilly suggests that the conjunction of the Moon with Jupiter is a "good argument of recovery" no matter in what sign Jupiter is placed. However, he tells us that the conjunction in Capricorn is the least favourable, because "neither the Moon or Jupiter have any delight therein".[9] In fact in a nocturnal chart the Moon has rulership over the earth triplicity.

I would suggest that a conjunction with a Fortune is always favourable, unless the Fortune rules an unfortunate house or is afflicted itself. However, a conjunction with an Infortune is unfortunate unless he is strong in essential dignities and there is some form of reception.

Conjunction through Retrogradation

Morin tells us that

> ...conjunctions which occur because of retrogradation realise their effects in extraordinary and unexpected ways, and consequently even more so if the two Planets in question should be simultaneously retrograde, and then the following, swifter one should overtake the preceding, slower one.[10]

An example of this would be Venus in Taurus retrograde in seventeen degrees and Mercury in Taurus retrograde in nineteen degrees. Mercury makes a conjunction with Venus (where Venus is retrograding more slowly). According to Morin, the same applies to departures by retrogradation (whether just one planet is retrograding or both are retrograding). The planet which is approaching, whether this is by direct or retrograde motion, will always "prevail over the other". In other words the approaching planet is stronger in terms of the Question for better or worse.

Conjunction with the Sun

There is no question that the conjunction of all the planets with the Sun is harmful and detrimental. The worst of all, according to Ibn Ezra, is the conjunction of the Sun with either Venus or the Moon. Ibn Ezra explains that Saturn and Mars "likewise exert a harmful influence with respect to the Sun when they enter into conjunction with it".[11] This implies that the combustion of Saturn and Mars makes their influence harmful to other planets. The conjunction of the Moon with Saturn and Mars is also harmful. As discussed in earlier chapters, the Sun is harmful to all planets in combustion, except when a planet is in the heart of the Sun (cazimi).

Combustion is one of the worst conditions to affect a planet, whether the chart under consideration is a Nativity, Question, Ingress, Election and so on. It could be argued that the effects of combustion are mitigated in a Nativity, because there is a whole lifetime to work through the relevant issues. However, in the case of a Question, there is no such mitigation. A combust significator is usually weakened beyond repair, particularly if the combustion is applying.

A planet under sunbeams is also weakened, especially when moving towards the Sun, when the outcome will be less promising than indicated. However, when a planet is moving away from sunbeams the outlook is better, especially in terms of a difficult situation, which starts to become far easier. A planet moving away from sunbeams can represent a person who has been very ill, but is getting better. The reverse might apply if that planet were moving towards the Sun. Bonatti tells us that a planet

> ...when he enters combustion he is like one who begins to grow sick. And when he is in the deepest combustion he is like a sick man when there is a paroxysm in his state, which is when the fever is about to overcome him and it is already in existence... And when [the planet] has separated from the Sun all the way to two degrees he is like a sick man who overcame the crisis, but is not yet completely over the things making up the crisis...[12]

However, when that planet has separated five degrees from the Sun up until he has separated from sunbeams

> ...he is like an ill man whose sickness ceases and is manifestly diminished... but he does not yet completely resume his pristine strength however he is now safe from that illness.

A planet emerging from sunbeams is very strong.

Sunbeams, Combustion and Cazimi

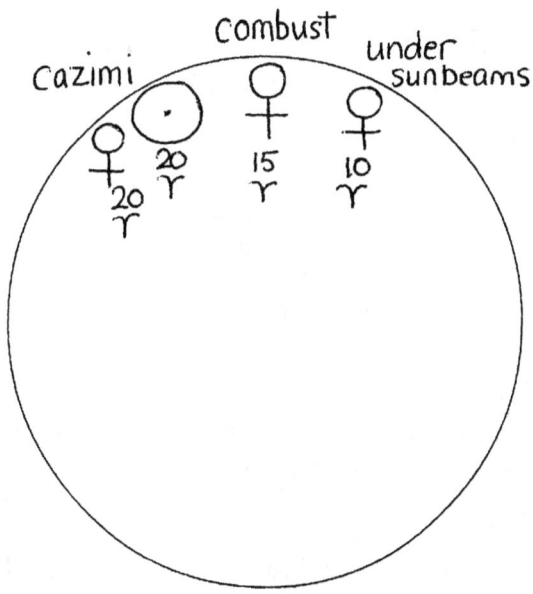

Square or Opposition

> When the Significators shall behold each other from hateful places of the Figure, or shall be in square or opposition of the Infortunes, its seldom known that upon such Positions any thing be brought to a good Conclusion.[13]

A square between two significators, with no essential dignity, no reception and in unfortunate houses, will hinder or prevent a positive outcome. Even if the significators behold one another with a good aspect, a square or opposition with an Infortune to one or both of them (especially when the latter is out of his essential dignities) prevents a successful outcome.

I would suggest that any opposition between significators is unfortunate, no matter whether it is between Fortunes or Infortunes (although it is always worse when an Infortune is involved). However, there is a possibility of some small success, if there is a strong mutual reception between the significators and a fortunate planet is translating light between them.

Destructive Oppositions

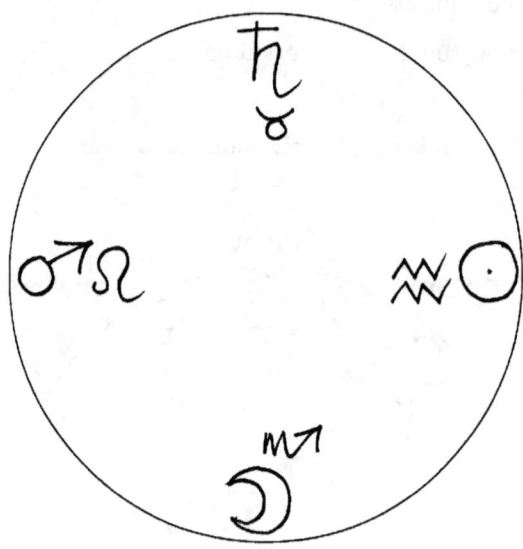

Bodily Prohibition

When two significators are applying to an aspect with each other, but before they come to exactitude (a partill aspect), another planet gets in the way, the matter is hindered and this can prevent the achievement of the outcome desired. As an example, if Venus is in seven degrees of Pisces and Jupiter is in twelve degrees of Pisces, Venus needs to perfect her aspect with Jupiter to bring about the desired outcome. However, if Mercury is in six degrees of Pisces and is moving more swiftly than Venus, he will overtake Venus and make a conjunction with Jupiter before Venus. This means that whatever was signified by the Venus-Jupiter conjunction is now prohibited by Mercury who first impedes Venus and then Jupiter, before they can come to a true conjunction. This is called bodily prohibition.

In practice, however, it may be the case that Jupiter actually collects the light of Mercury and Venus. It is also debatable whether Mercury could prevent a successful outcome to a Question where Fortunes are significators and where he is disposed of by Jupiter in his domicile and Venus in her exaltation. On a practical level, the matter may still be perfected, other testimonies being equal. However, if Jupiter in ten degrees of Leo is moving towards Saturn in twelve degrees of Leo and Mars in eight degrees of Leo overtakes Jupiter and makes a conjunction with Saturn, a negative outcome should be expected. This is even more certain because in this instance the Infortunes are involved. In fact, even if Jupiter were allowed to make his conjunction with Saturn, it is doubtful that much good would result from it.

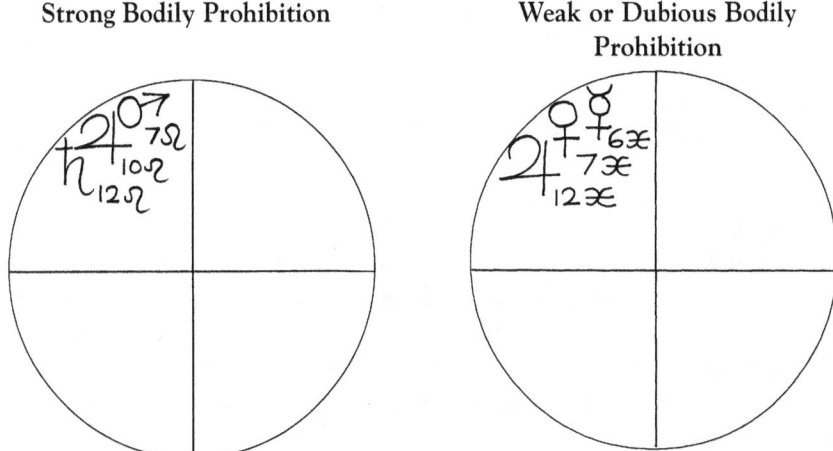

It should be emphasised that any configuration involving the Infortunes is likely to be unfortunate. Lilly and his contemporaries also put forward examples of prohibition involving the Sun. In these instances the outcome is certain to be unfortunate because the Sun causes these planets to be in combustion.

Prohibition through Aspect

Prohibition can also take place through sextile, square, trine or opposition aspect. As an example, Mars in seven degrees of Aries wants to perfect an aspect with Saturn in fifteen degrees of Aries. However, if the Sun is in five degrees of Gemini (and of course moves more quickly than Mars) the Sun will overtake Mars, making a sextile with Mars and then a sextile with Saturn. This takes place before Mars can make his conjunction with Saturn. This can also take place if the aspect is a square, trine or opposition. In an instance like this, it is possible that the lighter planet actually translates the light of the slower one, rather than prohibiting, even though this is not the strict definition of translation.

Bonatti also tells us that if a lighter planet is in conjunction with a heavier planet and another planet is aspecting the heavier planet, the planet in conjunction will prohibit this aspect. This is because a conjunction is stronger than an aspect (see *prevention*, on page 336).

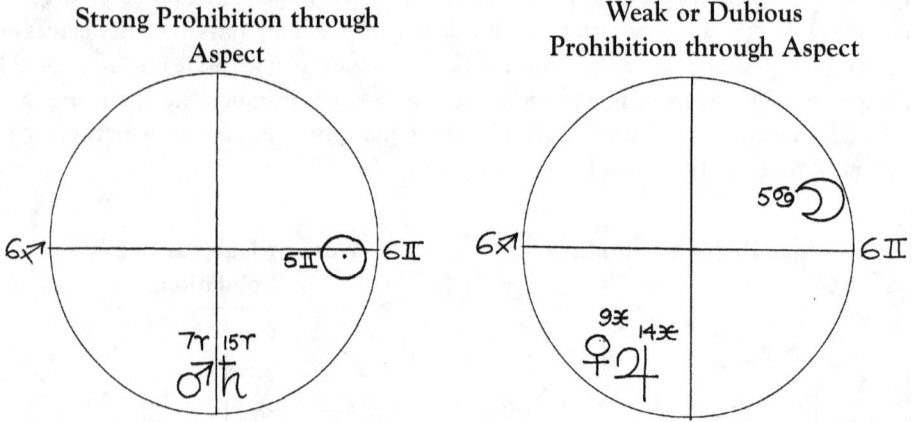

Refranation

If Mars in seven degrees of Aries is applying to a conjunction with Saturn in twelve degrees of Aries, but Mars turns retrograde at about nine or ten degrees of Aries, he cannot perfect his conjunction with Saturn who is still moving forward in that sign. So nothing signified by the potential of that conjunction will ever take place. Al Biruni explains that "the familiarity is said to be frustrated by refranation".[14] Bonatti calls this condition *restraint*.

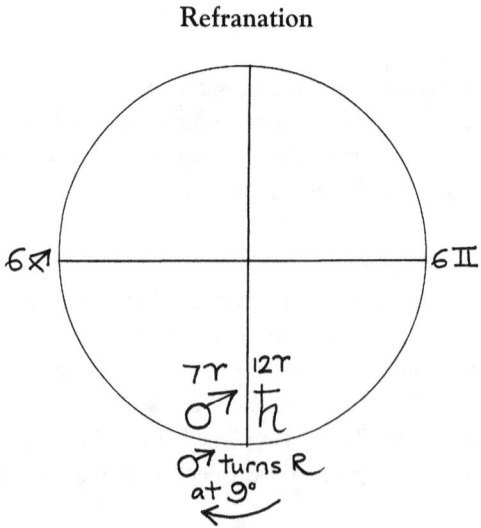

Return

The doctrine of 'return of virtue' has already been examined in chapter fourteen, where in certain instances this return can be beneficial and can assist in bringing about perfection in a Question. However, this return of virtue can also produce misfortune in a Question. When planets are applying to a conjunction, any other aspect, or an aspect through the antiscia, the collective name for this is familiarity. If, during this time of familiarity, a Superior is retrograde or under sunbeams, it is weak and "it cannot hold what is offered to it [from the Inferior], therefore returns and does not accept it". Thus is what Al Biruni and others call "return". However, if there is a reception between them or if the Inferior is in an angular or succedent house (or if both of them are) "the end of such return is satisfactory". If the Inferior is weak as described above, but the Superior is in an angle or succedent house, the result is destructive even if at the beginning there seemed to be hope. If both of them are weak, he tells us that from start to finish there is nothing but "destruction and ruin".[15]

Bonatti puts forward an example of a satisfactory return, where Mars in four degrees of Capricorn in the tenth house makes a square aspect with Jupiter in 10 degrees of Aries in the ascendant. Jupiter is retrograde and combust, but Mars receives Jupiter

Return

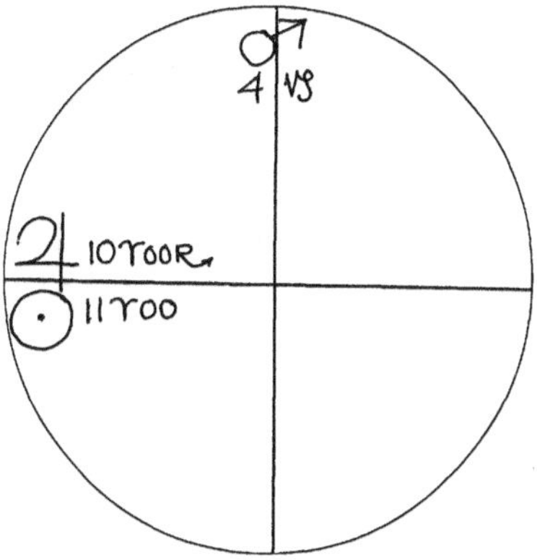

Satisfactory Return

♂ in an angle can retain the virtue returned to him by ♃. This is fortunate.

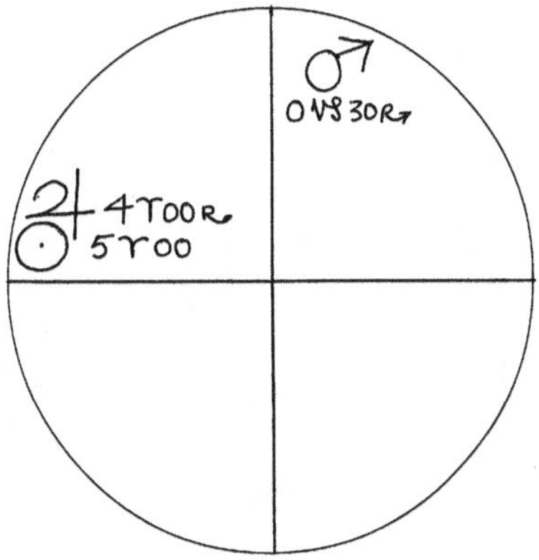

Unsatisfactory Return

♂, cadent and retrograde, cannot retain the virtue returned to him by ♃. This is unfortunate.

in his domicile. Mars commits his virtue and disposition to Jupiter, but because Jupiter is debilitated he cannot hold on to that virtue so he returns it to Mars. This, according to Bonatti, is "good, useful, and profitable" because Mars is in an angle and is able to retain the virtue returned to him by Jupiter. Thereafter, all of Mars' virtue remains so that the matter enquired about is brought to perfection by Mars.[16]

Frustration

Frustration occurs when a planet which is swift in motion moves towards a more ponderous (slow) planet, but before they can perfect their conjunction, the slower planet makes a conjunction with another planet. This means that the conjunction of the first planet is frustrated. For example, Mercury is in nine degrees of Gemini, Mars is in thirteen degrees of Gemini, Jupiter is in fourteen degrees of Gemini. Here Mercury hopes to make a conjunction with Mars, but Mars first completes his conjunction with Jupiter. This means that Mercury is frustrated in trying to perfect his conjunction with Mars. This is in line with what Lilly says when two dogs quarrel, but a third gets the bone.

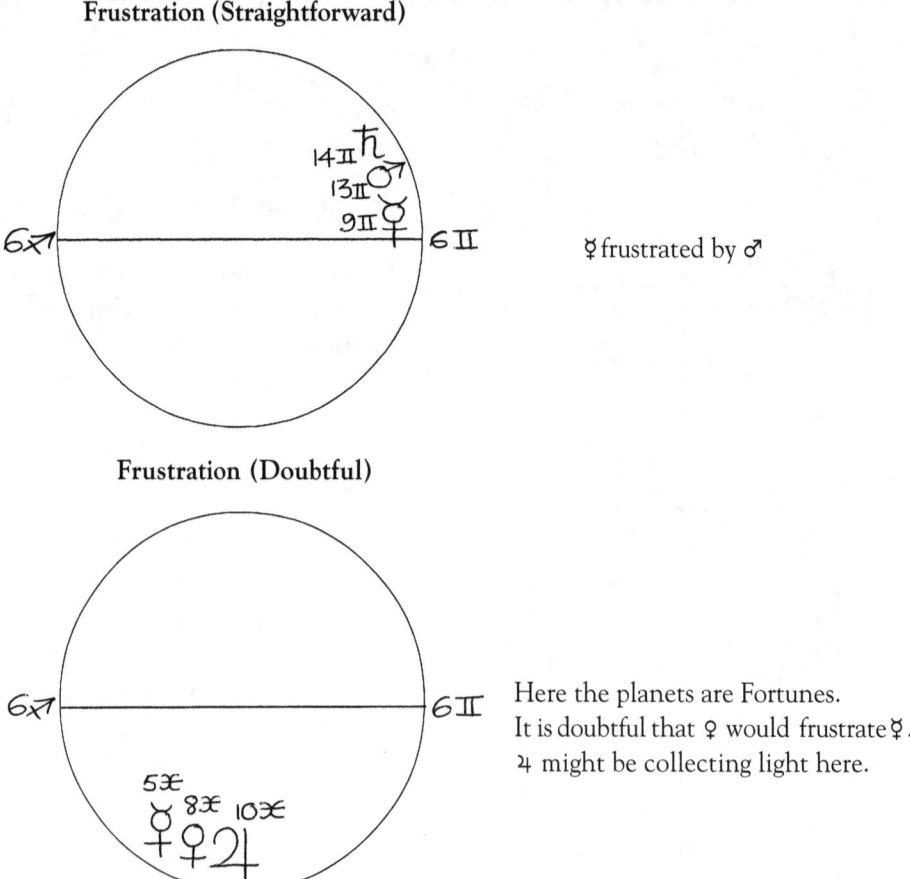

Frustration (Straightforward)

☿ frustrated by ♂

Frustration (Doubtful)

Here the planets are Fortunes. It is doubtful that ♀ would frustrate ☿. ♃ might be collecting light here.

Evasion

According to Al Biruni evasion takes place when an Inferior is about to make a conjunction with a Superior, but before that happens, the Superior moves out of the sign and the Inferior applies to another planet either in the same or another sign. In this instance, the first aspect is never completed. For example, Mercury in twenty-four degrees of Gemini applies to a conjunction with Saturn in twenty-nine degrees thirty minutes of Gemini. However, Saturn moves into Cancer and Mercury perfects his trine with Mars in twenty-eight degrees of Aquarius.[17]

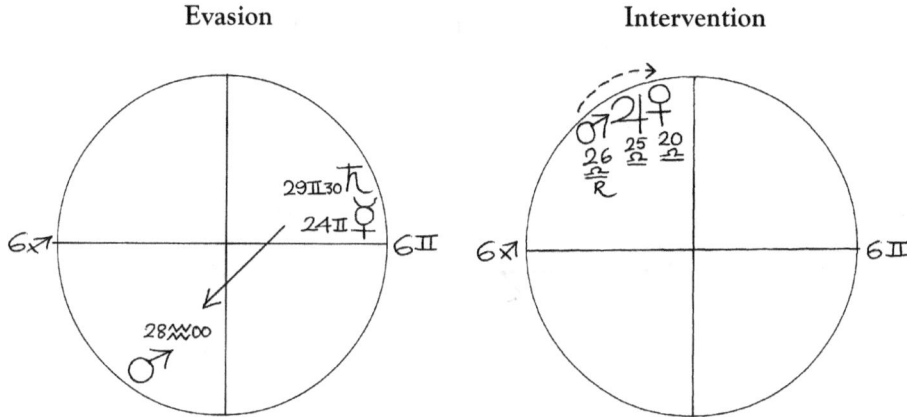

Intervention

Al Biruni tells us that intervention takes place when an Inferior is applying to a conjunction with a Superior. In the latter part of the same sign is placed a third planet, an Intermediate (in terms of motion). Before the Inferior completes the conjunction, this Intermediate planet retrogrades towards the Superior, passes it and makes a conjunction with the Inferior, so that the Inferior does not join with the Superior. For example, Venus in twenty degrees of Libra applies to a conjunction with Jupiter in twenty five degrees of Libra. However, Mars in twenty six degrees of Libra turns retrograde, passes Jupiter and makes a conjunction with Venus. Mars prevents Venus joining up with Jupiter.[18]

The Return, Abscission or Cutting off the Light

According to Al Biruni there are two methods of cutting off the light. The first takes place when the Intermediate planet, Mars (as in the example above), is in the adjacent sign to the Superior, Jupiter. Mars, the Intermediate, retrogrades back into the sign where the Superior is located. The text is not totally clear, but presumably Al Biruni means that Mars makes a conjunction with Jupiter and prevents Venus making her conjunction with Jupiter.

The second method is when an Inferior moves towards a conjunction with an Intermediate planet further on in the sign. There is a third planet even further on in later degrees of that sign. Before the Inferior can join with the Intermediate, the Intermediate moves to the Superior, makes a conjunction with him and moves on. The Inferior does not make a conjunction with the Intermediate, but with the Superior later.[19]

For example, Venus in ten degrees of Pisces applies to a conjunction with Mars in seventeen degrees of Pisces. However, Mars moves to a conjunction with Jupiter in twenty of Pisces. Here, Venus does not make her conjunction with Mars, but with Jupiter later.

Al Biruni's Cutting (Abscission) off the Light

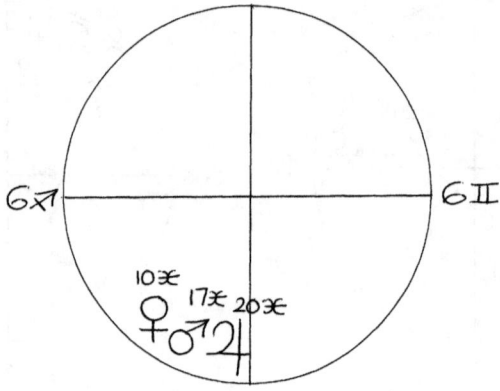

Bonatti tells us more about "the return of light and its abscission"

> This is when one planet seeks the conjunction of another but is not yet joined to it and another planet besides these two is joined to the first who sought the conjunction of the second and the third planet returns the light of the third to the first. This is called the return of light and its abscission.[20]

Bonatti gives as an example the Sun in twelve degrees of Cancer who is applying to a square with Saturn in eighteen degrees of Libra. However, Jupiter in fifteen degrees of Gemini makes his trine with Saturn before the Sun can make his square. Jupiter cuts off the light of the Sun from Saturn. This is called abscission of light, *abscissio luminis*. Bonatti explains that this is also called the return of light, because Saturn returns the light of the Sun which he had begun to receive and instead receives the light from Jupiter who is closer to him. Here, it appears that "the matter concerning which the question was made is able to be destroyed…"

Quite how the Sun's application to Saturn with a square could be fortunate, or bring about the desired outcome, is a matter for debate.

Bonatti's Cutting (Abscission) off the Light

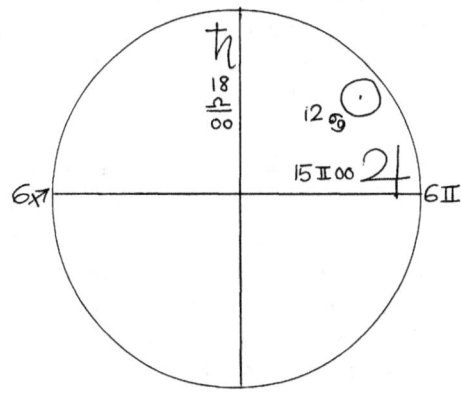

Bonatti gives a practical example of how a matter might be hindered in this way. He tells us that a merchant is intending to sell his goods to a particular buyer [A] and the buyer is keen to have the goods. However, a third party [B] comes along unexpectedly and offers more to the seller than the first person [A]. His offer is accepted and he buys the goods, thereby preventing the intended sale to the first person [A].[21]

> And this matter ought to be especially looked after in questions because many things are frustrated even after they seemed direct. And you ought to know that the returns of light are considered according to aspect, but translation of nature or virtue is considered according to corporal conjunction and according to aspect, but the most are according to corporal conjunction.

Abu Ma'shar tells us that cutting the light is of three kinds: firstly this can take place when an Inferior is "aiming at application" to a heavier planet in the same sign, but another planet is in the adjacent sign. Before the Inferior can perfect its conjunction, the planet in the adjacent sign retrogrades back into the sign and makes a conjunction with the heavier planet.[22]

For example Mercury in Aries is applying to a conjunction with Mars in Aries. Before Mercury reaches Mars, Venus in Taurus retrogrades back into Aries and makes a conjunction with Mars. Venus cuts the light from Mercury who was aiming at a conjunction with Mars.

Secondly this can take place where a lighter planet is applying to a conjunction with a heavier planet. The heavier planet is applying to a planet which is heavier still. Before the lighter planet can make its conjunction with the heavier planet, the latter has joined to the other planet and moved on, so the original conjunction does not take place. For example, Mercury is applying to Jupiter, a heavier planet and Jupiter "pushes" to a heavier planet Saturn, before Mercury can reach the degree of Jupiter. Jupiter applies to Saturn and passes Saturn. In this instance, the application is of Mercury to Saturn and the desired application of Mercury to Jupiter is "aborted".

The third method is where one planet applies to another planet, which is not the significator of the matter enquired about (what Abu Ma'shar calls the "Lord of the request"). As an example, Mercury applies to Mars when he wants to apply to Venus. Abu Ma'shar explains that this can also happen through translation, where the light of the planet is translated to another planet, which is not the significator of the matter enquired about.

Cutting off the light is also called frustrating the lights or *contrariety*. Bonatti gives an example of contrariety: Mars in fifteen degrees of Aquarius is applying to a conjunction with Saturn in twenty-four degrees of Aquarius. However, Jupiter in twenty-six degrees of Aquarius turns retrograde and makes a conjunction with Saturn. Jupiter then leaves Saturn behind and joins up with Mars. Jupiter "does not permit" Mars to make his conjunction with Saturn. This is called contrariety because the outcome which takes place is contrary to what was supposed to happen. In this instance, a matter enquired about and signified by Mars and Saturn is destroyed by the retrogradation of Jupiter. Bonatti tells us that Al-Qabisi calls such contrariety *Halintitad*.[23]

Prevention

According to Al Biruni, prevention takes place when, for example, Mars is placed in between an Inferior (Venus) and a Superior (Jupiter). Mars prevents their conjunction, until it itself has entered into a conjunction. He explains that when two planets are both in aspect with a third planet, one with a conjunction but the other with an aspect, the conjunction is more powerful than the aspect and will prohibit the aspect if they are in the same degrees. However, if their degrees are different and the one making an aspect is closer than the one applying to a conjunction, the planet in closest aspect is preferred. If however both planets apply by aspect to a third planet at the same time, the planet with a reception has the advantage. Al Biruni confirms that

> Certain aspects must have an advantage over others, just as corporal conjunction has over aspect, so that the more powerful aspect should interfere with the weaker.[24]

However, he concedes that "astrologers have not pronounced on this matter".

House Position

If the significator of the Querent or the Moon is not located in the house of the matter enquired about, nor aspecting that house, this casts some doubt over radicality. The astrologer must ask whether the Question is sincere. Perhaps the Querent is really thinking about something else, or perhaps this is a testimony of misfortune and/or the impossibility of achieving the desired outcome.

Notwithstanding the specific planetary configurations outlined above, there are other chart testimonies which also have a role in preventing or reducing good fortune in a chart.

Mars, Saturn and the South Node

Generally speaking, wherever you find the Infortunes (Mars and Saturn) not in any of their essential dignities, they hinder or prevent a successful outcome, particularly if they afflict the principal significators. Occasionally, strong aspects or mutual receptions elsewhere can help bring the matter to perfection, but the degree of success is diminished. An Infortune positioned in the house of the matter enquired about is unfortunate unless he is in any of his essential dignities, is received or benefits from a strong aspect with a Fortune or other benefic.

The south node brings misfortune when joined with a significator or with the Moon, if located in the house of the matter enquired about, or in the ascendant. I have found that in a Question, the south node in the ascendant either reduces any good that can be expected or, more commonly, prevents a positive outcome entirely. Even if the Fortunes are significators, Bonatti asks the reader to consider whether

> ...the Infortunes behold them with Opposition or Square; for that will much lessen their kind effects, and diminish the good they otherwise promised.[25]

Where a planet is afflicting a significator, the astrologer must consider whether this planet is a friend or not, what house that planet rules and in what house it is placed. This planet may represent the man, woman or thing which is hindering the Querent.

Bonatti tells us that if Mars is in any angle of the chart, in a Question or Nativity, especially in a fixed sign, or when Scorpio ascends, he "destroys all the good signified by that question, or at least much impedes and diminishes it..." However, if Jupiter beholds Mars with either a trine or sextile, the malice is "mitigated". The extent to which this takes place depends on Jupiter's power, that is, whether he is strong or weak.[26]

In a Question where the Querent is seeking a favour from another person, or if the Querent is hoping to get something from a secret hidden place, if either of the significators behold Saturn, are in conjunction with Saturn, or if Saturn is placed in the house of the thing asked about

> ...the business will hardly be done, or not without much labour and trouble, and more tediousness than the Querent can imagine.[27]

Besiegement

Any planet can be besieged, that is, located between two Infortunes

> ... so as to separate from one and be joined to another, without perfect reception of House, Exaltation, or two of the smaller Dignities, which are Term, Triplicity and Face.[28]

In terms of judgement this can represent a very bad situation indeed, especially if it is the Moon who is besieged. Abu Ma'shar calls this debility containment and tells us that there are two kinds of containment. The first is where a planet is positioned in between two malefics in the same sign. The second takes place where a planet is separating from a malefic with conjunction or aspect and is applying to another malefic with conjunction or aspect.[29]

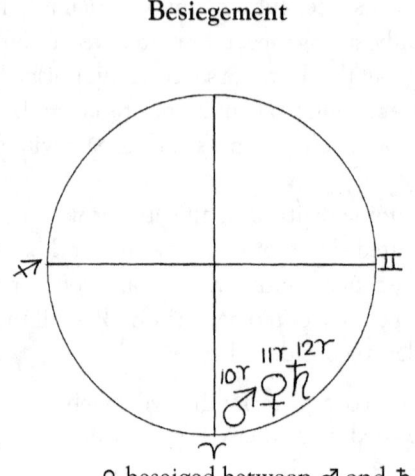 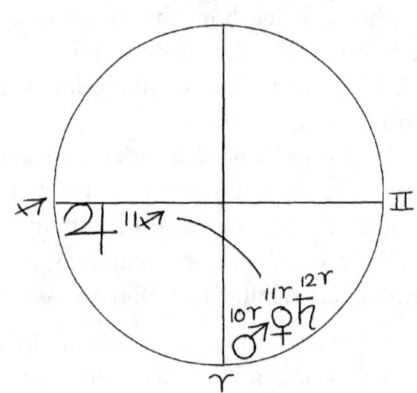

♀ beseiged between ♂ and ♄   ♃ releases some of the misfortune caused by the beseigement

Abu Ma'shar's second kind of containment occurs when

> ... a planet is in a sign, a malefic in its body or in its rays is in the second sign from it, and another malefic or its rays are in the twelfth sign from it. If there is no planet in it, and the situation of the ascendant or the other signs is like this, then the ascendant or that sign is contained.

Here Abu Ma'shar suggests that the ascendant or any other sign (house) can be contained, as well as a planet.

Abu Ma'shar tells us that in both of the above examples, if the Sun or one of the Fortunes aspects the besieged planet and there are less than seven degrees between the planet and the "rays", it indicates the release from that misfortune. Likewise, if a sign is besieged and one of the benefics or the Sun is in aspect, they release the misfortune. This is similar to Al Biruni's *benefactor* as discussed in chapter six, and also to the concept discussed in earlier chapters, where the power of a conjunction can be modified by other aspects.

Planetary Motion and Movement

A planet's first station before going retrograde is unfortunate, but not as unfortunate as being retrograde. Being retrograde is most unfortunate and shows "activity which is disturbed and slow, interruption and imperfection of effects". When a planet is slow, it can be an indication of delays and it causes the planet to become weaker. Morin explains that a planet which is slow in motion indicates "delay in the manifestation of events".[30] A planet slow in motion is unfortunate, although not as unfortunate as being in the first station or being retrograde. The Moon when slow in motion has been compared to a planet retrograde.

The End of a Sign

A planet near the very end of the sign does not have much strength in that sign. Bonatti tells us that if a significator, or the Moon, has passed the twenty-ninth degree of a sign and touches the thirtieth degree, it has "no strength in that sign but in the next". In this instance, if that planet signifies any misfortune, it can be avoided. In a similar way, any good promised by that planet will not happen.[31] Ibn Ezra explains that if a planet is at the end of a sign, "its force will be lost for the first sign, and all its force will pass to the sign into which it is to enter".[32] A planet in this position has no strength in that sign. However, if a planet is *in* the twenty-ninth degree of the sign

> ...its force stays in the sign where it is, because the planet exerts force in three degrees: in the degree in which it is, in the preceding degree, and in the subsequent degree.

Bonatti quotes Zael who appears to follow the same line of thought

> If a planet or the Moon be in the 29th degree of any Sign, its virtue is yet in that Sign wherein he is; because he has not yet wholly passed the 29th degree.[33]

Void of Course

In terms of judgement, a void of course Moon is an impediment to a positive outcome, unless the Moon is located in Taurus, Cancer, Sagittarius or Pisces. When she is in these signs Bonatti tells us that even if she is void she does not "prejudice so much in these places as elsewhere..."[34] However, if the Moon is void of course and not in any of the aforementioned signs, this is unfortunate in terms of a Question.

> ...for then it signifies an impediment to the thing in question it will not come to a good end, nor be accomplished; but the Querent shall be forced to desist with shame and loss.[35]

However, Bonatti suggests that if the ascendant ruler or significator of the thing enquired about are "in very good condition", the matter may then "be hindered, but not wholly frustrated". He tells us that a time like this is good for

> ...drinking, bathing, feasting, etc., and to use ointments for taking away of hair, especially if she [the Moon] be in Scorpio.[36]

Void of Course and Hopeful

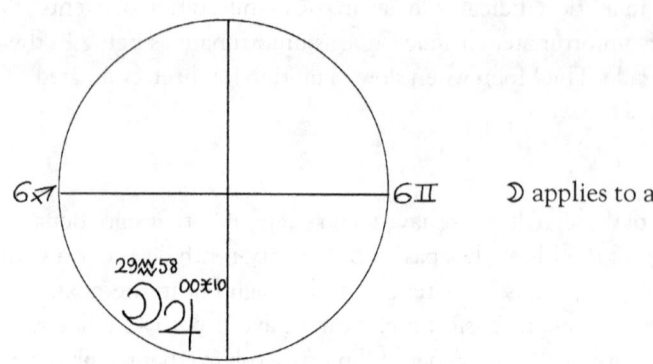

☽ applies to a conjunction with ♃

Void of Course and Hopeless

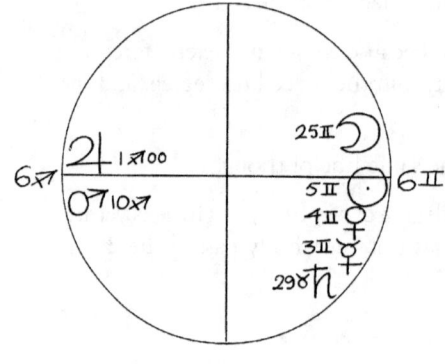

☽ applies to no planet in the next sign

A Note of Caution

I would suggest that caution is needed when analysing certain planetary configurations. It is possible that the configuration known as prohibition, for example, can be compared to translation or collection in terms of the outcome produced. This is especially true if the planets involved are Fortunes and not afflicted in any way. When Infortunes are involved, the outcome is more likely to be negative.

Care must be exercised and receptions noted, because these can significantly improve the outcome expected. Similarly, where a planet translates the light between two malefics, the outcome may be unfortunate, even if these planets are significators, unless they are all well dignified.

Example Charts

I include four examples of charts where perfection could not be achieved. I hope that these examples convey an idea of how certain unfortunate testimonies work out on a practical level in the context of a Question.

Will they rent my cottage?

The Querent hopes to let her cottage over the winter, but the Moon in the fourth house of the matter enquired about, is afflicted by her opposition with the Sun. The seventh house is afflicted by Saturn. The Fortunes, Venus and Jupiter are under sunbeams. After lengthy negotiations they did not rent the cottage.

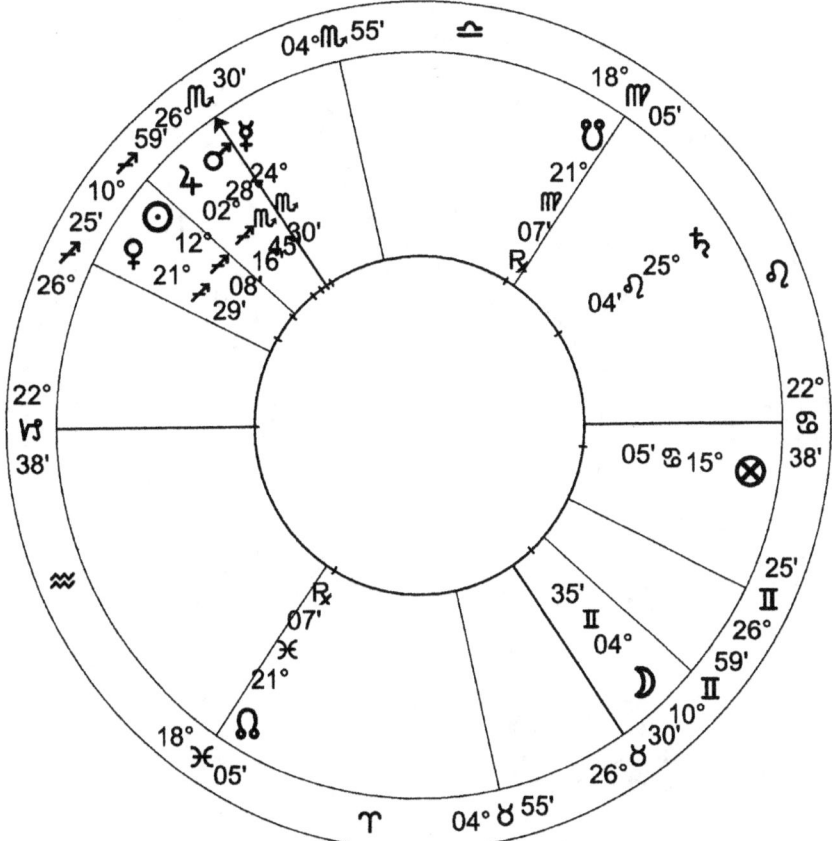

Should I sell and move?

The Querent is fed up in London and seriously considers moving, but the Moon opposes Saturn. Venus, ascendant ruler, is weak in dignity although she has a mixed reception with Saturn. Jupiter, a Fortune, is retrograde, incorrectly placed and disposed of by Mars who is in his detriment. The client was advised to take no action.

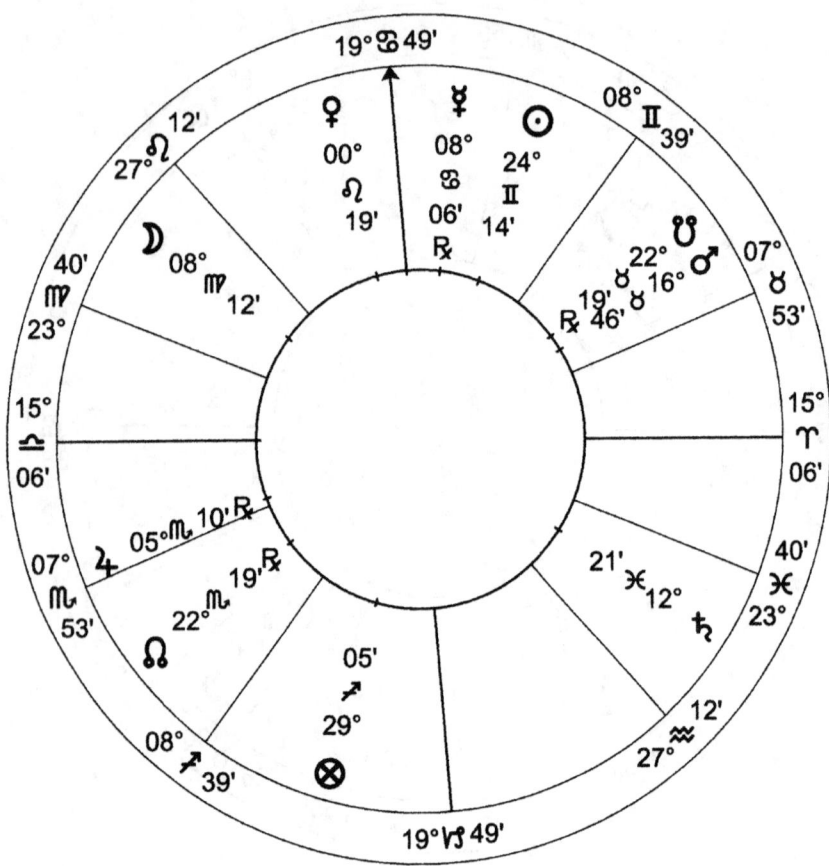

Will I win the prize?

The ascendant is afflicted by the south node and the midheaven is afflicted by Saturn in his detriment. Saturn is also retrograding towards an opposition with Mars. The ascendant ruler Venus is oriental of the Sun and will soon move into combustion. The dispositor of Venus is Saturn. The Querent did not win the prize.

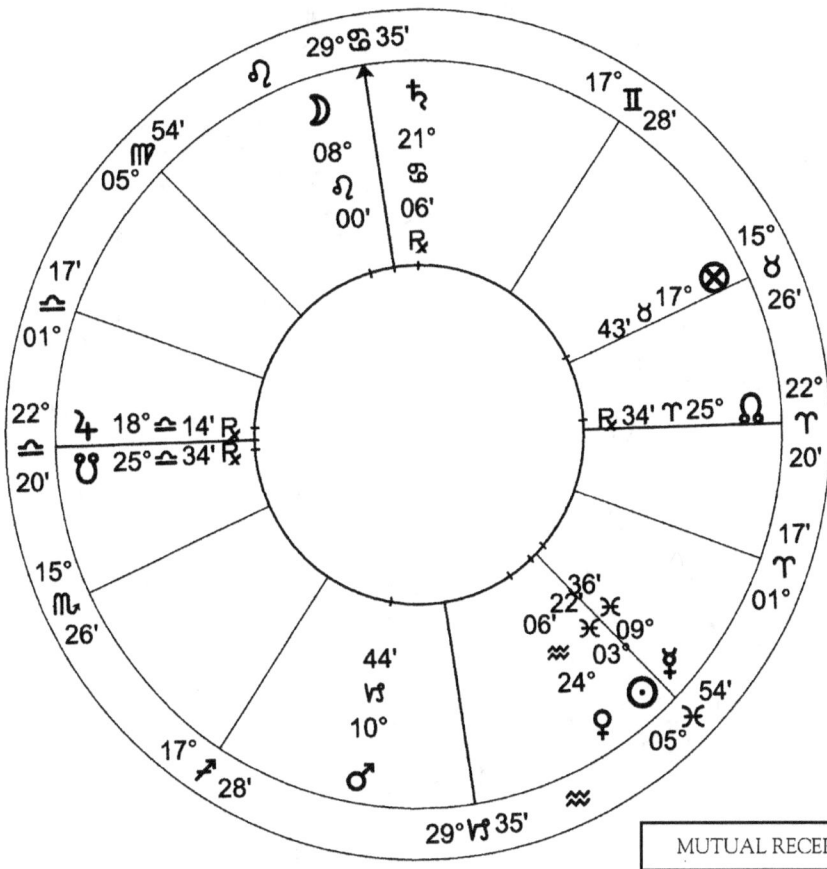

Is the friendship worth saving?

The Querent had fallen out with a friend and was sad. The eleventh house of friends is afflicted by Saturn in his fall opposing Mars in his detriment, although they have a

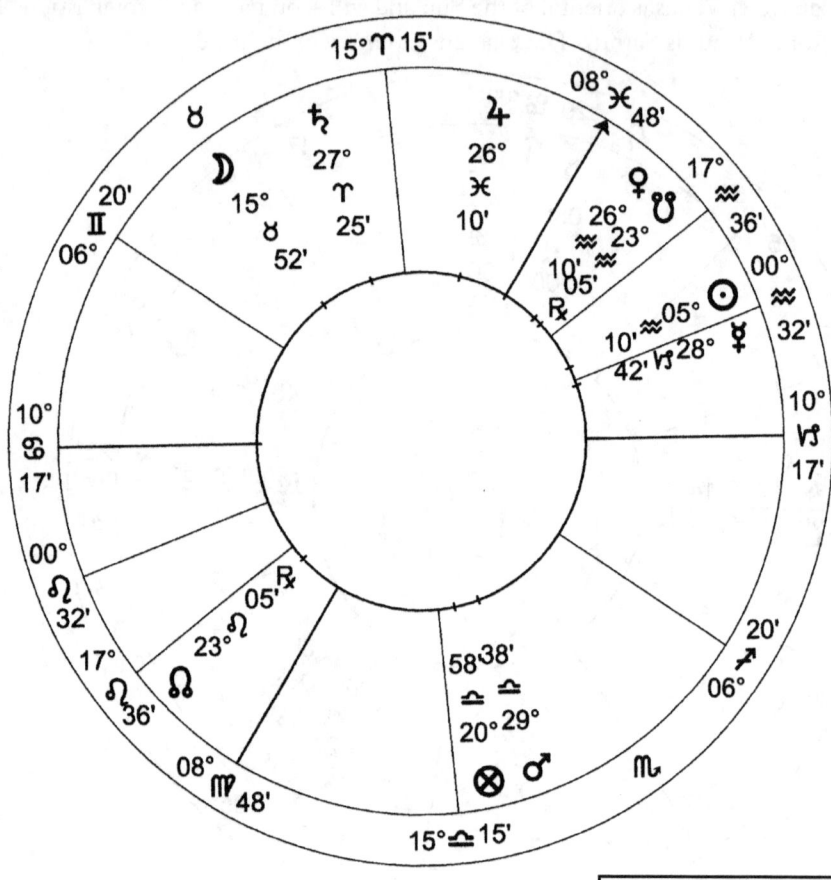

mutual reception. The Querent's significator is the Moon dignified in Taurus in the eleventh house of friends. This confirms her wish to be friends again, but the Moon makes no aspect with Mars ruler of the eleventh, nor with Saturn positioned in the eleventh. The Querent attempted a reconciliation, but to no avail.

All the information in the previous chapters can now be put together in a structured and logical manner. I hope that an understanding is developing as to how the various testimonies can either help to bring a matter to perfection, or prevent a matter being brought to perfection. I now move to Part Two of *Horary Astrology Re-Examined*, where I include over fifty chart examples covering different topics, ranging from Questions about money, property, pregnancy and health, to Questions about love, legal disputes, career and sport.

References

1. Ball p.62.
2. Dariot p.38.
3. Bonatus pp.6-8, 9th consideration.
4. ibid p.18, 51st consideration.
5. Masha'allah p.7.
6. Bonatus p.12, 17th consideration.
7. Ball p.62.
8. Morin p.77.
9. Lilly p.254.
10. Morin p.135.
11. Ibn Ezra, *The Beginning Of Wisdom* p.210.
12. Bonatus cited by Zoller in *Tools & Techniques of the Medieval Astrologers*, p.116.
13. Ball p.62.
14. Al Biruni pp.311-312 and editor's footnote.
15. ibid p..311.
16. Bonatus cited by Zoller in *Tools & Techniques of the Medieval Astrologers*, p.105.
17. Al Biruni p.311.
18. ibid pp. 311-312.
19. ibid p. 312.
20. Bonatus in *Tools & Techniques of the Medieval Astrologers*, by Robert Zoller, pp.100-102, Section V, Questions and Elections.
21. ibid p.102.
22. Abu Ma'shar p.29.
23. Bonatus in *Tools & Techniques of the Medieval Astrologers*, by Robert Zoller, p.108.
24. Al Biruni p.312.
25. Bonatus p.16, 37th consideration.
26. ibid p.30, 91st consideration.
27. ibid p.30, 93rd consideration.

28. Bonatus p.4, 6th consideration.
29. Abu Ma'shar pp.34-35.
30. Morin p.154.
31. Bonatus p.14, 30th consideration.
32. Ibn Ezra p.218.
33. Bonatus p.14, 30th consideration.
34. ibid p.23, 64th consideration.
35. ibid p.12, 19th consideration.
36. ibid p.23, 62nd consideration.

PART TWO

THE POSSIBILITY OR IMPOSSIBILITY OF THE MATTER PROPOUNDED: QUESTIONS AND JUDGEMENTS

> It is one thing to ferret out obscure or lost doctrines. It is quite another to separate those which are of value from those which are false or incomplete...[my] purpose in presenting this material is...the discovery, through experimentation and close observation, of worthwhile astrological methods.
>
> Robert Zoller, *Tools and Techniques of the Medieval Astrologers*, p.94

Part Two includes over fifty Questions, illustrating the tools and techniques discussed in Part One. I hope that I have selected some of the clearest and most straightforward charts and that the reader or student will benefit from the step by step approach, which I have adopted for the very first chart.

For the sake of clarity I would like to draw attention to the word "joyned". In some instances Lilly (and others) make it clear that this means a conjunction, where it is specifically stated that planets are "corporally joined together". In other instances it might be stated that a planet is "joyned by any aspect" which is also very clear. However, there are instances where Lilly and other authors do not make it clear and only use the word joyned. I have in some places offered my own interpretation; in others, I have simply left the word joyned in the text.

16

Second House Matters

Wealth and Possessions

The second house has signification over many different things, people or matters, but the focus of this chapter is on issues connected to money and possessions. Questions involving the latter are often linked to other enquiries, which may be related to career, job, moving house, renting property and so on.

Testimonies Relating to the Second House

Notwithstanding the chart testimonies discussed in previous chapters, the most important factors in the judgement of matters relating to the second house are:[1]

- The sign in the cusp of the second house.
- The second house ruler.
- Planets placed in the second house.
- Planets aspecting the ruler of the second house.
- Planets aspecting the second house cusp.
- The Lot of Fortune, its sign, position and the aspects it receives from the planets and luminaries.

The Lot of Fortune, like the nodes, has no "rays" and does not, in itself, influence any planet in terms of aspect.

Testimonies of Wealth

Lilly tells us that in general, "its one good signe of substance" if [2]

- All planets are angular.
- All planets are in succedent houses, direct and swift in motion.
- All planets are in good houses, direct but only moderately dignified.
  This is also "an hopefull argument of an Estate".

Any, or many, of the testimonies listed below, indicate that the Querent is likely to be well off and "shall not feare poverty". However, the amount of money will depend on the major testimonies.

- The ascendant ruler, or the Moon, in conjunction with the second house ruler.
- The ascendant ruler and the Moon in good aspect with the second house ruler.
- Jupiter and Venus in trine or sextile aspect with the ascendant ruler or the Moon.
- Jupiter or Venus in conjunction or friendly aspect with the Lot of Fortune.
- The second house ruler in the ascendant.
- The Moon in the ascendant.
- The ascendant ruler in the second house.
- Any planet translates the light from the ruler of the second house to the ruler of the ascendant.
- Fortunate planets in a sextile or trine aspect with the cusp of the ascendant or the Lot of Fortune.
- Any fixed star of the nature of Jupiter and Venus in the cusp of the second house.
- Any fixed star of the nature of Jupiter or Venus in conjunction with the Lot of Fortune.
- Jupiter ("natural significator of substance"), or Venus ("who is naturally a fortune"), or the north node, in the second house and no Infortune in aspect.
- All planets are direct and swift in motion.

The next step is to work out how the Querent might acquire wealth. Lilly gives several examples[3]

- If the ruler of the second house is in the second house, wealth comes through hard work.
- If the ruler of the second house is in the ascendant, a fortune can come unexpectedly without much work (here once more is the idea that when the significator of the matter enquired about is in the ascendant, it signifies the achieving of the matter without active seeking).
- If the ruler of the second house, or the Moon, promise wealth by an aspect between them, the house where the aspect takes place should be considered, as well as the house which the Moon rules. If the aspect between the ruler of the second house and the Moon does not promise wealth, the Lot of Fortune should be considered, as well as its dispositor and the house it rules.

- If the ruler of the third house makes a good aspect with the ruler of the second house, with the cusp of the second house, or with the Lot of Fortune, the Querent may receive help through a neighbour, a relative, a sibling, or perhaps a journey.

- If the significator, or fortunate planet which is assisting in the matter, is the ruler of the fourth house or is placed in the fourth house, the Querent will get rich through his father, by an elderly person (perhaps a grandfather), or through property, a farm, land or buildings. Alternatively, the Querent may get rich through money lent by a relative.

- If the ruler of the fifth house promises wealth, the Querent will become rich through gambling or working in entertainment. If a gentleman, wealth comes "by Play, Cards, Dice, Sports, Pastimes," If an "ordinary man" wealth comes

    ...by keeping a Victialling-house, as Ale-house, Inne, Taverne, Bowling-alley, or being a Door-keeper, Porer to some Gentleman...

The same can be applied to any house and its ruler, which is involved in the signification. If the eighth house promises wealth, this might come through an inheritance or through a partner's money. If the tenth house promises wealth, this might come through the Querent's career or perhaps through a mother or grandmother. Lilly tells us more[4]

- If the ascendant ruler and the Moon are "joyned"* to a Fortune, dignified in the sign ascending, or the sign intercepted in the ascendant the "matter will be effected". For example, if Pisces is ascending and the Moon is in conjunction with Jupiter in Pisces, this is testimony of the Querent being rich. In another example, let us suppose that Aquarius is rising and Pisces is intercepted in the first house. If in this instance the Moon is in conjunction with Jupiter in Pisces, the Querent will also be rich.

- If the ascendant ruler and the Moon are joyned to an Infortune, dignified in the ascendant, as long as the Infortune receives the ascendant ruler or the Moon, the Querent will be rich.

- If the ruler of the ascendant or the Moon are joyned to a Fortune and the Fortune is well placed in the tenth house or eleventh house (even without any reception) the Querent will be rich.

Lilly doesn't appear to include Fortunes which may be in the ascendant or first house, which do not have an aspect with the Moon or ascendant ruler. However, if Venus or Jupiter are well dignified in these places and not afflicted, it is an indication of good fortune.

---

* I understand Lilly to mean conjunction here.

Masha'allah tells us that in matters relating to the second house, the Querent will become rich, as long as there is an aspect between the Querent's significators and the ruler of the second house, even if that planet is an Infortune and even if there is no reception. This is because

> ...a joining together of the lord of the Ascendant with the lord of the matter sought for is a gain in and of itself, and nothing may prohibit its outcome...[5]

From his writings it would appear that reception is not essential, or at least is less important, in Questions about money and wealth.

As discussed previously, things come more easily (without active seeking) when the ruler of the second house (or any other significator of a sought for matter) applies to an aspect with the ruler of the ascendant rather than the other way around.

Bonatti tells us that in Nativities or Questions, if at the time of birth Taurus is ascending and the Moon is in the ascendant in "the very minute ascending" or if Leo is ascending and the Sun is in the "minute ascending" and is not afflicted by either of the Infortunes, this signifies that the native "shall get much money, and come to great preferment and honour..."[6] The opposite occurs if an Infortune is there (depending on his condition of course). From a reading of various sources it appears that the greater distance between the Fortune and the ascendant the less wealth is received proportionately.

As a point of interest, quite a number of wealthy people have similar configurations, including Mick Jagger who has the Sun in Leo in conjunction with a Leo ascendant.

A positive conclusion cannot be reached in any judgement without at least two strong and concurring testimonies. Furthermore, any positive testimony should not be outweighed by negative testimony. For example, if Jupiter is in the second house in his domicile, but afflicted by Saturn, much of the good fortune generated by Jupiter is removed. The examples below offer further clarification.

From the Horary Files

The evaluation of the testimonies in the very first chart in this chapter is presented in a more detailed manner, in order to present the reader or student with the step-by-step approach to judgement. In the majority of charts however, my aim is to present the student or reader with an immediate idea of the strength or otherwise of the chart in its entirety and to present the information in a more concise way. This helps to demonstrate whether the testimonies reveal the 'possibility or impossibility' of bringing the matter to perfection. A table of planetary dignities and a list of the most important mutual receptions accompany each chart.

In the very first example, I list all chart testimonies, broadly following William Lilly's scoring system as examined in chapter seven. However, I also list testimonies, which Lilly chose not to include, such as the correct or incorrect placing of a planet according to the diurnal or nocturnal nature of the chart. I do not consider a planet to be peregrine if it has a mutual reception with another planet between triplicity, or any other mixture of the stronger and weaker dignities. I assign a score of TWO to a planet aspecting the ascendant and a score of ONE to a planet not aspecting the ascendant, but who is aspecting another planet who is aspecting the ascendant. I give a score of ONE to a planet who is retrograde but about to turn direct (in the second station).

I would suggest that a harmonising of the ruler of the hour with the ascendant or ascendant ruler is not an absolute pre-requisite in establishing radicality. It would appear that this type of harmonisation is simply to be found in the most fortunate charts.

In order to retain confidentiality of my clients, I have not included their physical descriptions in most of the examples. However, these physical descriptions were supplied by the client and confirmation sought from the chart.

It is important to note that in any chart where a planet occupies a particular house, but does not rule that house, that planet can be a significator or co-significator of people or things pertaining to that house. Of course, the same planet also has signification in the house over which it has a rulership. As discussed in chapter ten, any planet can be a significator of more than one thing. For example, if Mars rules the tenth house and is in the ascendant, he becomes part significator of the Querent, as well as significator of the tenth house matter. If he is well dignified, this strengthens the Querent's position in regard to the Question. If not, the opposite is true.

The following charts do not ask specifically whether or not the Querent will be rich, but they are related to money and it is, therefore, the second house which is the main area under consideration. The Fortunes, of course, also have general signification in Questions concerning wealth.

Will I earn enough to move house?
6 August 1995 13.37 BST. 50N16 04W46

The Querent was working freelance and at the time of the Question was under contract. She wanted to move to a bigger house but wasn't sure whether the work would continue and whether she should take that risk.

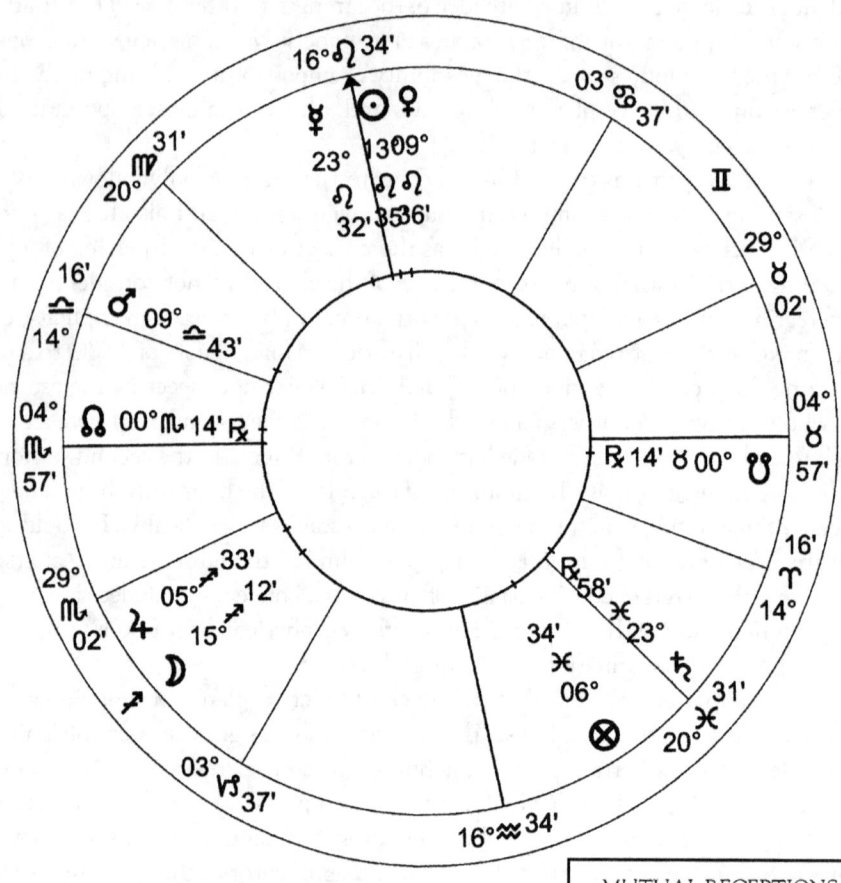

Saturn

Accidental & Essential Dignities

In mutual reception with Mars*	3
In the fifth house	3
Free from combustion	5
Oriental of the Sun	2
Aspecting the ascendant	2

Accidental & Essential Debilities

Retrograde	-5
Incorrectly placed	-2
Total	**8**

Jupiter

Accidental & Essential Dignities

In his domicile	5
In the second house	3
Direct	4
Free from combustion	5
Slow in motion but in his second station	1

Accidental & Essential Debilities

Occidental of the Sun	-2
Incorrectly placed	-2
Not aspecting the ascendant	-2
Total	**12**

Mars

Accidental & Essential Dignities

In mutual reception with Saturn*	3
Partill sextile with Venus	3
Direct	4
Free from combustion	5
Swift in motion	2
Not aspecting the ascendant, (but aspecting Venus)	1

Accidental & Essential Debilities

In the twelfth house	-5
In his detriment	-5

---

*   I assign a score of 3 to Saturn and Mars due to the mutual receptions between them. This does not follow Lilly's scoring system.

Occidental of the Sun	-2
Incorrectly placed	-2
Total	**4**

Sun
Accidental & Essential Dignities

In his domicile	5
In the midheaven	5
Swift in motion	2
Aspecting the ascendant	2
Correctly placed	2

Accidental & Essential Debilities
None

Total	**16**

Venus
Accidental & Essential Dignities

In the ninth house	2
Direct	4
Swift in motion	2
Aspecting the ascendant	2
In mutual reception with the Sun	2*

Accidental & Essential Debilities

Combust	-5
Oriental of the Sun	-2
Incorrectly placed	-2
Total	**3**

Mercury
Accidental & Essential Dignities

In the tenth house	5
Direct	4
Occidental of the Sun	2
Swift in motion	2
Aspecting the ascendant	2
Correctly placed	2

Accidental & Essential Debilities

Peregrine	-5

---

* she has two mutual receptions but they are weak.

Under sunbeams	-4
Total	**8**

Moon
Accidental & Essential Dignities

In her own face	1
In the second house	3
Free from combustion	5
Swift in motion	2
Increasing in light	2
Correctly placed	2
Not aspecting the ascendant (although she aspects Mercury who does aspect the ascendant)	1

Accidental & Essential Debilities
None

Total	**16**

The Lot of Fortune
Accidental & Essential Dignities

Fourth house	4

Accidental & Essential Debilities

In Pisces	5
Total	**9**

Signification

Querent
Significator: Ascendant, ascendant ruler Mars.
Co-significators: The Moon.

Quesited (Money)
Significator: Second house, second house ruler Mars.
Co-significators: Jupiter, the Moon.

Quesited (Work)
Significator: Tenth house, tenth house ruler, the Sun.
Co-significators: Venus, Mercury.

Mars, ruler of the hour harmonises with the ascendant. The chart is diurnal.

From the above listing it is clear that Jupiter, the Sun and the Moon achieve the highest scorings. In addition they are very well positioned in the houses of the matters enquired about.

Testimonies For
Jupiter is in the house of the matter enquired about, dignified in his domicile.
The Moon is in the house of the matter enquired about, is dignified in her face and disposed of by a very fortunate Jupiter.
The north node is in the ascendant.
The Lot of Fortune is angular and aspecting its dispositor, Jupiter.
The Moon is applying to a trine with Mercury in the tenth house.

Testimonies Against
Venus, a Fortune, is combust.

Judgement
With more than three concurring testimonies for an affirmative outcome and only one against, judgement is positive for the Querent.

Although the ascendant ruler Mars is in his detriment, he has strong mutual receptions with Saturn. Jupiter in his domicile, swift in motion and in the house of the matter enquired about (the second house) is a testimony of good fortune. The north node in conjunction with the ascendant is fortunate. The Moon is swift, in her own face and disposed of by a strong and dignified Jupiter. Her application to a trine with Mercury, in Mercury's terms, in the tenth house of career is fortunate. The Moon's eventual square with Saturn, fourth house ruler, is unfortunate, but Saturn has a mutual reception with Mars, which reduces his maleficity. Saturn's dispositor by domicile and term is Jupiter.

The Sun as principal significator of the Querent's career (and having a natural association with the tenth house) is very strong, with no affliction and in his hayyiz. However, Venus as co-significator is very weak and becoming weaker as she moves into sunbeams. Mercury, also a co-significator is becoming stronger as he emerges from sunbeams. The outlook career-wise, therefore, is a mixed picture, but the Querent will earn enough to move house as confirmed by the Lot of Fortune in the fourth house of property, disposed of by Jupiter. I would consider the Sun to be almuten of the Question and his position is most fortunate for the Querent.

Outcome
Over the following three years, the Querent managed to save a large deposit for a house. However, the amount of contract work fluctuated, with times when she earned well and times when she earned little. Had the Moon been applying to an aspect or conjunction with Jupiter or the Sun, the outlook career-wise and financially would have been a lot better.

Will I get my money back? When?
7 November 2007 7.13 GMT. 50N16 04W48

The Querent had been gambling on an internet site and had won a fair amount of money. That money, which should have been credited back to her credit card, apparently went missing. After four weeks and many complaints, she had heard nothing from the credit card company.

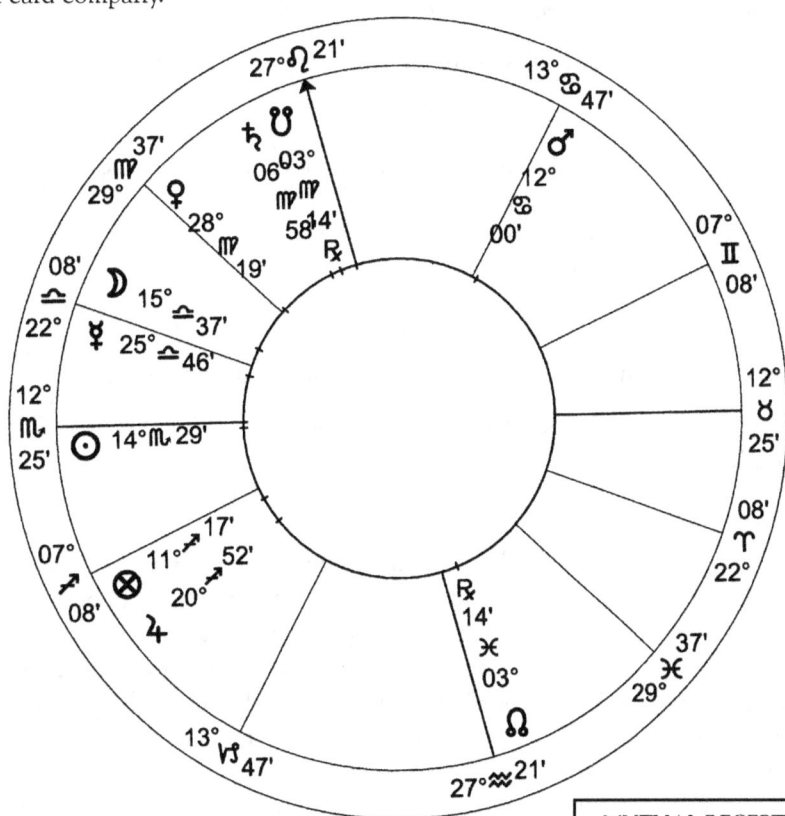

Signification

Querent
Significator: Ascendant and ascendant ruler Mars.
Co-significators: Sun in the ascendant, the Moon.

Quesited
Signifcator: Second house, second house ruler Jupiter, the Lot of Fortune.

The chart is nocturnal. The ruler of the hour Venus harmonises with the ascendant.

Testimonies For
The Moon applies to a sextile with Jupiter in his domicile in the house of the matter enquired about.
The Sun is in the ascendant, received by the ascendant ruler.
The Lot of Fortune is in the second house.

Testimonies Against
The Moon is slow in motion, in the via combusta and is decreasing in light.

With more than three strong and concurring testimonies, the Querent will get her money back.

Judgement
Saturn's position in the tenth house and in conjunction with the south node is unfortunate for the Question, but he is saved by his strong mutual reception with Mercury. The Moon, although partly afflicted by her recent square with Mars, disposes of Mars in her domicile. It is the Moon's application to a sextile with Jupiter, dignified in his domicile in the second house, together with the Lot of Fortune, which is undeniable testimony of good fortune for the Querent. The fact that Jupiter has no afflictions whatsoever suggests that the Querent will get all her money back, not just part of it. In addition, the Moon translates from Mars (significator of the Querent) to a sextile with Jupiter (the money), Mars being received by the Moon, the Moon received by Jupiter being in his terms. The Moon's mutual receptions with both Venus and Saturn give strong supporting testimony. She will get all the money back and within about five days (the Moon's application to a sextile with Jupiter is just over five degrees).

Outcome
The company called her the next day to say the money had been located and a cheque would be sent. A cheque arrived one week later.

Will I get a full student loan for my son and a grant?
22 July 2006 18.06 BST. 50N16 04W48

The Querent's son had not been awarded the full loan for his first year at University. The Querent complained to the local authority, but they needed a current set of accounts before they would consider a review. The Querent also applied for a grant for her son.

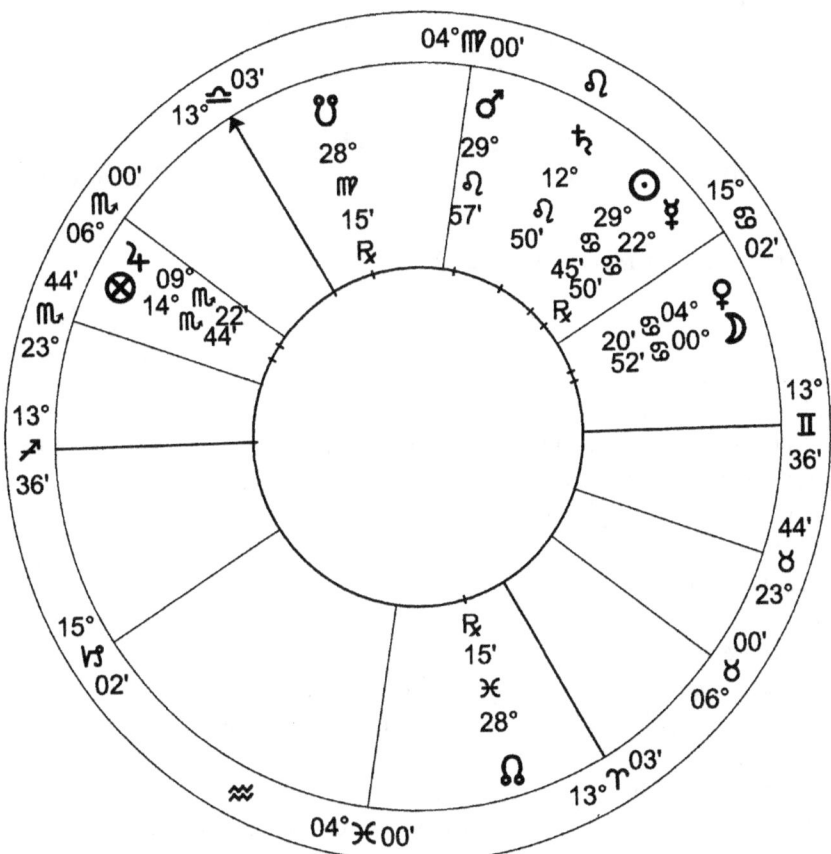

Signification
Querent
Significator: Ascendant and ascendant ruler Jupiter.
Co-significator: The Moon.

Querent's Son
Significator: Fifth house and fifth house ruler Venus.

Loan/Grant
Significator: Eighth house and eighth house ruler the Moon.
Co-significators: Mercury, Sun, and Saturn in the eighth house. The Fortunes, Venus and Jupiter.

The ruler of the hour, Mars, harmonises with the ascendant.

The chart is diurnal. Fortunes are significators.

Testimonies For
The Moon is dignified in her domicile in an angular house.
Venus is in an angular house in a sign of her own nature and in her face.
The ascendant ruler Jupiter is in the eleventh house, in his terms.
The Moon and Venus apply to a trine with Jupiter, both of them being received in his exaltation.
The Lot of Fortune is in the eleventh house.

Testimonies Against
The principal significators do not aspect the ascendant.
The Moon is decreasing in light, slow in motion and incorrectly placed.
Venus is incorrectly placed.
Jupiter is afflicted by his square with Saturn.
The Sun and Saturn afflict the house of the matter enquired about.

With such strong testimonies in favour of getting a loan the judgement is positive, but this must be modified due to other, less fortunate testimonies and especially the fact that Jupiter is afflicted by a square with Saturn, positioned in the house of the matter enquired about.

Judgement
It is important to note that the Moon's application to a conjunction with Venus is fortunate testimony in almost any chart. The Moon, ruler of the eighth house, is strong in her own domicile of Cancer and applies immediately to a conjunction with Venus, a Fortune, in less than three and a half degrees. Venus is received by the Moon being in her domicile. There is no frustration or other impediment, prior to the perfecting of this conjunction in an angular house. Jupiter, a Fortune, makes a trine with both the

Moon and Venus, receiving them both in his exaltation from a good house. Jupiter makes a conjunction with the Lot of Fortune, which is at the very degree of the Sun in the Querent's Nativity.

However, Jupiter makes a square with Saturn in the eighth house of loans. A combust, retrograde Mercury in the eighth house, together with the Sun and Saturn, do not bode well for getting all the money. However, she will get most of what she is asking for.

Outcome
The Querent received a letter on August 10th, just under three weeks later, to confirm that the loan would be upgraded and that the balance of the previous year's entitlement would be credited to her son's account. There would also be a grant to help with tuition fees, but there would be no grant for living expenses.

Will they pay me £1000?
21 March 2007 11.19 GMT. 50N16 04W48

The Querent had undertaken some work for a company, but had not agreed on a fee beforehand. She hoped they would send around £1000, which was the amount she believed the work was worth.

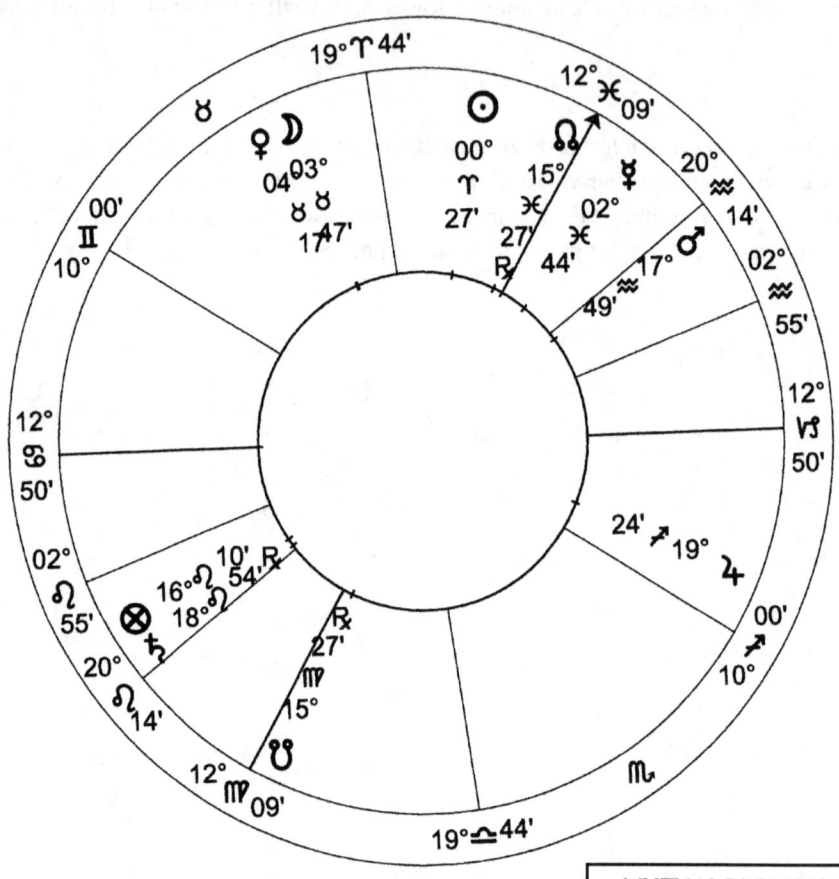

Signification

Querent
Significator: Ascendant and ascendant ruler the Moon.
Co-significators: Venus and Mercury (because of their very close aspect with the Moon).

Quesited (Money)
Significator: Second house and second house ruler the Sun.
Co-significators: The Lot of Fortune, Saturn.

The planetary hour ruler Mars harmonises with the ascendant.

The chart is diurnal. Fortunes are significators.

Testimonies For
The Moon is at the very degree of her exaltation in the eleventh house.
The Moon has a mutual reception with Venus and is applying to a conjunction with Venus.
Venus is in her own domicile in the eleventh house.
The Lot of Fortune is in the second house.
The Sun, ruler of the second house, is exalted and angular.

Testimonies Against
Saturn afflicts the house of the matter enquired about (the second house).
Saturn makes an opposition with Mars.

Due to the strength of the principal significators, the Querent will achieve the outcome desired, but with Saturn afflicting the second house her degree of success will be reduced.

Judgement
The Sun, second house ruler, is in his exaltation in the tenth house, aspecting the ascendant and correctly placed being in his hayyiz. The Sun makes a trine with the cusp of the second house and is the dispositor of the Lot of Fortune. The Moon applies to a conjunction with Venus, a Fortune, both swift in motion and dignified. From such positive testimony, the Querent should receive a large sum of money. However, the Moon, Venus and Mars are incorrectly placed above the horizon in a diurnal chart. Jupiter is cadent, not aspecting the ascendant and incorrectly placed. With Saturn in conjunction with the Lot of Fortune, afflicting the second house and opposing Mars, £1000 seemed unlikely.

Outcome
The Querent received £800.

Will I get my money back from the agent?
14 September 2006 9.52 BST. 50N16 04W48

The Querent owns a cottage and uses an agent for some of her holiday lets. The agency went into liquidation, owing her about a month's money. She recovered half the money, but wanted the remainder.

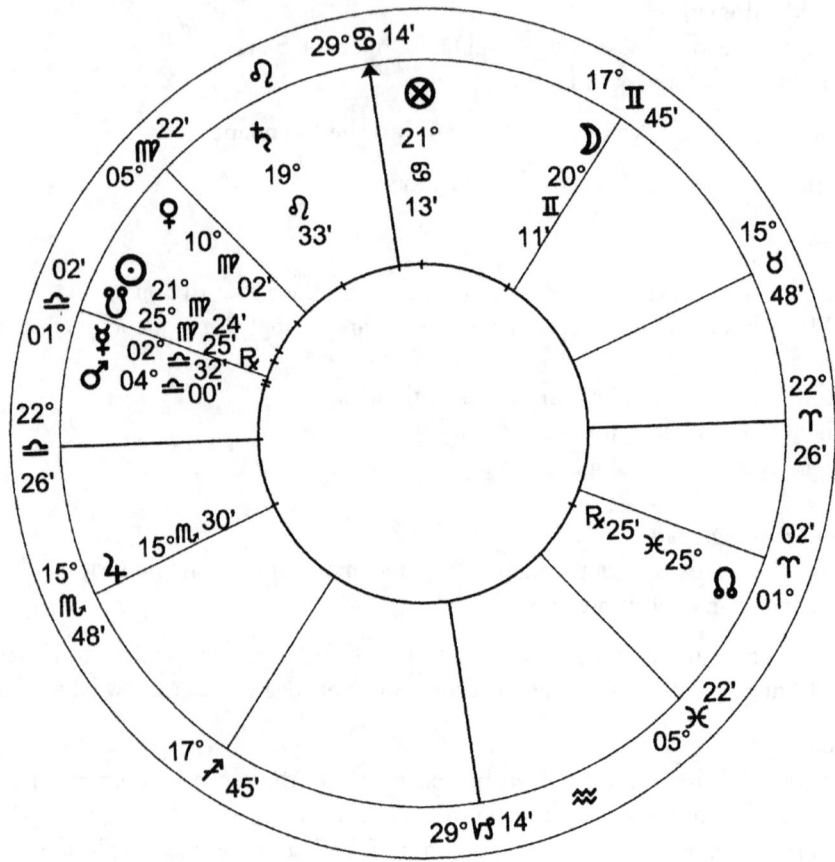

Signification

Querent
Significator: The ascendant and ascendant ruler, Venus.
Co-significator: The Moon.

Quesited
Significator: Second house, second house ruler Mars, Jupiter in the second house.

Owner of the Agency
Significator: Seventh house, seventh house ruler Mars.
Co-significators: The Sun, almuten of the seventh house, in conjunction with the south node.

The chart is diurnal.

Testimonies For
Jupiter is in the house of the matter enquired about.
Venus is applying to a sextile with Jupiter.

Testimonies Against
Jupiter is afflicted by his square with Saturn.
Saturn is weak and in the tenth house.
The Sun makes a conjunction with the south node.
Venus is under sunbeams.
The Moon is afflicted by her square with the Sun.

The lack of clear testimonies of good fortune confirm that there cannot be a positive outcome for the Querent.

Judgement
Although this Question did not ask about a thief, in fact the testimonies reveal that this is the most likely scenario. This may not be a theft in the usual sense, but it is a form of theft nonetheless. Lilly explains:

> The Lord of the seventh commonly signifies the Thief, but especially if he be peregrine in the ascendant, or in any other angle; but if he be not so, then behold if any other Planet be peregrine in any of the angles, call him the Thief; If none be peregrine in any of the angles, take the Lord of the hour, and call him the Thief, and if it happens that the Lord of the hour be Lord of the seventh, then it is more radicall...[7]

Later in *Christian Astrology*, Lilly tells us that in the opinion of "Master Allen of Oxford", the "true" significator of a thief is a planet in an angle or the second house, which beholds the seventh house. If there is no peregrine planet in an angle or the second house, the seventh house ruler is the thief providing that this planet beholds the seventh house. If there is no planet like this, the thief is signified by the planet to whom the Moon applies (providing that this planet beholds the seventh house) and this is especially true if the Moon has separated from the ascendant ruler. Lilly himself tells us that where there is more than one peregrine planet under consideration, it is the one closest to an angle which should be assigned signification of a thief.[8]

According to Lilly, in this chart Saturn would be considered peregrine, but I suggest that his mutual receptions with the Sun prevent him from being peregrine. However, the Sun in conjunction with the south node is more likely to represent a person who is untrustworthy. In *Christian Astrology*, Lilly tells us about a person signified by the Sun in conjunction with the south node, whom he calls "a Solar man, who was false".[9] In the chart under consideration now, the Sun, almuten of the seventh house, is also ruler of the hour and is the planet to whom the Moon applies. I would, therefore, assign the Sun as significator of the thief.

Although Jupiter in the second house and in direct motion is positive testimony of recovering the money, this can only be in part, because of his affliction with Saturn. Venus although in her own triplicity, terms and face is incorrectly placed above the horizon in a diurnal chart, is oriental of the Sun and under sunbeams. Venus applies to a sextile with Jupiter and has a mutual reception with Mercury, but Mercury is afflicted by his conjunction with Mars. The Moon applies to a square with the Sun.

The chart shows the impossibility of recovering all the money because the Fortunes are afflicted and the Infortunes have more power in the Question.

Outcome

The Querent could not get her money back. However, she did not pay an outstanding invoice for £200 from the agent.

Second House Matters

**Is this flat a good investment? Will I be able to get a mortgage?
Will I be able to resell?
2 April 1994 21.26 BST. 51N30 00W10**

The Querent was hoping to buy a flat in London, but as she already owned other properties, she was finding it difficult to raise another mortgage.

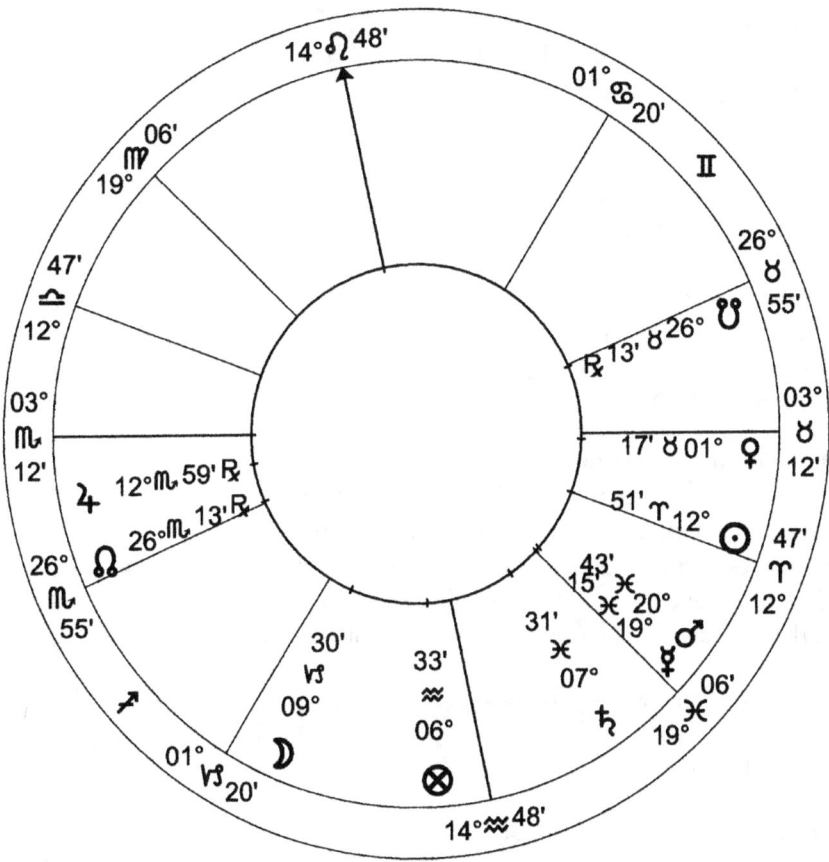

Signification
Querent
Significator: Ascendant and ascendant ruler Mars.
Co-significator: Jupiter, Moon.

Quesited (Mortgage)
Significator: Eighth house, eighth house ruler, Venus.
Co-significator: Mercury, co-ruler of the eighth house.

The Flat
Significator: Fourth house, fourth house ruler Saturn.
Co-significator: The Moon.

The Seller and the Possible Buyer
Significator: Seventh house, seventh house ruler Venus.

The chart is nocturnal.

Testimonies for a Good Investment
Fourth house ruler Saturn is placed in the fourth house.
Venus makes a sextile with Saturn and receives Saturn.
Jupiter makes a trine with Saturn and receives Saturn.
The Lot of Fortune is close to the fourth house cusp.
Mars, the ascendant ruler, has a mutual reception with Jupiter.

Testimonies against a Good Investment
Jupiter is retrograde.
The Moon is cadent.

Testimonies for Raising a Mortgage
Mercury, co-significator of the mortgage, is applying to a conjunction with Mars, the Querent, and is received by Mars in his triplicity.
Mercury and Mars are received by Venus, principal significator of the mortgage.
Mercury and Mars are aspecting the second house with a trine.
The north node is in conjunction with the second house cusp.

Testimonies against Raising a Mortgage
The south node afflicts the eighth house cusp.
The fixed star Caput Algol is in conjunction with the eighth house cusp.

Testimonies for Buying the Flat
Jupiter, co-significator of the Querent applies to a trine with Saturn, principal significator of the flat.

The Moon translates the light between Saturn and Jupiter.
Saturn collects the light of Venus (seller) and Jupiter.

Testimonies against Buying the Flat
None.
The testimonies for buying the flat are strong, but for raising a mortgage are weaker. However, the overall testimony is favourable for the Querent.

Judgement
This is a nocturnal chart but all the nocturnal planets, Moon, Venus and Mars, are incorrectly placed beneath the horizon. However, they all have dignity in their position. Mars as the Querent's significator is in his own triplicity, terms and face and has a mutual reception with Jupiter, a Fortune in the first house. Mars is aspecting the ascendant with a trine.

Venus, as principal significator of mortgages is dignified in her domicile, but makes no aspect with Mars. Venus applies to a sextile with Saturn, fourth house ruler and receives Saturn in her exaltation. Mercury, as co-significator of the eighth house, is applying to a conjunction with Mars. This shows the possibility of getting a mortgage but with difficulty as Mercury is in his detriment and fall, and besieged between Mars and Saturn.

Saturn, principal significator of the flat, is in his face and applies to Jupiter (co-significator of the Querent) with a trine and is received by Jupiter. The Moon translates the light between Saturn and Jupiter. Saturn, ruler of the fourth house and positioned in the fourth house, suggests that the flat is a good investment. This is confirmed by the trine with Jupiter and the sextile with Venus. The Lot of Fortune is near to the fourth house cusp and his dispositor is Saturn, well aspected.

I judged that the Querent would have difficulty getting a mortgage because the south node is in conjunction with the eighth house cusp and has great power there. The cusp is also within orb of the malefic fixed star Caput Algol. Venus opposes the ascendant, and Mercury is besieged between two Infortunes. Jupiter, co-significator, is retrograde. However, the strength of the principal significators and the Moon, together with their applications and mutual receptions is positive testimony. I judged the flat to be a good investment and that she would be able to buy it. I did not give judgement on a possible future sale.

Outcome
It took the Querent almost a year to raise a mortgage, but she bought the flat in 1995. The property proved to be a good investment and was actually resold at a profit ten years later to a young woman (Venus in the seventh house).

References

1. Lilly p.167.
2. ibid pp.167-168.
3. ibid pp.168-169.
4. ibid p.170.
5. Masha'allah p.23.
6. Bonatus p.40, 123rd consideration.
7. Lilly p.331.
8. ibid pp..394-395.
9. ibid p.457.

17

Fourth House Matters
Land and Property

The fourth house is associated with land, buildings, cities, towns, villages, farms, castles and property in general. Fathers and grandfathers also have signification here. Lilly tells us that this is the house of

> ...Parents, of Lands, Tenements, Hereditaments, Cities, Towns, Villages, Farmes, Manours, Castles, Treasure-trove, or any thing hid in the ground...[1]

Testimonies Relating to the Fourth House

In Questions concerning the buying or selling of land or property, we are told that the ascendant, ascendant ruler and the planet from whom the Moon has separated are significators of the buyer or Querent. The seventh house, the seventh house ruler and the planet to whom the Moon applies are assigned as significators of the seller (signification taken from the application or separation of the Moon isn't a rule which is consistently applied in *Christian Astrology*). The fourth house, any planet in the fourth house, the fourth house ruler and the Moon are significators of the property or land. The tenth house, tenth house ruler, and any planet in the tenth house, are significators of the price of the property or land to be sold.[2]

I would suggest that the Querent is always signified by the ascendant, whether buyer or seller.

Buying Property or Land

Lilly tells us that there will be a deal between a seller and a purchaser if

- The ascendant ruler and the seventh house ruler make any "amicable" aspect, especially if the seventh house ruler applies to an aspect or conjunction with the ascendant ruler. This is confirmation that the seller is keen to sell and to do business with the buyer or Querent. If the significators are placed in any of their essential dignities and there is a translation, other applying aspect, or a conjunction, they will agree easily and complete the deal with no hassle.

- The ascendant ruler or the Moon applies to an aspect or conjunction with the fourth house ruler.

- The fourth house ruler or the Moon applies to an aspect or conjunction with the ascendant ruler.
- The fourth house ruler applies to an aspect or conjunction with the ascendant ruler and is received in any of his dignities.
- The ascendant ruler is in the fourth house.
- The Moon is in the fourth house.
- The fourth house ruler is in the ascendant.
- There is no "dwelling in houses" as above, but the Moon translates the light of the fourth house ruler to the ascendant ruler. In this instance, the purchase will take place, but by agents or brokers (this happens almost routinely nowadays).

There will not be a deal between a seller and a purchaser if

- The application or translation is with a square or opposition. The parties will try to negotiate, but there will be a lot of hassle and the probability that the deal will not be concluded, having wasted a lot of time and money.

If either of the Infortunes (Saturn or Mars) is in the fourth house and is "very potent, or peregrine", or if the fourth house ruler is retrograde or unfortunate, in his fall or detriment, the house or land is not a good investment. In this instance, Lilly confirms that the Querent will "never continue long with ... [his] Posterity".[3] The south node in the fourth house is another unfortunate indication. However, if either of the Fortunes, Jupiter or Venus, or the north node is in the fourth house, or if the fourth house ruler is in the fourth house, the land or property is a good investment. The Querent will prosper from this investment. "...he shall have good encrease for his Money by that Bargaine".[4]

The tenth house ruler signifies the price of the land or property. If the tenth house ruler is angular, direct and strong in essential dignities, the price is going to be high. However, if the tenth house ruler is cadent, combust, retrograde, slow in motion or afflicted, "the price will not rise high".[5]

Simmonite asks "Is it Well to Purchase the Property?" He tells us that it is a yes if Venus, Jupiter or the north node are "on the 1st" or if the Lot of Fortune is unafflicted in the first house. It is also fortunate for the Querent if the second house ruler is in the first house, or if it is in sextile or trine with the degree in the first house cusp or the degree in the fourth house cusp (and not afflicted). It is the same if Venus, Jupiter or the north node are in the fourth house "or beholding the cusp favourably".[6]

Renting or Leasing Property or Land[7]
Again, Lilly assigns the ascendant and ascendant ruler as significators of the person who wishes to lease the house or property. He assigns the seventh house and the seventh house ruler as significators of the person doing the letting or leasing. I would suggest that the ascendant and ascendant ruler are always the significators of the Querent. The

Querent may be the person who wants to rent or lease a house or piece of land to another person, or the Querent may be the person who wants to rent or lease a house or piece of land from someone else. The seventh house and the seventh house ruler represent the other party.

Lilly explains that the tenth house signifies the profit, which might arise by letting the property. The fourth house and any planets in the fourth house show the end of the matter. In general the outcome to a Question like this is fortunate for the Querent if

- The ascendant ruler is in the ascendant or in the sign ascending, or makes a close trine or sextile aspect with the sign ascending, but especially if it aspects the degree ascending, within the moiety of his own orbs.
- There is a Fortune in the ascendant, whether essentially dignified or not.
- The Lot of Fortune is in the ascendant and not 'impeded'.

In general the other party will keep to their word but they will make a profit for themselves if

- The seventh house ruler is in the seventh house, or makes a harmonious aspect with the cusp of the seventh house.
- A fortunate planet is in the seventh house.
- A fortunate planet is in the tenth house or aspects the tenth house. Here the parties may have a few arguments, but the business will eventually be completed and the "House, Farme or Lands will be let to the Querent".[8]

The outcome overall is unfortunate if

- An Infortune is in the ascendant. Here the other party does not intend to keep their word and may lease the land or property to another person.
- An Infortune is in the seventh house and is not the ruler of the seventh house. Here, the other party (the landlord) is only concerned with his own profit and Lilly warns the reader to "have great care of the Covenants and Conditions to be drawne betwixt you..."[9]
- An unfortunate planet is in the tenth house, or aspecting the tenth house with a square or opposition. Here there will be no deal.

In regard to the end of the matter, if a Fortune is in the fourth house, or if the fourth house ruler is in the fourth house, or aspects the fourth house with a sextile or trine, there will be a good end to the matter and both parties will be pleased. If an Infortune is in the fourth house, the agreement probably won't take place, or if it does, neither party will be pleased with the outcome.

To Stay or Move?

Lilly explains how the Querent should decide whether it is best to stay or to move.[10] It is good for the Querent to stay where he or she is if

- The fourth house ruler is a good planet* and is in the seventh house and if both the ascendant ruler and the seventh house ruler are good planets (or if they are well placed in the chart, direct, swift in motion and in aspect with good planets).

It is good for the Querent to move if

- The seventh house ruler is with a good planet and the lord of the fourth house is with an evil planet.**

- The ascendant ruler has just separated from a square or opposition with the ruler of the sixth, eighth or twelfth house. The Moon must offer supporting testimony by separating from any bad aspect with the Infortunes, where they rule the fourth or seventh houses and they are "not Friends or Significators in the person of the Querent".

- An Infortune is in the ascendant peregrine or retrograde.

- A planet which is peregrine or retrograde is in the fourth house.

- The second house ruler is weak or badly placed.

- The sixth house ruler is in the ascendant or afflicts the ascendant ruler. Here, the Querent's health would suffer if he or she did not move, or the Querent's servants would not support him and his work would suffer as a result.

- The ascendant ruler or the Moon are afflicted by the twelfth house ruler. Here, the Querent would be slandered by wicked neighbours or people living in the community.

- The second house ruler is unfortunate or makes a square or opposition with the ascendant ruler, or if the Lot of Fortune is in the twelfth, eighth or sixth house. Here, the Querent's wealth would decrease and he would lose money.

- The ascendant ruler is afflicted by the tenth house ruler. The Querent's reputation would be damaged and his trade would suffer.

- The fourth house or fourth house ruler is unfortunate. In this case, the house is unlucky and very few people who lived there had prospered.

---

*   Lilly does not make it clear what he means by a good planet, but we must assume that it is a benefic as defined in Terms of Art.

**   Presumably an evil planet is in the opposite condition to a good planet, in other words, a malefic as defined in Terms of Art.

From the Horary Files

Will I receive a firm offer by the end of January?
21 November 2003 8.41 GMT. 50N16 04W48

The Querent had been trying to sell her flat for sometime, but with no luck.

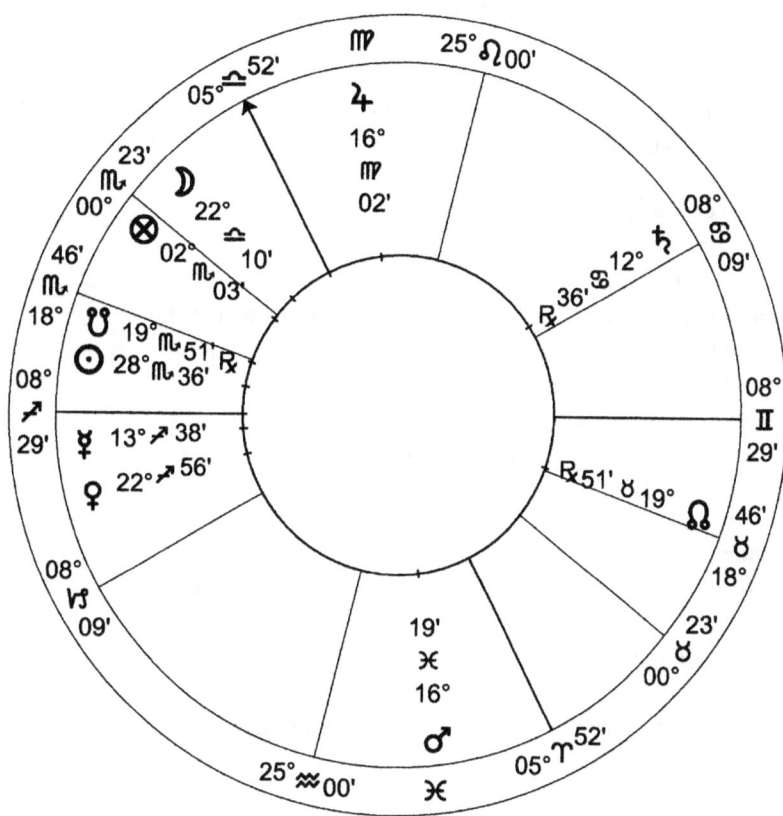

Signification

Querent (Seller)
Significator: Ascendant, ascendant ruler Jupiter.
Co-significator: Moon.

Quesited (Potential Buyer)
Significator: Seventh house, seventh house ruler Mercury.

The Flat
Significator: Fourth house, fourth house ruler, Mars.
Co-significator: Moon.

The chart is diurnal.

Testimonies For
The ruler of the seventh house, Mercury, is placed in the first house.
The ruler of the seventh house is applying to a square with Jupiter, the ruler of the first house.
Mercury and Jupiter have a mutual reception between domicile.
The Moon is applying to a sextile with Venus, a Fortune, in the first house. They have a reception.

Testimonies Against
The Moon is in the via combusta (although she is in conjunction with the benefic fixed star Spica).
Jupiter is afflicted by his opposition with Mars.

With strong testimonies in favour of a positive outcome, the Querent will sell her flat.

Judgement
Mercury in the first house, significator of the buyer, although applying to a square with Jupiter, significator of the seller, has a mutual reception with Jupiter between domicile. Mercury's position in the house of the Querent and applying to the Querent's significator shows the purchaser's eagerness for a deal and the ease with which a deal could be agreed. Mercury perfects his aspect with Jupiter in less than three degrees. The Moon in Libra applies to a sextile with Venus, a Fortune, in the first house and is received by Venus being in her domicile. The Moon aspects the ascendant and although she is in the via combusta, is close to the fortunate fixed star Spica. The Moon has a strong mutual reception with Saturn. Venus has a strong mutual reception with Jupiter. Mars afflicts Jupiter with his recent opposition, but is disposed of by Jupiter who is stronger in the chart than he.

Outcome

An offer was made within a week (the Moon's close application to a sextile with Venus), but completion did not take place for several months. A young woman bought the flat, but it was her mother who paid for it. It is interesting that Venus is in the first house, being the ruler of the tenth house of mothers in this chart, as well as the natural significator of mothers by day.

Will I buy the cottage?
8 August 2001 13.44 GMT. 51N30 00W00

The Querent was in the process of buying a cottage near the sea, but there were delays and a possibility that the purchase would not take place.

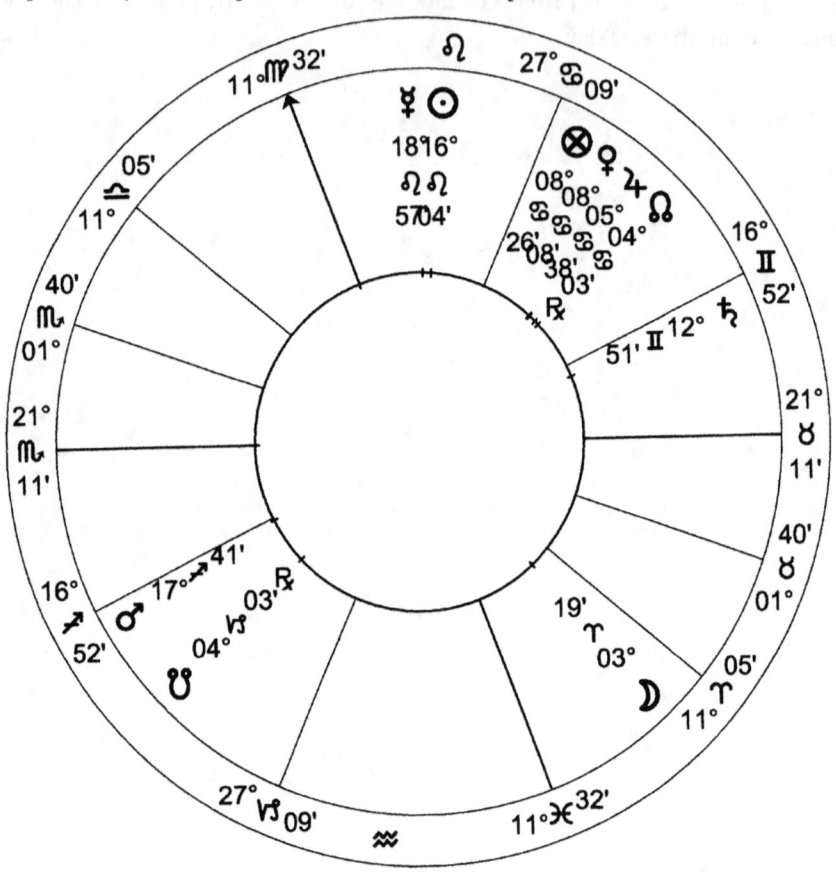

Signification

Querent (Buyer)
Significator: Ascendant, ascendant ruler Mars.
Co-significator: The Moon.

Quesited (Seller)
Significator: Seventh house, seventh house ruler, Venus.

The Cottage
Significator: Fourth house, fourth house ruler, Jupiter. The Moon.

The chart is diurnal.

Testimonies For
The Moon is in the house of the matter enquired about (the fourth house).
The Moon applies to a square with the fourth house ruler, Jupiter.
Moon and Jupiter have a mutual reception.
The fourth house ruler Jupiter is very strong in his exaltation, close to Venus, the Lot of Fortune and the north node.

Testimonies Against
Mars, ascendant ruler, is afflicted by his opposition with Saturn.
The fourth house ruler Jupiter is in the eighth house.
Venus and the north node are in the eighth house.

Testimonies of good fortune outweigh testimonies of misfortune so the Querent will achieve the outcome desired.

Judgement
Mars in the second house of finance is afflicted by his recent opposition with Saturn in the eighth house of loans and Mars does not aspect the ascendant. This signifies the difficulty the Querent was experiencing in trying to raise a mortgage. However, this aspect is separating. The Moon is in the fourth house applying to a square with Jupiter, fourth house ruler and they have a mutual reception. Despite his position in the eighth house, Jupiter is exalted, correctly placed and is aspecting the ascendant. Jupiter, Venus, the Lot of Fortune and the north node are co-significators of the mortgage and fortunate in this regard. The Querent will get her mortgage and buy the cottage.

Outcome
The transaction was completed on 5 October 2001, two months after the Question, (the Moon applies to an exact square with Jupiter in just over two degrees).

Will we agree on £x for the flat?
30 August 2007 21.02 BST. 50N16 04W48

The Querent wanted to buy a flat at about £10,000 less than the asking price, but her offer was refused. She hoped that in time the vendor would change his mind.

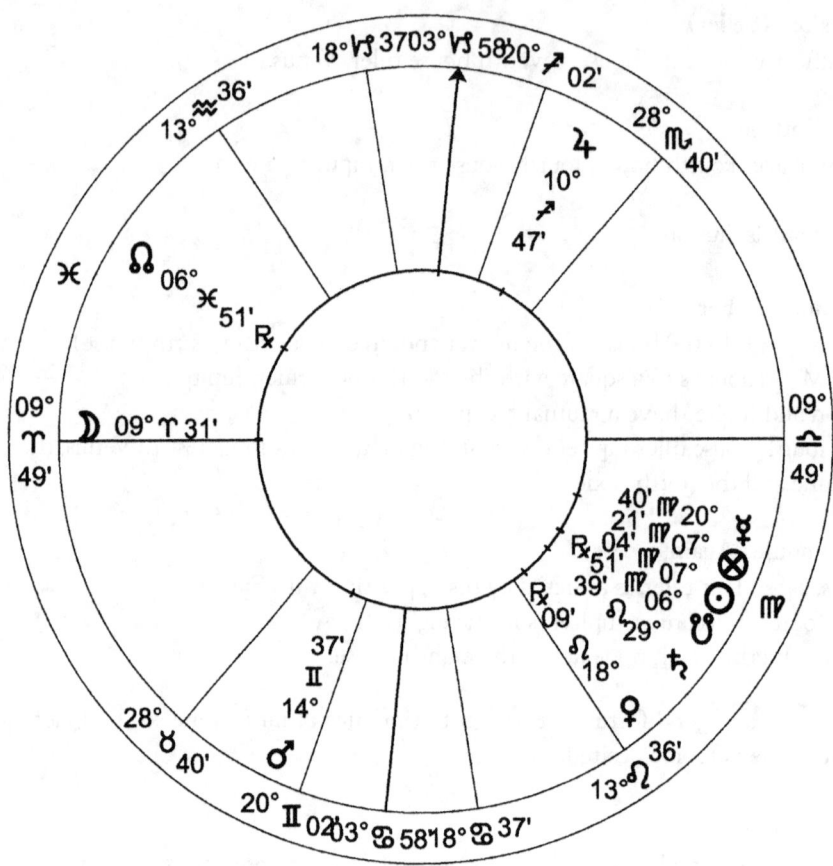

Signification

Querent (Buyer)
Significator: Ascendant and ascendant ruler Mars.
Co-significator: The Moon.

Quesited (Seller)
Significator: Seventh house and seventh house ruler Venus.

The Flat
Significator: Fourth house and fourth house ruler the Moon.

The chart is nocturnal.

Testimonies For
The Moon, fourth house ruler, is in the ascendant.
The Moon is applying to a sextile with Mars and is received.
Venus, ruler of the seventh house, is applying to a sextile with Mars.

Testimonies Against
Venus, significator of the seller, is in the sixth house and retrograde.
The application of Venus to a sextile with Mars is through retrogradation.

Testimonies of good fortune are stronger than those of misfortune, but the testimonies are weak nonetheless.

Judgement
The application to a trine between the principal significators of the potential buyer and seller, Venus and Mars, is hopeful. However, Venus is retrograde so this application is unfortunate. In addition, there is no mutual reception between Venus and Mars, although Mars in received by Venus being in her terms. The Moon, fourth house ruler is in conjunction with the ascendant and applies to a sextile with Mars, received by Mars in his domicile and face. From all of this I judged that the Querent could have the flat at the price she wanted to pay.

Outcome
The Querent's offer was accepted in early October, almost five weeks later (the Moon's application to a perfect sextile with Mars is five degrees). However, she changed her mind about the purchase and withdrew the offer at a later date. This was mainly due to the fact that she didn't think she could afford the mortgage repayments. Although the bank agreed to the mortgage (the Moon applies to a trine with Jupiter dignified in the eighth house of loans), with her second house ruler Venus retrograde and in the sixth house, pulling out of the deal proved to be a wise move.

Will she buy my house?
23 September 2006 12.26 BST. 50N30 04W48

An old friend of the Querent had expressed an interest in buying her house. They had known each other when they were younger, but were no longer close friends.

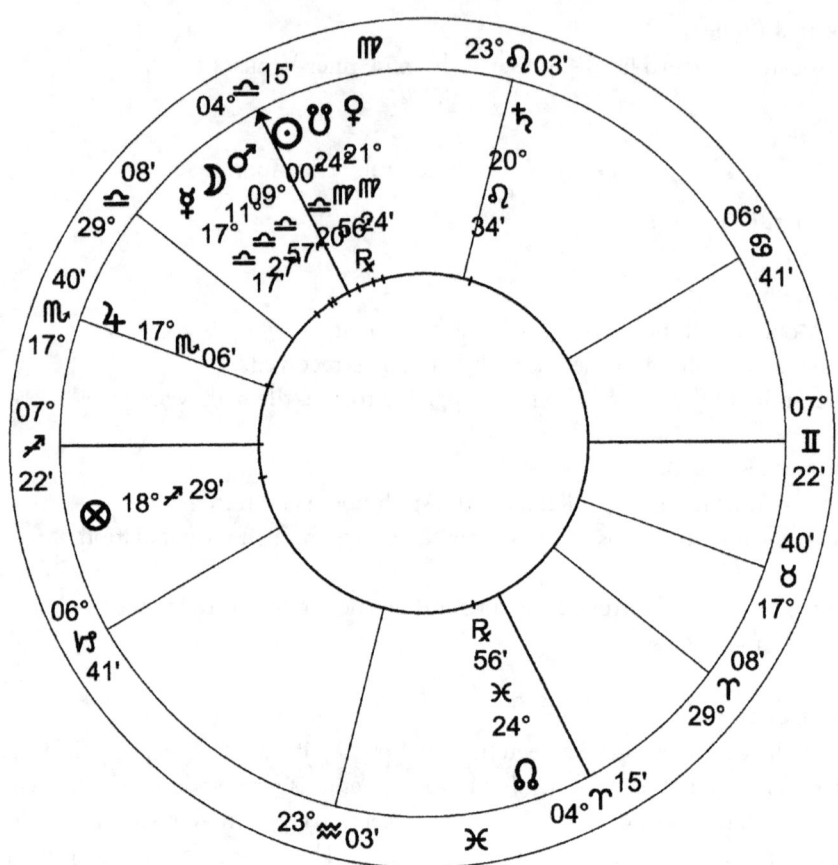

Signification

Querent
Significator: Ascendant, ascendant ruler Jupiter.
Co-significator: Moon.

Quesited (The Friend and Buyer)
Significator: Seventh house and seventh house ruler, Mercury. The eleventh house should also be considered.

The House
Significator: Fourth house, fourth house ruler Mars. The Moon.
Mars, fourth house ruler is in his detriment, under sunbeams, incorrectly placed and he has no strong mutual receptions. The house itself, which is made of red/brown timber, is in poor condition and requires a complete refurbishment (a condition not improving as the Sun moves closer).

The chart is diurnal.

Testimonies For
The Moon makes a conjunction with Mercury, the seventh house ruler, in a good house (the eleventh house).
There is a translation of light between the fourth house ruler Mars and the seventh house ruler Mercury.
Venus has a strong mutual reception with Mercury.

Testimonies Against
The ascendant ruler Jupiter is in the twelfth house.
The Moon is afflicted by her recent conjunction with Mars.

The testimonies in favour of a transaction are stronger than those against.

Judgement
The ascendant of the Question is Sagittarius. The Querent has Sagittarius ascending in her Nativity. Jupiter, principal significator of the Querent, is in the twelfth house and is applying to a square with Saturn. Jupiter does not aspect the ascendant and his dispositor Mars, is moving into combustion. The Querent has been suffering from depression.

The Querent's friend is partly signified by the eleventh house. However, the astrologer must also look at the seventh house for signification of the other party in the transaction. In fact, Venus, eleventh house ruler, has a mutual reception with Mercury (seventh house ruler) between domicile. Given that Mercury is also located in the eleventh house, Mercury is taken as principal significator of the buyer (and the friend).

The Moon is peregrine and Mars is under sunbeams, but Mercury is emerging from sunbeams, where he is very strong. The Sun has a mutual reception with Saturn, which is also very helpful. The Moon translates the light from Mars, ruler of the fourth house, to Mercury, the purchaser, in six degrees. The Moon is herself a co-significator of the property. I would expect the transaction to take place in about six weeks or perhaps more, because the Moon is slow in motion.

Outcome
Exchange took place just over six weeks later on 9 November 2006. Completion took place on 23 November 2006

Will I be able to agree on a lower price?
19 August 1991 19.25 BST. 51N30 00W00

The Querent was keen to buy an old Victorian house, but had a tight budget and could not afford to pay more than a certain sum.

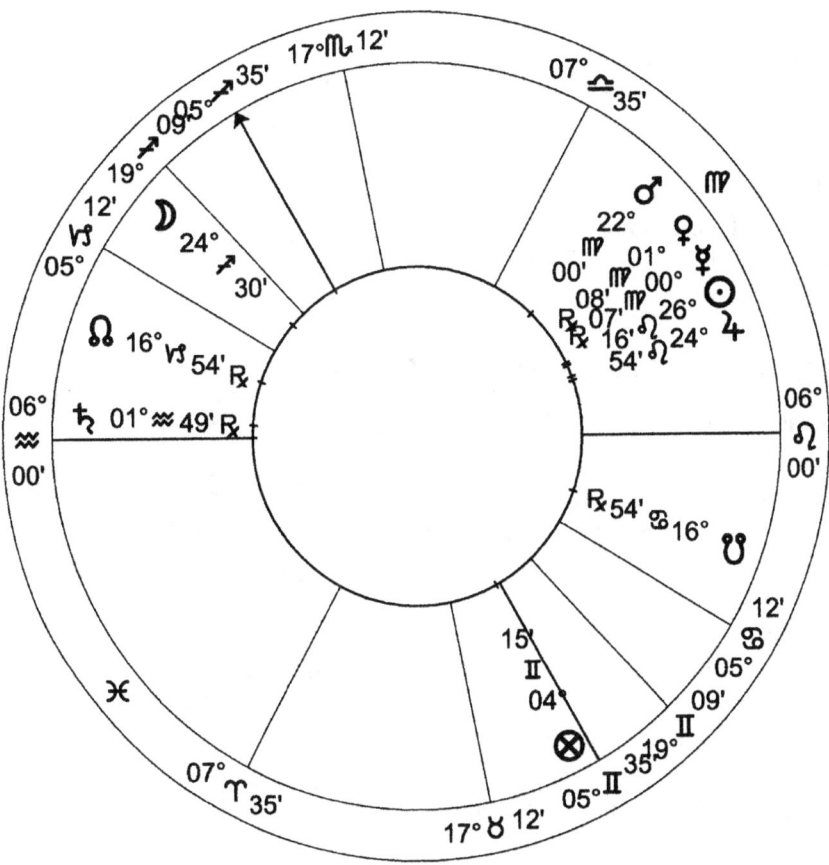

Signification

Querent
Significator: Ascendant, ascendant ruler Saturn.
Co-significator: The Moon.

Quesited (The Seller)
Significator: Seventh house, seventh house ruler, the Sun.
Co-significators: Jupiter, Mercury, Venus and Mars in the seventh house.

The House
Significator: Fourth house, fourth house ruler, Mercury.
Co-significator: The Lot of Fortune.

The Price
Significator: Tenth house, tenth house ruler, Jupiter

The chart is diurnal.

Testimonies For
The ascendant ruler Saturn is in the ascendant and in his domicile.
The Moon applies to a trine with the seventh house ruler, the Sun, from the fortunate eleventh house.
The Moon is received by Jupiter in his domicile and by the Sun in his triplicity.
The Lot of Fortune is in conjunction with the fourth house cusp.

Testimonies Against
Saturn is retrograde.
Mercury, fourth house ruler, is retrograde and moving towards combustion.

Testimonies for an agreement are stronger than those against.

Judgement
Saturn, significator of the Querent, is in the ascendant and makes a trine with the Lot of Fortune in the fourth house. Being in his own domicile, triplicity and term in a diurnal chart is fortunate for Saturn, although he loses some strength by his retrograde motion. Principal significator of the seller is the Sun, although there were several beneficiaries involved here, as signified by another four other planets in the seventh house. Jupiter, significator of the price, is combust, indicating that the beneficiaries might be willing to reduce the price for a quick sale.

    The Moon applies to Jupiter with a powerful dexter trine and is received by Jupiter being in his domicile. The Moon's next aspect is a dexter trine with the Sun and she is received by the Sun in his triplicity. This is confirmation of an agreement.

Outcome
The deal was agreed within two weeks, but exchange did not take place until the end of January 1992 (five months later). The application of the Moon to a partill aspect with Mercury is five and a half degrees. Mercury's poor condition reflects the condition of the old house and the amount of renovating required. The Querent did not lose money on the resale years later, but due to expensive works, did not gain. In the buoyant property market which followed, this was disappointing.

Will I be able to buy my flat?
12 October 1987 21.54 GMT. 51N30 00W10

The Querent, a single parent with little money, was hoping to buy her council flat under the right-to-buy scheme.

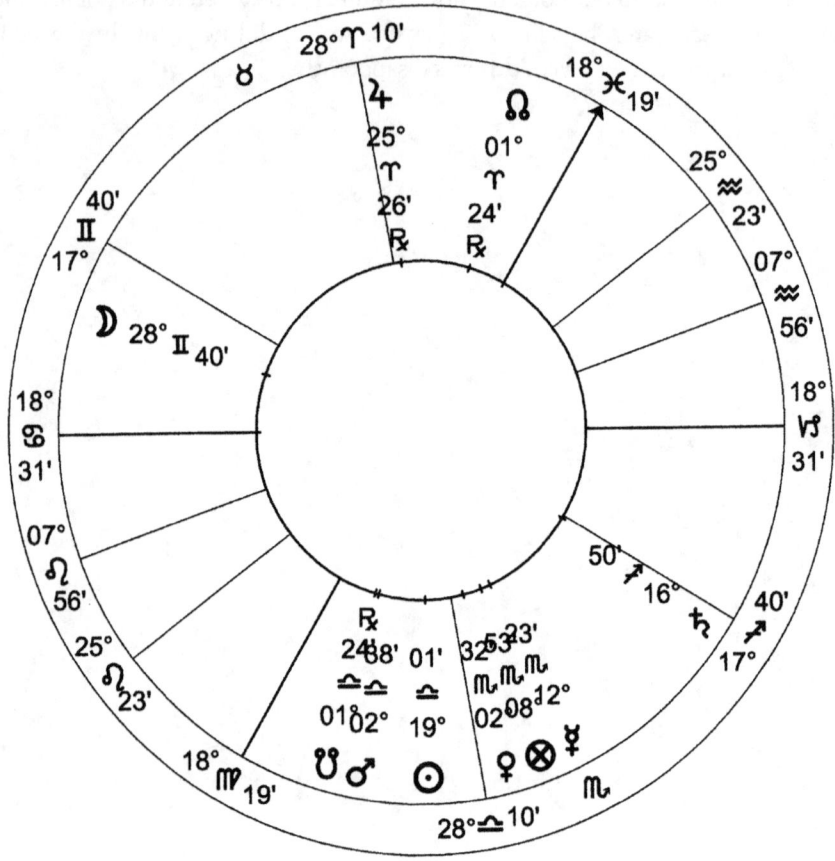

Signification

Querent
Significator: Ascendant, ascendant ruler the Moon.

Quesited (The Seller)
Significator: Seventh house, seventh house ruler, Saturn.

The Flat
Significator: Fourth house, fourth house ruler, Mercury.
Co-significator: South node, Mars, Sun.

The chart is nocturnal.

Testimonies For
None.

Testimonies Against
The Moon is in the twelfth house, void of course, and in late degrees of Gemini.
The Moon's aspect in the next sign is a square with Mars.
Infortunes are in the fourth house and ill-dignified.
Jupiter, a Fortune, is afflicted by his opposition with the Sun.

There are no testimonies of good fortune. The Querent cannot achieve the desired outcome.

Judgement

With the Moon peregrine in late degrees of Gemini, not aspecting the ascendant and void of course, the astrologer should refrain from judgement. I did not judge this chart; it was shown to me sometime later by the Querent. However, it is interesting to consider the chart in light of what took place.

The Moon has recently separated from a sextile with Jupiter and does not apply to the fourth house ruler Mercury, nor to the seventh house ruler Saturn. Although Mercury, fourth house ruler, has a mutual reception with Mars, Infortunes occupy the fourth house. Mars is in his detriment and in conjunction with the south node. The Sun is in his fall. The Infortunes strongly afflict the fourth house, indicating that there is a problem with the house. Although Mars has a mutual reception with Venus, they are both debilitated, so this reception is not very helpful. Chart testimonies confirm that the flat is not sound and that the buyer would not profit from the purchase.

Outcome

The Querent could not get a mortgage, because the building was subsiding. She did not buy the flat.

References

1. Lilly p.202.
2. ibid references to Lilly in this section from pp.204-205.
3. ibid p.206.
4. ibid p.206.
5. ibid p.208.
6. Simmonite p.101.
7. Lilly, references to Lilly in this section taken from pp.208-209.
8. ibid p.209.
9. ibid
10. ibid pp.212-214.

18

FIFTH HOUSE MATTERS
PREGNANCY AND CHILDREN

In any chart, it is the ascendant, the ascendant ruler, the fifth house and the fifth house ruler which have principal signification over children and pregnancy. Jupiter is the natural ruler of pregnancy and, together with Venus, also has signification in the matter. It must be emphasised however, that in any Question, particularly one concerning pregnancy, it is important to look at the Querent's Nativity. Lilly tells us very clearly

> ...if the Radix affirme Barrennesse, it's impossible any promising Horary Question can contradict its signification...[1]

In a similar way, when making a judgement as to whether there will be "unity" between the parents and the children, Lilly tells us that this is best judged from the Nativity, but adds a cautionary note

> ..because few among us are capable of judging one, I adventure somewhat by an Horary Question.[2]

Testimonies Relating to the Fifth House

Lilly tells us that in a Question relating to pregnancy and children, asked by a man or a woman long before marriage, or by "some ancient Batchelour, or Maid" the astrologer must consider whether any of the following testimonies are in place[3]

- If the sign ascending or the sign in the fifth house cusp is fruitful (Cancer, Scorpio or Pisces) and the ascendant ruler (no matter what sign it is in) or the Moon makes an aspect with the fifth house ruler through a conjunction, sextile, trine or square. However, the planet to whom the fifth house ruler is applying, or is in aspect with, "must be free from Combustion and other Accidental or Essential misfortunes". If these conditions are satisfied it is possible that the "good old Batchelour or stale Maid, or whoever propounds the Question, shall have Children or Issue ere they dye..."

- If the fifth house ruler or the Moon is in the ascendant or the ascendant ruler is in the fifth house. This is a strong indication of having children.

- If there is a rendering of virtue or of light between the ascendant ruler or the Moon and the fifth house ruler, or if there is a translation of light, or collection of light, by or from the principal significators. The Querent will still have children, but not as soon as in the first example.

- If the planet who receives the disposition of the significators is clear from affliction, that is, not retrograde, combust, nor cadent. This gives "great hopes…"

If there are no aspects between the significators as outlined above, it is unlikely there will be any children. If a woman who has been married for a long time has been unable to conceive and asks whether she will get pregnant, Lilly tells us that she will conceive if [4]

- The ascendant ruler is in the seventh house.
- The fifth house ruler is in the first house.
- The ascendant ruler is in the fifth house.
- The fifth house ruler is in the seventh house.
- The seventh house ruler is in the fifth house.
- The Moon makes a conjunction with the seventh house ruler.
- There are fortunate planets in the ascendant or with the fifth house ruler, or in any of the angles.

She will not conceive if

- None of the above testimonies are in place and there are barren signs and unfortunate planets in these places. In this instance, the woman is unlikely to be pregnant, nor will she be pregnant in the future.

- Fortunate and unfortunate planets are mixed. She may conceive or have children, but the children may not live.

- Leo or Virgo is in the cusp of the ascendant or fifth house. Here, the woman is unlikely to be pregnant, nor will she be pregnant in the future.

If the Querent believes she is pregnant and wants to be certain, Lilly tells us to "give Answer…as these following rules direct you".[5] If the following conditions are satisfied the Querent is pregnant

- Jupiter is in the first, fifth, eleventh or seventh house and not in aspect with Saturn or Mars, when they are slow in motion or retrograde.

- The ascendant ruler or fifth house ruler is aspecting a planet in an angle with reception.

- The ascendant ruler or the Moon beholds the fifth house ruler with any aspect or translation.

- The ascendant ruler and the Moon are in the fifth house, free from any bad aspects with the Infortunes, and are direct (of course the Moon cannot be retrograde). Here, Lilly explains that it is not only Mars, Saturn and the south node who are unfortunate. Any bad aspect with the rulers of the sixth, eighth or twelfth house (if they are in square or opposition with the fifth house ruler, the ascendant ruler or the Moon) is considered to be an affliction.

- The Moon has a reception with any planet in an angle that is essentially dignified, otherwise she is not, because "accidentall dignities in this manner of judgement, giveth hopes, but not reall assurance".

- The ascendant ruler aspects the ascendant with a friendly aspect from any good house.

- The Moon is in the seventh house and beholds the seventh house ruler in the eleventh house.

- The Moon is in the eleventh house and beholds the seventh house ruler in the seventh house.

- The ascendant ruler has a mutual reception (between domicile, exaltation, triplicity or term) with another planet.

- The Moon is giving virtue or rendering her light to a planet in the fifth house, or a planet which has essential dignities in the fifth house.

- The Moon is applying to an aspect or conjunction with the ascendant ruler or the fifth house ruler in the first or tenth house and "he not Cadent from his owne House or exaltation".*

- If the sign ascending is fixed and a Fortune is placed there, or if the fifth house ruler is strong in the ascendant or tenth house, it is an undeniable confirmation of pregnancy .

....the neerer a Fortune is to the Ascendant, the sooner the Querent may expect Children, the more remote the longer time must be allowed.[6]

Gadbury tells us that

> Mr Culpeper in his Directory for Midwives, averseth, That it is as easie for a woman to be cozened a Moneth, &c. in her time of being with child at the first, as for to mistake one shoue for another in the dark.[7]

---

*   For example, Mars in Aries is in his domicile and considered angular; Mars in Taurus is considered succedent and Mars in Gemini is considered to be cadent, that is, "Cadent as from his owne House". Lilly tells us that any planet is angular when in his domicile.

Gadbury puts forward a number of rules which should be observed in order to discover whether a woman is pregnant.[8] These are very similar to those of Lilly already discussed.

- If Jupiter, natural significator of children, is in the ascendant, fifth, seventh, or eleventh houses and is not in any way afflicted by the Infortunes, the woman is pregnant. But if Jupiter is afflicted by the Infortunes, is cadent, or is "sub radiis" the woman enquiring is not pregnant.

- Gadbury quotes Haly as saying that if the tenth house ruler and the Sun are in good places in the chart and are in a "friendly configuration with the Fortunes" the woman enquiring is pregnant.

- If the Moon and the rulers of the triplicity of the sign of the Moon are "well located in Signs of many children", such as Cancer, Scorpio, Pisces, the woman enquiring is pregnant.

- If Jupiter and Venus are angular and "free from the malicious Beams of the Infortunes" the woman enquiring is pregnant.

Lilly adds a note of caution

> In all Questions concerning Children, be carefull of the age of the Querent, or some other natural or hereditary infirmity incident to the Querent, and seldome conclude without two testimonies.[9]

If the testimonies reveal that the Querent may have a child or children and the Querent wants to know approximately when, this is calculated using the fifth house ruler.[10]

- If the fifth house ruler is in the ascendant or first house, she will be pregnant within one year.

- If the fifth house ruler is in the second house she will be pregnant in the second year.

- If in the tenth house the third year.

- If in the seventh house the fourth year.

- If in the fourth house she will be pregnant in the fifth year.

- If the fifth house ruler is swift in motion and in a moveable sign, this speeds up the time, a double-bodied sign slows things down, fixed signs prolong the matter.

- If the significator is swift in motion and direct, a pregnancy will happen far more quickly.

- In general terms, the astrologer must consider Jupiter who is the natural significator of children. If Jupiter is in the ascendant, third, fifth, ninth or eleventh house free from any affliction, the woman will become pregnant fairly quickly, perhaps the very next time she tries, or a little after, "and the matter seems as good as done".[11]

If a man or woman asks about a possible pregnancy, Lilly reports that the answer to this Question will be yes if [12]

- Fortunate planets aspect the ascendant and the ascendant ruler is in the ascendant, tenth, eleventh or fifth house and Jupiter is also well placed, together with the planet who is ruler of the triplicity ascending (as long as that planet is not combust or retrograde). In this case, you can judge that if a man asks the Question he may have children, or is capable of fathering them. If a woman asks, she is capable of conceiving and is not naturally barren.

- A fortunate planet is in the fifth house or is making a good aspect with the cusp of the fifth house. This indicates the probability of conceiving a child in just a small amount of time.

- An Infortune is in the fifth house as long as he is direct, swift in motion, oriental and in any of his essential dignities. The Querent will have even more children if Jupiter, Venus or the Sun is in sextile or trine aspect with the Infortune from good houses.

- If the ascendant ruler is in the fourth house or seventh house and Jupiter is in a fortunate house, there may be a child a long time after asking the Question.

- If Venus is not afflicted in the fifth house and "some other Fortune" is also in the fifth house, she will conceive very suddenly.

The answer to the above Question is no if

- The ascendant is afflicted by malevolent planets and the ascendant ruler is in an unfortunate house and Jupiter is cadent, in the eighth house, combust or under sunbeams. Here, there will only be a few children; they will be sickly, and not many of them will live.

- The Moon is unfortunate. This signifies "a great signe of non conception, or no capacity to conceive..."

- An Infortune is in the fifth house, ill dignified, combust, retrograde or slow in motion. Here, the Querent will have no children.

- Jupiter is afflicted in the ascendant, third, fifth, ninth or eleventh house. In this case, there will be no pregnancy or perhaps a miscarriage.

- Venus is afflicted by Saturn or Mars, is under sunbeams or combust. In this case, the Querent is not pregnant, (unless a Fortune is in the fifth house). However, there could still be problems before the birth.

- Either Saturn or Mars (and especially the south node), are in the fifth house, or Saturn or Mars make an opposition with the fifth house. Here, the woman is not pregnant. The square of the Infortunes to the fifth house seems to hinder conception.

The Sex of the Baby

Lilly explains that if the ascendant, the ascendant ruler, the fifth house and the fifth house ruler are in masculine signs, this indicates a male. If they are in feminine signs, this indicates a female. However, in most cases the indications are mixed and if this is the case, deciding the sex of a child can be really difficult. Lilly states that if the ascendant ruler is in a masculine sign and the fifth house ruler is in a feminine sign, one has to consider the Moon. One must note to which planet the Moon applies. If that planet is in a masculine sign the woman is likely to be pregnant with a boy. The masculine planets are Saturn, Jupiter, Mars and the Sun. The Moon and Venus are feminine planets. Mercury is judged according to his aspect or his conjunction with a masculine or feminine planet. Lilly confirms that Mercury is masculine when oriental of the Sun and feminine when occidental of the Sun.[13]

Judging the sex of a baby is not something I usually attempt as the degree of success to be expected is pretty limited. I include an example from William Lilly's *Christian Astrology*, but have no examples from my own practice.

If one were with Child of a Male or Female, and about what time she should be delivered?[14]

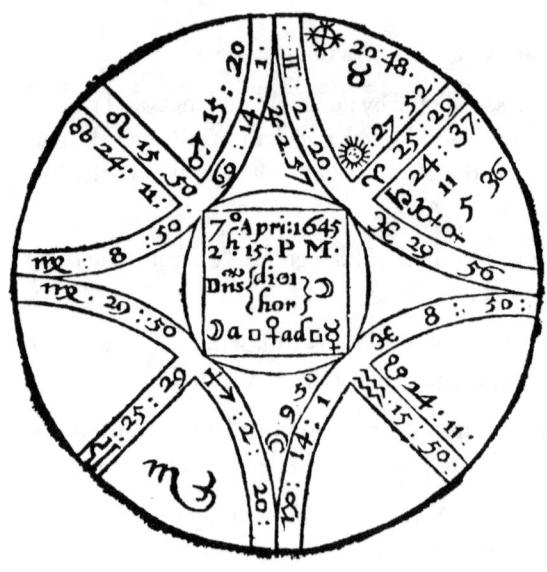

Significations of a girl

♍	Sign ascending	Feminine
♑	Sign of the fifth	Feminine
☽	In a sign	Feminine
☿	Lord of the ascendant with ♀	Feminine

Significations of a boy

☿	Lord of the ascendant in a sign	Masculine
♄	Lord of the fifth	Masculine
♄	Lord of the fifth in a sign	Masculine
☽	In a house	Masculine
♄	In a house	Masculine
♃	Lord of the hour	Masculine
♃	In a sign	Masculine
☿	Applying to a square with ♂	Masculine

With eight testimonies of a masculine child and four of a feminine, Lilly confirms that "the Lady was impregnated of a Man child, [and so it proved.]"

More than One Child

Lilly reports that if the ascendant is in a common sign (Pisces, Virgo, Gemini or Sagittarius) and both Jupiter and Venus are in the ascendant, or in conjunction with the fifth house cusp, or are in any of the twelve signs except Leo, it's likely that the woman is pregnant with twins. If the north node is also with Venus and Jupiter in the ascendant or fifth house, the woman may be pregnant with triplets.

If none of these planets are in the ascendant or fifth house, but make a sextile or trine aspect with the cusp of the fifth house or the degree ascending, the woman may conceive or is pregnant with more than one child.

However, if either a fixed or moveable sign is in the ascendant or fifth house and the Sun and Moon are also in a fixed or moveable sign (being in the fifth house or first house), the Querent is pregnant with only one child. Lilly adds another word of caution here when he says

> The Astrologer must not rashly adventure his Judgment without well considering his rules, or without knowledge had, whether it be not naturall or usuall for some of her Family to bring at one Birth more than one.[15]

From the Horary Files

The following chart examples are particularly interesting because they demonstrate that pregnancy is always a fifth house matter and that a chart cannot be turned in fifth house Questions.

If I try for a baby next year, will I get pregnant?
3 August 1993 11.07 BST. 51N34 00W00

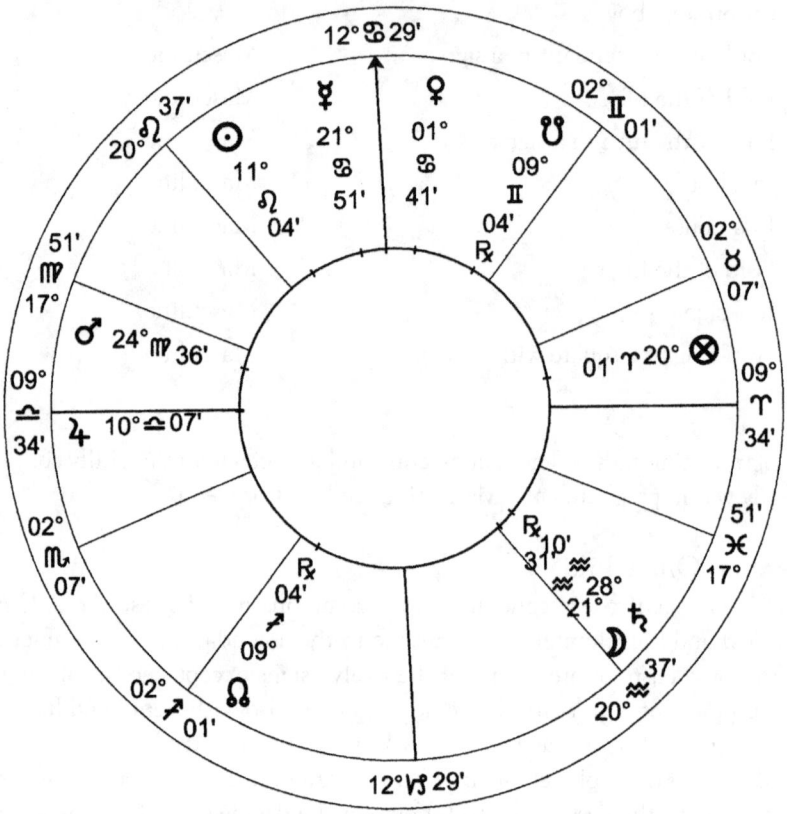

Signification
Querent
Significator: Ascendant, ascendant ruler Venus.
Co-significator: Moon and Jupiter, Saturn almuten of the ascendant.

Quesited (Baby)
Significator: Fifth house and fifth house ruler Saturn. Jupiter, natural significator of pregnancy.

The chart is diurnal.

Testimonies For
Jupiter, a Fortune, is in the ascendant.
Venus, a Fortune, is in the tenth house. (Venus is moving to angularity).
Jupiter has a mutual reception with Venus a Fortune.
The Moon is in the fifth house applying to a conjunction with the fifth house ruler Saturn in his domicile and joy.

Testimonies Against
The fifth house ruler, Saturn, is retrograde.

Testimonies of a pregnancy are strong and certain.

Judgement
The nearer a Fortune is to the ascendant, the sooner the Querent has children. As discussed above, Jupiter in conjunction with the ascendant shows that "the matter seems as good as done..." Moveable signs also speed up the timing. The Querent will be pregnant within a year. Jupiter has a mutual reception with the ascendant ruler Venus between domicile and exaltation. Jupiter is also received by the fifth house ruler Saturn in his exaltation, triplicity and face. Venus is moving towards angularity. The Moon in the fifth house applies to a conjunction with Saturn, fifth house ruler. Saturn is in his domicile and has a mutual reception with the Moon. However, Saturn is retrograde. The Moon is slightly afflicted by her opposition with the Sun, although separating by ten degrees. All significators are aspecting the ascendant.

    I judged that the Querent would be pregnant within the year. The Moon's application to a conjunction with Saturn is in seven degrees, the application of Venus to a square with Jupiter is just over eight degrees. The Moon is slow in motion so this may delay the matter slightly, but she should conceive in seven to eight months time.

Outcome
She conceived in late February/early March the following year, just over seven months later.

Will I get pregnant?
3 April 1986 11.45 BST. 51N30 00W00

The Querent is in her late thirties and has never had a pregnancy.

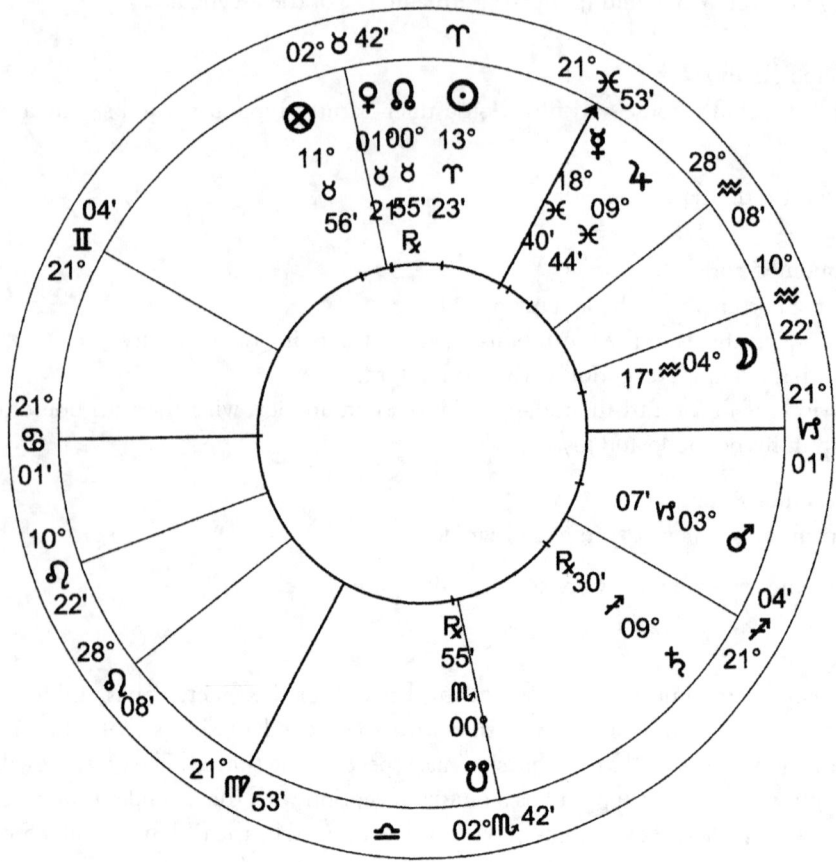

Signification

Querent
Significator: Ascendant and ascendant ruler the Moon.

Quesited (Baby)
Significator: Fifth house and fifth house ruler Mars.
Co-significators: Saturn in the fifth house, Jupiter, natural significator of pregnancy.

The chart is diurnal.

Testimonies For
Venus is in her domicile, applying to a trine with Mars and a sextile with Jupiter.
Jupiter is in his domicile.
Mars, fifth house ruler, is exalted.

Testimonies Against
Saturn is retrograde in the fifth house.
The south node is in conjunction with the fifth house cusp.
Jupiter, natural significator of pregnancy, is cadent and is afflicted by his square with Saturn.
The Moon is in a barren sign and moving into the eighth house.
Mars, fifth house ruler, is cadent.

The testimonies against a pregnancy are strong. A full-term pregnancy is not possible.

Judgement
Although Mars the ruler of the fifth house is exalted and applies to a sextile with Jupiter, both Jupiter and Mars are cadent. Jupiter is in his domicile of Pisces, but is afflicted by a recent square with a retrograde Saturn, ruler of the eighth house. They have a weak mutual reception which is helpful. Even if Jupiter were to be considered angular, he is unable to assist due to his affliction. The Moon is not in a fruitful sign, is peregrine, disposed of by Saturn and does not make an aspect with the ascendant. Venus is in her domicile of Taurus and applies to a trine with Mars.

Whatever hopes there may be from Venus, Mars and Jupiter, the south node is in conjunction with the fifth house cusp. This is most unfortunate in Questions concerning pregnancy. In addition, Saturn is retrograde in the fifth house and afflicts the fifth house by his presence. Saturn does not aspect the ascendant and is incorrectly placed beneath the horizon in a diurnal chart. Saturn becomes more malefic due to his rulership of the eighth house. There is unlikely to be a full-term pregnancy.

Outcome
A pregnancy followed and then a miscarriage. She had no children.

Will my sister be pregnant within the next two years?
30 May 1986 12.35 BST. 51N30 00W00

The Querent, who had recently had a baby, wanted to know if her sister would have a baby too.

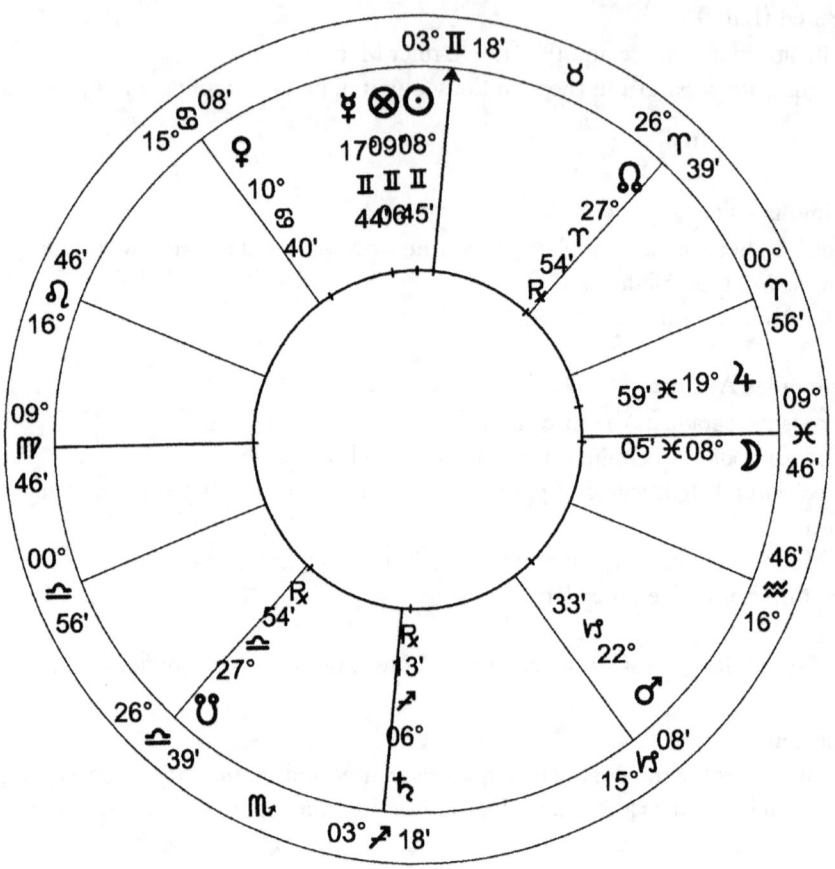

Signification

Querent
Significator: Ascendant, ascendant ruler Mercury.

Sister
Significator: Third house and third house ruler Venus.
Co-significator: Moon

Quesited (Baby)
Significator: Fifth house and fifth house ruler Saturn.
Co-significator: Jupiter, natural significator of pregnancy, and Mars in the fifth house.

The chart is diurnal.

Testimonies For
Venus is in a fruitful sign in the eleventh house and makes a trine with Jupiter.
Jupiter is angular and in his domicile. Jupiter and Venus have a strong mutual reception.
The Moon is in a fruitful sign, angular and makes a trine with Venus. They have a strong mutual reception.
The Moon applies to a conjunction with Jupiter.

Testimonies Against
The ascendant ruler Mercury is under sunbeams.
The south node afflicts the third house of the sister.
Venus is afflicted by her opposition with Mars (but they have a mutual reception and Jupiter interposes with his favourable aspect).

The strong mutual receptions between the Fortunes, together with their fortunate position, are clear and definite testimonies of pregnancy. It is rare to find the Fortunes as strong and well-dignified.

Judgement
This is a very fortunate and fruitful chart. The Querent's sister is capable of having children, as shown by her significator Venus in Cancer in mutual reception with both Jupiter and the Moon. Jupiter is dignified in his domicile and not afflicted by an Infortune. Jupiter and the Moon make a sextile with the fifth house cusp and the Moon applies to a conjunction with Jupiter, both in the prolific sign of Pisces. Although the Sun and Mercury apply to a square with Jupiter, Mercury is dignified in his domicile and the Sun is received by Jupiter being in his term and face.

Mars is not unfortunate in the fifth house, because he is essentially dignified in his exaltation and in good aspect with Jupiter. The fifth house ruler Saturn is unfortunate being retrograde, peregrine and in opposition with the Sun, but does not afflict the fifth house, nor can he undo the good fortune indicated elsewhere.* The south node in conjunction with the third house cusp suggests some misfortune for the Querent's sister. However, with the Fortunes so strong, a pregnancy is guaranteed. I judged pregnancy to be between nine and twelve months, based on the Moon's application to a conjunction with Jupiter in just under twelve degrees and Venus applying to a trine with Jupiter in just over nine degrees.

Outcome

The Querent's sister was pregnant in just under twelve months, but suffered some bleeding six weeks into the pregnancy. There were some anxious moments, but she gave birth to a healthy son in March 1988.

---

*   This is another clear example of a planet in a house being more important than an absent ruler. Mars exalted in the fifth house is more powerful in the Question than the fifth house ruler Saturn absent from the fifth house.

Will the pregnancy go well?
15 April 1990 5.08 BST. 51N30 00W00

The person enquired about was in her forties. This was her first pregnancy and as a colleague at the time, I was concerned. This is a third party Question but the chart is radical and describes the situation perfectly. The signification confirms that the chart should not be turned and that pregnancy is always a fifth house matter.

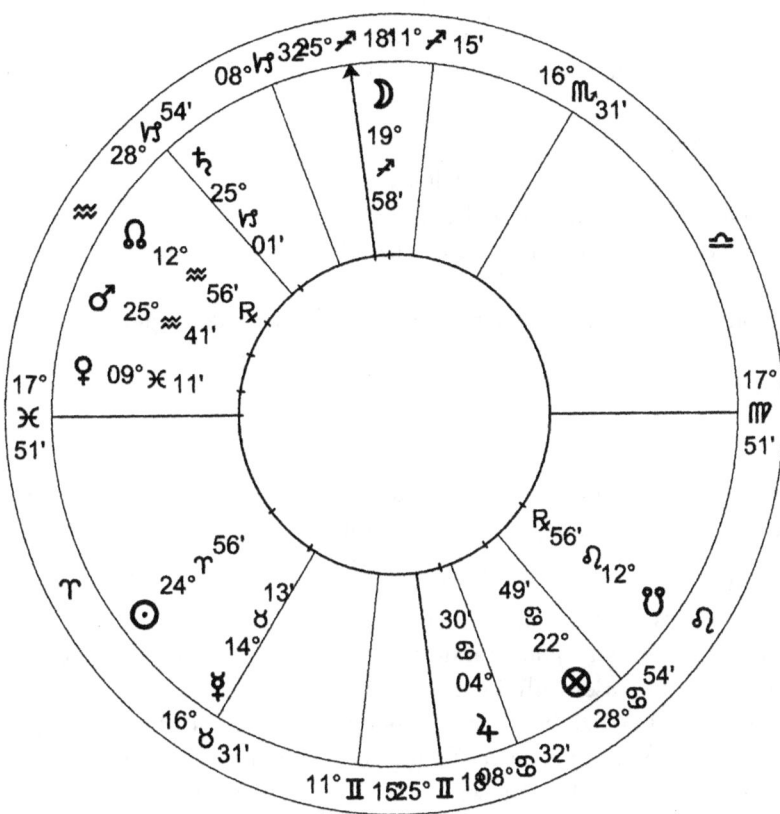

Signification

The Question
Significator: Ascendant, ascendant ruler Jupiter.
Co-significators: The Moon. Venus who is applying to a conjunction with the ascendant.

Quesited (Baby)
Significator: Fifth house, fifth house ruler the Moon, and Jupiter in the fifth house.

The chart is nocturnal. Fortunes are significators.
Jupiter, ruler of the hour, harmonises with the ascendant.

Testimonies For
Jupiter is in the fifth house in his exaltation.
Venus is close to the ascendant in her exaltation.
Venus is received by Jupiter in his domicile, Jupiter is received by Venus in her face.
The Lot of Fortune is in the fifth house.
The Moon and Jupiter have a mutual reception between domicile.

Testimonies Against
None

This is probably one of the most fortunate charts I have judged and there is no doubt whatsoever that a pregnancy will be successful.

Judgement
Horaries like this are rare. This is a very fruitful chart, with every planet being in at least one of its essential dignities and/or in a strong mutual reception. The ruler of the hour, Jupiter, harmonises with the ascendant.

Venus, Jupiter and the Sun are in their exaltation. The Moon and Jupiter have a mutual reception between domicile. Saturn is in his domicile and has a mutual reception between exaltation and domicile with Mars. The Moon applies to a trine with the Sun in the first house in his exaltation. Jupiter is in conjunction with the fifth house cusp having a great deal of power in this position. The Moon, Venus and Mars are nocturnal planets, placed correctly above the horizon in a nocturnal chart. Venus and Mars are in their hayyiz. The Sun is afflicted by Saturn but they both have dignity where they are.

The Moon, Venus and ascendant are placed in common signs and together with the good fortune signified by Venus and Jupiter, provide strong testimony of more than one baby. It is interesting to note that Venus, as in the first chart example above, is several degrees away from the angle, but she still has great power in the Question. I would count Venus as angular in this chart.

Outcome
She had a full term pregnancy and twin boys with no problems.

Is she pregnant?
18 May 1986 17.40 BST. 51N30 00W00

The Querent asks about her sister in-law. In line with the discussion in chapter twelve, it is interesting to note that the action taken by the person enquired about is implicit in this chart, although that person knew nothing about the Question. The chart also demonstrates that pregnancy is always a fifth house matter. The chart is not turned.

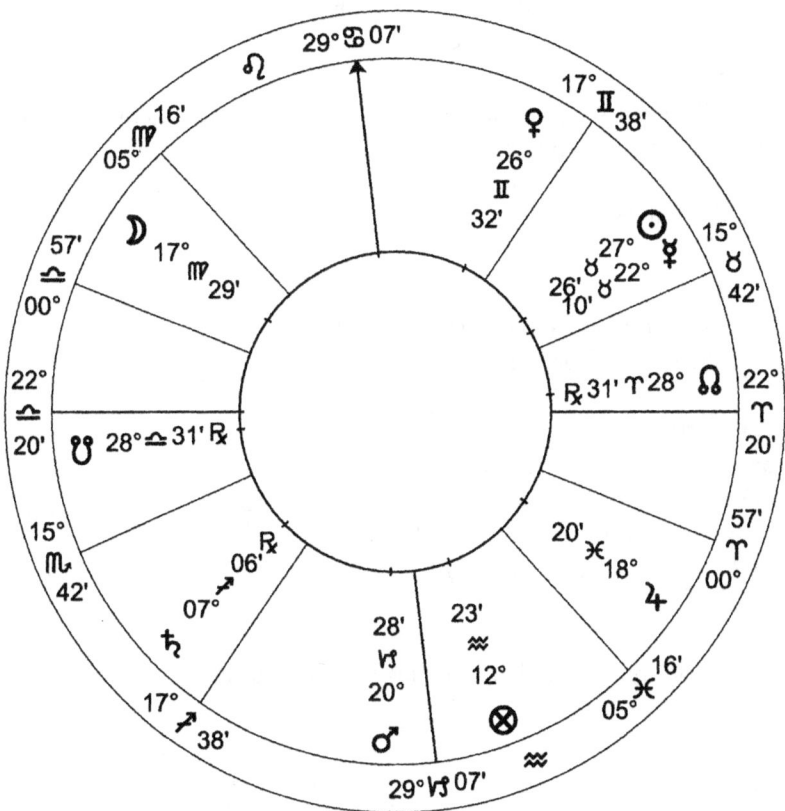

Signification

Querent
Significator: Ascendant, ascendant ruler Venus.
Co-significator: The Moon and the south node.

Quesited (Baby)
Significator: Fifth house and fifth house ruler, Jupiter.

Sister-in-Law
Significator: Ninth house (third house from the seventh house, as in husband's sister) and ninth house ruler Mercury; partly Venus in the ninth house.

The chart is diurnal. Fortunes are significators.

Testimonies For
Jupiter rules the fifth house and is positioned in the fifth house.
Jupiter is dignified in his domicile.

Testimonies Against
The Moon is in opposition with Jupiter.
The south node is in the ascendant.
The dispositor of the Moon is Mercury who is combust.
The Sun and Mercury are in the eighth house and in conjunction with the malefic fixed star Caput Algol.

Testimonies show a pregnancy, but other testimonies indicate that it is unsustainable.

Judgement
The Querent's significator Venus is in the house of her sister-in-law and, consequently, shows her concern. Both Venus and the Moon have a mutual reception with Mercury, confirmation of their friendship. Jupiter in the fifth house, in his domicile of Pisces, clearly indicates a pregnancy. However, the Moon's opposition with Jupiter is unfortunate and Saturn makes a square with the fifth house cusp.

Mercury is combust and in conjunction with the malefic fixed star Caput Algol in the eighth house. The south node in conjunction with the ascendant is further unfortunate testimony. Jupiter receives no support from any planet. The pregnancy is under threat.

Outcome
The sister-in-law was pregnant but had a termination. The Querent tried to convince her to keep the baby, but failed.

Will his wife have a baby?
27 June 1986 14.55 BST. 51N30 00W00

The couple had been trying for a baby for many years. The Question was asked by a friend. The chart describes the situation perfectly and the ruler of the hour harmonises with the ascendant. This chart is yet another example confirming that pregnancy is a fifth house matter.

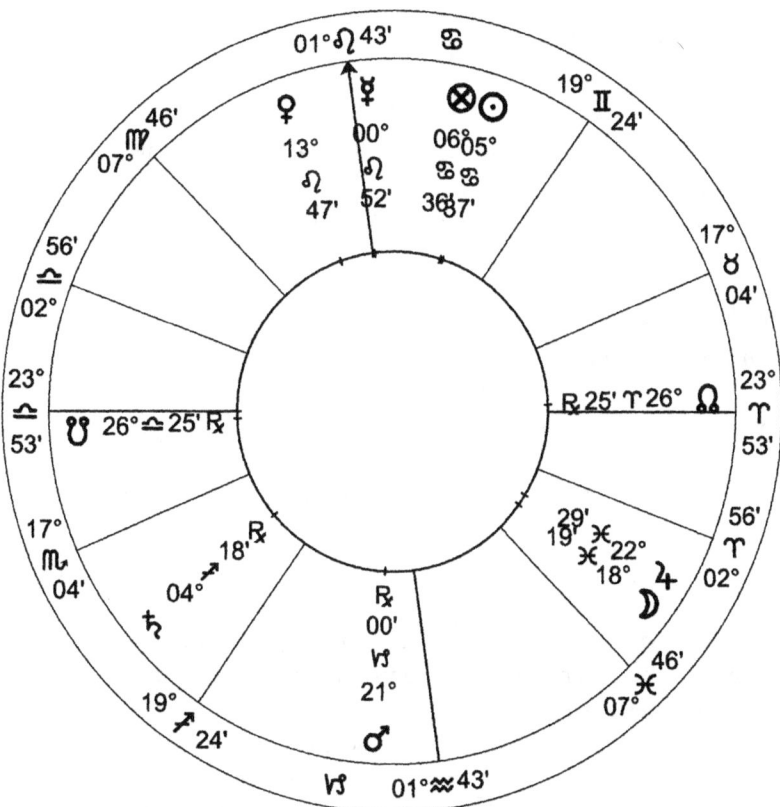

Signification

The Question
Significator: Ascendant, ascendant ruler Venus.
Co-significator: The Moon and the south node.

Quesited (Baby)
Significator: Fifth house and fifth house ruler, Jupiter.

The chart is diurnal. Fortunes are significators.

Testimonies For
The Moon is in the fifth house applying to a conjunction with Jupiter in the fifth house.
The Moon and Jupiter are in the prolific sign of Pisces.
Jupiter is in his domicile of Pisces.

Testimonies Against
Venus is in Leo, an infertile sign.
The south node is in the ascendant.
Saturn makes a square with the fifth house cusp.

Testimonies are mixed, but the testimonies for a pregnancy are stronger than those against.

Judgement
Libra is the sign ascending which is not fruitful, the south node in the ascendant is unfortunate and the ascendant ruler Venus is placed in a barren sign. These are unfortunate chart testimonies. However, the Moon in the fifth house applying to a conjunction with Jupiter in his domicile of Pisces is very positive testimony. Jupiter is incorrectly placed beneath the horizon in a diurnal chart and is not aspecting the ascendant, but is strong nevertheless. The Moon first applies to a sextile with Mars, received by him in his triplicity. However, given the testimony of the Moon and Jupiter, I would expect a pregnancy perhaps within about four months because the Moon applies to a conjunction with Jupiter in four degrees. However, other more unfortunate testimony throws doubt on the timing and the ease with which she might get pregnant.

Outcome
She conceived four years later and had a baby boy.

References

1. Lilly p.240.
2. ibid p.234.
3. ibid references to Lilly in this section are from pp.222-223.
4. ibid p.223.
5. ibid p..226-228.
6. ibid p.225.
7. Gadbury p.265.
8. ibid p.265.
9. Lilly p.225.
10. ibid p.224.
11. ibid p.226.
12. ibid pp..224-226.
13. ibid p.230.
14. ibid pp..240-241.
15. ibid p.230.

19

Sixth House Matters
Health and Sickness

Lilly tells us that the sixth house has signification over "Sicknesse, Servants, small Cattle".[1] The sixth house also has signification over employees and perhaps colleagues or work-mates, although this should be confirmed by supporting testimony. Small animals such as cats and dogs are also signified by the sixth house. However, the focus of this chapter is sickness. For further reading I refer the reader to Culpeper's *Astrologicall Judgment of Diseases*.

Testimonies Relating to the Sixth House
Lilly, together with many other authorities, reports that the potent moment for drawing up a chart relating to sickness is when the patient is forced to lie down or go to bed. A chart drawn up at this moment is known as a *decumbiture*. If that moment is unknown, it is the time when the sick person's urine is carried to somebody, usually a doctor, so as to "enquire about the Disease". If neither is available, it is the time when the doctor first speaks to the patient, or when the urine is brought to him. At this time a decumbiture is drawn up and the following observed in order to discover the whereabouts of the disease in the body

> First, the ascendant, what Planet or Planets are therein placed. Secondly, the sixth house, and what Planet or Planets are therein posited. Thirdly, the Signe and house wherein the Moon is. Fourthly, how she is affected or afflicted, by what Planet, in what house that Planet is, what house of the Figure that Planet is Lord of.[2]

In a decumbiture or a Question about health and sickness, it is the ascendant and the sixth house which are the main areas of focus. Even if the Question relates to another person's sickness, the ascendant and the sixth house are places of principal signification. For example, if the Question is about a sister's illness, the sixth house from the third house (the eighth house) may be important, but the sixth house of the original chart takes precedence. In an overall sense, it is usually the ascendant which has signification over the sick person. If the Fortunes are stronger than the Infortunes, the sick person will recover from the illness.

The timing of events in Questions relating to sickness is a little different to other Questions. For example, in the majority of charts, if significators are angular, this speeds up the timing of an event. As a general guide, the matter enquired about may take place within weeks if significators are in angular houses; months if they are in succedent houses or years if in cadent houses. However, in judgements relating to sickness, the angles do not accelerate death or the spread of a disease but "shew that life and nature are strong, and a possibility of overcoming the malignity of the humour afflicting".[3] In other words if signifcators of the sick person are angular it can be fortunate for that person.

As ever, it is the Nativity which takes precedence over the Question. Bonatti tells us that it is important to have details of the Nativity, if these are available.

> When you find the Figure at the beginning of a grievous distemper to appear much more mild and favourable than the distemper, you may conclude the disease contracts its malignity from the Nativity, the principal places fall upon some disastrous configurations.[4]

Culpeper confirms that next to the Nativity, "the Decumbiture is the safest and surest ground for you to build your judgement upon..." [5]

The Influence of the Moon

The role of the Moon is of fundamental importance in charts relating to sickness.

> A chronical disease (that is a disease which usually continues above a month) is ruled by the motion of the Sun; acute diseases (which are more sharp and violent but less lasting) by the motion of the Moon, according to whose swifter or slower motion the critical times are either hastened or retarded...[6]

One must also look to the Sun and Moon in a Nativity, because if the luminaries fall in a place where there is currently an Eclipse (at the time of the sickness) or close to an important conjunction, this is unfortunate.

If the Moon is essentially dignified and in a fortunate house, not afflicted by the Infortunes, it is positive testimony for the sick person and offers great assistance in terms of a positive outcome.

Signification and Parts of the Body

Lilly tells us that if the first house is afflicted by the presence of an Infortune or unfortunate planet and this planet is retrograde, combust, peregrine, slow in motion, or in square or opposition with any planet which rules the fourth, sixth, eighth or twelfth house, the disease is in the head. Alternatively the disease is in those parts of the body signified by the planet or planets in the sign ascending.[7] I refer the reader to Lilly's table reproduced in chapter three.

As an example, if Cancer is ascending and Saturn is in Cancer, the person has a sickness connected to the head, because the first house signifies the head. However, that person may also have stomach problems and/or a bad cough because Saturn in

Cancer also rules those parts of the body. This is even more certain if the ascendant ruler, the Moon, the sign in the sixth house cusp, or the sixth house ruler is also in a sign which signifies the same part of the body as Saturn.

These rules can be applied to the sixth house, that is, the sign in the sixth house cusp and any planets placed in the sixth house. These can be related to the parts of the body. It is also important to observe from which planet the sixth house ruler has separated and to which planet he applies, as well as the sign and position of the Moon, together with her separating and applying aspects.

Generally speaking, significators in fire signs show fevers, in earth signs, long and tedious illnesses or depression, in air signs show blood diseases and gout, in water signs coughs and stomach problems. A brief summary follows showing the diseases signified by house, sign and planet.[8]

Diseases Signified by the Houses

First House	Head, eyes, face, ears, bad breath, sore mouth
Second House	Throat, neck
Third House	Shoulders, arms, hands
Fourth House	Stomach, breast, lungs
Fifth House	Back, back of shoulders, stomach, liver, heart, sides
Sixth House	Lower belly, guts, liver
Seventh House	Small intestine, bladder, genitals
Eighth House	Back bone, backside, groin
Ninth House	Hips
Tenth House	Knees, hamstring
Eleventh House	The leg from knee to ankle, shinbone
Twelfth House	The feet and all diseases connected to them

Diseases Signified by the Signs

Aries	All diseases connected to the head (as signified by the first house) pocks, pimples.
Taurus	Diseases of the neck and throat, sometimes due to depression.
Gemini	Shoulders, arms, hands, often due to problems in the blood.
Cancer	Breast cancer, problems with the breast, poor digestion, spleen, lungs, upper belly, arising from cold and moisture.
Leo	Back bone, sides, ribs, heart, lower part of breast and infirmities arising from "Choller and excesse of Blood".
Virgo	Depression, disease in the guts, stomach aches, wind, cholic.
Libra	Back problems, kidney stones, problems from eating or drinking too much, or from sex, diseases in the buttocks and joints.
Scorpio	Groin, genitals, backside, piles, the arse, bladder, stones in the bladder.

Sagittarius	Hips, buttocks, itches, sciatica.
Capricorn	Knees, hamstring, scurfs and itches in and around the knees, depressive illnesses.
Aquarius	Legs, shin bones, calves of the legs, ankles.
Pisces	Ankle bone and feet, gout, swelling in ankles.

Diseases Signified by the Planets

Saturn	Rumbling in the right ear and head, deafness, tooth-ache, arthritis and rheumatism, problems with bladder, depression, coughs, pneumonia.
Jupiter	Lungs, ribs, liver, arteries, convulsions, inflammation of the liver, heart problems, diseases in the head, veins, diseases of the blood.
Mars	Left ear, genitals, stones, wounds in the face, burning fevers, epilepsy, jaundice.
Sun	Brain, heart, eye sight, right eye of man, left eye of a woman, cramps, heart murmurs.
Venus	Genitals, throat, liver, sperm in man, ovaries in a woman, gonorrhoea, weakness of stomach and liver, problems with having children, vomiting, heart burn.
Mercury	Brain, mind, spirits, imagination, speech, tongue, fingers, hands, madness, lethargy, stammering, hoarseness, coughs.
Moon	Left eye of man, right eye of woman, brain, intestines, small guts, the bladder, menstruation.

The Length of the Illness

Lilly tells us that if the sign in the sixth house is fixed, it indicates an illness which is long lasting and won't go away without a lot of time and difficulty. If the sign is moveable, it signifies an illness which is short. If the sign is common, the illness is neither short nor long, but there can be a change in the disease and a return of it once again. If the last degrees of any sign are in the cusp of the sixth house, the disease is almost at an end, or is altering for better of worse. However, fixed signs indicate that the illness won't go away easily and it may take a lot of time.[9]

When the sixth house ruler is unfortunate and is placed in the sixth house, it's an indication of a long-lasting and nasty sickness, but if a Fortune is in the sixth house, the illness will soon be cured. When the sixth house ruler is stronger than the ascendant ruler, the illness is likely to increase and the sick person needs medication, because nature is weaker than the illness. If the sixth house ruler is weaker than the ascendant ruler, nature will be able to overcome the malignity of the illness, without much assistance from a doctor. When Saturn is the sixth house ruler and is in a fixed sign, or is slow in motion or retrograde, the illness is prolonged. However, if Saturn is placed in a moveable sign and is in his terms or swift in motion, he not as unfortunate, nor will the illness be prolonged. The common signs prolong the illness more than moveable signs, except for Pisces which is more equivalent to a moveable sign.

There are many factors relating to the judgement of illness and, together with Culpeper's work as mentioned above, I refer the reader to *Christian Astrology*, the "Astrologicall Aphorismes beneficiall for Physicians".[10]

Most Important Testimonies

The most important chart testimonies relating to an illness are summarised below:[11]

- Saturn, Mars, or any unfortunate planet in the sixth house is dangerous, but if well aspected or essentially dignified, the illness happened suddenly and has not arisen from any serious problem.
- If there is a benevolent planet, well aspected and in some of its essential dignities in the sixth house and is not significator of the illness, the illness is only temporary.
- If the sixth house ruler is in the ascendant, the illness will continue, but if in a cadent house, the illness is not serious and won't last.
- Fortunate planets in the sixth house promise a good end to the illness, but unfortunate planets indicate the contrary.
- If the ascendant ruler and the Moon do not make a square or opposition with Saturn or Mars or any unfortunate planet and are direct, not combust, swift in motion, not peregrine, not in their fall or detriment, nor in the eighth or sixth house (nor in any aspect with the rulers of the twelfth, sixth or eighth houses) it's a good indication of health and recovery.
- If the ascendant ruler is in an angle, not badly aspected and in a good house, not under sunbeams, nor retrograde, the Querent is in no danger.
- If the ascendant ruler is applied to by a malevolent planet, it delays the cure and prolongs the illness.
- If the Fortunes are stronger than the Infortunes, there should be recovery. If Mars is the ascendant ruler and in the sixth house, but makes a trine or sextile with Venus, there's no danger; in fact the same applies to a square or opposition with Venus.
- There's usually no danger if, at the time of the Question, the Moon is strong and the ascendant ruler is not badly aspected and in no aspect with the ruler of the sixth house.

Testimonies that a Person will Recover from an Illness[12]

- If the Moon is separating from a malevolent, weak planet who is ill dignified and is applying to a Fortune powerfully strong.

- If there is any reception between the ascendant ruler and the eighth house ruler and "neither of them infortunated by the malignant Planets, after desperation, there will be recovery."
- If the ascendant ruler has a reception with the eighth house ruler between domicile or triplicity and the Fortunes are helping with either a trine or sextile aspect with the degree ascending, to the sixth house, or to the Moon.
- If the ascendant ruler is a benevolent planet and placed in the first, tenth, eleventh, fifth or third house, not in a bad aspect with an Infortune. Lilly says that this "prenotes sanity". Another fortunate indication is when the Fortunes are in the midheaven or first house.
- If the Sun, Jupiter, Venus or the Moon are in the ascendant of the Question, not badly aspected by the rulers of eighth or sixth houses. This is more certain if the significators are in good signs, for example, Jupiter in Pisces or Sagittarius, or Jupiter in Cancer or Leo (in a nocturnal chart).
- If the Moon is in Cancer, or in the domicile of Jupiter or Venus and makes an aspect with either of them and makes no bad aspect with Saturn and Mars.
- If the Moon makes a conjunction with Jupiter (whatever sign Jupiter is in), although any good fortune produced is less in Capricorn than other signs.
- If the Moon is applying to the ascendant ruler with a trine or sextile, "clear of all misfortune" and not afflicted by the rulers of the eighth or sixth houses.
- If the Moon is well aspected in a succedent house, providing she is increasing in light and motion and not in conjunction with Saturn or Mars, nor "infected with their Rayes".
- If the Moon is in the first, ninth, tenth, eleventh, second, third or fifth house in a trine or sextile with the ascendant ruler or with his antiscium, even if this is an Infortune, as long as the Moon and the ascendant ruler have no other affliction.
- If benevolent planets are more potent than malevolent, they give "assured hopes of life..."

A person is not ill if [13]
- No unfortunate planet is in the sixth house.
- The ascendant is not afflicted.
- The ascendant ruler is not afflicted, nor out of his essential dignities, nor in any bad aspect with Mars, Saturn or the sixth house ruler.
- The Moon is not afflicted in the eighth or twelfth house.
- Jupiter, Venus or north node are in the ascendant.

- The Sun is in the sixth house.
- The Moon and the ascendant ruler are in any good aspect with each other.
- Jupiter or Venus are in trine or sextile aspect with the cusp of the ascendant or sixth house.

If the above testimonies are in place, it is unlikely that the person is sick at that time and that no sickness is likely to develop after the Question.

Saturn naturally shows, or causes, depression and a disturbed mind. A person is not well mentally if [14]

- Saturn is the ascendant ruler, the ruler of the hour, or the ruler of the twelfth or sixth house.
- The Moon separates from Saturn.
- Saturn is in the sixth house, in the ascendant, or in conjunction, square or opposition with the ascendant ruler.

The opposite effect comes from Jupiter: Jupiter never causes illnesses in the mind, but illnesses in the body. In a similar way to Saturn, Mercury represents fearful imagination, so wherever you find Mercury as significator and afflicted, the person is mistrustful, fearful and probably worried over nothing.

If, in a Question, the ascendant ruler is moving out of one sign into another and has essential dignities in the sign he is moving into, the person recovers or at least feels an improvement. Bonatti confirms that if the ruler of the seventh house and the seventh house itself are "free from impediments" the sick person can safely trust himself to the care of a doctor, because in this instance the "medicines will do very well". But if there are afflictions to these places, "Ptolemy saith 'The Physician must be changed, for neither his physic nor care will do any good' ".[15]

One of the most important considerations in these Questions is the aspect between Jupiter and the Sun. If Jupiter is in good aspect with the Sun, the person who is ill will not die from the illness. According to Lilly this holds good, even if the ascendant ruler applies to the eighth house ruler.[16]

Of major importance in judgement are mutual receptions, which can make the difference between recovery and no recovery or between a quick recovery and a slow recovery.

> If the Moon be swift in course, and encreasing in light, and by a sextile or trine apply to the Lord of the ascendant, though under the earth, it hastens the cure, the more easily if any Reception be...[17]

In an overall sense, in any Question relating to sickness, the following should always be observed:

> In sickness, the Ascendant [and its ruler] shall signify the Patient, the seventh house the disease,* the Luminaries the Patient's strength, the Infortunes the strength of the disease, but the eighth house has always a share in the signification.[18]

Lilly tells us

> The Sun in the ascendant brings usually health immediately ... the Sun is the candle or light of Heaven, and that Spirit which clarifies and beautifies those Signes he is in, destroying natures enemies.[19]

In a diurnal chart, the Lot or Part of Sickness is calculated using the degrees of the ascendant plus those of Mars, minus those of Saturn. In a nocturnal chart, Mars and Saturn are reversed. This is in line with Abu Ma'shar's calculation of the Lots in *The Abbreviation of the Introduction to Astrology*.[20]

It is worth noting that in the Middle Ages, astrological considerations played a central role in medical practice. Robert Zoller tells us that the two arts of medicine and astrology were closely interwoven: many of the best astrologers were physicians, and many of the best physicians were astrologers.[21]

---

* It is unclear why Bonatti should assign the seventh house to the illness. The seventh house is usually significator of the doctor. Or is this a mis-translation?

From the Horary Files

Will my mother survive this illness? Should I go to America to see her?
14 March 1993 12.30 GMT. 51N30 00W10

The Querent's mother was critically ill in intensive care in an American hospital. The nature of the illness was not discussed by the Querent.

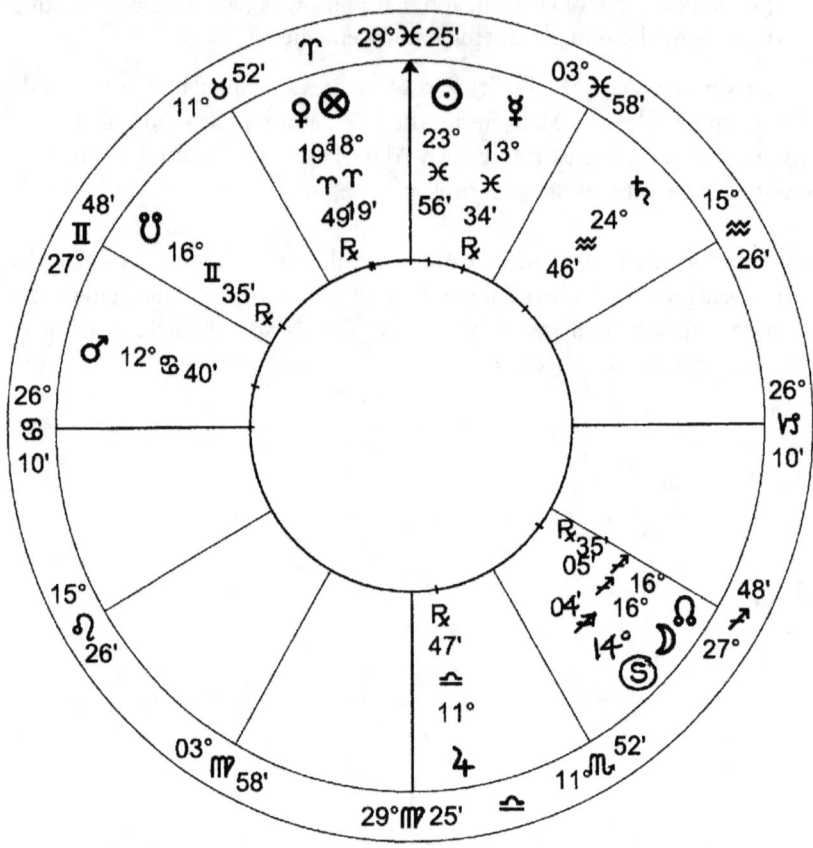

Signification

Querent
Significator: Ascendant and ascendant ruler the Moon.

Querent's Mother
Significators: Venus in the tenth house (Venus is also natural significator of mothers by day), Mars ruler of Aries intercepted in the tenth house, the Moon, the Sun in the tenth house, the Lot of Fortune.
Co-significator: Tenth house and tenth house ruler Jupiter.
The luminaries are natural significators of a patient's strength.

Illness
Significator: Sixth house and sixth house ruler Jupiter.

The chart is diurnal. Fortunes are significators.
The ruler of the hour harmonises with the ascendant.

Testimonies For
Venus and the Lot of Fortune make a conjunction with each other in the tenth house
Venus has a mutual reception with the Sun
The Sun makes a conjunction with the tenth house cusp
The Moon is applying to a trine with Venus.

Testimonies Against
Jupiter, tenth house ruler, is retrograde
Venus is retrograde
The Moon makes a conjunction with the Lot of Sickness

With such strong and concurring testimonies, the mother's recovery is certain.

Judgement
The Fortunes are stronger than the Infortunes. Venus in the tenth house and having a strong mutual reception with the Sun indicates a recovery. The Moon in Sagittarius applies to a trine with Venus, powerfully strong, and the Sun is applying to a conjunction with the tenth house cusp. Although Venus is retrograding towards a square with Mars, she is received by Mars. In addition, Mars is part ruler of the tenth house and, as the ruler of the hour, also harmonises with the ascendant. Jupiter is not considered to be principal significator of the mother, because of the very late degrees of his domicile, Pisces, in the tenth house cusp.

Venus turns direct six weeks after the Question and the Sun moves into his exaltation in six degrees, which suggests that in six weeks there may be a change for the better. Late degrees in the sixth house cusp indicate that the disease is almost at an end. Jupiter as sixth house ruler is retrograde, but is a Fortune and is in his terms. He is disposed of by Venus stronger and elevated. Whether the significator of the sickness is considered to be Jupiter ruler of the sixth house, the Moon moving towards the sixth house, or Mercury, ruler of the mother's sixth house, the significators of the mother are stronger than any of these.

Outcome
Nine days later the Querent called to say her mother had taken a turn for the better. She was discharged six and a half weeks later.

Will he recover?
10 March 2006 15.19 GMT. 50N16 04W48

An elderly neighbour of the Querent was in hospital, having undergone heart surgery. It seemed that he might not recover. The Querent was very friendly with his wife and was worried.

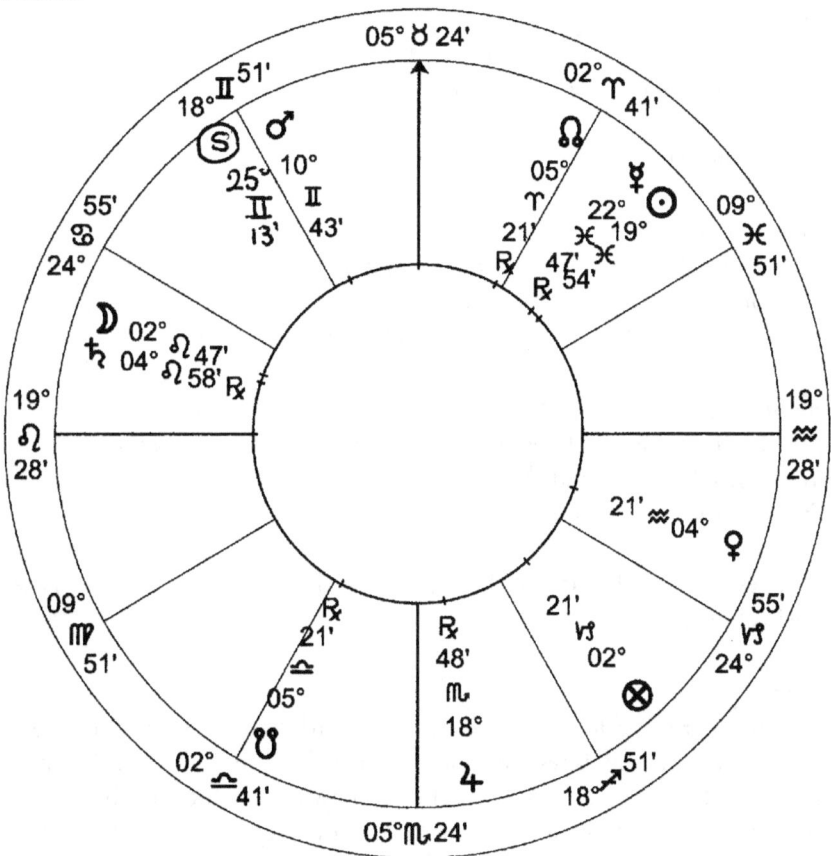

Signification
Elderly Man
Significator: The Sun, ascendant ruler and the Moon.
Co-significator: Saturn

Illness
Significator: Sixth house and sixth house ruler Saturn.
Co-significator: Venus in the sixth house

The chart is diurnal.

Testimonies For
Ascendant ruler the Sun makes a trine with Jupiter.
Venus, a Fortune, is in the sixth house
Saturn is free from combustion and not badly aspected.

Testimonies Against
The Moon is in the twelfth house moving to a conjunction with Saturn.
Saturn is in his detriment and retrograde
The Sun is in the eighth house

With the testimonies of illness so strong, I feared the worst, but hoped that the Sun's aspect with Jupiter might save him.

Judgement
Saturn in his detriment and retrograde in the twelfth house describes an elderly man sick in hospital and establishes radicality in the chart. Leo is also the sign associated with the heart. The situation looks very serious. The Moon is afflicted by her conjunction with Saturn in the twelfth house. There is little assistance from Venus, she being cadent and only dignified by face. However, she is a Fortune and is positioned in the sixth house, being received by Saturn in his domicile, triplicity and term.

The Sun is the dispositor of the Moon and Saturn. The Sun's trine with Jupiter, although separating, is hopeful because the Sun is received by Jupiter, is unafflicted and correctly placed above the horizon. Unfortunately, the Sun does not aspect the ascendant. However, Saturn has dignity by term and face and makes no bad aspect with any planet. The testimonies for recovery are not very strong but I was hopeful.

Outcome
It was touch and go for many weeks, but against the odds he recovered slowly.

What is wrong with X? Will she be OK?
21 January 2007 21.27 GMT. 50N16 04W48

A friend of the Querent had been bleeding a lot more than usual each month and was not feeling at all well. She was going into hospital for an investigation.

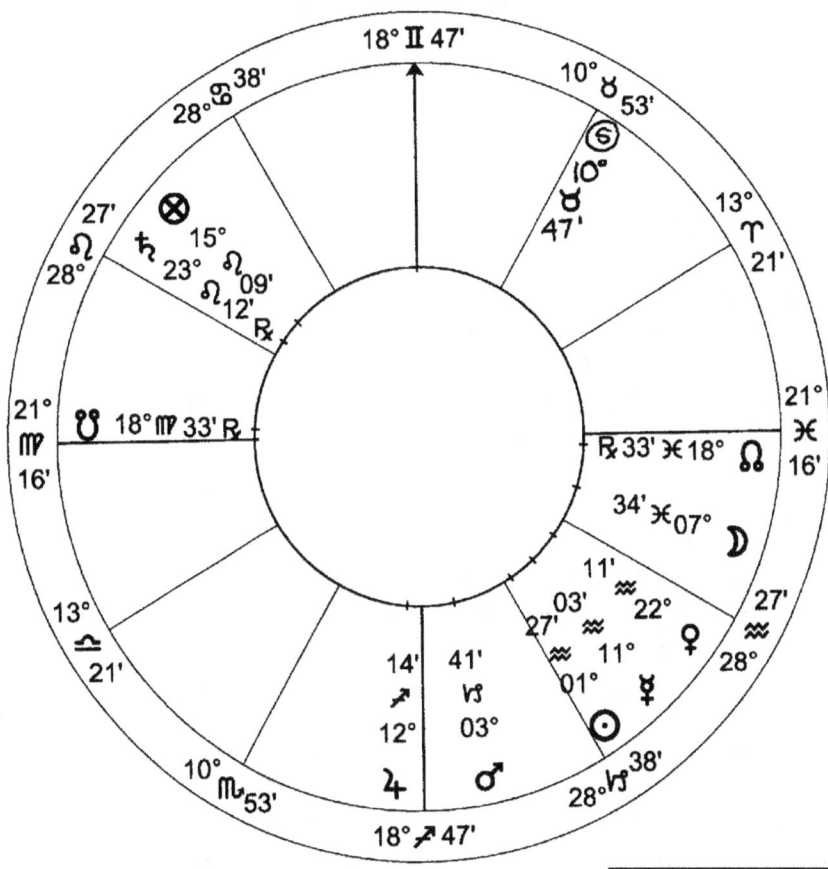

Signification

The Question
Significator: Ascendant and ascendant ruler Mercury.
Co-significator: Eleventh house (the friend) and eleventh house ruler the Moon. Lot of Fortune, and Saturn retrograding back into the eleventh house.

Sickness
Significator: Sixth house and sixth house ruler Saturn. Venus in conjunction with the sixth house cusp.

The chart is nocturnal.

Testimonies For
Jupiter is angular and in his own domicile and triplicity.
The Sun makes a sextile with Jupiter.
The ascendant ruler Mercury is in his triplicity and makes a sextile with Jupiter.
The Moon makes a square with Jupiter and is received by him in his domicile.
Venus, a Fortune, is moving into the sixth house.

Testimonies Against
The south node is in conjunction with the ascendant.
Venus is afflicted by her opposition with Saturn.
All planets except Saturn are under the earth.

Testimonies of good fortune are stronger than those of misfortune and confirm that the sick person will recover.

Judgement
The Moon in the sixth house is confirmation of a sickness, but the Moon is not afflicted, makes an aspect with Jupiter and they have a mutual reception between domicile and face. She also has a mutual reception with Mars between triplicity.

Jupiter is strong in his domicile and angular. Venus as co-significator of the illness is associated with the reproductive organs and she is the dispositor by domicile of the Lot of Sickness.

I considered the ascendant as principal significator of the sick person (the friend) together with the ascendant ruler, Mercury. Mercury's recent position in combustion confirms the anxiety and fear of the sick person, but his separation from combustion is one testimony of recovery. Mercury is direct, in his triplicity in the fifth house and makes a sextile with a Fortune, Jupiter. The Sun is applying to a sextile with Jupiter, an indication that this is not a serious health problem.

Venus moves towards the sixth house and in this position would usually be considered fortunate in terms of an illness, but she is afflicted by her opposition with Saturn. However, Saturn as significator of the illness, has a mutual reception with the Sun and is retrograding towards a trine with a Fortune, Jupiter. Saturn's retrograde motion reduces his power. The south node in conjunction with the ascendant is unfortunate. In an overall sense, the Fortunes are more powerful and show that the condition is treatable.

Outcome

She was diagnosed with a chronic inflammation of the uterus lining, which was treated and settled down.

What is wrong with X? Is she very ill? Will she be OK?
16 March 2007 6.52 GMT. 51N30 00W10

The Querent asked about her friend who had been taken to hospital seriously ill with a suspected brain tumour.

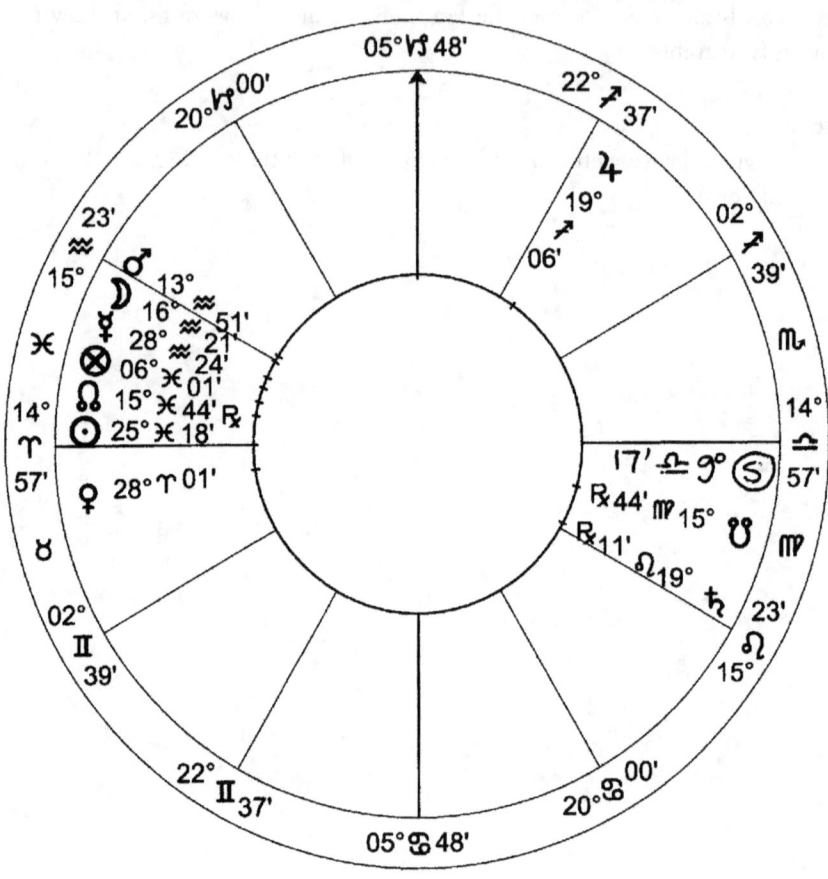

Signification

Sick Friend
Significator: Ascendant and ascendant ruler Mars.
Co-significator: The Moon, Venus, and Saturn, eleventh house ruler.

Illness
Significator: Sixth house and sixth house ruler the Sun.
Co-significators: Saturn, south node.

The chart is diurnal. Infortunes are significators.

Testimonies For
Venus is in the first house.
Venus has a strong mutual reception with the Sun.
Jupiter makes harmonious aspects with the Moon, Mars and Saturn.
Jupiter, although ruler of the eighth house, is correctly placed and aspects the ascendant with a trine.

Testimonies Against
Saturn is in his detriment in a fixed sign and in the sixth house.
The south node is in the sixth house.
The Moon and Mars are in the twelfth house and apply to an opposition with Saturn.
The Moon and Mars are in fixed signs.
The Sun is in the twelfth house.

With such strong testimonies against recovery the situation looks very serious. However, with assistance from the Fortunes the illness should not be life threatening.

Judgement
As a sick person in hospital, principal signification is taken from Mars, ascendant ruler, in the twelfth house, and the Moon. Aries ascending confirms that the illness is connected to the head. The Moon and Mars are both peregrine and incorrectly placed above the horizon in a diurnal chart. Their dispositor is Saturn, in his detriment, fixed, retrograde and in opposition with the Moon and Mars. This confirms that the illness is serious and long lasting.

However, an angular Venus in the ascendant of the Question and in mutual reception with the Sun is clear testimony of life for the sick person. Although Jupiter is the ruler of the eighth house, he makes a trine with the degree ascending and a sextile with the ascendant ruler Mars and the Moon. Jupiter has a mutual reception with the Sun and makes a partill trine with Saturn, and thereby helps to remove the malice of Saturn. The mutual reception between Venus and the Sun, together with the fortunate influence of Jupiter indicates that this illness is unlikely to be terminal, but is a less serious, treatable condition. In addition, the Moon and Mars aspect the ascendant with a sextile and Saturn aspects the ascendant with a trine. Good aspects with the ascendant signify planets who are not enemies, but are friends of the ascendant.

Outcome

She did not have a brain tumour, but a chronic inflammation behind her eyes. This is a serious, long-term and unpleasant illness, but is treatable.

Should Caleb have the eye operation? Will it be successful?
31 October 1992 9.28 GMT. 51N30 00W10

My mother's dog was fairly old and had been almost blind for sometime. An operation could help, but my mother was anxious as to whether Caleb would survive the operation under anaesthetic.

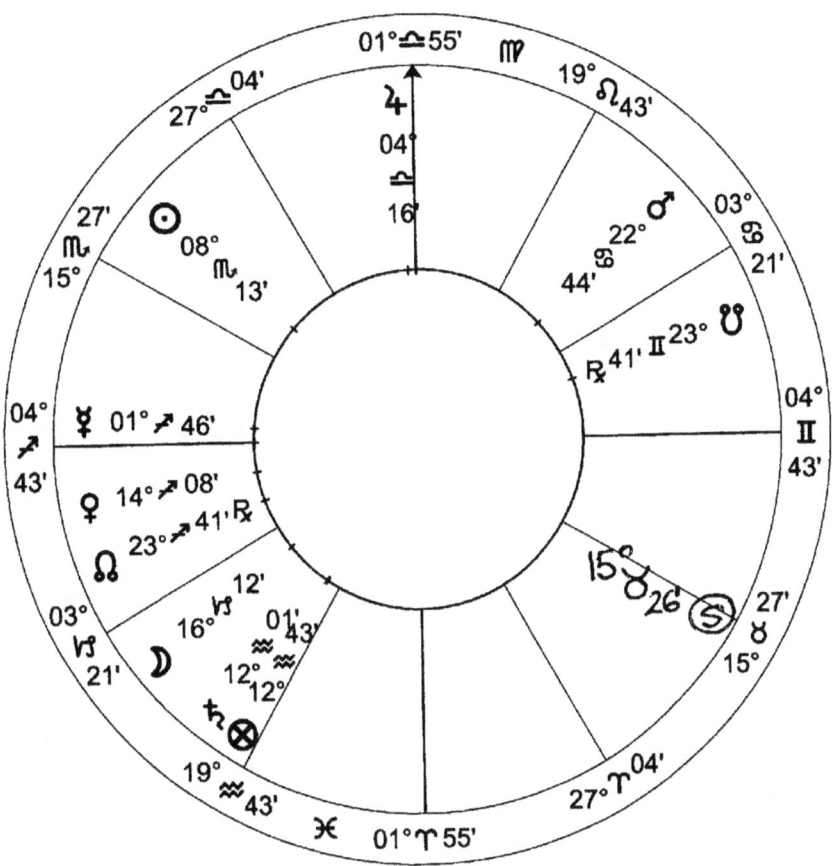

Signification
Caleb
Significator: Sixth house and sixth house ruler, Venus.
Co-significator: The Moon

His Illness
Significator: Partly Caleb's sixth house (eleventh) and the Sun in the eleventh house.

The chart is diurnal. The ruler of the hour harmonises with the ascendant. Fortunes are significators.

Testimonies For
Venus is in the first house.
Jupiter is in the tenth house.
Venus has a mutual reception with Jupiter.
The north node is in the first house.
Jupiter makes a very close sextile with the ascending degree.

Testimonies Against
The Moon and Mars are in their detriment and fall.
The Moon makes an opposition with Mars from the second house to the eighth house.
The Sun makes a square with Saturn.

Strong and fortunate testimonies of life confirm that Caleb will survive the operation. However, the testimonies for an improvement in his eyesight are poor.

Judgement
Due to the fact that Venus, principal significator of the dog, is angular in the first house and has a mutual reception with Jupiter, angular in the cusp of the tenth house, there is no doubt that Caleb will survive the operation. However, the Sun, always important in health questions, is afflicted by his square with Saturn. Just as importantly, the Moon in the second house opposes Mars in the eighth house. Any afflictions to the Moon can cause problems with the eyes. We also learnt in chapter two that Al Biruni gives signification over eyesight to the second house.

Although there is a strong mutual reception between the Moon and Mars, they are in their detriment and fall respectively. This does not bode well for the success of the operation. I am unsure as to why Mercury is in the ascendant and suggest that Mercury is the doctor performing the operation since he is the ruler of the seventh house. Being in his detriment, it appears as if Mercury cannot bring about the hoped for improvement in Caleb's eyesight.

Outcome
Caleb was fine after the operation but his eyesight was not much improved. The operation was mostly unsuccessful.

Will Beau the Wolf recover?
13 July 2006 19.55 PDT. 44N34 123W16

A student of mine from America, Zane Maser, sent this chart during work for her QHP (Qualifying Horary Practitioner). The wolf was being looked after in a sanctuary, because he was not well.

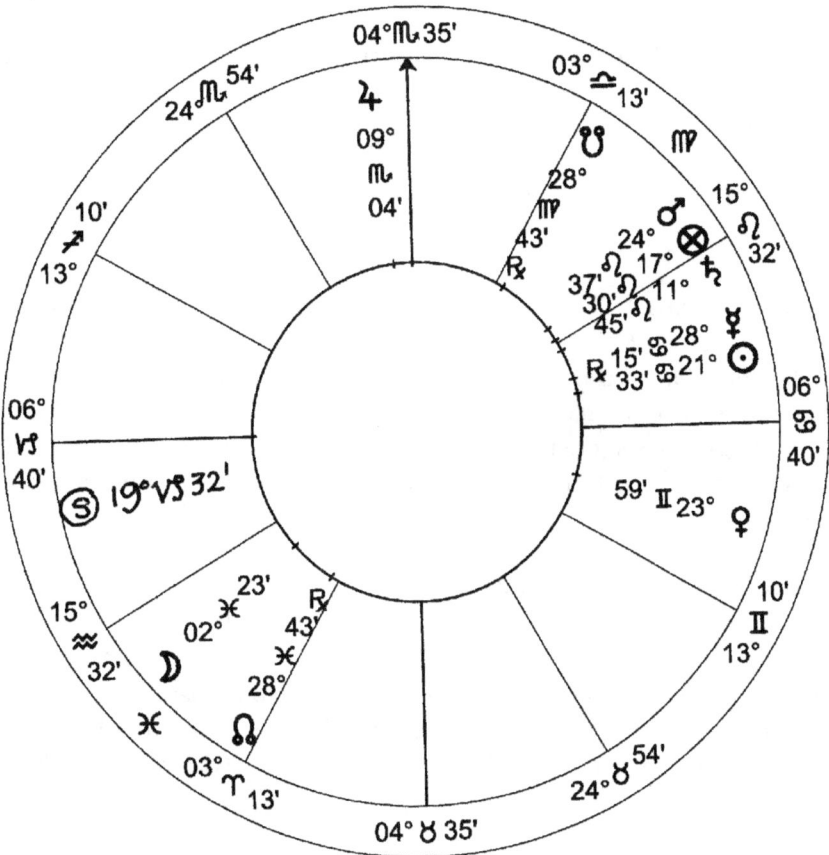

Signification
Beau the Wolf
Significator: Sixth house and sixth house ruler, Mercury.
Co-significator: The Moon.

Illness
Signifcator: His sixth house (eleventh house) and ruler of the eleventh house Mars.

The chart is diurnal.

Testimonies For
None

Testimonies Against
Mercury significator of the wolf is retrograde and combust.
Ascendant ruler Saturn is in his detriment in the eighth house.
There is no assistance from the Fortunes.
The Lot of Sickness is in the first house.
The dispositor of the Lot of Sickness is Saturn in conjunction with the cusp of the eighth house.

There is no hope of recovery in this chart.

Judgement
Mercury, principal significator of the wolf is in opposition with the ascendant, retrograde and moving towards the Sun and combustion. There is no real assistance from the Fortunes, although Venus is located in the sixth house. The Sun is ruler of the eighth house. There can be no recovery.

Outcome
Beau the wolf died a few days after the Question was asked.

References

1. Lilly p.243.
2. ibid p.243.
3. ibid pp.243-296.
4. Bonatus p.78 no.6 Aphorisms relating to Decumbitures.
5. Culpeper p.i.
6. Bonatus p.82 no 42.
7. Lilly pp.243-244.
8. ibid pp..245-247.
9. ibid p.248.
10. ibid pp.282-286 Aphorisms.
11. ibid pp.251-253.
12. ibid pp.253-255.
13. ibid p.259.
14. ibid p.264.
15. Bonatus p.24 68th consideration.
16. Lilly p.285 Aphorism 38.
17. ibid p.284 Aphorism 20.
18. Bonatus p.77 Aphorism 1.
19. Lilly p.285 Aphorisms no 36 and 37.
20. Abu Ma'shar, p.45.
21. Robert Zoller, *Tools & Techniques of the Medieval Astrologers*, p.33.

20

SEVENTH HOUSE MATTERS
MARRIAGE AND RELATIONSHIPS

Lilly explains that matters relating to the seventh house require more consideration than those of the other houses and are also more difficult to judge. He tells us that signification taken from the seventh house includes "Marriage, open Enemies, Law-suits, Controversies, Contracts, Warres, Bargaines, Fugitives, Thefts..." [1]

It is beyond the scope of this book to cover all of these matters, but instead, the focus of this chapter is marriage and relationships. The seventh house matter of law-suits and disputes is covered in chapter twenty one.

In his section on seventh house matters, Lilly quotes various authors, but it is not always clear which are Lilly's opinions and which are not. I have, where possible drawn attention to the different authors.

Testimonies Relating to Marriage and Relationships

The main points noted in this chapter are those which I have found to be most reliable in terms of Questions concerning relationships.[2]

The ascendant, ascendant ruler and the Moon are significators of the Querent. The seventh house and the seventh house ruler are significators of the Quesited (the person enquired about). Al-Kindi tells us that in a Question about marriage, if a man asks the Question, his significators are the ascendant ruler, the Moon, the planet from whom the Moon has separated and the Sun, natural significator of men. In the same Question, the significators of the woman are the seventh house ruler, the planet to whom the Moon is applying, any planet in the seventh house and Venus, natural significator of women.[3] Lilly also confirms that the Sun is natural significator of men and Venus is the natural significator of women.[4]

I cannot confirm that the planet from whom the Moon separates or applies should be taken as significator. I have not found this method to be reliable.

Coley tells us that in a man's Nativity, in addition to the main significators, the Moon and Venus are general significators of marriage. In a woman's Nativity the Sun and Mars are general significators of marriage.[5] I would suggest that in terms of a Question, this additional rulership is not necessarily required, but occasionally these planets help when the resolution of the Question is not clear from the accidental rulers.

Lilly outlines all sorts of issues connected to marriage, such as the time of marriage, how many husbands a woman shall have, who shall be master of the two, whether the marriage is legitimate, how they shall agree after marriage, whether she is a maid or whether she is chaste, whether a woman "trades" with any but her husband, if the Querent's lover or wife has a lover besides himself or whether the child conceived is the son of the man reputed to be the father.[6] However, in terms of my own practice, the most frequently asked Question is whether a relationship will actually take place or if it will last. According to Lilly, a relationship or marriage will take place if:[7]

- The ascendant ruler or the Moon makes a conjunction with the ruler of the seventh house (in any of the dignities of the ruler of the seventh house). This should take place in the ascendant, eleventh or tenth house, but not the seventh house.

- The significators aspect each other with a trine or sextile and are positioned in the ascendant and eleventh houses, ninth and seventh houses, or seventh and fifth houses (with or without reception). However, there must not be any prohibition, frustration or retrogradation of these significators before the aspect perfects. With mutual reception the process is a lot easier.

- The ruler of the ascendant or the Moon applies to an aspect with the ruler of the seventh house. However, in this instance, it won't be easy for the Querent. This emphasises a theme noted several times in this book, where it is demonstrated that the Querent achieves the desired outcome with more difficulty if his or her significators are those that are applying.

- The ruler of the seventh house applies to an aspect with the ruler of the ascendant, or if the ruler of the seventh house is in the ascendant. With this sort of application, the Querent gets a result easily and a lot of goodwill is generated (especially if the application is with a trine or sextile). Again, we see the idea that the outcome is achieved without 'active seeking' if the significator of the matter enquired about applies to the significator of the Querent.

- The significators aspect each other with a square and there is reception. Here, the desired outcome is not achieved easily, but if there is no reception, the matter comes to nothing.

- The significators do not make an aspect with each other, but a planet translates the influence from one to another with a trine or sextile. Here there will be a good outcome, brought about by a person described by the translating planet. A masculine diurnal planet indicates a man. A feminine nocturnal planet indicates a woman.

- The Moon is in the tenth house and translating the light between significators. This signifies that a positive outcome may be brought about by friends or acquaintances.

- There is an applying aspect between the Moon and Venus. Here, a relationship or marriage is brought about through the help of friends. Al-Kindi tells us that this is more certain if the Moon is strong, increasing in motion and in some of her essential dignities. The same applies to Venus.[8]

- If Venus beholds the Sun and the Sun has dignity in the ascendant and beholds the ruler of the sign where he is placed (his dispositor). Here Lilly is quoting Al-Kindi. I have never seen this type of perfection. Given that the Sun and Venus cannot be in major aspect, perhaps Al-Kindi means the conjunction (where Venus by definition would be combust) or perhaps Venus is beholding the Sun through her antiscium?[9]

- The Moon, Sun, Venus, the seventh house ruler and ascendant ruler are angular and are beholding one another, or if their dispositors behold them even with a square or opposition. Here there will be despair followed by the achievement of the desired outcome.

When the ruler of seventh house is in the ascendant, the Quesited usually loves the most. When the ruler of the ascendant is in the seventh house, the Querent loves the most. In fact, those significator(s) that apply represent the person who loves the most.

A marriage or relationship will not take place if:

- The significators make an opposition with each other, even if there is reception. If there is a relationship the Querent will regret it.

- The ruler of the seventh house is in the seventh house especially in one of his own domiciles. This indicates that the person asked about is not in love, is not interested in a relationship, nor in getting married and that if there is consent it is given unwillingly.

- The significator of the person asked about does not aspect the significator of the Querent. This indicates that the person asked about is in love with somebody else, or even that he or she doesn't like the Querent at all.

- The application of the two significators is frustrated. If the application is frustrated by the ruler of the second house, for example, there may be money problems. If the ruler of the fifth house or eleventh house frustrates the application, a friend may be the cause.

- Significators are cadent and especially if they do not make an aspect with their dispositors.

Gadbury asks the reader to consider

...the position of the Lord of the Ascendant, the Moon and Venus, and the Part of Marriage, and their position; for they all have signification of the Party enquiring in this case. If either all, or the major part of them shall be in prolifical or fruitful Signs; It is a very great Argument that the Party enquiring shall marry.[10]

In addition, if the ascendant ruler or the Moon makes a good aspect with the Sun, or either of the Fortunes, or "neer fixed Stars of their Natures," there is the possibility of marriage for the Querent.

Gadbury confirms that if the ascendant ruler, the Moon or Venus are in the seventh house, or in the dignities of the seventh house ruler, and the seventh house ruler is either in the ascendant or in trine or sextile with the above significators, "the Querent no question will Marry". However, if all the (above) significators of marriage are in "Sterile Signs" and make a square or opposition with the seventh house ruler, or the seventh house itself, "you may conclude the Party enquiring is averse to Marriage; and in plain terms, he or she will not Marry".

The Time of Marriage

In working out the time of a marriage, Lilly points to the number of degrees between the application of the Moon to the Sun or to Venus, or the degrees between the ascendant ruler and the seventh house ruler or the seventh house ruler and the ascendant ruler. The number of degrees shows the amount of time between the Question and the marriage. If this takes place in moveable signs, it will probably happen within days, in common signs, months, in fixed signs years. However, this can only take place where there are strong testimonies of marriage and the significators are swift in motion.[11]

Lilly tells us how to find out whether a marriage is "legitimate". If either of the main significators are

> ..vitiated or joyned to Saturn or Mars, and they not Significators in the Question, or if they be with south node, it sheweth unlawfull Marriage, viz, there hath been some wrangling or claime laid to the party by some former man or woman.[12]

When he asks whether a woman is "chaste" Lilly tells us that if the significators are in moveable signs with Infortunes beholding them, the woman might be very keen on a particular man, but that she restrains herself. He concludes by saying "yet it is not to trust always to this judgment, because the nature of women is changeable". [13]

From the Horary Files

It is unusual to be asked a Question about a relationship or marriage when all is going well. For this reason, an astrologer is unlikely to have many charts on this subject which are strong and fortunate. However, in this section I include some of the clearest, although not necessarily the most fortunate, charts on this matter.

Will we get back together? Should I use a mediator? Or will I meet someone else?
5 October 2007 12.26 BST. 50N16 04W48

The Querent was living apart from her long-term partner and was anxious to know whether she might get back with him and whether a mediator could help. If that didn't work, she asked whether she might meet someone else.

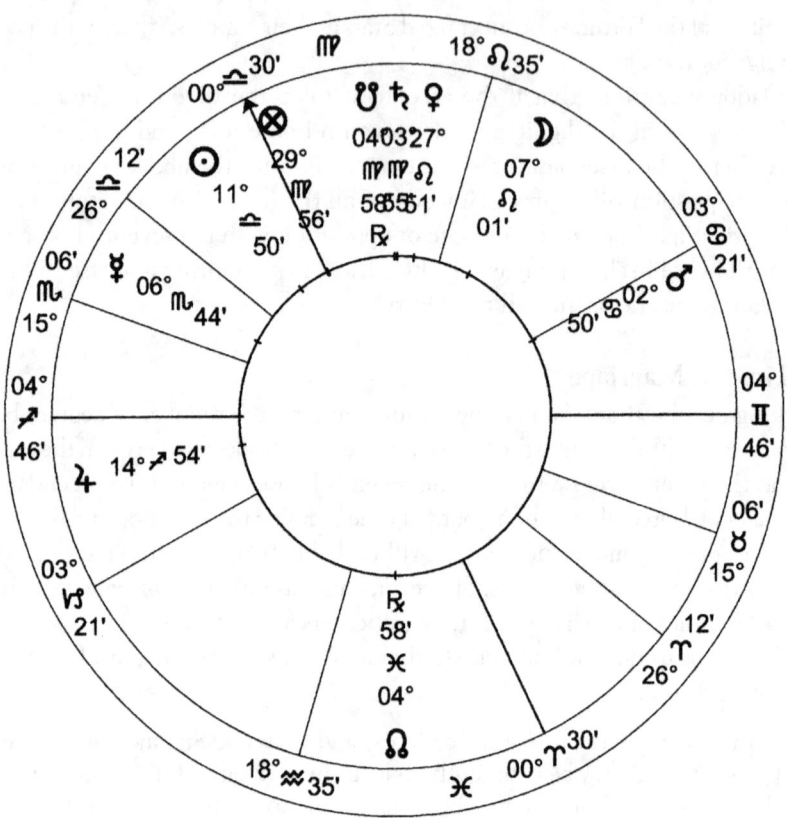

Signification

Querent
Significator: Ascendant, ascendant ruler Jupiter.
Co-significator: Moon

Quesited
Significator: Seventh house and seventh house ruler Mercury.

Possible New Partner
Significator: Sun, natural significator of men.

The chart is diurnal. Fortunes are significators.
The ruler of the hour harmonises with the ascendant.

Testimonies for Getting Back Together
None.

Testimonies against Getting Back Together
Principal significators Mercury and Jupiter make no aspect with each other.
The Moon has separated from Mercury, seventh house ruler, and applies to a sextile with the Sun (another man).

Testimonies for a New Relationship
The Sun is angular and has a mutual reception with Venus.
The Sun is applying to a sextile with Jupiter and they have a reception.
Jupiter is in his domicile and angular.
The Moon is applying to a sextile with the Sun and they have a reception.

Testimonies against a New Relationship
None

With such strong testimonies supporting a new relationship and none against, the Querent can expect the start of a new relationship. There are no testimonies to support a reconciliation with the previous partner at this point in time.

Judgement
The Querent's significator is Jupiter, very strong in his own domicile and in the first house. Although he is incorrectly placed beneath the horizon in a diurnal chart, he is nevertheless the most powerful planet in the chart. However, Jupiter does not aspect Mercury, significator of her partner, and the Moon has separated from Mercury, so there seemed no possibility of a reconciliation at the time of the Question. However, the

Moon applies to a sextile with the Sun and is received by the Sun, being in his domicile, with no frustration before perfection. The Sun is powerfully placed in the tenth house and although in his fall, has a mutual reception with Venus. The Sun aspects the ascendant and applies to a sextile with Jupiter, receiving Jupiter in his triplicity.

It appeared as if someone with an important, well paid job might be interested in the Querent. This is because of the Sun's position in the tenth house, together with the Lot of Fortune exactly in conjunction with the midheaven. The Sun's application to Jupiter suggests that he will be the keener. The Sun's mutual reception with Venus indicates an involvement with someone else, but that their relationship is not solid, because there is no aspect between them.

Outcome

There was no reconciliation at that time with the long-term partner, but a relationship with a man described as above started about four to five weeks after the Question.

Will she get married next year?
8 October 1992 18.03 GMT. 51N30 00W00

There had been rumours about a marriage for Princess Anne. The editor of a weekly magazine asked if I could confirm this.

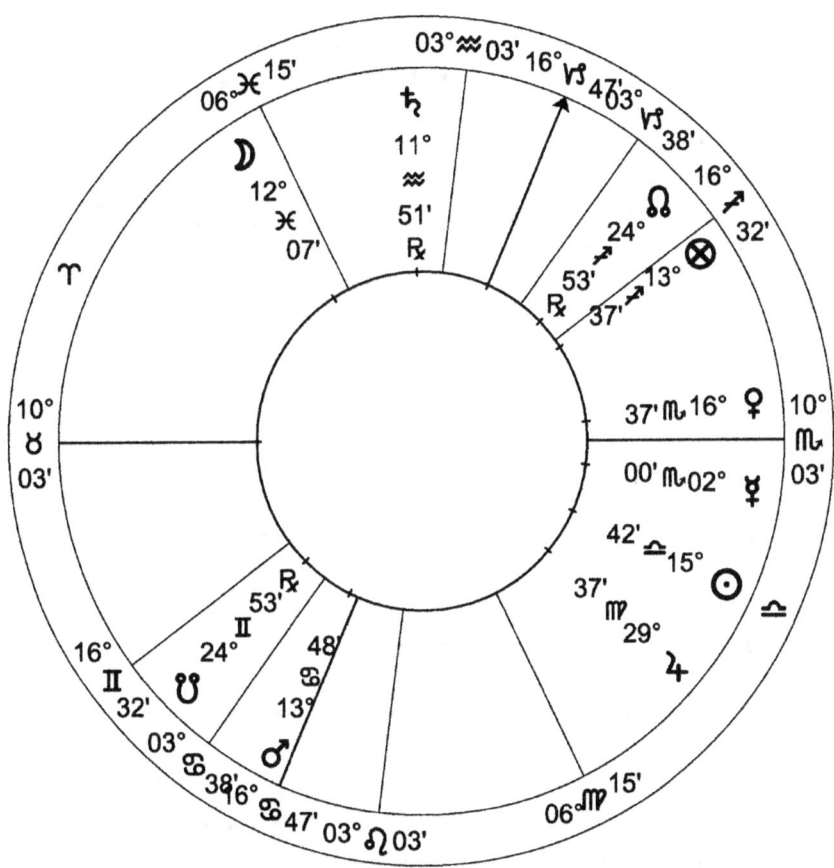

Signification

Princess Anne
Significator: Tenth house and tenth house ruler Saturn.
Co-significator: Moon, Venus.

Husband to Be
Significator: Seventh house from the tenth house (fourth house) and fourth house ruler the Moon.
Co-significator: Mars

Signification of the relationship is also taken from the first house and the seventh house of the unturned chart.

The chart is nocturnal.
The ruler of the hour harmonises with the ascendant.

Testimonies For
The Moon is applying to a trine with Venus in the seventh house.
The Moon is received by Venus in her exaltation.
The Moon applies to a trine with Mars. They have a strong mutual reception.

Testimonies Against
No aspect between the principal significators

The testimonies supporting a marriage are stronger than those preventing it.

Judgement
There is no aspect between the principal significators, the Moon and Saturn, but marriage is indicated by the Moon's application to a trine with Venus in the seventh house, Venus being in her own terms and receiving the Moon in her exaltation. The Moon and Venus are in their hayyiz, being above the horizon in a nocturnal chart and in a feminine sign.

The turned chart supports the former testimony, where the Moon applies to a trine with Mars on the Princess's seventh house cusp. In *Christian Astrology*, Lilly tells us that Mars represents "all manner of Souldiers".[14] The husband to be (Tim Lawrence) is a Commander in the army. There is a mutual reception between the Moon and Mars between domicile and triplicity. With the Moon applying to a trine with Mars, it is likely that she is the keener, for as we know "...those [significators] that apply argue most love..." [15]

Added confirmation is derived from Venus, ascendant ruler, in the seventh and in the dignities of the seventh house ruler. The Moon is just under two degrees from her trine with Mars, which suggests two weeks or two months until the time of the marriage. However, as the Moon and Mars are slow in motion, months seemed more likely than weeks.

Outcome

They married just over two months later on Saturday 12 December 1992, when the Moon and Mars made a conjunction, but Mars was retrograde.

Will they get back together?
17 July 2007 10.26 BST. 50N16 04W48

The Querent's close friend had run off with another man and appeared to have left her husband.

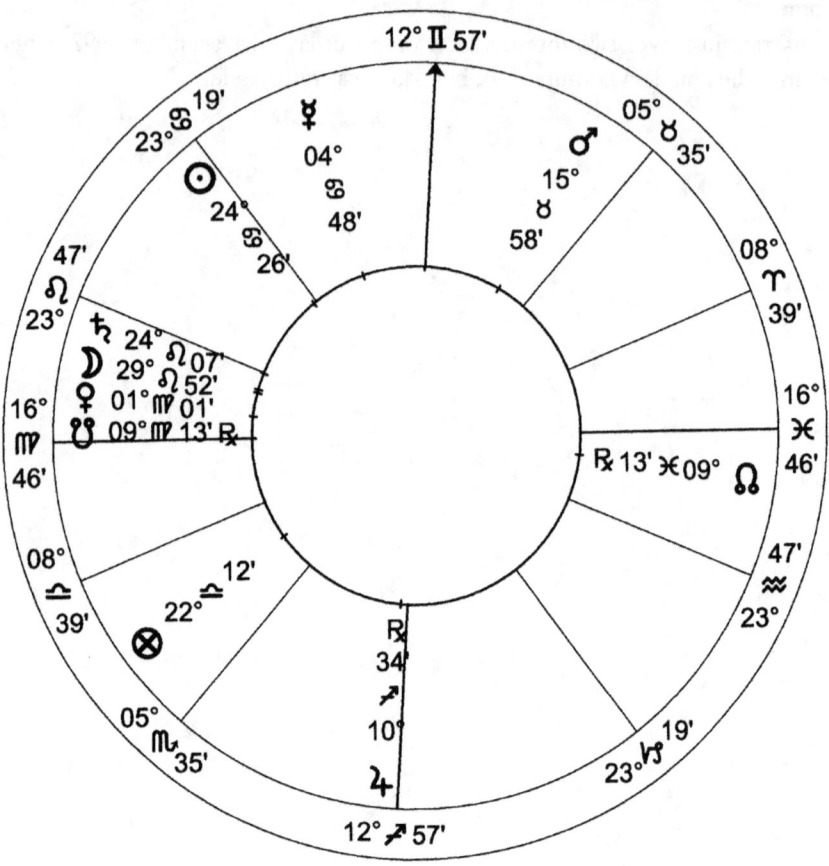

Signification

Querent's Friend
Significator: Eleventh house and eleventh house ruler, the Moon.
Co-significator: The Sun in the eleventh house (or possibly co-significator of the husband).

Friend's Husband
Significator: Seventh house from eleventh house which is fifth house and fifth house ruler Saturn.

Signification of the marriage is also taken from the first and seventh houses of the unturned chart.

The chart is diurnal. The ruler of the hour harmonises with the ascendant.

Testimonies For
None

Testimonies Against
The principal significators are separating.
The Moon is void of course and applying to another planet, which is not significator of the husband.
There is no assistance by way of translation or collection between the principal significators.
There is no assistance from the Fortunes.

With such strong testimonies against the marriage and none for its continuation, the marriage is at an end.

Judgement
Principal significator of the friend, the Moon, is void of course and in late degrees. The Moon is separating from Saturn in his detriment, principal significator of her husband. Mars, who is 'out of sect' afflicts Saturn. The relationship was not a happy one.

I allow the next aspect the Moon makes because it is so close. The Moon is about to change sign, moving from her position where she has a mutual reception with the Sun, to one where she has no dignity. She will join Venus in her fall and the unfortunate south node in the twelfth house. Venus describes the lover who is fairly tall, slim and quite feminine in character. The Moon and Venus are incorrectly placed above the horizon in a diurnal chart. The Moon is 'out of sect'. As co-significators in the Question and as further supporting testimony, Mercury and Jupiter (first and seventh house rulers) make no aspect with each other. They will not get back together.

Outcome
The husband filed for divorce. The affair did not last and the Querent's friend was left alone.

Will he come home soon? What will happen between him and his wife?
3 February 1989 11.45 GMT. 51N30 00W00

The Querent's friend's marriage was in trouble. The Querent was deeply upset. Her friend's husband was seeing another woman.

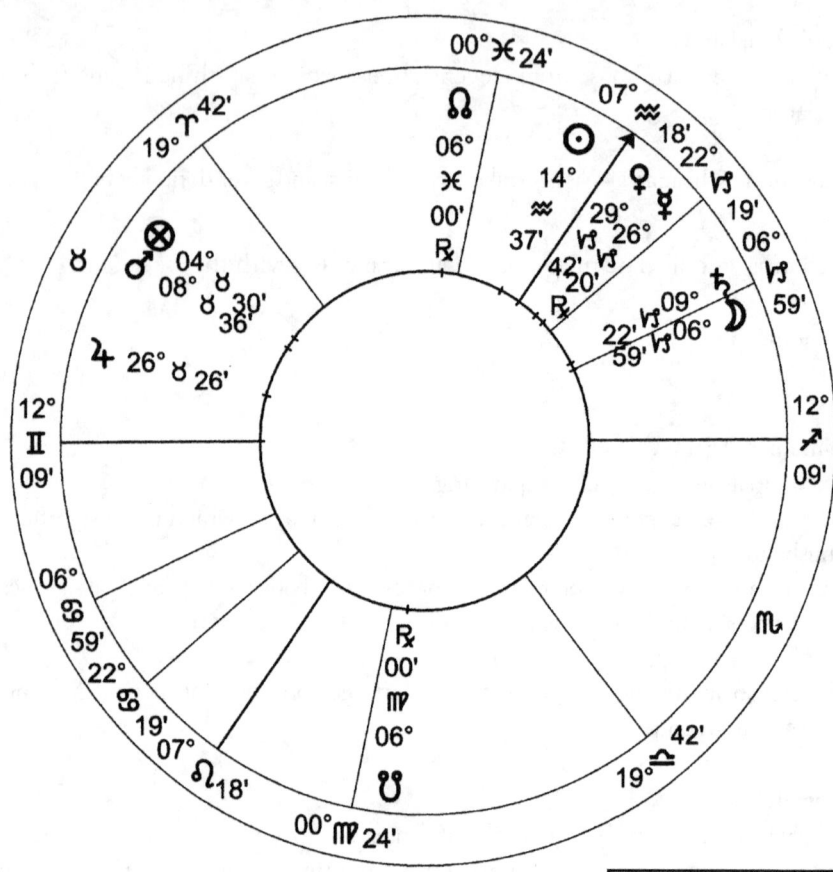

Signification

The Friend
Significator: Eleventh house and eleventh house ruler, Jupiter.
Co-significator: The Moon

Friend's Husband
Significator: Seventh house from the eleventh house (fifth house) and ruler of the fifth house, Mercury.

The Other Woman
Significator: Venus

The chart is diurnal. The Fortunes are significators.
Signification taken from the unturned chart is the same as the turned chart.

Testimonies For
The principal significators Mercury and Jupiter will perfect a trine aspect.
Mercury is retrograding away from Venus, the other woman.

Testimonies Against
The Moon is in conjunction with Saturn.
The Moon and Saturn are in the eighth house.
Jupiter is debilitated and has no reception with Mercury, who is retrograde.
Mercury and Jupiter are cadent and make no aspect with the ascendant.

Testimonies suggest that a reconciliation is possible, but with such strong opposing testimonies, no good can come of it.

Judgement
Jupiter in the twelfth house in conjunction with the malefic fixed star Caput Algol clearly describes the Querent's friend (the wife) who is unwell, and spends a lot of time in hospital having kidney dialysis. Mercury's proximity to Venus describes her husband, living with another woman. However, Mercury is retrograding away from Venus (the other woman). The affair is over. Despite the fact that Mercury is also retrograding away from Jupiter (his wife) he turns direct two days after the Question and perfects a trine with Jupiter four days after that. Note: Mercury does not perfect with Venus, who is about to change sign position and enter Aquarius.

However, the principal significators are cadent and only have dignity through some of the weaker mutual receptions. Neither of the significators, nor the Moon, makes an aspect with the ascendant. Venus and the Moon are incorrectly placed above the horizon in a diurnal chart and Mars is out of sect. The Moon and Mars are in their detriment and although the Moon acquires strength through her mutual reception with Mars, she applies to a conjunction with Saturn in the eighth house. The relationship could never work.

Outcome
He came back for a few months, but the marriage did not work out.

Seventh House Matters - Relationships

What will happen between them? Will they stay together?
9 July 2006 15.20 BST. 51N30 00W10

The Querent asks about her son, whose marriage seemed to be in difficulty.

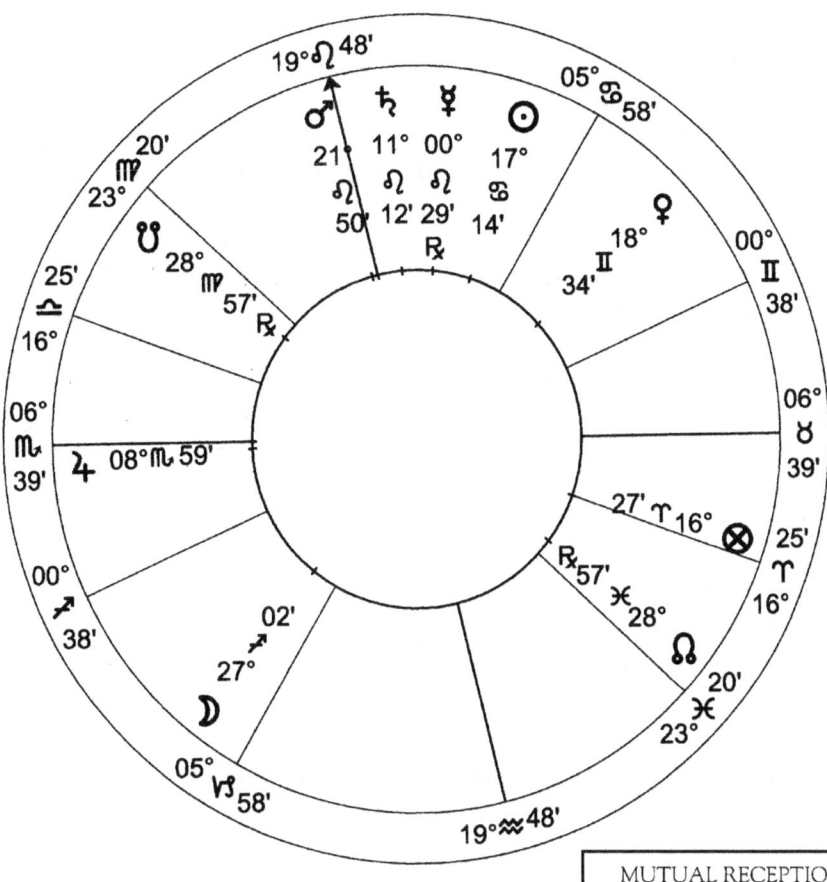

Signification

Querent
Significator: Ascendant and ascendant ruler, Mars.

Her Son
Significator: Fifth house and fifth house ruler Jupiter.

Her Son's Partner
Significator: Seventh house from the fifth house, which is the eleventh house, and eleventh house ruler Mercury.

The first and seventh houses and their rulers are part significators. The Moon has chief signification over the Question.

Lilly says that the Moon can sometimes perform in Sagittarius despite being void of course. He gives an example in *Christian Astrology* where the Moon is in late degrees of Sagittarius, but has a mutual reception with the Sun between domicile and triplicity.

The chart is diurnal.

Testimonies For
Venus applies to a sextile with Mars.
The Sun and the Moon have a mutual reception.

Testimonies Against
There is no aspect between the principal significators Mercury and Jupiter.
Jupiter applies to a square with Saturn in his detriment.
The Moon is void of course.
The Moon is applying to an opposition with the Sun.
Mars and Saturn, the Infortunes, are angular, elevated and make a square with the ascendant.

With only two weak testimonies to support the marriage, it seemed as if it was over.

Judgement
Although the Moon is void of course, radicality is confirmed by the Moon's position in exactly the same sign and degree as the Querent's son in his Nativity. I informed the Querent that I wasn't sure whether the Moon could perform here, as she does not immediately make an aspect after changing sign. However Lilly and other authorities judged the Moon to be strong in Sagittarius even if void. In addition the Moon has a mutual reception with the Sun.

Notwithstanding the Moon's position, the outlook is not good for the Querent's son. Mercury and Jupiter make no aspect. Mercury, principal significator of his partner is cadent, besieged between the Sun and Saturn, retrograde and about to change sign. The south node afflicts her house: she is very unhappy.

The Querent's son is unhappy: although he has the north node in his house and Jupiter, his principal significator, is in the ascendant in his own terms, Jupiter is afflicted by Saturn. Once the Moon enters the sign of Capricorn she makes a sextile with Jupiter, but later applies to an opposition with the Sun, which is unfortunate.

Mars, ascendant ruler and dispositor of Jupiter, is incorrectly placed above the horizon in a diurnal chart and in the tenth house. Mars cannot, therefore, offer much help in terms of the Question. Saturn moving into the tenth house is in his detriment and also unfortunate. Infortunes ill-dignified in angles are always unfortunate.

I judged that with Mercury changing sign position in about half a degree (half a year) together with the Moon changing sign and moving to a Full Moon, the relationship would flounder by the end of the year. However, the fact that the Moon is received by Jupiter and will complete a sextile with Jupiter, suggested that they would continue to get on well.

Outcome

They separated, but lived amicably together for a few months in the same house and then divorced.

Are we splitting up?
31 August 2007 9.43 BST. 50N16 04W48

The Querent's long-term partner had just packed his bags and left.

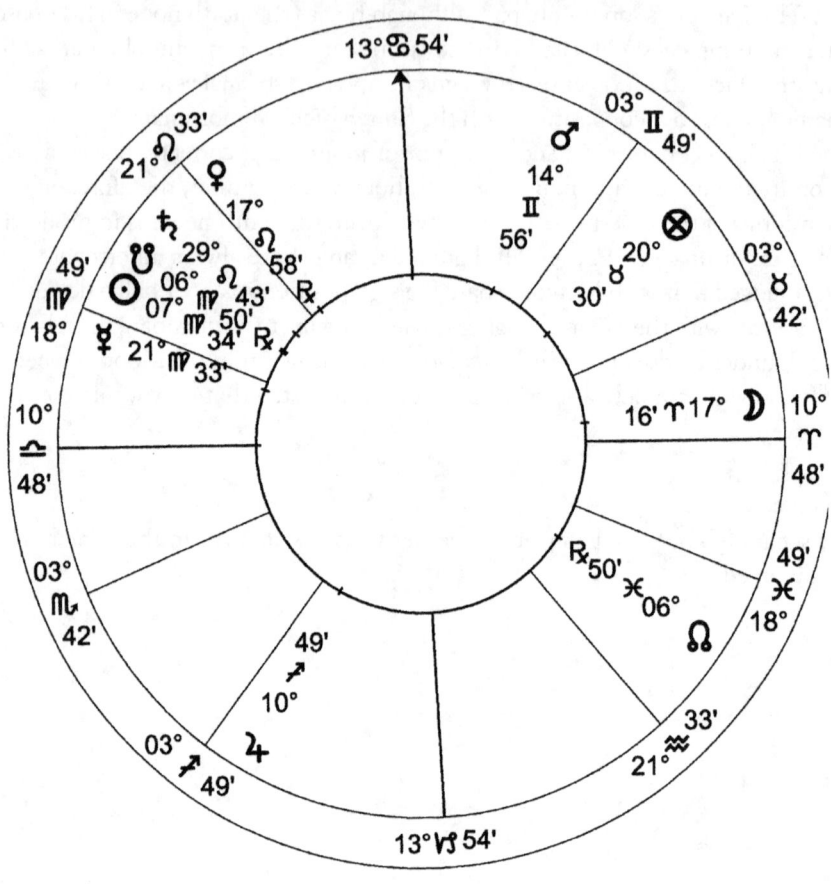

Signification
Querent
Significator: Ascendant and ascendant ruler Venus.
Co-significator: Moon

Quesited
Significator: Seventh house and seventh house ruler Mars

The chart is diurnal.

Testimonies for Staying Together
Venus is applying to a sextile with Mars, receiving him in her terms.
The Moon is translating the light between Venus and Mars.

Testimonies Against
There are no mutual receptions between the principal significators.
Mars is cadent and weak in dignity.
Venus, principal significator, is retrograde.

With two concurring testimonies, I believed that there was some hope of a reconciliation, but so far this has proved to be incorrect.

Judgement
Venus principal significator of the Querent is retrograde. This signifies great changes at hand. Although she is dignified in her own terms, has a strong mutual reception with the Sun and is aspecting the ascendant, Venus is 'out of sect'. Her application to a dexter sextile with Mars shows her wish for them to be together. However, there is no mutual reception between them. Mars is cadent and only has dignity in his face, although he makes an aspect with the ascendant.

The Moon is translating the light of Mars to Venus, where the Moon is received by Mars being in his domicile. However, the Moon is 'out of sect'. The very close trine between the Moon and Venus made me think that this was not a permanent split and that he might return within about three weeks or three months.

Outcome
He did not return. The Querent started a new relationship a few months later. The Moon's position in the seventh house applying to a trine with Venus signifies this new relationship, not the rejuvenation of the old one as I had previously thought. The mutual reception between Venus and the Sun offers further testimony in support of this new relationship. Whether there might be a reconciliation in the future remains to be seen.

The following charts demonstrate that the position of Mars or Saturn in the seventh house is unfortunate in terms of seventh house Questions, even if either of them are significators. In Questions about relationships, the matter cannot be brought to perfection when the seventh house is afflicted. In some instances the relationship or marriage does take place, but subsequently turns out to be unhappy. I have not seen a Question with Mars or Saturn positioned in the seventh house, which produces a happy outcome for the Querent. The same is true in the case of Nativities, unless there is some strong assistance from a Fortune or other benefic.

Does she really want to marry B?
24 January 2007 14.22. 50N16 04W48

The Querent asks about a third party.

Judgement
Despite the fact that the Moon, ascendant ruler, applies to a trine with Saturn, seventh house ruler, they have no reception, so this application can only give hopes. Although the Moon applies to a sextile with Venus, Venus is peregrine and cadent, afflicted by her recent opposition with Saturn. The boyfriend had recently left his wife (Saturn separating from Venus). Superseding all of this is the fact that Mars is in the seventh house. This is overriding testimony of misfortune, even more so in a diurnal chart when Mars is above the horizon and out of sect.

Outcome
No marriage

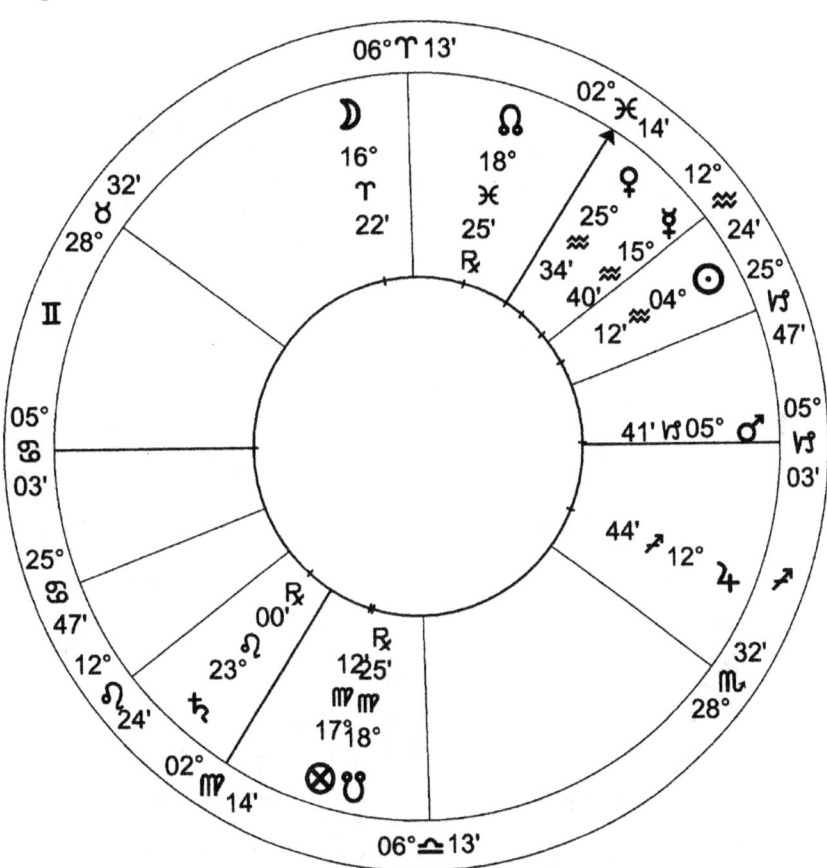

Will there be a marriage?
17 April 1986 9.45 BST. 51N30 00W00

The Querent asks about two close friends.

Judgement

There is no aspect between the ascendant ruler and seventh house ruler, the Moon and Saturn, nor between the eleventh house ruler (the friend) and the fifth house ruler, Venus and Mars, as significators in the turned chart. The Sun and Moon are strong in essential dignity and although the Moon's application to the Sun with a square is promising, they have no reception. The fact that Mars afflicts the seventh house by his presence and is unfortunate being out of sect, is conclusive testimony that there can be no positive outcome.

Outcome

No marriage

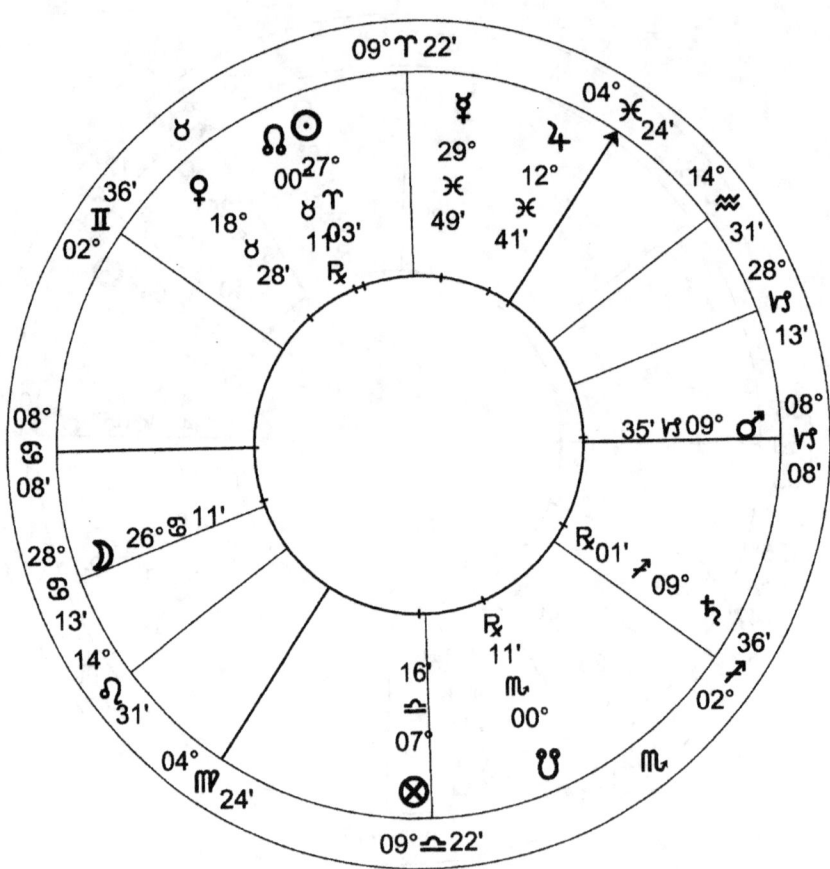

How long will we stay together? What will happen?
22 July 1992 13.20 BST. 51N30 00W10

The Querent had a baby but her son's father wasn't interested in the relationship. They were not getting on.

Judgement

I would not usually judge a chart with the Moon in late degrees of Aries, but she has a mutual reception with Mars and perfects a square with the Sun on changing sign. Mars in the seventh house confirms the difficulties in the relationship and establishes radicality in the Question. Mars in his detriment, out of sect and in conjunction with the malefic fixed star Caput Algol afflicts the seventh house. Mars is unfortunate in this position in a diurnal chart. The Moon is in late degrees and is void of course. Venus and Mars, as principal significators, make no aspect with each other.

Outcome

They split up shortly afterwards.

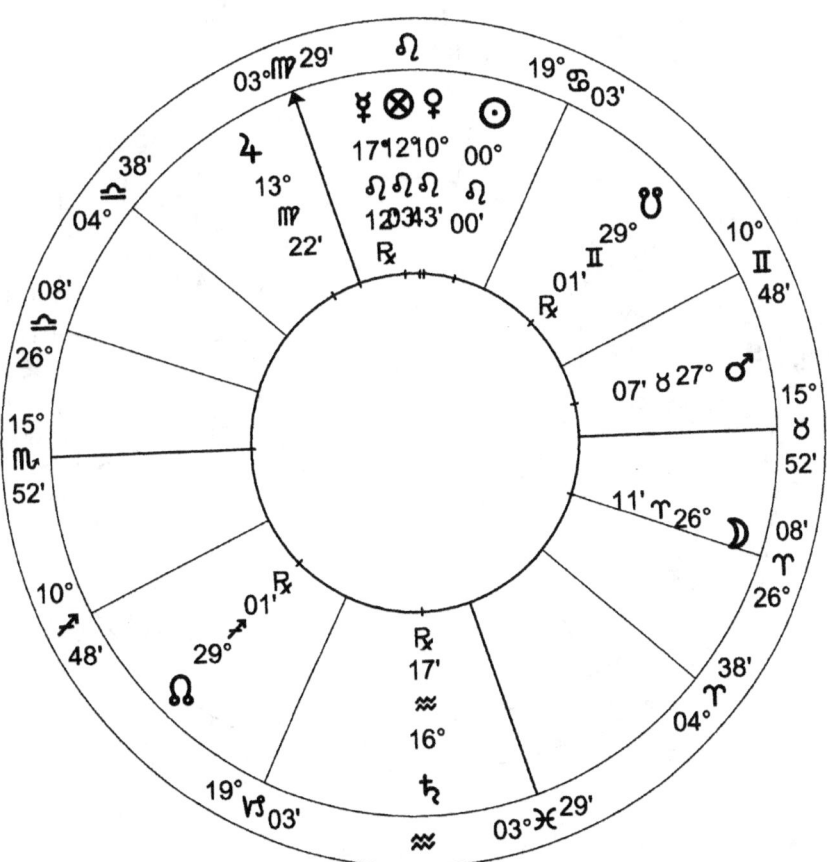

Is it good to stay in the relationship?
20 Oct 2005 7.29 GMT. 51N30 00W10

The Querent felt that the relationship was not going well.

Judgement
Mars and Venus are principal significators in the Question. The Moon in the eighth house applies to an opposition with Venus with no strong reception. Mercury in the first house applies to an opposition with Mars. Mars retrogrades towards a square with Saturn. Despite the strong mutual reception between the Fortunes, Venus and Jupiter, Jupiter is combust. Most importantly, Mars in the seventh house always causes a problem for relationships and he is out of sect in this diurnal chart.

Outcome
It didn't work out.

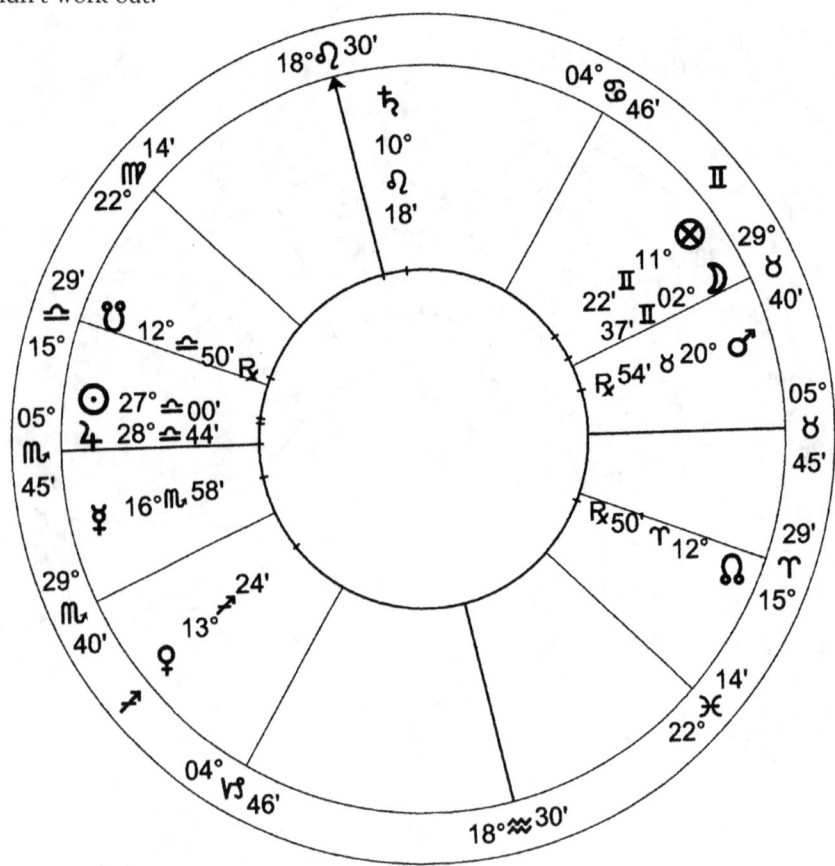

References

1. Lilly p.297.
2. ibid pp.298-319.
3. Al Kindi cited in *Christian Astrology* p.304.
4. Lilly p.319.
5. Coley p.550.
6. Lilly pp.298-319.
7. ibid, this section based on pp. 317-318 and pp.302-305.
8. Al Kindi in *Christian Astrology* p.303.
9. ibid
10. Gadbury pp.273-274.
11. Lilly p.307.
12. ibid p.309.
13. ibid p.312.
14. ibid p.67.
15. ibid p.305.

21

SEVENTH HOUSE MATTERS
LAWSUITS AND DISPUTES

The evaluation of testimonies relating to legal matters is slightly different in comparison with other Questions. Here the strength of a planet is greater in its exaltation than in its domicile. However, in all other Questions, a planet has greatest strength in its domicile.[1]

Testimonies Relating to Law-Suits and Disputes

In any Question about a law-suit or dispute, the ascendant, the ascendant ruler and the Moon are significators of the Querent. The seventh house and seventh house ruler represent the adversary. The significator of the judge is the tenth house ruler. The end of the matter is represented by the fourth house ruler. In chapter two it was noted that in the matter of lawsuits without any foundation, Al Biruni assigns signification to the eighth house.

The following points should be observed in matters which are related to a law-suit or dispute:[2]

- If the ascendant ruler or the Moon makes a conjunction with the seventh house ruler, or a sextile or trine, and they have a mutual reception, the parties will easily sort the matter out amongst themselves, without the help of anyone else.

- If the same conditions apply as above, but one planet receives the other planet and the one that is received does not receive the other (for example, Jupiter in Scorpio and Mars in Capricorn), they will agree without going to court. However, this agreement will not take place without the intervention of a third party (or more). The person intervening is likely to be a friend or acquaintance, represented by the planet which does the receiving.

- If the ascendant ruler and the seventh house ruler aspect each other with a square or opposition and have a mutual reception, or with a trine or sextile without reception, the matter will be resolved. However, there will be one little legal battle beforehand. A compromise is usually offered by the person whose significator is the lighter planet and who commits his disposition to the other planet. This is even more certain if both significators receive each other.

- If the lighter planet is in conjunction with a heavier planet and does not receive the heavier planet, but instead the heavier planet receives the lighter planet, this indicates that the person represented by the heavier planet would like to settle the matter. The person represented by the planet who does the receiving is the person who would like to settle, whether or not the adversary would like to do the same. An example of this is Mercury in Pisces in conjunction with Jupiter in Pisces, where Jupiter would like to settle.

- If the ascendant ruler is applying to a conjunction with the seventh house ruler (or the other way around) and if the ruler of the tenth house frustrates their conjunction, this is an indication that the two parties will not reach an agreement before going to court. In fact, the judge (or lawyer) may be at fault, because he won't allow the two people to settle their differences. If the Moon or any other planet translates the light between the ascendant ruler and the seventh house ruler, it's possible that some other person will help towards an agreement, even though the parties concerned may be in the middle of a legal dispute.

- The person represented by the significator who is most powerful wins the lawsuit or dispute. The strongest person is represented by a planet in an angle and in some of his essential dignities. The more essential dignities that planet has, the stronger he is. If that planet is also received by any another planet, it indicates that this particular person is more competent and has more friends to help him. If you find that there is the possibility of an agreement, the person represented by the lighter planet who commits his disposition to the heavier planet, will make the first move. If the ascendant ruler is the lighter planet and the seventh house ruler the heavier planet, the first person to try to settle things will be the Querent and vice versa.

- A planet in a cadent house is weak if not received or assisted by the aspect of another planet.

- If the seventh house ruler is in the ascendant, the Querent will definitely win the dispute.

- If the ascendant ruler is retrograde, it indicates that the Querent is weak, he won't stand firm, he won't tell the truth, nor really believe that he has any right to the thing in question. If the seventh house ruler is retrograde it indicates the same thing about the adversary.

   ...for if the lord of the ascendant be retrograde, it argues the weakness of the querent, and that he will not stand to it stoutly, that he will deny the truth to his Adversary nor will he beleeve that he hath any right to the thing in question...[3]

- If the tenth house ruler (the judge) is direct and beholds the significators, he will proceed according to the law, will try to speed things up and find a resolution. If the tenth house ruler is retrograde it is an indication that the judge will not proceed according to the law, nor will he want to bring the matter to an end. He may even prolong it longer than he should.

- If the ascendant ruler is separating from the seventh house ruler, or vice versa, it means that one of the parties is not interested in finding a solution and would like to prolong the matter.

- If the ascendant ruler makes an aspect with the Sun or Moon, or if either of them is in conjunction with the ascendant ruler (not the Sun unless that planet is cazimi) and no other planet is hindering their aspect, the Querent is stronger than the adversary.

- If the ascendant ruler is in either of the domiciles of the luminaries (Sun and Moon) or if the Sun and Moon are in the ascendant, the Querent is stronger. Judge in the same way for the adversary.

- If the ascendant ruler makes a conjunction with the tenth house ruler, the Querent will get to know the judge and may even attempt to bribe the judge. If the tenth house ruler receives the second house ruler, the judge will take money for his efforts.

- If the tenth house ruler receives the ascendant ruler, the judge will be sympathetic towards the Querent.

- If the tenth house ruler is lighter than the ascendant ruler and they make a conjunction, he will judge favourably for the Querent.

- If the seventh house ruler makes a conjunction with the tenth house ruler, the adversary approaches the judge. If the tenth house ruler receives the seventh house ruler, the judge will assist him and if the tenth house ruler receives the eighth house ruler, he will take his money.

- If the tenth house ruler receives both significators, the judge will sort things out before the matter goes to trial.

- If the tenth house ruler is in the tenth house and in his domicile, he will do justice and judge the case honourably (unless that planet is Saturn).

- If the tenth house ruler only has dignity in his terms or triplicity, the judge won't care which way it goes.

- If a planet is in the tenth house with no dignity, or has no reception with the tenth house ruler, it indicates that the two people in the legal dispute will be worried about the judge and would prefer a different judge.

- If more planets are in the ascendant and the second house (than the seventh or eight house), the Querent has most friends and vice versa.

- If both significators "give their virtue to one Planet" there will be a person who intervenes.[4]

- If the sign ascending and the sign in the seventh house are fixed, both the Querent and the adversary are determined to proceed in the lawsuit. If they are in moveable signs, they probably won't want to carry on and will end it shortly. If they are in common signs they will continue the dispute for a long time and go from one courtroom to another.

- Where you find an Infortune, you will find the person who experiences the most misfortune and trouble arising out of the dispute.

- If the seventh house ruler and the ascendant ruler are both in angular houses, neither party wins the lawsuit.[5]

- If any planet is joined to an Infortune in a cadent house, the person represented by that planet is beaten.

- If both of the planets representing the Querent and the adversary are joined to Infortunes, "both Parties will be undone by the Suit, or receive infinite prejudice" because of the lawsuit.

To sum up

> ...the Planet that is most strong, and best posited, is the best man, and most likely to carry the victory, and hath the best Cause.[6]

At the end of his discussion about legal matters, Lilly explains that in this type of judgement, the planet from whom the Moon separates and the planet to whom she applies are "equally significant, as the ascendant and seventh house..." Perhaps this is just an afterthought by Lilly or perhaps he is quoting from another source, but it is doubtful that these planets would have equal signification with the ascendant and seventh house rulers in a dispute.[7] Earlier in the chapter, where he touches upon the matter, he does not confirm that these planets have signification.

From the Horary Files

Will I keep all the money or part of it?
16 January 1997 11.38 GMT. 50N16 04W48

The Querent, a contractor, had been overpaid by a substantial amount. After some months the company were in contact to ask for the money back and were threatening legal action.

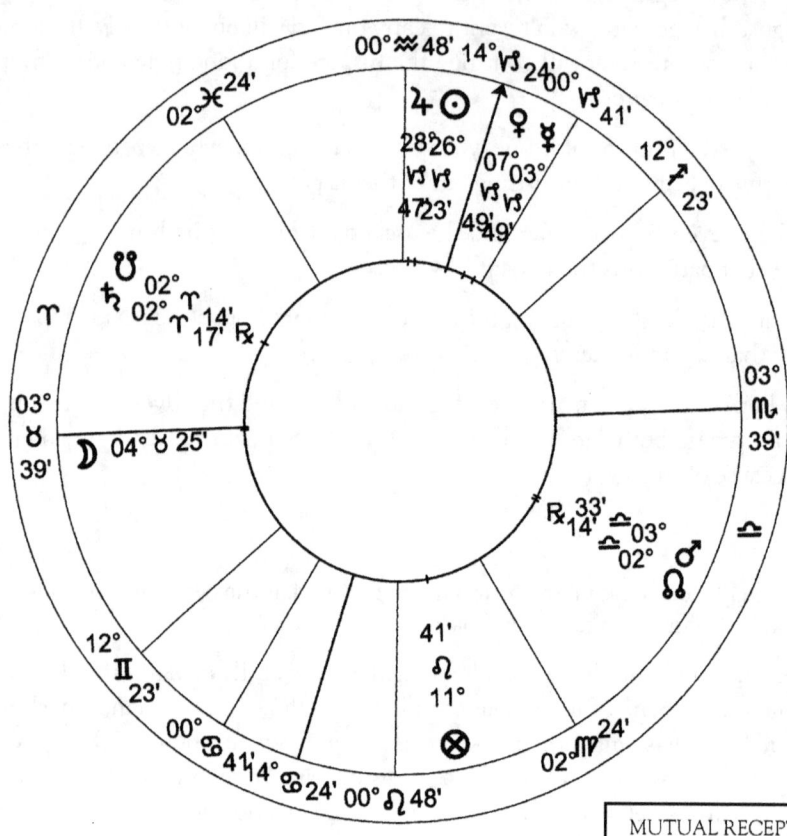

Signification

Querent
Significator: Ascendant and ascendant ruler Venus.
Co-Significator: The Moon.

Adversary
Significator: Seventh house and seventh house ruler Mars.

Querent's Solicitor
Significator: Tenth house and tenth house ruler Saturn.

The chart is diurnal. The ruler of the hour harmonises with ascendant.

Testimonies For
Venus, the ascendant ruler, is angular, in her triplicity, and has a mutual reception with Mars.
The Moon is in the ascendant and in her exaltation.
The Moon is applying to a trine with Venus.
Mercury is translating the light between Venus and Mars.
Mars, the adversary, is in his detriment and cadent.

Testimonies Against
Venus is oriental and moving into sunbeams.
Venus is afflicted by recent squares with Mars and Saturn.

With such strong testimonies in favour of the Querent, she will achieve some measure of success, but not total success because of the afflictions to the ascendant ruler.

Judgement
Although the dispute was between the Querent and the company, it was the Querent's solicitor who became more involved, represented here by Saturn in opposition with Mars. The Querent's solicitor has a serious physical disability, accurately described by Saturn's unfortunate condition. However, Saturn has a strong mutual reception with Mars, which helps to facilitate an agreement.

The principal significators, Venus and Mars, are separating from a square, but have a mutual reception between domicile and exaltation. Mercury separates from a square with Mars and moves to a conjunction with Venus, thereby translating the light from Mars to Venus, Mercury being in the triplicity of Venus and the exaltation of Mars.

Because Venus (and the Moon) are the lighter planets, it was the Querent who first offered to compromise and return some of the money. Ironically, the strongest person in the chart is the Querent, represented by Venus close to the tenth house cusp. Her co-significator the Moon is angular, in conjunction with the ascendant and close to the very degree of her exaltation. The Moon's first application is a trine with Venus, being received by Venus in her domicile. The adversary (Mars) is cadent and in his detriment, although he has two strong mutual receptions with Venus and Saturn. The Sun also has a strong mutual reception with Saturn.

Due to the strength of the Fortunes, Moon and Venus, together with their application to each other with a trine, I judged that the Querent would keep a large part of the money, but not all of it, because Venus is moving into sunbeams and is afflicted by both Saturn and Mars. Mercury, ruler of the second house (and intermediary in the matter) is a great help, but is afflicted by his recent square with Saturn and Mars.

Outcome

The Querent returned a large sum, but it was agreed that she could keep the remainder. However, the company appeared to be unaware of other overpayments and the Querent did very well out of the business.

Seventh House Matters - Lawsuits and Disputes

Will X take me to court? Will I win the case? What will happen?
16 March 1994 9.30 GMT. 51N30 00W10

The Querent was having work done on her holiday home. In her absence the men were doing very little, but were submitting large invoices. A Quantity Surveyor was hired who confirmed that she had overpaid the men substantially and should make no further payments. The builder was angry and threatened court action.

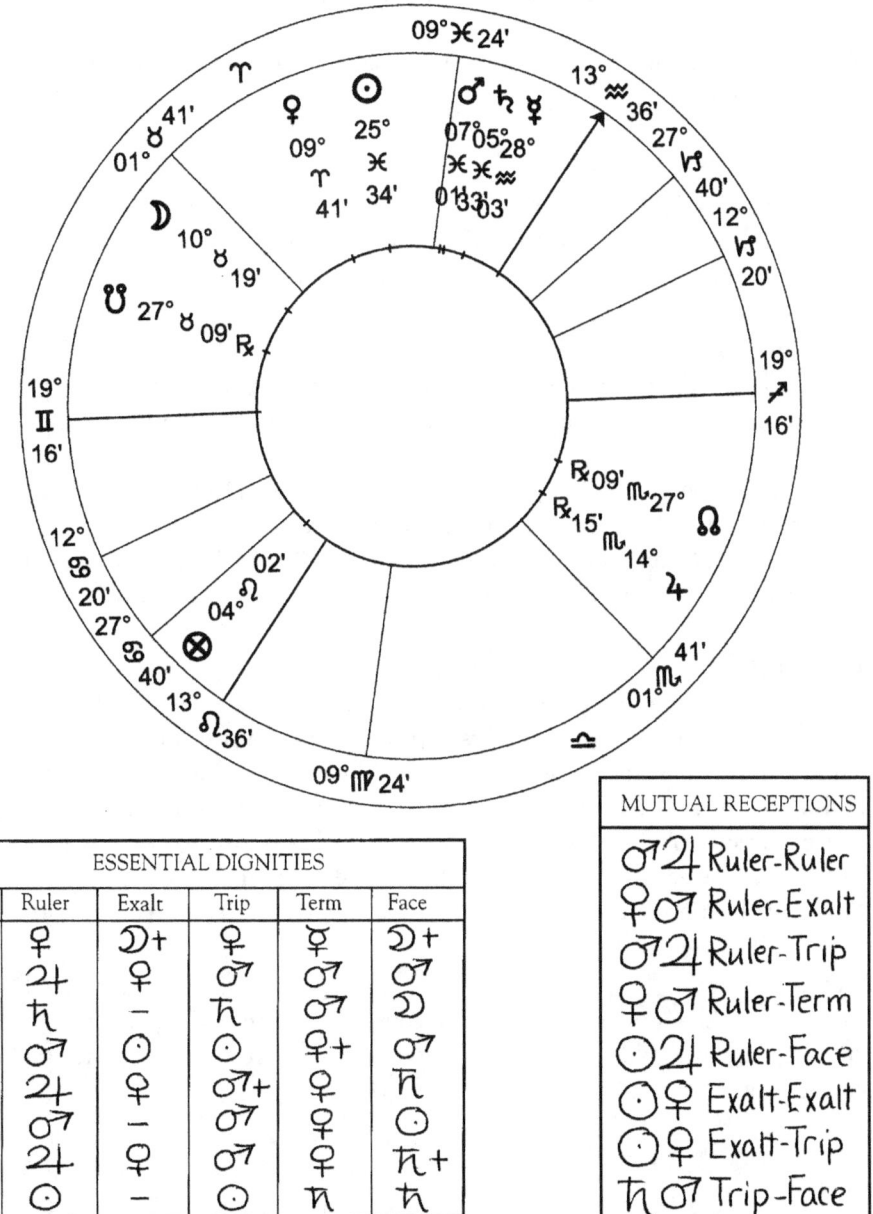

Signification

Querent
Significator: Ascendant and ascendant ruler Mercury.
Co-significator: The Moon.

Adversary
Significator: Seventh house and seventh house ruler Jupiter.

The chart is diurnal. The ruler of the planetary hour harmonises with the ascendant. Fortunes are significators.

Testimonies For
The Moon is exalted.
Mercury ascendant ruler is angular, direct and in his hayyiz.
Jupiter, the adversary, is retrograde, cadent and 'out of sect'.

Testimonies Against
The Moon is cadent and in opposition with Jupiter. They have no mutual reception.
Jupiter, the adversary, acquires strength through his mutual reception with Mars.

Due to the strength of Mercury's position in an angle, the Querent will be successful. If the significator of the Querent is stronger in essential and accidental dignities than the adversary, the Querent does best. If there is any trouble or misfortune arising out of the dispute, the person whose significator is in a cadent house suffers most.

Judgement
Although Mercury is not essentially dignified, he is accidentally dignified by virtue of his position in the tenth house, in his hayyiz and aspecting the ascendant with a trine. The Moon is exalted in Taurus. However, the Moon opposes Jupiter ("perfect enmity"). Although Jupiter benefits from his mutual reception with Mars he is cadent, retrograde and incorrectly placed. Jupiter does not aspect the ascendant, which confirms the weakness of the adversary and the hostility of the adversary towards the Querent. The Moon's application to a conjunction with the south node is unfortunate for the Querent.

Outcome
The builder did not take the Querent to court. The Querent did not pay the final bill demanded by the builder. The builder was furious and spread lies about her around the community.

Seventh House Matters - Lawsuits and Disputes

What will happen in court? Will I win?
5 November 1996 12.04 GMT. 50N16 04W48

The Querent had several invoices outstanding against a local company, which had not been paid. She took out a claim against the owner of a company in the small claims court.

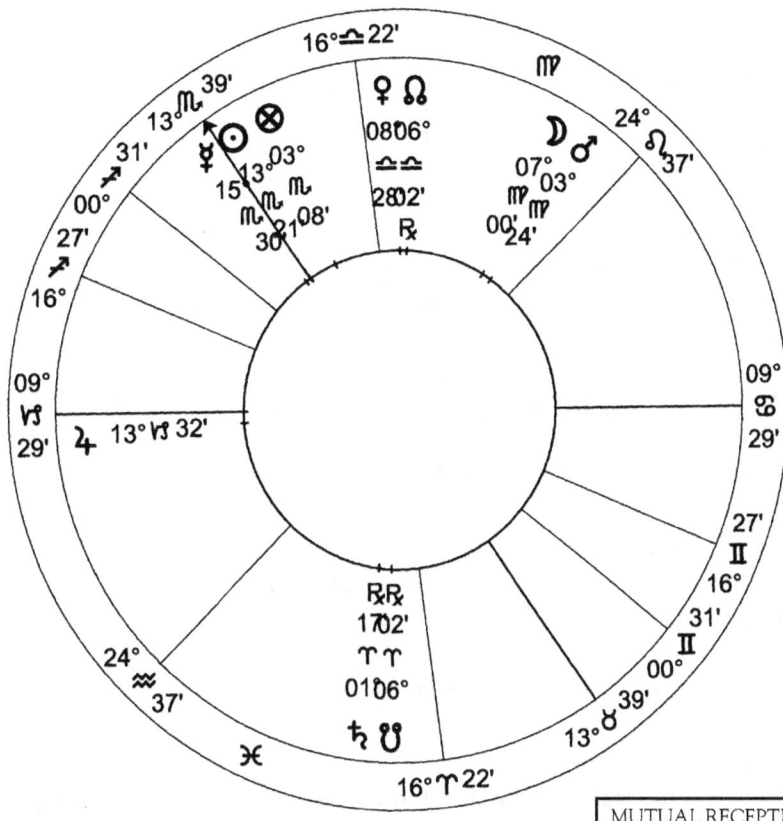

Signification
Querent
Significator: First house and first house ruler Saturn.
Co-significator: Jupiter in the ascendant.

Adversary
Significator: Seventh house and seventh house ruler the Moon.

The chart is diurnal.

Testimonies For
Jupiter, a Fortune, is in the ascendant in his terms.
The Moon, significator of the adversary is succedent, and afflicted by her recent conjunction with Mars.
The Sun aspects the ascendant with a sextile.
The Moon is aspecting the ascendant with a trine and is applying to a trine with the Sun.
The Moon applies to a trine with Jupiter.

Testimonies Against
Ascendant ruler Saturn is in a succedent house, in his fall, retrograde and in conjunction with the south node.

The testimonies in favour of a successful outcome outweigh the one testimony against.

Judgement
The Querent's principal significator, Saturn, is in his fall, retrograde, incorrectly placed, close to the south node and in her second house. Saturn's position in the second house confirms radicality in this Question about money and of course confirms the Querent's weak position financially. However, Jupiter in the ascendant is the Querent's co-significator or perhaps principal significator. Jupiter is in his own terms, is accidentally dignified and has a mutual reception with Saturn.

The Moon, significator of the adversary, makes no aspect with Saturn but applies to a sextile with the Sun in the midheaven and later to Jupiter. The Sun is moving to a partill sextile with Jupiter. Although the Sun might be seen as frustrating the Moon's trine with Jupiter, the Sun in the tenth house represents the judge who might help in the matter. Lilly assigns the ruler of the tenth house to the judge, but in this instance it is clear that the Sun exactly in conjunction with the tenth house cusp is the person who has power in the matter.

All significators have a reception with the Sun. The Sun is in the domicile of Mars, in the term of Jupiter and receives Saturn in his exaltation and triplicity. In addition Jupiter collects the light of the Moon, Venus and the Sun.

Due to the fact that the Moon is a lighter planet than either Jupiter or Saturn, I judged that the adversary would be the first to compromise and that there would be some sort of agreement. I judged that the Querent would get some money, but not very much, because Saturn and the south node afflict the second house. Saturn also afflicts Venus, a Fortune, with an opposition. Although Mars has a mutual reception with Mercury, Mars afflicts the adversary's second house. He has very little money.

Outcome

Before the hearing the judge spoke to both parties and advised them to try to settle beforehand. The adversary offered part of the money in cash to the Querent. She accepted.

If I write to the Chair will I get my money?
9 September 1997, 11.31 BST. 50N16 04W48

The Querent (the author) had co-written an astrology book, but extracts from it had been reproduced without permission by a national daily newspaper. Legal action was underway but proving costly. I decided to write directly to the Chair for compensation and damages.

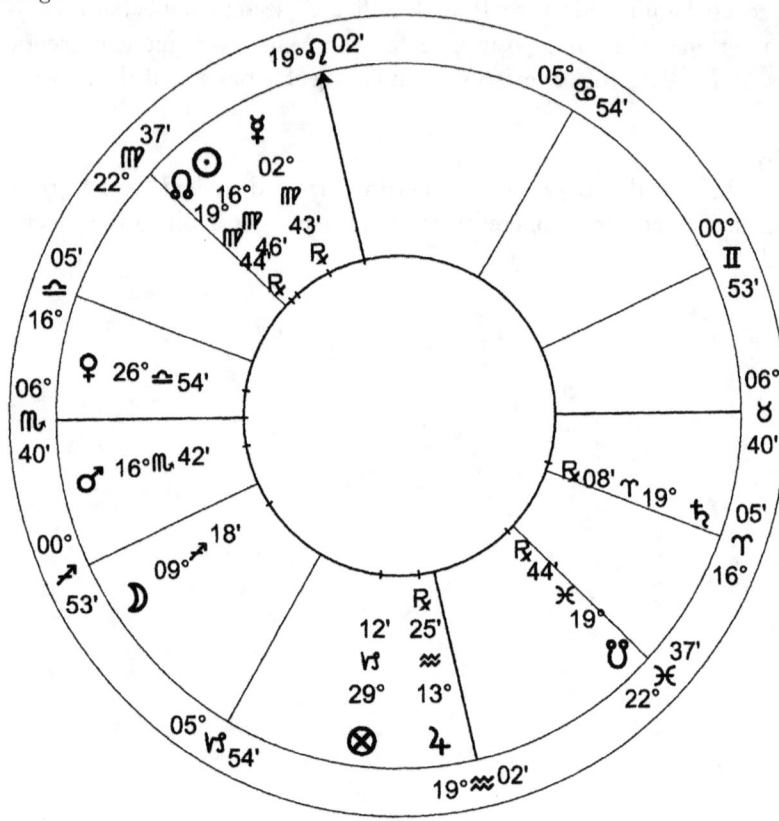

Signification

Querent
Significator: Ascendant and ascendant ruler Mars.
Co-significator: The Moon

Her Money
Significator: Second house and second house ruler Jupiter. The Moon.

Chair
Significator: Tenth house and tenth house ruler the Sun.
Co-significator: Mercury in the tenth house.

The chart is diurnal. The ruler of the hour harmonises with the ascendant.

Testimonies For
Mars, principal signifcator of the Querent, is almuten.
The Moon is in the second house applying to a sextile with Jupiter, second house ruler.
The Moon is translating the light between Mercury and Jupiter.

Testimonies Against
Jupiter is retrograde.
Jupiter's dispositor is Saturn in his fall, cadent and retrograde.

With three concurring testimonies I judged that I would get some money but not as much as I was hoping for because Jupiter is weak.

Judgement
Mars, principal significator of the Querent, is almuten of the chart being essentially dignified in his domicile and triplicity, correctly placed and located in the ascendant. There is a sextile aspect between Mars and the Sun, but it is separating. However, the Moon is in the second house applying to the ruler of the second house, Jupiter, with a sextile and no interference.

Mercury clearly signifies someone in authority but not the Chair who is the Sun. Having separated from Mercury, co-significator of the tenth house, the Moon translates the light of Mercury to Jupiter. Jupiter is retrograde, incorrectly placed and disposed of by a very unfortunate Saturn. Venus, a Fortune, makes no aspect with the principal significators and is afflicted by her opposition from Saturn. I believed, therefore, that I would get some money in compensation and damages, but not all.

Outcome
The Chair of the company referred the matter to a manager who apparently was reprimanded for not having sorted it out previously (Mercury retrograde and under

sunbeams). He called me before Christmas (about three months later) with a view to resolving the matter. We agreed on a sum, which was less than we hoped for, but enough to cover all legal costs and provide adequate compensation.

Seventh House Matters - Lawsuits and Disputes

Will he take me to court? Will I be able to get rid of him?
14 September 2007 8.58 BST. 50N16 04W48

The Querent had a new kitchen installed in 2004, but the builder did not complete the work, so did not get paid in full. Some months later he called to demand the remainder of the money. The Querent agreed, but only after the kitchen was finished. He claimed that it was finished and threatened court action. He contacted debt collectors, but his

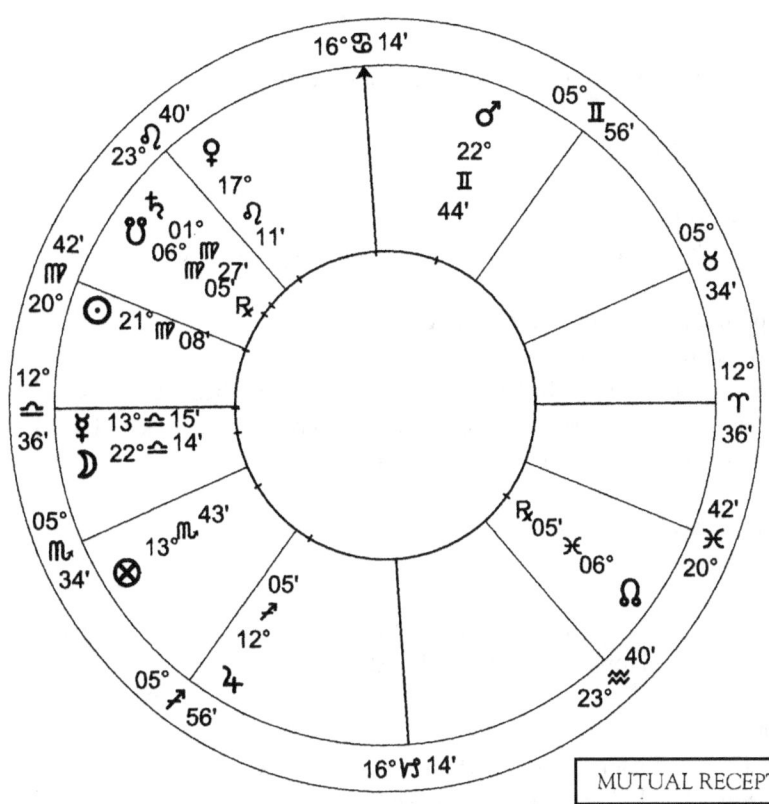

case was thrown out. Two years later he contacted new debt collectors, who contacted the Querent. The Querent refused to pay the balance.

Signification

Querent
Significator: Ascendant and ascendant ruler Venus.
Co-significator: The Moon and Mercury in the ascendant.

Adversary
Significator: Seventh house and seventh house ruler Mars.

The chart is diurnal.

Testimonies For
Ascendant ruler Venus is in the eleventh house and has a mutual reception with the Sun.
Venus applies to a sextile with the adversary, Mars.
The Moon is in the first house.
The Moon is translating light between the principal significators Venus and Mars.
Mercury is in the first house and is dignified through his mutual reception with Saturn.
Mars, the adversary, is cadent and out of his essential dignities.

Testimonies Against
None

The outcome will be in the Querent's favour, because of the strong and concurring testimonies of good fortune and none of misfortune.

Judgement
Venus is stronger by house position than her adversary Mars and has a mutual reception with the Sun. The Moon in the first house is supporting positive testimony. Although in the via combusta, the Moon is close to the benefic fixed star Spica. Mars, the adversary, is cadent, out of his essential dignities, incorrectly placed and afflicted by a square with the Sun. Mercury, dispositor of Mars, is in the ascendant and has a strong mutual reception with Saturn. The Querent is far stronger and will win. As the lighter planet, the Querent will make the first move or an intermediary will (as represented by the Moon translating the light from Venus to Mars).

Outcome
The Querent wrote to the debt collectors with details of the contract, including details of the specification as agreed between them, as well as details of what was actually built. She claimed that the discrepancies between the two constituted a breach of the contract. The debt collectors agreed. She did not hear from the builder again.

Seventh House Matters - Lawsuits and Disputes

Will I be able to negotiate?
14 February 1997 16.59 GMT. 50N16 04W48

There was a dispute about money. The Querent was hoping to settle the matter in her favour before going to court.

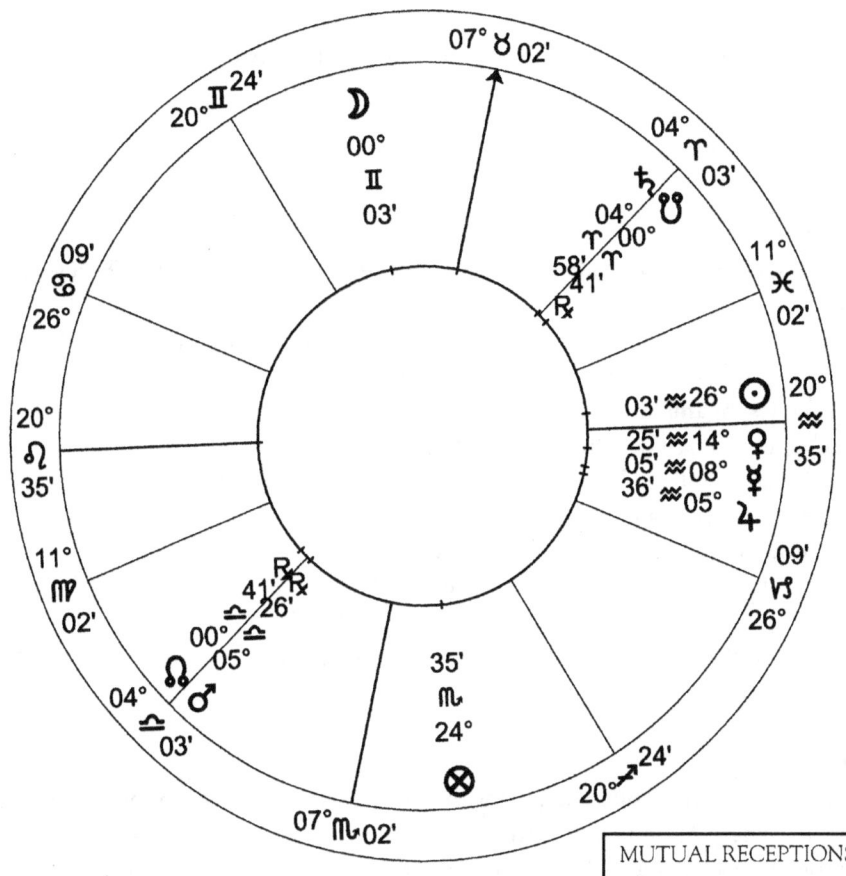

Signification

Querent
Significator: Ascendant and ascendant ruler the Sun.
Co-significator: The Moon

Adversary
Significator: Seventh house and seventh house ruler Saturn.
Co-Significator: Venus close to the seventh house cusp.

Chart is diurnal.

Testimonies For
The principal significators, the Sun and Saturn, have strong mutual receptions with each other.
The Moon applies to a sextile with Saturn, received in his triplicity.

Testimonies Against
The Querent, the Sun, is in the seventh house.
The angles are in fixed signs.
The Sun and Venus are in fixed signs.
There is no aspect between the Sun and Saturn.
The Sun and Saturn are in their detriment and fall.

The testimonies for the Querent being able to negotiate favourably are weaker than those against.

Judgement
The angles are in fixed signs, indicating that neither party is willing to concede. However, the Sun, principal significator of the Querent, is in the seventh house, a clear indication that the Querent is more willing to negotiate and would give in under pressure. Although the Moon applies to a sextile with Saturn, the adversary, and is received in his triplicity, Saturn is afflicted by Mars. Despite his mutual reception with Mars, Saturn is an Infortune and becomes more unfortunate due to his conjunction with the south node. The Moon and Sun are lighter planets and are therefore the first to compromise. The mutual reception between the Sun and Saturn is fortunate, but there is no aspect between them. The Querent's lawyer, signified by Venus, is also in the seventh house and disposed of by Saturn.

Outcome
The Querent did not manage any negotiating. The adversary was very difficult, a bully and unwilling to even discuss the matter. She paid up.

Business Partnerships[8]

The ascendant and ascendant ruler are the significators of the Querent. The seventh house and the seventh house ruler are significators of the potential business partner. Lilly warns us to take careful note of any planet in the seventh house or near to the cusp of the seventh house and to consider whether this planet describes the person asked about. The astrologer must consider whether the planet more accurately describing the person is the planet in the seventh house or the seventh house ruler. That planet who describes the person most accurately is the significator of that person (the intended partner). Lilly tells us that the Moon is "partner in the signification..." Here Lilly appears to emphasise the importance of house position, where a planet in the seventh house may take precedence over the ruler of the seventh house. Lilly does not confirm whether or not the ruler of the seventh house should be present in the seventh house.

The tenth house shows what success may come of the partnership. To find out whether the partnership will be fortunate or unfortunate, consider the fourth house, the fourth house ruler, any planets in the fourth house and the planet to whom the Moon applies.

If the ascendant ruler and the Moon are in moveable signs without any reception between domicile, exaltation, triplicity or term, they will disagree, but they may later be reconciled and the partnership will hold. However, they won't trust each other, nor will much good come of the partnership. If the significators are in fixed signs, the partnership will continue for a long time, but if they have no reception, neither of them will make much profit. If they buy any type of stock or goods, it will be on their hands for a long time. If the significators are in common signs, the partnership should be reasonably profitable and they will be loyal to each other. If one significator is in a moveable sign and the other in a fixed sign, any problems arising will be less than initially feared.

If Infortunes aspect both significators (the ascendant ruler and the seventh house ruler), the partnership will be bad for both of them and neither of them will play fair. A malefic in the first house indicates that the Querent is at fault. If a malefic is in the seventh house, the partner is at fault.

If the Moon separates from a benefic and applies to another benefic, the partnership will begin well and end well, even if neither of them becomes rich. If the Moon separates from a benefic and applies to a malefic, the partnership will begin well, but will end with strife and hatred. If the Moon separates from one malefic and applies to another, they will begin their partnership with grumbles and regrets, continue with distrust and jealousy and end it with a lawsuit.

A benefic in the tenth house shows that the partnership will enjoy a good reputation and the partners will enjoy each other's company. A benefic in the second house shows that the Querent will do best; in the seventh house the partner will do best. A malefic in the second house (or the south node), signifies that the Querent will not gain very much and will be cheated, or trust too much and get into debt.

If the fourth house ruler applies to the eleventh house ruler with a sextile or trine, or if a benefic is in the fourth house, or if the eleventh house and fourth house rulers have a reception, or if benefics make a sextile or trine with the rulers of the ascendant and seventh house, a good outcome may be expected from the partnership.

Also consider the condition of the Lot of Fortune and how it is aspected. If the seventh house ruler or the eighth house ruler make a square or opposition with the Lot of Fortune, the Querent cannot expect too much from the partner, because there is a strong possibility that he will steal from the partnership or steal goods.

References

1. Lilly p. 369. Lilly is not totally clear on the role of a planet in its exaltation. Here Lilly says that a planet exalted is stronger in Questions about disputes, but later in the text Lilly says the stronger the dignity the better, that is, the domicile (sign).
2. ibid pp. 372-376.
3. ibid p. 373.
4. ibid p. 375.
5. ibid. The rest of this small section from p. 369.
6. ibid p. 375.
7. ibid p. 376.
8. ibid, this section based on pp. 377–379.

22

TENTH HOUSE MATTERS
CAREER AND ACHIEVEMENT

The tenth house is a very important and powerful house. If, in a Question or Nativity, the tenth house is occupied by a Fortune well dignified, this can have a beneficial effect on the entire chart. If on the other hand the tenth house is occupied by an Infortune, in his detriment, fall, or peregrine, this can have a detrimental effect on the entire chart.

Matters which fall under the rulership of the tenth house are those concerning a job, career, achievement, honour, promotion, exam results or anything to do with status. This is the house of kings, prime ministers, generals and mothers among other things. Lilly tells us that the tenth house is connected to "Government, Office, Dignity, Preferment, or any place of Command or Trust..." [1]

Testimonies Relating to the Tenth House

The first house, the ruler of the first house and the Moon are significators of the Querent. The tenth house and the ruler of the tenth house are significators of the "Place, Office, Preferment, Command, Honour... enquired after..." [2] Bonatti also tells us

> To regard in Nativities and Questions, the Significators of the Querent's and Native's estate and also of his preferment, calling or profession; which thou mayest take to be the Lord of the Tenth, or of the Ascendant, if the other shall not be fit to signify the same ...[3]

Here, Bonatti is suggesting that the ascendant may, in certain instances, acquire a signification over the profession of the Native or Querent. This highlights once more the theme emphasised throughout this book: it is the chart in its entirety which is important in terms of the life pattern for the Native and in terms of the outcome of a Question. Clearly, a Fortune, or other benefic, in the ascendant of a Nativity, has a beneficial effect upon the life of an individual. A Fortune in the ascendant of a Question has the same beneficial effect on the outcome of a Question, no matter what that Question may be.

Summarising the main points from *Christian Astrology*, Lilly tells us that the Querent will achieve the desired outcome if:[4]

- The ruler of the ascendant and the Moon are joyned to the Sun, or to the ruler of the tenth house (or either of them). The ruler of the tenth house should aspect the tenth house or better still be placed in the tenth house. However, it will not be easy to achieve the desired outcome. The Querent must get moving and use all the contacts available.

- The ruler of the ascendant or the Moon is in the tenth house and not afflicted in any way.

- The ruler of the tenth house is in the first house and is a lighter planet than the ruler of the first house. A positive outcome can be expected, even if there is no aspect between them. Again we see the idea that if the ruler of the matter enquired about is in the house of the Querent, or applying to the significator of the Querent, the desired outcome is accomplished easily and without active seeking. Of course, this happens even more easily if the ruler of the tenth house is in the ascending degree and applying to a sextile or trine aspect with the ruler of the first house.

- The ruler of the tenth house makes any aspect with Jupiter or Venus and the ruler of the tenth house is in the ascendant. Achieving the desired outcome will be an easy process.

- The ruler of the tenth house is joyned with Saturn or Mars and they (or either of them) are in the ascendant, in their own domicile, or exaltation, are oriental and direct and not in opposition with each other. However, in this instance, a positive outcome is only achieved with difficulty.

- The ruler of the tenth house receives the ruler of the ascendant or the Moon by any reception and in any sign. This will be brought about easily and will be to the Querent's advantage.

- Any planet translates the light of the ruler of the ascendant to the ruler of the tenth house. Here, the Querent will achieve the outcome desired, but only with the help of another person. This person, represented by the translating planet, is probably acquainted with the relevant person in connection with the position. In this case, it's best that the Querent should approach the person described in the Question and ask for assistance.

- The ascendant ruler is applying to a conjunction with the ruler of the tenth house, without any frustration before this conjunction. However, this process will not be easy. The Querent will have to work really hard.

- The ascendant ruler and the tenth house ruler commit their disposition to any planet in an angle with any aspect, with or without reception, whether the receiving planet is a Fortune or Infortune (as long as the receiver is not retrograde, combust, cadent nor changes sign before he makes a conjunction with the ascendant ruler or tenth house ruler). If, in addition, the Moon is joyned to the ascendant ruler or the tenth house ruler, the Querent "shall achieve the preferment expected".[5]

- The ascendant ruler is joyned to the ruler of the fourth house, or the ruler of the fourth house is joyned to the ascendant ruler. Here, the outcome desired will be achieved. However, if the ascendant ruler is joyned to the ruler of the fourth house and the ruler of the fourth house is joyned to the ruler of the tenth house, there will be so much struggling and delay that the Querent will not believe that it will ever happen. Although Lilly claims that it will eventually turn out well for the Querent, I do not have a clear example of this type of perfection.

- The ascendant ruler and the ruler of the tenth house are joyned together and the Moon applies to either of them. This happens most easily when the Moon separates from the ruler of the tenth house and applies to the ruler of the ascendant. Lilly tells us that this is agreed by all astrologers.

It is always important to consider whether any of the significators are placed in the tenth house, or at least aspect the tenth house or the cusp of the tenth house. If not, the chances of a positive outcome to a tenth house Question are much reduced. If the significators are angular, there is a speedy outcome. If they are succedent, the matter proceeds slowly. If they are cadent, the matter goes backwards and backwards, but there may be success eventually.

Gadbury tells us that if:

- The ascendant ruler or the Moon are positioned in the tenth house or if the tenth house ruler or the Sun are in the ascendant and neither of them 'impedited', "the Querent shall obtain the Honour and Office... that he seeks after".[6]

- The ascendant ruler or the Moon are in conjunction with the Sun or with the tenth house ruler, or behold the tenth house with a trine or a sextile aspect, the Querent will achieve the desired outcome by his own efforts.

- There are fortunate planets in the tenth house, or if they are in conjunction, sextile or trine with the tenth house ruler, who has dignities in the ascendant, the Querent will get what he is seeking.

- Saturn or Mars are strong, placed in the ascendant and are

   ...joyned to the Lord of the Tenth, either by body or good Aspect; it presages good hopes of the Preferment sought after, and that it will be gained, although after much seeking.

The Querent will not get what is asked for if:

- An unfortunate planet aspects the ascendant ruler or the Moon with a square or opposition and there is no reception.

- Saturn, Mars or the south node are unfortunate in the ascendant. However, if they are strong and are in good aspect with the ruler of the tenth house, either with a conjunction or good aspect, there is the possibility of a positive outcome, but this will only be achieved with difficulty.

I am often asked how long a job will last and this is something which is not easy to judge. However, there are certain rules that can be applied.[7] In a general sense the Querent will continue in the position if:

- The ascendant ruler and the tenth house ruler make any aspect with each other, or are near to a conjunction. If the heavier planet of the two (the receiver of the disposition) is in any angle (except the fourth house) the Querent will not lose his job or other position until the appointed time, for example, at the end of a contract. However, if the receiver of the disposition is under the earth, close to the seventh house cusp, or part of the sixth house, the Querent will leave the job temporarily, but shall return again even stronger. If the receiver of the disposition is received again, the Querent returns with even more honour and very quickly.

- The ascendant ruler is joyned to the ruler of the third house or the ninth house, or to a planet in one of those houses, and after separation is joyned to any planet in an angle, except the fourth house. However, if they are separated from each other, there will be no return, the job is lost and the Querent will leave for good.

- The ascendant ruler, tenth house ruler, or the Moon commit their disposition to any planet in an angle, apart from the fourth house, and that planet is slow in motion. The Querent won't be asked to leave the job until the receiver of that planet turns retrograde, approaches combustion or goes out of its current sign into a new one.

- The Moon is joyned to the ruler of the tenth house and that planet is in the tenth house.

- Either the ascendant ruler or the Moon are joyned to the ruler of the tenth house and the ruler of the tenth house is heavier than either of them and in a good house, (the tenth, eleventh or fifth) and free from affliction, even if he does not behold the tenth house. Here, the Querent will be transferred to some other job. However, if the ruler of the tenth house beholds the tenth house, the Querent will continue in the same job.

Gadbury tells us that the Querent keeps the job if:[8]

- The ascendant ruler or the Moon and the tenth house ruler make a conjunction, sextile or trine with each other, or if there is any reception between the two chief significators.

- The ascendant ruler makes a sextile or trine with either of the two Fortunes in the tenth house and there is no affliction from the Infortunes.

- The ascendant ruler is in the tenth house or the tenth house ruler is in the ascendant.

The Querent will not keep the job if:

- The ascendant ruler and the Moon are positioned in angles, the angles are in moveable signs and the Moon is not joyned to the ruler of the exaltation of the sign that she is positioned in.
- The Moon is joyned to a planet that is not in any of its essential dignities, even though that planet is received (unless he is received by a Fortune and the aspect is with a sextile or trine and the Fortune is in the third or ninth house).
- The ruler of the fourth house, or the Moon, is in the fourth house and the sign in the fourth house cusp is Aries, Cancer, Libra or Capricorn. This is even more certain if the Moon is joyned to the ruler of the fourth house and the ruler of the fourth house is peregrine.
- The Moon is joyned to a planet who is in the opposite sign to the exaltation or domicile that the Moon is placed in, or if the Moon is in Capricorn or is void of course.
- The ascendant ruler is retrograde or combust. This shows the Querent

    ...to have incurr'd the displeasure of those that have power over him, and that they will take away the Office or Employment he holds from him therefore.

- The ascendant ruler or the Moon make a square or opposition with the tenth house ruler or the Sun and they have no reception.
- The ascendant ruler or the Moon is separating from the tenth house ruler or the Sun, but most especially if after separating they apply to the "maliciousAspects of the Infortunes."

Below is an example of a tenth house matter reproduced from *Christian Astrology*, showing a masterly judgement from William Lilly, together with his wonderful descriptions of the people involved.[9]

If attaine the Preferment desired?

The ascendant and Venus are for the querent, the tenth house for the Office or place of preferment he expects.

Finding the moon placed in the tenth, which is the house of the thing looked after, viz. Preferment, it was one argument the querent should have it.

In the next place, the moon applied to a trine of Saturn, who hath Exaltation in the ascendant, and who receives Venus, and is received of her again.

Besides, the moon applying to Saturn, who is Lord of the fourth, argued, that in the end he should obtaine the Office: but because the Sun was in the seventh house in opposition to the ascendant, and with the south node, and was Lord of the eleventh, I judged he did employ as a Friend, a Solar man, who was false, and did rather envy then affect him. I concluded for the reasons above-named, that with some difficulty he should obtain the Dignity, notwithstanding the opposition a pretended Friend did make; and so it came to passe within lesse three weeks, and he then discovered that his Friend was false, who had a great scarre in his Face, was not of bright or yellow Haire, but of a blackish, dark colour, occasioned by the Sun his neernesse to the south node: the separation of the moon from a square of Mercury, argued, he had delivered many Petitions about it, but hitherto without successe.

Tenth House Matters - Career and Achievement

From the Horary Files

Will he get the job?
26 February 2007 12.21 GMT. 50N16 04W48

I received a text from a close friend about her son's recent job application.

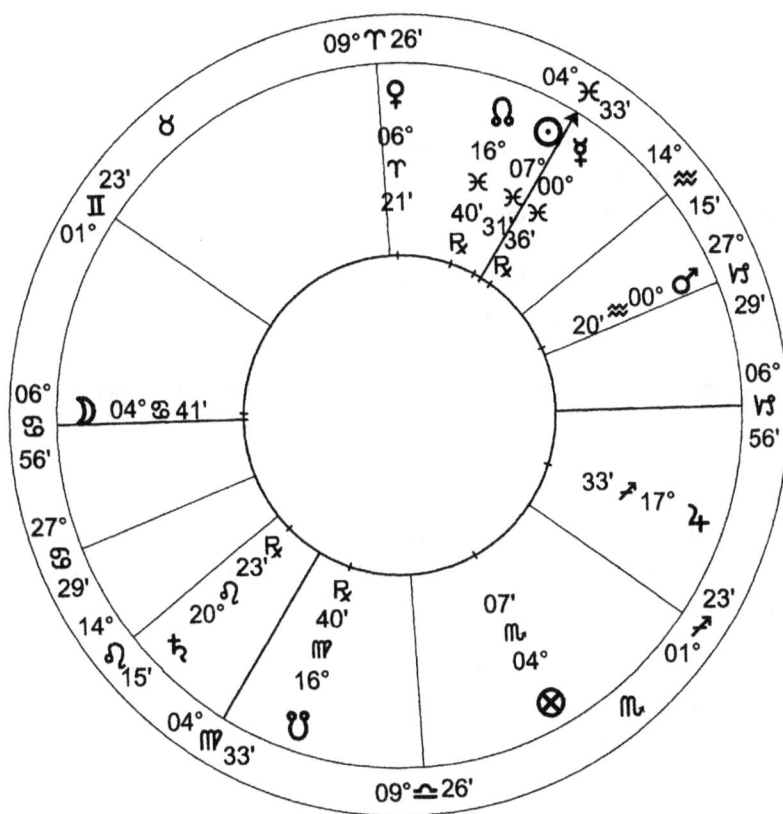

Signification

Querent
Significator: Ascendant and ascendant ruler, the Moon.

Son
Significator: The fifth house and fifth house ruler Venus. The Moon.
Co-significator: Mars, ruler of Scorpio intercepted in the fifth house.

Job
Significator: The Sun in the tenth house.
Co-significator: Tenth house and tenth house ruler Jupiter.
Mercury and the north node in the tenth house.

The chart is diurnal. The planetary ruler of the hour Venus harmonises with the ascendant. Fortunes are significators.

This chart shows very clearly that the original chart takes precedence over the turned chart.

Testimonies For
The Moon is in the ascendant and in her domicile.
The Moon is applying to a trine with the Sun in the tenth house.
Venus, fifth house ruler, applies to a trine with Jupiter, tenth house ruler.
The Sun has a mutual reception with Venus.
The Lot of Fortune is in the fifth house.
The north node is in the tenth house.

Testimonies Against
None

With strong testimonies for and none against, the young man will get the job, although it won't be easy.

Judgement
The Moon is angular, dignified in her domicile and applies directly to a trine with the Sun in conjunction with the tenth house cusp. The Sun aspects the ascending degree exactly and has a mutual reception with Venus. Venus applies to a trine with Jupiter, tenth house ruler dignified in his domicile (although cadent and not aspecting the ascendant). The Lot of Fortune is in the fifth house in exact trine with the Moon and in close trine with the Sun and Mercury.

Although Jupiter is the ruler of the tenth house, Jupiter is absent from that house.

The Sun in the tenth house takes on the role of principal significator (as well as being natural significator of tenth house matters). A planet in a house is worth more than an absent ruler.

Due to the fact that the ascendant ruler (the Moon) and Venus are the applying planets, it won't be easy to get the job; the young man will have to work hard for it.

Outcome

After several interviews and written tests he was offered the job three weeks later.

Will I get the job?
5 October 2007 12.22 BST. 50N16 04W48

The Querent had been told of the possibility of a job offer, but had not actually applied for that job. She was waiting for news.

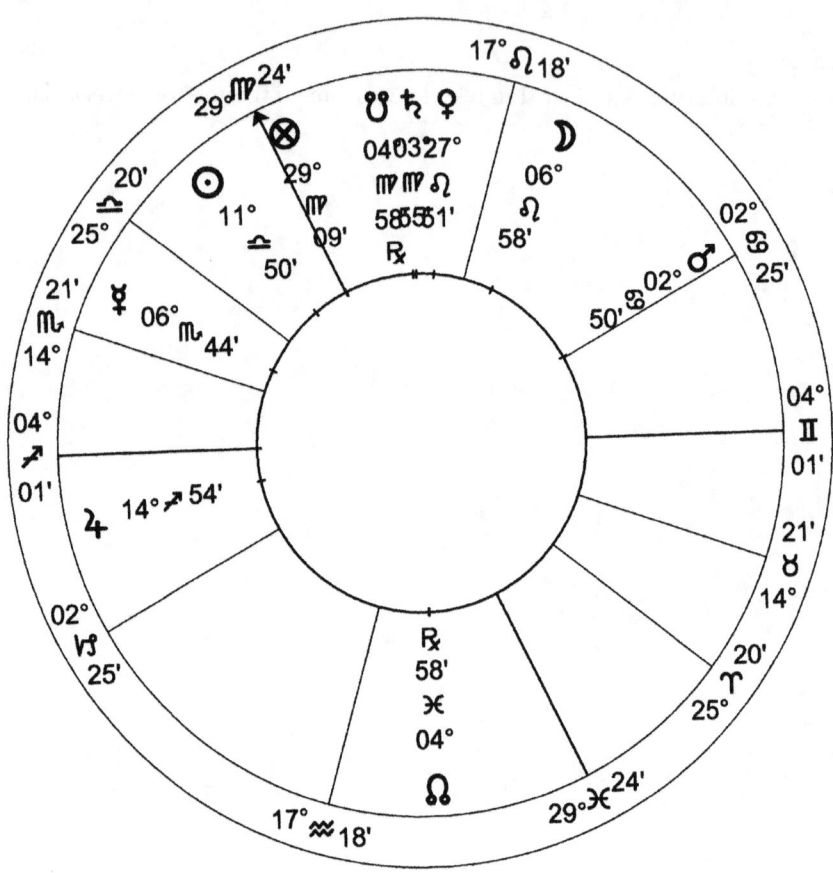

Signification

Querent
Significator: Ascendant and ascendant ruler Jupiter.
Co-significator: The Moon.

The Job
Significator: The Sun in the tenth house.
Co-significators: The tenth house and its ruler Mercury, and Venus, part ruler. The Lot of Fortune.

The chart is diurnal. The planetary hour ruler Mars harmonises with the ascendant. Fortunes are significators.

Testimonies For
The Sun is in the tenth house.
The Sun is applying to a sextile with the ascendant ruler Jupiter.
The Sun has a mutual reception with Venus.
The ascendant ruler Jupiter is in the ascendant and is dignified in his domicile.
The Moon is applying to a sextile with the Sun in the tenth house.

Testimonies Against
None

With such strong supporting testimony, the Querent will be offered the job without any effort on her part.

Judgement
A chart as clear and unambiguous as this is rare. The Sun in the tenth house, the lighter planet, applies to a sextile with the ascendant ruler Jupiter and receives him in his triplicity. Jupiter strong in his domicile and angular receives the Sun in his term. The Moon applies to a sextile with the Sun and is received by the Sun in his domicile. Although the Sun is in his fall, he has a strong mutual reception between domicile with a Fortune, Venus, who is part ruler of the tenth house. With the Lot of Fortune exactly in conjunction with the tenth house cusp, I judged that she would get the job easily.

Outcome
The Querent was offered the job with no hassle whatsoever and with no "active seeking". She signed a contract and started work three months later. The Sun's application to a sextile with Jupiter is three degrees.

Will I get that really good job?
22 October 1992 10.19 GMT. 51N30 00W10

The Querent was aiming high, hoping to get a top job.

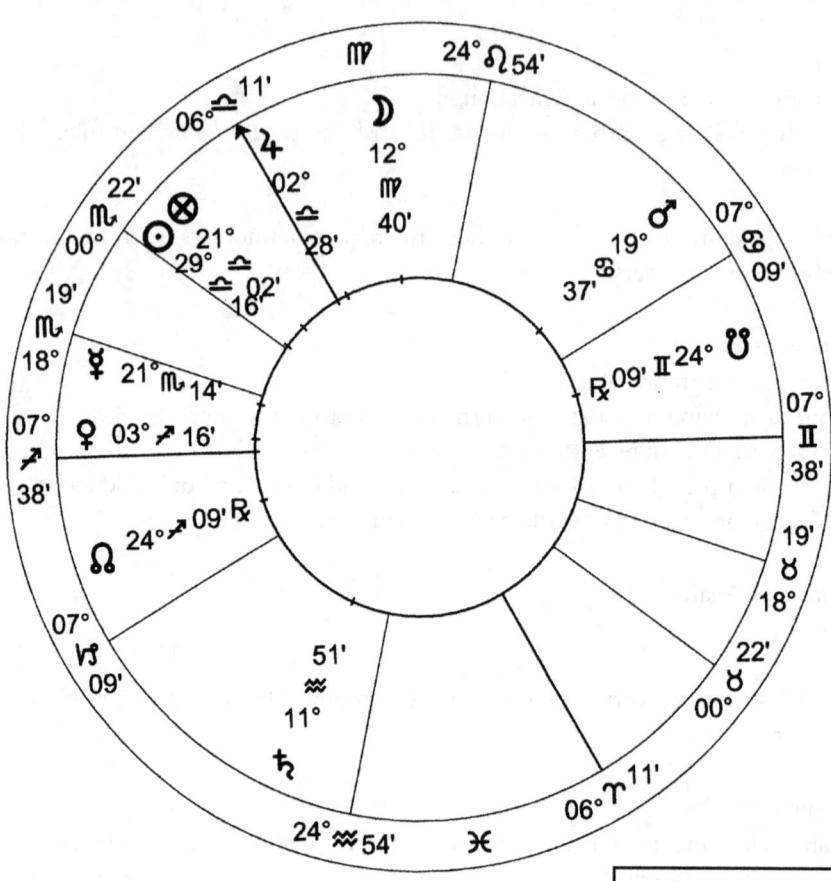

Signification

Querent
Significator: Ascendant and ascendant ruler Jupiter.
Co-significator: The Moon.

The Job
Significator: Tenth house and tenth house ruler Venus.
Co-significator: The Sun

The chart is diurnal. Fortunes are Significators.

Testimonies For
Venus, tenth house ruler, is in conjunction with the ascendant.
Jupiter, ascendant ruler, is in conjunction with the tenth house cusp.
Venus and Jupiter have a mutual reception between domicile.
The Lot of Fortune is in the tenth house.

Testimonies Against
There is no applying aspect between the principal significators Venus and Jupiter.

There is certain to be a positive outcome with such strong and concurring testimonies.

Judgement
This is a really interesting and very rare example of the ascendant ruler being in the house of the matter enquired about, the significator of the matter enquired about being in the ascendant and both of them having a mutual reception between domicile. In fact, both the significators are in conjunction with the cusp of the house so they have even more power.

With the Fortunes as principal significators and so strong, the outcome will be positive for the Querent, despite the fact that the aspect is separating. The Lot of Fortune is in the tenth house and disposed of by Venus in the ascendant. I could not be sure whether the Moon's application to a sextile with Mercury or a sextile with Mars (neither of whom have principal signification in the matter), would be important in the timing. The Sun is about to move out of the sign where she has a mutual reception with Venus. This is also significant.

Outcome
The Querent was offered the job two years later! I was unable to work out the time accurately.

Will I keep the job?
8 July 2004 10.50 BST. 51N30 00W10

The Querent had been working freelance for a company for five years, but there had been management changes and she was concerned that she might lose her job.

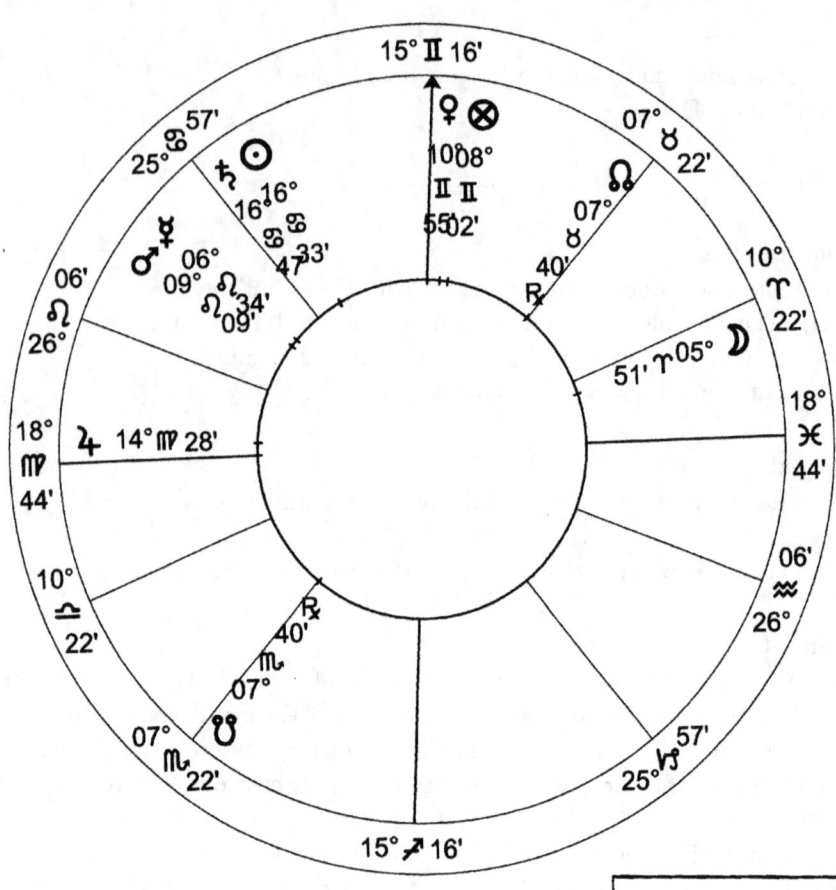

Signification
Querent
Significator: Ascendant and ascendant ruler Mercury.
Co-significator: The Moon, Jupiter.

The Job
Significator: Venus in the tenth house.
Co-significator: Mercury, the tenth house ruler, the Sun, and the Lot of Fortune.

The chart is diurnal. The planetary hour ruler harmonises with the ascendant. Fortunes are significators.

Testimonies For
Venus, a Fortune, makes a conjunction with the tenth house cusp.
Jupiter, a Fortune, makes a conjunction with the ascendant.
Venus and Jupiter have a weak mutual reception.
The Moon has a mutual reception with the Sun.
Mercury and the Moon apply to a sextile with Venus in the tenth house.

Testimonies Against
Mercury is afflicted by his conjunction with Mars.
The Sun and Saturn are unfortunate in their conjunction in Cancer.
The Moon applies to a square with Saturn.

With the Fortunes stronger than the Infortunes the Querent will keep her job.

Judgement
The Moon applies to a trine with Mercury, co-ruler of the tenth house. The Moon has a strong mutual reception with the Sun. Mercury, ascendant ruler, is making an aspect with the third house ruler Mars, and after separation perfects a sextile with Venus, a heavier planet in an angle (tenth house). In this chart, I consider Venus as principal significator, rather than Mercury, because Venus is positioned in the tenth house and Mercury is absent. However, Mercury receives Venus and Jupiter in his domicile.

Whenever Jupiter, a Fortune, is in conjunction with the ascendant and in at least one or more of his dignities the outcome is usually positive for the Querent. Here, Jupiter is in his terms, has a mutual reception with Venus between triplicity and term, is direct, free from combustion and unafflicted by any unfortunate planet. The overall chart testimonies indicate that the Querent shall not lose the job until the appointed time (the end of a contract or commission).

However, with Mercury afflicted by Mars and the Moon afflicted by Saturn, I judged that there might be some sort of crisis in about eleven months when the Moon perfects her square with Saturn.

Outcome
Within the year the Querent was asked to undertake some extra work which proved to be very time consuming and for which she is paid very little money. However, as of the time of publication (2009) the Querent still works in the same job and has recently been offered another freelance contract with the same company.

Tenth House Matters – Career and Achievement

Will I be able to show that I am the best candidate for the job?
9 September 1994 11.52 BST. 51N16 04W48

The Querent was mostly unemployed, had very little money and really needed this job. There were over one hundred applicants and she had been out of the workplace for fifteen years.

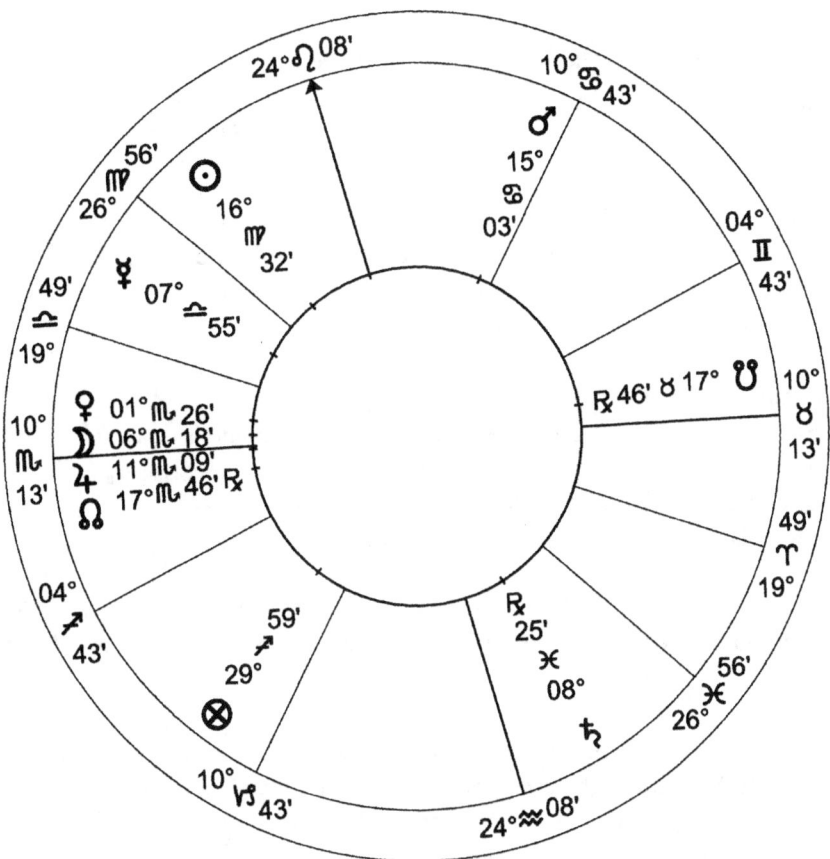

Signification

Querent
Significator: Ascendant and ascendant ruler Mars.
Co-significator: The Moon, Venus and Jupiter.

The Job
Significator: Tenth house and tenth house ruler the Sun.

The chart is diurnal.

Testimonies For
The Sun is in the tenth house.
The Moon is besieged between two Fortunes and the north node.
The Moon has a mutual reception with ascendant ruler Mars.
Jupiter has a mutual reception with ascendant ruler Mars.

Testimonies Against
The Sun is afflicted by his recent opposition with Saturn and is peregrine.
The ascendant ruler Mars and the Sun are separating from a sextile aspect.
Mars and the Moon are in their fall.
The Moon is applying to an Infortune retrograde.

With the testimonies fairly evenly balanced the judgement is not easy, but with no reception nor applying aspect between the Sun and Mars, success seems unlikely.

Judgement
The presence of the Fortunes in the ascendant is positive testimony for the Querent. However, the Sun, although making a sextile with the ascendant ruler Mars, is separating from him and they have no mutual reception. The Sun is accidentally dignified in the tenth house, but has no essential dignity and is afflicted by his recent opposition with Saturn. Mars is afflicted by an approaching dexter square with Mercury with no reception, although Mars is aspecting the ascendant which is helpful.

The Moon in her fall and in the via combusta applies to a sextile with the Sun in the tenth house, but firstly has to make a trine with Saturn, retrograde and incorrectly placed, as well as a conjunction with Jupiter. Notwithstanding the mutual receptions between Mars/Moon and Mars/Jupiter, Mars is cadent, in his fall and out of sect. The Fortunes have no dignity except for Jupiter being in his terms. I judged that she would come very close to getting the job, but would not actually get the job.

Outcome
The Querent was short-listed to the final three but did not get the job. I wonder if Venus, Moon and Jupiter angular are also representative of the three final candidates?

Tenth House Matters - Career and Achievement

Will I pass my driving test?
20 June 1992 13.40 BST. 51N30 00W10

The Querent had failed her driving test three times and still lacked confidence, but her test was due.

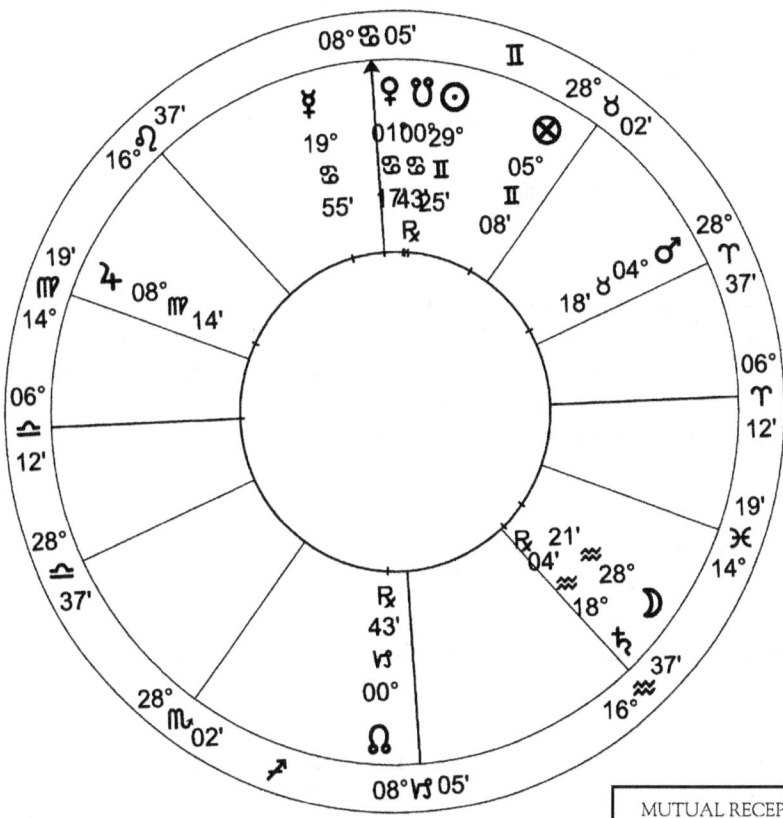

Signification
Querent
Significator: Ascendant and ascendant ruler Venus.
Co-Significator: The Moon.

The Driving Test
Significator: Tenth house and tenth house ruler, the Moon.
Co-significator: Venus, Mercury, the Sun and the south node.

The chart is diurnal. Fortunes are significators.

Testimonies For
Venus makes a conjunction with the tenth house cusp.
Venus is applying to a sextile with Jupiter and they have a mutual reception.
Venus is applying to a sextile with Mars and they have a mutual reception.
Jupiter has a mutual reception with Mercury in the tenth house.
The Moon is applying to a trine with the Sun.

Testimonies Against
Venus and the Sun make a conjunction with the south node.
The Moon is in late degrees of Aquarius.

With strong concurring testimonies, the Querent will pass the driving test.

Judgement
The position of the ascendant ruler Venus in the tenth house is promising. Venus applies to a sextile with Mars and they have a strong mutual reception. Venus also applies later to a sextile with Jupiter and they have a strong mutual reception. This is strong supporting testimony. Jupiter has a mutual reception with Mercury. Although in late degrees, the Moon applies to a trine with the Sun, natural ruler of tenth house matters. The Sun's dispositor is Mercury in the tenth house. The unfortunate south node close to the tenth house cusp is a big concern, but the strength of Venus is enough to outweigh this negative testimony.

Outcome
She was very nervous but passed the test.

References

1. Lilly p. 444.
2. ibid.
3. Bonatus p. 40 124th consideration.
4. Lilly pp. 444-447.
5. ibid p.446.
6. Gadbury pp. 288-289.
7. Lilly pp. 447-448.
8. Gadbury pp. 289-290.
9. Lilly pp. 456-457.

23

TENTH HOUSE MATTERS

SPORT

Arriving at a correct judgement in relation to Questions about sport is not at all easy. This is due to a number of reasons, but mainly because these Questions are often asked by a third party and there can be concerns about radicality. In view of this, the considerations before judgement are particularly important. The best and most accurate charts are produced when the Querent is either directly involved in the matter enquired about, such as a manager of a team, or is a very keen fan.

It is not usually possible, nor appropriate, to set up a chart for every team in a tournament, every horse in a race, or every individual in a competition. This is not the purpose of horary astrology. It is best if judgement is limited to those Questions with which the Querent has some involvement. My son who is a keen football supporter asks Questions which are radical and clear. Friends or clients who ask a Question simply in order to place a bet seldom produce a chart which is radical or clear.

I have found that in competitive charts, the testimonies (fortunate or unfortunate) are often only relevant for the team enquired about. The strength or otherwise of the opposing team may not necessarily be represented. At times, the testimonies relating to these competitive charts are similar to those which are applicable to seventh house matters such as law-suits or disputes, but not always. The astrologer must be guided by the chart.

As discussed throughout this book, in the best and most fortunate charts, the planets are angular (best of all in the cusp of a house) in some of their dignities, have a strong mutual reception, and are direct, swift in motion and free from combustion. The Lot of Fortune is also very important: in the most fortunate charts the Lot of Fortune is found in conjunction with a principal significator, rather than having an aspect only.

In order to establish radicality, the chart ought to confirm the timing of an event. If the final of a football tournament is, for example, two weeks away, but the aspects do not confirm this, the chart is not describing the situation and caution must be exercised.

From the Horary Files

Will England win the 2003 Rugby World Cup tomorrow?
21 November 2003 8.23 GMT. 50N16 04W48

A friend was very excited about the World Cup tournament and asked if England would win the next day.

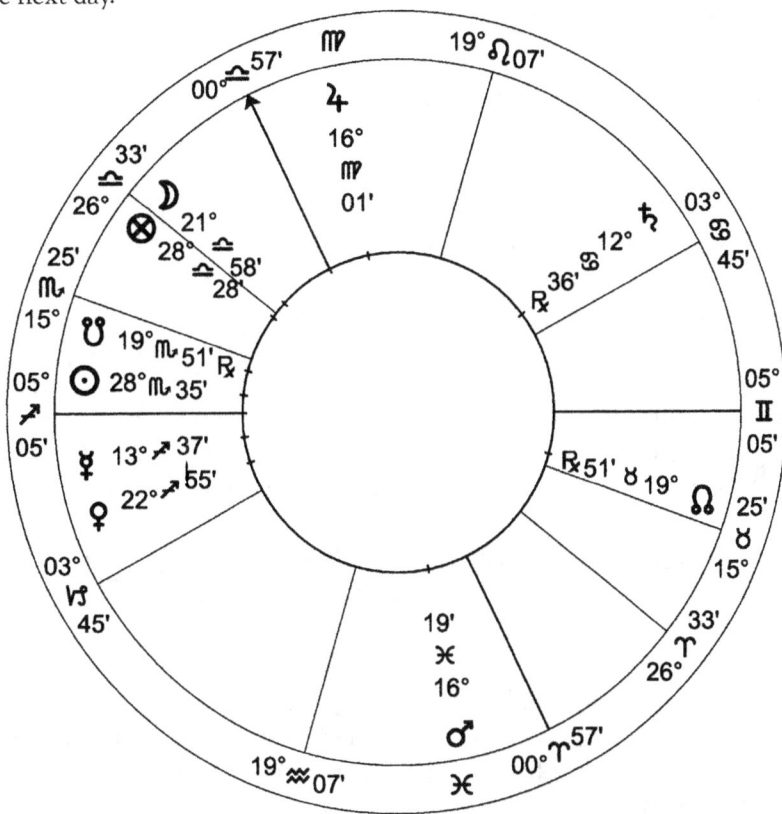

Signification
England Rugby Team
Significator: Ascendant and ascendant ruler Jupiter.
Co-significator: The Moon and Mercury.

The Win
Significator: Tenth house and tenth house ruler Venus.

The chart is diurnal. Fortunes are significators.

Testimonies For
The tenth house ruler Venus, a lighter planet, is in the first house.
Venus and the ascendant ruler Jupiter have a mutual reception.
The Moon applies to a sextile with the tenth house ruler and is received.
The Moon applies to a conjunction with the Lot of Fortune.
Jupiter has a mutual reception with Mercury in the first house.

Testimonies Against
Jupiter is in his detriment and cadent.
Jupiter is afflicted by his recent opposition with Mars (although received).

With such strong concurring testimonies, as well as the Moon's perfection with Venus in one degree, a win for England the very next day looked certain.

Judgement
The ascendant ruler Jupiter, although cadent by house position and in his detriment, has a mutual reception between domicile with Mercury in the first house. The Moon applies to a partill sextile with the tenth house ruler Venus, with no interference. The Moon is received by Venus, with perfection of this aspect taking place in less then one degree. Moreover, Venus, a lighter planet than Jupiter, is in the first house of the England team.

The Moon, although in the via combusta, is close to the fixed star Spica. If one were to take significance from Mercury as the opposing team (being the seventh house ruler), Mercury is in the first house of the England team and, therefore, certain to be beaten. The Moon applies to a conjunction with the Lot of Fortune in the eleventh house. Jupiter is afflicted by a recent opposition with Mars, but is the more elevated planet and is the dispositor of Mars.

Outcome
They won the next day.

Tenth House Matters - Sport

Will England beat Australia in the Quarter Final of the 2007 Rugby World Cup?
5 October 2007 13.25 BST. 50N16 04W46

In the following rugby World Cup four years later, I had already predicted that England would do a lot better in the tournament than had been suggested. A friend, who is a keen fan, asked me how they would perform in the quarter finals.

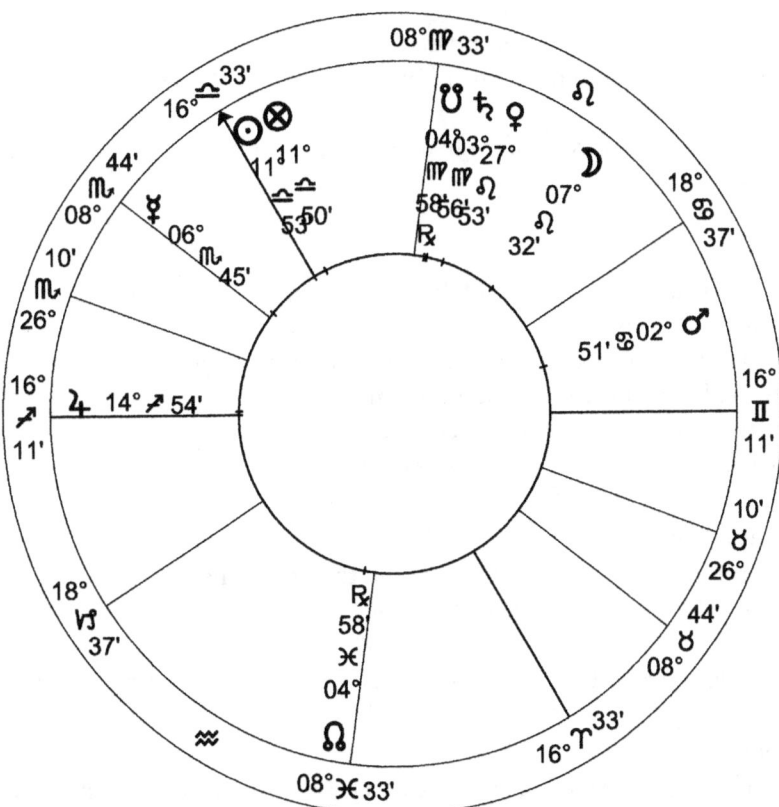

Signification

England Rugby Team
Significator: Ascendant and ascendant ruler Jupiter.
Co-significator: The Moon.

The Win
Significator: The Sun in the tenth house.
Co-significator: The tenth house ruler Venus and the Lot of Fortune.

The chart is diurnal. The ruler of the hour harmonises with the ascendant. Fortunes are significators.

Testimonies For
Jupiter, ascendant ruler, is almuten of the chart, being in the ascendant in the cusp, and in his domicile and joy.
The Sun is in the tenth house applying to a sextile with the ascendant ruler Jupiter.
The Sun and Jupiter have a mutual reception.
The Sun and Venus have a mutual reception.
The Moon is applying to a sextile with the Sun.

Testimonies Against
Mars is in the seventh house (although not in the sign in the cusp).
The Moon and Venus are in the eighth house.

A win for England is certain with this number of strong and concurring testimonies.

Judgement
This is an amazing chart for England. The Sun has a mutual reception with Venus, is in the tenth house cusp and in partill conjunction with the Lot of Fortune. The Sun applies directly to a sextile with Jupiter, ruler of the ascendant in the ascendant and in his own domicile, free from any affliction. The Sun and Jupiter have a mutual reception, where Jupiter is in the triplicity of the Sun and the Sun is in Jupiter's terms.

The Moon applies to a sextile with the Sun and the Lot of Fortune. Mars in the seventh house is unfortunate but he is not in the same sign as the sign in the cusp and receives the seventh house ruler Mercury. Jupiter is almuten of this chart and signifies without any doubt a win for England.

Outcome
A great win for England.

Tenth House Matters - Sport

Will Italy win the (football) World Cup 2006?
13 June 2006 10.12 BST. 50N16 04W46

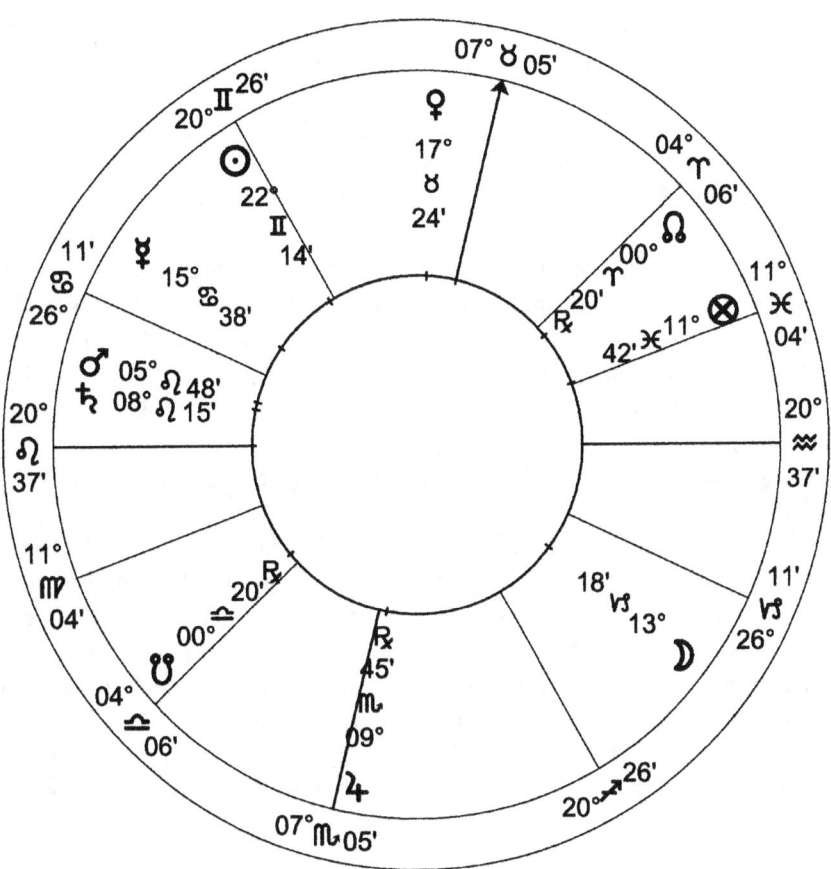

This article first appeared in the *Astrological Journal* 2006. The tournament had just started. An initial horary was drawn up to narrow down the options and allow me to focus on the most likely part of the world that the winning team would come from. So this first Question focused on the possible nationality and colours of the winning team. The chart produced the Moon in the tenth house in Sagittarius. This was a good omen in that the tenth house is the house of the win and described the situation. Sagittarius corresponds approximately to Eastern Croatia, Czech Republic, Spain, Hungary and Poland. The colours of the Moon are white, pale yellow, pale green and silver. I decided to focus on European teams, possibly those playing in white, as no team plays in pale yellow or pale green.

To get the degree of accuracy required, horary maps were then drawn up. I knew that once a really clear horary presented, I need not look any further, because only one team can have such a chart! When I came to Italy, I knew this was the winner.

The Moon in Capricorn is in the fifth house of the game. The Moon applies to a trine with Venus, ruler of the tenth house, positioned in the tenth house. This is a win! Venus is strong in her domicile. There is the added confirmation of a mutual reception, Venus being in the exaltation of the Moon and the Moon being in the diurnal triplicity of Venus.

Mercury's opposition with the Moon causes no hindrance because of the reception (Mercury being in the domicile of the Moon). The Infortunes, Mars and Saturn, are cadent. Jupiter is in poor condition but cannot interfere with play. The Sun, ascendant ruler, is well placed in the eleventh house, free from affliction, has a mutual reception with Saturn between triplicity and is casting a sextile aspect with the degree ascending.

For absolute confirmation Lilly lists, among others, the cities of Parma and Mantua (in Italy) and the area of Campania (in Italy) being associated with the sign of Taurus.

The Italian team won the tournament on 9 July 2006, almost four weeks later. The Moon perfects her application with Venus in four degrees.

Note

The Italians played in blue. Venus and the Moon are in the term of Jupiter. Jupiter's own colour is "Azure", which is a strong blue. Jupiter is associated with "a colour mixed with red and greene", Venus with white, Taurus "white mixed with Citrine". The Sun, ascendant ruler, is in Gemini. Gemini is associated with "white mixed with red".[1] Interestingly the Italian flag is red, white and green. The colours of the Italian away kit is white.

It is easy to be clever about colours after the event, but it is really difficult to work this out from the multitude of significators available. I did not consider this in my judgement. Interestingly, the Moon is exactly in conjunction with the sign and degree of the Moon in my Nativity and in exactly the same sign and degree as William Lilly's Moon.

Will Arsenal win the 2006 Champions League final against Barcelona?
16 May 2006 9.32 BST. 50N16 04W48

The Champions' League final was almost upon us and my son asked the Question, being a very strong Arsenal supporter.

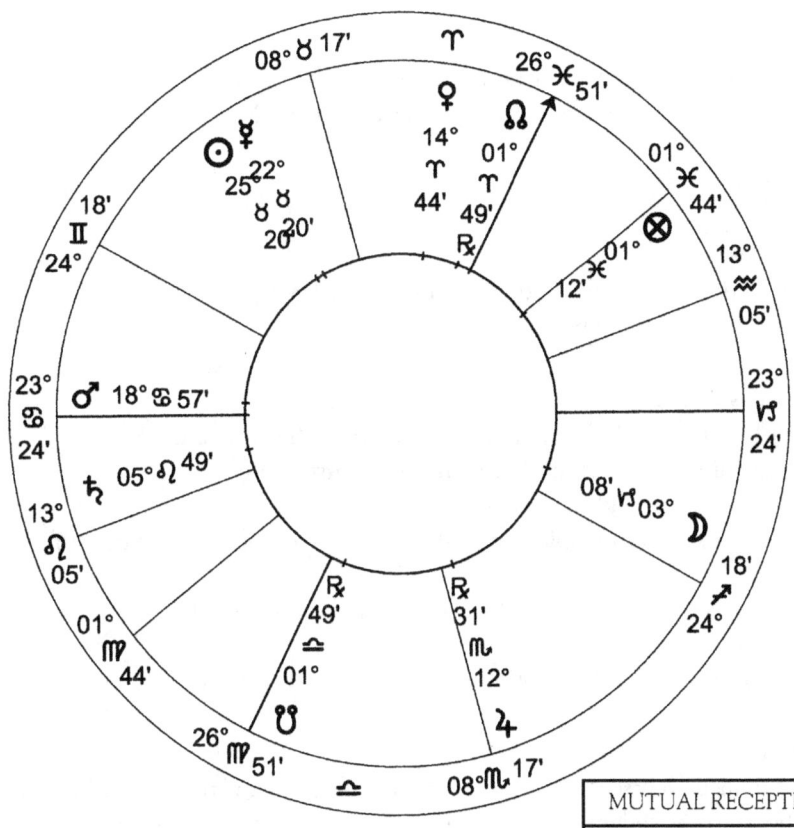

Signification
Arsenal
Significator: Ascendant and ascendant ruler the Moon.
Co-significator: Mars and Saturn.

The Win
Significator: Venus in the tenth house and the north node.
Co-significator: Tenth house ruler Jupiter, the Sun and Mars.

The chart is diurnal.

Testimonies For
Venus is in the tenth house and has strong mutual receptions with the Sun.
The north node is in the tenth house.

Testimonies Against
Mars, an Infortune, is in his fall, in conjunction with the ascendant.
Saturn, an Infortune, is in his detriment in the first house.
The Moon is cadent and in her detriment.
The Fortunes, Venus and Jupiter, are afflicted by squares with the the Infortunes, Saturn and Mars.
The Sun is in conjunction with the malefic fixed star Caput Algol.

With strong and concurring testimonies against a win, Arsenal cannot be successful.

Judgement
One can immediately see the contrast between this chart and those described previously. Here the Moon is cadent by house and in her detriment, although she has a mutual reception with Mars. Jupiter, co-significator of the win, is positioned in the fifth house of the game, has a mutual reception with Mars, but is retrograde, afflicted by Saturn and 'out of sect'.

Venus in the tenth house, significator of the win, although having a mutual reception with the Sun, is afflicted by Mars. The Sun makes a conjunction with the malefic fixed star Caput Algol.

No matter what the strength or otherwise of the principal significators, Saturn is in his detriment, incorrectly placed and afflicts the first house by his presence. Mars, co-ruler of the tenth house, is in his fall, out of sect, in conjunction with the ascendant and will ultimately oppose the Moon.

Outcome
Arsenal lost the match.

The 2007 Premiership

I now take a brief look at the charts drawn up in 2006 for the favourite four in the Barclays Premiership 2007. In all cases the ascendant and ascendant ruler, plus the Moon represent the team enquired about. The tenth house, tenth house ruler, planets in the tenth house and the Sun represent the win.

Will Arsenal win the Premiership next year (2006/2007)?
17 July 2006 15.09 BST. 50N16 04W48

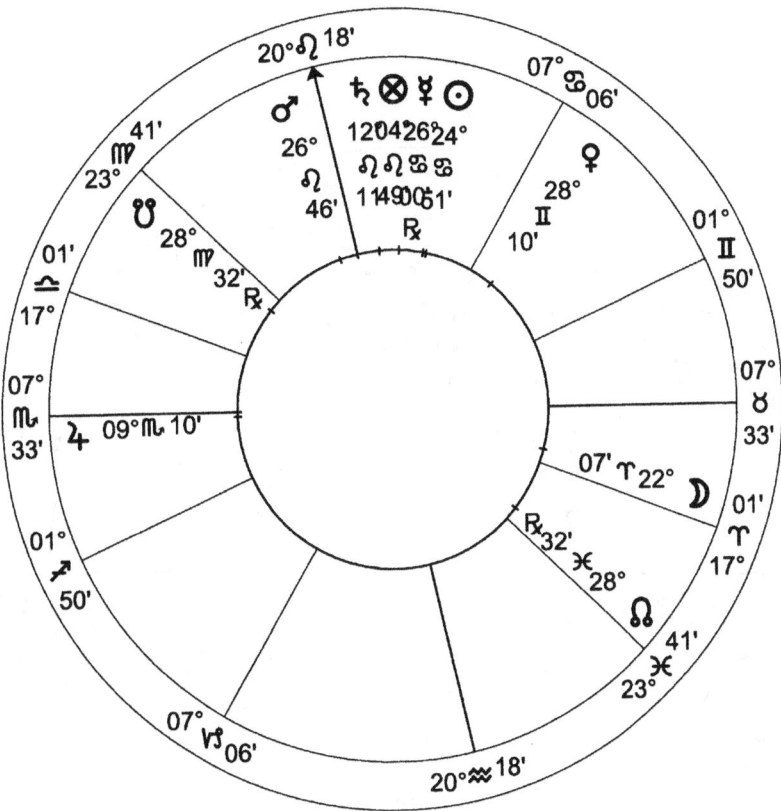

The Ascendant ruler is an Infortune.

Mars, ascendant ruler, is positioned in the tenth house close to the fixed star Regulus, which is positive testimony. However, Mars is incorrectly placed and is an Infortune. The Moon, although having a mutual reception with the Sun, is in a cadent house and does not make an aspect with the ascendant. She applies to the Sun, tenth house ruler, with a square and later, Mars in the tenth house with a trine. Jupiter, a Fortune, in conjunction with the ascendant, bodes well. However, Jupiter is afflicted by his square with Saturn and Saturn afflicts the tenth house by his presence. I judged that Arsenal would not win the Premiership in 2007. Nor did they.

Will Chelsea win the Premiership next year (2006/2007)?
2 August 2006 13.51 BST. 50N16 04W48

The Ascendant ruler is an Infortune.

Despite the promising testimony of having Jupiter and the Moon in the ascendant, they are both afflicted by a square with the Sun and Saturn in the tenth house. The ascendant ruler Mars is in the tenth house, but Mars is out of sect. Saturn afflicts the tenth house, being in his detriment and combust. The Sun, tenth house ruler, is afflicted by Saturn. I judged that Chelsea would not win the Premiership in 2007 and nor did they.

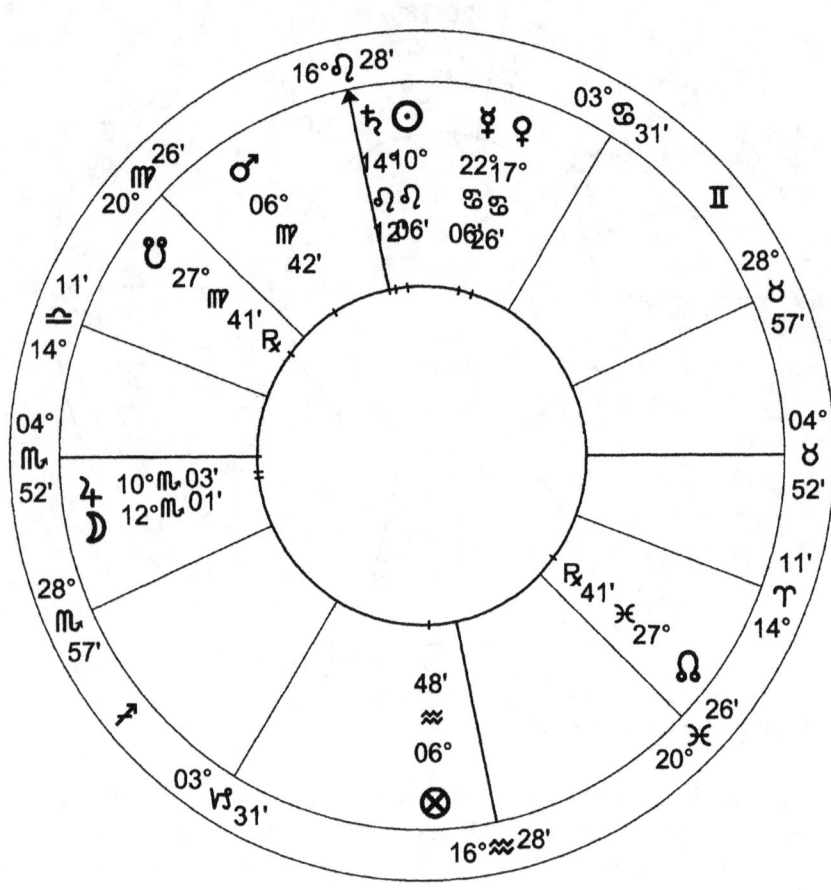

Will Liverpool win the Premiership next year (2006/2007)?
10 August 2006 15.09 BST. 50N16 04W48

The Ascendant ruler is an Infortune.

The ascendant ruler Mars is in the tenth house and has a mutual reception with the tenth house ruler Mercury, but Mars is out of sect and makes no aspect with Mercury. Mercury is cadent and weak in late degrees. The tenth house is also afflicted by the presence of the south node. The Moon is afflicted by her applying opposition with Mars. Judgement for a no-win given. They did not win.

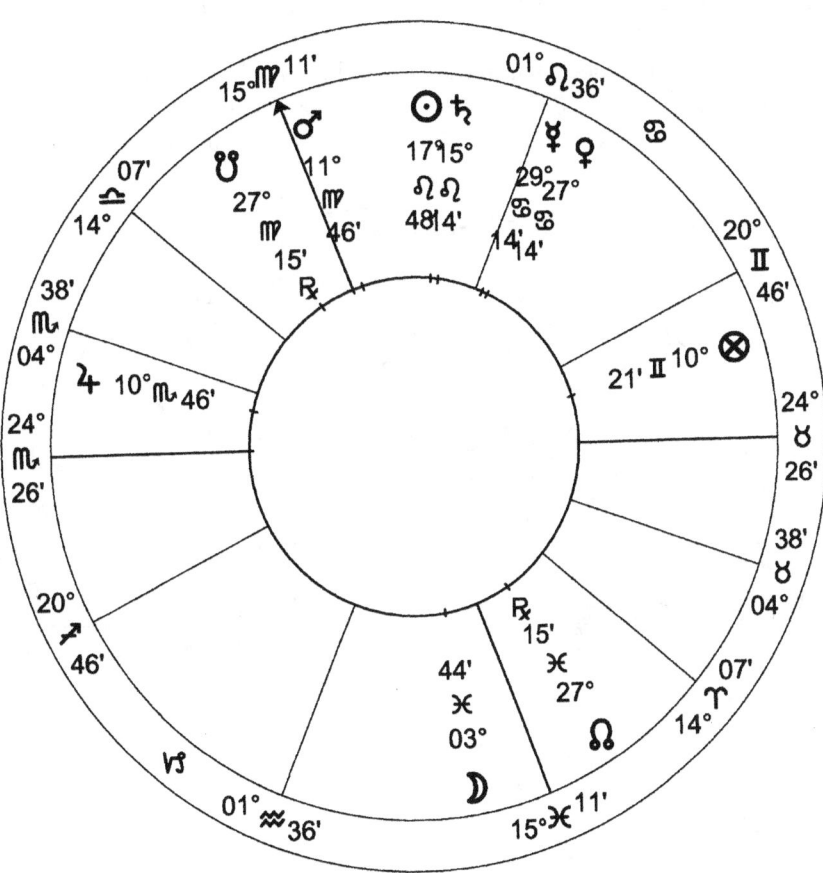

Will Manchester United win the Premiership next year (2006/2007)?
19 July 2006 11.55 BST. 50N16 04W48

The Ascendant ruler is a Fortune.

Although the ascendant is afflicted by the south node, they are in different signs. The ascendant ruler Venus is incorrectly placed, but is in conjunction with the tenth house cusp, has a strong mutual reception with the Moon and is applying to a trine with Jupiter. The Moon applies to a sextile with Mercury and with the Sun in the tenth house, both in conjunction with the Lot of Fortune. The tenth house is not afflicted. Although this chart is not very strong, it is significantly more promising than the other three charts, so judgement for a win was given. Manchester United duly won the title in 2007.

It is interesting to note that in the case of the three losing teams, the ascendant ruler is Mars, an Infortune, and is located in the tenth house. In the chart of the winning team, a Fortune, Venus, is the ascendant ruler and is located in the tenth house.

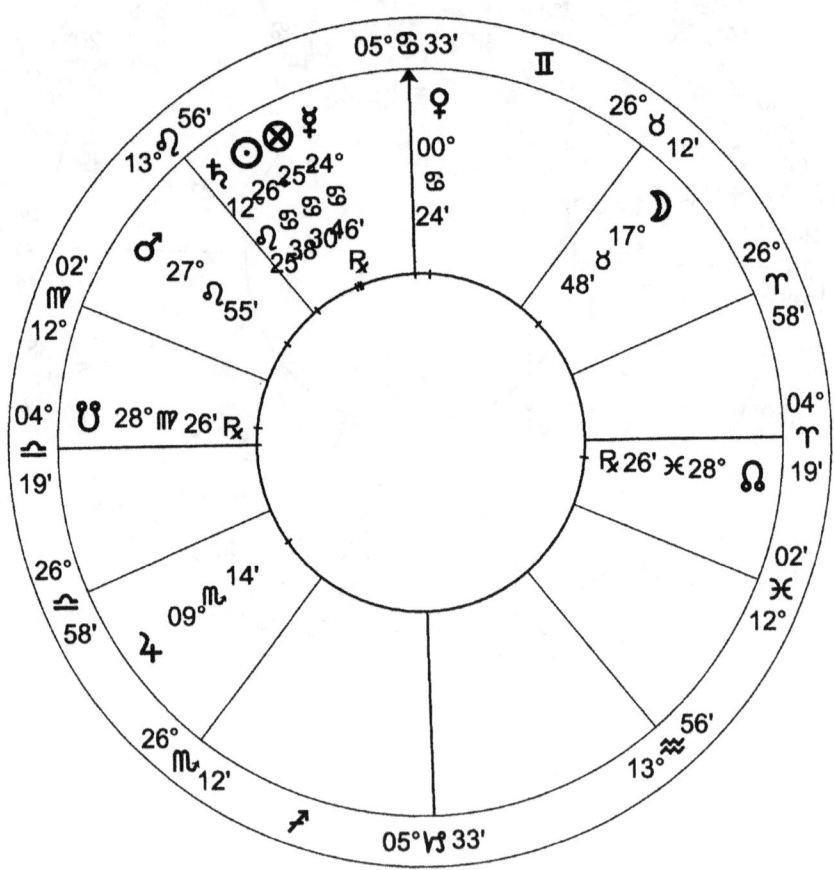

Tenth House Matters - Sport   519

The Champions League 2007

My son gave me the names of the eight remaining teams in the Champions League at the end of March 2007, the final due to take place in May 2007. I considered the Questions for Chelsea, PSV Eindhoven, Liverpool, Manchester United, Bayern Munich, Roma, Valencia and AC Milan. The chart which showed a win and which I picked was for AC Milan.

Will AC Milan win the Champions League?
5 April 2007 13.07 BST. 50N16 04W48

The Sun, ascendant ruler, is in his exaltation and makes a conjunction with the tenth house cusp. The power of a planet in conjunction with a cusp cannot be underestimated. The Sun applies to a trine with powerful Jupiter dignified in his domicile in the fortunate fifth house. Jupiter is received by the Sun, being in his triplicity. This is sufficient testimony to produce a win.

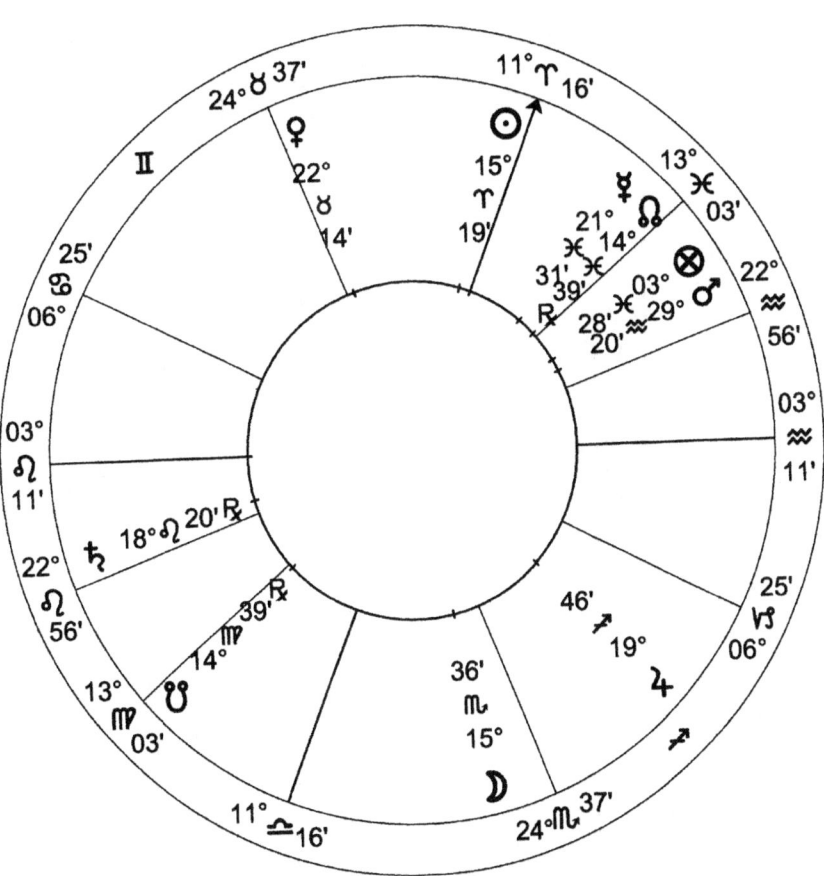

Although the Moon applies to a square with Saturn and an opposition with Venus, the Sun makes a trine with Saturn and they have a reception, which helps remove the ill-will of Saturn. In addition, Jupiter's trine with Saturn (although separating), is helpful. Venus is not a hindrance because she is dignified and received by the Moon in her exaltation.

This chart was the best of all the remaining eight charts and was, therefore, chosen as the winner. And so it was. Most importantly, unlike the remaining charts, this chart reflects the timing accurately, because the Moon perfects her aspect with Venus in seven degrees: the final was seven weeks after the Question.

AC Milan won 2-1 against Liverpool on Wednesday 23 May 2007.

References

1. Lilly p.86.

Afterword

I hope that the reader or student has derived useful insights from this book: from the writings of astrologers before us and from an understanding of their methods. These methods can be applied successfully to charts of the present and future, just as they could in the past.

The amount of information to process in the evaluation of any chart can be confusing, but with time and experience, the process becomes clearer and easier. I have little to add, except to emphasise once more that it is the chart in its entirety which contains the good fortune or otherwise. I believe that Ptolemy is right when he states that it is the ascendant, the Sun, the Moon, the Lot of Fortune and their rulers, which are most important and which are the principal places of significance.

In an overall sense however, chart judgement is derived from a careful evaluation of the strength of the Fortunes (including any benefics), as compared with the strength of the Infortunes (including any malefics).

> Fortunate Planets in fortunate Places of the Figure, befriending the Significators, give hopes of the business enquired after: If infortunate Planets being in unfortunate Places of the Figure, shall afflict the Significators of the business, it will not come to anything.[1]

As astrologers, we need to carefully evaluate the methods of the past and adapt them to the present. It is of course true, as Annabella Kitson reminds us, that

> The past was not all admirable, nor are those who explore astrology's history rejecting the present or the need for adapting to it. [2]

However, it is also true that if we wish to incorporate astrology's history in any way at all, we need to have a thorough knowledge of that history. This is a theme which I have attempted to take up, expand upon and emphasise throughout this book.

Robert Zoller in his *Tools & Techniques of the Medieval Astrologers*, tells us why it is so important to reinvestigate the methods of past astrologers

> In this way, we reconnect with the perceptual mode of the ancients and are instructed thereby in the principles underlying their world.[3]

He tells us that we do not do this in order to re-enter the past, but instead, to re-enter the future and "...to do homage to those who went before us thereby making our efforts possible".

To conclude on an optimistic note, I would like to believe that the future for traditional astrology and astrologers is as hopeful as Annabella Kitson envisages

> For memory of things past is a means of formulating and enhancing selfhood. I suggest that the astrological community needs this enhancement, will earn it abundantly, and will pass on a rich inheritance to those who come after us.[4]

References

1. Gadbury p.288.
2. Annabella Kitson, 'The Uses and Abuses of the History of Astrology: The Astrologer's Reputation, Motivation and Roles, Part II', *The Astrological Journal*, March/April 1995, Vol.37, No.2, p.129.
3. Robert Zoller, *Tools & Techniques of the Medieval Astrologers*, p.134.
4. Kitson, as above.

BIBLIOGRAPHY

Abu 'Ali Al-Khayyat. *The Judgments of Nativities*. Tr. James H Holden from the Latin version of John of Seville. The American Federation of Astrologers, AZ., 1988.

Abu Ma'shar. *The Abbreviation of the Introduction to Astrology*. Ed. and tr. Charles Burnett (1994). Additional Annotations Charles Burnett, Geoffrey Cornelius, Graeme Tobyn, Vernon Wells. ARHAT Publications, Restmont, VA., 1997.

Al Biruni, Abu'l-Rayhan Muhammad Ibn Ahmad. *The Book of Instruction in the Elements of the Art of Astrology* (1029). Tr. R Ramsay Wright, University of Toronto. Luzac and Co. London, 1934.

Ball, Richard. *An Astrolo-Physical Compendium or A Brief Introduction to Astrology* (1697). Ballantrae Reprint, Ontario, Canada.

Barclay, Olivia. *Horary Astrology Rediscovered. A Study in Classical Astrology*. Schiffer, PA., 1990.

―――― 'The Need for Traditional Astrology'. Transcript of the Carter Memorial lecture delivered at the 1996 Exeter conference. *The Astrological Journal*, Vol 39, no 1. Jan/Feb 1997.

―――― 'A Natal Astrologer's Guide To Horary'. *Transit*, The Magazine of the Astrological Association. Issue No. 42 August 1983 and Issue No. 44 February 1984.

Bonatus, Guido. *The Astrologer's Guide or Anima Astrologiae*. Tr. Henry Coley, 1675. Ed. William Lilly. Republished W.C.E. Serjeant 1886. Republished by The National Astrological Library, WA., 1953.

Boudet, Jean-Patrice. 'From Baghdad to Civitas Solis', from a handout at the Warburg Institute conference, London, November 2008.

Campion, Nicholas. *The Astrologers' Quarterly*, The Astrological Lodge of London Summer 1993.

―――― 'An Introduction to the History of Astrology'. Institute For The Study Of Cycles In World Affairs, Bromley, 1982.

―――― *The Great Year. Astrology, Millenarianism and History in the Western Tradition*. Penguin Arkana, London, 1994.

Carter, Charles. *The Astrological Aspects*. L N Fowler Ltd, London, 1930.

―――― *The Zodiac and The Soul*. The Theosophical Publishing House Ltd, London, 1928.

Coley, Henry. *Clavis Astrologiae Elimata, or A Key to the whole Art of Astrology* (1676). Ballantrae Reprints, Canada, 1988.

Cornelius, Geoffrey. *The Moment of Astrology, Origins in Divination*, Penguin Arkana, London, 1994.

Culpeper, Nicholas. *Astrologicall Judgement of Diseases From the Decumbiture of the sick* (1655). Ballantrae Reprint, Ontario, Canada.

Curry, Patrick. *A Confusion of Prophets. Victorian and Edwardian Astrology.* Collins and Brown Ltd, London, 1992.

_____ *Prophecy and Power. Astrology in Early Modern England.* Polity Press, Cambridge UK, in association with Basil Blackwell, Oxford, 1989.

Dariot, Claudius. *A breefe and most easie Introduction to the Astrologicall judgement of the Starres.* Tr. Fabian Wither, Thomas Purfoote, London, 1598.

Dorotheus of Sidon. *Carmen Astrologicum.* Tr. and ed. David Pingree. BSB B.G. Teubner Verlagsgesellschaft, Leipzig, 1976.

_____*Carmen Astrologicum.* Tr. David Pingree. Ascella Publications, 1993.

Ezra, Abraham Ibn. *Sefer Ha'Moladot.* Translation and commentary by Meira Epstein. From a handout at the Warburg Institute conference London, November, 2008.

_____ *The Beginning Of Wisdom.* Ed. Raphael Levy and Francisco Cantera. The John Hopkins Press and Oxford University Press 1939, reprinted by Ascella Publications.

Fagan, Cyril. *Zodiacs Old and New.* Robert Anscombe and Co, London, 1951.

Gadbury, John. *The Doctrine of Nativities.* Giles Calvert, William Larnar and Daniel White, London, 1658.

Gauquelin, Michel. *Astrology and Science,* Tr. James Hughes. Peter Davies, London, 1966.

_____ *The Cosmic Clocks.* Peter Owen, London, 1967.

Granite, Robert Hurzt. *The Fortunes of Astrology.* Astro Computing Services, CA.,1981.

Hand, Robert. *Night and Day. Planetary Sect in Astrology.* ARHAT Publications, Restmont, VA., 1995.

Heindel, Max and Heindel, August Foss. *The Message of the Stars. An Esoteric Exposition of Medical and Natal Astrology, Explaining the Arts of Prediction and Diagnosis of Disease.* The Rosicrucian Fellowship, L N Fowler & Co, London, 1919.

Jeans, James, 1948. *The Stars In Their Courses.* Cambridge University Press, Cambridge and London, 1948.

Kennedy, E. S. and Pingree, David. *The Astrological History of Masha'allah.* Harvard University Press, Cambridge, MA., 1971.

Kitson, Annabella, ed. *History and Astrology, Clio and Urania confer.* Unwin Hyman, London, 1989.

Lehman, J. Lee. *Essential Dignities.* Whitford Press, PA., 1989.

_____ 'Horary Two Generations before Lilly: A Review and Discussion', *The Astrologers' Quarterly,* Spring 1992 Vol. 62 No. 2.

Lilly, William. *Christian Astrology.* Tho. Brudenell for John Partridge and Humphrey Blunden, London, 1647.

_____*Christian Astrology.* Regulus Publishing, 1984.

Lindsay, Jack. *Origins of Astrology.* Frederick Muller Ltd, London, 1971.

Maimonides, Moses. *The Correspondence Between the Rabbis of Southern France and Maimonides about Astrology.* Tr. with annotations by Meira B. Epstein. ARHAT Publications, Restmont, VA., 1998.

Manilius, Marcus. *Astronomica*. Tr. G P Goold. Loeb Classical Library, VT., 1977.

Masha'allah. *On Reception*. Ed. and tr. Robert Hand. ARHAT, Reston, VE. 1998.

Maternus, Firmicus. *Ancient Astrology Theory and Practice. Matheseos Libri VIII.* Tr. Jean Rhys Bram, Noyes Press, NJ., 1975.

McCaffery, Ellen. *Astrology: Its History and Influence in the Western World*. Charles Scribner's Sons, New York, 1942.

Morin de Villefranche, Jean Baptiste. The 21st Book of *The Astrologia Gallica* published as *Astrosynthesis: The Rational System of Horoscope Interpretation*. Tr. Lucy Little, Emerald Books, New York, 1974.

—— *Cornerstones of Astrology*. Friedrich "Sinbad" Schwickert and Adolf Weiss Series, Morin de Villefranche, Sangreal Foundation Inc, TX, 1972.

Neugebauer and van Hoesen. *Greek Horoscopes*. The American Philosophical Society, PA., 1959.

North, J. D. *Horoscopes and History*. Warburg Institute, University of London, London, 1986.

Pagan, Isabelle. *From Pioneer to Poet*. The Theosophical Publishing House, London, 1954.

Partridge, John. *Opus Reformatum or a Treatise of Astrology* (1693). Awnshank and John Churchill. Reprinted by Ascella Publications.

—— *Vade Mecum*, (1679). William Bromwich, London, reprinted by Ascella Publications.

Placidus de Titis. *Primum Mobile* (1657). Tr. John Cooper. Introduction by Michael Baigent, The Institute for the Study of Cycles in World Affairs, Bromley, 1983.

Proctor, Richard A. *Easy Star Lessons*. Chatto and Windus, London, 1882.

Ptolemy, Claudius. *Tetrabiblos*. Tr. F E Robbins, Loeb Classical Library, MA., 1980.

Ptolemy, Claudius. *Tetrabiblos*. Tr. J M Ashmand. Foulsham & Co, London.

Ramesey, William. *Astrologia Restaurata or Astrology Restored: Being An Introduction to the General and Chief Part of the Language of the Stars* (1653). Ascella Publications.

Saunders, Richard. *The Astrological Judgement and Practice of Physick* (1677). Ballantrae Reprints, Canada.

Simmonite, W. J. *Horary Astrology, the key to scientific prediction, being the prognostic astronomer*. Additions by John Story and further edited by Ernest A Grant. American Federation of Astrologers, AZ.,1950.

Simmonite, W. *Complete Arcana of Astral Philosophy or the Celestial Philosopher*.

Smith, R.C. *The Astrologer of the Nineteenth Century or the Master Key of Futurity, being a Complete System of Astrology, Geomancy & Occult Science*. William Charlton Wright, London, 1825.

Thorndike, Lynn. *A History of Magic and Experimental Science*. The Sixteenth Century Columbia University Press, New York, 1941.

Volguine, Alexandre. *The Ruler of the Nativity*. ASI Publishers Inc, New York, 1973.

Ward, Sue. 'The Houses in Traditional Astrology', *The Astrological Journal*, Vol. 44 No. 4 July/August 2002.

Wharton, George. *Gesta Britannorum*, (1657). London.

Worsdale, John. *Celestial Philosophy or Genethliacal Astronomy*, Longman & Co, London,1798.

Zadkiel, *An Introduction to Astrology and A Grammar of Astrology*. George Bell & Sons, London and New York, 1893.

Zoller, Robert. *The Lost Key to Prediction: The Arabic Parts in Astrology*. Inner Traditions, New York, 1980.

―――― *Tools & Techniques of the Medieval Astrologers*. Ascella Publications.

INDEX

A

abscissio luminis, 334, *see also* abscission or return of light
abscission, 310, 333-336, *see also* return
Abu Ali Al-Khayyat, 34, 51-52, 277, 285-286, 315, 316, 317
Abu Mashar, viii, 11-15, 16-29, 65-71, 97, 103-104, 108, 138-140, 145-146, 149, 159, 170, 263, 274, 302, 303, 305, 306, 307, 309-311, 315, 335-336, 337-338, 421
accidental debility, xxi, (table 135), 136-145, 153-159, 161-163, 355-357
accidental dignity, xxi, 10, 135-152, (table 135), 161-163, 264, 294, 317, 355-357, 395
Adelard of Bath, 170
adulthood, 36, 61, *see also* quarter
afflicted, xxi
afterword, 521
Al Biruni, viii, xx, xiv, 1, 2, 5, 6, 7, 8, 9, 16, 18, 20, 26, 28, 29, 39, 41, 44-49, 52, 63, 76, 79, 80, 81, 83, 90, 92, 95, 101-102, 105, 106, 114, 117, 119, 122-124, 128, 130, 136, 138, 140, 153, 157, 158, 170-171, 181, 214, 274, 285, 293-294, 307, 308, 330, 331, 333-334, 336, 462
Alchabitius, *see* Al Qabasi
house, 33
Aldebaran, 317
Al Kindi, xi, 236, 438, 440
almutem, 188, *see also* almuten
almuten, xxi, 152, 163, 185-193, 226-227
of a chart, xxi, 185-189
of a house, xxi, 189-193
Al Qabasi, 137, 138, 336
angle, xxi, 34-35, 40-42, 91, 93, 146, 158, 271, 277, 296, 301, 304-305, 332
distant from, 153
animal, 16-28
Antares, 317
Antiochus, 139
antiscia, xxi, 93-94, table 94, chart 95, 147, 163, 265, 331
antiscion, *see* antiscia
aphorism, 418
appearance, 16-28, 44, 222-226, *see also* description
application, xxi, 97, 101-102, 104-105
direct, 101
relaying of, 280
through retrograde motion, 101
through mutual application, 102
Aquarius, 70, 71
Arabian, iii, 236
Arabic, xi, xii, xxi, 33, 50, 182
Arabs, 190
Aries, 65, 66
ascendant, *see* ascending degree
ascending degree, xxii, 34
early or late, 233-234
Saturn in, 236-237
ascension,
long or right, 65, 305-306
short or oblique, 65, 305-306
aspect, xxii, 35, 90-108, 153, 169, 265, 278, 279-280, 299-300, 300-306, 325
and approach and departure, 271
and beholding, 297, 298, 324, 325
and denial of perfection, 325-328
and dignity, 145-146
and perfection, 300-306
and reception, 177-178
order of in time, 280
partill and platick, 99, 100
relaying of applications, 280
signification through, 212-213, 215-216
the power of, 274-277, 278
with benevolent fixed stars, 148
with houses and house cusps, 281
with Jupiter or Venus, 149
with malevolent fixed stars, 157-158
with reception and mutual reception, 177-178

with Saturn, Mars or the south node, 158
with the Lot of Fortune, 150-151
with the Moon, 268
with the north node, 149
with the Sun, 136-140, 232
Asteratus, 122
autumnal, 39, 61, *see also* quarter

B

Babylonian, vii, 1, 23, 122, 128
Bad Daemon, 38, 43, *see also* house
Bad Fortune, 38, 43, *see also* house
Baigent, Michael, 1
baleful, 51, 303
Ball, Richard, 213, 235, 240, 325
Barclay, Olivia, x, viii, xv, 17, 18, 22, 28, 48, 65-71, 73, 100, 119, 132, 231, 245
Beginning of Death, 38, 43, *see also* house
behold, 96, 173, 297, 298, 324, 325
Bellatrix, 317
benefactor, 130
benefic, xxii, 272, 283, 315
beneficent, xx, 5-6, *see also* benefic
besiegement, xxii, 150, 153, 158, 315, 337-338
bicorporeal, 61
bird, 16-28
blood, 213
body,
    signs and parts of, 59
    signs, planets and parts of (table), 60
Bonatti, Guido, viii, x, xiv, 2-3, 5-6, 46, 62, 63, 80, 100, 103, 104, 106, 112, 130-131, 137, 138, 148-149, 150, 154-156, 183, 229-230, 233-234, 236-238, 245-246, 261, 262, 264-265, 267, 270, 280-281, 287, 294-297, 298, 308-310, 311, 315-317, 319, 322-325, 327, 330, 331-332, 334, 336, 337, 339, 352, 415, 420, 485
Boudet, Jean-Patrice, 149
Burnett, Charles, 97-98, 139, 140, 170, 303
business partnerships, 483-484
Bustros, Michel, 187

C

cadent house, xxii, 40-42, 155, 305, 321, 323-324, 331
cadent planet, xxii,
    from its domicile, 155, 395
camino solis, 138, *see also* cazimi
Campanella, Tommaso, 149
Campanus house, 33
Campion, Nicholas, x, 258
Cancer, 67
Capricorn, 70
Caput Algol, 149, 151, 157, 323, 461
Caput Draconis, xxiii, *see also* north node
Cardan, Jerome, 25, 29, 147, 216, 261
cardine, 35-36, 293
cardinal point, 34, *see also* cardine
career, *see* tenth house
Cauda Draconis, xxiii, *see also* south node
cazimi, xviii, 138, 139, 140, 141, 304, 327
celestial spheres, xx
Centiloquium, 148, 294
Chaldean, (terms), 122
chart, xxiii,
childhood, 61 *see also* quarter
choler, 213
choleric, 39, *see also* quarter
cities, 65-71
Civitas Solis, 149
cold and dry, 39
Coley, Henry, x, xiii, xv, 46, 167, 181, 185, 219-220, 222, 261-262, 438
collection of light, xxiii, 310, 312, 313, 332
colours, 43
    and houses, 44-50
    and planets, 4, 16-28
    and signs, 62
combust, *see* combustion
combustion, xxiii, 86-87, 137, 139, 140, 144-145, 153, 154, 164, 232, 237-238, 304, 311, 321-322, 331, 326-327, 343
committing disposition, xxiii, 90, 103, 174, 267, 309, 311, 331
common,
    planet, (Mercury), xx
    ruler, 50-52, 76-77
    sign, xxii, 61-62, 287

communion, 173, 303, *see also* reception
congenial, 115, 128, 155,
  quarter or quadrant, 148,
conjunction, xxiv, 90, 92, 137, 148, 149, 150, 151, 157, 274-277, 278, 301-303, 325-327
considerations before judgement, 229-238, 246
containment, *see* besiegement
contention, 83, 157
contra-antiscion or contra-antiscium, *see* contra-antiscia
contra-antiscia, xxiv, 93, 163
contrariety, 336
co-operation, 9-10, 91-92, 267
Copernicus, vii
corde solis, 138, *see also* cazimi
Cor Leonis, *see* Regulus
Cornelius, Geoffrey, x, xiv, xv, 229, 245, 248-256
co-significator, *see* signification
countries, 16-29, 65-71
Culpeper, Nicholas, 39, 59, 65, 395, 414, 415
Curry, Patrick, x
cusp, xxiv, 146-147, 277, 281, 284, 296-297
cutting, abscission or return of light, 333-336

D

Daemonie, 37, *see also* house
Daemonium, 37-38, *see also* house
Dariot, Claudius, 17, 50-51, 52, 53-55, 76, 80, 111, 157, 172, 173, 181, 190-193, 198, 221, 250, 262, 309-311
  chart 310, 313-314
day, xxiv
  of week, 16-29
Dea, 37, *see also* house
debilis receptio, 173, *see also* reception
debility, see essential debility and accidental debility
decanate, 111, 124, *see also* face
declination, xxiv
decreasing,
  in light, 118, 141
  quarter or quadrant, 39-40
decumbiture, xxiv, 414
degree, xxiv,
  ascending, late or early, 233-234

azimene, pitted, smoky, dark, 156
  bright and dark, 65
  combust, 154
  increasing or diminishing in fortune, 65
  injurious to the eyes, 65
  late degrees, Moon in, 234
  male and female, 65
  masculine and feminine, 190
dejection, 130, 179 *see also* essential debility
desart, 155
descension, 154
description, 30, 219
  and radicality, 213, 230-232
  and signs, 63-65, 65-71
determinism, 248-254, chart 249
detriment, xxv, 128-129
Deus, 37, *see also* house
dexter, xxv, 92, 96, 97
dignities, *see* essential dignity and accidental dignity
direct, xxv, 100, 147
direct or indirect Question, 241
direction,
  and houses, 40
  and signs, 62
disease and sickness, 16-28, 60, 64, 65-71, 203, 232, 414-421, *see also* sixth house
  Questions concerning, 422-436
disharmony between planets, 9-10
dishonor, 131
dispositor, xxv, 44, 129, 152, 174, 179-181, 223, 317, 325, 343
dispute, 47, 128, 305, 306, 464-467, *see also* seventh house
  Questions concerning, 468-482
Ditis Ianua, 37, *see also* house
diurnal, xx, xxv, 1, 50-53, 76-78, 79, 80-82, 83-85, 86, 113, 116, 120-122, 144, 190
division, 34, 57
dodecatropos, 37
domicile, xxv, 111, 114-116, 128, 169, 238, 324
dominium, 190, *see also* almuten
Dorotheus, 6, 41, 50, 54, 94, 139-140, 152
dragon's head, *see* north node

dragon's tail, *see* south node
Dunlop, Archie, 237-238

E

eclipse, 164, 266, 288, 321
ecliptic, 27
Egyptian, 122-123, (system of terms)
eighth house, 48
Election, ix, xiv, xxv, 38, 55, 154, 219, 293-294, 321
elevated, xxvi
eleventh house, 49
Elliot, Rose, 257
enmity between planets, 7-9
Epstein, Meira, ix, xv, 258
Equal house, 33
equipollent, 95
essential debility, xxvi, 10,111,128-132, 161-163, 355-357
    mutual reception in debility, 175-177
essential dignity, xxvi, 10, 111-128, 161-163, 264, 265, 294, 317, 355-357, 395,
    table, 113
estivall, 39, 61, *see also* quarter
evasion, 333
evasus, 138
evening star, 85
exaltation, xxvi, 117-119, 128
exchange of places, 181-182 *see also* reception

F

face, xxvi, 124-125, 128
    table of, 125
Fagan, Cyril, 119
fall, xxvi, 129-130
fallen amiss, 40, *see also* house
falling house, 40, 321
familiarity, 330, 331
family ties and social connections, 11
feminine
    degree, 190
    planet, 80-83, 131, 190
    quarter, xxvi, 39, 157
    sign, xx, xxvi, 39, 58, 80-83, 113, 131
feral, xxvi, 108, 155, 159

fertility, 63, 195, 393-399, *see also* pregnancy
fifth house, 46-47, 393
    Questions concerning, 400-412
first house, 43-44, 268
    almuten of, 192-193
first lord of the triplicity, *see* triplicity
fixed sign, xxvii, 61-62, 267, 287, 298, 337
fixed star, 21, 148, 151, 153, 157, 222, 224, 295-296, 316-317, 322-323, 441
fortis receptio, 173, *see also* reception
fortitudes, *see* essential dignities and accidental dignities
Fortuna, 37, *see also* house
Fortuna Felix, 37, *see also* house
Fortune (⊕), xxvii, 5-6, 104, 112-113, 132, 137, 145-147, 149, 150, 158, 177-178, 197, 199, 217-219, 225, 227, 230, 238, 242-243, 248, 252, 265, 268, 270, 272-273, 274, 275, 282-283, 293, 298, 299, 312, 315, 324, 325, 326, 328, 329, 332, 340, 341, 342, 351-352, 353, 374, 376, 395, 414, 520
fourth house, 45-46, 314, 373,
    almuten of, 191-192
    Questions concerning, 377-391
friendship (between planets), 7-9
fruitful, 393, *see also* prolific
frustration, xxvii, 332
fusion, 303

G

Gadbury, John, 17, 19, 21, 23, 46, 138, 148, 181, 230, 231, 232, 236, 263, 273, 287, 395-396, 440-441, 487-489
Galileo, vii
Gate of Hades, 38, *see also* house
Gauquelin, Michel, 48, 256-257, 268
Gemini, 66
geniture, 36, *see also* Nativity
giving back, *see* rendering
God, 37, 43, *see also* house
Goddess, 38, 43, *see also* house
Good Daemon, 37, 43, 49, *see also* house
Good Fortune, 38, 43, *see also* house
Greater Fortune, 17, 49, 91, *see also* Fortune

Greater Infortune, 16, 91, *see also* Infortune
Greek, 76, 93, 98, 108, 119, 124, 187, 188, 245

H

halb, 81, 146, 147
Haly, xii, 396
Hand, Robert, xi, xiii, 23, 40, 46, 54, 76, 79, 98, 120, 130, 138, 150, 167, 174, 176-177, 182, 204-205, 210, 235, 243, 250
hayyiz, xxvii, 80-82, 112, 130, 147, 148
    in a contrary, 82, 153
hayz, *see* hayyiz
head of the dragon, *see* north node
health and sickness,
    Questions concerning, 422-437
Heller, Joachim, 315
helper, 294-297
    manifest, 296-297
    secret, 295-296
Hephaestio of Thebes, 98
herbs, 16-28
Hercules, 317
Hesperus, 23
hibernal, 61, *see also* quarter
hinderer, 322-324
    manifest, 323
    secret, 323
Hindu, 8, 117, 122, 124, 129
Holden, James, 34, 285-286, 317
honor, 111, 131
horizon, 39, 78, 298
horoscope, xxvii, 43, 150
horoskopos, 34
house, xxvii, 33-55, 146-147, 156, 205-210, 220-222, 268, 273, 280-281, 284-285, 313-315, 336-337
Hyde, Maggie, 257
hylegiacall, 196

I

Ibn Ezra, Abraham, xv, xxii, xxxi, 42, 51, 92, 94, 147, 156, 170, 171, 188, 231, 267, 301, 302, 303, 304, 339
ill-dignified, 16-28
illness, *see* disease
impedited, xxvii, 299

imum coeli, 46
inconjunct, xxvii, 96, 128, 153
increasing
    in light, 141, 163
    quarter or quadrant, 39
indications (planetary), 6-7, *see also* testimony
infancy, 36, *see also* quarter
infant, 39, *see also* quarter
Inferior, xxvii, 1, 85-87, 138, 141-144, 148, 157, 159, 170-171, 269, 280, 308, 312, 331, 333-338
Infortune (An), xxviii, 5-6, 98, 104, 112-113, 132, 137, 145-146, 153, 154, 155, 156, 158, 177-178, 197, 199, 200, 225, 227, 230, 238, 242-243, 268, 272-273, 275, 282-283, 293, 298, 299, 312, 317, 319, 321, 323, 324, 325, 326, 328, 329, 337, 340, 351-352, 374-376, 397, 398, 414, 441, 467
intercepted sign, 214, 351
    and signification, 214
interrogation, ix, 177, 182, 240
intervalla, 36
intervention, 333

J

Joy, xxviii, 1, 2-4, 117, 147-148
    by house, 3, 44-50
    by position, 3
    by quarter, 4
    by sign, 3
joyned, 92, 347
judge, 466
judgement, 285-286, 287-288, 289, 317, *see also* Part Two
    caution in, 285, 340

K

katarche, 249, 251, 252, 254
Kitson, Annabella, xiii, xv, 521
Kollerstrom, Nicholas, 66

L

Laboris, 38, *see also* house
lady, (of a house), xxviii

latitude, xxviii
law-suit, *see* dispute
Lehman, Lee, 54, 179, 182
Leo, 67, 68
Leovitius, 223-224
Lesser Fortune, 23, 91, 116, *see also* Fortune
Lesser Infortune, 19, 47, 91, 116, *see also* Infortune
liberality, 171, *see also* reception
Libra, 68, 69
lights, *see* luminaries
Lilly, William, viii, ix, x, xi, xii, xiv, 15-29, 34, 39, 43-50, 52, 54, 63, 65-71, 80, 81, 98, 99, 100, 102, 104, 105-106, 107, 116, 119, 121, 124, 125, 129, 131, 136-138, 141, 146, 147, 149, 150, 156, 157, 159-163, 174, 178, 181-183, 185, 188, 204, 207, 209, 212, 215-216, 220-221, 222-226, 229, 232, 233-238, 241, 244, 245, 248-256, 261-264, 274-275, 281, 287-288, 299-301, 304-308, 311-312, 319, 323, 326, 349-351, 367, 373-376, 393-399, 414-421, 438-441, 464-467, 485-490, 483-484
limit, 111, *see also* term
longitude, xxviii, 105, 150
lord,
    of the geniture, 185, 226, *see also* almuten
    of a house, xviii, 190
    of a triplicity, 53-54
lot, xxviii, 34, 76
Lot of Fortune, xxviii, 10, 34, 128, 135, 149, 150-152, table 151, 163, 196, 227, 266, 281, 282, 315-316, 349, 521
Lot of Sickness, 421
Lower Midheaven, 37, 43 *see also* house
Lucifer, 23
luminaries, xx, xxviii, 115, 135-136, 222, 224, 266, 316
    relationship with, 91

M

Maimonides, Moses, ix, 258
malefic, xxix, 5, 35, 153, 272, 283, 315
maleficent, xx, 5-6, *see also* malefic
manhood, 39, *see also* quarter

Manilius, Marcus, 35-38
marriage, 47, 195, 201-202, 210-211, 226, 251-252, 255, 311-312, 438-441
    Questions concerning, 442-462
masculine,
    degree, 190
    planet, xx, xxix, 80-83, 131, 190
    quarter, xxix, 39, 157
    sign, xxix, 58, 80-83, 113, 131
Masha'allah, viii, xii, 40, 41, 42, 46, 98, 99, 107, 130, 156, 159, 167, 169, 176-178, 182, 203-206, 209-210, 235, 240-241, 243-244, 245, 250, 257, 262, 273, 280, 304-305, 308, 314, 324, 352
Maternus, Firmicus, 77, 83-85, 87, 93-94, 112, 119, 179-180, 187-188, 290
matutine, 85-87, 143
medieval, ix, xi
medium coeli, 49
melancholic, 39, *see also* quarter
melancholy, 213
meridian, 39
Midheaven, 37, 43, 163, *see also* house
Miller, Kaye, 257
mineral, 16-28
Mirach, 267
mirth, 265
missing
    animals, 72-73
    items, 71-72, 92
moiety, 98, *see also* orb
Montulmo, xii, 46
Moon, 26-29, 140-141, 153-156, 201, 203-204, 204-206, 231, 234-235, 266-268, 269, 415
    and ascendant ruler, 204-206
    phases of, 140
Morin, Jean-Baptiste, viii, xii, 2, 7, 9-15, 29, 42, 43-49, 52, 57, 76, 91-94, 108, 116, 121-122, 129, 130, 131, 138, 147, 159, 172-173, 175, 180-181, 186, 198, 206-207, 214, 216-219, 254, 265-267, 268-273, 277-280, 281-285, 288, 302, 303, 315, 325-326
Morinus house, 33
morning star, 85

motion, 4, 16-29, 100, 106, 147, 156, 160, 315, 319, 338-339
moveable sign, xxix, 61-62, 287
Muller, Johannes, 33, *see also* Regiomontanus
multiple Questions, 247-248
mutual reception, *see* reception

N

nadir, 35, 46, 153
Nativity, vii, ix, xiv, xxix, 24, 38, 44-50, 51, 55, 63, 92, 94, 108, 112, 130, 131, 132, 138, 140, 148, 150, 154, 164, 167, 179, 185, 187, 188, 195, 196, 203, 207, 213, 216-217, 219, 224, 227, 229, 236, 262-263, 266, 276-277, 278, 279, 285-286, 290, 293, 301, 312, 315, 321, 337
nature,
    of a contrary, 153, 294, 322
    of houses, 42-50
    of planets, 2, 15-29, 130
    of signs, 65-71
    of signs and sect, 79-80
ninth house, 48-49
nocturnal, 1, 50-53, 76-78, 79, 80-83, 83-85, 86, 113, 115, 120-122, 132, 144, 190, 256
    chart, xxix
    planet, xx, xxx
    sign, xxx
north node, 10, 27, 46, 149, 151, 153, 155, 213, 374

O

oblique or short ascension, 65
occident, 37
occidental, xxx, 39, 141-144,
    its affect on appearance, 222-223
    (table 143), 270
occupation and profession, 11-13, 485-490
    Questions concerning, 491-504
oecodespotes, 187
old age, 36, 39, 61, *see also* quarter
opposition, 91, 92, 136-137, 238, 306, 328
orb, xxx, 16-29, 97-99, 104-108
oriental, xxx, 39, 141-144
    affect on appearance, 222-223
    (table 143), 270

Origanus, xii, 44
out of sect, 82-83, 459, 460, 462

P

part, 35, *see also* place
partill, xxx, 99-100, 213
Partridge, John, 149, 158, 181, 213, 222-224, 287
parts of the body, 59-60, (table 60), 415-416
Paulus, Alexandrinus, 98, 105, 150
peregrine, xi, xxx, 111, 128, 130-131, 164, 179, 325
perfection, xxx, 243, 300-318
    denial of, 325-337
Persian, 119, 124, 128, 144
phlegm, 213
phlegmatic, 39, *see also* quarter
Pico, Giovanni (Mirandola), xi
Pisces, 71
place, 35-38, *see also* house
places, 16-28, 65-71, 73-74
Placidus de Tito, 1
Placidus house, 33
planet, xx, 1-31, 91-92, 111-132, 135-159
    according to sect, 83-85
    angular and in the cusp, 277
    approach and departure, 271
    aspects with houses and house cusps, 281
    changes in situation and action, 144-145
    conflicting influences, 286
    in opposition with own domicile, 238
    in the same house, 284-285
    motion and movement, 4, 100-106, 147, 156, 160, 315, 319, 338-339
    natural properties and signification, 15-29
    natural rank, 269
    position, 146-147, 156, 206-211, 265, 266, 273, 284-285, 313-315, 336-337
    prevailing, 271
    principal signification and analogies, 10-15
    ruling two houses, 280-281
    strength, 161-164, 178-179, 268-271
    their terrestrial state, 270-271
    their zodiacal state, 270
planetary ruler of the hour, 30-31
    harmonising with, 232-233, 353

plants, 16-28
platick, 99-100
poles, 42 *see also* house
Porphyry house, 33
Porta Laboris, 37, *see also* house
Portal of Toil, 38, *see also* house
precedence of dignity, 126, 128
pregnancy, 46-47, 63, 195, 198-199, 200, 218-219, 274-275, 393-399
    year of, 16-29
    Questions concerning, 400-412
prevention, 330, 336
prison, 113, *see also* essential debility
Proctor, Richard, 157
prohibition, xxx, 340
    bodily, 328-329
    through aspect, 329-330
prolific, 63, 195
property, 46, 373-391
prorogative, 150, 196, 227, 266, 521
psychological horary, 254-257
Ptolemy, Claudius, vii, viii, xi, xxviii, 1, 5, 29, 30, 35-38, 42, 43, 48, 50, 52, 77, 93, 105, 114, 117-119, 120, 122, 123-124, 148, 150, 155, 196-197, 216, 227, 235, 266, 294, 304, 305, 521
pushing counsel, 104
pushing nature, 103
pushing power, 103
pushing two natures, 103-104

Q

quadrant, *see* quarter
quality, 9-10
    antagonistic, 9
    of sign, 65-71
    vital, 9
quarter, 34, 36, 39-40, 61, 145, 147-148, 153
    decreasing, 39
    increasing, 39
    planets in congenial, 148
    planets in uncongenial, 157
Querent, xi, xxx, 175, 176, 201-203, 229-231, 240-258, 262, 313, *see also* charts in Part Two

Quesited, xii, xxxi, 220, 231
Question, ix, 196, 240-258, 263

R

radical, 213, 229-238, 244-245, 230-232, 232-233
radix, 54
Ramesey, William, xiv-xv, 21, 91, 99, 100-101, 104, 115-116, 117-119, 120-125, 174, 181, 185, 189, 262, 306
rank, wealth and life events, 13-15
reception, xxix, xxxi, 126, 131-132, 167-183, 312-313
refranation, xxxi, 330
Regiomontanus, xxxi, 33-34, 40, 214
Regulus, 148-149, 151, 163, 316-317
rejoicing, 77
relationships, 438-441
    Questions concerning, 442-462
rendering, reflection, giving back or return of light, 309-311, 394
rendering up, giving back or return of virtue, 103, 251, 309, 310, 311-312, 331-332, 394, 467
restraint, 330, *see also* refranation
retrograde, xxxi, 100, 156-157, 311, 321-322, 326, 331, 335, 338
return, *see also* rendering
    satisfactory, 331
    unsatisfactory, 331
Rigel, 267
royal sign, *see* Regulus
ruler, 214-215, 266, 280-281
    and sign, 57,
    and signification, 195, 205
    common (partner or participating), 76-77
    natural, xxix, 215-219, 438
    of the ascendant, 204-205
    of the chart, 187, 193
    of the hour, 30, 232, 353
    of the triplicity, 50-54, 113, 120-122
rulership, 16-28, 206-211

S

Sagittarius, 69, 70
samim, 141, *see also* cazimi

sanguine, 39 *see also* quarter
Saunders, Richard, 173, 181
Scorpio, 69
season,
    and quarter, 61
    and signs, 61
second house, 44-45, 349
    almuten of, 190
    Questions concerning, 354-371
second lord of the triplicity, *see* triplicity
sect, xxxi, 76-87, 82-83
separation, xxxi, 104-106
Serjeant, William Eldon, xiii
seventh house, 47, 235-236, 438, 464
    Questions concerning, 218, 442-462, 468-482
sextile, 90-91, 92, 136, 149, 151, 304-305
Sibley, Ebenezer, 15-29
sign (zodiacal), xx, 38-39, 57-74, 339
sign-house, 34
signification, xxiv, xxxi, 10-15, 15-29, 29-30, 38, 41, 42-50, 50-53, 54-55, 63-65, 65-71, 195-227, 357, 360, 362, 365, 367, 370, 378, 381, 383, 385, 388, 391, 401, 403, 405, 408, 410, 412, 415, 423, 426, 428, 431, 434, 436, 438, 443, 446, 449, 451, 454, 457, 469, 472, 474, 477, 480, 482, 492, 495, 497, 499, 502, 504, 508, 510, 514,
significator, *see* signification
Simmonite, William Joseph, 197, 273, 374
Simpson, Shepherd, 34
sincerity, 246
sinister, xxxii, 92, 96, 97
Sirius, 267
sixth house, 47, 197, 414
    Questions concerning, 422-436
solitary, 108, 159
south node, 10, 27, 49, 151, 153, 155, 158, 213, 321, 337, 374
spaces, 36, *see also* house
Spica, 148, 151, 234-235, 297
sport, 506-520
square, 91, 136-137, 305-306, 328
station, 100, 101, 141, 157
    first, 100

    second, 100-101
stationary, xxxii, 157
Stilbon, 37
stones, 16-29
Story, John, 197
substitutes, 312
succedent house, xxxii, 40-42
Sun, 20-22, 136-140, 154, 266-268, 269, 326-327, 333-338
sunbeams, xxxii, 86-87, 137-138, 139, 153, 154, 327
Superior, xxxii, 1, 85-87, 138, 141-144, 148, 157, 159, 170-171, 269, 280, 303, 308, 312, 331, 336
supports, 42, *see also* house
suspect, *see* suspicion
suspicion, 153, *see also* accidental debility
symbol, *see* signification

T

tail of the dragon, *see* south node
tasmim, 144, *see also* cazimi
taste, 16-28
Taurus, 66
temple, 34, 36
tenth house, 49, 195, 208, 212, 231, 268, 269, 282, 314, 485
    almuten of, 189
    Questions concerning, 218-219, 491-504, 507-520
term, xxxii, 122-124, (table 123), 128, 154, 155, 321
terrestrial state, 270-271
testimony, (*see also* perfection), xxxii, 1, 159, 199, 241-243, 248, 263-265, 285-286, 288, 337, 358, 360, 362, 365, 367, 370-371, 378, 381, 383, 385, 388, 391, 401, 403, 405, 408, 410, 412, 423, 426, 428, 431, 434, 436, 443, 446, 449, 451, 454, 457, 469, 472, 474, 477, 480, 482, 492, 495, 497, 499, 502, 504, 508, 510, 514
    concurring, 317
    of good fortune, 293-300, 314-319
    of misfortune, 321-324, 336-340
    Questions to illustrate, 318, 344, 342, 317-319, 343, 341

relating to fifth house and pregnancy, 393-399
relating to fourth house and property, 373-376
relating to second house and wealth, 349-352
relating to seventh house and business partnerships, 483-484
relating to seventh house and disputes and lawsuits, 464-467
relating to seventh house and relationships, 438-441
relating to sixth house and health and sickness, 414-421
relating to sport, 506
relating to tenth house and career and achievement, 485-490
thief, 47, 130, 367-368
third house, 45
third lord of the triplicity, *see* triplicity
third party Questions, 257-258
throne, 113, 119, *see also* essential dignities
timing, 244, 287-288
and location, 248
translation of light, xxxii, 103, 307-309, 336
trees, 16-28
trine, 90-91, 92, 136, 149, 151, 304-305
triplicity, xxxii, 58, 120, 128
triplicity ruler, 50-54, 76-77, 120-122
turned chart, 54-55, 220-222
twelfth house, 50
Typhonis Sedes, 37, *ee also* house

U

uncongenial,
quarter or quadrant, 157

V

Valens, Vettius, 40, 54, 122, 132
vazirate, 144, *see also* oriental
vernall, 39, 61 *see also* quarter
vespertine, 85-87, 143
via combusta, xxxiii, 155, 234-235
Virgo, 68
void of course, xxxiii, 106-107, 155-156, 159, 235, 339-340
Volguine, Alexander, 185-186

W

wanes, 42, *see also* house
Ward, Sue, 234
wealth, 44-45, 51, 349-352
Questions concerning, 354-371
weather, 16-29
well-dignified, 16-28
Wharton, George, 38, 164
wild, xxxiii, 108, 159
winter, 39
Worsdale, John, x,

Y

yielding of light, *see* rendering of light
yielding of virtue, *see* rendering of virtue
youth, 36, 61, *see also* quarter
youthful, 39, *see also* quarter

Z

Zael, xi, xii, 5, 104, 262, 298, 324, 339,
zaminium, 138, *see also* cazimi
zodiac, xx, xxxiii, 10, 26, 57, 61, 309-310
zodiacal state, 10-11, 267, 268, 270
Zoller, Robert, xi, xiii, 50, 150, 188, 263, 266, 308-309, 347, 421, 521

Other books by
The Wessex Astrologer

The Essentials of Vedic Astrology
Lunar Nodes - Crisis and Redemption
Personal Panchanga and the Five Sources of Light
Komilla Sutton

Astrolocality Astrology
From Here to There
Martin Davis

The Consultation Chart
Introduction to Medical Astrology
Wanda Sellar

The Betz Placidus Table of Houses
Martha Betz

Astrology and Meditation
Greg Bogart

Patterns of the Past
Karmic Connections
Good Vibrations
Soulmates and why to avoid them
Judy Hall

The Book of World Horoscopes
Nicholas Campion

The Moment of Astrology
Geoffrey Cornelius

Life After Grief - An Astrological Guide to Dealing with Loss
AstroGraphology
Darrelyn Gunzburg

The Houses: Temples of the Sky
Deborah Houlding

Temperament: Astrology's Forgotten Key
Dorian Geiseler Greenbaum

Astrology, A Place in Chaos
Star and Planet Combinations
Bernadette Brady

Astrology and the Causes of War
Jamie Macphail

Flirting with the Zodiac
Kim Farnell

The Gods of Change
Howard Sasportas

Astrological Roots: The Hellenistic Legacy
Joseph Crane

The Art of Forecasting using Solar Returns
Anthony Louis

Horary Astrology Re-Examined
Barbara Dunn

Living Lilith - Four Dimensions of the Cosmic Feminine
Kelley Hunter

www.wessexastrologer.com

www.ingramcontent.com/pod-product-compliance
Lightning Source LLC
Chambersburg PA
CBHW071231300426
44116CB00008B/991